INTERNATIONAL CRIMINA

INTERNATIONAL CRIMINAL LAW

A Collection of International and
European Instruments

Edited by

CHRISTINE VAN DEN WYNGAERT

Professor of Law, University of Antwerp

and

Guy Stessens (assistant editor)

Lecturer in Law, University of Antwerp

KLUWER LAW INTERNATIONAL
THE HAGUE / LONDON / BOSTON

A C.I.P. Catalogue record for this book is available from the Library of Congress

ISBN 90-411-0303-1 (HB)
ISBN 90-411-0304-X (PB)

Published by Kluwer Law International,
P.O. Box 85889, 2508 CN The Hague, The Netherlands.

Sold and distributed in the U.S.A. and Canada
by Kluwer Law International,
675 Massachusetts Avenue, Cambridge, MA 02139, U.S.A.

In all other countries, sold and distributed
by Kluwer Law International,
P.O. Box 85889, 2508 CN The Hague, The Netherlands.

Printed on acid-free paper

All Rights Reserved
© 1996 Christine Van den Wyngaert
Kluwer Law International incorporates the publishing programmes of
Graham & Trotman Ltd, Kluwer Law and Taxation Publishers,
and Martinus Nijhoff Publishers.

No part of the material protected by this copyright notice may be reproduced or
utilized in any form or by any means, electronic or mechanical,
including photocopying, recording, or by any information storage and
retrieval system, without written permission from the copyright owner.

Printed in the Netherlands

Contents

Foreword ix

1. INTERNATIONAL CRIMES 1
   1.1. War Crimes 3
      Geneva Conventions of 12 August 1949 (excerpts) (1949) 5
      Protocol additional to the Geneva Conventions of 12 August 1949, and relating to the Protection of Victims of International Armed Conflicts (Protocol I) (excerpts) (1977) 17
      Protocol additional to the Geneva Conventions of 12 August 1949, and Relating to the Protection of Victims of Non-International Armed Conflicts (Protocol II) (excerpts) (1977) 25
      Convention on the Non-applicability of Statutory Limitations to War Crimes and Crimes against Humanity (1968) 27
      European Convention on the Non-applicability of Statutory Limitation to Crimes against Humanity and War Crimes (1974) 29
   1.2. Crimes against Humanity 33
      Convention on the Prevention and Suppression of the Crime of Genocide (1948) 35
      International Convention on the Suppression and Punishment of the Crime of Apartheid (excerpts) (1973) 37
   1.3. Terrorism 39
      Convention for the Suppression of Unlawful Seizure of Aircraft (1970) . 41
      Convention for the Suppression of Unlawful Acts against the Safety of Civil Aviation (excerpts) (1971) 45
      International Convention against the Taking of Hostages (excerpts) (1979) 47
      Convention on the Prevention and Punishment of Crimes against Internationally Protected Persons including Diplomatic Agents (excerpts) (1973) 49
      Convention for the Suppression of Unlawful Acts against the Safety of Maritime Navigation (excerpts) (1988) 51
   1.4. Physical Protection of Nuclear Material 53
      Convention on the Physical Protection of Nuclear Material 55
   1.5. Torture 63
      Convention against Torture and Other Cruel, Inhuman or Degrading Treatment or Punishment (1984) 65
      European Convention for the Prevention of Torture and Inhuman or Degrading Treatment or Punishment (1987) 75
   1.6. Drug Offences and Money Laundering 81
      Convention against Illicit Traffic in Narcotic Drugs and Psychotropic Substances (1988) 83
      Convention on Laundering, Search, Seizure and Confiscation of the Proceeds from Crime (1990) 107
      Schengen Convention - Title III - Chapter VI (excerpts) (1990) 123
      EC Council Directive No 91/308 of 10 June 1991 on Prevention of the Use of the Financial System for the Purpose of Money Laundering (1991) 125
   1.7. Crimes against the Environment 133
      Council of Europe Draft Convention for the Protection of the Environment through Criminal Law (1996) 135
   1.8. Fraud 143
      Convention on the Protection of the European Communities' Financial Interests (1995) 145
      Council Regulation (EC, EURATOM) No 2988/95 of 18 December 1995 on the Protection of the European Communities' Financial Interests (1995) 151

1.9. Corruption 157
  Inter-American Convention against Corruption (1996) 159
1.10. Insider Dealing 167
  Convention on Insider Trading (1989) 169
  Protocol to the Convention on Insider Trading (1989) 175
  EC Council Directive No 89/592 of 13 November 1989 coordinating
    Regulations on Insider Dealing (1989) 177

2. EXTRADITION 183
  2.1. United Nations 185
    UN Model Treaty on Extradition (1990) 187
  2.2. Council of Europe 195
    European Convention on Extradition (1957) 197
    (First) Additional Protocol to the European Convention on Extradition
      (excerpts) (1975) 207
    Second Additional Protocol to the European Convention on Extradition
      (excerpts) (1978) 209
    European Convention on the Suppression of Terrorism (1977) ... 211
    Recommendation No. R (80) 7 of the Committee of Ministers to Member States Concerning the Practical Application of the European
      Convention on Extradition (1980) 215
    Recommendation No. R (80) 9 of the Committee of Ministers to Member States Concerning Extradition to States not Party to the
      European Convention on Human Rights 217
  2.3. Schengen Group 219
    Schengen Convention - Title III - Chapter IV (excerpts) (1990) ... 221
  2.4. Commonwealth 223
    Commonwealth Scheme for the Rendition of Fugitive Offenders (1966) . 225
  2.5. Bilateral Extradition Treaties 235
    Convention between Belgium and the United States of America concerning the Mutual Extradition of Fugitive Offenders (1901) 237
    Supplementary Treaty concerning the Extradition Treaty between the Government of the United States of America and the Government of the United Kingdom of Great Britain and Northern Ireland signed at London on 8 June 1972 (excerpts) (1985) 243

3. MUTUAL ASSISTANCE 245
  3.1. Police Cooperation 247
    Constitution of Interpol (1956) 249
    Schengen Convention - Title III - Chapter I and Title IV - Chapters I to
      IV (excerpts) (1990) 257
    Europol Convention (1995) 275
  3.2. Administrative Cooperation 307
    EC Council Regulation No 1468/81 of 19 May 1981 on Mutual Assistance between the Administrative Authorities of the Member States and Cooperation between the Latter and the Commission to Ensure the Correct Application of the Law on Customs or
      Agricultural Matters (1981) 309
  3.3. Judicial Cooperation 317
    UN Model Treaty on Mutual Assistance in Criminal Matters (1990) ... 319
    Optional Protocol to the UN Model Treaty on Mutual Assistance in
      Criminal Matters concerning the Proceeds of Crime (1990) 327
    European Convention on Mutual Assistance in Criminal Matters (1959) 329
    Additional Protocol to the European Convention on Mutual Assistance
      in Criminal Matters (excerpts) (1978) 337
    Recommendation No. R (80)8 of the Committee of Ministers to Member States concerning the Practical application of the European
      Convention on Mutual Assistance in Criminal Matters 339
    Schengen Convention - Title III - Chapters II and III (excerpts) (1990) . 341
    Scheme Relating to Mutual Assistance in Criminal Matters within the Commonwealth including Amendments made by Law Ministers
      in April 1990 345

4. TRANSFER OF PROCEEDINGS, OF EXECUTION AND OF PRISONERS ... 357
4.1. Transfer of Proceedings ... 359
UN Model Treaty on the Transfer of Proceedings in Criminal Matters (1990) ... 361
European Convention on the Transfer of Proceedings in Criminal Matters (1972) ... 365
4.2. Transfer of Execution ... 377
European Convention on the International Validity of Criminal Judgments (1970) ... 379
4.3. Transfer of Prisoners ... 399
UN Model Agreement on the Transfer of Foreign Prisoners ... 401
UN Model Treaty on the Transfer of Supervision of Offenders Conditionally Sentenced or Conditionally Released (1990) ... 403
Convention on the Transfer of Sentenced Persons (1983) ... 407
Schengen Convention - Title III - Chapter V (excerpts) (1990) ... 415

5. INTERNATIONAL CRIMINAL COURT ... 417
Nuremberg Charter: Charter of International Military Tribunal, adopted by the Big Four Powers (1945) ... 419
Statute of the International Tribunal for the Former Yugoslavia (1993) . 427
Rules of Procedure and Evidence of the International Tribunal for the Former Yugoslavia (1994) ... 437
Statute of the International Tribunal for Rwanda (1994) ... 467
International Law Commission - Draft Statute for an International Criminal Court (1994) ... 477

6. INTERNATIONAL CRIMINAL CODE ... 499
Nuremberg Principles: Principles of International Law Recognized in the Charter of the Nuremberg Tribunal and in the Judgment of the Tribunal (1950) ... 501
International Law Commission - Draft Code of Offences against the Peace and Security of Mankind (excerpts) (1954) ... 503
International Law Commission - Draft Code of Crimes against the Peace and Security of Mankind (1991) ... 505
International Law Commission - Draft Code of Crimes against the Peace and Security of Mankind (1996) ... 515
International Law Commission - Draft Articles on State Responsibilty (excerpts) (1976) ... 523

7. THE EUROPEAN UNION AND THE CRIMINAL LAW ... 525
EEC-Treaty (excerpts) (1957) ... 527
Treaty on the European Union (excerpts) (1992) ... 531

8. GENERAL HUMAN RIGHTS INSTRUMENTS AND INTERNATIONAL CRIMINAL LAW ... 539
8.1. United Nations ... 541
International Covenant on Civil and Political Rights (1966) ... 543
Second Optional Protocol to the International Covenant on Civil and Political Rights, aiming at the Abolition of the Death Penalty (1989) ... 557
8.2. Council of Europe ... 559
European Convention on the Protection of Human Rights and Fundamental Freedoms (1950) ... 561
First Protocol to the Convention for the Protection of Human Rights and Fundamental Freedoms (1952) ... 573
Protocol No.6 to the Convention for the Protection of Human Rights and Fundamental Freedoms concerning the Abolition of the Death Penalty (1983) ... 575
Protocol No.7 to the Convention for the Protection of Human Rights and Fundamental Freedoms (1984) ... 577

9. TRANSFER OF DATA AND INTERNATIONAL CRIMINAL LAW 581
        Convention for the Protection of Individuals with regard to Automatic Processing of Personal Data (1981) 583
        Recommendation No. R(87) 15 of the Committee of Ministers to Member States Regulating the Use of Personal Data in the Police Sector (1987) 593
        EC Directive No 95/46 of 24 October 1995 of the European Parliament and of the Council on the Protection of Individuals with regard to the Processing of Personal Data and on the Free Movement of such Data (1995) 599

Index of International Instruments 615

Subject Index 621

Foreword

The fact that many scholars are sceptical about the question whether there is such a thing as an international criminal law, let alone a legal discipline of that name, does not seem to bother treaty makers. In recent years there has been an exponential growth in the number of international instruments that fall within this "discipline". In the United Nations and its specialised agencies and in the various European organisations (Council of Europe, European Union, Schengen-countries) there has been a dramatic increase in the number of conventions dealing with various aspects of international criminal law. In recent years so many instruments have been drafted that it has become very difficult to find one's way in the labyrinth of international criminal law treaties. This collection is intended to guide students of international criminal law through this labyrinth. Its focus is on international (universal) and European instruments, and in most cases on multilateral international treaties.

Selecting and arranging conventions is a hazardous exercise. In this book the following structure has been adopted. The first chapter is a selection of the most important *international crimes*, as they emerge from international conventions, including war crimes, crimes against humanity, terrorism, torture, drug offences and money laundering, crimes against the environment, fraud, corruption and insider dealing. The second, third and fourth chapters deal with the different forms of international co-operation in criminal matters (*extradition, mutual assistance, transfer of proceedings, execution and prisoners*). They encompass the "horizontal approach" to international criminal law, that is the approach based on the view that international criminal is a means for states to help each other in the application of their respective domestic criminal laws. The fifth and sixth chapters contain the instruments of a more "vertical" nature, that aim at developing a supranational perspective on the criminal law: they include the texts on the *International Criminal Court* and the *International Criminal Code*. Despite the fact that the *European Union* has no powers in the field of the criminal law, chapter 7 lists a number of texts that may constitute the legal basis for such powers, exercised by organs of the European Community or by member states. The last two chapters deal with the *human rights dimension of international criminal law*. Whereas within national legal systems the dichotomy between the repressive and the protective side of the criminal law is usually finely balanced, most international criminal law instruments are principally directed towards enhancing the supression of crime, thus leaving a lacuna in respect of the protection of persons (suspects, convicts, victims, witnesses) involved in international criminal proceedings. International human rights instruments are increasingly important in filling this lacuna. Chapter 8 contains the most important *General Human Rights Instruments* relevant to international criminal law. Chapter 9 on *Transfer of Data and International Criminal Law* contains the instruments that have further developed one particular human right, the right to privacy.

Arranging the material has proved to be particularly difficult. For example, the Nuremberg Charter could be placed either in the opening chapter, dealing with international crimes or in the fifth chapter, together with the instruments on the International Criminal Court. I preferred the second option, as the Nuremberg Charter was the legal basis of the International Military Tribunal. Also, titles of conventions may be misleading. For example, the European Convention on the Suppression of Terrorism has not been placed in the section on terrorist offences, but in the section on extradition. Despite its title, this convention does not punish terrorism, but only modifies the extradition arrangements between the member states of the Council of Europe. Another example is art.209a of the EC-Treaty, dealing with EC-fraud, which could have been placed in the section on fraud, but was placed with the instruments on the European Union instead. There are many other examples throughout the book. In order to find the links between topics that transcend more than one chapter, the reader is advised to use the index.

The collection is limited in time and space. In time, it is limited to the period after the second world war. In space, the focus is on universal and on European instruments. As a rule only conventions, and not draft conventions, have been listed. Again, there are several exceptions to this rule. For example, the drafts of the International Law Commission on both the International Criminal Court (1994) and the Code of Crimes against the Peace and Security of Mankind (1996) have been included, despite the fact that these texts are likely to undergo substantial changes in the near future, as they are in the process of being discussed in the appropriate organs of the United Nations. Another example is the Council of Europe's Draft Convention for the Protection of the Environment through the Criminal Law (1996), wich had just been finalised when the manuscript for this book was completed.

A rule guiding the selection of the texts that are contained in this book is that only conventions are included, not international instruments of a non-treaty nature. Again, there are some exceptions to this rule. For example, the section on police co-operation includes the Interpol Statute, which is not a convention, and there are also a number of Recommendations of the Committee of Ministers of the Council of Europe that are included because they contain important guidelines for the practical application of the conventions that they address.

It was, of course, impossible to include *all* international criminal law instruments within a book of this size. There are, quite obviously, many more international crimes than those listed in the first chapter. For example, there are no entries for aggression, counterfeiting, slavery, trade in human beings, obscene publications, theft of archeological treasures and crimes against United Nations and associated personnel (a "new" international crime that was introduced by the International Law Commission in July 1996). And, in respect of the crimes that were selected, not *all* conventions could be included, mainly for reasons of space. For example, in the section on drug offences and money laundering, the 1961 Single Convention on Narcotic Drugs is omitted and so is the 1972 Protocol to the same convention. Likewise, in the chapters on international co-operation in criminal matters, I have, for reasons of space, omitted the numerous conventions on the subject that have been concluded within the framework of European Political Co-operation. In the same vein, I have not included the rules of evidence of the Rwanda-Tribunal in the chapter on the International Criminal Court as these rules are substantially similar to those drafted for the tribunal for the former Yugoslavia. For reasons of space, several instruments have been reduced to their most important provisions. In the section on terrorism, only the Hague convention on aircraft hijacking (1970) has been included in full. The other anti-terrorist conventions, which follow the same general pattern (jurisdiction-clause, extradition-clause, aut dedere aut judicare-clause, etc.), have only been included in the form of excerpts. For the same reason, the preambles to the conventions have, with some exceptions, not been included.

I wish to extend my special gratitude to John Dugard, professor of international law at the University of the Witwatersrand and at present Director of the Research Centre for International Law at the University of Cambridge. The collection of instruments in this book complements another book that we are producing together to assist us in our respective courses on international criminal law. The idea of producing the present book arose from the many discussions we have had on the subject of international criminal law as co-rapporteurs of the International Law Association's Subcommittee on Extradition and Human Rights. John Dugard commented on the earlier drafts of this collection and gave me many helpful ideas and suggestions.

I wish to thank Guy Stessens, lecturer at the University of Antwerp, who teaches the International Criminal Law course with me. He has helped me to collect the instruments contained in this book, made useful comments, checked the references and helped in the production of the book. His contribution is acknowledged by describing him as an assistant editor.

James Crawford, Whewell professor of international law at the University of Cambridge, Philippe De Koster, administrator at the anti-fraud unit of the European Commission (UCLAF), Hans Nilsson, formerly Director of Legal Affairs at the Secretariat General of the Council of Europe and at present Head of Division of Directorate General H at the Secretariat General of the Council of the European Union, and Patrick Zanders, Head of the section International Co-operation of the Belgian Algemene Politie Steundienst, kindly supplied me with the most recent versions of documents that, without their help, I would have had great difficulty in finding. I also wish to thank Julian Schutte, director at the Legal Service of the Council of the European Union, who pointed me to some lacunae in the list.

Ingrid Billiaert typed the manuscript with great care and enthusiasm. Steve Cosyn, who graduated in 1996 from the Department of Law at the University of Antwerp, did the proofreading. Bart De Smet and Eric Verbert have helped with the index. My thanks also extend to them.

Christine Van den Wyngaert
10 July 1996

1. INTERNATIONAL CRIMES

1.1. War Crimes

Geneva Conventions of 12 August 1949 (excerpts) (1949)[*]

Geneva, 12 August 1949

Convention for the Amelioration of the Condition of the Wounded and Sick in Armed Forces in the Field (excerpts)

Chapter I

General Provisions

Article 1

The High Contracting Parties undertake to respect and to ensure respect for the present Convention in all circumstances.

Article 2

In addition to the provisions which shall be implemented in peacetime, the present Convention shall apply to all cases of declared war or of any other armed conflict which may arise between two or more of the High Contracting Parties, even if the state of war is not recognized by one of them.

The Convention shall also apply to all cases of partial or total occupation of the territory of a High Contracting Party, even if the said occupation meets with no armed resistance.

Although one of the Powers in conflict may not be a party to the present Convention, the Powers who are parties thereto shall remain bound by it in their mutual relations. They shall furthermore be bound by the Convention in relation to the said Power, if the latter accepts and applies the provisions thereof.

Article 3

In the case of armed conflict not of an international character occurring in the territory of one of the High Contracting Parties, each Party to the conflict shall be bound to apply, as a minimum, the following provisions:

1. Persons taking no active part in the hostilities, including members of armed forces who have laid down their arms and those placed *hors de combat* by sickness, wounds, detention, or any other cause, shall in all circumstances be treated humanely, without any adverse distinction founded on race, colour, religion or faith, sex, birth or wealth, or any other similar criteria.

To this end, the following acts are and shall remain prohibited at any time and in any place whatsoever with respect to the above-mentioned persons:

(a) violence to life and person, in particular murder of all kinds, mutilation, cruel treatment and torture;

(b) taking of hostages;

(c) outrages upon personal dignity, in particular humiliating and degrading treatment;

---

[*] *United Nations Treaty Series*, vol.75, 31.

(d) the passing of sentences and the carrying out of executions without previous judgment pronounced by a regularly constituted court, affording all the judicial guarantees which are recognized as indispensable by civilized peoples.

2. The wounded and sick shall be collected and cared for.

An impartial humanitarian body, such as the International Committee of the Red Cross, may offer its services to the Parties to the conflict.

The Parties to the conflict should further endeavour to bring into force, by means of special agreements, all or part of the other provisions of the present Convention.

The application to the preceding provisions shall not affect the legal status of the Parties to the conflict.

Article 4

Neutral Powers shall apply by analogy the provisions of the present Convention to the wounded and sick, and to members of the medical personnel and to chaplains of the armed forces of the Parties to the conflict, received or interned in their territory, as well as to dead persons found.

Article 5

For the protected persons who have fallen into the hands of the enemy, the present Convention shall apply until their final repatriation.

Article 6

In addition to the agreements expressly provided for in Articles 10, 15, 23, 28, 31, 36, 37, and 52, the High Contracting Parties may conclude other special agreements for all matters concerning which they may deem it suitable to make separate provision. No special agreement shall adversely affect the situation of the wounded and sick, of members of the medical personnel or of chaplains, as defined by the present Convention, nor restrict the rights which it confers upon them.

Wounded and sick, as well as medical personnel and chaplains, shall continue to have the benefit of such agreements as long as the Convention is applicable to them, except where express provisions to the contrary are contained in the aforesaid or in subsequent agreements, or where more favourable measures have been taken with regard to them by one or other of the Parties to the conflict.

Article 7

Wounded and sick, as well as members of the medical personnel and chaplains, may in no circumstances renounce in part or in entirety the rights secured to them by the present Convention, and by the special agreements referred to in the foregoing Article, if such there be.

Article 8

The present Convention shall be applied with the cooperation and under the scrutiny of the Protecting Powers whose duty it is to safeguard the interests of the Parties to the conflict. For this purpose, the Protecting Powers may appoint, apart from their diplomatic or consular staff, delegates from amongst their own nationals or the nationals of other neutral Powers. The said delegates shall be subject to the approval of the Power with which they are to carry out their duties.

The Parties to the conflict shall facilitate to the greatest extent possible, the task of the representatives or delegates of the Protecting Powers.

The representatives or delegates of the Protecting Powers shall not in any case exceed their mission under the present Convention. They shall, in particular, take account of the imperative necessities of security of the State wherein they carry out their duties. Their activities shall only be restricted as an exceptional and temporary measure when this is rendered necessary by imperative military necessities.

[...]

Chapter IX

Repression of Abuses and Infractions

Article 49

The High Contracting Parties undertake to enact any legislation necessary to provide effective penal sanctions for persons committing, or ordering to be committed, any of the grave breaches of the present Convention defined in the following Article.

Each High Contracting Party shall be under the obligation to search for persons alleged to have committed, or to have ordered to be committed, such grave breaches, and shall bring such persons, regardless of their nationality, before its own courts. It may also, if it prefers, and in accordance with the provisions of its own legislation, hand such persons over for trial to another High Contracting Party concerned provided such High Contracting Party has made out a *prima facie* case.

Each High Contracting Party shall take measures necessary for the suppression of all acts contrary to the provisions of the present Convention other than the grave breaches, defined in the following Article.

In all circumstances, the accused persons shall benefit by safeguards of proper trial and defence, which shall not be less favourable than those provided by Article 105 and those following of the Geneva Convention relative to the Treatment of Prisoners of War of 12 August 1949.

Article 50

Grave breaches to which the preceding Article relates shall be those involving any of the following acts, if committed against persons or property protected by the Convention: wilful killing, torture or inhuman treatment, including biological experiments, wilfully causing great suffering or serious injury to body or health, and extensive destruction and appropriation of property, not justified by military necessity and carried out unlawfully and wantonly.

Article 51

No High Contracting Party shall be allowed to absolve itself or any other High Contracting Party of any liability incurred by itself or by another High Contracting Party in respect of breaches referred to in the preceding Article.

Article 52

At the request of a Party to the conflict, an enquiry shall be instituted, in a manner to be decided between the interested Parties, concerning any alleged violation of the Convention.

If agreement has not been reached concerning the procedure for the enquiry, the Parties should agree on the choice of an umpire who will decide upon the procedure to be followed.

Once the violation has been established, the Parties to the conflict shall put an end to it and shall repress it with the least possible delay.

Article 53

The use by individuals, societies, firms or companies either public or private, other than those entitled thereto under the present Convention, of the emblem or the designation "Red Cross" or "Geneva Cross" or any sign or designation constituting an imitation thereof, whatever the object of such use, and irrespective of the date of its adoption, shall be prohibited at all times.

By reason of the tribute paid to Switzerland by the adoption of the reversed Federal colours, and of the confusion which may arise between the arms of Switzerland and the distinctive emblem of the Convention, the use by private individuals, societies or firms, of the arms of the Swiss Confederation or of marks constituting an imitation thereof, whether as trademarks or commercial marks, or as parts of such marks, or for a purpose contrary to commercial honesty, or in circumstances capable of wounding Swiss national sentiment, shall be prohibited at all times.

Nevertheless, such High Contracting Parties as were not party to the Geneva Convention of 27 July 1929, may grant to prior users of the emblems, designations, signs or marks designated in the first paragraph, a time limit not to exceed three years from the coming into force of the present Convention to discontinue such use, provided that the said use shall not be such as would appear, in time of war, to confer the protection of the Convention.

The prohibition laid down in the first paragraph of the present Article shall also apply, without effect on any rights acquired through prior use, to the emblems and marks mentioned in the second paragraph of Article 38.

Article 54

The High Contracting Parties shall, if their legislation is not already adequate, take measures necessary for the prevention and repression, at all times, of the abuses referred to under Article 53.

[...]

Convention for the Amelioration of the Condition of the Wounded, Sick and Shipwrecked Members of Armed Forces at Sea (excerpts) (1949)[*]

Chapter VIII

Repression of Abuses and Infractions

Article 50

The High Contracting Parties undertake to enact any legislation necessary to provide effective penal sanctions for persons committing, or ordering to be committed, any of the grave breaches of the present Convention defined in the following Article.

Each High Contracting Party shall be under the obligation to search for persons alleged to have committed, or to have ordered to be committed, such grave breaches, and shall bring such persons, regardless of their nationality, before its own courts. It may also, if it prefers, and in accordance with the provisions of its own legislation, hand such persons over for trial to another High Contracting Party concerned, provided such High Contracting Party has made out a *prima facie* case.

Each High Contracting Party shall take measures necessary for the suppression of all acts contrary to the provisions of the present Convention other than the grave breaches defined in the following Article.

In all circumstances, the accused persons shall benefit by safeguards of proper trial and defence, which shall not be less favourable than those provided by Article 105 and those following of the Geneva Convention relative to the Treatment of Prisoners of War of 12 August 1949.

Article 51

Grave breaches to which the preceding Article relates shall be those involving any of the following acts, if committed against persons or property protected by the Convention: wilful killing, torture or inhuman treatment, including biological experiments, wilfully causing great suffering or serious injury to body or health, and extensive destruction and appropriation of property, not justified by military necessity and carried out unlawfully and wantonly.

[...]

---

[*] *United Nations Treaty Series*, vol. 75, 85.

Convention relative to the Treatment of Prisoners of War (excerpts) (1949)[*]

Part III

Captivity

[...]

Section VI

Relation between Prisoners of War and the Authorities

[...]

Chapter III

Penal and Disciplinary Sanctions

[...]

Article 105

1. The prisoner of war shall be entitled to assistance by one of his prisoner comrades, to defence by a qualified advocate or counsel of his own choice, to the calling of witnesses and, if he deems necessary, to the services of a competent interpreter. He shall be advised of these rights by the Detaining Power in due time before the trial.

2. Failing a choice by the prisoner of war, the Protecting Power shall find him an advocate or counsel, and shall have at least one week at its disposal for the purpose. The Detaining Power shall deliver to the said Power, on request, a list of persons qualified to present the defence. Failing a choice of an advocate or counsel by the prisoner of war or the Protecting Power, the Detaining Power shall appoint a competent advocate or counsel to conduct the defence.

3. The advocate or counsel conducting the defence on behalf of the prisoner of war shall have at his disposal a period of two weeks at least before the opening of the trial, as well as the necessary facilities to prepare the defence of the accused. He may, in particular, freely visit the accused and interview him in private. He may also confer with any witnesses for the defence, including prisoners of war. He shall have the benefit of these facilities until the term of appeal or petition has expired.

4. Particulars of the charge or charges on which the prisoner of war is to be arraigned, as well as the documents which are generally communicated to the accused by virtue of the laws in force in the armed forces of the Detaining Power, shall be communicated to the accused prisoner of war in a language which he understands, and in good time before the opening of the trial. The same communication in the same circumstances shall be made to the advocate or counsel conducting the defence on behalf of the prisoner of war.

5. The representatives of Protecting Power shall be entitled to attend the trial of the case, unless, exceptionally, this is held in camera in the interest of State security. In such a case the Detaining Power shall advise the Protecting Power accordingly.

Article 106

Every prisoner of war shall have, in the same manner as the members of the armed forces of the Detaining Power, the right of appeal or petition from any sentence pronounced

---

[*] *United Nations Treaty Series*, vol.75, 135.

upon him, with a view to the quashing or revising of the sentence or the re-opening of the trial. He shall be fully informed of his right to appeal or petition and of the time limit within which he may do so.

Article 107

1. Any judgment and sentence pronounced upon a prisoner of war shall be immediately reported to the Protecting Power in the form of a summary communication, which shall also indicate whether he has the right of appeal with a view to the quashing of the sentence or the re-opening of the trial. This communication shall likewise be sent to the prisoners' representative concerned. It shall also be sent to the accused prisoner of war in a language he understands, if the sentence was not pronounced in his presence. The Detaining Power shall also immediately communicate to the Protecting Power the decision of the prisoner of war to use or to waive his right of appeal.

2. Furthermore, if a prisoner of war is finally convicted or if a sentence pronounced against a prisoner of war in the first instance is a death sentence, the Detaining Power shall as soon as possible address to the Protecting Power a detailed communication containing:

(a) the precise wording of the finding and sentence:

(b) a summarized report of any preliminary investigation and of the trial, emphasizing in particular the elements of the prosecution and the defence.

(c) notification, where applicable, of the establishment where the sentence will be served.

3. The communications provided for in the foregoing subparagraphs shall be sent to the Protecting Power at the address previously made known to the Detaining Power.

Article 108

1. Sentences pronounced on prisoners of war after a conviction has become duly enforceable, shall be served in the same establishments and under the same conditions as in the case of members of the armed forces of the Detaining Power. These conditions shall in all cases conform to the requirements of health and humanity.

2. A woman prisoner of war on whom such a sentence has been pronounced shall be confined in separate quarters and shall be under the supervision of women.

3. In any case, prisoners of war sentenced to a penalty depriving them of their liberty shall retain the benefit of the provisions of Articles 78 and 126 of the present Convention. Furthermore, they shall be entitled to receive and despatch correspondence, to receive at least one relief parcel monthly, to take regular exercise in the open air, to have the medical care required by their state of health, and the spiritual assistance they may desire. Penalties to which they may be subjected shall be in accordance with the provisions of Article 87, third paragraph.

[...]

Part VI

Execution of the Convention

Section I

General Provisions

[...]

Article 129

The High Contracting Parties undertake to enact any legislation necessary to provide effective penal sanctions for persons committing, or ordering to be committed, any of the grave breaches of the present Convention defined in the following Article.
Each High Contracting Party shall be under the obligation to search for persons alleged to have committed, or to have ordered to be committed, such grave breaches, and shall bring such persons, regardless of their nationality, before its own courts. It may also, if it prefers, and in accordance with the provisions of its own legislation, hand such persons over for trial to another High Contracting Party concerned, provided such High Contracting Party has made out a *prima facie* case.

Each High Contracting Party shall take measures necessary for the suppression of all acts contrary to the provisions of the present Convention other than the grave breaches defined in the following Article.

In all circumstances, the accused persons shall benefit by safeguards of proper trial and defence, which shall not be less favourable than those provided by Article 105 and those following of the present Convention.

Article 130

Grave breaches to which the preceding Article relates shall be those involving any of the following acts, if committed against persons or property protected by the Convention: wilful killing, torture or inhuman treatment, including biological experiments, wilfully causing great suffering or serious injury to body or health, compelling a prisoner of war to serve in the forces of the hostile Power, or wilfully depriving a prisoner of war of the rights of fair and regular trial prescribed in this Convention.

[...]

Convention relative to the Protection of Civilian Persons in Time of War (excerpts) (1949)[*]

Part IV

Execution of the Convention

Section I

General Provisions

Article 146

The High Contracting Parties undertake to enact any legislation necessary to provide effective penal sanctions for persons committing, or ordering to be committed, any of the grave breaches of the present Convention defined in the following Article.
Each High Contracting Party shall be under the obligation to search for persons alleged to have committed, or to have ordered to be committed, such grave breaches, and shall bring such persons, regardless of their nationality, before its own courts. It may also, if it prefers, and in accordance with the provisions of its own legislation, hand such persons over for trial to another High Contracting Party concerned, provided such High Contracting Party has made out a *prima facie* case.

Each High Contracting Party shall take measures necessary for the suppression of all acts contrary to the provisions of the present Convention other than the grave breaches defined in the following Article.

In all circumstances, the accused persons shall benefit by safeguards of proper trial and defence, which shall not be less favourable than those provided by Article 105 and those following of the Geneva Convention relative to the Treatment of Prisoners of War of 12 August 1949.

Article 147

Grave breaches to which the preceding Article relates shall be those involving any of the following acts, if committed against persons or property protected by the present Convention: wilful killing, torture or inhuman treatment, including biological experiments, wilfully causing great suffering or serious injury to body or health, unlawful deportation or transfer or unlawful confinement of a protected person, compelling a protected person to serve in the forces of a hostile Power, or wilfully depriving a protected person of the rights of fair and regular trial prescribed in the present Convention, taking of hostages and extensive destruction and appropriation of property, not justified by military necessity and carried out unlawfully and wantonly.

[...]

---

[*] *United Nations Treaty Series*, vol.75, 287.

Protocol additional to the Geneva Conventions of 12 August 1949, and relating to the Protection of Victims of International Armed Conflicts (Protocol I) (excerpts) (1977)[*]

Geneva, 8 June 1977

Part I

General provisions

Article 1

General principles and scope of application

1. The High Contracting Parties undertake to respect and to ensure respect for this Protocol in all circumstances.

2. In cases not covered by this Protocol or by other international agreements, civilians and combatants remain under the protection and authority of the principles of international law derived from established custom, from the principles of humanity and from the dictates of public conscience.

3. This Protocol, which supplements the Geneva Conventions of 12 August 1949 for the protection of war victims, shall apply in the situations referred to in Article 2 common to those Conventions.

4. The situations referred to in the preceding paragraph include armed conflicts in which peoples are fighting against colonial domination and alien occupation and against racist regimes in the exercise of their right of self-determination, as enshrined in the Charter of the United Nations and the Declaration on Principles of International Law concerning Friendly Relations and Co-operation among States in accordance with the Charter of the United Nations.

[...]

Article 11

Protection of persons

1. The physical or mental health and integrity of persons who are in the power of the adverse Party or who are interned, detained or otherwise deprived of liberty as a result of a situation referred to in Article 1 shall not be endangered by any unjustified act or omission. Accordingly, it is prohibited to subject the persons described in this Article to any medical procedure which is not indicated by the state of health of the person concerned and which is not consistent with generally accepted medical standards which would be applied under similar medical circumstances to persons who are nationals of the Party conducting the procedure and who are in no way deprived of liberty.

2. It is, in particular, prohibited to carry out on such persons, even with their consent:

    (a)   physical mutilations;

    (b)   medical or scientific experiments;

    (c)   removal of tissue or organs for transplantation,

---

[*] *United Nations, General Assembly*, A/32/144, 15 August 1977.

except where these acts are justified in conformity with the conditions provided for in paragraph 1.

3. Exceptions to the prohibition in paragraph 2 (c) may be made only in the case of donations of blood for transfusion or of skin for grafting, provided that they are given voluntarily and without any coercion or inducement, and then only for therapeutic purposes, under conditions consistent with generally accepted medical standards and controls designed for the benefit of both the donor and the recipient.

4. Any wilful act or omission which seriously endangers the physical or mental health or integrity of any person who is in the power of a Party other than the one on which he depends and which either violates any of the prohibitions in paragraphs 1 and 2 or fails to comply with the requirements of paragraph 3 shall be a grave breach of this Protocol.

5. The persons described in paragraph 1 have the right to refuse any surgical operation. In case of refusal, medical personnel shall endeavour to obtain a written statement to that effect, signed or acknowledged by the patient.

6. Each Party to the conflict shall keep a medical record for every donation of blood for transfusion or skin for grafting by persons referred to in paragraph 1, if that donation is made under the responsibility of that Party. In addition, each Party to the conflict shall endeavour to keep a record of all medical procedures undertaken with respect to any person who is interned, detained or otherwise deprived of liberty as a result of a situation referred to in Article 1. These records shall be available at all times for inspection by the Protecting Power.

[...]

Article 75

Fundamental guarantees

1. In so far as they are affected by a situation referred to in Article 1 of this Protocol, persons who are in the power of a Party to the conflict and who do not benefit from more favourable treatment under the Conventions or under this Protocol shall be treated humanely in all circumstances and shall enjoy, as a minimum, the protection provided by this Article without any adverse distinction based upon race, colour, sex, language, religion or belief, political or other opinion, national or social origin, wealth, birth or other status, or on any other similar criteria. Each Party shall respect the person, honour, convictions and religious practices of all such persons.

2. The following acts are and shall remain prohibited at any time and in any place whatsoever, whether committed by civilian or by military agents:

    (a) violence, to the life, health, or physical or mental well-being of persons, in particular:

        (i) murder;

        (ii) torture of all kinds, whether physical or mental:

        (iii) corporal punishment; and

        (iv) mutilation;

    (b) outrages upon personal dignity, in particular humiliating and degrading treatment, enforced prostitution and any form of indecent assault;

    (c) the taking of hostages;

    (d) collective punishments; and

    (e) threats to commit any of the foregoing acts.

3. Any person arrested, detained or interned for actions related to the armed conflict shall be informed promptly, in a language he understands, of the reasons why these measures have been taken. Except in cases of arrest or detention for penal offences, such persons shall be released with the minimum delay possible and in any event as soon as the circumstances justifying the arrest, detention or internment have ceased to exist.

4. No sentence may be passed and no penalty may be executed on a person found guilty of a penal offence related to the armed conflict except pursuant to a conviction pronounced by an impartial and regularly constituted court respecting the generally recognized principles of regular judicial procedure, which include the following:

   (a) the procedure shall provide for an accused to be informed without delay of the particulars of the offence alleged against him and shall afford the accused before and during his trial all necessary rights and means of defence;

   (b) no one shall be convicted of an offence except on the basis of individual penal responsibility;

   (c) no one shall be accused or convicted of a criminal offence on account of any act or omission which did not constitute a criminal offence under the national or international law to which he was subject at the time when it was committed; nor shall a heavier penalty be imposed than that which was applicable at the time when the criminal offence was committed; if, after the commission of the offence, provision is made by law for the imposition of a lighter penalty, the offender shall benefit thereby;

   (d) anyone charged with an offence is presumed innocent until proved guilty according to law;

   (e) anyone charged with an offence shall have the right to be tried in his presence;

   (f) no one shall be compelled to testify against himself or to confess guilt;

   (g) anyone charged with an offence shall have the right to examine, or have examined, the witnesses against him and to obtain the attendance and examination of witnesses on his behalf under the same conditions as witnesses against him;

   (h) no one shall be prosecuted or punished by the same Party for an offence in respect of which a final judgement acquitting or convicting that person has been previously pronounced under the same law and judicial procedure;

   (i) anyone prosecuted for an offense, shall have the right to have the judgement pronounced publicly; and

   (j) a convicted person shall be advised on conviction of his judicial and other remedies and of the time-limit within which they may be exercised.

5. Women whose liberty has been restricted for reasons related to the armed conflict shall be held in quarters separated from men's quarters. They shall be under the immediate supervision of women. Nevertheless, in cases where families are detained or interned, they shall, whenever possible, be held in the same place and accommodated as family units.

6. Persons who are arrested, detained or interned for reasons related to the armed conflict shall enjoy the protection provided by this Article until their final release, repatriation or re-establishment, even after the end of the armed conflict.

7. In order to avoid any doubt concerning the prosecution and trial of persons accused of war crimes, or crimes against humanity, the following principles shall apply:

   (a) persons who are accused of such crimes should be submitted for the purpose of prosecution and trial in accordance with the applicable rules of international law; and

(b) any such persons who do not benefit from more favourable treatment under the Conventions or this Protocol shall be accorded the treatment provided by this Article, whether or not the crimes of which they are accused constitute grave breaches of the Conventions or of this Protocol.

8. No provision of this Article may be construed as limiting or infringing any other more favourable provision granting protection,, under any applicable rules of international law, to greater persons covered by paragraph 1.

[...]

Section II

Repression of breaches of the conventions and of this protocol

Article 85

Repression of breaches of this Protocol

1. The provisions of the Conventions relating to the repression of breaches and grave breaches, supplemented by this Section, shall apply to the repression of breaches and grave breaches of this Protocol.

2. Acts described as grave breaches in the Conventions are grave breaches of this Protocol if committed against persons in the power of an adverse party protected by Articles 44, 45 and 73 of this Protocol, or against the wounded, sick and shipwrecked of the adverse Party who are protected by this Protocol, or against those medical or religious personnel, medical units or medical transports which are under the control of the adverse Party and are protected by this Protocol.

3. In addition to the grave breaches defined in Article 11, the following acts shall be regarded as grave breaches of this Protocol, when committed wilfully in violation of the relevant provisions of this Protocol, and causing death or serious injury to body or health:

(a) making the civilian population or individual the object of attack:

(b) launching an indiscriminate attack affecting the civilian population or civilian objects in the knowledge that such attack will cause excessive loss of life, injury to civilians or damage to civilian objects, as defined in Article 57, paragraph 2 (a) (iii);

(c) launching an attack against works or installations containing dangerous forces in the knowledge that such attack will cause excessive loss of life, injury to civilians or damage to civilian objects, as defined in Article 57, paragraph 2 (a) (iii);

(d) making non-defended localities and demilitarized zones the object of attack;

(e) making a person the object of attack in the knowledge that he is *hors de combat*;

(f) the perfidious use, in violation of Article 37, of the distinctive emblem of the red cross, red crescent or red lion and sun or of other protective signs recognized by the Conventions or this Protocol.

4. In addition to the grave breaches defined in the preceding paragraphs and in the Conventions, the following shall be regarded as grave breaches of this Protocol, when committed wilfully and in violation of the Conventions or the Protocol:

(a) the transfer by the Occupying Power of parts of its own civilian population into the territory it occupies, or the deportation or transfer of all or parts of the population of the occupied territory within or outside this territory, in violation of Article 49 of the Fourth Convention;

(b) unjustifiable delay in the repatriation of prisoners of war or civilians;

(c) practices of *apartheid* and other inhuman and degrading practices involving outrages upon personal dignity, based on racial discrimination;

(d) making the clearly recognized historic monuments, works of art or places of worship which constitute the cultural or spiritual heritage of peoples and to which special protection has been given by special arrangement, for example, within the framework of a competent international organization, the object of attack, causing as a result extensive destruction thereof, where there is no evidence of the violation by the adverse Party of Article 53, sub-paragraph (b), and when such historic monuments, works of art and places of worship are not located in the immediate proximity of military objectives;

(e) depriving a person protected by the Conventions or referred to in paragraph 2 of this Article of the rights of fair and regular trial.

5. Without prejudice to the application of the Conventions and of this Protocol, grave breaches of these instruments shall be regarded as war crimes.

Article 86

Failure to act

1. The High Contracting Parties and the Parties to the conflict shall repress grave breaches, and take measures necessary to suppress all other breaches, of the Conventions or of this Protocol which result from a failure to act when under a duty to do so.

2. The fact that a breach of the Conventions or of this Protocol was committed by a subordinate does not absolve his superiors from penal or disciplinary responsibility, as the case may be, if they knew, or had information which should have enabled them to conclude in the circumstances at the time, that he was committing or was going to commit such a breach and if they did not take feasible measures within their power to prevent or repress the breach.

Article 87

Duty of commanders

1. The High Contracting Parties and the Parties to the conflict shall require military commanders, with respect to members of the armed forces under their command and other persons under their control, to prevent and, where necessary, to suppress and to report to competent authorities breaches of the Conventions and of this Protocol.

2. In order to prevent and suppress breaches, High Contracting Parties and Parties to the conflict shall require that, commensurate with their level of responsibility, commanders ensure that members of the armed forces under their command are aware of their obligations under the Conventions and this Protocol.

3. The High Contracting Parties and Parties to the conflict shall require any commander who is aware that subordinates or other persons under his control are going to commit or have committed a breach of the Conventions or of this Protocol, to initiate such steps as are necessary to prevent such violations of the Conventions or this Protocol, and, where appropriate, to initiate disciplinary or penal action against violators thereof.

Article 88

Mutual assistance in criminal matters

1. The High Contracting Parties shall afford one another the greatest measure of assistance in connection with criminal proceedings brought in respect of grave breaches of the Conventions or of this Protocol.

2. Subject to the rights and obligations established in the Conventions and in Article 85, paragraph 1, of this Protocol, and when circumstances permit, the High Contracting Parties shall co-operate in the matter of extradition. They shall give due consideration to the request of the State in whose territory the alleged offence has occurred.

3. The law of the High Contracting Party requested shall apply in all cases. The provisions of the preceding paragraphs shall not, however, affect the obligations arising from the provisions of any other treaty of a bilateral or multilateral nature which governs or will govern the whole or part of the subject of mutual assistance in criminal matters.

Article 89

Co-operation

In situation of serious violations of the Conventions or of this Protocol, the High Contracting Parties undertake to act, jointly or individually, in co-operation with the United Nations and in conformity with the United Nations Charter.

Article 90

International Fact-Finding Commission

1. (a) An International Fact-Finding Commission (hereinafter referred to as "the Commission") consisting of fifteen members of high moral standing and acknowledged impartiality shall be established.

   (b) When not less than twenty High Contracting Parties have agreed to accept to competence of the Commission pursuant to paragraph 2, the depositary shall then, and at intervals of five years thereafter, convene a meeting of representatives of those High Contracting Parties for the purpose of electing the members of the Commission. At the meeting, the representatives shall elect the members of the Commission by secret ballot from a list of persons to which each of those High Contracting Parties may nominate one person.

   (c) The members of the Commission shall serve in their personal capacity and shall hold office until the election of new members at the ensuing meeting.

   (d) At the election, the High Contracting Parties shall ensure that the persons to be elected to the Commission individually possess the qualifications required and that, in the Commission as a whole, equitable geographical representation is assured.

   (e) In the case of a casual vacancy, the Commission itself shall fill the vacancy, having due regard to the provisions of the preceding sub-paragraphs.

   (f) The depositary shall make available to the Commission the necessary administrative facilities for the performance of its functions.

2. (a) The High Contracting Parties may at the time of signing, ratifying or acceding to the Protocol, or at any other subsequent time, declare that they recognize ipso facto and without special agreement, in relation to any other High Contracting Party accepting the same obligation, the competence of the Commission to enquire into allegations by such other Party, as authorized by this Article.

   (b) The declarations referred to above shall be deposited with the depositary, which shall transmit copies thereof to the High Contracting Parties.

   (c) The Commission shall be competent to:

      (i) enquire into any facts alleged to be a grave breach as defined in the Conventions and this Protocol or other serious violation of the Conventions or of this Protocol.

- (ii) facilitate, through its good offices, the restoration of an attitude of respect for the Conventions and this Protocol.

(d) In other situations, the Commissions shall institute an enquiry at the request of a Party to the conflict only with the consent of the other Party or Parties concerned.

(e) Subject to the foregoing provisions of this paragraph, the provisions of Article 52 of the First Convention, Article 53 of the Second Convention, Article 132 of the Third Convention and Article 149 of the Fourth Convention shall continue to apply to any alleged violation of the Conventions and shall extend to any alleged violation of this Protocol.

3. (a) Unless otherwise agreed by the Parties concerned, all enquiries shall be undertaken by a Chamber consisting of seven members appointed as follows:

- (i) five members of the Commission, not nationals of any Party to the conflict, appointed by the President of the Commission on the basis of equitable representation of the geographical areas, after consultation with the Parties to the conflict;
- (ii) two *ad hoc* members, not nationals of any Party to the conflict, one to be appointed by each side.

(b) Upon receipt of the request for an enquiry, the President of the Commission shall specify an appropriate time-limit for setting up a Chamber. If any *ad hoc* member has not been appointed within the time-limit, the President shall immediately appoint such additional member or members of the Commission as may be necessary to complete the membership of the Chamber.

4. (a) The Chamber set up under paragraph 3 to undertake an enquiry shall invite the Parties to the conflict to assist it and to present evidence. The Chamber may also seek such other evidence as it deems appropriate and may carry out an investigation of the situation in loco.

(b) All evidence shall be fully disclosed to the Parties, which shall have the right to comment on it to the Commission.

(c) Each Party shall have the right to challenge such evidence.

5. (a) The Commission shall submit to the Parties a report on the findings of fact of the Chamber, with such recommendations as it may deem appropriate.

(b) If the Chamber is unable to secure sufficient evidence for factual and impartial findings, the Commission shall state the reasons for that inability.

(c) The Commission shall not report its findings publicly, unless all the Parties to the conflict have requested the Commission to do so.

6. The Commission shall establish its own rules, including rules for the presidency of the Commission and the presidency of the Chamber. Those rules shall ensure that the functions of the President of the Commission are exercised at all times and that, in the case of an enquiry, they are exercised by a person who is not a national of a Party to the conflict.

7. The administrative expenses of the Commission shall be met by contributions form the High Contracting Parties which made declarations under paragraph 2, and by voluntary contributions. The Party or Parties to the conflict requesting an enquiry shall advance the necessary funds for expenses incurred by a Chamber and shall be reimbursed by the Party or Parties against which the allegations are made to the extent of fifty per cent of the costs of the Chamber. Where there are counter-allegations before the Chamber each side shall advance fifty per cent of the necessary funds.
[...]

Protocol additional to the Geneva Conventions of 12 August 1949, and Relating to the Protection of Victims of Non-International Armed Conflicts (Protocol II) (excerpts) (1977)[*]

Geneva, 8 June 1977

Article 1

Material field of application

1. This Protocol, which develops and supplements Article 3 common to the Geneva Conventions of 12 August 1949 without modifying its existing conditions of application, shall apply to all armed conflicts which are not covered by Article 1 of the Protocol Additional to the Geneva Conventions of 12 August 1949, and relating to the Protection of Victims of International Armed Conflicts (Protocol I) and which take place in the territory of a High Contracting Party between its armed forces and dissident armed forces or other organized armed groups which, under responsible command, exercise such control over a part of its territory as to enable them to carry out sustained and concerted military operations and to implement this Protocol.

2. This Protocol shall not apply to situations of internal disturbances and tensions, such as riots, isolated and sporadic acts of violence and other acts of a similar nature, as not being armed conflicts.

[...]

Article 6

Penal prosecutions

1. This Article applies to the prosecution and punishment of criminal offences related to the armed conflict.

2. No sentence shall be passed and no penalty shall be executed on a person found guilty of an offence except pursuant to a conviction pronounced by a court offering the essential guarantees of independence and impartiality. In particular:

 (a) the procedure shall provide for an accused to be informed without delay of the particulars of the offence alleged against him and shall afford the accused before and during his trial all necessary rights and means of defence;

 (b) no one shall be convicted of an offence except on the basis of individual penal responsibility;

 (c) no one shall be held guilty of any criminal offence on account of any act or omission which did not constitute a criminal offence, under the law, at the time when it was committed; nor shall a heavier penalty be imposed than that which was applicable at the time when the criminal offence was committed; if, after the commission of the offence, provision is made by law for the imposition of a lighter penalty, the offender shall benefit thereby;

 (d) anyone charged with an offence is presumed innocent until proven guilty according to law;

 (e) anyone charged with an offence shall have the right to be tried in his presence;

---

[*] *United Nations, General Assembly*, A/32/144, 15 August 1977.

(f) no one shall be compelled to testify against himself or to confess guilt.

3. A convicted person shall be advised on conviction of his judicial and other remedies and of the time-limits within which they may be exercised.

4. The death penalty shall not be pronounced on persons who were under the age or eighteen years at the time of the offence and shall not be carried out on pregnant women or mothers of young children.

5. At the end of hostilities, the authorities in power shall endeavour to grant the broadest possible amnesty to persons who have participated in the armed conflict, or those deprived of their liberty for reasons related to the armed conflict, whether they are interned or detained.

[...]

Convention on the Non-applicability of Statutory Limitations to War Crimes and Crimes against Humanity (1968)

Adopted by Resolution 2391 (XXIII) of the United Nations General Assembly on 26 November 1968[*]

Article 1

No statutory limitation shall apply to the following crimes, irrespective of the date of their commission:

(a) War crimes as they are defined in the Charter of the International Military Tribunal, Nuremberg, of 8 August 1945 and confirmed by resolutions 3 (I) of 13 February 1946 and 95 (I) of 11 December 1946 of the General Assembly of the United Nations, particularly the 'grave breaches' enumerated in the Geneva Conventions of 12 August 1949 for the protection of war victims;

(b) Crimes against humanity whether committed in time of war or in time of peace as they are defined in the Charter of the International Military Tribunal, Nuremberg, of 8 August 1945 and confirmed by resolutions 3 (I) of 13 February 1946 and 95 (I) of 11 December 1946 of the General Assembly of the United Nations, eviction by armed attack or occupation and inhuman acts resulting from the policy of apartheid and the crime of genocide as defined in the 1948 Convention on the Prevention and Punishment of the Crime of Genocide even if such acts do not constitute a violation of the domestic law of the country in which they were committed.

Article 2

If any of the crimes mentioned in Article 1 is committed, the provisions of this Convention shall apply to representatives of the State authority and private individuals who, as principals or accomplices, participate in or who directly incite others to the commission of any of those crimes, or who conspire to commit them, irrespective of the degree of completion, and to representatives of the State authority who tolerate their commission.

Article 3

The States Parties to the present Convention undertake to adopt all necessary domestic measures, legislative or otherwise, with a view to making possible the extradition in accordance with international law, of the persons referred to in Article 2 of this Convention.

Article 4

The States Parties to the present Convention undertake to adopt, in accordance with their respective constitutional processes, any legislative or other measures necessary to ensure that statutory or other limitations shall not apply to the prosecution and punishment of the crimes referred to in Articles 1 and 2 of this Convention and that, where they exist, such limitations shall be abolished.

Article 5

This Convention shall, until 31 December 1969, be open for signature by any State member of the United Nations or member of any of its specialized agencies or of the International Atomic Energy Agency, by any State Party to the Statute of the International Court of Justice, and by any other State which has been invited by the General Assembly of the United Nations to become a Party to this Convention.

---

[*] *International Legal Materials*, 1969, 68.

Article 6

This Convention is subject to ratification. Instruments of ratification shall be deposited with the Secretary-General of the United Nations.

Article 7

This Convention shall be open to accession by any State referred to in Article 5. Instruments of accession shall be deposited with the Secretary-General of the United Nations.

Article 8

1. This Convention shall enter into force on the ninetieth day after the date of the deposit with the Secretary-General of the United Nations of the tenth instrument of ratification or accession.

2. For each State ratifying this Convention or acceding to it after the deposit of the tenth instrument of ratification or accession, the Convention shall enter into force on the ninetieth day after the date of the deposit of its own instrument of ratification or accession.

Article 9

1. After the expiry of a period of ten years from the date on which this Convention enters into force, a request for the revision of the Convention may be made at any time by any Contracting Party by means of a notification in writing addressed to the Secretary-General of the United Nations.

2. The General Assembly of the United Nations shall decide upon the steps, if any, to be taken in respect of such a request.

Article 10

1. This Convention shall be deposited with the Secretary-General of the United Nations.

2. The Secretary-General of the United Nations shall transmit certified copies of this Convention to all States referred to in Article 5.

3. The Secretary-General of the United Nations shall inform all States referred to in Article 5 of the following particulars:

(a) Signatures of this Convention, and instruments of ratification and accession deposited under Articles 5, 6 and 7;

(b) The date of entry into force of this Convention in accordance with Article 8;

(c) Communications received under Article 9.

Article 11

This Convention, of which the Chinese, English, French, Russian and Spanish texts are equally authentic, shall bear the date of 26 November 1968.

In witness whereof the undersigned, being duly authorized for that purpose, have signed this Convention.

European Convention on the Non-applicability of Statutory Limitation to Crimes against Humanity and War Crimes (1974)*

Strasbourg, 25 January 1974

The member States of the Council of Europe, signatory hereto,

Considering the necessity to safeguard human dignity in time of war and in time of peace:

Considering that crimes against humanity and the most serious violations of the laws and customs of war constitute a serious infraction of human dignity;

Concerned in consequence to ensure that the punishment of those crimes is not prevented by statutory limitations whether in relation to prosecution or to the enforcement of the punishment;

Considering the essential interest in promoting a common criminal policy in the field, the aim of the Council of Europe being to achieve greater unity between her members,

Have agreed as follows:

Article 1

Each Contracting State undertakes to adopt any necessary measures to the secure statutory limitation shall not apply to the prosecution of the following offences, and to the enforcement of the sentences imposed for such offences, in so far as they are punishable under its domestic law:

1. the crimes against humanity specified in the Convention on the Prevention and Punishment of the Crime of Genocide adopted on 9 December 1948 by the General Assembly of the United Nations;

   (a) the violations specified in Article 50 of the 1949 Geneva Convention for the Amelioration of the Condition of the Wounded and sick in Armed Forces in the Field, Article 51 of the 1949 Geneva Convention for the Amelioration of the Condition of Wounded, Sick and Shipwrecked Members of Armed Forces at Sea, Article 130 of the 1949 Geneva Convention relative to the Treatment of Prisoners of War and Article 147 of the 1949 Geneva Convention relative to the Protection of Civilian Persons in Time of War,

   (b) any comparable violations of the laws of war having effect at the time when this Convention enters into force and of customs of war existing at that time, which are not already provided for in the above-mentioned provisions of the Geneva Conventions,

2. when the specific violation under consideration is of a particularly grave character by reason either of its factual and intentional elements or of the extent of its foreseeable consequences;

3. any other violation of a rule or custom of international law which may hereafter be established and which the Contracting State concerned considers according to a declaration under Article 6 as being of a comparable nature to those referred to in paragraph 1 or 2 of this Article.

---

* *European Treaty Series*, No.82.

Article 2

1. The present Convention applies to offences committed after its entry into force in respect of the Contracting State concerned.

2. It applies also to offences committed before such entry into force in those cases where the statutory limitation period had not expired at that time.

Article 3

1. This Convention shall be open to signature by the member States of the Council of Europe. It shall be subject to ratification or acceptance. Instruments of ratification or acceptance shall be deposited with the Secretary General of the Council of Europe.

2. The Convention shall enter into force three months after the date of deposit of the third instrument of ratification or acceptance.

3. In respect of a signatory State ratifying or accepting subsequently, the Convention shall come into force three months after the date of the deposit of its instrument of ratification or acceptance.

Article 4

1. After the entry into force of this Convention, the Committee of Ministers of the Council of Europe may invite any non-member State to accede thereto, provided that the resolution containing such invitation receives the unanimous agreement of the Members of the Council who have ratified the Convention.

2. Such accession shall be effected by depositing with the Secretary General of the Council of Europe an instrument of accession which shall take effect three months after the date of its deposit.

Article 5

1. Any State may, at the time of signature or when depositing its instrument of ratification, acceptance or accession, specify the territory or territories to which this Convention shall apply.

2. Any State may, when depositing its instrument of ratification, acceptance or accession or at any later date, by declaration addressed to the Secretary General of the Council of Europe, extend this Convention to any other territory or territories specified in the declaration and for whose international relations it is responsible or on whose behalf it is authorised to give undertakings.

3. Any declaration made in pursuance of the preceding paragraph may, in respect of any territory mentioned in such declaration, be withdrawn according to the procedure laid down in Article 7 of this Convention.

Article 6

1. Any Contracting State may, at any time, by declaration addressed to the Secretary General of the Council of Europe, extend this Convention to any violations provided for in Article 1, paragraph 3 of this Convention.

2. Any declaration made in pursuance of the preceding paragraph may be withdrawn according to the procedure laid down in Article 7 of this Convention.

Article 7

1. This Convention shall remain in force indefinitely.

2. Any Contracting State may, insofar as it is concerned, denounce this Convention by means of a notification addressed to the Secretary General of the Council of Europe.

3. Such denunciation shall take effect six months after the date of receipt by the Secretary General of such notification.

Article 8

The Secretary General of the Council of Europe shall notify the member States of the Council and any State which has acceded to this Convention of:

(a) any signature;

(b) any deposit of an instrument of ratification, acceptance or accession;

(c) any date of entry into force of this Convention in accordance with Article 3 thereof;

(d) any declaration received in pursuance of the provisions of Article 5 or Article 6;

(e) any notification received in pursuance of the provisions of Article 7 and the date on which the denunciation takes effect.

In witness whereof the undersigned, being duly authorised thereto, have signed this Convention.

1.2. Crimes against Humanity

Convention on the Prevention and Suppression of the Crime of Genocide (1948)[*]

Paris, 9 December 1948

Article 1

The Contracting Parties confirm that genocide, whether committed in time of peace or in time of war, is a crime under international law which they undertake to prevent and to punish.

Article 2

In the present Convention, genocide means any of the following acts committed with intent to destroy, in whole or in part, a national, ethnical, racial, or religious group, as such:

(a) Killing members of the group;

(b) Causing serious bodily or mental harm to members of the group;

(c) Deliberately inflicting on the group, conditions of life calculated to bring about its physical destruction in whole or in part;

(d) Imposing measures intended to prevent births within the group;

(e) Forcibly transferring children of the group to another group.

Article 3

The following acts shall be punishable:

(a) Genocide;

(b) Conspiracy to commit genocide;

(c) Direct and public incitement to commit genocide;

(d) Attempt to commit genocide;

(e) Complicity in genocide.

Article 4

Persons committing genocide or any of the other acts enumerated in article III shall be punished, whether they are constitutionally responsible rulers, public officials, or private individuals.

Article 5

The Contracting Parties undertake to enact, in accordance with their respective Constitutions, the necessary legislation to give effect to the provisions of the present Convention and, in particular, to provide effective penalties for persons guilty of genocide or of any of the other acts enumerated in article III.

---

[*] *United Nations Treaty Series*, vol.78, 277.

Article 6

Persons charges with genocide or any of the other acts enumerated in article III shall be tried by a competent tribunal of the State in the territory of which the act was committed, or by such international penal tribunal as may have jurisdiction with respect to those Contracting Parties which shall have accepted its jurisdiction.

Article 7

Genocide and the other acts enumerated in article III shall not be considered as political crimes for the purpose of extradition.

The Contracting Parties pledge themselves in such cases to grant extradition in accordance with their laws and treaties in force.

Article 8

Any Contracting Party may call upon the competent organs of the United Nations to take such action under the Charter of the United Nations as they consider appropriate for the prevention and suppression of acts of genocide or any of the other acts enumerated in article III.

Article 9

Disputes between the Contracting Parties relating to the interpretation, application, or fulfilment of the present Convention, including those relating to the responsibility of a State for genocide or for any of the other acts enumerated in article III, shall be submitted to the International Court of Justice at the request of any of the parties to the dispute.

International Convention on the Suppression and Punishment of the Crime of Apartheid (excerpts) (1973)[*]

Adopted and opened for signature and ratification by General Assembly resolution 3068 (XXVIII) of 30 November 1973

Article 1

1. The States Parties to the present Convention declare that *apartheid* is a crime against humanity and that inhuman acts resulting from the policies and practices of apartheid and similar policies and practices of racial segregation and discrimination, as defined in article II of the Convention, are crimes violating the principles of international law, in particular the purposes and principles of the Charter of the United Nations, and constituting a serious threat to international peace and security.

2. The States Parties to the present Convention declare criminal those organizations, institutions and individuals committing the crime of *apartheid*.

Article 2

For the purpose of the present Convention, the term "the crime of apartheid", which shall include similar policies and practices of racial segregation and discrimination as practised in southern Africa, shall apply to the following inhuman acts committed for the purpose of establishing and maintaining domination by one racial group of persons over any other racial group of persons and systematically oppressing them:

(a) Denial to a member or members of a racial group or groups of the right to life and liberty of person:

  (i) By murder of members of a racial group or groups;

  (ii) By the infliction upon the members of a racial group or groups of serious bodily or mental harm, by the infringement of their freedom or dignity, or by subjecting them to torture or to cruel, inhuman or degrading treatment or punishment;

  (iii) By arbitrary arrest and illegal imprisonment of the members of a racial group or groups;

(b) Deliberate imposition on racial group or groups of living conditions calculated to cause its or their physical destruction in whole or in part;

(c) Any legislative measures and other measures calculated to prevent a racial group or groups from participation in the political, social, economic and cultural life of the country and the deliberate creation of conditions preventing the full development of such a group or groups, in particular by denying to members of a racial group or groups basic human rights and freedoms, including the right to work, the right to form recognized trade unions, the right to education, the right to leave and to return to their country, the right to a nationality, the right to freedom of movement and residence, the right to freedom of opinion and expression, and the right to freedom of peaceful assembly and association:

(d) Any measures, including legislative measures, designed to divide the population along racial lines by the creation of separate reserves and ghettos for the members of a racial group or groups, the prohibition of mixed marriages among

---

[*] *International Legal Materials*, 1974, 50.

members of various racial groups, the expropriation of landed property belonging to a racial group or groups or to members thereof;

(e) Exploitation of the labour of the members of a racial group or groups, in particular by submitting them to forced labour;

(f) Persecution of organizations and persons, by depriving them of fundamental rights and freedoms, because they oppose *apartheid*.

Article 3

International criminal responsibility shall apply, irrespective of the motive involved, to individuals, members of organizations and institutions and representatives of the State, whether residing in the territory of the State in which the acts are perpetrated or in some other State, whenever they:

(a) Commit, participate in, directly incite or conspire in the commission of the acts mentioned in article II of the present Convention:

(b) Directly abet, encourage or co-operate in the commission of the crime of *apartheid*.

[...]

1.3. Terrorism

Convention for the Suppression of Unlawful Seizure of Aircraft (1970)[*]

The Hague, 16 December 1970

Article 1

Any person who on board an aircraft in flight:

(a) unlawfully, by force or threat thereof, or by any other form of intimidation, seizes, or exercises control of, that aircraft, or attempts to perform any such act, or

(b) is an accomplice of a person who performs or attempts to perform any such act commits an offense (hereinafter referred to as "the offense").

Article 2

Each Contracting State undertakes to make the offense punishable by severe penalties.

Article 3

1. For the purposes of this Convention, an aircraft is considered to be in flight at any time from the moment when all its external doors are closed following embarkation until the moment when any such door is opened for disembarkation. In the case of a forced landing, the flight shall be deemed to continue until the competent authorities take over the responsibility for the aircraft and for persons and property on board.

2. This Convention shall not apply to aircraft used in military, customs or police services.

3. This Convention shall apply only if the place of take-off or the place of actual landing of the aircraft on board which the offense is committed is situated outside the territory of the State of registration of that aircraft; it shall be immaterial whether the aircraft is engaged in an international or domestic flight.

4. In the cases mentioned in Article 5, this Convention shall not apply if the place of take-off and the place of actual landing of the aircraft on board which the offense is committed are situated within the territory of the same State where that State is one of those referred to in that Article.

5. Notwithstanding paragraphs 3 and 4 of this Article, Articles 6, 7, 8 and 10 shall apply whatever the place of take-off or the place of actual landing of the aircraft, if the offender or the alleged offender is found in the territory of a State other than the State of registration of that aircraft.

Article 4

1. Each Contracting State shall take such measures as may be necessary to establish its jurisdiction over the offense and any other act of violence against passengers or crew committed by the alleged offender in connection with the offense, in the following cases:

(a) when the offense is committed on board an aircraft registered in that State;

(b) when the aircraft on board which the offense is committed lands in its territory with the alleged offender still on board;

---

[*] *International Legal Materials*, 1971, 133.

(c) when the offense is committed on board an aircraft leased without crew to a lessee who has his principal place of business or, if the lessee has no such place of business, his permanent residence, in that State.

2. Each Contracting State shall likewise take such measures as may be necessary to establish its jurisdiction over the offense in the case where the alleged offender is present in its territory and it does not extradite him pursuant to Article 8 to any of the States mentioned in paragraph 1 of this Article.

3. This Convention does not exclude any criminal jurisdiction exercised in accordance with national law.

Article 5

The Contracting States which establish joint air transport operating organizations or international operating agencies, which operate aircraft which are subject to joint or international registration shall, by appropriate means, designate for each aircraft the State among them which shall exercise the jurisdiction and have the attributes of the State of registration for the purpose of this Convention and shall give notice thereof to the International Civil Aviation Organization which shall communicate the notice to all States Parties to this Convention.

Article 6

1. Upon being satisfied that the circumstances so warrant, any Contracting State in the territory of which the offender or the alleged offender is present, shall take him into custody or take other measures to ensure his presence. The custody and other measures shall be as provided in the law of the State but may only be continued for such time as is necessary to enable any criminal or extradition proceedings to be instituted.

2. Such State shall immediately make a preliminary inquiry into the facts.

3. Any person in custody pursuant to paragraph 1 of this Article shall be assisted in communicating immediately with the nearest appropriate representative of the State of which he is a national.

4. When a State, pursuant to this Article, has taken a person into custody, it shall immediately notify the State of registration of the aircraft, the State mentioned in Article 4, paragraph 1 (c), the State of nationality of the detained person and, if it considers it advisable, any other interested States of the fact that such person is in custody and of the circumstances which warrant his detention. The State which makes the preliminary inquiry contemplated in paragraph 2 of this Article shall promptly report its findings to the said States and shall indicate whether it intends to exercise jurisdiction.

Article 7

The Contracting State in the territory of which the alleges offender is found shall, if it does not extradite him, be obliged, without exception whatsoever and whether or not the offense was committed in its territory, to submit the case to its competent authorities for the purpose of prosecution. Those authorities shall take their decision in the same manner as in the case of any ordinary offense of a serious nature under the law of that State.

Article 8

1. The offense shall be deemed to be included as an extraditable offense in any extradition treaty existing between Contracting States. Contracting States undertake to include the offense as an extraditable offense in every extradition treaty to be concluded between them.

2. If a Contracting State which makes extradition conditional on the existence of a treaty receives a request for extradition from another Contracting State with which it has no extradition treaty, it may at its option consider this Convention as the legal basis for extradition in respect of the offense. Extradition shall be subject to the other conditions provided by the law of the requested State.

3. Contracting States which do not make extradition conditional on the existence of a treaty shall recognize the offense as an extraditable offense between themselves subject to the conditions provided by the law of the requested State.

4. The offense shall be treated, for the purpose of extradition between Contracting States, as if it had been committed not only in the place in which it occurred but also in the territories of the States required to establish their jurisdiction in accordance with Article 4, paragraph 1.

Article 9

1. When any of the acts mentioned in Article 1 (a) has occurred or is about to occur, Contracting States shall take all appropriate measures to restore control of the aircraft to its lawful commander or to preserve his control of the aircraft.

2. In the cases contemplated by the preceding paragraph, any Contracting State in which the aircraft or its passengers or crew are present shall facilitate the continuation of the journey of the passengers and crew as soon as practicable, and shall without delay return the aircraft and its cargo to the persons lawfully entitled to possession.

Article 10

1. Contracting States shall afford one another the greatest measure of assistance in connection with criminal proceedings brought in respect of the offense and other acts mentioned in Article 4. The law of the State requested shall apply in all cases.

2. The provisions of paragraph 1 of this Article shall not affect obligations under any other treaty, bilateral of multilateral, which governs or will govern, in whole or in part, mutual assistance in criminal matters.

Article 11

Each Contracting State shall in accordance with its national law report to the Council of the International Civil Aviation Organization as promptly as possible any relevant information in its possession concerning:

(a) the circumstances of the offense;

(b) the action taken pursuant to Article 9;

(c) the measures taken in relation to the offender or the alleged offender, and, in particular, the results of any extradition proceedings or other legal proceedings.

Article 12

1. Any dispute between two or more Contracting States concerning the interpretation or application of this Convention which cannot be settled through negotiation, shall, at the request of one of them, be submitted to arbitration. If within six months from the date of the request for arbitration the Parties are unable to agree on the organization of the arbitration, any one of those Parties may refer the dispute to the International Court of Justice by request in conformity with the Statute of the Court.

2. Each State may at the time of signature or ratification of this Convention or accession thereto, declare that it does not consider itself bound by the preceding paragraph. The other Contracting States shall not be bound by the preceding paragraph with respect to any Contracting State having made such a reservation.

3. Any Contracting State having made a reservation in accordance with the preceding paragraph may at any time withdraw this reservation by notification to the Depositary Governments.

Article 13

1. This Convention shall be open for signature at The Hague on December 16, 1970, by States participating in the International Conference on Air Law held at The Hague from December 1 to 16, 1970 (hereinafter referred to as The Hague Conference). After December 31, 1970, the Convention shall be open to all States for signature in Moscow, London and Washington. Any State which does not sign this Convention before its entry into force in accordance with paragraph 3 of this Article may accede to it at any time.

2. This Convention shall be subject to ratification by the signatory States. Instruments of ratification and instruments of accession shall be deposited with the Governments of the Union of Soviet Socialist Republics, the United Kingdom of Great Britain and Northern Ireland, and the United States of America, which are hereby designated the Depositary Governments.

3. This Convention shall enter into force thirty days following the date of the deposit of instruments of ratification by ten States signatory to this Convention which participated in The Hague Conference.

4. For other States, this Convention shall enter into force on the date of entry into force of this Convention in accordance with paragraph 3 of this Article, or thirty days following the date of deposit of their instruments of ratification or accession, whichever is later.

5. The Depository Governments shall promptly inform all signatory and acceding States of the date of each signature, the date of deposit of each instrument of ratification or accession, the date of entry into force of this Convention, and other notices.

6. As soon as this Convention comes into force, it shall be registered by the Depositary Governments pursuant to Article 102 of the Charter of the United Nations and pursuant to Article 83 of the Convention on International Civil Aviation (Chicago, 1944).

Article 14

1. Any Contracting State may denounce this Convention by written notification to the Depository Governments.

2. Denunciation shall take effect six months following the date on which notification is received by the Depositary Governments.

Convention for the Suppression of Unlawful Acts against the Safety of Civil Aviation (excerpts) (1971)[*]

Montreal, 23 September 1971

Article 1

1. Any person commits an offence if he unlawfully and intentionally:

    (a) performs an act of violence against a person on board an aircraft in flight if that act is likely to endanger the safety of that aircraft; or

    (b) destroys an aircraft in service or causes damage to such an aircraft which renders it incapable of flight or which is likely to endanger its safety in flight; or

    (c) places or causes to be placed on an aircraft in service, by any means whatsoever, a device or substance which is likely to destroy that aircraft, or to cause damage to it which renders it incapable of flight, or to cause damage to it which is likely to endanger its safety in flight; or

    (d) destroys or damages air navigation facilities or interferes with their operation, if any such act if likely to endanger the safety of aircraft in flight; or

    (e) communicates information which he knows to be false, thereby endangering the safety of an aircraft in flight.

2. Any person also commits an offence if he:

    (a) attempts to commit any of the offences mentioned in paragraph 1 of this article; or

    (b) is an accomplice of a person who commits or attempts to commit any such offence.

[...]

---

[*] *International Legal Materials*, 1971, 1151.

International Convention against the Taking of Hostages (excerpts) (1979)[*]

New York, 17 December 1979

Article 1

1. Any person who seizes or detains and threatens to kill, to injure or to continue to detain another person (hereinafter referred to as the "hostage") in order to compel a third party, namely, a State, an international intergovernmental organization, a natural or juridical person, or a group of persons, to do or abstain from doing any act as an explicit or implicit condition for the release of the hostage commits the offence of taking of hostages ("hostage-taking") within the meaning of this Convention.

2. Any person who:

   (a) Attempts to commit an act of hostage-taking; or

   (b) Participates as an accomplice of anyone who commits or attempts to commit an act of hostage-taking;

   likewise commits an offence for the purpose of this Convention.

[...]

---

[*] *International Legal Materials*, 1979, 1456.

Convention on the Prevention and Punishment of Crimes against Internationally Protected Persons including Diplomatic Agents (excerpts) (1973)[*]

New York, 14 December 1973

Article 2

1. The intentional commission of:

    (a) a murder, kidnapping or other attack upon the person or liberty of an internationally protected person;

    (b) a violent attack upon the official premises, the private accommodation or the means of transport of an internationally protected person likely to endanger his person or liberty; and

    (c) a threat to commit any such attack;

    (d) an attempt to commit any such attack;

    (e) an act constituting participation as an accomplice in any such attack;

    shall be made by each State Party a crime under its internal law.

2. Each State Party shall make these crimes punishable by appropriate penalties which take into account their grave nature.

3. Paragraphs 1 and 2 of this article in no way derogate from the obligations of States Parties under international law to take all appropriate measures to prevent other attacks on the person, freedom or dignity of an internationally protected person.

[...]

---

[*] *International Legal Materials*, 1974, 41.

Convention for the Suppression of Unlawful Acts against the Safety of Maritime Navigation (excerpts) (1988)[*]

Rome, 10 March 1988

Article 3

1. Any person commits an offence if that person unlawfully and intentionally:

    (a) seizes or exercises control over a ship by force or threat thereof or any other form of intimidation; or

    (b) performs an act of violence against a person on board a ship if that act is likely to endanger the safe navigation of that ship; or

    (c) destroys a ship or causes damage to a ship or to its cargo which is likely to endanger the safe navigation of that ship; or

    (d) places or causes to be placed on a ship, by any means whatsoever, a device or substance which is likely to destroy that ship, or cause damage to that ship or its cargo which endangers or is likely to endanger the safe navigation of that ship; or

    (e) destroys or seriously damages maritime navigational facilities or seriously interferes with their operation, if any such act is likely to endanger the safe navigation of a ship; or

    (f) communicates information which he knows to be false, thereby endangering the safe navigation of a ship; or

    (g) injures or kills any person, in connection with the commission or the attempted commission of any of the offences set forth in subparagraphs (a) to (f).

2. Any person also commits an offence if that person:

    (a) attempts to commit any of the offences set forth in paragraph 1; or

    (b) abets the commission of any of the offences set forth in paragraph 1 perpetrated by any person or is otherwise an accomplice of a person who commits such an offence; or

    (c) threatens with or without a condition, as is provided for under national law, aimed at compelling a physical or juridical person to do or refrain from doing any act, to commit any of the offences set forth in paragraph 1, subparagraphs (b), (c) and (e), if that threat is likely to endanger the safe navigation of the ship in question.

[...]

---

[*] *International Legal Materials*, 1988, 668.

1.4. Physical Protection of Nuclear Material

Convention on the Physical Protection of Nuclear Material[*]

Vienna and New York, 3 March 1980

Article 1

For the purpose of this Convention:

(a) "Nuclear material" means plutonium except that with isotopic concentration exceeding 80% in plutonium-238; uranium-233; uranium enriched in the isotope 235 or 233; uranium containing the mixture of isotopes as occurring in nature other than in the form of ore or ore-residue; any material containing one or more of the foregoing;

(b) "Uranium enriched in the isotope 235 or 233" means uranium containing the isotope 235 or 233 or both in an amount such that the abundance ratio of the sum of these isotopes to the isotope 238 is greater than the ratio of the isotope 235 tot the isotope 238 occurring in nature;

(c) "International nuclear transport" means the carriage of a consignment of nuclear material by any means of transportation intended to go beyond the territory of the State where the shipment originates beginning with the departure from a facility of the shipper in that State and ending with the arrival at a facility of the receiver within the State of ultimate destination

Article 2

1. This Convention shall apply to nuclear material used for peaceful purposes while in international nuclear transport.

2. With the exception of articles 3 and 4 and paragraph 3 of article 5, this Convention shall also apply to nuclear material used for peaceful purposes while in domestic use, storage and transport.

3. Apart from the commitments expressly undertaken by States Parties in the articles covered by paragraph 2 with respect to nuclear material used for peaceful purposes while in domestic use, storage and transport, nothing in this Convention shall be interpreted as affecting the sovereign rights of a State regarding the domestic use, storage and transport of such nuclear material.

Article 3

Each State Party shall take appropriate steps within the framework of its national law and consistent with international law to ensure as far as practicable that, during international nuclear transport, nuclear material within its territory, or on board a ship or aircraft under its jurisdiction insofar as such ship or aircraft is engaged in the transport to or from that State, is protected at the levels described in Annex 1.

Article 4

1. Each State Party shall not export or authorize the export of nuclear material unless the State Party has received assurances that such material will be protected during the international nuclear transport at the levels described in Annex I.

---

[*] *Selected Multilateral Treaties in the Field of the Environment*, RUMMEL-BULSKA, I. and OSAFO, S. (ed.), Volume II, Cambridge, Grotius Publications Limited, 1991, 75.

2. Each State Party shall not import or authorize the import of nuclear material from a State not party to this Convention unless the State Party has received assurances that such material will during the international nuclear transport be protected at the levels described in Annex 1.

3. A State Party shall not allow the transit of its territory by land or internal waterways or through its airports or seaports of nuclear material between States that are not parties to this Convention unless the State Party has received assurances as far as practicable that this nuclear material will be protected during international nuclear transport at the levels described in Annex I.

4. Each State Party shall apply within the framework of its national law the levels of physical protection described in Annex I to nuclear material being transported from a part of that State to another part of the same State through international waters or airspace.

5. The State Party responsible for receiving assurances that the nuclear material will be protected at the levels described in Annex I according tot paragraphs 1 to 3 shall identify and inform in advance States which the nuclear material is expected to transit by land or internal waterways, or whose airports or seaports it is expected to enter.

6. The responsibility for obtaining assurances referred to in paragraph 1 may be transferred, by mutual agreement, to the State Party involved in the transport as the importing State.

7. Nothing in this article shall be interpreted as in any way affecting the territorial sovereignty and jurisdiction of a State, including that over its airspace and territorial sea.

Article 5

1. States Parties shall identify and make known to each other directly or through the International Atomic Energy Agency their central authority and point of contact having responsibility for physical protection of nuclear material and for co-ordinating recovery and response operations in the event of any unauthorized removal, use or alteration of nuclear material or in the event of credible threat thereof.

2. In the case of theft, robbery of any other unlawful taking of nuclear material or of credible threat thereof, States Parties shall, in accordance with their national law, provide co-operation and assistance to the maximum feasible extent in the recovery and protection of such material to any State that so requests. In particular:

    (a) A State Party shall take appropriate steps to inform as soon as possible other States, which appear to it to be concerned, of any theft, robbery or other unlawful taking of nuclear material or credible threat thereof and to inform, where appropriate, international organizations;

    (b) As appropriate, the States Parties concerned shall exchange information with each other or international organizations with a view tot protecting threatened nuclear material, verifying the integrity of the shipping container, or recovering unlawfully taken nuclear material and shall:
    (i) co-ordinate their efforts through diplomatic and other agreed channels;
    (ii) render assistance, if requested;
    (iii) ensure the return of nuclear material stolen or missing as a consequence of the above-mentioned events.

The means of implementation of this co-operation shall be determined by the States Parties concerned.

3. States Parties shall co-operate and consult as appropriate, with each other directly or through international organizations, with a view to obtaining guidance on the design, maintenance and improvement of systems of physical protection of nuclear material in international transport.

Article 6

1. States Parties shall take appropriate measures consistent with their national law to protect the confidentiality of any information which they receive in confidence by virtue of the provisions of this Convention from another State Party of through participation in an activity carried out for the implementation of this Convention. If States Parties provide information to international organizations in confidence, steps shall be taken to ensure that the confidentiality of such information is protected.

2. States Parties shall not be required by this Convention to provide any information which they are not permitted to communicate pursuant to national law or which would jeopardize the security of the State concerned or the physical protection of nuclear material.

Article 7

1. The intentional commission of:

    (a) an act without lawful authority which constitutes the receipt, possession, use, transfer, alteration, disposal or dispersal of nuclear material and which causes or is likely to cause death or serious injury to any person or substantial damage to property;

    (b) a theft or robbery of nuclear material;

    (c) an embezzlement or fraudulent obtaining of nuclear material;

    (d) an act constituting a demand for nuclear material by threat or use of force or by any other form of intimidation;

    (e) a threat:
    (i) to use nuclear material to cause death or serious injury to any person or substantial property damage, or
    (ii) to commit an offence described in subparagraph (b) in order to compel a natural or legal person, international organization or State to do or to refrain from doing any act;

    (f) an attempt to commit any offence described in paragraphs (a), (b) or (c); and

    (g) an act which constitutes participation in any offence described in paragraphs (a) to (f)

    shall be made a punishable offence by each State Party under its national law.

2. Each State Party shall make the offences described in this article punishable by appropriate penalties which take into account their grave nature.

Article 8

1. Each State Party shall take such measures as may be necessary to establish its jurisdiction over the offences set fort in Article 7 in the following cases:

    (a) when the offence is committed in the territory of that State or on board a ship or aircraft registered in that State;

    (b) when the alleged offender is a national of that State.

2. Each State Party shall likewise take such measures as may be necessary to establish its jurisdiction over these offences in cases where the alleged offender is present in its territory and it does not extradite him pursuant to Article 11 to any of the States mentioned in paragraph 1.

3. This Convention does not exclude any criminal jurisdiction exercised in accordance with national law.

4. In addition to the States Parties mentioned in paragraphs 1 and 2, each State Party may, consistent with international law, establish its jurisdiction over the offences set fort in Article 7 when it is involved in international nuclear transport as the exporting or importing State.

Article 9

Upon being satisfied that the circumstances so warrant, the State Party in whose territory the alleged offender is present shall take appropriate measures, including detention, under its national law to ensure his presence for the purpose of prosecution or extradition. Measures taken according to this article to establish jurisdiction pursuant to Article 8 and, where appropriate, all other States concerned.

Article 10

The State Party in whose territory the alleged offender is present shall, if it does not extradite him, submit, without exception whatsoever and without undue delay, the case to its competent authorities for the purpose of prosecution, through proceedings in accordance with the laws of that State.

Article 11

1. The offences in Article 7 shall be deemed to be included as extraditable offences in any extradition treaty existing between States Parties. States Parties undertake to include those offences as extraditable offences in every future extradition treaty to be concluded between them.

2. If a State Party which makes extradition conditional on the existence of a treaty receives a request for extradition from another State Party with which it has no extradition treaty, it may at its option consider this Convention as the legal basis for extradition in respect of those offences. Extradition shall be subject to the other conditions provided by the law of the requested State.

3. States Parties which do not make extradition conditional on the existence of a treaty shall recognize those offences as extraditable offences between themselves subject to the conditions provided by the law of the requested State.

4. Each of the offences shall be treated, for the purpose of extradition between States Parties, as if it had been committed not only in the place in which it occurred but also in the territories of the States Parties required to establish their jurisdiction in accordance with paragraph 1 of Article 8.

Article 12

Any person regarding whom proceedings are being carried out in connection with any of the offences set fort in Article 7 shall be guaranteed fair treatment at all stages of the proceedings.

Article 13

1. States Parties shall afford one another the greatest measure of assistance in connection with criminal proceedings brought in respect of the offences set forth in Article 7, including the supply of evidence at their disposal necessary for the proceedings. The law of the State requested shall apply in all cases.

2. The provisions of paragraph 1 shall not affect obligations under any other treaty, bilateral of multilateral, which governs or will govern, in whole or in part, mutual assistance in criminal matters.

Article 14

1. Each State Party shall inform the depositary of its laws and regulations which give effect to this Convention. The depositary shall communicate such information periodically to all States Parties.

2. The State Party where an alleged offender is prosecuted shall, wherever practicable, first communicate the final outcome of the proceedings to the States directly concerned. The State Party shall also communicate the final outcome to the depositary who shall inform all States.

3. Where an offence involves nuclear material used for peaceful purposes in domestic use, storage or transport, and both the alleged offender and the nuclear material remain in the territory of the State Party in which the offence was committed, nothing in this Convention shall be interpreted as requiring that State Party to provide information concerning criminal proceedings arising out of such an offence.

Article 15

The Annexes constitute an integral part of this Convention.

Article 16

1. A conference of States Parties shall be convened by the depositary five years after the entry into force of this Convention to review the implementation of the Convention and its adequacy as concerns the preamble, the whole of the operative part and the annexes in the light of the then prevailing situation.

2. At intervals of not less than five years thereafter, the majority of States Parties may obtain, by submitting a proposal to this effect to the depositary, the convening of further conferences with the same objective.

Article 17

1. In the event of a dispute between two or more States Parties concerning the interpretation or application of this Convention, such States Parties shall consult with a view to the settlement of the dispute by negotiation, or by any other peaceful means of settling disputes acceptable to all parties to the dispute.

2. Any dispute of this character which cannot be settled in the manner prescribed in paragraph 1 shall, at the request of any party to such dispute, be submitted to arbitration or referred to the International Court of Justice for decision. Where a dispute is submitted to arbitration, if, within six months from the date of the request, the parties to the dispute are unable to agree on the organization of the arbitration, a party may request the President of the International Court of Justice or the Secretary-General of the United Nations to appoint one or more arbitrators. In case of conflicting requests by the parties to the dispute, the request to the Secretary-General of the United Nations shall have priority.

3. Each State Party may at the time of signature, ratification, acceptance or approval of this Convention or accession thereto declare that it does not consider itself bound by either or both of the dispute settlement procedures provided for in paragraph 2. The other States Parties shall not be bound by a dispute settlement procedure provided for in paragraph 2, with respect to a State Party which has made a reservation to that procedure.

4. Any State Party which has made a reservation in accordance with paragraph 3 may at any time withdraw that reservation by notification to the depositary.

Article 18

1. This Convention shall be open for signature by all States at the Headquarters of the International Atomic Energy Agency in Vienna and at the Headquarters of the United Nations in New York from 3 March 1980 until its entry into force.

2. This Convention is subject to ratification, acceptance or approval by the signatory States.

3. After its entry into force, this Convention will be open for accession by all States.

4. (a) This Convention shall be open for signature or accession by international organizations and regional organizations of an integration or other nature, provided that any such organization is constituted by sovereign States and has competence in respect of the negotiation, conclusion and application of international agreements in matters covered by this Convention.

(b) In matters within their competence, such organizations shall, on their own behalf, exercise the rights and fulfil the responsibilities which this Convention attributes to States Parties.

(c) When becoming party to this Convention such an organization shall communicate to the depositary a declaration indicating which States are members thereof and which Articles of this Convention do not apply to it.

(d) Such an organization shall not hold any vote additional to those of its Member States.

5. Instruments or ratification, acceptance, approval or accession shall be deposited with the depositary.

Article 19

1. This Convention shall enter into force on the thirtieth day following the date of deposit of the twenty-first instrument of ratification, acceptance or approval with the depositary.

2. For each State ratifying, accepting, approving or acceding to the Convention after the date of deposit of the twenty-first instrument of ratification, acceptance or approval, the Convention shall enter into force on the thirtieth day after the deposit by such State of its instrument of ratification, acceptance, approval or accession.

Article 20

1. Without prejudice to Article 16 a State Party may propose amendments to this Convention. The proposed amendment shall be submitted to the depositary who shall circulate it immediately to all States Parties. If a majority of States Parties request the depositary to convene a conference to consider the proposed amendments, the depositary shall invite all States Parties to attend such a conference to begin not sooner than thirty days after the invitations are issued. Any amendment adopted at the conference by a two-thirds majority of all States Parties shall be promptly circulated by the depositary to all States Parties.

2. The amendment shall enter into force for each State Party that deposits its instrument of ratification, acceptance or approval of the amendment on the thirtieth day after the date on which two thirds of the States Parties have deposited their instruments of ratification, acceptance or approval with the depositary. Thereafter, the amendment shall enter into force for any other State Party on the day on which that State Party deposits its instrument of ratification, acceptance or approval of the amendment.

Article 21

1. Any State Party may denounce this Convention by written notification to the depositary.

2. Denunciation shall take effect one hundred and eighty days following the date on which notification is received by the depositary.

Article 22

The depositary shall promptly notify, all State of:

(a) each signature of this Convention;

(b) each deposit of an instrument or ratification, acceptance, approval or accession;

(c) any reservation or withdrawal in accordance with Article 17;

(d) any communication made by an organization in accordance with paragraph 4(c) of Article 18;

(e) the entry into force of this Convention;

(f) the entry into force of any amendment to this Convention; and

(g) any denunciation made under Article 21.

Article 23

The original of this Convention, of which the Arabic. Chinese, English, French, Russian and Spanish texts are equally authentic, shall be deposited wit the Director General of the International Atomic Energy Agency who shall send certified copies thereof to all States.

In witness whereof, the undersigned, being duly authorized, have signed this Convention, opened for signature at Vienna and at New York on 3 March 1980.

1.5. Torture

Convention against Torture and Other Cruel, Inhuman or Degrading Treatment or Punishment (1984)*

New York, 10 December 1984

Part I

Article 1

1. For the purposes of this Convention, "torture" means any act by which severe pain or suffering, whether physical or mental, is intentionally inflicted on a person for such purposes as obtaining from him or a third person information or a confession, punishing him for an act he or a third person has committed or is suspected of having committed, or intimidating or coercing him or a third person, or for any reason based on discrimination of any kind, when such pain or suffering is inflicted by or at the instigation of or with the consent or acquiescence of a public official or other person acting in an official capacity. It does not include pain or suffering arising only from, inherent in, or incidental to lawful sanctions.

2. This article is without prejudice to any international instrument or national legislation which does or may contain provisions of wider application.

Article 2

1. Each State Party shall take effective legislative, administrative, judicial or other measures to prevent acts of torture in any territory under its jurisdiction.

2. No exceptional circumstances whatsoever, whether a state of war or a threat of war, internal political instability or any other public emergency, may be invoked as a justification of torture.

3. An order from a superior officer or a public authority may not be invoked as a justification of torture.

Article 3

1. No State Party shall expel, return ("*refouler*") or extradite a person to another State where there are substantial grounds for believing that he would be in danger of being subjected to torture.

2. For the purpose of determining whether there are such grounds, the competent authorities shall take into account all relevant considerations including, where applicable, the existence in the State concerned of a consistent pattern of gross, flagrant or mass violations of human rights.

Article 4

1. Each State Party shall ensure that all acts of torture are offences under its criminal law. The same shall apply to an attempt to commit torture and to an act by any person which constitutes complicity or participation in torture.

2. Each State Party shall make these offences punishable by appropriate penalties which take into account their grave nature.

---

* *International Legal Materials*, 1984, 1027 with changes in *International Legal Materials*, 1985, 535.

Article 5

1. Each State Party shall take such measures as may be necessary to establish its jurisdiction over the offences referred to in article 4 in the following cases:

    (a) When the offences are committed in any territory under its jurisdiction or on board a ship or aircraft registered in that State;

    (b) when the alleged offender is a national of that State;

    (c) When the victim is a national of that State if that State considers it appropriate.

2. Each State Party shall likewise take such measures as may be necessary to establish its jurisdiction over such offences in cases where the alleged offender is present in any territory under its jurisdiction and it does not extradite him pursuant to article 8 to any of the States mentioned in paragraph 1 of this article.

3. This Convention does not exclude any criminal jurisdiction exercised in accordance with internal law.

Article 6

1. Upon being satisfied, after an examination of information available to it, that the circumstances so warrant, any State Party in whose territory a person alleged to have committed any offence referred to in article 4 is present, shall take him into custody or take other legal measures to ensure his presence. The custody and other legal measures shall be as provided in the law of that State but may be continued only for such time as is necessary to enable any criminal or extradition proceedings to be instituted.

2. Such State shall immediately make a preliminary inquiry into the facts.

3. Any person in custody pursuant to paragraph 1 of this article shall be assisted in communicating immediately with the nearest appropriate representative of the State of which he is a national, or, if he is a stateless person, to the representative of the State where he is usually resides.

4. When a State, pursuant to this article, has taken a person into custody, it shall immediately notify the States referred to in article 5, paragraph 1, of the fact that such person is in custody and of the circumstances which warrant his detention. The State which makes the preliminary inquiry contemplated in paragraph 2 of this article shall promptly report its findings to the said States and shall indicate whether it intends to exercise jurisdiction.

Article 7

1. The State Party in territory under whose jurisdiction a person alleged to have committed any offence referred to in article 4 is found, shall in the cases contemplated in article 5, if it does not extradite him, submit the case to its competent authorities for the purpose of prosecution.

2. These authorities shall take their decision in the same manner as in the case of any ordinary offence of a serious nature under the law of that State. In the cases referred to in article 5, paragraph 2, the standards of evidence required for prosecution and conviction shall in no way be less stringent than those which apply in the cases referred to in article 5, paragraph 1.

3. Any person regarding whom proceedings are brought in connection with any of the offences referred to in article 4 shall be guaranteed fair treatment at all stages of the proceedings.

Article 8

1. The offences referred to in article 4 shall be deemed to be included as extraditable offences in any extradition treaty existing between States Parties. States Parties undertake to

include such offences as extraditable offences in every extradition treaty to be concluded between them.

2.   If a State Party which makes extradition conditional on the existence of a treaty receives a request for extradition from another State Party with which it has no extradition treaty, it may consider this Convention as the legal basis for extradition in respect of such offences. Extradition shall be subject to the other conditions provided by the law of the requested State.

3.   States Parties which do not make extradition conditional on the existence of a treaty shall recognize such offences as extraditable offences between themselves subject to the conditions provided by the law of the requested State.

4.   Such offences shall be treated, for the purpose of extradition between States Parties, as if they had been committed not only in the place in which they occurred but also in territories of the States required to establish their jurisdiction in accordance with article 5, paragraph 1.

Article 9

1.   States Parties shall afford one another the greatest measure of assistance in connection with criminal proceedings brought in respect of any of the offences referred to in article 4, including the supply of all evidence at their disposal necessary for the proceedings.

2.   States Parties shall carry out their obligations under paragraph 1 of this article in conformity with any treaties on mutual judicial assistance that may exist between them.

Article 10

1.   Each State Party shall ensure that education and information regarding the prohibition against torture are fully included in the training of law enforcement personnel, civil or military, medical personnel, public officials and other persons who may be involved in the custody, interrogation or treatment of any individual subjected to any form of arrest, detention or imprisonment.

2.   Each State Party shall include this prohibition in the rules or instructions issued in regard to the duties and functions of any such persons.

Article 11

Each State Party shall keep under systematic review interrogation rules, instructions, methods and practices as well as arrangements for the custody and treatment of persons subjected to any form of arrest, detention, or imprisonment in any territory under its jurisdiction, with a view to preventing any cases of torture.

Article 12

Each State Party shall ensure that its competent authorities proceed to a prompt and impartial investigation, wherever there is reasonable ground to believe that an act of torture has been committed in any territory under its jurisdiction.

Article 13

Each State Party shall ensure that any individual who alleges he has been subjected to torture in any territory under its jurisdiction has the right to complain to and to have his case promptly and impartially examined by its competent authorities. Steps shall be taken to ensure that the complainant and witnesses are protected against all ill-treatment or intimidation as a consequence of his complaint or any evidence given.

Article 14

1.   Each State Party shall ensure in its legal system that the victim of an act of torture obtains redress and has an enforceable right to fair and adequate compensation including the

means for as full rehabilitation as possible. In the event of the death of the victim as a result of an act of torture, his dependants shall be entitled to compensation.

2. Nothing in this article shall affect any right of the victim or other persons to compensation which may exist under national law.

Article 15

Each State Party shall ensure that any statement which is established to have been made as a result of torture shall not be invoked as evidence in any proceedings, except against a person accused of torture as evidence that the statement was made.

Article 16

1. Each State Party shall undertake to prevent in any territory under its jurisdiction other acts of cruel, inhuman or degrading treatment or punishment which do not amount to torture as defined in article 1, when such acts are committed by or at the instigation of or with the consent or acquiescence of a public official or other person acting in an official capacity. In particular, the obligations contained in articles 10, 11, 12 and 13 shall apply with the substitution for references to torture or references to other forms of cruel, inhuman or degrading treatment or punishment.

2. The provisions of this Convention are without prejudice to the provisions of any other international instrument or national law which prohibit cruel, inhuman or degrading treatment or punishment or which relate to extradition or expulsion.

Part II

Article 17

1. There shall be established a Committee against Torture (hereinafter referred to as the Committee) which shall carry out the functions hereinafter provided. The Committee shall consist of 10 experts of high moral standing and recognized competence in the field of human rights, who shall serve in their personal capacity. The experts shall be elected by the States Parties, consideration being given to equitable geographical distribution and to the usefulness of the participation of some persons having legal experience.

2. The members of the Committee shall be elected by secret ballot from a list of persons nominated by States Parties. Each State Party may nominate one person from among its own nationals. States Parties shall bear in mind the usefulness of nominating persons who are also members of the Human Rights Committee established under the International Covenant on Civil and Political Rights and are willing to serve on the Committee against Torture.

3. Elections of the members of the Committee shall be held at biennial meetings of States Parties convened by the Secretary-General of the United Nations. At those meetings, for which two thirds of the States Parties shall constitute a quorum, the persons elected to the Committee shall be those who obtain the largest number of votes and an absolute majority of the votes of the representatives of States Parties present and voting.

4. The initial election shall be held no later than six months after the date of the entry into force of this Convention. At least four months before the date of each election, the Secretary-General of the United Nations shall address a letter to the States Parties inviting them to submit their nominations within three months. The Secretary-General shall prepare a list in alphabetical order of all persons thus nominated, indicating the States Parties which have nominated them, and shall submit it to the States Parties.

5. The members of the Committee shall be elected for a term of four years. They shall be eligible for re-election if renominated. However, the term of five of the members elected at the first election shall expire at the end of two years: immediately after the first election the names of these five members shall be chosen by lot by the chairman of the meeting referred to in paragraph 3.

6. If a member of the Committee dies or resigns for any other cause can no longer perform his Committee duties, the State Party which nominated him shall appoint another expert from among its nationals to serve for the remainder of his term, subject to the approval of the majority of the States Parties. The approval shall be considered given unless half or more of the States Parties respond negatively within six weeks after having been informed by the Secretary-General of the United Nations of the proposed appointment.

7. States Parties shall be responsible for the expenses of the members of the Committee while they are in performance of Committee duties.

Article 18

1. The Committee shall elect its officers for a term of two years. They may be re-elected.

2. The Committee shall establish its own rules of procedure, but these rules shall provide, *inter alia*, that:

   (a) Six members shall constitute a quorum;

   (b) Decisions of the Committee shall be made by a majority vote of the members present.

3. The Secretary-General of the United Nations shall provide the necessary staff and facilities for the effective performance of the functions of the Committee under this Convention.

4. The Secretary-General of the United Nations shall convene the initial meeting of the Committee. After its initial meeting, the Committee shall meet at such times as shall be provided in its rules of procedure.

5. The State Parties shall be responsible for expenses incurred in connection with the holding of meetings of the States Parties and of the Committee, including reimbursement to the United Nations for any expenses, such as the cost of staff and facilities, incurred by the United Nations pursuant to paragraph 3 above.

Article 19

1. The States Parties shall submit to the Committee, through the Secretary-General of the United Nations, reports on the measures they have taken to give effect to their undertakings under this Convention, within one year after the entry into force of this Convention for the State Party concerned. Thereafter the States Parties shall submit supplementary reports every four years on any new measures taken, and such other reports as the Committee may request.

2. The Secretary-General shall transmit the reports to all States Parties.

3. Each report shall be considered by the Committee which may make such comments or suggestions on the report as it may consider appropriate, and shall forward these to the State Party concerned. That State Party may respond with any observations it chooses to the Committee.

4. The Committee may, at its discretion, decide to include any comments or suggestions made by it in accordance with paragraph 3, together with the observations thereon received from the State Party concerned, in its annual report made in accordance with article 24. If so requested by the State Party concerned, the Committee may also include a copy of the report submitted under paragraph 1.

Article 20

1. If the Committee receives reliable information which appears to it to contain well-founded indications that torture is being systematically practised in the territory of a State Party, the Committee shall invite that State to (co-operate in the examination of the information and to this end) submit observations with regard to the information concerned.

2. Taking into account any observations which may have been submitted by the State Party concerned as well as any other relevant information available to it, the Committee may, if it decides that this is warranted, designate one or more of its members to make a confidential inquiry and to report to the Committee urgently.

3. If an inquiry is made in accordance with paragraph 2, the Committee shall seek the co-operation of the State Party concerned. In agreement with that State Party, such an inquiry may include a visit to its territory.

4. After examining the findings of its member or members submitted in accordance with paragraph 2, the Committee shall transmit these findings to the State Party concerned together with any comments or suggestions which seem appropriate in view of the situation.

5. All the proceedings of the Committee referred to in paragraphs 1 to 4 (of this article) shall be confidential, (and at all stages of the proceedings the co-operation of the State Party shall be sought). After such proceedings have been completed with regard to an inquiry made in accordance with paragraph 2, the Committee may, (after consultations with the State Party concerned), decide to include a summary account of the results of the proceedings in its annual report made in accordance with article 24.

Article 21

1. A State Party to this Convention may at any time declare under this article that it recognizes the competence of the Committee to receive and consider communications to the effect that a State Party claims that another State Party is not fulfilling its obligations under this Convention. Such communications may be received and considered according to the procedures laid down in this article only if submitted by a State Party which has made a declaration recognizing in regard to itself the competence of the Committee. No communication shall be dealt with by the Committee under this article if it concerns a State Party which has not made such a declaration. Communications received under this article shall be dealt with in accordance with the following procedure:

(a) If a State Party considers that another State Party is not given effect to the provisions of this Convention, it may, by written communication, bring the matter to the attention of that State Party. Within three months after the receipt of the communication the receiving State shall afford the State which sent the communication an explanation or any other statement in writing clarifying the matter which should include, to the extent possible and pertinent, reference to domestic procedures and remedies taken, pending, or available in the matter.

(b) If the matter is not adjusted to the satisfaction of both States Parties concerned within six months after the receipt by the receiving State of the initial communication, either State shall have the right to refer the matter to the Committee, by notice given to the Committee and to the other State.

(c) The Committee shall deal with a matter referred to it under this article only after it has ascertained that all domestic remedies have been invoked and exhausted in the matter, in conformity with the generally recognized principles of international law. This shall not be the rule where the application of the remedies is unreasonably prolonged or is unlikely to bring effective relief to the person who is the victim of the violation of this Convention.

(d) The Committee shall hold closed meetings when examining communications under this article.

(e) Subject to the provisions of subparagraph (c), the Committee shall make available its good offices to the States Parties concerned with a view to a friendly solution of the matter on the basis of respect for the obligations provided for in the present Convention. For this purpose, the Committee may, when appropriate, set up an *ad hoc* conciliation commission.

(f) In any matter referred to it under this article, the Committee may call upon the States Parties concerned, referred to in subparagraph (b), to supply any relevant information.

(g) The States Parties concerned, referred to in subparagraph (b), shall have the right to be represented when the matter is being considered by the Committee and to make submissions orally and/or in writing.

(h) The Committee shall, within 12 months after the date of receipt of notice under subparagraph (b), submit a report.

(i) If a solution within the terms of subparagraph (e) is reached, the Committee shall confine its report to a brief statement of the facts and of the solution reached.

(ii) If a solution within the terms of subparagraph (e) is not reached, the Committee shall confine its report to a brief statement of the facts; the written submissions and record of the oral submissions made by the States Parties concerned shall be attached to the report.

In every matter, the report shall be communicated to the States Parties concerned.

2. The provisions of this article shall come into force when five States Parties to this Convention have made declarations under paragraph 1 of this article. Such declarations shall be deposited by the States Parties with the Secretary-General of the United Nations, who shall transmit copies thereof to the other States Parties. A declaration may be withdrawn at any time by notification to the Secretary-General. Such a withdrawal shall not prejudice the consideration of any matter which is the subject of a communication already transmitted under this article; no further communication by any State Party shall be received under this article after the notification of withdrawal of the declaration has been received by the Secretary-General, unless the State Party concerned has made a new declaration.

Article 22

1. A State Party to this Convention may at any time declare under this article that it recognizes the competence of the Committee to receive and consider communications from or on behalf of individuals subject to its jurisdiction who claim to be victims of a violation by a State Party of the provisions of the Convention. No communication shall be received by the Committee if it concerns a State Party to the Convention which has not made such a declaration.

2. The Committee shall consider inadmissible any communication under this article which is anonymous, or which it considers to be an abuse of the right of submission of such communications or to be incompatible with the provisions of this Convention.

3. Subject to the provisions of paragraph 2, the Committee shall bring any communications submitted to it under this article to the attention of the State Party to this Convention which has made a declaration under paragraph 1 and is alleged to be violating any provisions of the Convention. Within six months, the receiving State shall submit to the Committee written explanations or statements clarifying the matter and the remedy, if any, that may have been taken by that State.

4. The Committee shall consider communications received under this article in the light of all information made available to it by or on behalf of the individual and by the State Party concerned.

5. The Committee shall not consider any communications from an individual under this article unless it has ascertained that:

(a) The same matter has not been, and is not being, examined under another procedure of international investigation or settlement;

(b) The individual has exhausted all available domestic remedies; this shall not be the rule where the application of the remedies is unreasonably prolonged or is unlikely to bring effective relief to the person who is the victim of the violation of this Convention.

6. The Committee shall hold closed meetings when examining communications under this article.

7. The Committee shall forward its views to the State Party concerned and to the individual.

8. The provisions of this article shall come into force when five States Parties to this Convention have made declarations under paragraph 1 of this article. Such declarations shall be deposited by the States Parties with the Secretary-General of the United Nations, who shall transmit copies thereof to the other States Parties. A declaration may be withdrawn at any time by notification to the Secretary-General. Such a withdrawal shall not prejudice the consideration of any matter which is the subject of a communication already transmitted under this article; no further communication by or on behalf of an individual shall be received under this article after the notification of withdrawal of the declaration has been received by the Secretary-General, unless the State Party concerned has made a new declaration.

Article 23

The members of the Committee, and of the *ad hoc* conciliation commissions which may be appointed under article 21, paragraph 1 (e), shall be entitled to the facilities, privileges and immunities of experts on mission for the United Nations as laid down in the relevant sections of the Convention on the Privileges and Immunities of the United Nations.

Article 24

The Committee shall submit and annual report on its activities under this Convention to the States Parties and to the General Assembly of the United Nations.

Part III

Article 25

1. This Convention is open for signature by all States.

2. This Convention is subject to ratification. Instruments of ratification shall be deposited with the Secretary-General of the United Nations.

Article 26

This Convention is open to accession by all States. Accession shall be effected by the deposit of an instrument of accession with the Secretary-General of the United Nations.

Article 27

1. This Convention shall enter into force on the thirtieth day after the date of the deposit with the Secretary-General of the United Nations of the twentieth instrument of ratification or accession.

2. For each State ratifying this Convention or acceding to it after the deposit of the twentieth instrument of ratification or accession, the Convention shall enter into force on the thirtieth day after the date of the deposit of its own instrument of ratification or accession.

Article 28

1. Each State may, at the time of signature or ratification of this Convention or accession thereto, declare that it does not recognize the competence of the Committee provided for in article 20.

2. Any Party State having made a reservation in accordance with paragraph 1 of this article may, at any time, withdraw this reservation by notification to the Secretary-General of the United Nations.

Article 29

1. Any dispute between two or more States Parties concerning the interpretation or application of this Convention which cannot be settled through negotiation, shall, at the request of one of them, be submitted to arbitration. If within six months from the date of the request for arbitration the Parties are unable to agree on the organisation of the arbitration, any one of those Parties may refer the dispute to the International Court of Justice by request in conformity with the Statute of the Court.

2. Each State may at the time of signature or ratification of this Convention or accession thereto, declare that it does not consider itself bound by the preceding paragraph. The other States Parties shall not be bound by the preceding paragraph with respect to any State Party having made such a reservation.

3. Any State Party having made a reservation in accordance with the preceding paragraph may at any time withdraw this reservation by notification to the Secretary-General of the United Nations.

Article 30

1. A State Party may denounce this Convention by written notification to the Secretary-General of the United Nations. Denunciation becomes effective one year after the date of receipt of the notification by the Secretary-General.

2. Such a denunciation shall not have the effect of releasing the State Party from its obligations under this Convention in regard to any act or omission which occurs prior to the date at which the denunciation becomes effective. Nor shall denunciation prejudice in any way the continued consideration of any matter which is already under consideration by the Committee prior to the date at which the denunciation becomes effective.

3. Following the date at which the denunciation of a State Party becomes effective, the Committee shall not commence consideration of any new matter regarding that State.

Article 31

The Secretary-General of the United Nations shall inform all members of the United Nations and all States which have signed this Convention or acceded to it, or the following particulars:

(a) Signatures, ratifications and accessions under articles 25 and 26;

(b) The date of entry into force of this Convention under article 27, and the date of the entry into force of any amendments under article 28;

(c) Denunciations under article 30.

Article 32

1. This Convention, of which the Arabic, Chinese, English, French, Russian and Spanish texts are equally authentic, shall be deposited in the archives of the United Nations.

2. The Secretary-General of the United Nations shall transmit certified copies of this Convention to all States.

European Convention for the Prevention of Torture and Inhuman or Degrading Treatment or Punishment (1987)[*]

Strasbourg, 26 November 1987

Chapter I

Article 1

There shall be established a European Committee for the Prevention of Torture and Inhuman or Degrading Treatment or Punishment (hereinafter referred to as "the Committee). The Committee shall, by means of visits, examine the treatment of persons deprived of their liberty with a view to strengthening, if necessary, the protection of such persons from torture and from inhuman or degrading treatment or punishment.

Article 2

Each Party shall permit visits, in accordance with this Convention, to any place within its jurisdiction where persons are deprived of their liberty by a public authority.

Article 3

In the application of this Convention, the Committee and the competent national authorities of the Party concerned shall co-operate with each other.

Chapter II

Article 4

1. The Committee shall consist of a number of members equal to that of the Parties.

2. The members of the Committee shall be chosen from among persons of high moral character, known for their competence in the field of human rights or having professional experience in the areas covered by this Convention.

3. No two members of the Committee may be nationals of the same State.

4. The members shall serve in their individual capacity, shall be independent and impartial, and shall be available to serve the Committee effectively.

Article 5

1. The members of the Committee shall be elected by the Committee of Ministers of the Council of Europe by an absolute majority of votes, from a list of names drawn up by the Bureau of the Consultative Assembly of the Council of Europe; each national delegation of the Parties in the Consultative Assembly shall put forward three candidates, of whom two at least shall be its nationals.

2. The same procedure shall be followed in filling casual vacancies.

3. The members of the Committee shall be elected for a period of four years. They may only be re-elected once. However, among the members elected at the first election, the terms of three members shall expire at the end of two years. The members whose terms are to expire at the end of the initial period of two years shall be chosen by lot by the Secretary General of the Council of Europe immediately after the first election has been completed.

---

[*] *European Treaty Series*, No.126.

Article 6

1. The Committee shall meet in camera. A quorum shall be equal to the majority of its members. The decisions of the Committee shall be taken by a majority of the members present, subject to the provisions of Article 10, paragraph 2.

2. The Committee shall draw up its own rules of procedure.

3. The Secretariat of the Committee shall be provided by the Secretary General of the Council of Europe.

Chapter III

Article 7

1. The Committee shall organise visits to places referred to in Article 2. Apart from periodic visits, the Committee may organise such other visits as appear to it to be required in the circumstances.

2. As a general rule, the visits shall be carried out by at least two members of the Committee. The Committee may, if it considers it necessary, be assisted by experts and interpreters.

Article 8

1. The Committee shall notify the Government of the Party concerned of its intention to carry out a visit. After such notification, it may at any time visit any place referred to in Article 2.

2. A Party shall provide the Committee with the following facilities to carry out its task:

   (a) access to its territory and the right to travel without restriction

   (b) full information on the places where persons deprived of their liberty are being held;

   (c) unlimited access to any place where persons are deprived of their liberty, including the right to move inside such places without restriction;

   (d) other information available to the Party which is necessary for the Committee to carry out its task. In seeking such information, the Committee shall have regard to applicable rules of national law and professional ethics.

3. The Committee may interview in private persons deprived of their liberty.

4. The Committee may communicate freely with any person whom it believes can supply relevant information.

5. If necessary, the Committee may immediately communicate observations to the competent authorities of the Party concerned.

Article 9

1. In exceptional circumstances, the competent authorities of the Party concerned may make representations to the Committee against a visit at the time or to the particular place proposed by the Committee.

Such representations may only be made on grounds of national defence, public safety, serious disorder in places where persons are deprived of their liberty, the medical conditions of a person or that an urgent interrogation relating to a serious crime is in progress.

2. Following such representations, the Committee and the Party shall immediately enter into consultations in order to clarify the situation and seek agreement on arrangements to enable the Committee to exercise its functions expeditiously. Such arrangements may include the transfer to another place of any person whom the Committee proposed to visit. Until the visit takes place, the Party shall provide information to the Committee about any person concerned.

Article 10

1. After each visit, the Committee shall draw up a report on the facts found during the visit, taking account of any observations which may have been submitted by the Party concerned. It shall transmit to the latter its report containing any recommendations it considers necessary. The Committee may consult with the Party with a view to suggesting, if necessary, improvements in the protection of persons deprived of their liberty.

2. If the Party fails to co-operate or refuses to improve the situation in the light of the Committee's recommendations, the Committee may decide, after the Party has had an opportunity to make known its views, by a majority of two-thirds of its members to make a public statement on the matter.

Article 11

1. The information gathered by the Committee in relation to a visit, its report and its consultations with the Party concerned shall be confidential.

2. The Committee shall publish its report, together with any comments of the Party concerned, whenever requested to do so by that Party.

3. However, no personal data shall be published without the express consent of the person concerned.

Article 12

Subject to the rules of confidentiality in Article 11, the Committee shall every year submit to the Committee of Ministers a general report on its activities which shall be transmitted to the Consultative Assembly and made public.

Article 13

The members of the Committee, experts and other persons assisting the Committee are required, during and after their terms of office, to maintain the confidentiality of the facts or information of which they have become aware during the discharge of their functions.

Article 14

1. The names of persons assisting the Committee shall be specified in the notification under Article 8, paragraph 1.

2. Experts shall act on the instructions and under the authority of the Committee. They shall have particular knowledge and experience in the areas covered by this Convention and shall be bound by the same duties of independence, impartiality and availability as the members of the Committee.

3. A Party may exceptionally declare that an expert or other person assisting the Committee may not be allowed to take part in a visit to a place within its jurisdiction.

Chapter IV

Article 15

Each Party shall inform the Committee of the name and address of the authority competent to receive notifications to its Government, and of any liaison officer it may appoint.

Article 16

The Committee, its members and experts referred to in Article 7, paragraph 2, shall enjoy the privileges and immunities set out in the annex to this Convention.

Article 17

1. This Convention shall not prejudice the provisions of domestic law or any international agreement which provide greater protection for persons deprived of their liberty.

2. Nothing in this Convention shall be construed as limiting or derogating from the competence of the organs of the European Convention on Human Rights or from the obligations assumed by the Parties under that Convention.

3. The Committee shall not visit places which representatives or delegates of protecting powers or the International Committee of the Red Cross effectively visit on a regular basis by virtue of the Geneva Convention of 12 August 1949 and the Additional Protocols of 8 June 1977 thereto.

Chapter V

Article 18

This Convention shall be open for signature by the member States of the Council of Europe. It is subject to ratification, acceptance or approval. Instruments of ratification, acceptance or approval shall be deposited with the Secretary General of the Council of Europe.

Article 19

1. This Convention shall enter into force on the first day of the month following the expiration of a period of three months after the date on which seven member States of the Council of Europe have expressed their consent to be bound by the Convention in accordance with the provisions of Article 18.

2. In respect of any member State which subsequently expresses its consent to be bound by it, the Convention shall enter into force on the first day of the month following the expiration of a period of three months after the date of the deposit of the instrument of ratification, acceptance or approval.

Article 20

1. Any State may at the time of signature or when depositing its instrument of ratification, acceptance or approval, specify the territory or territories to which this Convention shall apply.

2. Any State may at any later date, by a declaration addressed to the Secretary General of the Council of Europe, extend the application of this Convention to any other territory specified in the declaration. In respect of such territory the Convention shall enter into force on the first day of the month following the expiration of a period of three months after the date of receipt of such declaration by he Secretary General.

3. Any declaration made under the two preceding paragraphs may, in respect of any territory specified in such declaration, be withdrawn by a notification addressed to the Secretary General. The withdrawal shall become effective on the first day of the month following the expiration of a period of three months after the date of receipt of such notification by the Secretary General.

Article 21

No reservation may made in respect of the provisions of this Convention.

Article 22

1. Any Party may, at any time, denounce this Convention by means of a notification addressed to the Secretary General of the Council of Europe.

2. Such denunciation shall become effective on the first day of the month following the expiration of a period of twelve months after the date of receipt of the notification by the Secretary General.

Article 23

The Secretary General of the Council of Europe shall notify the member States of the Council of Europe of:

- (a) any signature;

- (b) the deposit of any instrument of ratification, acceptance or approval;

- (c) any date of entry into force of this Convention in accordance with Articles 19 and 20;

- (d) any other act, notification or communication relating to this Convention, except for action taken in pursuance of Articles 8 and 10.

Annex

Privileges and immunities

Article 16

1. For the purpose of this annex, references to members of the Committee shall be deemed to include references to experts mentioned in Article 7, paragraph 2.

2. The members of the Committee shall, while exercising their functions and during journeys made in the exercise of their functions, enjoy the following privileges and immunities:

- (a) immunity from personal arrest or detention and from seizure of their personal baggage and, in respect of words spoken or written and all acts done by them in their official capacity, immunity from legal process of every kind;

- (b) exemption from any restrictions on their freedom of movement: on exit from and to their country of residence, and entry into and exit from the country in which they exercise their functions, and from alien registration in the country which they are visiting or through which they are passing in the exercise of their functions.

3. In the course of journeys undertaken in the exercise of their functions, the members of the Committee shall, in the matter of customs and exchange control, be accorded:

- (a) by their own government, the same facilities as those accorded to senior officials travelling abroad on temporary official duty;

- (b) by the governments of other Parties, the same facilities as those accorded to representatives of foreign governments on temporary official duty.

4. Documents and papers of the Committee, insofar as they relate to the business of the Committee, shall be inviolable.

The official correspondence and other official communications of the Committee may not be held up or subjected to censorship.

5. In order to secure for the members of the Committee complete freedom of speech and complete independence in the discharge of their duties, the immunity from legal process in respect of words spoken or written and all acts done by them in discharging their duties shall continue to be accorded, notwithstanding that the persons concerned are no longer engaged in the discharge of such duties.

6. Privileges and immunities are accorded to the members of the Committee, not for the personal benefit of the individuals themselves but in order to safeguard the independent exercise of their functions. The Committee alone shall be competent to waive the immunity of its members; it has not only the right, but is under a duty, to waive the immunity of one of its members in any case where, in its opinion, the immunity would impede the course of justice, and where it can be waived without prejudice to the purpose for which the immunity is accorded.

1.6. Drug Offences and Money Laundering

Convention against Illicit Traffic in Narcotic Drugs and Psychotropic Substances (1988)*

Vienna, 20 December 1988

Article 1

Definitions

Except where otherwise expressly indicated or where the context otherwise requires, the following definitions shall apply throughout this Convention:

(a) "Board" means the International Narcotics Control Board established by the Single Convention on Narcotic Drugs, 1961, and that Convention as amended by the 1972 Protocol Amending the Single Convention on Narcotic Drugs, 1961;

(b) "Cannabis plant" means any plant of the genus Cannabis;

(c) "Coca bush" means the plant of any species of the genus Erythroxylon;

(d) "Commercial carrier" means any person or any public, private or other entity engaged in transporting persons, goods or mails for remuneration, hire or any other benefit;

(e) "Commission" means the Commission on Narcotic Drugs of the Economic and Social Council of the United Nations;

(f) "Confiscation", which includes forfeiture where applicable, means the permanent deprivation of property by order of a court or other competent authority;

(g) "Controlled delivery" means the technique of allowing illicit or suspect consignments of narcotic drugs, psychotropic substances, substances in Table I and Table II annexed to this Convention, or substances substituted for them, to pass out, through or into the territory of one or more countries, with the knowledge and under the supervision of their competent authorities, with a view to identifying persons involved in the commission of offences established in accordance with article 3, paragraph 1 of the Convention;

(h) "1961 Convention" means the Single Convention on Narcotic Drugs, 1961;

(i) "1961 Convention as amended" means the Single Convention on Narcotic Drugs, 1961, as amended by the 1972 Protocol Amending the Single Convention on Narcotic Drugs, 1961;

(j) "1971 Convention" means the Convention on Psychotropic Substances, 1971;

(k) "Council" means the Economic and Social Council of the United Nations;

(l) "Freezing" or "seizure" means temporarily prohibiting the transfer, conversion, disposition or movement of property or temporarily assuming custody or control of property on the basis of an order issued by a court or a competent authority;

(m) "Illicit traffic" means the offences set forth in article 3, paragraphs 1 and 2, of this Convention;

---

* *International Legal Materials*, 1989, 493.

(n) "Narcotic drug" means any of the substances, natural or synthetic, in Schedules I and II of the Single Convention on Narcotic Drugs, 1961, and that Convention as amended by the 1972 Protocol Amending the Single Convention on Narcotic Drugs, 1961;

(o) "Opium poppy" means the plant of the species *Papaver somniferum* L;

(p) "Proceeds" means any property derived from or obtained, directly or indirectly, through the commission of an offenses established in accordance with article 3, paragraph 1;

(q) "Property" means assets of every kind, whether corporeal or incorporeal, movable or immovable, tangible or intangible, and legal documents or instruments evidencing title to, or interest in, such assets;

(r) "Psychotropic substance" means any substance, natural or synthetic, or any natural material in Schedules I, II, III and IV of the Convention on Psychotropic Substances, 1971;

(s) "Secretary-General" means the Secretary-General of the United Nations;

(t) "Table I" and "Table II" mean the correspondingly numbered lists of substances annexed to this Convention, as amended from time to time in accordance with article 12;

(u) "Transit State" means a State through the territory of which illicit narcotic drugs, psychotropic substances and substances in Table I and Table II are being moved, which is neither the place of origin nor the place of ultimate destination thereof.

Article 2

Scope of the Convention

1. The purpose of this Convention is to promote co-operation among the Parties so that they may address more effectively the various aspects of illicit traffic in narcotic drugs and psychotropic substances having an international dimension. In carrying out their obligations under the Convention, the Parties shall take necessary measures, including legislative and administrative measures, in conformity with the fundamental provisions of their respective domestic legislative systems.

2. The Parties shall carry out their obligations under this Convention in a manner consistent with the principles of sovereign equality and territorial integrity of States and that of non-intervention in the domestic affairs of other States.

3. A Party shall not undertake in the territory of another Party the exercise of jurisdiction and performance of functions which are exclusively reserved for the authorities of that other Party by its domestic law.

Article 3

Offences and Sanctions

1. Each Party shall adopt such measures as may be necessary to establish as criminal offences under its domestic law, when committed intentionally:

(a) (i) The production, manufacture, extraction, preparation, offering, offering for sale, distribution, sale, delivery on any terms whatsoever, brokerage, dispatch, dispatch in transit, transport, importation or exportation of any narcotic drug or any psychotropic substance contrary to the provisions of the 1961 Convention, the 1961 Convention as amended or the 1971 Convention;

- (ii) The cultivation of opium poppy, coca bush or cannabis plant for the purpose of the production of narcotic drugs contrary to the provisions of the 1961 Convention and the 1961 Convention as amended;

- (iii) The possession or purchase of any narcotic drug or psychotropic substance for the purpose of any of the activities enumerated in (i) above;

- (iv) The manufacture, transport or distribution of equipment, materials or of substances listed in Table I and Table II, knowing that they are to be used in or for the illicit cultivation, production or manufacture of narcotic drugs or psychotropic substances;

- (v) The organization, management or financing of any of the offenses enumerated in (i), (ii), (iii) or (iv) above;

(b)
- (i) The conversion or transfer of property, knowing that such property is derived from any offence or offences established in accordance with subparagraph (a) of this paragraph, or from an act of participation in such offence or offences, for the purpose of concealing or disguising the illicit origin of the property or of assisting any person who is involved in the commission of such an offence or offences to evade the legal consequences of his actions;

- (ii) The concealment or disguise of the true nature, source, location, disposition, movement, rights with respect to, or ownership of property, knowing that such property is derived from an offence or offences established in accordance with subparagraph (a) of this paragraph or from an act of participation in such an offence or offences;

(c) Subject to its constitutional principles and the basic concepts of its legal system:

- (i) The acquisition, possession or use of property, knowing, at the time of receipt, that such property was derived from an offence or offences established in accordance with subparagraph (a) of this paragraph or from an act of participation in such offence or offences;

- (ii) The possession of equipment or materials or substances listed in Table I and Table II, knowing that they are being or are to be used in or for the illicit cultivation, production or manufacture of narcotic drugs of psychotropic substances;

- (iii) Publicly inciting or inducing others, by any means, to commit any of the offences established in accordance with this article or to use narcotic drugs or psychotropic substances illicitly;

- (iv) Participation in, association or conspiracy to commit, attempts to commit and aiding, abetting, facilitating and counselling the commission of any of the offences established in accordance with this article.

2. Subject to its constitutional principles and the basic concepts of its legal system, each Party shall adopt such measures as may be necessary to establish as a criminal offence under its domestic law, when committed intentionally, the possession, purchase or cultivation of narcotic drugs or psychotropic substances for personal consumption contrary to the provisions of the 1961 Convention, the 1961 Convention as amended or the 1971 Convention.

3. Knowledge, intent or purpose required as an element of an offence set forth in paragraph 1 of this article may be inferred from objective factual circumstances.

4. (a) Each Party shall make the commission of the offences established in accordance with paragraph 1 of this article liable to sanctions which take into account the grave nature of these offences, such as imprisonment or other forms of deprivation of liberty, pecuniary sanctions and confiscation.

(b) The Parties may provide, in addition to conviction or punishment, for an offence established in accordance with paragraph 1 of this article, that the offender shall undergo measures such as treatment, education, aftercare, rehabilitation or social reintegration.

(c) Notwithstanding the preceding subparagraphs, in appropriate cases of a minor nature, the Parties may provide, as alternatives to conviction or punishment, measures such as education, rehabilitation or social reintegration, as well as, when the offender is a drug abuser, treatment and aftercare.

(d) The Parties may provide, either as an alternative to conviction or punishment, or in addition to conviction or punishment of an offence established in accordance with paragraph 2 of this article, measures for the treatment, education, aftercare, rehabilitation or social reintegration of the offender.

5. The Parties shall ensure that their courts and other competent authorities having jurisdiction can take into account factual circumstances which make the commission of the offences established in accordance with paragraph 1 of this article particularly serious, such as:

(a) The involvement in the offence of an organized criminal group to which the offender belongs;

(b) The involvement of the offender in other international organized criminal activities;

(c) The involvement of the offender in other illegal activities facilitated by commission of the offence;

(d) The use of violence or arms by the offender;

(e) The fact that the offender holds a public office and that the offence is connected with the office in question;

(f) The victimization or use of minors;

(g) The fact that the offence is committed in a penal institution or in an educational institution or social service facility or in their immediate vicinity or in other places to which school children and students resort for educational, sports and social activities;

(h) Prior conviction, particularly for similar offenses, whether foreign or domestic, to the extent permitted under the domestic law of a Party.

6. The Parties shall endeavour to ensure that any discretionary legal powers under their domestic law relating to the prosecution of persons for their offences established in accordance with this article are exercised to maximize the effectiveness of law enforcement measures in respect of those offences and with due regard to the need to deter the commission of such offences.

7. The Parties shall ensure that their courts or other competent authorities bear in mind the serious nature of the offences enumerated in paragraph 1 of this article and the circumstances enumerated in paragraph 5 of this article when considering the eventuality of early release or parole of persons convicted of such offences.

8. Each Party shall, where appropriate, establish under its domestic law a long statute of limitations period in which to commence proceedings for any offence established in accordance with paragraph 1 of this article, and a longer period where the alleged offender has evaded the administration of justice.

9. Each Party shall take appropriate measures, consistent with its legal system, to ensure that a person charged with or convicted of an offence established in accordance with para-

graph 1 of this article, who is found within its territory, is present at the necessary criminal proceedings.

10. For the purpose of co-operation among the Parties under this Convention, including, in particular, co-operation under articles 5, 6, 7 and 9, offences established in accordance with this article shall not be considered as fiscal offences or as political offenses or regarded as politically motivated, without prejudice to the constitutional limitations and the fundamental domestic law of the Parties.

11. Nothing contained in this article shall affect the principle that the description of the offenses to which it refers and of legal defences thereto is reserved to the domestic law of a Party and that such offenses shall be prosecuted and punished in conformity with that law.

Article 4

Jurisdiction

1. Each Party:

    (a) Shall take such measures as may be necessary to establish its jurisdiction over the offenses it has established in accordance with article 3, paragraph 1, when:

    (i) The offence is committed in its territory;

    (ii) The offence is committed on board a vessel flying its flag or an aircraft which is registered under its laws at the time the offence is committed;

    (b) May take such measures as may be necessary to establish its jurisdiction over the offenses it has established in accordance with article 3, paragraph 1, when:

    (i) The offence is committed by one of its nationals or by a person who has his habitual residence in its territory;

    (ii) The offence is committed on board a vessel concerning which that Party has been authorized to take appropriate action pursuant to article 17, provided that such jurisdiction shall be exercised only on the basis of agreements or arrangements referred to in paragraphs 4 and 9 of that article;

    (iii) The offence is one of those established in accordance with article 3, paragraph 1, subparagraph (c)(iv), and is committed outside its territory with a view to the commission, within its territory, of an offence established in accordance with article 3, paragraph 1.

2. Each Party:

    (a) Shall also take such measures as may be necessary to establish its jurisdiction over the offences it has established in accordance with article 3, paragraph 1, when the alleged offender is present in its territory and it does not extradite him to another Party on the ground:

    (i) That the offence has been committed in its territory or on board a vessel flying its flag or an aircraft which was registered under its law at the time the offence was committed; or

    (ii) That the offence has been committed by one of its nationals;

    (b) May also take such measures as may be necessary to establish its jurisdiction over the offences it has established in accordance with article 3, paragraph 1, when the alleged offender is present in its territory and it does not extradite him to another Party;

3. This Convention does not exclude the exercise of any criminal jurisdiction established by a Party in accordance with its domestic law.

Article 5

Confiscation

1. Each Party shall adopt such measures as may be necessary to enable confiscation of:

    (a) Proceeds derived from offences established in accordance with article 3, paragraph 1, or property the value of which corresponds to that of such proceeds;

    (b) Narcotic drugs and psychotropic substances, materials and equipment or other instrumentalities used in or intended for use in any manner in offences established in accordance with article 3, paragraph 1.

2. Each Party shall also adopt such measures as may be necessary to enable its competent authorities to identify, trace, and freeze or seize proceeds, property, instrumentalities or any other things referred to in paragraph 1 of this article, for the purpose of eventual confiscation.

3. In order to carry out the measures referred to in this article, each Party shall empower its courts or other competent authorities to order that bank, financial or commercial records be made available or be seized. A Party shall not decline to act under the provisions of this paragraph on the ground of bank secrecy.

4. (a) Following a request made pursuant to this article by another Party having jurisdiction over an offence established in accordance with article 3, paragraph 1, the Party in whose territory proceeds, property, instrumentalities or any other things referred to in paragraph 1 of this article are situated shall:

    (i) Submit the request to its competent authorities for the purpose of obtaining an order of confiscation and, if such order is granted, give effect to it; or

    (ii) Submit to its competent authorities, with a view to giving effect to it to the extent requested, an order of confiscation issued by the requesting Party in accordance with paragraph 1 of this article, in so far as it relates to proceeds, property, instrumentalities or any other things referred to in paragraph 1 situated in the territory of the requested Party.

   (b) Following a request made pursuant to this article by another Party having jurisdiction over an offence established in accordance with article 3, paragraph 1, the requested Party shall take measures to identify, trace, and freeze or seize proceeds, property, instrumentalities or any other things referred to in paragraph 1 of this article for the purpose of eventual confiscation to be ordered either by the requesting Party or, pursuant to a request under subparagraph (a) of this paragraph, by the requested Party.

   (c) The decisions or actions provided for in subparagraphs (a) and (b) of this paragraph shall be taken by the requested Party, in accordance with and subject to the provisions of its domestic law and its procedural rules or any bilateral or multilateral treaty, agreement or arrangement to which it may be bound in relation to the requesting Party.

   (d) The provisions of article 7, paragraphs 6 to 19 applicable mutatis mutandis. In addition to the information specified in article 7, paragraph 10, requests made pursuant to this article shall contain the following:

    (i) In the case of a request pertaining to subparagraph (a)(i) of this paragraph, a description of the property to be confiscated and a statement of the facts relied upon by the requesting Party sufficient to enable the requested Party to seek the order under its domestic law;

(ii) In the case of a request pertaining to subparagraph (a)(ii), a legally admissible copy of an order of confiscation issued by the requesting Party upon which the request is based, a statement of the facts and information as to the extent to which the execution of the order is requested;

(iii) In the case of a request pertaining to subparagraph (b), a statement of the facts relied upon by the requesting Party and a description of the actions requested.

(e) Each Party shall furnish to the Secretary-General the text of any of its laws and regulations which give effect to this paragraph and the text of any subsequent changes to such laws and regulations.

(f) If a Party elects to make the taking of the measures referred to in subparagraphs (a) and (b) of this paragraph conditional on the existence of a relevant treaty, that Party shall consider this Convention as the necessary and sufficient treaty basis.

(g) The Parties shall seek to conclude bilateral and multilateral treaties, agreements or arrangements to enhance the effectiveness of international co-operation pursuant to this article.

5. (a) Proceeds or property confiscated by a Party pursuant to paragraph 1 or paragraph 4 of this article shall be disposed of by that Party according to its domestic law and administrative procedures.

(b) When acting on the request of another Party in accordance with this article, a Party may give special consideration to concluding agreements on:

(i) Contributing the value of such proceeds and property, or funds derived from the sale of such proceeds or property, or a substantial part thereof, to intergovernmental bodies specializing in the fight against illicit traffic in and abuse of narcotic drugs and psychotropic substances;

(ii) Sharing with other Parties, on a regular or case-by-case basis, such proceeds or property, or funds derived from the sale of such proceeds or property, in accordance with its domestic law, administrative procedures or bilateral or multilateral agreements entered into for this purpose.

6. (a) If proceeds have been transformed or converted into other property, such property shall be liable to the measures referred to in this article instead of the proceeds.

(b) If proceeds have been intermingled with property acquired from legitimate sources, such property shall, without prejudice to any powers relating to seizure or freezing, be liable to confiscation up to the assessed value of the intermingled proceeds.

(c) Income or other benefits derived from:

(i) Proceeds;

(ii) Property into which proceeds have been transformed or converted; or

(iii) Property with which proceeds have been intermingled

shall also be liable to the measures referred to in this article, in the same manner and to the same extent as proceeds.

7. Each Party may consider ensuring that the onus of proof be reversed regarding the lawful origin of alleged proceeds or other property liable to confiscation, to the extent that

such action is consistent with the principles of its domestic law and with the nature of the judicial and other proceedings.

8. The provisions of this article shall not be construed as prejudicing the rights of bona fide third parties.

9. Nothing contained in this article shall affect the principle that the measures to which it refers shall be defined and implemented in accordance with and subject to the provisions of the domestic law of a Party.

Article 6

Extradition

1. This article shall apply to the offenses established by the Parties in accordance with article 3, paragraph 1.

2. Each of the offences to which this article applies shall be deemed to be included as an extraditable offence in any extradition treaty existing between Parties. The Parties undertake to include such offences as extraditable offenses in every extradition to be concluded between them.

3. If a Party which makes extradition conditional on the existence of a treaty receives a request for extradition from another Party with which it has no extradition treaty, it may consider this Convention as the legal basis for extradition in respect of any offence to which this article applies. The Parties which require detailed legislation in order to use this Convention as a legal basis for extradition shall consider enacting such legislation as may be necessary.

4. The Parties which do not make extradition conditional on the existence of a treaty shall recognize offences to which this article applies as extraditable offences between themselves.

5. Extradition shall be subject to the conditions provided for by the law of the requested Party or by applicable extradition treaties, including the grounds upon which the requested Party may refuse extradition.

6. In considering requests received pursuant to this article, the requested State may refuse to comply with such requests where there are substantial grounds leading its judicial or other competent authorities to believe that compliance would facilitate the prosecution or punishment of any person on account of his race, religion, nationality or political opinions, or would cause prejudice for any of those reasons to any person affected by the request.

7. The Parties shall endeavour to expedite extradition procedures and to simplify evidentiary requirements relating thereto in respect of any offence to which this article applies.

8. Subject to the provisions of its domestic law and its extradition treaties, the requested Party may, upon being satisfied that the circumstances so warrant and are urgent, and at the request of the requesting Party, take a person whose extradition is sought and who is present in its territory into custody or take other appropriate measures to ensure his presence at extradition proceedings.

9. Without prejudice to the exercise of any criminal jurisdiction established in accordance with its domestic law, a Party in whose territory an alleged offender is found shall:

    (a) If it does not extradite him in respect of an offence established in accordance with article 3, paragraph 1, on the grounds set forth in article 4, paragraph 2, subparagraph (a), submit the case to its competent authorities for the purposes of prosecution, unless otherwise agreed with the requesting Party;

    (b) If it does not extradite him in respect of such an offence and has established its jurisdiction in relation to that offence in accordance with article 4, paragraph 2, subparagraph (b), submit the case to its competent authorities for the purpose of prosecution, unless otherwise requested by the requesting Party for the purposes of preserving its legitimate jurisdiction.

10. If extradition, sought for purposes of enforcing a sentence, is refused because the person sought is a national of the requested Party, the requested Party shall, if its law so permits and in conformity with the requirements of such law, upon application of the requesting Party, consider the enforcement of the sentence which has been imposed under the law of the requesting Party, or the remainder thereof.

11. The Parties shall seek to conclude bilateral and multilateral agreements to carry out or to enhance the effectiveness of extradition.

12. The Parties may consider entering into bilateral or multilateral agreements, whether *ad hoc* or general, on the transfer to their country of persons sentenced to imprisonment and other forms of deprivation of liberty for offences to which this article applies, in order that they may complete their sentences there.

Article 7

Mutual Legal Assistance

1. The Parties shall afford one another, pursuant to this article, the widest measure of mutual legal assistance in investigations, prosecutions and judicial proceedings in relation to criminal offences established in accordance with article 3, paragraph 1.

2. Mutual legal assistance to be afforded in accordance with this article may be requested for any of the following purposes:

- (a) Taking evidence or statements from persons;
- (b) Effecting service of judicial documents;
- (c) Executing searches and seizures;
- (d) Examining objects and sites;
- (e) Providing information and evidentiary items;
- (f) Providing originals or certified copies of relevant documents and records, including bank, financial, corporate or business records;
- (g) Identifying or tracing proceeds, property, instrumentalities or other things for evidentiary purposes.

3. The Parties may afford one another any other forms of mutual legal assistance allowed by the domestic law of the requested Party.

4. Upon request, the Parties shall facilitate or encourage, to the extent consistent with their domestic law and practice, the presence or availability of persons, including persons in custody, who consent to assist in investigations or participate in proceedings.

5. A Party shall not decline to render mutual legal assistance under this article on the ground of bank secrecy.

6. The provisions of this article shall not affect the obligations under any other treaty, bilateral or multilateral, which governs or will govern, in whole or in part, mutual legal assistance in criminal matters.

7. Paragraphs 8 to 19 of this article shall apply to requests made pursuant to this article if the Parties in question are not bound by a treaty of mutual legal assistance. If these Parties

are bound by such a treaty, the corresponding provisions of that treaty shall apply unless the Parties agree to apply paragraphs 8 to 19 of this article in lieu thereof.

8. Parties shall designate an authority, or when necessary authorities, which shall have the responsibility and power to execute requests for mutual legal assistance or to transmit them to the competent authorities for execution. The authority or the authorities designated for this purpose shall be notified to the Secretary-General. Transmission of requests for mutual legal assistance and any communication related thereto shall be effected between the authorities designated by the Parties; this requirement shall be without prejudice to the right of a Party to require that such requests and communications be addressed to it through the diplomatic channel and, in urgent circumstances, where the Parties agree, through channels of the International Criminal Police Organization, if possible.

9. Requests shall be made in writing in a language acceptable to the requested Party. The language of languages acceptable to each Party shall be notified to the Secretary-General. In urgent circumstances, and where agreed by the Parties, requests may be made orally, but shall be confirmed in writing forthwith.

10. A request for mutual legal assistance shall contain:

   (a) The identity of the authority making the request;

   (b) The subject matter and nature of the investigation, prosecution or proceeding to which the request relates, and the name and the functions of the authority conducting such investigation, prosecution or proceeding;

   (c) A summary of the relevant facts, except in respect of requests for the purpose of service of judicial documents;

   (d) A description of the assistance sought and details of any particular procedure the requesting Party wishes to be followed;

   (e) Where possible, the identity, location and nationality of any person concerned;

   (f) The purpose for which the evidence, information or action is sought.

11. The requested Party may request additional information when it appears necessary for the execution of the request in accordance with its domestic law or when it can facilitate such execution.

12. A request shall be executed in accordance with the domestic law of the requested Party and, to the extent not contrary to the domestic law of the requested Party and where possible, in accordance with the procedures specified in the request.

13. The requesting Party shall not transmit nor use information or evidence furnished by the requested Party for investigations, prosecutions or proceedings other than those stated in the request without the prior consent of the requested Party.

14. The requesting Party may require that the requested Party keep confidential the fact and substance of the request, except to the extent necessary to execute the request. If the requested Party cannot comply with the requirement of confidentiality, it shall promptly inform the requesting Party.

15. Mutual legal assistance may be refused:

   (a) If the request is not made in conformity with the provisions of this article;

   (b) If the requested Party considers that execution of the request is likely to prejudice its sovereignty, security, *ordre public* or other essential interests;

   (c) If the authorities of the requested Party would be prohibited by its domestic law from carrying out the action requested with regard to any similar offence, had it been subject to investigation, prosecution or proceedings under their own jurisdiction;

(d) If it would be contrary to the legal system of the requested Party relating to mutual legal assistance for the request to be granted.

16. Reasons shall be given for any refusal of mutual legal assistance.

17. Mutual legal assistance may be postponed by the requested Party on the ground that it interferes with an ongoing investigation, prosecution or proceeding. In such a case, the requested Party shall consult with the requesting Party to determine if the assistance can still be given subject to such terms and conditions as the requested Party deems necessary.

18. A witness, expert or other person who consents to give evidence in a proceeding or to assist in an investigation, prosecution or judicial proceeding in the territory of the requesting Party, shall not be prosecuted, detained, punished or subjected to any other restriction of his personal liberty in that territory in respect of acts, omissions or convictions prior to his departure from the territory of the requested Party. Such safe conduct shall cease when the witness, expert or other person having had, for a period of fifteen consecutive days, or for any period agreed upon by the Parties, from the date on which he has been officially informed that his presence is no longer required by the judicial authorities, an opportunity of leaving, has nevertheless remained voluntarily in the territory or, having left it, has returned of his own free will.

19. The ordinary costs of executing a request shall be borne by the requested Party, unless otherwise agreed by the Parties concerned. If expenses of a substantial or extraordinary nature are or will be required to fulfil the request, the Parties shall consult to determine the terms and conditions under which the request will be executed as well as the manner in which the costs shall be borne.

20. The Parties shall consider, as may be necessary, the possibility of concluding bilateral or multilateral agreements or arrangements that would serve the purposes of, give practical effect to, or enhance the provisions of this article.

Article 8

Transfer of Proceedings

The Parties shall give consideration to the possibility of transferring to one another proceedings for criminal prosecution of offenses established in accordance with article 3, paragraph 1, in cases where such transfer is considered to be in the interests of a proper administration of justice.

Article 9

Other Forms of Co-operation and Training

1. The Parties shall co-operate closely with one another, consistent with their respective domestic legal and administrative systems, with a view to enhancing the effectiveness of law enforcement action to suppress the commission of offences established in accordance with article 3, paragraph 1. They shall, in particular, on the basis of bilateral or multilateral agreements or arrangements:

(a) Establish and maintain channels of communication between their competent agencies and services to facilitate the secure and rapid exchange of information concerning all aspects of offenses established in accordance with article 3, paragraph 1, including, if the Parties concerned deem it appropriate, links with other criminal activities;

(b) Co-operate with one another in conducting enquiries, with respect to offences established in accordance with article 3, paragraph 1, having an international character, concerning:

- (i) The identity, whereabouts and activities of persons suspected of being involved in offences established in accordance with article 3, paragraph 1;

- (ii) The movement of proceeds or property derived from the commission of such offenses;

- (iii) The movement of narcotic drugs, psychotropic substances, substances in Table I and Table II of this Convention and instrumentalities used or intended for use in the commission of such offenses;

(c) In appropriate cases and if not contrary to domestic law, establish joint teams, taking into account the need to protect the security of persons and of operations, to carry out the provisions of this paragraph. Officials of any Party taking part in such teams shall act as authorized by the appropriate authorities of the Party in whose territory the operation is to take place; in all such cases, the Parties involved shall ensure that the sovereignty of the Party on whose territory the operation is to take place is fully respected;

(d) Provide, when appropriate, necessary quantities of substances for analytical or investigative purposes;

(e) Facilitate effective co-ordination between their competent agencies and services and promote the exchange of personnel and other experts, including the posting of liaison officers.

2. Each Party shall, to the extent necessary, initiate, develop or improve specific training programmes for its laws enforcement and other personnel, including customs, charged with the suppression of offenses established in accordance with article 3, paragraph 1. Such programmes shall deal, in particular, with the following:

(a) Methods used in the detection and suppression of offenses established in accordance with article 3, paragraph 1;

(b) Routes and techniques used by persons suspected of being involved in offenses established in accordance with article 3, paragraph 1, particularly in transit States, and appropriate countermeasures;

(c) Monitoring of the import and export of narcotic drugs, psychotropic substances and substances in Table I and Table II;

(d) Detection and monitoring of the movement of proceeds and property derived from, and narcotic drugs, psychotropic substances and substances in Table I and Table II, and instrumentalities used or intended for use in, the commission of offences established in accordance with article 3, paragraph 1;

(e) Methods used for the transfer, concealment or disguise of such proceeds, property and instrumentalities;

(f) Collection of evidence;

(g) Control techniques in free trade zones and free ports;

(h) Modern law enforcement techniques.

3. The Parties shall assist one another to plan and implement research and training programmes designed to share expertise in the areas referred to in paragraph 2 of this article and, to this end, shall also, when appropriate, use regional and international conferences and seminars to promote co-operation and stimulate discussion on problems of mutual concern, including the special problems and needs of transit States.

Article 10

International Co-operation and Assistance for Transit States

1. The Parties shall co-operate, directly or through competent international or regional organizations, to assist and support transit States and, in particular, developing countries in need of such assistance and support, to the extent possible, through programmes of technical co-operation on interdiction and other related activities.

2. The Parties may undertake, directly or through competent international or regional organizations, to provide financial assistance to such transit States for the purpose of augmenting and strengthening the infrastructure needed for effective control and prevention of illicit traffic.

3. The Parties may conclude bilateral or multilateral agreements or arrangements to enhance the effectiveness of international co-operation pursuant to this article and may take into consideration financial arrangements in this regard.

Article 11

Controlled delivery

1. If permitted by the basic principles of their respective domestic legal systems, the Parties shall take the necessary measures, within their possibilities, to allow for the appropriate use of controlled delivery at the international level, on the basis of agreements or arrangements mutually consented to, with a view to identifying persons involved in offenses established in accordance with article 3, paragraph 1, and to taking legal action against them.

2. Decisions to use controlled delivery shall be made on a case-by-case basis and may, when necessary, take into consideration financial arrangements and understandings with respect to the exercise of jurisdiction by the Parties concerned.

3. Illicit consignments whose controlled delivery is agreed to may, with the consent of the Parties concerned, be intercepted and allowed to continue with the narcotic drugs or psychotropic substances intact or removed or replaced in whole or in part.

Article 12

Substances Frequently used in the Illicit Manufacture of Narcotic Drugs or Psychotropic Substances

1. The Parties shall take the measures they deem appropriate to prevent diversion of substances in Table I and Table II used for the purpose of illicit manufacture of narcotic drugs or psychotropic substances, and shall co-operate with one another to this end.

2. If a Party or the Board has information which in its opinion may require the inclusion of a substance in Table I or Table II, it shall notify the Secretary-General and furnish him with the information in support of that notification. The procedure described in paragraphs 2 to 7 of this article shall also apply when a Party or the Board has information justifying the deletion of a substance from Table I or Table II, or the transfer of a substance from one Table to the other.

3. The Secretary-General shall transmit such notification, and any information which he considers relevant, to the Parties, to the Commission, and, where notification is made by a Party, to the Board. The Parties shall communicate their comments concerning the notification to the Secretary-General, together with all supplementary information which may assist the Board in establishing an assessment and the Commission in reaching a decision.

4. If the Board, taking into account the extent, importance and diversity of the licit use of the substance, and the possibility and ease of using alternate substances both for licit purposes and for the illicit manufacture of narcotic drugs or psychotropic substances, finds:

(a) That the substance is frequently used in the illicit manufacture of a narcotic drug or psychotropic substance;

(b) That the volume and extent of the illicit manufacture of a narcotic drug or psychotropic substance creates serious public health or social problems, so as to warrant international action, it shall communicate to the Commission an assessment of the substances, including the likely effect of adding the substance to either Table I or Table II on both licit use and illicit manufacture, together with recommendations of monitoring measures, if any, that would be appropriate in the light of its assessment.

5. The Commission, taking into account the comments submitted by the Parties and the comments and recommendations of the Board, whose assessment shall be determinative as to scientific matters, and also taking into due consideration any other relevant factors, may decide by a two-thirds majority of its members to place a substance in Table I or Table II.

6. Any decision of the Commission taken pursuant to this article shall be communicated by the Secretary-General to all States and other entities which are, or which are entitled to become, Parties to this Convention, and to the Board. Such decision shall become fully effective with respect to each Party one hundred and eighty days after the date of such communication.

7. (a) The decisions of the Commission taken under this article shall be subject to review by the Council upon the request of any Party filed within one hundred and eighty days after the date of notification of the decision. The request for review shall be sent to the Secretary-General, together with all relevant information upon which the request for review is based.

(b) The Secretary-General shall transmit copies of the request for review and the relevant information to the Commission, to the Board and to all the Parties, inviting them to submit their comments within ninety days. All comments received shall be submitted to the Council for consideration.

(c) The Council may confirm or reverse the decision of the Commission. Notification of the Council's decision shall be transmitted to all States and other entities which are, or which are entitled to become, Parties to this Convention, to the Commission and to the Board.

8. (a) Without prejudice to the generality of the provisions contained in paragraph 1 of this article and the provisions of the 1961 Convention, the 1961 Convention as amended and the 1971 Convention, the Parties shall take the measures they deem appropriate to monitor the manufacture and distribution of substances in Table I and Table II which are carried out within their territory.

(b) To this end, the Parties may:

(i) Control all persons and enterprises engages in the manufacture and distribution of such substances;

(ii) Control under licence the establishment and premises in which such manufacture or distribution may take place;

(iii) Require that licensees obtain a permit for conducting the aforesaid operations;

(iv) Prevent the accumulation of such substances in the possession of manufacturers and distributors, in excess of the quantities required for the normal conduct of business and the prevailing market conditions.

9. Each Party shall, with respect to substances in Table I and Table II, take the following measures:

(a) Establish and maintain a system to monitor international trade in substances in Table I and Table II in order to facilitate the identification of suspicious transactions. Such monitoring systems shall be applied in close co-operation with manufacturers, importers, exporters, wholesalers and retailers, who shall inform the competent authorities of suspicious orders and transactions.

(b) Provide for the seizure of any substance in Table I or Table II if there is sufficient evidence that it is for use in the illicit manufacture of a narcotic drug or psychotropic substance.

(c) Notify, as soon as possible, the competent authorities and services of the Parties concerned if there is reason to believe that the import, export or transit of a substance in Table I or Table II is destined for the illicit manufacture of narcotic drugs or psychotropic substances, including in particular information about the means of payment and any other essential elements which led to that belief.

(d) Require that imports and exports be properly labelled and documented. Commercial documents such as invoices, cargo manifests, customs, transport and other shipping documents shall include the names, as stated in Table I or Table II, of the substances being imported or exported, the quantity being imported or exported, and the name and address of the exporter, the importer and, when available, the consignee.

(e) Ensure that documents referred to in subparagraph (d) of this paragraph are maintained for a period of not less than two years and may be made available for inspection by the competent authorities.

10. (a) In addition to the provisions of paragraph 9, and upon request to the Secretary-General by the interested Party, each Party from whose territory a substance in Table I is to be exported shall ensure that, prior to such export, the following information is supplied by its competent authorities to the competent authorities of the importing country:

(i) Name and address of the exporter and importer and, when available, the consignee;

(ii) Name of the substance in Table I;

(iii) Quantity of the substance to be exported;

(iv) Expected point of entry and expected date of dispatch;

(v) Any other information which is mutually agreed upon by the Parties.

(b) A Party may adopt more strict or severe measures of control than those provided by this paragraph if, in its opinion, such measures, are desirable or necessary.

11. Where a Party furnishes information to another Party in accordance with paragraphs 9 and 10 of this article, the Party furnishing such information may require that the Party receiving it keep confidential any trade, business, commercial or professional secret or trade process.

12. Each Party shall furnish annually to the Board, in the form and manner provided for by it and on forms made available by it, information on:

(a) The amounts seized of substances in Table I and Table II and, when known, their origin;

(b) Any substance not included in Table I or Table II which is identified as having been used in illicit manufacture of narcotic drugs or psychotropic substances, and which is deemed by the Party to be sufficiently significant to be brought to the attention of the Board;

(c) Methods of diversion and illicit manufacture.

13. The Board shall report annually to the Commission on the implementation of this article and the Commission shall periodically review the adequacy and propriety of Table I and Table II.

14. The provisions of this article shall not apply to pharmaceutical preparations, nor to other preparations containing substances in Table I or Table II that are compounded in such a way that substances cannot be easily used or recovered by readily applicable means.

Article 13

Materials and Equipment

The Parties shall take such measures as they deem appropriate to prevent trade in and the diversion of materials and equipment for illicit production or manufacture of narcotic and psychotropic substances and shall co-operate to this end.

Article 14

Measures to Eradicate Illicit Cultivation of Narcotic Pplants and to Eliminate Illicit Demand for Narcotic Drugs and Psychotropic Substances

1. Any measures taken pursuant to this Convention by Parties shall not be less stringent that the provisions applicable to the eradication of illicit cultivation of plants containing narcotic and psychotropic substances and to the elimination of illicit demand for narcotic drugs and psychotropic substances under the provisions of the 1961 Convention, the 1961 Convention as amended and the 1971 Convention.

2. Each Party shall take appropriate measures to prevent illicit cultivation of and to eradicate plants containing narcotic or psychotropic substances, such as opium poppy, coca bush and cannabis plants, cultivated illicitly in its territory. The measures adopted shall respect fundamental human rights and shall take due account of traditional licit uses, where there is historic evidence of such use, as well as the protection of the environment.

3. (a) The Parties may co-operate to increase the effectiveness of eradication efforts. Such co-operation may, *inter alia*, include support, when appropriate, for integrated rural development leading to economically viable alternatives to illicit cultivation. Factors such as access to markets, the availability of resources and prevailing socio-economic conditions should be taken into account before such rural development programmes are implemented. The Parties may agree on any other appropriate measures of co-operation.

    (b) The Parties shall also facilitate the exchange of scientific and technical information and the conduct of research concerning eradication.

    (c) Whenever they have common frontiers, the Parties shall seek to co-operate in eradication programmes in their respective areas along those frontiers.

4. The Parties shall adopt appropriate measures aimed at eliminating or reducing illicit demand for narcotic drugs and psychotropic substances, with a view to reducing human suffering and eliminating financial incentives for illicit traffic. These measures may be based, *inter alia*, on the recommendations of the United Nations, specialized agencies of the United Nations such as the World Health Organization, and other competent international organizations, and on the Comprehensive Multidisciplinary Outline adopted by the International Conference on Drug Abuse and Illicit Trafficking, held in 1987, as it pertains to governmental and non-governmental agencies and private efforts in the fields of prevention, treatment and rehabilitation. The Parties may enter into bilateral or multilateral agreements or arrangements

aimed at eliminating or reducing illicit demand for narcotic drugs and psychotropic substances.

5. The Parties may also take necessary measures for early destruction or lawful disposal of the narcotic drugs, psychotropic substances and substances in Table I and Table II which have been seized or confiscated and for the admissibility as evidence of duly certified necessary quantities of such substances.

Article 15

Commercial Carriers

1. The Parties shall take appropriate measures to ensure that means of transport operated by commercial carriers are not used in the commission of offences established in accordance with article 3, paragraph 1; such measures may include special arrangements with commercial carriers.

2. Each Party shall require commercial carriers to take reasonable precautions to prevent the use of their means of transport for the commission of offences established in accordance with article 3, paragraph 1. Such precautions may include:

 (a) If the principal place of business of a commercial carrier is within the territory of the Party:

 (i) Training of personnel to identify suspicious consignments or persons;

 (ii) Promotion of integrity of personnel;

 (b) If a commercial carrier is operating within the territory of the Party:

 (i) Submission of cargo manifests in advance, whenever possible;

 (ii) Use of tamper-resistant, individually verifiable seals on containers;

 (iii) Reporting to the appropriate authorities at the earliest opportunity all suspicious circumstances that may be related to the commission of offences established in accordance with article 3, paragraph 1.

3. Each Party shall seek to ensure that commercial carriers and the appropriate authorities at points of entry and exit and other customs control areas co-operate, with a view to preventing unauthorized access to means of transport and cargo and to implementing appropriate security measures.

Article 16

Commercial Documents and Labelling of Exports

1. Each Party shall require that lawful exports of narcotic drugs and psychotropic substances be properly documented. In addition to the requirements for documentation under article 31 of the 1961 Convention, article 31 of the 1961 Convention as amended and article 12 of the 1971 Convention, commercial documents such as invoices, cargo manifests, customs, transport and other shipping documents shall include the names of the narcotic drugs and psychotropic substances being exported as set out in the respective Schedules of the 1961 Convention, the 1961 Convention as amended and the 1971 Convention, the quantity being exported, and the name and address of the exporter, the importer and, when available, the consignee.

2. Each Party shall require that consignments of narcotic drugs and psychotropic substances being exported be not mislabelled.

Article 17

Illicit Traffic by Sea

1. The Parties shall co-operate to the fullest extent possible to suppress illicit traffic by sea, in conformity with the international law of the sea.

2. A Party which has reasonable grounds to suspect that a vessel flying its flag or not displaying a flag or marks of registry is engaged in illicit traffic may request the assistance of other Parties in suppressing its use for that purpose. The Parties so requested shall render such assistance within the means available to them.

3. A Party which has reasonable grounds to suspect that a vessel exercising freedom of navigating in accordance with international law and flying the flag or displaying marks of registry of another Party is engaged in illicit traffic may so notify the flag State, request confirmation of registry and, in confirmed, request authorization from the flag State to take appropriate measures in regard to that vessel.

4. In accordance with paragraph 3 or in accordance with treaties in force between them or in accordance with any agreement or arrangement otherwise reached between those Parties, the flag State may authorize the requesting State to, *inter alia*:

    (a) Board the vessel;

    (b) Search the vessel;

    (c) If evidence of involvement in illicit traffic is found, take appropriate action with respect to the vessel, persons and cargo on board.

5. Where action is taken pursuant to this article, the Parties concerned shall take due account of the need not to endanger the safety of life at sea, the security of the vessel and the cargo or to prejudice the commercial and legal interests of the flag State or any other interested State.

6. The flag State may, consistent with its obligations in paragraph 1 of this article, subject its authorization to conditions to be mutually agreed between it and the requesting Party, including conditions relating to responsibility.

7. For the purposes of paragraphs 3 and 4 of this article, a Party shall respond expeditiously to a request from another Party to determine whether a vessel that is flying its flag is entitled to do so, and to requests for authorization made pursuant to paragraph 3. At the time of becoming a Party to this Convention, each Party shall designate an authority or, when necessary, authorities to receive and respond to such requests. Such designation shall be notified through the Secretary-General to all other Parties within one month of the designation.

8. A Party which has taken any action in accordance with this article shall promptly inform the flag State concerned of the results of that action.

9. The Parties shall consider entering into bilateral or regional agreements or arrangements to carry out, or to enhance the effectiveness of, the provisions of this article.

10. Action pursuant to paragraph 4 of this article shall be carried out only by warships or military aircraft, or other ships or aircraft clearly marked and identifiable as being on government service and authorized to that effect.

11. Any action taken in accordance with this article shall take due account of the need not to interfere with or affect the rights and obligations and the exercise of jurisdiction of coastal States in accordance with the international law of the sea.

Article 18

Free Trade Zones and Free Ports

1. The Parties shall apply measures to suppress illicit traffic in narcotic drugs, psychotropic substances and substances in Table I and Table II in free trade zones and in free ports that are no less stringent than those applied in other parts of their territories.

2. The Parties shall endeavour:

   (a) To monitor the movement of goods and persons in free trade zones and free ports, and, to that end, shall empower the competent authorities to search cargoes and incoming and outgoing vessels, including pleasure craft and fishing vessels, as well as aircraft and vehicles and, when appropriate, to search crew members, passengers and their baggage;

   (b) To establish and maintain a system to detect consignments suspected of containing narcotic drugs, psychotropic substance and substances in Table I and Table II passing into or out of free trade zones and free ports;

   (c) To establish and maintain surveillance systems in harbour and dock areas and at airports and border control points in free trade zones and free ports.

Article 19

The Use of the Mails

1. In conformity with their obligations under the Conventions of the Universal Postal Union, and in accordance with the basic principles of their domestic legal systems, the Parties shall adopt measures to suppress the use of the mails for illicit traffic and shall co-operate with one another to that end.

2. The measures referred to in paragraph 1 of this article shall include, in particular:

   (a) Co-ordinated action for the prevention and repression of the use of the mails for illicit traffic;

   (b) Introduction and maintenance by authorized law enforcement personnel of investigative and control techniques designed to detect illicit consignments of narcotic drugs, psychotropic substances and substances in Table I and Table II in the mails;

   (c) Legislative measures to enable the use of appropriate means to secure evidence required for judicial proceedings.

Article 20

Information to be Furnished by the Parties

1. The Parties shall furnish, through the Secretary-General, information to the Commission on the working of this Convention in their territories and, in particular:

   (a) The text of laws and regulations promulgated in order to give effect to the Convention;

   (b) Particulars of cases of illicit traffic within their jurisdiction which they consider important because of new trends disclosed, the quantities involved, the sources from which the substances are obtained, or the methods employed by persons so engaged.

2. The Parties shall furnish such information in such a manner and by such dates as the Commission may request.

Article 21

Functions of the Commission

The Commission is authorized to consider all matters pertaining to the aims of this convention and, in particular:

(a) The Commission shall, on the basis of the information submitted by the Parties in accordance with Article 20, review the operation of this Convention;

(b) The Commission may make suggestions and general recommendations based on the examination of the information received from the Parties;

(c) The Commission may call the attention of the Board to any matters which may be relevant to the functions of the Board;

(d) The Commission shall, on any matter referred to it by the Board under article 22, paragraph 1 (b), take such action as it deems appropriate;

(e) The Commission may, in conformity with the procedures laid down in article 12, amend Table I and Table II;

(f) The Commission may draw the attention of non-Parties to decisions and recommendations which it adopts under this Convention, with a view to their considering taking action in accordance therewith.

Article 22

Functions of the Board

1. Without prejudice to the functions of the Commission under article 21, and without prejudice to the functions of the Board and the Commission under the 1961 Convention, the 1961 Convention as amended and the 1971 Convention:

(a) If, on the basis of its examination of information available to it, to the Secretary-General or to the Commission, or of information communicated by United Nations organs, the Board has reason to believe that the aims of this Convention, in matters related to its competence are not being met, the Board may invite a Party or Parties to furnish any relevant information;

(b) With respect to article 12, 13 and 16:

(i) After taking action under subparagraph (a) of this article, the Board, if satisfied that it is necessary to do so, may call upon the Party concerned to adopt such remedial measures as shall seem under the circumstances to be necessary for the execution of the provisions of articles 12, 13 and 16;

(ii) Prior to taking action under (iii) below, the Board shall treat as confidential its communications with the Party concerned under the preceding subparagraphs;

(iii) If the Board finds that the Party concerned has not taken remedial measures which it has been called upon to take under this subparagraph, it may call the attention of the Parties, the Council and the Commission to the matter. Any report published by the Board under this subparagraph shall also contain the views of the Party concerned if the latter so requests.

2. Any Party shall be invited to be represented at a meeting of the Board at which a question of direct interest to it is to be considered under this article.

3. If in any case a decision of the Board which is adopted under this article is not unanimous, the views of the minority shall be stated.

4. Decisions of the Board under this article shall be taken by a two-thirds majority of the whole number of the Board.

5. In carrying out its functions pursuant to subparagraph 1(a) of this article, the Board shall ensure the confidentiality of all information which may come into its possession.

6. The Board's responsibility under this article shall not apply to the implementation of treaties or agreements entered into between Parties in accordance with the provisions of this Convention.

7. The provisions of this article shall not be applicable to disputes between Parties falling under the provisions of article 32.

Article 23

Reports of the Board

1. The Board shall prepare an annual report on its work containing an analysis of the information at its disposal and, in appropriate cases, an account of the explanations, if any, given by or required of Parties, together with any observations and recommendations which the Board desires to make.

The Board may make such additional reports as it considers necessary. The reports shall be submitted to the Council through the Commission which may make such comments as it sees fit.

2. The reports of the Board shall be communicated to the Parties and subsequently published by the Secretary-General. The Parties shall permit their unrestricted distribution.

Article 24

Application of Stricter Measures than those Required by This Convention

A Party may adopt more strict or severe measures than those provided by this Convention if, in its opinion, such measures are desirable or necessary for the prevention or suppression of illicit traffic.

Article 25

Non-derogation from Earlier Treaty Rights and Obligations

The provisions of this Convention shall not derogate from any rights enjoyed or obligations undertaken by Parties to this Convention under the 1961 Convention, the 1961 Convention as amended and the 1971 Convention.

Article 26

Signature

This Convention shall be open for signature at the United Nations Office at Vienna, from 20 December 1988 to 28 February 1989, and thereafter at the Headquarters of the United Nations at New York, until 20 December 1989, by:

    (a)   All States;

    (b)   Namibia, represented by the United Nations Council for Namibia;

(c) Regional economic integration organizations which have competence in respect of the negotiation, conclusion and application of international agreements in matters covered by this Convention, references under the Convention to Parties, States or national services being applicable to these organizations within the limits of their competence.

Article 27

Ratification, Acceptance, Approval or Act of Formal Confirmation

1. This Convention is subject to ratification, acceptance or approval by States and by Namibia, represented by the United Nations Council for Namibia, and to acts of formal confirmation by regional economic integration organizations referred to in article 26, subparagraph (c). The instruments of ratification, acceptance or approval and those relating to acts of formal confirmation shall be deposited with the Secretary-General.

2. In their instruments of formal confirmation, regional economic integration organizations shall declare the extent of their competence with respect to the matters governed by this Convention. These organizations shall also inform the Secretary-General of any modification in the extent of their competence with respect to the matters governed by the Convention.

Article 28

Accession

1. This Convention shall remain open for accession by any State, by Namibia, represented by the United Nations Council for Namibia, and by regional economic integration organizations referred to in article 26, subparagraph (c).
Accession shall be effected by the deposit of an instrument of accession with the Secretary-General.

2. In their instruments of accession, regional economic integration organizations shall declare the extent of their competence with respect to the matters governed by this Convention. These organizations shall also inform the Secretary-General of any modification in the extent of their competence with respect to the matters governed by the Convention.

Article 29

Entry into force

1. This Convention shall enter into force on the ninetieth day after the date of the deposit with the Secretary-General of the twentieth instrument of ratification, acceptance, approval or accession by States or by Namibia, represented by the Council for Namibia.

2. For each State or for Namibia, represented by the Council for Namibia, ratifying, accepting, approving or acceding to this Convention after the deposit of the twentieth instrument of ratification, acceptance, approval or accession, the Convention shall enter into force on the ninetieth day after the date of the deposit of its instrument of ratification, acceptance, approval or accession.

3. For each regional economic integration organization referred to in article 26, subparagraph (c) depositing an instrument relating to an act of formal confirmation or an instrument of accession, this Convention shall enter into force on the ninetieth day after such deposit, or at the date the Convention enters into force pursuant to paragraph 1 of this article, whichever is later.

Article 30

Denunciation

1. A Party may denounce this Convention at any time by a written notification addressed to the Secretary-General.

2. Such denunciation shall take effect for the Party concerned one year after the date of receipt of the notification by the Secretary-General.

Article 31

Amendments

1. Any Party may propose an amendment to this Convention. The text of any such amendment and the reasons therefor shall be communicated by that Party to the Secretary-General, who shall communicate it to the other Parties and shall ask them whether they accept the proposed amendment. If a proposed amendment so circulated has not been rejected by any Party within twenty-four months after it has been circulated, it shall be deemed to have been accepted and shall enter into force in respect of a Party ninety days after that Party has deposited with the Secretary-General an instrument expressing its consent to be bound by that amendment.

2. If a proposed amendment has been rejected by any Party, the Secretary-General shall consult with the Parties and, if a majority so requests, he shall bring the matter, together with any comments made by the Parties, before the Council which may decide to call a conference in accordance with Article 62, paragraph 4, of the Charter of the United Nations. Any amendment resulting from such a Conference shall be embodied in a Protocol of Amendment. Consent to be bound by such a Protocol shall be required to be expressed specifically to the Secretary-General.

Article 32

Settlement of disputes

1. If there should arise between two or more Parties a dispute relating to the interpretation or application of this Convention, the Parties shall consult together with a view to the settlement of the dispute by negotiation, enquiry, mediation, conciliation, arbitration, recourse to regional bodies, judicial process or other peaceful means of their own choice.

2. Any such dispute which cannot be settled in the manner prescribed in paragraph 1 of this article shall be referred, at the request of any one of the States Parties to the dispute, to the International Court of Justice for decision.

3. If a regional economic integration organization referred to in article 26, subparagraph (c) is a Party to a dispute which cannot be settled in the manner prescribed in paragraph 1 of this article, it may, through a State Member of the United Nations, request the Council to request an advisory opinion of the International Court of Justice in accordance with article 65 of the Statute of the Court, which opinion shall be regarded as decisive.

4. Each State, at the time of signature or ratification, acceptance or approval of this Convention or accession thereto, or each regional economic integration organization, at the time of signature or deposit of an act of formal confirmation or accession, may declare that it does not consider itself bound by paragraphs 2 and 3 of this article. The other Parties shall not be bound by paragraphs 2 and 3 with respect to any Party having made such a declaration.

5. Any Party having made a declaration in accordance with paragraph 4 of this article may at any time withdraw the declaration by notification to the Secretary-General.

Article 33

Authentic Texts

The Arabic, Chinese, English, French, Russian and Spanish texts of this Convention are equally authentic.

Article 34

Depositary

The Secretary-General shall be the depositary of this Convention.

Convention on Laundering, Search, Seizure and Confiscation of the Proceeds from Crime (1990)[*]

Strasbourg, 8 November 1990

Chapter I

Use of terms

Article 1

Use of Terms

For the purposes of this Convention:

a. "proceeds" means any economic advantage from criminal offences. It may consist of any property as defined in sub-paragraph b of this article;

b. "property" includes property of any description, whether corporeal or incorporeal, movable or immovable, and legal documents or instruments evidencing title to, or interest in such property;

c. "instrumentalities" means any property used or intended to be used, in any manner, wholly or in part, to commit a criminal offence or criminal offences;

d. "confiscation" means a penalty or a measure, ordered by a court following proceedings in relation to a criminal offence or criminal offences resulting in the final deprivation of property;

e. "predicate offence" means any criminal offence as a result of which proceeds were generated that may become the subject of an offence as defined in Article 6 of this Convention.

Chapter II

Measures to be taken at national level

Article 2

Confiscation measures

1. Each Party shall adopt such legislative and other measures as may be necessary to enable it to confiscate instrumentalities and proceeds or property the value of which corresponds to such proceeds.

2. Each Party may, at the time of signature or when depositing its instrument of ratification, acceptance, approval or accession, by a declaration addressed to the Secretary General of the Council of Europe, declare that paragraph 1 of this article applies only to offences or categories of offences specified in such declaration.

---

[*] *European Treaties Series*, No.141.

Article 3

Investigative and provisional measures

Each Party shall adopt such legislative and other measures as may be necessary to enable it to identify and trace property which is liable to confiscation pursuant to Article 2, paragraph 1, and to prevent any dealing in, transfer or disposal of such property.

Article 4

Special investigative powers and techniques

1. Each Party shall adopt such legislative and other measures as may be necessary to empower its courts or other competent authorities to order that bank, financial or commercial records be made available or be seized in order to carry out the actions referred to in Articles 2 and 3. A Party shall not decline to act under the provisions of this article on grounds of bank secrecy.

2. Each Party shall consider adopting such legislative and other measures as may be necessary to enable it to use special investigative techniques facilitating the identification and tracing of proceeds and the gathering of evidence related thereto. Such techniques may include monitoring orders, observation, interception of telecommunications, access to computer systems and orders to produce specific documents.

Article 5

Legal remedies

Each Party shall adopt such legislative and other measures as may be necessary to ensure that interested parties affected by measures under Article 2 and 3 shall have effective legal remedies in order to preserve their rights.

Article 6

Laundering offences

1. Each Party shall adopt such legislative and other measures as may be necessary to establish as offences under its domestic law, when committed intentionally:

    (a) the conversion or transfer of property, knowing that such property is proceeds, for the purpose of concealing or disguising the illicit origin of the property or of assisting any person who in involved in the commission of the predicate offence to evade the legal consequences of his actions;

    (b) the concealment or disguise of the true nature, source, location, disposition, movement, rights with respect to, or ownership of, property, knowing that such property is proceeds;

    and, subject to its constitutional principles and the basic concepts of its legal system:

    (c) the acquisition, possession or use of property, knowing, at the time of receipt, that such property was proceeds;

    (d) participation in, association or conspiracy to commit, attempts to commit and aiding, abetting, facilitating and counselling the commission of any of the offences established in accordance with this article.

2. For the purposes of implementing or applying paragraph 1 of this article:

    (a) it shall not matter whether the predicate offence was subject to the criminal jurisdiction of the Party;

(b) it may be provided that the offences set forth in that paragraph do not apply to the persons who committed the predicate offence;

(c) knowledge, intent or purpose required as a element of an offence set forth in that paragraph may be inferred from objective, factual circumstances.

3. Each Party may adopt such measures as it considers necessary to establish also as offences under its domestic law all or some of the acts referred to in paragraph 1 of this article, in any or all of the following cases where the offender:

(a) ought to have assumed that the property was proceeds;

(b) acted for the purpose of making profit;

(c) acted for the purpose of promoting the carrying on of further criminal activity.

4. Each Party may, at the time of signature or when depositing its instrument of ratification, acceptance, approval or accession, by declaration addressed to the Secretary General of the Council of Europe declare that paragraph 1 of this article applies only to predicate offences or categories of such offences specified in such declaration.

Chapter III

International Co-operation

Section 1

Principles of international co-operation

Article 7

General principles and measures for international co-operation

1. The Parties shall co-operate with each other to the widest extent possible for the purposes of investigations and proceedings aiming at the confiscation of instrumentalities and proceeds.

2. Each Party shall adopt such legislative or other measures as may be necessary to enable it to comply, under the conditions provided for in this chapter, with requests:

(a) for confiscation of specific items of property representing proceeds or instrumentalities, as well as for confiscation of proceeds consisting in a requirement to pay a sum of money corresponding to the value of proceeds;

(b) for investigative assistance and provisional measures with a view to either form of confiscation referred to under a above.

Section 2

Investigative assistance

Article 8

Obligation to assist

The Parties shall afford each other, upon request, the widest possible measure of assistance in the identification and tracing of instrumentalities, proceeds and other property liable to confiscation. Such assistance shall include any measure providing and securing evidence as to the existence, location or movement, nature, legal status or value of the aforementioned property.

Article 9

Execution of assistance

The assistance pursuant to Article 8 shall be carried out as permitted by and in accordance with the domestic law of the requested Party and, to the extent not incompatible with such law, in accordance with the procedures specified in the request.

Article 10

Spontaneous information

Without prejudice to its own investigations or proceedings, a Party may without prior request forward to another Party information on instrumentalities and proceeds, when it considers that the disclosure of such information might assist the receiving Party in initiating or carrying out investigations or proceedings or might lead to a request by that Party under this chapter.

Section 3

Provisional measures

Article 11

Obligation to take provisional measures

1. At the request of another Party which has instituted criminal proceedings or proceedings for the purpose of confiscation, a Party shall take the necessary provisional measures, such as freezing or seizing, to prevent any dealing in, transfer or disposal of property which, at a later stage, may be the subject of a request for confiscation or which might be such as to satisfy the request.

2. A Party which has received a request for confiscation pursuant to Article 13 shall, if so requested, take the measures mentioned in paragraph 1 of this article in respect of any property which is the subject of the request or which might be such as to satisfy the request.

Article 12

Execution of provisional measures

1. The provisional measures mentioned in Article 11 shall be carried out as permitted by and in accordance with the domestic law of the requested Party and, to the extent not incompatible with such law, in accordance with the procedures specified in the request.

2. Before lifting any provisional measure taken pursuant to this article, the requested Party shall, wherever possible, give the requesting Party an opportunity to present its reasons in favour of continuing the measure.

Section 4

Confiscation

Article 13

Obligation to confiscate

1. A Party, which has received a request made by another Party for confiscation concerning instrumentalities or proceeds, situated in its territory, shall:

    (a)   enforce a confiscation order made by a court of a requesting Party in relation to such instrumentalities or proceeds: or

(b) submit the request to its competent authorities for the purpose of obtaining an order of confiscation and, if such order is granted, enforce it.

2. For the purposes of applying paragraph 1, b of this article, any Party shall whenever necessary have competence to institute confiscation proceedings under its own law.

3. The provisions of paragraph 1 of this article shall also apply to confiscation consisting in a requirement to pay a sum of money corresponding to the value of proceeds, if property on which the confiscation can be enforced is located in the requested Party. In such cases, when enforcing confiscation pursuant to paragraph 1, the requested Party shall, if payment is not obtained, realise the claim on any property available for that purpose.

4. If a request for confiscation concerns a specific item of property, the Parties may agree that the requested Party may enforce the confiscation in the form of a requirement to pay a sum of money corresponding to the value of the property.

Article 14

Execution of confiscation

1. The procedures for obtaining and enforcing the confiscation under Article 13 shall be governed by the law of the requested Party.

2. The requested Party shall be bound by the findings as to the facts in so far as they are stated in a conviction or judicial decision of the requesting Party or in so far as such conviction or judicial decision is implicitly based on them.

3. Each Party may, at the time of signature or when depositing its instrument of ratification, acceptance, approval or accession, by a declaration addressed to the Secretary General of the Council of Europe, declare that paragraph 2 of this article applies only subject to its constitutional principles and the basic concepts of its legal system.

4. If the confiscation consists in the requirements to pay a sum of money, the competent authority of the requested Party shall convert the amount thereof into the currency of that Party at the rate of exchange ruling at the time when the decision to enforce the confiscation is taken.

5. In the case of Article 13, paragraph 1a, the requesting Party alone shall have the right to decide on any application for review of the confiscation order.

Article 15

Confiscated property

Any property confiscated by the requested Party shall be disposed of by that Party in accordance with its domestic law, unless otherwise agreed by the Parties concerne(d)

Article 16

Right of enforcement and maximum amount of confiscation

1. A request for confiscation made under Article 13 does not affect the right of the requesting Party to enforce itself the confiscation order.

2. Nothing in this Convention shall be so interpreted as to permit the total value of the confiscation to exceed the amount of the sum of money specified in the confiscation order. If a Party finds that this might occur, the Parties concerned shall enter into consultations to avoid such an effect.

Article 17

Imprisonment in default

The requested Party shall not impose imprisonment in default or any other measure restricting the liberty of a person as a result of a request under Article 13, if the requesting Party has so specified in the request.

Section 5

Refusal and postponement of co-operation

Article 18

Grounds for refusal

1. Co-operation under this chapter may be refused if:

    (a) the action sought would be contrary to the fundamental principles of the legal system of the requested Party; or

    (b) the execution of the request is likely to prejudice the sovereignty, security, ordre public or other essential interests of the requested Party; or

    (c) in the opinion of the requested Party, the importance of the case to which the request relates does not justify the taking of the action sought; or

    (d) the offence to which the request relates is a political or fiscal offence: or

    (e) the requested Party considers that compliance with the action sought would be contrary to the principle of ne bis in idem; or

    (f) the offence to which the request relates would not be an offence under the law of the requested Party if committed within its jurisdiction. However, this ground for refusal applies to co-operation under Section 2 only in so far as the assistance sought involves coercive action.

2. Co-operation under Section 2, in so far as the assistance sought involves coercive action, and under Section 3 of this chapter, may also be refused if the measures sought could not be taken under the domestic law of the requested Party for the purposes of investigations or proceedings, had it been a similar domestic case.

3. Where the law of the requested Party so requires, co-operation under Section 2, in so far as the assistance sought involves coercive action, and under Section 3 of this chapter may also be refused if the measures sought or any other measures having similar effects would not be permitted under the law of the requesting Party, or, as regards the competent authorities of the requesting Party, if the request is not authorised by either a judge or another judicial authority, including public prosecutors, any of these authorities acting in relation to criminal offences.

4. Co-operation under Section 4 of this chapter may also be refused if:

    (a) under the law of the requested Party confiscation is not provided for in respect of the type of offence to which the request relates; or

    (b) without prejudice to the obligation pursuant to Article 13, paragraph 3, it would be contrary to the principles of the domestic laws of the requested Party concerning the limits of confiscation in respect of the relationship between an offence and:

        (i) an economic advantage that might be qualified as its proceeds; or

(ii) property that might be qualified as its instrumentalities; or

(c) under the law of the requested Party confiscation may no longer be imposed or enforced because of the lapse of time; or

(d) the request does not relate to a previous conviction, or a decision of a judicial nature or a statement in such a decision that an offence or several offences have been committed, on the basis of which the confiscation has been ordered or is sought; or

(e) confiscation is either not enforceable in the requesting Party, or it is still subject to ordinary means of appeal: or

(f) the request relates to a confiscation order resulting from a decision rendered in absentia of the person against whom the order was issued and, in the opinion of the requested Party, the proceedings conducted by the requesting Party leading to such decision did not satisfy the minimum rights of defence recognised as due to everyone against whom a criminal charge is made.

5. For the purposes of paragraph 4.f of this article a decision is not considered to have been rendered in absentia if:

(a) it has been confirmed or pronounced after opposition by the person concerned; or

(b) it has been rendered on appeal, provided that the appeal was lodged by the person concerned

6. When considering, for the purposes of paragraph 4.f of this article, if the minimum rights of defence have been satisfied, the requested Party shall take into account the fact that the person concerned has deliberately sought to evade justice or the fact that that person, having had the possibility of lodging a legal remedy against the decision made in absentia, elected not to do so. The same will apply when the person concerned, having been duly served with the summons to appear, elected not to do so nor to ask for adjournment.

7. A Party shall not invoke bank secrecy as a ground to refuse any co-operation under this chapter. Where its domestic law so requires, a Party may require that a request for co-operation which would involve the lifting of bank secrecy be authorised by either a judge or another judicial authority, including public prosecutors, any of these authorities acting in relation to criminal offences.

8. Without prejudice to the ground for refusal provided for in paragraph 1.a of this article:

(a) the fact that the person under investigation or subjected to a confiscation order by the authorities of the requesting Party is a legal person shall not be invoked by the requested Party as an obstacle to affording any co-operation under this chapter;

(b) the fact that the natural person against whom an order of confiscation of proceeds has been issued has subsequently died or the fact that a legal person against whom an order of confiscation of proceeds has been issued has subsequently been dissolved shall not be invoked as an obstacle to render assistance in accordance with Article 13, paragraph 1.(a)

Article 19

Postponement

The requested Party may postpone action on a request if such action would prejudice investigations or proceedings by its authorities.

Article 20

Partial or conditional granting of a request

Before refusing or postponing co-operation under this chapter, the requested Party shall, where appropriate after having consulted the requesting Party, consider whether the request may be granted partially or subject to such conditions as it deems necessary.

Section 6

Notification and protection of third parties' rights

Article 21

Notification of documents

1. The Parties shall afford each other the widest measure of mutual assistance in the serving of judicial documents to persons affected by provisional measures and confiscation.

2. Nothing in this article is intended to interfere with:

    (a) the possibility of sending judicial documents, by postal channels, directly to persons abroad;

    (b) the possibility for judicial officers, officials or other competent authorities of the Party of origin to effect service of judicial documents directly through the consular authorities of that Party or through judicial officers, officials or other competent authorities of the Party of destination,

    unless the Party of destination makes a declaration to the contrary to the Secretary General of the Council of Europe at the time of signature or when depositing its instrument of ratification, acceptance, approval or accession.

3. When serving judicial documents to persons abroad affected by provisional measures or confiscation orders issued in the sending Party, this Party shall indicate what legal remedies are available under its law to such persons.

Article 22

Recognition of foreign decisions

1. When dealing with a request for co-operation under Section 3 and 4, the requested Party shall recognise any judicial decision taken in the requesting Party regarding rights claimed by third parties.

2. Recognition may be refused if:

    (a) third parties did not have adequate opportunity to assert their rights; or

    (b) the decision is incompatible with a decision already taken in the requested Party on the same matter; or

    (c) it is incompatible with the ordre public of the requested Party; or

    (d) the decision was taken contrary to provisions on exclusive jurisdiction provided for by the law of the requested Party.

Section 7

Procedural and other general rules

Article 23

Central authority

1. The Parties shall designate a central authority or, if necessary, authorities, which shall be responsible for sending and answering requests made under this chapter, the execution of such requests or the transmission of them to the authorities competent for their execution.

2. Each Party shall, at the time of signature or when depositing its instrument of ratification, acceptance, approval or accession, communicate to the Secretary General of the Council of Europe the names and addresses of the authorities designated in pursuance of paragraph 1 of this article.

Article 24

1. The central authorities shall communicate directly with one another.

2. In the event of urgency, requests or communications under this chapter may be sent directly by the judicial authorities, including public prosecutors, of the requesting Party to such authorities of the requested Party. In such cases a copy shall be sent at the same time to the central authority of the requested Party through the central authority of the requesting Party.

3. Any request or communication under paragraphs 1 and 2 of this article may be made through the International Criminal Police Organisation (Interpol).

4. Where a request is made pursuant to paragraph 2 of this article and the authority is not competent to deal with the request, it shall refer the request to the competent national authority and inform directly the requesting Party that it has done so.

5. Requests or communications under Section 2 of this chapter, which do not involve coercive action, may be directly transmitted by the competent authorities of the requesting Party to the competent authorities of the requested Party.

Article 25

Form of request and languages

1. All requests under this chapter shall be made in writing. Modern means of telecommunications, such as telefax, may be used.

2. Subject to the provisions of paragraph 3 of this article, translations of the requests or supporting documents shall not be required.

3. At the time of signature or when depositing its instrument of ratification, acceptance, approval or accession, any Party may communicate to the Secretary General of the Council of Europe a declaration that it reserves the right to require that requests made to it and documents supporting such requests be accompanied by a translation into its own language or into one of the official languages of the Council of Europe or into such one of these languages as it shall indicate. It may on that occasion declare its readiness to accept translations in any other language as it may specify. The other Parties may apply the reciprocity rule.

Article 26

Legislation

Documents transmitted in application of this chapter shall be exempt from all legislation formalities.

Article 27

Content of request

1. Any request for co-operation under this chapter shall specify:

    (a) the authority making the request and the authority carrying out the investigation or proceedings;

    (b) the object of and the reason for the request;

    (c) the matters, including the relevant facts (such as date, place and circumstances of the offence) to which the investigations or proceedings relate, except in the case of a request for notification;

    (d) in so far as the co-operation involves coercive action:

    (i) the text of the statutory provisions or, where this is not possible, a statement of the relevant law applicable; and

    (ii) an indication that the measure sought or any other measures having similar effects could be take in the territory of the requesting Party under its own law;

    (e) where necessary and in so far as possible:

    (i) details of the person or persons concerned, including name, date and place of birth, nationality and location, and, in the case of a legal person, its seat; and

    (ii) the property in relation to which co-operation is sought, its location, its connection with the person or persons concerned, any connection with the offence, as well as any available information about other persons' interests in the property; and

    (f) any particular procedure the requesting Party wishes to be followed.

2. A request for provisional measures under Section 3 in relation to seizure of property on which a confiscation order consisting in the requirement to pay a sum of money be realised shall also indicate a maximum amount for which recovery is sought in that property.

3. In addition to the indications mentioned in paragraph 1, any request under Section 4 shall contain:

    (a) in the case of Article 13, paragraph 1.a:

    (i) a certified true copy of the confiscation order made by the court in the requesting Party and a statement of the grounds on the basis of which the order was made, if they are not indicated in the order itself;

    (ii) an attestation by the competent authority of the requesting Party that the confiscation order is enforceable and not subject to ordinary means of appeal;

    (iii) information as to the necessity of taking any provisional measures;

    (b) in the case of Article 13, paragraph 1.b, a statement of the facts relied upon by the requesting Party sufficient to enable the requested Party to seek the order under its domestic law;

    (c) when third parties have had the opportunity to claim rights, documents demonstrating that this has been the case.

Article 28

Defective requests

1. If a request does not comply with the provisions of this chapter or the information supplied is not sufficient to enable the requested Party to deal with the request, that Party may ask the requesting Party to amend the request or to complete it with additional information.

2. The requested Party may set a time-limit for the receipt of such amendments or information.

3. Pending receipt of the requested amendments or information in relation to a request under Section 4 of this chapter, the requested Party may take any of the measures referred to in Sections 2 or 3 of this chapter.

Article 29

Plurality of requests

1. Where the requested Party receives more than one request under Sections 3 or 4 of this chapter in respect of the same person or property, the plurality of requests shall not prevent that Party from dealing with the requests involving the taking of provisional measures.

2. In the case of plurality of requests under Section 4 of this chapter, the requested Party shall consider consulting the requesting Parties.

Article 30

Obligations to give reasons

The requested Party shall give reasons for any decision to refuse, postpone or make conditional any co-operation under this chapter.

Article 31

Information

1. The requested Party shall promptly inform the requesting Party of:

    (a) the action initiated on a request under this chapter;

    (b) the final result of the action carried out on the basis of the request;

    (c) a decision to refuse, postpone or make conditional, in whole or in part, any co-operation under this chapter;

    (d) any circumstances which render impossible the carrying out of the action sought or are likely to delay it significantly; and

    (e) in the event of provisional measures taken pursuant to a request under Sections 2 or 3 of this chapter, such provisions of its domestic law as would automatically lead to the lifting of the provisional measure.

2. The requesting Party shall promptly inform the requested Party of:

    (a) any review, decision or any other fact by reason of which the confiscation order ceases to be wholly or partially enforceable; and

    (b) any development, factual or legal, by reason of which any action under this chapter is no longer justified.

3. Where a Party, on the basis of the same confiscation order, requests confiscation in more that one Party, it shall inform all Parties which are affected by an enforcement of the order about the request.

Article 32

Restriction of use

1. The requested Party may make the execution of a request dependent on the condition that the information or evidence obtained will not, without its prior consent, be used or transmitted by the authorities of the requesting Party for investigations or proceedings other than those specified in the request.

2. Each Party may, at the time of signature or when depositing its instrument of ratification, acceptance, approval or accession, by declaration addressed to the Secretary General of the Council of Europe, declare that, without its prior consent, information or evidence provided by it under this chapter may not be used or transmitted by the authorities of the requesting Party in investigations or proceedings other than those specified in the request.

Article 33

Confidentiality

1. The requesting Party may require that the requested Party keep confidential the facts and substance of the request, except to the extent necessary to execute the request. If the requested Party cannot comply with the requirement of confidentiality, it shall promptly inform the requesting Party.

2. The requesting Party shall, if not contrary to basic principles of its national law and if so requested, keep confidential any evidence and information provided by the requested Party, except to the extent that its disclosure is necessary for the investigation or proceedings described in the request.

3. Subject to the provisions of its domestic law, a Party which has received spontaneous information under Article 10 shall comply with any requirement of confidentiality as required by the Party which supplies the information. If the other Party cannot comply with such requirement, it shall promptly inform the transmitting Party.

Article 34

Costs

The ordinary costs of complying with a request shall be borne by the requested Party. Where costs of a substantial or extraordinary nature are necessary to comply with a request, the Parties shall consult in order to agree the conditions on which the request is to be executed and how to costs shall be borne.

Article 35

Damages

1. When legal action on liability for damages resulting from an act or omission in relation to co-operation under this chapter has been initiated by a person, the Parties concerned shall consider consulting each other, where appropriate, to determine how to apportion any sum of damages due.

2. A party which has become subject of a litigation for damages shall endeavour to inform the other Party of such litigation if that Party might have an interest in the case.

Chapter IV

Final Provisions

Article 36

Signature and entry into force

1. This Convention shall be open for signature by the member States of the Council of Europe and non-member States which have participated in its elaboration. Such States may express their consent to be bound by:

    (a)   signature without reservation as to ratification, acceptance or approval; or

    (b)   signature subject to ratification, acceptance or approval, followed by ratification, acceptance or approval.

2. Instruments of ratification, acceptance or approval shall be deposited with the Secretary General of the Council of Europe.

3. This Convention shall enter into force on the first day of the month following the expiration of a period of three months after the date on which three States, of which at least two are member States of the Council of Europe, have expressed their consent to be bound by the Convention in accordance with the provisions of paragraph 1.

4. In respect of any signatory State which subsequently expresses its consent to be bound by it, the Convention shall enter into force on the first day of the month following the expiration of a period of three months after the date of the expression of its consent to be bound by the Convention in accordance with the provisions of paragraph 1.

Article 37

Accession to the Convention

1. After the entry into force of this Convention, the Committee of Ministers of the Council of Europe, after consulting the Contracting States to the Convention, may invite any State not a member of the Council and not having participated in its elaboration to accede to this Convention, by a decision taken by the majority provided for in Article 20.d of the Statute of the Council of Europe and by the unanimous vote of the representatives of the Contracting States entitled to sit on the Committee.

2. In respect of any acceding State the Convention shall enter into force on the first day of the month following the expiration of a period of three months after the date of deposit of the instrument of accession with the Secretary General of the Council of Europe.

Article 38

Territorial application

1. Any State may, at the time of signature or when depositing its instrument of ratification, acceptance, approval or accession, specify the territory or territories to which this Convention shall apply.

2. Any State may, at any later date, by a declaration addressed to the Secretary General of the Council of Europe, extend the application of this Convention to any other territory specified in the declaration. In respect of such territory the Convention shall enter into force on the first day of the month following the expiration of a period of three months after the date of receipt of such declaration by the Secretary General.

3. Any declaration made under the two preceding paragraphs may, in respect of any territory specified in such declaration, be withdrawn by a notification addressed to the Secretary General. The withdrawal shall become effective on the first day of the month following

the expiration of a period of three months after the date of receipt of such notification by the Secretary General.

Article 39

Relationship to other conventions and agreements

1. This Convention does not affect the rights and undertakings derived from international multilateral conventions concerning special matters.

2. The Parties to the Convention may conclude bilateral or multilateral agreements with one another on the matters dealt with in this Convention, for purposes of supplementing or strengthening its provisions or facilitating the application of the principles embodied in it.

3. If two or more Parties have already concluded an agreement or treaty in respect of a subject which is dealt with in this Convention or otherwise have established their relations in respect of that subject, they shall be entitled to apply that agreement or treaty or to regulate those relations accordingly, in lieu of the present Convention, if it facilitates international co-operation.

Article 40

Reservations

1. Any State may, at the time of signature or when depositing its instrument of ratification, acceptance, approval or accession, declare that it avails itself of one or more of the reservations provided for in Article 2, paragraph 2, Article 6, paragraph 4, Article 14, paragraph 3, Article 21, paragraph 2, Article 25, paragraph 3 and Article 32, paragraph 2. No other reservation may be made.

2. Any State which has made a reservation under the preceding paragraph may wholly or partly withdraw it by means of a notification addressed to the Secretary General of the Council of Europe. The withdrawal shall take effect on the date of receipt of such notification by the Secretary General.

3. A Party which has made a reservation in respect of a provision of this Convention may not claim the application of that provision by any other Party; it may, however, if its reservation is partial or conditional, claim the application of that provision in so far as it has itself accepted it.

Article 41

Amendments

1. Amendments to this Convention may be proposed by any Party, and shall be communicated by the Secretary General of the Council of Europe to the member States of the Council of Europe and to every non-member State which has acceded to or has been invited to accede to this Convention in accordance with the provisions of Article 37.

2. Any amendment proposed by a Party shall be communicated to the European Committee on Crime Problems which shall submit to the Committee of Ministers its opinion on that proposed amendment.

3. The Committee of Ministers shall consider the proposed amendment and the opinion submitted by the European Committee on Crime Problems and may adopt the amendment.

4. The text of any amendment adopted by the Committee of Ministers in accordance with paragraph 3 of this article shall be forwarded to the Parties for acceptance.

5. Any amendment adopted in accordance with paragraph 3 of this article shall come into force on the thirtieth day after all Parties have informed the Secretary General of their acceptance thereof.

Article 42

Settlement of disputes

1. The European Committee on Crime Problems of the Council of Europe shall be kept informed regarding the interpretation and application of this Convention.

2. In case of a dispute between Parties as to the interpretation or application of this Convention, they shall seek a settlement of the dispute through negotiation or any other peaceful means of their choice, including submission of the dispute to the European Committee on Crime Problems, to an arbitral tribunal whose decisions shall be binding upon the Parties, or to the International Court of Justice, as agreed upon by the Parties concerned.

Article 43

Denunciation

1. Any Party may, at any time, denounce this Convention by means of a notification addressed to the Secretary General of the Council of Europe.

2. Such denunciation shall become effective on the first day of the month following the expiration of a period of three months after the date of receipt of the notification by the Secretary General.

3. The present Convention shall, however, continue to apply to the enforcement under Article 14 of confiscation for which a request has been made in conformity with the provisions of this Convention before the date on which such a denunciation takes effect.

Article 44

Notifications

The secretary General of the Council of Europe shall notify the member States of the Council and any State which has acceded to this Convention of:

(a) any signature

(b) the deposit of any instrument of ratification, acceptance, approval or accession;

(c) any date of entry into force of this Convention in accordance with Articles 36 and 37;

(d) any reservation made under Article 40, paragraph 1;

(e) any other act, notification or communication relating to this Convention.

Schengen Convention - Title III - Chapter VI (excerpts) (1990)[*]

Schengen, 19 June 1990

Title III

Police and Security

Chapter VI

Narcotic Drugs

Article 70

1. The Contracting Parties shall set up a permanent working party to examine common problems relating to the combating of offenses involving narcotic drugs and to draw up proposals, where necessary, to improve the practical and technical aspects of co-operation between the Contracting Parties. The working party shall submit its proposals to the Executive Committee.

2. The working party referred to in paragraph 1, the members of which are nominated by the relevant national authorities, shall include representatives of the police and of the customs authorities.

Article 71

1. The Contracting Parties undertake as regards the direct or indirect sale of narcotic drugs and psychotropic substances of whatever type, including cannabis, and the possession of such products and substances for sale or export, to take, in compliance with the existing United Nations Conventions all measures necessary for the prevention and punishment of the illicit traffic in narcotic drugs and psychotropic substances.

2. The Contracting Parties undertake to prevent and to punish by administrative and penal measures the illegal export of narcotic drugs and psychotropic substances, including cannabis, as well as the sale, supply and handling of such products and substances, without prejudice to the relevant provisions of Article 74, 75 and 76.

3. To combat the illegal importation of narcotic drugs and psychotropic substances, including cannabis, the Contracting Parties shall strengthen the checks on the movement of persons and goods and of means of transport at their external borders. Such measures shall be drawn up by the working party provided for in Article 70. This working party shall consider inter alia the reassignment of some of the police and customs staff released from internal border duty, as well as recourse to modern drug-detection methods and sniffer dogs.

4. To ensure compliance with this Article, the Contracting Parties shall specifically maintain surveillance on places known to be used for drug trafficking.

5. The Contracting Parties shall do all in their power to prevent and combat the negative effects of the illicit demand for narcotic drugs and psychotropic substances of whatever kind, including cannabis. The measures adopted to this end shall be the responsibility of each Contracting Party.

---

[*] Convention of 19 June 1990, applying the Schengen Agreement of 14 June 1985 between the Governments of the States of the Benelux Economic Union, the Federal Republic of Germany and the French Republic, on the Gradual Abolition of Checks at their Common Borders, *International Legal Materials*, 1991, 84.

Article 72

The Contracting Parties shall in accordance, with their constitution and their national legal system, ensure that legislation is enacted to permit the seizure and confiscation of assets deriving from illicit traffic in narcotic drugs and psychotropic substances.

Article 73

1. The Contracting Parties undertake, in accordance with their constitution and their national legal system, to take measures to allow monitored deliveries to take place in the illicit traffic in narcotic drugs and psychotropic substances.

2. In each individual case, a decision to allow monitored deliveries will be taken on the basis of prior authorization by each of the Contracting Parties concerned.

3. Each contracting Party shall retain responsibility for and control over the operation on its own territory and shall be empowered to intervene.

Article 74

With respect to legal trade in narcotic drugs and psychotropic substances, the Contracting Parties agree to transfer inside the country, wherever possible, checks conducted at the border and arising from obligations under the United Nations Conventions listed in Article 71.

Article 75

1. As regards the movement of travellers to the territory of the Contracting Parties or within such territory, individuals may carry narcotic drugs and psychotropic substances in connection with medical treatment, provided they produce at any check a certificate issued or authenticated by a competent authority of the State of residence.

2. The Executive Committee shall adopt the form and content of the certificate referred to in paragraph 1 and issued by one of the Contracting Parties, with particular reference to the data regarding the nature and quantity of the products and substances and the duration of the journey.

3. The Contracting Parties shall notify each other of the authorities responsible for the issue and authentication of the certificate referred to in paragraph 2;

Article 76

1. The Contracting Parties shall, if necessary, and in accordance with their medical, ethical and practical usage, adopt the appropriate measures for the monitoring of narcotic drugs and psychotropic substances subjected in the territory of one or more Contracting Party to more rigorous checks than in their own territory so that the effectiveness of such checks is not prejudiced.

2. Paragraph 1 shall also apply to substances frequently used for the manufacture of narcotic drugs and psychotropic substances.

3. The Contracting Parties shall notify each other of the measured taken in order to monitor the legal trade in the substances referred to in paragraphs 1 and 2

4. Problems experienced in this connection shall be regularly raised in the Executive Committee.

[...]

EC Council Directive No 91/308 of 10 June 1991 on Prevention of the Use of the Financial System for the Purpose of Money Laundering (1991)[*]

Luxembourg, 10 June 1991.

THE COUNCIL OF THE EUROPEAN COMMUNITIES.

HAVING REGARD to the Treaty establishing the European Economic Community, and in particular Article 57 (2), first and third sentences, and Article 100a thereof,

HAVING REGARD to the proposal from the Commission.

IN COOPERATION with the European Parliament.

HAVING REGARD to the opinion of the Economic and Social Committee.

WHEREAS when credit and financial institutions are use to launder proceeds from criminal activities (hereinafter referred to as 'money laundering'), the soundness and stability of the institution concerned and confidence in the financial system as a whole could be seriously jeopardized, thereby losing the trust of the public;

WHEREAS lack of Community action against money laundering could lead Member States, for the purpose of protecting their financial systems, to adopt measures which could be inconsistent with completion of the single market; whereas, in order to facilitate their criminal activities, launderers could try to take advantage of the freedom of capital movement and freedom to supply financial services which the integrated financial area involves, if certain coordinating measures are not adapted at Community level;

WHEREAS money laundering has an evident influence on the rise of organized crime in general and drug trafficking in particular; whereas there is more and more awareness that combating money laundering is one of the most effective means of opposing this form of criminal activity, which constitutes a particular threat to Member States societies;

WHEREAS money laundering must be combated mainly by penal means and within the framework of international cooperation among judicial and law enforcement authorities, as has been undertaken, in the field of drugs, by the United Nations Convention Against Illicit Traffic in Narcotic Drugs and Psychotropic Substances, adopted on 19 December 1988 in Vienna (hereinafter referred to as the 'Vienna Convention') and more generally in relation to all criminal activities, by the Council of Europe Convention on laundering, tracing, seizure and confiscation of proceeds of crime, opened for signature on 8 November 1990 in Strasbourg;

WHEREAS a penal approach should, however, not be the only way to combat money laundering, since the financial system can play a highly effective role: whereas reference must be made in this context to the recommendation of the Council of Europe of 27 June 1980 and to the declaration of principles adopted in December 1988 in Basle by the banking supervisory authorities of the Group of Ten, both of which constitute major steps towards preventing the use of the financial system for money laundering;

WHEREAS money laundering is usually carried out in an international context so that the criminal origin of the funds can be better disguised; whereas measures exclusively adopted at a national level, without taking account of international coordination and cooperation, would have very limited effects;

---

[*] *Official Journal of the European Communities* No L 166, 28.6.1991, p.77.

WHEREAS any measures adopted by the Community in this field should be consistent with other action undertaken in other international fora; whereas in this respect any Community action should take particular account of the recommendations adopted by the financial action task force on money laundering, set up in July 1989 by the Paris summit of the seven most developed countries;

WHEREAS the European Parliament has requested, in several resolutions, the establishment of a global Community programme to combat drug trafficking, including provisions on prevention of money laundering;

WHEREAS for the purposed of this Directive the definition of money laundering is taken from that adopted in the Vienna Convention; whereas, however, since money laundering occurs not only in relation to the proceeds of drug-related offences but also in relation to the proceeds of other criminal activities (such as organized crime and terrorism), the Member States should, within the meaning of their legislation, extend the effects of the Directive to include the proceeds of such activities, to the extent that they are likely to result in laundering operations justifying sanctions on that basis;

WHEREAS prohibition of money laundering in Member States' legislation backed by appropriate measures and penalties is a necessary condition for combating this phenomenon;

WHEREAS ensuring that credit and financial institutions require identification of their customers when entering into business relations or conducting transactions, exceeding certain thresholds, are necessary to avoid launderers' taking advantage of anonymity to carry out their criminal activities; whereas such provisions must also be extended, as far as possible, to any beneficial owners;

WHEREAS credit and financial institutions must keep for at least five years copies or references of the identification documents required as well as supporting evidence and records consisting of documents relating to transactions or copies thereof similarly admissible in court proceedings under the applicable national legislation for use as evidence in any investigation into money laundering;

WHEREAS ensuring that credit and financial institutions examine with special attention any transaction which they regard as particularly likely, by its nature, to be related to money laundering is necessary, in order to preserve the soundness and integrity of the financial system as well as to contribute to combating this phenomenon; whereas to this end they should pay special attention to transactions with third countries which do not apply comparable standards against money laundering to those established by the Community or to other equivalent standards set out by international fora and endorsed by the Community;

WHEREAS, for those purposed, Member States may ask credit and financial institutions to record in writing the results of the examination they are required to carry out and to ensure that those results are available to the authorities responsible for efforts to eliminate money laundering;

WHEREAS preventing the financial system from being used for money laundering is a task which cannot be carried out by the authorities responsible for combating this phenomenon without the cooperation of credit and financial institutions and their supervisory authorities; whereas banking secrecy must be lifted in such cases; whereas a mandatory system of reporting suspicious transactions which ensures that information is transmitted to the abovementioned authorities without alerting the customers concerned, is the most effective way to accomplish such cooperation; whereas a special protection clause is necessary to exempt credit and financial institutions, their employees and their directors from responsibility for breaching restrictions on disclosure of information;

WHEREAS the information received by the authorities pursuant to this Directive may be used only in connection with combating money laundering: whereas Member States may nevertheless provide that this information may be used for other purposes;

WHEREAS establishment by credit and financial institutions of procedures of internal control and training programmes in this field are complementary provisions without which the other measures contained in this Directive could become ineffective;

WHEREAS, since money laundering can be carried out not only through credit and financial institutions but also through other types of professions and categories of undertakings, Member States must extend the provisions of this Directive in whole or in part, to include those professions and undertakings whose activities are particularly likely to be used for money laundering purposes;

WHEREAS it is important that the Member States should take particular care to ensure that coordinated action is taken in the Community where there are strong grounds for believing that professions or activities the conditions governing the pursuit of which have been harmonized at Community level are being used for laundering money;

WHEREAS the effectiveness of efforts to eliminate money laundering is particularly dependent on the close coordination and harmonization of national implementing measures; whereas such coordination and harmonization which is being carried out in various international bodies requires, in the Community context, cooperation between Member States and the Commission in the framework of a contact committee;

WHEREAS it is for each Member State to adopt appropriate measures and to penalize infringement of such measures in an appropriate manner to ensure full application of this Directive,

HAS ADOPTED THIS DIRECTIVE:

Article 1

For the purpose of this Directive:

- 'credit institution' means a credit institution, as defined as in the first indent of Article 1 of Directive 77/780/EEC [1], as last amended by Directive 89/646/EEC [2], and includes branches within the meaning of the third indent of that Article and located in the Community, of credit institutions having their head offices outside the Community,

- 'financial institution' means an undertaking other than a credit institution whose principal activity is to carry out one or more of the operations included in numbers 2 to 12 and number 14 of the list annexed to Directive 89/464/EEC, or an insurance company duly authorized in accordance with Directive 79/267/EEC [3], as last amended by Directive 90/619/EEC [4], in so far as it carries out activities covered by that Directive; this definition includes branches located in the Community of financial institutions whose head offices are outside the Community.

- 'money laundering' means the following conduct when committed intentionally:

- the conversion or transfer of property, knowing that such property is derived from criminal activity or from an act of participation in such activity, for the purpose of concealing or disguising the illicit origin of the property or of assisting any person who is involved in the commission of such activity to evade the legal consequences of his action,

- the concealment or disguise of the true nature, source, location, disposition, movement, rights with respect to, or ownership of property, knowing that such property is derived from criminal activity or from an act of participation in such activity.

---

[1] *Official Journal of the European Communities* No L 322, 17.12.1977, p. 30.
[2] *Official Journal of the European Communities* No L 386, 30.12.1989, p. 1.
[3] *Official Journal of the European Communities* No L 63, 13.3.1979, p. 1.
[4] *Official Journal of the European Communities* No L 330, 29.11.1990, p. 50.

- the acquisition, possession or use of property, knowing, at the time of receipt, that such property was derived from criminal activity or from an act of participation in such activity.

- participation in, association to commit, attempts to commit and aiding, abetting, facilitating and counselling the commission of any of the actions mentioned in the foregoing paragraphs.

Knowledge, intent or purpose required as an element of the abovementioned activities may be inferred from objective factual circumstances.

Money laundering shall be regarded as such even where the activities which generated the property to be laundered were perpetrated in the territory of another Member State or in that of a third country.

- 'Property' means assets of every kind, whether corporeal or incorporeal, movable or immovable, tangible or intangible, and legal documents or instruments evidencing title to or interests in such assets.

- 'Criminal activity' means a crime specified in Article 3 (1) (a) of the Vienna Convention and any other criminal activity designated as such for the purposes of this Directive by each Member State.

- 'Competent authorities' means the national authorities empowered by law or regulation to supervise credit or financial institutions.

Article 2

Member States shall ensure that money laundering as defined in this Directive is prohibited.

Article 3

1. Member States shall ensure that credit and financial institutions require identification of their customers by means of supporting evidence when entering into business relations, particularly when opening an account or savings accounts, or when offering safe custody facilities.

2. The identification requirement shall also apply for any transaction with customers other than those referred to in paragraph 1, involving a sum amounting to ECU 15.000 or more, wether the transaction is carried out in a single operation or in several operations which seems to be linked. Where the sum is not known at the time when the transaction is undertaken, the institution concerned shall proceed with identification as soon as it is apprised of the sum and establishes that the threshold has been reached.

3. By way of derogation from paragraphs 1 and 2, the identification requirements with regard to insurance policies written by insurance undertakings within the meaning of Directive 79/267/EEC, where they perform activities which fall within the scope of that Directive shall not be required where the periodic premium amount or amounts to be paid in any given year does or do not exceed ECU 1 000 or where a single premium is paid amounting to ECU 2 500 or less. If the periodic premium amount or amounts to be paid in any given year is or are increased so as to exceed the ECU 1 000 threshold, identification shall be required.

4. Member States may provide that the identification requirement is not compulsory for insurance policies in respect of pension schemes taken out by virtue of a contract of employment or the insured's occupation, provided that such policies contain no surrender clause and may not be used as collateral for a loan.

5. In the event of doubt as to whether the customers referred to in the above paragraphs are acting on their own behalf, or where it is certain that they are not acting on their own, behalf, the credit and financial institutions shall take reasonable measures to obtain information as to the real identity of the persons on whose behalf those customers are acting.

6. Credit and financial institutions shall carry out identification, even where the amount of the transaction is lower than the threshold laid down, wherever there is suspicion of money laundering.

7. Credit and financial institutions shall not be subject to the identification requirements provided for in this Article where the customer is also a credit or financial institution covered by this Directive.

8. Member States may provide that the identification requirements regarding transactions referred to in paragraphs 3 and 4 are fulfilled when it is established that the payment for the transaction is to be debited from an account opened in the customer's name with a credit institution subject to this Directive according to the requirements of paragraph 1.

Article 4

Member States shall ensure that credit and financial institutions keep the following for use as evidence in any investigation into money laundering:

- in the case of identification, a copy or the references of the evidence required, for a period of at least five years after relationship with their customer has ended,

- in the case of transactions, the supporting evidence and records, consisting of the original documents or copies admissible in court proceedings under the applicable national legislation for a period of at least five years following execution of the transactions.

Article 5

Member States shall ensure that credit and financial institutions examine with special attention any transaction which they regard as particularly likely, by its nature, to be related to money laundering.

Article 6

Member States shall ensure that credit and financial institutions and their directors and employees cooperate fully with the authorities responsible for combating money laundering:

- by informing those authorities, on their own initiative, of any fact which might be an indication of money laundering.

- by furnishing those authorities, at their request, with all necessary information, in accordance with the procedures established by the applicable legislation.

The information referred to in the first paragraph shall be forwarded to the authorities responsible for combating money laundering of the Member State in whose territory the institution forwarding the information is situated. The person or persons designated by the credit and financial institutions in accordance with the procedures provided for in Article 11 (1) shall normally forward the information.

Information supplied to the authorities in accordance with the first paragraph may be used only in connection with the combating of money laundering. However, Member States may provide that such information may also be used for other purposes.

Article 7

Member States shall ensure that credit and financial institutions refrain from carrying out transactions which they know or suspect to be related to money laundering until they have apprised the authorities referred to in Article 6. Those authorities may, under conditions determined by their national legislation, give instruction not to execute the operation. Where such a transaction is suspected of giving rise to money laundering and where to refrain in such manner is impossible or is likely to frustrate efforts to pursue the beneficiaries of a suspected money-laundering operation, the institutions concerned shall apprise the authorities immediately afterwards.

Article 8

Credit and financial institutions and their directors and employees shall not disclose to the customer concerned nor to other third persons that information has been transmitted to the authorities in accordance with Articles 6 and 7 or that a money laundering investigation is being carried out.

Article 9

The disclosure in good faith to the authorities responsible for combating money laundering by an employee or director of a credit or financial institution of the information referred to in Articles 6 and 7 shall not constitute a breach of any restriction on disclosure of information imposed by contract or by any legislative, regulatory or administrative provision, and shall not involve the credit or financial institution, its directors or employees in liability of any kind.

Article 10

Member States shall ensure that if, in the course of inspections carried out in credit or financial institutions by the competent authorities, or in any other way, those authorities discover facts that could constitute evidence of money laundering, they inform the authorities responsible for combating money laundering.

Article 11

Member States shall ensure that credit and financial institutions:

1. establish adequate procedures of internal control and communication in order to forestall and prevent operations related to money laundering.

2. take appropriate measures so that their employees are aware of the provisions contained in this Directive. These measures shall include participation of their relevant employees in special training programmes to help them recognize operations which may be related to money laundering as well as to instruct them as to how to proceed in such cases.

Article 12

Member States shall ensure that the provisions of this Directive are extended in whole or in part to professions and to categories of undertakings, other than the credit and financial institutions referred to in Article 1, which engage in activities which are particularly likely to be used for money-laundering purposes.

Article 13

1. A contact committee (hereinafter referred to as 'the Committee') shall be set up under the aegis of the Commission. Its function shall be:

   (a) without prejudice to Articles 169 and 170 of the Treaty, to facilitate harmonized implementation of this Directive through regular consultation on any practical problems arising from its application and on which exchanges of view are deemed useful;

   (b) to facilitate consultation between the Member States on the more stringent or additional conditions and obligations which they may lay down at national level;

   (c) to advise the Commission, if necessary, on any supplements or amendments to be made to this Directive or on any adjustments deemed necessary, in particular to harmonize the effects of Article 12;

(d) to examine whether a profession or a category of undertaking should be included in the scope of Article 12 where it has been established that such profession or category of undertaking has been used in a Member State for money laundering.

2. It shall not be the function of the Committee to appraise the merits of decisions taken by the competent authorities in individual cases.

3. The Committee shall be composed of persons appointed by the Member States and of representatives of the Commission. The secretariat shall be provided by the Commission. The chairman shall be a representative of the Commission. It shall be convened by its chairman, either on his own initiative or at the request of the delegation of a Member State.

Article 14

Each Member State shall take appropriate measures to ensure full application of all the provisions of this Directive and shall in particular determine the penalties to be applied for infringement of the measures adopted pursuant to this Directive.

Article 15

The Member States may adopt or retain in force stricter provisions in the field covered by this Directive to prevent money laundering.

Article 16

1. Member States shall bring into force the laws, regulations and administrative decisions necessary to comply with this Directive before 1 January 1993 at the latest.

2. Where Member States adopt these measures, they shall contain a reference to this Directive or shall be accompanied by such reference on the occasions of their official publication. The methods of making such a reference shall be laid down by the Member States.

3. Member States shall communicate to the Commission the text of the main provisions of national law which they adopt in the field governed by this Directive.

Article 17

One year after 1 January 1993, whenever necessary and at least at three yearly intervals thereafter, the Commission shall draw up a report on the implementation of this Directive and submit it to the European Parliament and the Council.

Article 18

This Directive is addressed to the Member States.

Statement by the representatives of the Governments of the Member States meeting within the Council

The representatives of the Governments of the Member States, meeting within the Council,

Recalling that the Member States signed the United Nations Convention against illicit traffic in narcotic drugs and psychotropic substances, adopted on 19 December 1988 in Vienna;

Recalling also that most Member States have already signed the Council of Europe Convention on laundering, tracing, seizure and confiscation of proceeds of crime on 8 November 1990 in Strasbourg;

Conscious of the fact that the description of money laundering contained in Article 1 of Council Directive 91/308/EEC derives its wording from the relevant provisions of the aforementioned Conventions;

Hereby undertake to take all necessary steps by 31 December 1992 at the latest to enact criminal legislation enabling them to comply with their obligations under the aforementioned instruments.

1.7. Crimes against the Environment

Council of Europe Draft Convention for the Protection of the Environment through Criminal Law (1996)[*]

SECTION I - USE OF TERMS

Article 1

Definitions

For the purposes of this Convention:

(a) "unlawful" means infringing a law, an administrative regulation or a decision taken by a competent authority, aiming at the protection of the environment;

(b) "water" means groundwater and surface water including the water of lakes, rivers, oceans and seas;

SECTION II - MEASURES TO BE TAKEN AT NATIONAL LEVEL

Article 2

Intentional offences

1. Each Party shall adopt such appropriate measures as may be necessary to establish as criminal offences under its domestic law :

   (a) the discharge, emission or introduction of a quantity of substances or ionising radiation into air, soil or water, which

   (i) causes death or serious injury to any person, or
   (ii) creates a significant risk of causing death or serious injury to any person;

   (b) the unlawful discharge, emission or introduction of a quantity of substances or ionising radiation into air, soil or water, which causes or is likely to cause their lasting deterioration, or death or serious injury to any person or substantial damage to protected monuments, other protected objects, property, animals or plants;

   (c) the unlawful disposal, treatment, storage, transport, export or import of hazardous waste, which causes or is likely to cause death or serious injury to any person or substantial damage to the quality of air, soil, water, animals or plants;

   (d) the unlawful operation of a plant in which a dangerous activity is carried out and which causes or is likely to cause death or serious injury to any person or substantial damage to the quality of air, soil, water, animals or plants;

   (e) the unlawful manufacture, treatment, storage, use, transport, export or import of nuclear materials or other hazardous radio-active substances which causes or is likely to cause death or serious injury to any person or substantial damage to the quality of air, soil, water, animals or plants;

   when committed intentionally.

2. Each Party shall adopt such appropriate measures as may be necessary to establish as criminal offences under its domestic law aiding or abetting the commission of any of the offences established in accordance with paragraph 1 of this Article.

---

[*] Council of Europe, *Addendum to Doc CDPC(96) 12 and 13* (6 June 1996).

Article 3

Negligent offences

1. Each Party shall adopt such appropriate measures as may be necessary to establish as criminal offences under its domestic law, when committed with negligence, the offences enumerated in Article 2, subparagraph 1 a - e.

2. Each Party may, at the time of signature or when depositing its instrument of ratification, acceptance, approval or accession, by a declaration addressed to the Secretary General of the Council of Europe, declare that subparagraph 1 of this Article, in part or in whole, shall only apply to offences which were committed with gross negligence.

3. Each Party may, at the time of signature or when depositing its instrument of ratification, acceptance, approval or accession, by a declaration addressed to the Secretary General of the Council of Europe, declare that subparagraph 1 of this Article, in part or in whole, shall not apply to:

- subparagraph 1 a. ii of Article 2,

- subparagraph 1 b of Article 2, in so far as the offence relates to protected monuments, other protected objects or property.

Article 4

Other criminal offences or administrative offences

In so far as these are not covered by the provisions of Articles 2 and 3, each Party shall adopt such appropriate measures as may be necessary to establish as criminal offences or administrative offences, liable to sanctions or other measures under its domestic law, when committed intentionally or with negligence:

(a) the unlawful discharge, emission or introduction of a quantity of substances or ionising radiation into air, soil or water;

(b) the unlawful causation of noise;

(c) the unlawful disposal, treatment, storage, transport, export or import of waste;

(d) the unlawful operation of a plant;

(e) the unlawful manufacture, treatment, use, transport, export or import of nuclear materials, other radio-active substances or hazardous chemicals;

(f) the unlawful causation of changes detrimental to natural components of a national park, nature reserve, water conservation area or other protected areas;

(g) the unlawful possession, taking, damaging, killing or trading in protected wild flora and fauna species.

Article 5

Jurisdiction

1. Each Party shall adopt such appropriate measures as may be necessary to establish jurisdiction over a criminal offence established in accordance with this convention when the offence is committed:

(a) in its territory; or

(b) on board a ship or an aircraft registered in it or flying its flag; or

(c) by one of its nationals if the offence is punishable under criminal law where it was committed or if the place where it was committed does not fall under any territorial jurisdiction.

2. Each Party shall adopt such appropriate measures as may be necessary to establish jurisdiction over a criminal offence established in accordance with this convention, in case where an alleged offender is present in its territory and it does not extradite him to another Party after a request for extradition.

3. This Convention does not exclude any criminal jurisdiction exercised in accordance with national law.

4. Each Party may, at the time of signature or when depositing its instrument of ratification, acceptance, approval or accession, by a declaration addressed to the Secretary General of the Council of Europe, declare that sub-paragraphs 1 (c) and 2 of this Article, in part or in whole, shall not apply.

Article 6

Sanctions for environmental offences

Each Party shall adopt, in accordance with the relevant international instruments, such appropriate measures as may be necessary to enable it to make the offences established in accordance with Articles 2 and 3 punishable by criminal sanctions which take into account the serious nature of these offences. The sanctions available shall include imprisonment and pecuniary sanctions and may include reinstatement of the environment.

Article 7

Confiscation measures

1. Each Party shall adopt such appropriate measures as may be necessary to enable it to confiscate instrumentalities and proceeds or property the value of which corresponds to such proceeds, in respect of offences enumerated in Articles 2 and 3.

2. Each Party may, at the time of signature or when depositing its instrument of ratification, acceptance, approval or accession, by a declaration addressed to the Secretary General of the Council of Europe, declare that it will not apply paragraph 1 of this Article either in respect of offences specified in such declaration or in respect of certain categories of instrumentalities, proceeds or property the value of which corresponds to such proceeds.

Article 8

Reinstatement of the environment

Each Party may, at any time, in a declaration, addressed to the Secretary General of the Council of Europe, declare that it will provide for reinstatement of the environment according to the following provisions of this Article:

(a) The competent authority may order the reinstatement of the environment in relation to an offence established in accordance with this convention. Such an order may be made subject to certain conditions.

(b) Where an order of the reinstatement of the environment has not been complied with, the competent authority may, in accordance with national law, make it executable at the expense of the person subject to the order or that person may be liable to other criminal sanctions instead of or in addition to it.

Article 9

Corporate liability

1. Each Party shall adopt such appropriate measures as may be necessary to enable it to impose criminal or administrative sanctions or measures on legal persons on whose behalf an offence referred to in Articles 2 or 3 has been committed by its organ, a member of its organ or another representative.

2. Corporate liability under subparagraph 1 of this Article shall not exclude criminal proceedings against a natural person.

3. Each Party may, at the time of signature or when depositing its instrument of ratification, acceptance, approval or accession, by a declaration addressed to the Secretary General of the Council of Europe, declare that it reserves the right not to apply paragraph 1 of this Article or any part thereof or that it applies only to offences specified in such declaration.

Article 10

Cooperation between authorities

1. Each Party shall adopt such appropriate measures as may be necessary to ensure that those of its authorities responsible for environmental protection cooperate with those of its authorities responsible for investigating and prosecuting criminal offences:

   (a) by informing the latter authorities, on their own initiative, where there are reasonable grounds to believe that an offence under Article 2 has been committed;

   (b) by providing, upon request, to the latter authorities all necessary information, in accordance with national law.

2. Each Party may, at the time of signature or when depositing its instrument of ratification, acceptance, approval or accession, by a declaration addressed to the Secretary General of the Council of Europe, declare that it reserves the right not to apply paragraph 1 a) of this Article or that it applies only to offences specified in such declaration.

Article 11

Rights for groups to participate in proceedings

Each Party may, at any time, in a declaration, addressed to the Secretary General of the Council of Europe, declare that it will, in accordance with national law, grant any group, foundation or association which, according to its statutes, aims at the protection of the environment the right to participate in proceedings concerning criminal offences established in accordance with this Convention.

SECTION III - MEASURES TO BE TAKEN AT INTERNATIONAL LEVEL

Article 12

International co-operation

1. The Parties shall afford each other, in accordance with the provisions of relevant international instruments on international co-operation in criminal matters and their national law, the widest measure of co-operation in investigations and proceedings relating to criminal offences established in accordance with this Convention.

2. The Parties may afford each other assistance in investigations and proceedings relating to those acts defined in Article 4 of this Convention which are not covered by paragraph 1 of this Article.

SECTION IV - FINAL CLAUSES

Article 13

Signature and entry into force

1. This Convention shall be open for signature by the member States of the Council of Europe and non-member States which have participated in its elaboration. Such States may express their consent to be bound by:

   (a) signature without reservation as to ratification, acceptance or approval; or

   (b) signature subject to ratification, acceptance or approval, followed by ratification, acceptance or approval.

2. Instruments of ratification, acceptance or approval shall be deposited with the Secretary General of the Council of Europe.

3. This Convention shall enter into force on the first day of the month following the expiration of a period of three months after the date on which three States have expressed their consent to be bound by the Convention in accordance with the provisions of paragraph 1.

4. In respect of any signatory State which subsequently expresses its consent to be bound by it, the Convention shall enter into force on the first day of the month following the expiration of a period of three months after the date of the expression of its consent to be bound by the Convention in accordance with the provisions of paragraph 1.

Article 14

Accession to the Convention

1. After the entry into force of this Convention, the Committee of Ministers of the Council of Europe, after consulting the Contracting States to the Convention, may invite any State not a member of the Council to accede to this Convention, by a decision taken by the majority provided for in Article 20.d. of the Statute of the Council of Europe and by the unanimous vote of the representatives of the Contracting States entitled to sit on the Committee.

2. In respect of any acceding State the Convention shall enter into force on the first day of the month following the expiration of a period of three months after the date of deposit of the instrument of accession with the Secretary General of the Council of Europe.

Article 15

Territorial application

1. Any State may, at the time of signature or when depositing its instrument of ratification, acceptance, approval or accession, specify the territory or territories to which this Convention shall apply.

2. Any State may, at any later date, by a declaration addressed to the Secretary General of the Council of Europe, extend the application of this Convention to any other territory specified in the declaration. In respect of such territory the Convention shall enter into force on the first day of the month following the expiration of a period of three months after the date of receipt of such declaration by the Secretary General.

3. Any declaration made under the two preceding paragraphs may, in respect of any territory specified in such declaration, be withdrawn by a notification addressed to the Secretary General. The withdrawal shall become effective on the first day of the month following the expiration of a period of three months after the date of receipt of such notification by the Secretary General.

Article 16

Relationship to other conventions and agreements

1. This Convention does not affect the rights and undertakings derived from international multilateral conventions concerning special matters.

2. The Parties to the Convention may conclude bilateral or multilateral agreements with one another on the matters dealt with in this Convention, for purposes of supplementing or strengthening its provisions or facilitating the application of the principles embodied in it.

3. If two or more Parties have already concluded an agreement or treaty in respect of a subject which is dealt with in this Convention or otherwise have established their relations in respect of that subject, they shall be entitled to apply that agreement or treaty or to regulate those relations accordingly, in lieu of the present Convention, if it facilitates international co-operation.

Article 17

Reservations

1. Any State may, at the time of signature or when depositing its instrument of ratification, acceptance, approval or accession, declare that it avails itself of one or more of the reservations provided for in Article 3, paragraphes 2 and 3, Article 5, paragraph 4, Article 7, paragraph 2, Article 9, paragraph 3 and Article 10, paragraph 2. No other reservation may be made.

2. Any State which has made a reservation under the preceding paragraph may wholly or partly withdraw it by means of a notification addressed to the Secretary General of the Council of Europe. The withdrawal shall take effect on the date of receipt of such notification by the Secretary General.

3. A Party which has made a reservation in respect of a provision of this Convention may not claim the application of that provision by any other Party; it may, however, if its reservation is partial or conditional, claim the application of that provision in so far as it has itself accepted it.

Article 18

Amendments

1. Amendments to this Convention may be proposed by any Party, and shall be communicated by the Secretary General of the Council of Europe to the member States of the Council of Europe and to every non-member State which has acceded to or has been invited to accede to this Convention in accordance with the provisions of Article 14.

2. Any amendment proposed by a Party shall be communicated to the European Committee on Crime Problems which shall submit to the Committee of Ministers its opinion on that proposed amendment.

3. The Committee of Ministers shall consider the proposed amendment and the opinion submitted by the European Committee on Crime Problems and may adopt the amendment.

4. The text of any amendment adopted by the Committee of Ministers in accordance with paragraph 3 of this article shall be forwarded to the Parties for acceptance.

5. Any amendment adopted in accordance with paragraph 3 of this article shall come into force on the thirtieth day after all Parties have informed the Secretary General of their acceptance thereof.

Article 19

Settlement of disputes

1. The European Committee on Crime Problems of the Council of Europe shall be kept informed regarding the interpretation and application of this Convention.

2. In case of a dispute between Parties as to the interpretation or application of this Convention, they shall seek a settlement of the dispute through negotiation or any other peaceful means of their choice, including submission of the dispute to the European Committee on Crime Problems, to an arbitral tribunal whose decisions shall be binding upon the Parties, or to the International Court of Justice, as agreed upon by the Parties concerned.

Article 20

Denunciation

1. Any Party may, at any time, denounce this Convention by means of a notification addressed to the Secretary General of the Council of Europe.

2. Such denunciation shall become effective on the first day of the month following the expiration of a period of three months after the date of receipt of the notification by the Secretary General.

Article 21

Notifications

The Secretary General of the Council of Europe shall notify the member States of the Council and any State which has acceded to this Convention of:

(a) any signature;

(b) the deposit of any instrument of ratification, acceptance, approval or accession;

(c) any date of entry into force of this Convention in accordance with Articles 13 and 14;

(d) any reservation made under Article 17, paragraph 1;

(e) any other act, notification or communication relating to this Convention.

In witness whereof the undersigned, being duly authorised thereto, have signed this Convention.

Done at Strasbourg, the ....1996, in English and in French, both texts being equally authentic, in a single copy which shall be deposited in the archives of the Council of Europe. The Secretary General of the Council of Europe shall transmit certified copies to each member State of the Council of Europe and to any State invited to accede to it.

1.8. Fraud

Convention on the Protection of the European Communities' Financial Interests (1995)[*]

Brussels, 26 July 1995

THE COUNCIL OF THE EUROPEAN UNION

HAVING REGARD to the Treaty on European Union, and in particular Article K.3(2)(c) thereof,

WHEREAS, for the purposes of achieving the objectives of the Union, the Member States regard the combating of fraud affecting the European Communities' financial interests as a matter of common interest coming under the co-operation provided for in Title VI of the Treaty;

WHEREAS, in order to combat such fraud with the utmost vigour, it is necessary to draw up a first agreement, to be supplemented shortly afterwards by another legal instrument, in such a way as to improve the effectiveness of protection under criminal law of the European Communities' financial interests;

HAVING DECIDED that the Convention, the text of which is given in the Annex and which is signed today by the Representatives of the Governments of the Member States of the Union, is hereby drawn up;

RECOMMENDS that it be adopted by the Member States in accordance with their respective constitutional requirements.

ANNEX

CONVENTION DRAWN UP ON THE BASIS OF ARTICLE K.3 OF THE TREATY ON EUROPEAN UNION, ON THE PROTECTION OF THE EUROPEAN COMMUNITIES' FINANCIAL INTERESTS

THE HIGH CONTRACTING PARTIES to this Convention, Member States of the European Union,

REFERRING to the Act of the Council of the European Union of 26 July 1995;

DESIRING to ensure that their criminal laws contribute effectively to the protection of the financial interests of the European Communities;

NOTING that fraud affecting Community revenue and expenditure in many cases is not confined to a single country and is often committed by organized criminal networks;

CONVINCED that protection of the European Communities' financial interests calls for the criminal prosecution of fraudulent conduct injuring those interests and requires, for that purpose, the adoption of a common definition,

CONVINCED of the need to make such conduct punishable with effective, proportionate and dissuasive criminal penalties, without prejudice to the possibility of applying other penalties in appropriate cases, and of the need, at least in serious cases, to make such conduct punishable with deprivation of liberty which can give rise to extradition,

---

[*] Council Act of 26 July 1995 Drawing up the Convention on the Protection of the European Communities' Financial Interests, *Official Journal of the European Communities* No C 316, 27.11.1995, p.48.

RECOGNIZING that businesses play an important role in the areas financed by the European Communities and that those with decision-making powers in business should not escape criminal responsibility in appropriate circumstances,

DETERMINED to combat together fraud affecting the European Communities' financial interests by undertaking obligations concerning jurisdiction, extradition, and mutual cooperation,

HAVE AGREED on the following provisions:

Article 1

General provisions

1. For the purposes of this Convention, fraud affecting the European Communities' financial interests shall consist of:

    (a) in respect of expenditure, any intentional act or omission relating to:

    - the use or presentation of false, incorrect or incomplete statements of documents, which has as its effect the misappropriation or wrongful retention of funds from the general budget of the European Communities or budgets managed by, or on behalf of, the European Communities;

    - non-disclosure of information in violation of a specific obligation, with the same effect;

    - the misapplication of such funds for purposes other than those for which they were originally granted;

    (b) in respect of revenue, any intentional act or omission relating to:

    - the use or presentation of false, incorrect or incomplete statements or documents, which has as its effect the illegal diminution of the resources of the general budget of the European Communities or budgets managed by, or on behalf of, the European Communities;

    - non-disclosure of information in violation of a specific obligation, with the same effect;

    - misapplication of a legally obtained benefit, with the same effect.

2. Subject to Article 2(2), each Member State shall take the necessary and appropriate measures to transpose paragraph 1 into their national criminal law in such a way that the conduct referred to therein constitutes criminal offences.

3. Subject to Article 2(2), each Member State shall also take the necessary measures to ensure that the intentional preparation or supply of false, incorrect of incomplete statements or documents having the effect described in paragraph 1 constitutes a criminal offence if it is not already punishable as a principal offence or as participation in, instigation of, or attempt to commit, fraud as defined in paragraph 1.

4. The intentional nature of an act or omission as referred to in paragraphs 1 and 3 may be inferred from objective, factual circumstances.

Article 2

Penalties

1. Each Member State shall take the necessary measures to ensure that the conduct referred to in Article 1, and participating in, instigating, or attempting the conduct referred to in Article 1(1), are punishable by effective, proportionate and dissuasive criminal penalties,

including, at least in cases of serious fraud, penalties involving deprivation of liberty which can give rise to extradition, it being understood that serious fraud shall be considered to be fraud involving a minimum amount to be set in each Member State. This minimum amount may not be set at a sum exceeding ECU 50 000.

2. However in cases of minor fraud involving a total amount of less than ECU 4 000 and not involving particularly serious circumstances under its laws, a Member State may provide for penalties of a different type from those laid down in paragraph 1.

3. The Council of the European Union, acting unanimously, may alter the amount referred to in paragraph 2.

Article 3

Criminal liability of heads of businesses

Each Member State shall take the necessary measures to allow heads of businesses or any persons having power to take decisions or exercise control within a business to be declared criminally liable in accordance with the principles defined by its national law in cases of fraud affecting the European Community's financial interests, as referred to in Article 1, by a person under their authority acting on behalf of the business.

Article 4

Jurisdiction

1. Each Member State shall take the necessary measures to establish its jurisdiction over the offences it has established in accordance with Article 1 and 2(1) when:

- fraud, participation in fraud or attempted fraud affecting the European Communities' financial interests is committed in whole or in part within its territory, including fraud for which the benefit was obtained in that territory;

- a person within its territory knowingly assists or induces the commission of such fraud within the territory of any other State;

- the offender is a national of the Member State concerned, provided that the law of that Member State may require the conduct to be punishable also in the country where it occurred.

2. Each Member State may declare, when giving the notification referred to in Article 11(2), that it will not apply the rule laid down in the third indent of paragraph 1 of this Article.

Article 5

Extradition and prosecution

1. Any Member State which, under its law, does not extradite its own nationals shall take the necessary measures to establish its jurisdiction over the offences it has established in accordance with Articles 1 and 2(1), when committed by its own nationals outside its territory.

2. Each Member State shall, when one of its nationals is alleged to have committed in another Member State a criminal offence involving the conduct described in Articles 1 and 2(1), and it does not extradite that person to that other Member State solely on the ground of his or her nationality, submit the case to its competent authorities for the purpose of prosecution if appropriate. In order to enable prosecution to take place, the files, information and exhibits relating to the offence shall be transmitted in accordance with the procedures laid down in Article 6 of the European Convention on Extradition. The requesting Member State shall be informed of the prosecution initiated and of its outcome.

3. A Member State may not refuse extradition in the event of fraud affecting the European Communities' financial interests for the sole reason that it concerns a tax or customs duty offence.

4. For the purposes of this Article, a Member State's own nationals shall be construed in accordance with any declaration made by it under Article 6(1)(b) of the European Convention on Extradition and with paragraph 1(c) of that Article.

Article 6

Co-operation

1. If a fraud as defined in Article 1 constitutes a criminal offence and concerns at least two Member States, those States shall co-operate effectively in the investigation, the prosecution and in carrying out the punishment imposed by means, for example, of mutual legal assistance, extradition, transfer of proceedings or enforcement of sentences passed in another Member State.

2. Where more that one Member State has jurisdiction and has the possibility of viable prosecution of an offence based on the same facts, the Member States involved shall co-operate in deciding which shall prosecute the offender or offenders with a view to centralizing the prosecution in a single Member State where possible.

Article 7

Ne bis in idem

1. Member States shall apply in their national criminal laws the "ne bis in idem" rule, under which a person whose trial has been finally disposed of in Member State may not be prosecuted in another Member State in respect of the same facts, provided that if a penalty was imposed, it has been enforced, is actually in the process of being enforced or can no longer be enforced under the laws of the sentencing State.

2. A Member State may, when giving the notification referred to in Article 11(2), declare that it shall not be bound by paragraph 1 of this Article in one or more of the following cases:

(a) if the facts which were the subject of the judgement rendered abroad took place on its own territory either in whole or in part; in the latter case this exception shall not apply if those facts took place partly on the territory of the Member State where the judgment was rendered;

(b) if the facts which were the subject of the judgment rendered abroad constitute an offence directed against the security or other equally essential interests of that Member State;

(c) if the facts which were the subject of the judgment rendered abroad were committed by an official of that Member State contrary to the duties of his offence.

3. The exceptions which may be the subject of a declaration under paragraph 2 shall not apply if the Member State concerned in respect of the same facts requested the other Member State to bring the prosecution or granted extradition of the person concerned.

4. Relevant bilateral or multilateral agreements concluded between Member States and relevant declarations shall remain unaffected by this Article.

Article 8

Court of Justice

1. Any dispute between Member States on the interpretation or application of this Convention must in an initial stage be examined by the Council in accordance with the procedure set out in Title VI of the Treaty on European Union with a view to reaching a solution.

2. If no solution is found within six months, the matter may be referred to the Court of Justice of the European Communities by a party to the dispute.

3. Any dispute between one or more Member States and the Commission of the European Communities concerning the application of this Convention which it has proved impossible to settle through negotiation may be submitted to the Court of Justice.

Article 9

Internal provisions

No provision in this Convention shall prevent Member States from adopting internal legal provisions which go beyond the obligations deriving from this Convention.

Article 10

Transmission

1. Member States shall transmit to the Commission of the European Communities the text of the provisions transposing into their domestic law the obligations imposed on them under the provisions of this Convention.

2. For the purposes of implementing this Convention, the High Contracting Parties shall determine, within the Council of the European Union, the information to be communicated or exchanged between the Member States or between the Member States and the Commission, and also the arrangements for doing so.

Article 11

Entry into force

1. This convention shall be subject to adoption by the Member States in accordance with their respective constitutional requirements.

2. Member States shall notify the Secretary-General of the Council of the European Union of the completion of their constitutional requirements for adopting this Convention.

3. This Convention shall enter into force ninety days after the notification, referred to in paragraph 2, by the last Member State to fulfil that formality.

Article 12

Accession

1. This Convention shall be open to accession by any State that becomes a member of the European Union.

2. The text of this Convention in the language of the acceding State, drawn up by the Council of the European Union, shall be authentic.

3. Instruments of accession shall be deposited with the depositary.

4. This Convention shall enter into force with respect to any State that accedes to it ninety days after the deposit of its instrument of accession or on the date of entry into force of the

Convention if it has not already entered into force at the time of expiry of the said period of ninety days.

Article 13

Depositary

1. The Secretary-General of the Council of the European Union shall act as depositary of this Convention.

2. The depositary shall publish in the Official Journal of the European Communities information on the progress of adoptions and accessions, declarations and reservations, and also any other notification concerning this Convention.

IN WITNESS WHEREOF, the undersigned Plenipotentiaries have hereunto set their hands.

DONE at Brussels, this twenty-sixth day of July in the year one thousand nine hundred and ninety-five in a single original, in the German, English, Danish, Spanish, Finnish, French, Greek, Irish, Italian, Dutch, Portuguese and Swedish languages, each text being equally authentic, such original remaining deposited in the archives of the General Secretariat of the Council of the European Union.

Council Regulation (EC, EURATOM) No 2988/95 of 18 December 1995 on the Protection of the European Communities' Financial Interests (1995)*

Brussels, 18 December 1995

THE COUNCIL OF THE EUROPEAN UNION,

HAVING REGARD to the Treaty establishing the European Community, and in particular Article 235 thereof,

HAVING REGARD to the Treaty establishing the European Atomic Energy Community, and in particular Article 203 thereof,

HAVING REGARD to the proposal from the Commission,

HAVING REGARD to the opinion of the European Parliament,

WHEREAS the general budget of the European Communities is financed by own resources and administered by the Commission within the limit of the appropriations authorized and in accordance with the principle of sound financial management; whereas the Commission works in close co-operation with the Member States to that end;

WHEREAS more than half of Community expenditure is paid to beneficiaries through the intermediary of the Member States;

WHEREAS detailed rules governing this decentralized administration and the monitoring of their use are the subject of differing detailed provisions according to the Community policies concerned; whereas acts detrimental to the Communities' financial interests must, however, be countered in all areas;

WHEREAS the effectiveness of the combating of fraud against the Communities' financial interests calls for a common set of legal rules to be enacted for all areas covered by Community policies;

WHEREAS irregular conduct, and the administrative measures and penalties relating thereto, are provided for in sectoral rules in accordance with this Regulation;

WHEREAS the aforementioned conduct includes fraudulent actions as defined in the Convention on the protection of the European Communities' financial interests;

WHEREAS Community administrative penalties must provide adequate protection for the said interests; whereas it is necessary to define general rules applicable to these penalties;

WHEREAS Community law has established Community administrative penalties in the framework of the common agricultural policy: whereas such penalties must be established in other fields as well;

WHEREAS Community measures and penalties laid down in pursuance of the objectives of the common agricultural policy form an integral part of the aid systems; whereas they pursue their own ends which do not affect the assessment of the conduct of the economic operators concerned by the competent authorities of the Member States from the point of view of criminal law; whereas their effectiveness must be ensured by the immediate effect of Community rules and by applying in full Community measures as a whole, where the adoption of preventive measures has not made it possible to achieve that objective;

---

* *Official Journal of the European Communities* No C 321, 23.12.1995, p.1.

WHEREAS not only under the general principle of equity and the principle of proportionality but also in the light of the principle of *ne bis in idem*, appropriate provisions must be adopted while respecting the *acquis communautaire* and the provisions laid down in specific Community rules existing at the time of entry into force of this Regulation, to prevent any overlap of Community financial penalties and national criminal penalties imposed on the same persons for the same reasons;

WHEREAS, for the purposes of applying this Regulation, criminal proceedings may be regarded as having been completed where the competent national authority and the person concerned come to an arrangement;

WHEREAS this Regulation will apply without prejudice to the application of the Member States' criminal law;

WHEREAS Community law imposes on the Commission and the Member States an obligation to check that Community budget resources are used for their intended purpose; whereas there is a need for common rules to supplement existing provisions;

WHEREAS the Treaties make no provision for the specific powers necessary for the adoption of substantive law of horizontal scope on checks, measures and penalties with a view to ensuring the protection of the Communities' financial interests; whereas recourse should therefore be had to Article 235 of the EC Treaty and to Article 203 of the EAEC Treaty;

WHEREAS additional general provisions relating to checks and inspections on the spot will be adopted at a later stage,

HAS ADOPTED this regulation:

Title I

General principles

Article 1

1. For the purposes of protecting the European Communities' financial interests, general rules are hereby adopted relating to homogenous checks and to administrative measures and penalties concerning irregularities with regard to Community law.

2. 'Irregularity' shall mean any infringement of a provision of Community law resulting from an act or omission by an economic operator, which has, or would have, the effect of prejudicing the general budget of the Communities or budgets managed by them, either by reducing or losing revenue accruing from own resources collected directly on behalf of the Communities, or by an unjustified item of expenditure.

Article 2

1. Administrative checks, measures and penalties shall be introduced in so far as they are necessary to ensure the proper application of Community law. They shall be effective, proportionate and dissuasive so that they provide adequate protection for the Communities' financial interests.

2. No administrative penalty may be imposed unless a Community act prior to the irregularity has made provision for it. In the event of a subsequent amendment of the provisions which impose administrative penalties and are contained in Community rules, the less severe provisions shall apply retroactively.

3. Community law shall determine the nature and scope of the administrative measures and penalties necessary for the correct application of the rules in question, having regard to the nature and seriousness of the irregularity, the advantage granted or received and the degree of responsibility.

4. Subject to the Community law applicable, the procedures for the application of Community checks, measures and penalties shall be governed by the laws of the Member States.

Article 3

1. The limitation period for proceedings shall be four years as from the time when the irregularity referred to in Article 1 (1) was committed. However, the sectoral rules may make provision for a shorter period which may not be less than three years.

In the case of continuous or repeated irregularities, the limitation period shall run from the day on which the irregularity ceases. In the case of multiannual programmes, the limitation period shall in any case run until the programme is definitively terminated.

The limitation period shall be interrupted by any act of the competent authority, notified to the person in question, relating to investigation or legal proceedings concerning the irregularity. The limitation period shall start again following each interrupting act.

However, limitation shall become effective at the latest on the day on which a period equal to twice the limitation period expires without the competent authority having imposed a penalty, except where the administrative procedure has been suspended in accordance with Article 6 (1).

2. The period for implementing the decision establishing the administrative penalty shall be three years. That period shall run from the day on which the decision becomes final.

Instances of interruption and suspension shall be governed by the relevant provisions of national law.

3. Member States shall retain the possibility of applying a period which is longer than that provided for in paragraphs 1 and 2 respectively.

Title II

Administrative measures and penalties

Article 4

1. As a general rule, any irregularity shall involve withdrawal of the wrongly obtained advantage:

- by an obligation to pay or repay the amounts due or wrongly received,

- by the total or partial loss of the security provided in support of the request for an advantage granted or at the time of the receipt of an advance.

2. Application of the measures referred to in paragraph 1 shall be limited to the withdrawal of the advantage obtained plus, where so provided for, interest which may be determined on a flat-rate basis.

3. Acts which are established to have as their purpose the obtaining of an advantage contrary to the objectives of the Community law applicable in the case by artificially creating the conditions required for obtaining that advantage shall result, as the case shall be, either in failure to obtain the advantage or in its withdrawal.

4. The measures provided for in this Article shall not be regarded as penalties.

Article 5

1. Intentional irregularities or those caused by negligence may lead to the following administrative penalties:

  (a) payment of an administrative fine;

(b) payment of an amount greater than the amounts wrongly received or evaded, plus interest where appropriate; this additional sum shall be determined in accordance with a percentage to be set in the specific rules, and may not exceed the level strictly necessary to constitute a deterrent;

(c) total or partial removal of an advantage granted by Community rules, even if the operator wrongly benefited from only a part of that advantage;

(d) exclusion from, or withdrawal of, the advantage for a period subsequent to that of the irregularity;

(e) temporary withdrawal of the approval or recognition necessary for participation in a Community aid scheme;

(f) the loss of a security or deposit provided for the purpose of complying with the conditions laid down by rules or the replenishment of the amount of a security wrongly released;

(g) other penalties of a purely economic type, equivalent in nature and scope, provided for in the sectoral rules adopted by the Council in the light of the specific requirements of the sectors concerned and in compliance with the implementing powers conferred on the Commission by the Council.

2. Without prejudice to the provisions laid down in the sectoral rules existing at the time of entry into force of this Regulation, other irregularities may give rise only to those penalties not equivalent to a criminal penalty that are provided for in paragraph 1, provided that such penalties are essential to ensure correct application of the rules.

Article 6

1. Without prejudice to the Community administrative measures and penalties adopted on the basis of the sectoral rules existing at the time of entry into force of this Regulation, the imposition of financial penalties such as administrative fines may be suspended by decision of the competent authority if criminal proceedings have been initiated against the person concerned in connection with the same facts. Suspension of the administrative proceedings shall suspend the period of limitation provided for in Article 3.

2. If the criminal proceedings are not continued, the suspended administrative proceedings shall be resumed.

3. When the criminal proceedings are concluded, the suspended administrative proceedings shall be resumed, unless that is precluded by general legal principles.

4. Where the administrative procedure is resumed, the administrative authority shall ensure that a penalty at least equivalent to that prescribed by Community rules is imposed, which may take into account any penalty imposed by the judicial authority on the same person in respect of the same facts.

5. Paragraphs 1 to 4 shall not apply to financial penalties which form an integral part of financial support systems and may be applied independently of any criminal penalties, if and in so far as they are not equivalent to such penalties.

Article 7

Community administrative measures and penalties may be applied to the economic operators referred to in Article 1, namely the natural or legal persons and the other entities on which national law confers legal capacity who have committed the irregularity and to those who are under a duty to take responsibility for the irregularity or to ensure that it is not committed.

Title III

Checks

Article 8

1. In accordance with their national laws, regulations and administrative provisions, the Member States shall take the measures necessary to ensure the regularity and reality of transactions involving the Communities' financial interests.

2. Measures providing for checks shall be appropriate to the specific nature of each sector and in proportion to the objectives pursued. They shall take account of existing administrative practice and structures in the Member States and shall be determined so as not to entail excessive economic constraints or administrative costs.

The nature and frequency of the checks and inspections on the spot to be carried out by the Member States and the procedure for performing them shall be determined as necessary by sectoral rules in such a way as to ensure uniform and effective application of the relevant rules and in particular to prevent and detect irregularities.

3. The sectoral rules shall include the provisions necessary to ensure equivalent checks through the approximation of procedures and checking methods.

Article 9

1. Without prejudice to the checks carried out by the Member States in accordance with their national laws, regulations and administrative provisions and without prejudice to the checks carried out by the Community institutions in accordance with the EC Treaty, and in particular Article 188c thereof, the Commission shall, on its responsibility, have checks carried out on:

   (a) the conformity of administrative practices with Community rules;

   (b) the existence of the necessary substantiating documents and their concordance with the Communities' revenue and expenditure as referred to in Article 1;

   (c) the circumstances in which such financial transactions are carried out and checked.

2. In addition, it may carry out checks and inspections on the spot under the conditions laid down in the sectoral rules.

Before carrying out such checks and inspections, in accordance with the rules in force, the Commission shall inform the Member State concerned accordingly in order to obtain any assistance necessary.

Article 10

Additional general provisions relating to checks and inspections on the spot shall be adopted later in accordance with the procedures laid down in Article 235 of the EC Treaty and Article 203 of the EAEC Treaty.

Article 11

This Regulation shall enter into force on the third day following its publication in the *Official Journal of the European Communities*.

This Regulation shall be binding in its entirety and directly applicable in all Member States.

1.9. Corruption

Inter-American Convention against Corruption (1996)[*]

Caracas, 29 March 1996

Article 1

Definitions

For the purposes of this Convention:

"Public functions" means any temporary or permanent, paid or honorary activity, performed by a natural person in the name of the State or in the service of the State or its institutions, at any level of its hierarchy.

"Public official", "government official", or "public servant" means any official or employee of the State or its agencies, including those who have been selected, appointed, or elected to perform activities or functions in the name of the State or in the service of the State, at any level of its hierarchy.

"Property" means assets of any kind, whether movable or immovable, tangible or intangible, and any document or legal instrument demonstrating, purporting to demonstrate, or relating to ownership or other rights pertaining to such assets.

Article 2

Purposes

The purposes of this Convention are:

(a) To promote and strengthen the development by each of the States Parties of the mechanisms needed to prevent, detect, punish and eradicate corruption; and

(b) To promote, facilitate and regulate cooperation among the States Parties to ensure the effectiveness of measures and actions to prevent, detect, punish and eradicate corruption in the performance of public functions and acts of corruptions specifically related to such performance.

Article 3

Preventive Measures

For the purposes set forth in Article 2 of this Convention, the States Parties agree to consider the applicability of measures within their own institutional systems to create, maintain and strengthen:

(a) Standards of conduct for the correct, honorable, and proper fulfillment of public functions. These standards shall be intended to prevent conflicts of interest and mandate the proper conservation and use of resources entrusted to government officials in the performance of their functions. These standards shall also establish measures and systems requiring government officials to report to appropriate authorities acts of corruption in the performance of public functions. Such measures should help preserve the public's confidence in the integrity of public servants and government processes.

(b) Mechanisms to enforce these standards of conduct.

---

[*] OAE/Ser.K/XXXIV.1 CICOR/doc.14/96 rev.2.

(c) Instruction to government personnel to ensure proper understanding of their responsibilities and the ethical rules governing their activities.

(d) Systems for registering the income, assets and liabilities of persons who perform public functions in certain posts as specified by law and, where appropriate, for making such registrations public.

(e) Systems of government hiring and procurement of goods and services that assure the openness, equity and efficiency of such systems.

(f) Government revenue collection and control systems that deter corruption.

(g) Laws that deny favorable tax treatment for any individual or corporation for expenditures made in violation of the anticorruption laws of the States Parties.

(h) Systems for protecting public servants and private citizens who, in good faith, report acts of corruption, including protection of their identities, in accordance with their Constitutions and the basic principles of their domestics legal systems.

(i) Oversight bodies with a view to implementing modern mechanisms for preventing, detecting, punishing and eradicating corrupt acts.

(j) Deterrents to the bribery of domestic and foreign government officials, such as mechanisms to ensure that publicly held companies and other types or associations maintain books and records which, in reasonable detail, accurately reflect the acquisition and disposition of assets, and have sufficient internal accounting controls to enable their officers to detect corrupt acts.

(k) Mechanisms to encourage participation by civil society and nongovernmental organizations in efforts to prevent corruption.

(l) The study of further preventive measures that take into account the relationship between equitable compensation and probity in public service.

Article 4

Scope

This Convention is applicable provided that the alleged act of corruption has been committed or has effects in a State Party.

Article 5

Jurisdiction

1. Each State Party shall adopt such measures as may be necessary to establish its jurisdiction over the offenses it has established in accordance with this Convention when the offense in question is committed in its territory.

2. Each State Party may adopt such measures as may be necessary to establish its jurisdiction over the offenses it has established in accordance with this Convention when the offense is committed by one of its nationals or by a person who habitually resides in its territory.

3. Each State Party shall adopt such measures as may be necessary to establish its jurisdiction over the offenses is has established in accordance with this Convention when the alleged criminal is present in its territory and it does not extradite such person to another country on the ground of the nationality of the alleged criminal.

4. This Convention does not preclude the application of any other rule of criminal jurisdiction established by a State Party under its domestic law.

Article 6

Acts of Corruption

1. This Convention is applicable to the following acts of corruption:

    (a) The solicitation or acceptance, directly or indirectly, by a government official or a person who performs public functions, of any article of monetary value, or other benefit, such as a gift, favor, promise or advantage for himself or for another person or entity, in exchange for any act or omission in the performance of his public functions:

    (b) The offering or granting, directly or indirectly, to a government official or a person who performs public functions, of any article of monetary value, or other benefit, such as a gift, favor, promise or advantage for himself or for another person or entity, in exchange for any act or omission in the performance of his public functions:

    (c) Any act or omission in the discharge of his duties by a government official or a person who performs public functions for the purpose of illicitly obtaining benefits for himself or for a third party:

    (d) The fraudulent use or concealment of property derived from any of the acts referred to in this article; and

    (e) Participation as a principal, coprincipal, instigator, accomplice or accessory after the fact, or in any other manner, in the commission or attempted commission of, or in any collaboration or conspiracy to commit, any of the acts referred to in this article.

    (f) This Convention shall also be applicable by mutual agreement between or among two or more States Parties with respect to any other act of corruption not described herein.

Article 7

Domestic Law

The States Parties that have not yet done so shall adopt the necessary, legislative or other measures to establish as criminal offenses under their domestic law the acts of corruption described in Article 6(1) and to facilitate cooperation among themselves pursuant to this Convention.

Article 8

Transnational Bribery

Subject to its Constitution and the fundamental principles of its legal system, each State Party shall prohibit and punish the offering or granting, directly or indirectly, by its nationals, persons having their habitual residence in its territory, and businesses domiciled there, to a government official of another State, of any article of monetary value, or other benefit, such as a gift, favor, promise or advantage, in connection with any economic or commercial transaction in exchange for any act or omission in the performance of that official's public functions.

Among those States Parties that have established transnational bribery as an offense, such offense shall be considered an act of corruption for the purposes of this Convention.

Any State Party that has not established transnational bribery as an offense shall, insofar as its laws permit, provide assistance and cooperation with respect to this offense as provided in this Convention.

Article 9

Illicit Enrichment

Subject to its Constitution and the fundamental principles of its legal system, each State Party that has not yet done so shall take necessary measures to establish under its laws as an offense a significant increase in the assets of a government official that he cannot reasonably explain in relation to his lawful earnings during the performance of his functions.

Among those State Parties that have established illicit enrichment as an offense, such offense shall be considered an act of corruption for the purposes of this Convention.

Any State Party that has not established illicit enrichment as an offense shall, insofar as its laws permit, provide assistance and cooperation with respect to this offense as provided in this Convention.

Article 10

Notification

When a State Party adopts the legislation referred to in paragraph 1 of articles 8 and 9, it shall notify the Secretary General of the Organization of American States, who shall in turn notify the other States Parties. For the purposes of this Convention, the crimes of transnational bribery and illicit enrichment shall be considered acts of corruption for that State Party thirty days following the date of such notification.

Article 11

Progressive Development

1. In order to foster the development and harmonization of their domestic legislation and the attainment of the purposes of this Convention, the States Parties view as desirable, and undertake to consider, establishing as offenses under their laws the following acts:

    (a) The improper use by a government official or a person who performs public functions for his own benefit or that of a third party, of any kind of classified or confidential information which that official or person who performs public functions has obtained because of, or in the performance of, his functions:

    (b) The improper use by a government official or a person who performs public functions for his own benefit or that of a third party, of any kind or property belonging to the State or to any firm or institution in which the State has a proprietary interest, to which that official or person who performs public functions has access because of, or in the performance of, his functions:

    (c) Any act or omission by any person who, personally or through a third party, or acting as an intermediary, seeks to obtain a decision from a public authority whereby he illicitly obtains for himself or for another person any benefit or gain, whether or not such act or omission harms State property; and

    (d) The diversion by a government official, for purposes unrelated to those for which they were intended, for his own benefit, or that of a third party, of any movable or immovable property, monies or securities belonging to the State, to an independent agency, or to an individual, that such official has received by virtue of his position for purposes of administration, custody or for other reasons.

2. Among those States Parties that have established these offenses, such offenses shall be considered acts of corruption for the purposes of this Convention.

3. Any State Party that has not established these offenses shall, insofar as its laws permit, provide assistance and cooperation with respect to these offenses as provided in this Convention.

Article 12

Effect on State Property

For application of this Convention, it shall not be necessary that the acts of corruption harm State property.

Article 13

Extradition

1. This article shall apply to the offenses established by the States Parties in accordance with this Convention.

2. Each of the offenses to which this article applies shall be deemed to be included as an extraditable offense in any extradition treaty existing between or among the States Parties. The States Parties undertake to include such offenses as extraditable offenses in every extradition treaty to be concluded between or among them.

3. If a State Party that makes extradition conditional on the existence of a treaty receives a request for extradition from another State Party with which it does not have an extradition treaty, it may consider this Convention as the legal basis for extradition with respect to any offense to which this article applies.

4. States Parties that do not make extradition conditional on the existence of a treaty shall recognize offenses to which this article as extraditable offenses between themselves.

5. Extradition shall be subject to the conditions provided for by the law of the Requested State or by applicable extradition treaties, including the grounds on which the Requested State may refuse extradition.

6. If extradition for an offense to which this article applies is refused solely on the basis of the nationality of the person sought, or because the Requested State deems that it has jurisdiction over the offense, the Requested State shall submit the case to its competent authorities for the purpose of prosecution unless otherwise agreed with the Requesting State, and shall report the final outcome to the Requesting State in due course.

7. Subject to the provisions of its domestic law and its extradition treaties, the Requested State may, upon being satisfied that the circumstances so warrant and are urgent, and at the request of the Requesting State, take into custody a person whose extradition is sought and who is present in its territory, or take other appropriate measures to ensure his presence at extradition proceedings.

Article 14

Assistance and Cooperation

1. In accordance with their domestic laws and applicable treaties, the States Parties shall afford one another the widest measure of mutual assistance by processing requests from authorities that, in conformity with their domestic laws, have the power to investigate or prosecute the acts of corruption described in this Convention to obtain evidence and take other necessary action to facilitate legal proceedings and measures regarding the investigation or prosecution of acts of corruption.

2. The States Parties shall also provide each other with the widest measure of mutual technical cooperation on the most effective ways and means of preventing, dedecting, investigating and punishing acts of corruption. To that end, they shall foster exchanges of experiences by way of agreements and meetings between competent bodies and institutions, and

shall pay special attention to methods and procedures of citizen participation in the fight against corruption.

Article 15

Measures Regarding Property

1. In accordance with their applicable domestic laws and relevant treaties or other agreements that may be in force between or among them, the States Parties shall provide each other the broadest possible measure of assistance in the identification, tracing, freezing, seizure and forfeiture of property or proceeds obtained, derived from or used in the commission of offenses, established in accordance with this Convention.

2. A State Party that enforces its own or another State Party's forfeiture judgment against property or proceeds described in paragraph 1 of this Article shall dispose of the property or proceeds in accordance with its laws. To the extent permitted by a State Party's laws and upon such terms as it deems appropriate, it may transfer all or part of such property or proceeds to another State Party that assisted in the underlying investigation or proceedings.

Article 16

Bank Secrecy

1. The Requested State shall not invoke bank secrecy as a basis for refusal to provide the assistance sought by the Requesting State. The Requested State shall apply this article in accordance with its domestic law, its procedural provisions, or bilateral or multilateral agreements with the Requesting State.

2. The Requesting State shall be obligated not to use any information received that is protected by bank secrecy for any purpose other than the proceeding for which that information was requested, unless authorized by the Requested State.

Article 17

Nature of the Act

For the purposes of articles 13, 14, 15 and 16 of this Convention, the fact that the property obtained or derived from an act of corruption was intended for political purposes, or that it is alleged that an act of corruption was committed for political motives or purposes, shall not suffice in and of itself to qualify the act as a political offense or as a common offense related to a political offense.

Article 18

Central Authorities

1. For the purposes of international assistance and cooperation provided under this Convention, each State Party may designate a central authority or may rely upon such central authorities as are provided for in any relevant treaties or other agreements.

2. The central authorities shall be responsible for making and receiving the requests for assistance and cooperation referred to in this Convention.

3. The central authorities shall communicate with each other directly for the purposes of this Convention.

Article 19

Temporal Application

Subject to the constitutional principles and the domestic laws of each State and existing treaties between the States Parties, the fact that the alleged act of corruption was committed before this Convention entered into force shall not preclude procedural cooperation in criminal matters between the States Parties. This provision shall in no case affect the principle of non-retroactivity in criminal law, nor shall application of this provision interrupt existing statutes of limitations relating to crimes committed prior to the date of the entry into force of this Convention.

Article 20

Other Agreements or Practices

No provision of this Convention shall be construed as preventing the States Parties from engaging in mutual cooperation within the framework of other international agreements, bilateral or multilateral, currently in force or concluded in the future, or pursuant to any other applicable arrangement or practice.

Article 21

Signature

This Convention is open for signature by the Member States of the Organizations of American States.

Article 22

Ratification

This Convention is subject to ratification. The instruments of ratification shall be deposited with the General Secretariat of the Organization of American States.

Article 23

Accession

This Convention shall remain open for accession by any other State. The instruments of accession shall be deposited with the General Secretariat of the Organization of American States.

Article 24

Reservations

The States Parties may, at the time of adoption, signature, ratification, or accession, make reservations to this Convention, provided that each reservation concerns one or more specific provisions and is not incompatible with the object and purpose of the Convention.

Article 25

Entry Into Force

This Convention shall enter into force on the thirtieth day following the date of deposit of the second instrument of ratification. For each State ratifying or acceding to the Convention after the deposit of the second instrument of ratification, the Convention shall enter into force on the thirtieth day after deposit by such State of its instrument of ratification or accession.

Article 26

Denunciation

This Convention shall remain in force indefinitely, but any of the States Parties may denounce it. The instrument of denunciations shall be deposited with the General Secretariat of the Organization of American States. One year from the date of deposit of the instrument of denunciation, the Convention shall cease to be in force for the denouncing State, but shall remain in force for the other States Parties.

Article 27

Additional Protocols

Any State Party may submit for the consideration of other States Parties meeting at a General Assembly of the Organization of American States draft additional protocols to this Convention to contribute to the attainment of the purposes set forth in Article 2 thereof.

Each additional protocol shall establish the terms for its entry into force and shall apply only to those States that become Parties to it.

Article 28

Deposit of Original Instrument

The original instrument of this Convention, the English, French, Portuguese, and Spanish texts of which are equally authentic, shall be deposited with the General Secretariat of the Organization of American States, which shall forward an authenticated copy of its text to the Secretariat of the United Nations for registration and publication in accordance with Article 102 of the United Nations Charter, The General Secretariat of the Organization of American States shall notify its Member States and the States that have acceded to the Convention of signatures of the deposit of instruments of ratification, accession, or denunciation and of reservations, if any.

1.10. Insider Dealing

Convention on Insider Trading (1989)[*]

Strasbourg, 20 April 1989

Chapter I

Definitions

Article 1

1. For the purposes of this Convention an irregular operation of insider trading means an irregular operation carried out by a person:

    (a) who is the president or chairman, or a member of a board of directors or other administrative or supervisory organ, or is the authorised agent or in the employment of an issuer of securities, and has effected or caused to be effected an operation on an organised stock market knowingly using information not yet disclosed to the public, the possession of which he obtained by reason of his occupation and the disclosure of which was likely to have significant influence on the stock market, with a view to securing an advantage for himself or a third party;

    (b) who has entered into the transactions described above knowingly using not yet disclosed information which he obtained in the performance of his duties or in the course of his occupation;

    (c) who has entered into the transactions described above knowingly using not yet disclosed information communicated to him by one of the persons mentioned in *a* or *b* above.

2. For the purposes of applying this Convention:

    (a) the expression "organised stock market" signifies stock markets subject to regulations established by authorities recognised by the government for the purpose;

    (b) the term "stock" signifies transferable securities issued according to the national legislation of each Party by business firms or companies or other issuers, where such securities may be bought and sold on a market organised in accordance with the provisions of paragraph a above, as well as other transferable securities admitted on that market in conformity with the national rules applicable to it;

    (c) the expression "operation" signifies any act on an organised stock market which gives or may give entitlement to stock as provided for in paragraph b above.

Chapter II

Exchange of information

Article 2

The Parties undertake, in accordance with the provisions of this chapter, to provide each other with the greatest possible measure of mutual assistance in the exchange of information relating to matters establishing or giving rise to the belief that irregular operations of insider trading have been carried out.

---

[*] *European Treaty Series*, No.130.

Article 3

Each Party may, by a declaration to the Secretary General of the Council of Europe, undertake to provide other Parties, subject to reciprocity, with the greatest possible measure of mutual assistance in the exchange of information necessary for the surveillance of operations carried out in the organised stock markets which could adversely affect equal access to information for all users of the stock market or the quality of the information supplied to investors in order to ensure honest dealing.

Article 4

1. Each Party shall designate one or more authorities actually responsible for submitting any request for assistance, and for receiving and taking action on requests for assistance from the corresponding authorities designated by each Party.

2. Each Party shall, in a declaration addressed to the Secretary General of the Council of Europe, indicate the name and address of the authority or authorities designated in accordance with the provisions of this Article and any modification thereto.

3. The Secretary General shall notify these declarations to the other Parties.

Article 5

1. Reasons shall be given for making a request for assistance.

2. The request shall contain a description of the facts establishing or giving rise to the belief that irregular operations of insider trading have been carried out or, if assistance is requested according to the rules laid down by Parties under Article 3, reference to the principles mentioned in that Article which have been violated.

3. The request shall contain reference to the provisions by virtue of which the operations are irregular in the State of the requesting authority.

4. The request shall be in or translated into one of the official languages of the State of the requested authority, or in one of the official languages of the Council of Europe.

5. The request shall specify:

    (a) the requesting authority and the requested authority;

    (b) the information sought by the requesting authority, the persons or bodies which may be in possession of it, or the place where it may be available;

    (c) the reasons for and the purpose of the requesting authority's application, and the use it will make of the information under its national law; and

    (d) how soon a response is required and, in cases of urgency, the reasons therefor.

Article 6

1. The executions of requests for assistance by the requested authority is carried out in accordance with the rules and procedures laid down by the law of the Party in which that authority operates.

2. When the search for information so requires, and in the absence of specific provisions, the rules laid down by national law for obtaining evidence shall be capable of being applied by the requested authority or on its behalf. Sanctions laid down for breaches of professional secrecy shall not apply in regard to the information provided compulsorily in the course of enquiries.

3. These provisions shall not prejudice the rights accorded to the defendant by national law.

4. Save to the extent strictly necessary to carry out the request, the requested authority and the persons seeking the information requested are bound to maintain secrecy about the request, the component parts of the request and the information so gathered.

5. However, at the time of the designation of the authority, provided for by Article 4, each Party shall declare the derogations to the principle set forth in paragraph 4 of this Article possibly imposed or permitted by national law:

   (a) either to guarantee free access of citizens to the files of the administration;

   (b) or when the designated authority is obliged to denounce to other administrative or judicial authorities information communicated or gathered within the framework of the request;

   (c) or, provided the requesting authority has been informed, to investigate violations of the law of the requested Party or to secure compliance with such law.

Article 7

1. The requesting authority may not use the information supplied for purposes other than those set out in its request.

2 The requested authority may refuse to supply the requested information or subsequently oppose its use for purposes set out in the request or fix certain conditions unless:

   (a) the facts are within the scope of Article 1, and

   (b) the purposes set out are in conformity with the aims defined in Article 2, and

   (c) the facts constitute in each State an irregularity as regards the rules of both States.

3. When the requesting authority wishes to use the information supplied for purposes other than those set out in the initial request it must inform in advance the requested authority who may refuse to consent to such use unless the conditions in paragraph 2 above are fulfilled.

4. The information supplied may be used before a criminal court only in cases where it could have been obtained by application of Chapter III.

5. No authority of the requesting Party may use or transmit this information for tax, customs or currency purposes unless otherwise provided in a declaration by the requested Party.

Article 8

The requested authority may refuse to give effect to the request for assistance or to supply the information obtained, if:

   (a) the request is not in conformity with this Convention;

   (b) the communication of the information obtained might constitute an infringement of the sovereignty, security, essential interests or public policy (ordre public) of the requested Party;

   (c) the irregularities to which the requested information relates or the sanctions provided for such irregularities are time-barred under the law of the requesting or of the requested Party;

   (d) the requested information relates to matters which arose before the Convention entered into force for the requesting or the requested Party;

(e) proceedings have already been commenced before the authorities in the requested Party in respect of the same matters and against the same persons, or if they have been finally adjudicated upon in respect of the same matters by the competent authorities of the requested Party;

(f) the authorities of the requested Party have decided not to commence proceedings or to stop proceedings in respect of the same matters.

Article 9

The requested authority shall, in so far as it is able to do so, supply the information requested by the requesting authority in the form desired by that authority or in the form currently in use between them.

Article 10

1. Any Party which has ascertained that there has been a substantial breach by the requesting authority of the confidentiality of the information provided may suspend the application of Chapter II of this Convention with respect to the Party which has failed to discharge its obligation and shall notify the Secretary General of the Council of Europe of its decision. The Party may lift the suspension at any time and shall notify the Secretary General accordingly.

2. Any Party which intends to make use of the procedure provided for in paragraph 1 must first give an opportunity to the Party concerned to make observations on the alleged breach of confidentiality.

3. The Secretary General of the Council of Europe shall inform the member States and the Parties to this Convention of any use made of the procedure provided for in paragraph 1.

Article 11

Parties may agree that, notwithstanding the provisions of paragraph 4 of Article 5, requests for assistance and replies thereto may be drawn up in the language of their choice and made according to simplified procedures or by employing means of communication other than the exchange of written correspondence.

Chapter III

Mutual assistance in criminal matters

Article 12

1. The Parties undertake to afford each other the widest measure of mutual assistance in criminal matters relating to offences involving insider trading.

2. Nothing in this Convention shall be construed as restricting or prejudicing the application of the European Convention on Mutual Assistance in Criminal Matters and the Additional Protocol thereto among States party to these instruments or of specific agreements or arrangements on mutual assistance in criminal matters in force between Parties.

Chapter IV

Final provisions

Article 13

This Convention shall be open for signature by the member States of the Council of Europe. It shall be subject to ratification, acceptance or approval. Instruments of ratification, acceptance or approval shall be deposited with the Secretary General of the Council of Europe.

Article 14

1. This Convention shall enter into force on the first day of the month following the expiration of a period of three months after the date on which three member States of the Council of Europe have expressed their consent to be bound by the Convention in accordance with the provisions of Article 13.

2. In respect of any member State which subsequently expresses its consent to be bound by it, the Convention shall enter into force on the first day of the month following the expiration of a period of three months after the date of the deposit of the instrument of ratification, acceptance or approval.

Article 15

1. After the entry into force of this Convention, the Committee of Ministers of the Council of Europe may invite any State not a member of the Council of Europe or any international intergovernmental organisation to accede to this Convention, by a decision taken by the majority provided for in Article 20.d of the Statute of the Council of Europe and by the unanimous vote of the representatives of the Contracting States entitled to sit on the Committee.

2. In respect of any acceding State or international intergovernmental organisation, the Convention shall enter into force on the first day of the month following the expiration of a period of three months after the date of deposit of the instrument of accession with the Secretary General of the Council of Europe.

Article 16

1. Any State may, at the time of signature or when depositing its instrument of ratification, acceptance, approval or accession, specify the territory or territories, to which this Convention shall apply.

2. Any State may, at any later date, by a declaration addressed to the Secretary General of the Council of Europe, extend the application of this Convention to any other territory specified in the declaration. In respect of such territory the Convention shall enter into force on the first day of the month following the expiration of a period of three months after the date of receipt of such declaration by the Secretary General.

3. Any declaration made under the two preceding paragraphs may, in respect of any territory specified in such declaration, be withdrawn by a notification addressed to the Secretary General. The withdrawal shall become effective on the first day of the month following the expiration of a period of three months after the date of receipt of such notification by the Secretary General.

Article 17

Without prejudice to the application of Article 6, no reservation may be made to the Convention.

Article 18

1. After the entry into force of the present Convention, a group of experts representing the Parties to the Convention and the member States of the Council of Europe not being Parties to the Convention shall be convened at the request of at least two Parties or on the initiative of the Secretary General of the Council of Europe.

2. This group shall have the task of preparing an evaluation of the application of the Convention and making appropriate suggestions.

Article 19

Difficulties with regard to the interpretation and application of this Convention shall be settled by direct consultation between the competent administrative authorities and, if the need arises, through diplomatic channels.

Article 20

1. Any Party may at any time denounce this Convention by means of a notification addressed to the Secretary General of the Council of Europe.

2. Such denunciation shall become effective on the first day of the month following the expiration of a period of three months after the date of receipt of the notification by the Secretary General; denunciation shall not prejudice requests already in progress at the time of denunciation.

Article 21

The Secretary General of the Council of Europe shall notify the member States of the Council of Europe and any Party to this Convention of:

(a) any signature;

(b) the deposit of any instrument of ratification, acceptance, approval or accession;

(c) any date of entry into force of this Convention in accordance with Articles 14, 15 and 16;

(d) any other act, notification or communication relating to this Convention.

In witness whereof, the undersigned, being duly authorised thereto, have signed this Convention.

Done at Strasbourg, this 20th day of April 1989, in English and French, both texts being equally authentic, in a single copy which shall be deposited in the archives of the Council of Europe. The Secretary General of the Council of Europe shall transmit certified copies to each member state of the Council of Europe and to any state and any international intergovernmental organisation invited to accede to this Convention.

Protocol to the Convention on Insider Trading (1989)[*]

Strasbourg, 11 September 1989

The member States of the Council of Europe signatories to the Convention on Insider Trading (hereinafter called "the Convention") and to this Protocol,

Having regard to the undertakings contained in Chapters II and III of the Convention relating to exchange of information and mutual assistance in criminal matters respectively;

Considering that between States members of the European Economic Community the application of Community rules should be reserved,

Have agreed as follows:

Article 1

The following provision shall be inserted in the Convention:

"Article 16 bis

In their mutual relations, Parties which are members of the European Economic Community shall apply Community rules and shall therefore not apply the rules arising form this Convention except in so far as there is no Community rule governing the particular subject concerned."

Article 2

This Protocol shall be open for signature by the member States of the Council of Europe signatories to the Convention. It shall be subject to ratification, acceptance or approval. Instruments of ratification, acceptance or approval shall be deposited with the Secretary General of the Council of Europe.

Article 3

This Protocol shall enter into force:

- either on the same date as the Convention, if on that date all Contracting States to the Convention have expressed their consent to be bound by this Protocol in accordance with the provisions of Article 2;

- or subsequently, on the first day of the month after the date on which all Contracting States to the Convention have expressed their consent to be bound by this Protocol in accordance with the provisions of Article 2.

Article 4

The Secretary General of the Council of Europe shall notify the member States of the Council of Europe of:

(a) any signature;

(b) the deposit of any instrument of ratification, acceptance or approval;

(c) the date of entry into force of this Protocol in accordance with the provisions of Article 3;

---

[*] *European Treaty Series*, No.130.

(d) any other act, declaration, notification or communication relating to this Protocol.

In witness whereof, the undersigned, being duly authorised thereto, have signed this Protocol.

Done at Strasbourg, this 11th day of September 1989, in English and French, both texts being equally authentic, in a single copy which shall be deposited in the archives of the Council of Europe. The Secretary General of the Council of Europe shall transmit certified copies to each member state of the Council of Europe.

EC Council Directive No 89/592 of 13 November 1989 coordinating Regulations on Insider Dealing (1989)[*]

Brussels, 13 November 1989

THE COUNCIL OF THE EUROPEAN COMMUNITIES,

HAVING REGARD to the Treaty establishing the European Economic Community, and in particular Article 100a thereof,

HAVING REGARD to the proposal from the Commission,

IN COOPERATION with the European Parliament,

HAVING REGARD to the opinion of the Economic and Social Committee,

WHEREAS Article 100a (1) of the Treaty states that the Council shall adopt the measures for the approximation of the provisions laid down by law, regulation or administrative action in Member States which have as their object the establishment and functioning of the internal market;

WHEREAS the secondary market in transferable securities plays an important role in the financing of economic agents;

WHEREAS, for that market to be able to play its role effectively, every measure should be taken to ensure that market operates smoothly;

WHEREAS the smooth operation of that market depends to a large extent on the confidence it inspires in investors;

WHEREAS the factors on which such confidence depends include the assurance afforded to investors that they are placed on an equal footing and that they will be protected against the improper use of inside information;

WHEREAS, by benefiting certain investors as compared with others, insider dealing is likely to undermine that confidence and may therefore prejudice the smooth operation of the market;

WHEREAS the necessary measures should therefore be taken to combat insider dealing;

WHEREAS in some Member States there are no rules or regulations prohibiting insider dealing and whereas the rules or regulations that do exist differ considerably from one Member State to another;

WHEREAS it is therefore advisable to adopt coordinated rules at a Community level in this field;

WHEREAS such coordinated rules also have the advantage of making it possible, through cooperation by the competent authorities, to combat transfrontier insider dealing more effectively;

WHEREAS, since the acquisition or disposal of transferable securities necessarily involves a prior decision to acquire or to dispose taken by the person who undertakes one or other of these operations, the carrying-out of this acquisition or disposal does not constitute in itself the use of inside information;

---

[*] *Official Journal of the European Communities* No L 334, 18.12.1989, p.30.

WHEREAS insider dealing involves taking advantage of inside information; whereas the mere fact that market-makers, bodies authorized to act as *contrepartie*, or stockbrokers with inside information confine themselves, in the first two cases, to pursuing their normal business of buying or selling securities, or , in the last, to carrying out an order should not in itself be deemed to constitute use of such inside information; whereas likewise the fact of carrying out transactions with the aim of stabilizing the price of new issues or secondary offers of transferable securities should not in itself be deemed to constitute use of inside information;

WHEREAS estimates developed from publicly available data cannot be regarded as inside information and whereas, therefore, any transaction carried out on the basis of such estimates does not constitute insider dealing within the meaning of this Directive;

WHEREAS communication of inside information to an authority, in order to enable it to ensure that the provisions of this Directive or other provisions in force are respected, obviously cannot be covered by the prohibitions laid down by this Directive,

HAS ADOPTED THIS DIRECTIVE:

Article 1

For the purposes of this Directive:

1. 'inside information' shall mean information which has not been made public of a precise nature relating to one or several issuers of transferable securities or to one or several transferable securities, which, if it were made public, would be likely to have a significant effect on the price of the transferable security or securities in question;

2. 'transferable securities' shall mean:

    (a) shares and debt securities, as well as securities equivalent to shares and debt securities;

    (b) contracts or rights to subscribe for, acquire or dispose of securities referred to in (a);

    (c) futures contracts, options and financial futures in respect of securities referred to in (a);

    (d) index contracts in respect of securities referred to in (a),

when admitted to trading on a market which is regulated and supervised by authorities recognized by public bodies, operates regularly and is accessible directly or indirectly to the public.

Article 2

1. Each Member shall prohibit any person who:

    (a) by virtue of his membership of the administrative, management or supervisory bodies of the issuer,

    (b) by virtue of his holding in the capital of the issuer, or

    (c) because he has access to such information by virtue of the exercise of his employment, profession or duties,

possesses inside information from taking advantage of that information with full knowledge of the facts by acquiring or disposing of for his own account or for the account of a third party, either directly or indirectly, transferable securities of the issuer or issuers to which that information relates.

2. Where the person referred to in paragraph 1 is a company or other type of legal person, the prohibition laid down in that paragraph shall apply to the natural persons who take part in the decision to carry out the transaction for the account of the legal person concerned.

3. The prohibition laid down in paragraph 1 shall apply to any acquisition or disposal of transferable securities effected through a professional intermediary,

Each Member State may provide that this prohibition shall not apply to acquisitions of disposals of transferable securities effected without the involvement of a professional intermediary outside a market as defined in Article 1 (2) *in fine*;

4. This Directive shall not apply to transactions carried out in pursuit of monetary, exchange-rate or public debt-management policies by a sovereign State, by its central bank or any other body designated to that effect by the State, or by any person acting on their behalf. Member States may extend this exemption to their federated States or similar local authorities in respect of the management of their public debt.

Article 3

Each Member State shall prohibit any person subject to the prohibition laid down in Article 2 who possesses inside information from:

(a) disclosing that inside information to any third party unless such disclosure is made in the normal course of the exercise of his employment, profession or duties;

(b) recommending or procuring a third party, on the basis of that inside information, to acquire or dispose of transferable securities admitted to trading on its securities markets as referred to in Article 1 (2) *in fine*.

Article 4

Each Member State shall also impose the prohibition provided for in Article 2 on any person other that those referred to in that Article who with full knowledge of the facts possesses inside information, the direct or indirect source of which could not be other that a person referred to in Article 2.

Article 5

Each Member State shall apply the prohibitions provided for in Articles 2, 3 and 4, at least to actions undertaken within its territory to the extent that the transferable securities concerned are admitted to trading on a market of a Member State. In any event, each Member State shall regard transaction as carried out within its territory if it is carried out on a market, as defined in Article 1 (2) *in fine*, situated or operating within that territory.

Article 6

Each Member State may adopt provisions more stringent than those laid down by this Directive or additional provisions, provided that such provisions are applied generally. In particular it may extend the scope of the prohibition laid down in Article 2 and impose on persons referred to in Article 4 the prohibitions laid down in Article 3.

Article 7

The provisions of Schedule C.5 (a) of the Annex to Directive 79/279/EEC [1] shall also be apply to companies and undertakings the transferable securities of which, whatever their nature, are admitted to trading on a market as referred to in Article 1 (2) *in fine* of this Directive.

Article 8

1. Each Member State shall designate, the administrative authority or authorities competent, if necessary in collaboration with other authorities to ensure that the provisions adopted pursuant to this Directive are applied. It shall so inform the Commission which shall transmit that information to all Member States.

2. The competent authorities must be given all supervisory and investigatory powers that are necessary for the exercise of their functions, where appropriate in collaboration with other authorities.

Article 9

Each Member State shall provide that all persons employed of formerly employed by the competent authorities referred to in Article 8 shall be bound by professional secrecy. Information covered by professional secrecy may not be divulged to any person or authority except by virtue of provisions laid down by law.

Article 10

1. The competent authorities in the Member States shall cooperate with each other whenever necessary for the purpose of carrying out their duties, making use of the powers mentioned in Article 8 (2). To this end, and notwithstanding Article 9 they shall exchange any information required for that purpose, including information relating to actions prohibited, under the options given to Member States by Article 5 and by the second sentence of Article 6, only by the Member State requesting cooperation. Information thus exchanged shall be covered by the obligation of professional secrecy to which the persons employed or formerly employed by the competent authorities receiving the information are subject.

2. The competent authorities may refuse to act on a request for information:

    (a) where communication of the information might adversely affect the sovereignty, security or public policy of the State addressed;

    (b) where judicial proceedings have already been initiated in respect of the same actions and against the same persons before the authorities of the State addressed or where final judgment has already been passed on such persons for the same actions by the competent authorities of the State addressed.

3. Without prejudice to the obligations to which they are subject in judicial proceedings under criminal law, the authorities which receive information pursuant to paragraph 1 may use it only for the exercise of their functions within the meaning of Article 8 (1) and in the context of administrative or judicial proceedings specifically relating to the exercise of those functions. However, where the competent authority communicating information consents thereto, the authority receiving the information, may use it for other purposes or forward it to other States' competent authorities.

Article 11

The Community may, in conformity with the Treaty, conclude agreements with non-member countries on the matters governed by this Directive.

---

[1] *Official Journal of the European Communities* No L 66, 16.3.1979, p. 21.

Article 12

The Contact Committee set up by Article 20 of Directive 79/279/EEC shall also have as its function:

(a) to permit regular consultation on any practical problems which arise from the application of this Directive and on which exchanges of view are deemed useful;

(b) to advise the Commission, if necessary, on any additions or amendments to be made to this Directive.

Article 13

Each Member State shall determine the penalties to be applied for infringement of the measures taken pursuant to this Directive. The penalties shall be sufficient to promote compliance with those measures.

Article 14

1. Member States shall take the measures necessary to comply with this Directive before 1 June 1992. They shall forthwith inform the Commission thereof.

2. Member States shall communicate to the Commission the provisions of national law which they adopt in the field governed by this Directive.

Article 15

This Directive is addressed to the Member States.

2. EXTRADITION

2.1. United Nations

UN Model Treaty on Extradition (1990)[*]

New York, 14 December 1990

Article 1

Obligation to extradite

Each Party agrees to extradite to the other, upon request and subject to the provisions of the present Treaty, any person who is wanted in the requesting State for prosecution for an extraditable offence or for the imposition or enforcement of a sentence in respect of such an offence. [1]

Article 2

Extraditable offences

1. For the purposes of the present Treaty, extraditable offences are offences that are punishable under the laws of both Parties by imprisonment or other deprivation of liberty for a maximum period of at least [one/two] year(s), or by a more severe penalty. Where the request for extradition relates to a person who is wanted for the enforcement of a sentence of imprisonment or other deprivation of liberty imposed for such an offence, extradition shall be granted only if a period of at least [four/six] months of such sentence remains to be served.

2. In determining whether an offence is an offence punishable under the laws of both Parties, it shall not matter whether:

   (a) The laws of the Parties place the acts or omissions constituting the offence within the same category of offence or denominate the offence by the same terminology;

   (b) Under the laws of the Parties the constituent elements of the offence differ, it being understood that the totality of the acts or omissions as presented by the requesting State shall be taken into account.

3. Where extradition of a person is sought, for an offence against a law relating to taxation, customs duties, exchange control or other revenue matters, extradition may not be refused on the ground that the law of the requested State does not impose the same kind of tax or duty or does not contain a tax, customs duty or exchange regulation of the same kind as the law of the requesting State. [2]

4. If the request for extradition includes several separate offences each of which is punishable under the laws of both Parties, but some of which do not fulfil the other conditions set out in paragraph 1 of the present article, the requested Party may grant extradition for the latter offences provided that the person is to be extradited for at least one extraditable offence.

---

[*] General Assembly resolution 45/116 of 14 December 1990, *Compendium of United Nations Standards and Norms in Crime Prevention and Criminal Justice*, New York, United Nations, 1992, 48; *International Legal Materials*, 1991, 1407.

[1] Reference to the imposition of a sentence may not be necessary for all countries.

[2] Some countries may wish to omit this paragraph or provide an optional ground for refusal under article 4.

Article 3

Mandatory grounds for refusal

Extradition shall not be granted in any of the following circumstances:

(a) If the offence for which extradition is requested is regarded by the requested State as an offence of a political nature; [3]

(b) If the requested State has substantial grounds for believing that the request for extradition has been made for the purpose of prosecuting or punishing a person on account of that person's race, religion, nationality, ethnic origin, political opinions, sex or status, or that that person's position may be prejudiced for any of those reasons;

(c) If the offence for which extradition is requested is an offence under military law, which is not also an offence under ordinary criminal law;

(d) If there has been a final judgement rendered against the person in the requested State in respect of the offence for which the person's extradition is requested;

(e) If the person whose extradition is requested has, under the law of either Party, become immune from prosecution or punishment for any reason, including lapse of time or amnesty; [4]

(f) If the person whose extradition is requested has been or would be subjected in the requesting State to torture or cruel, inhuman or degrading treatment or punishment or if that person has not received or would not receive the minimum guarantees in criminal proceedings, as contained in the International Covenant on Civil and Political Rights, article 14; [5]

(g) If the judgement of the requesting State has been rendered *in absentia*, the convicted person has not had sufficient notice of the trial or the opportunity to arrange for his or her defence and he has not had or will not have the opportunity to have the case retried in his or her presence. [6]

Article 4

Optional grounds for refusal

Extradition may be refused in any of the following circumstances:

(a) If the person whose extradition is requested is a national of the requested State. Where extradition is refused on this ground, the requested State shall, if the other State so requests, submit the case to its competent authorities with a view to taking appropriate action against the person in respect of the offence for which extradition had been requested;

---

[3] Some countries may wish to add the following text: "Reference to an offence of a political nature shall not include any offence in respect of which the Parties have assumed an obligation, pursuant to any multilateral convention, to take prosecutorial action where they do not extradite, or any other offence that the Parties have agreed is not an offence of a political character for the purposes of extradition."

[4] Some countries may wish to make this an optional ground for refusal under article 4.

[5] See resolution 2200 A (xxi), annex.

[6] Some countries may wish to add to article 3 the following ground for refusal: "If there is insufficient proof, according to the evidentiary standards of the requested State, that the person whose extradition is requested is a party to the offence". (See also footnote 9.)

(b) If the competent authorities of the requested State have decided either not to institute or to terminate proceedings against the person for the offence in respect of which extradition is requested;

(c) If a prosecution in respect of the offence for which extradition is requested is pending in the requested State against the person whose extradition is requested;

(d) If the offence for which extradition is requested carries the death penalty under the law of the requesting State, unless that State gives such assurance as the requested State considers sufficient that the death penalty will not be imposed or, if imposed, will not be carried out; [7]

(e) If the offence for which extradition is requested has been committed outside the territory of either Party and the law of the requested State does not provide for jurisdiction over such an offence committed outside its territory in comparable circumstances;

(f) If the offence for which extradition is requested is regarded under the law of the requested State as having been committed in whole or in part within that State. [8] Where extradition is refused on this ground, the requested State shall, if the other State so requests, submit the case to its competent authorities with a view to taking appropriate action against the person for the offence for which extradition had been requested;

(g) If the person whose extradition is requested has been sentenced or would be liable to be tried or sentenced in the requesting State by an extraordinary or *ad hoc* court or tribunal;

(h) If the requested State, while also taking into account the nature of the offence and the interests of the requesting State, considers that, in the circumstances of the case, the extradition of that person would be incompatible with humanitarian considerations in view of age, health or other personal circumstances of that person.

Article 5

Channels of communication and required documents

1. A request for extradition shall be made in writing. The request, supporting documents and subsequent communications shall be transmitted through the diplomatic channel, directly between the ministries of justice or any other authorities designated by the Parties.

2. A request for extradition shall be accompanied by the following:

(a) In all cases,

(i) As accurate a description as possible of the person sought, together with any other information that may help to establish that person's identity, nationality and location;

(ii) The text of the relevant provision of the law creating the offence or, where necessary, a statement of the law relevant to the offence and a statement of the penalty that can be imposed for the offence;

---

[7] Some countries may wish to apply the same restriction to the imposition of a life, or indeterminate, sentence.
[8] Some countries may wish to make specific reference to a vessel under its flag or an aircraft registered under its laws at the time of the commission of the offence.

(b) If the person is accused of an offence, by a warrant issued by a court or other competent judicial authority for the arrest of the person or a certified copy of that warrant, a statement of the offence for which extradition is requested and a description of the acts or omissions constituting the alleged offence, including an indication of the time and place of its commission; [9]

(c) If the person has been convicted of an offence, by a statement of the offence for which extradition is requested and a description of the acts or omissions constituting the offence and by the original or certified copy of the judgement or any other document setting out the conviction and the sentence imposed, the fact that the sentence is enforceable, and the extent to which the sentence remains to be served;

(d) If the person has been convicted of an offence in his or her absence, in addition to the documents set out in paragraph 2 (c) of the present article, by a statement as to the legal means available to the person to prepare his or her defence or to have the case retried in his or her presence;

(e) If the person has been convicted of an offence but no sentence has been imposed, by a statement of the offence for which extradition is requested and a description of the acts or omissions constituting the offence and by a document setting out the conviction and a statement affirming that there is an intention to impose a sentence.

3. The documents submitted in support of a request for extradition shall be accompanied by a translation into the language of the requested State or in another language acceptable to that State.

Article 6

Simplified extradition procedure

The requested State, if not precluded by its law, may grant extradition after receipt of a request for provisional arrest, provided that the person sought explicitly consents before a competent authority.

Article 7

Certification and authentication

Except as provided by the present Treaty, a request for extradition and the documents in support thereof, as well as documents or other material supplied in response to such a request, shall not require certification or authentication. [10]

Article 8

Additional information

If the requested State considers that the information provided in support of a request for extradition is not sufficient, it may request that additional information be furnished within such reasonable time as it specifies.

---

[9] Countries that require a judicial assessment of the sufficiency of evidence may wish to add the following clause: "and sufficient proof in form acceptable under the law of the requested State, establishing, according to the evidentiary standards of that State, that the person is a party to the offence". (See also footnote 6.)

[10] The laws of some countries require authentication before documents transmitted from other countries can be admitted in their courts and, therefore, would require a clause setting out the authentication required.

Article 9

Provisional arrest

1. In case of urgency the requesting State may apply for the provisional arrest of the person sought pending the presentation of the request for extradition. The application shall be transmitted by means of the facilities of the International Criminal Police Organization, by post or telegraph or by any other means affording a record in writing.

2. The application shall contain a description of the person sought, a statement that extradition is to be requested, a statement of the existence of one of the documents mentioned in paragraph 2 of article 5 of the present Treaty, authorizing the apprehension of the person, a statement of the punishment that can be or has been imposed for the offence, including the time left to be served and a concise statement of the facts of the case, and a statement of the location, where known, of the person.

3. The requested State shall decide on the application in accordance with its law and communicate its decision to the requesting State without delay.

4. The person arrested upon such an application shall be set at liberty upon the expiration of [40] days from the date of arrest if a request for extradition, supported by the relevant documents specified in paragraph 2 of article 5 of the present Treaty, has not been received. The present paragraph does not preclude the possibility of conditional release of the person prior to the expiration of the [40] days.

5. The release of the person pursuant to paragraph 4 of the present article shall not prevent rearrest and institution of proceedings with a view to extraditing the person sought if the request and supporting documents are subsequently received.

Article 10

Decision on the request

1. The requested State shall deal with the request for extradition pursuant to procedures provided by its own law, and shall promptly communicate its decision to the requesting State.

2. Reasons shall be given for any complete or partial refusal of the request.

Article 11

Surrender of the person

1. Upon being informed that extradition has been granted, the Parties shall, without undue delay, arrange for the surrender of the person sought and the requested State shall inform the requesting State of the length of time for which the person sought was detained with a view to surrender.

2. The person shall be removed from the territory of the requested State within such reasonable period as the requested State specifies and, if the person is not removed within that period, the requested State may release the person and may refuse to extradite that person for the same offence.

3. If circumstances beyond its control prevent a Party from surrendering or removing the person to be extradited, it shall notify the other Party. The two Parties shall mutually decide upon a new date of surrender, and the provisions of paragraph 2 of the present article shall apply.

Article 12

Postponed or conditional surrender

1. The requested State may, after making its decision on the request for extradition, postpone the surrender of a person sought, in order to proceed against that person, or, if that person has already been convicted, in order to enforce a sentence imposed for an offence other than that for which extradition is sought. In such a case the requested State shall advise the requesting State accordingly.

2. The requested State may, instead of postponing surrender, temporarily surrender the person sought to the requesting State in accordance with conditions to be determined between the Parties.

Article 13

Surrender of property

1. To the extent permitted under the law of the requested State and subject to the rights of third parties, which shall be duly respected, all property found in the requested State that has been acquired as a result of the offence or that may be required as evidence shall, if the requesting State so requests, be surrendered if extradition is granted.

2. The said property may, if the requesting State so requests, be surrendered to the requesting State even if the extradition agreed to cannot be carried out.

3. When the said property is liable to seizure or confiscation in the requested State, it may retain it or temporarily hand it over.

4. Where the law of the requested State or the protection of the rights of third parties so require, any property so surrendered shall be returned to the requested State free of charge after the completion of the proceedings, if that State so requests.

Article 14

Rule of speciality

1. A person extradited under the present Treaty shall not be proceeded against, sentenced, detained, re-extradited to a third State, or subjected to any other restriction of personal liberty in the territory of the requesting State for any offence committed before surrender other than:

 (a) An offence for which extradition was granted;

 (b) Any other offence in respect of which the requested State consents. [11] Consent shall be given if the offence for which it is requested is itself subject to extradition in accordance with the present Treaty. [12]

2. A request for the consent of the requested State under the present article shall be accompanied by the documents mentioned in paragraph 2 of article 5 of the present Treaty and a legal record of any statement made by the extradited person with respect to the offence.

3. Paragraph 1 of the present article shall not apply if the person has had an opportunity to leave the requesting State and has not done so within [30/45] days of final discharge in respect of the offence for which that person was extradited or if the person has voluntarily returned to the territory of the requesting State after leaving it.

---

[11] Some countries may wish to add, as a third case, explicit consent of the person.

[12] Some countries may not wish to assume that obligation and may wish to include other grounds in determining whether or not to grant consent.

Article 15

Transit

1. Where a person is to be extradited to a Party from a third State through the territory of the other Party, the Party to which the person is to be extradited shall request the other Party to permit the transit of that person through its territory. This does not apply where air transport is used and no landing in the territory of the other Party is scheduled.

2. Upon receipt of such a request, which shall contain relevant information, the requested State shall deal with this request pursuant to procedures provided by its own law. The requested State shall grant the request expeditiously unless its essential interests would be prejudiced thereby. [13]

3. The State of transit shall ensure that legal provisions exist that would enable detaining the person in custody during transit.

4. In the event of an unscheduled landing, the Party to be requested to permit transit may, at the request of the escorting officer, hold the person in custody for [48] hours, pending receipt of the transit request to be made in accordance with paragraph 1 of the present article.

Article 16

Concurrent requests

If a Party receives requests for extradition for the same person from both the other Party and a third State it shall, at its discretion, determine to which of those States the person is to be extradited.

Article 17

Costs

1. The requested State shall meet the cost of any proceedings in its jurisdiction arising out of a request for extradition.

2. The requested State shall also bear the costs incurred in its territory in connection with the seizure and handing over of property, or the arrest and detention of the person whose extradition is sought. [14]

3. The requesting State shall bear the costs incurred in conveying the person from the territory of the requested State, including transit costs.

Article 18

Final provisions

1. The present Treaty is subject to [ratification, acceptance or approval]. The instruments of [ratification, acceptance or approval] shall be exchanged as soon as possible.

2. The present Treaty shall enter into force on the thirtieth day after the day on which the instruments of [ratification, acceptance or approval] are exchanged.

---

[13] Some countries may wish to agree on other grounds for refusal, which may also warrant refusal for extradition, such as those related to the nature of the offence (e.g. political, fiscal, military) or to the status of the person (e.g. their own nationals).
[14] Some countries may wish to consider reimbursement of costs incurred as a result of withdrawal of a request for extradition or provisional arrest.

3. The present Treaty shall apply to requests made after its entry into force, even if the relevant acts or omissions occurred prior to that date.

4. Either Contracting Party may denounce the present Treaty by giving notice in writing to the other Party. Such denunciation shall take effect six months following the date on which such notice is received by the other Party.

2.2. Council of Europe

European Convention on Extradition (1957)*

Paris, 13 December 1957

Article 1

Obligation to Extradite

The Contracting Parties undertake to surrender to each other, subject to the provisions and conditions laid down in this Convention, all persons against whom the competent authorities of the requesting Party are proceeding for an offence or who are wanted by the said authorities for the carrying out of a sentence or detention order.

Article 2

Extraditable Offences

1. Extradition shall be granted in respect of offences punishable under the laws of the requesting Party and of the requested Party by deprivation of liberty or under a detention order for a maximum period of at least one year or by a more severe penalty. Where a conviction and prison sentence have occurred or a detention order has been made in the territory of the requesting Party the punishment awarded must have been for a period of a least four months.

2. If the request for extradition includes several separate offences each of which is punishable under the laws of the requesting Party and the requested Party by deprivation of liberty or under a detention order, but of which some do not fulfil the condition with regard to the amount of punishment which may be awarded, the requested Party shall also have right to grant extradition for the latter offences.

3. Any Contracting Party whose law does not allow extradition for certain of the offences referred to in paragraph 1 of this Article may, in so far as it is concerned, exclude such offences from the application of this Convention.

4. Any Contracting Party which wishes to avail itself of the right provided for in paragraph 3 of this Article shall, at the time of the deposit of its instrument of ratification or accession, transmit to the Secretary-General of the Council of Europe either a list of the offences for which extradition is allowed or a list of those for which it is excluded and shall at the same time indicate the legal provisions which allow or exclude extradition. The Secretary-General of the Council shall forward these lists to the other signatories.

5. If extradition is subsequently excluded in respect of other offences by the law of a Contracting Party, that Party shall notify the Secretary-General. The Secretary-General shall inform the other signatories. Such notification shall not take effect until three months from the date of its receipt by the Secretary-General.

6. Any Party which avails itself of the right provided for in paragraphs 4 or 5 of this Article may at any time apply this Convention to offences which have been excluded from it. It shall inform the Secretary-General of the Council of such changes, and the Secretary-General shall inform the other signatories.

7. Any Party may apply reciprocity in respect of any offences excluded from the application of the Convention under this Article.

---

* *European Treaty Series*, No.24.

Article 3

Political Offences

1. Extradition shall not be granted if the offence in respect of which it is requested is regarded by the requested Party as a political offence or as an offence connected with a political offence.

2. The same rule shall apply if the requested Party has substantial grounds for believing that a request for extradition for an ordinary criminal offence has been made for the purpose of prosecuting or punishing a person on account of his race, religion, nationality or political opinion, or that that person's position may be prejudiced for any of these reasons.

3. The taking or attempted taking of the life of a Head of State or a member of his family shall not be deemed to be a political offence for the purpose of this Convention.

4. This Article shall not affect any obligations which the Contracting Parties may have undertaken or may undertake under any other international convention of a multilateral character.

Article 4

Military Offences

Extradition for offences under military law which are not offences under ordinary criminal law is excluded from the application of this Convention.

Article 5

Fiscal Offences

Extradition shall be granted, in accordance with the provisions of this Convention, for offences in connection with taxes, duties, customs and exchange only if the Contracting Parties have so decided in respect of any such offence or category of offences.

Article 6

Extradition of Nationals

1. (a) A Contracting Party shall have the right to refuse extradition of its nationals.

   (b) Each Contracting Party may, by a declaration made at the time of signature or of deposit of its instrument of ratification or accession, define as far as it is concerned the term "nationals" within the meaning of this Convention.

   (c) Nationality shall be determined as at the time of the decision concerning extradition. If, however, the person claimed is first recognised as a national of the requested Party during the period between the time of the decision and the time contemplated for the surrender, the requested Party may avail itself of the provision contained in sub-paragraph (a) of this Article.

2. If the requested Party does not extradite its national, it shall at the request of the requesting Party submit the case to its competent authorities in order that proceedings may be taken if they are considered appropriate. For this purpose, the files, information and exhibits relating to the offences shall be transmitted without charge by the means provided for in Article 12, paragraph 1. The requesting Party shall be informed of the result of its request.

Article 7

Place of Commission

1. The requested Party may refuse to extradite a person claimed for an offence which is regarded by its law as having been committed in whole or in part in its territory or in a place treated as its territory.

2. When the offence for which extradition is requested has been committed outside the territory of the requesting Party, extradition may only be refused if the law of the requested Party does not allow prosecution for the same category of offence when committed outside the latter Party's territory or does not allow extradition for the offence concerned.

Article 8

Pending Proceedings for the Same Offences

The requested Party may refuse to extradite the person claimed if the competent authorities of such Party are proceeding against him in respect of the offence or offences for which extradition is requested.

Article 9

Non Bis in Idem

Extradition shall not be granted if final judgment has been passed by the competent authorities of the requested Party upon the person claimed in respect of the offence or offences for which extradition is requested. Extradition may be refused if the competent authorities of the requested Party have decided either not to institute or to terminate proceedings in respect of the same offence or offences.

Article 10

Lapse of time

Extradition shall not be granted when the person claimed has, according to the law of either the requesting or the requested Party, become immune by reason of lapse of time from prosecution or punishment.

Article 11

Capital Punishment

If the offence for which extradition is requested is punishable by death under the law of the requesting Party, and if in respect of such offence the death-penalty is not provided for by the law of the requested Party or is not normally carried out, extradition may be refused unless the requesting Party gives such assurance as the requested Party considers sufficient that the death-penalty will not be carried out.

Article 12

The Request and Supporting Documents

1. The request shall be in writing and shall be communicated through the diplomatic channel. Other means of communication may be arranged by direct agreement between two or more Parties.

2. The request shall be supported by:

    (a) the original or an authenticated copy of the conviction and sentence or detention order immediately enforceable or of the warrant of arrest or other order having the same effect and issued in accordance with the procedure laid down in the law of the requesting Party;

(b) a statement of the offences for which extradition is requested. The time and place of their commission, their legal descriptions and a reference to the relevant legal provisions shall be set out as accurately as possible; and

(c) a copy of the relevant enactments or, where this is not possible, a statement of the relevant law and as accurate a description as possible of the person claimed, together with any other information which will help to establish his identity and nationality.

Article 13

Supplementary Information

If the information communicated by the requesting Party is found to be insufficient to allow the requested Party to make a decision in pursuance of this Convention, the latter Party shall request the necessary supplementary information and may fix a time-limit for the receipt thereof.

Article 14

Rule of Speciality

1. A person who has been extradited shall not be proceeded against, sentenced or detained with a view to the carrying out of a sentence or detention order for any offence committed prior to his surrender other than that for which he was extradited, nor shall he be for any other reason restricted in his personal freedom, except in the following cases:

    (a) When the Party which surrendered him consents. A request for consent shall be submitted, accompanied by the documents mentioned in Article 12 and a legal record of any statement made by the extradited person in respect of the offence concerned. Consent shall be given when the offence for which it is requested is itself subject to extradition in accordance with the provisions of this Convention;

    (b) when that person, having had an opportunity to leave the territory of the Party to which he has been surrendered, has not done so within 45 days of his final discharge, or has returned to that territory after leaving it.

2. The requesting Party may, however, take any measures necessary to remove the person from its territory, or any measures necessary under its law, including proceedings by default, to prevent any legal effects of lapse of time.

3. When the description of the offence charged is altered in the course of proceedings, the extradited person shall only be proceeded against or sentenced in so far as the offence under its new description is shown by its constituent elements to be an offence which would allow extradition.

Article 15

Re-extradition to a Third State

Except as provided for in Article 14, paragraph 1 (b), the requesting Party shall not, without the consent of the requested Party, surrender to another Party or to a third State a person surrendered to the requesting Party and sought by the said other Party or third State in respect of offences committed before his surrender. The requested Party may request the production of the documents mentioned in Article 12, paragraph 2.

Article 16

Provisional arrest

1. In case of urgency the competent authorities of the requesting Party may request the provisional arrest of the person sought. The competent authorities of the requested Party shall decide the matter in accordance with its law.

2. The request for provisional arrest shall state that one of the documents mentioned in Article 12, paragraph 2 (a), exists and that it is intended to send a request for extradition. It shall also state for what offence extradition will be requested and when and where such offence was committed and shall so far as possible give a description of the person sought.

3. A request for provisional arrest shall be sent to the competent authorities of the requested Party either through the diplomatic channel or direct by post or telegraph or through the International Criminal Police Organisation (Interpol) or by any other means affording evidence in writing or accepted by the requested Party. The requesting authority shall be informed without delay of the result of its request.

4. Provisional arrest may be terminated if, within a period of 18 days after arrest, the requested Party has not received the request for extradition and the documents mentioned in Article 12. It shall not, in any event, exceed 40 days from the date of such arrest. The possibility of provisional release at any time is not excluded, but the requested Party shall take any measures which it considers necessary to prevent the escape of the person sought.

5. Release shall not prejudice re-arrest and extradition if a request for extradition is received subsequently.

Article 17

Conflicting requests

If extradition is requested concurrently by more than one State, either for the same offence or for different offences, the requested Party shall make its decision having regard to all the circumstances and especially the relative seriousness and place of commission of the offences, the respective dates of the requests, the nationality of the person claimed and the possibility of subsequent extradition to another State.

Article 18

Surrender of the Person to be Extradited

1. The requested Party shall inform the requesting Party by the means mentioned in Article 12, paragraph 1 of its decision with regard to the extradition.

2. Reasons shall be given for any complete or partial rejection.

3. If the request is agreed to, the requesting Party shall be informed of the place and date of surrender and of the length of time for which the person claimed was detained with a view to surrender.

4. Subject to the provisions of paragraph 5 of this Article, if the person claimed has not been taken over on the appointed date, he may be released after the expiry of 15 days and shall in any case be released after the expiry of 30 days. The requested Party may refuse to extradite him for the same offence.

5. If circumstances beyond its control prevent a Party from surrendering or taking over the person to be extradited, it shall notify the other Party. The two Parties shall agree a new date for surrender and the provisions of paragraph 4 of this Article shall apply.

Article 19

Postponed or Conditional Surrender

1. The requested Party may, after making its decision on the request for extradition, postpone the surrender of the person claimed in order that he may be proceeded against by that Party or, if he has already been convicted, in order that he may serve his sentence in the territory of that Party for an offence other than that for which extradition is requested.

2. The requested Party may, instead of postponing surrender, temporarily surrender the person claimed to the requesting Party in accordance with conditions to be determined by mutual agreement between the Parties.

Article 20

Handing over of Property

1. The requested Party shall, in so far as its law permits and at the request of the requesting Party, seize and hand over property:

    (a) which may be required as evidence or

    (b) which has been acquired as a result of the offence and which, at the time of the arrest, is found in the possession of the person claimed or is discovered subsequently.

2. The property mentioned in paragraph 1 of this Article shall be handed even if extradition, having been agreed to, cannot be carried out owing to the death or escape of the person claimed.

3. When the said property is liable to seizure or confiscation in the territory of the requested Party, the latter may, in connection with pending criminal proceedings, temporarily retain it over on condition that it is returned.

4. Any rights which the requested Party or third parties may have acquired in the said property shall be preserved. Where these rights exist, the property shall be returned without charge to the requested Party as soon as possible after the trial.

Article 21

Transit

1. Transit through the territory of one of the Contracting Parties shall be granted on submission of a request by the means mentioned in Article 12, paragraph 1, provided that the offence concerned is not considered by the Party requested to grant transit as an offence of a political or purely military character having regard to Articles 3 and 4 of this Convention.

2. Transit of a national, within the meaning of Article 6, of a country requested to grant transit may be refused.

3. Subject to the provisions of paragraph 4 of this Article, it shall be necessary to produce the documents mentioned in Article 12, paragraph 2.

4. If air transport is used, the following provisions shall apply:

    (a) when it is not intended to land, the requesting Party shall notify the Party over whose territory the flight is to be made and shall certify that one of the documents mentioned in Articled 12, paragraph 2 (a) exists. In the case of an unscheduled landing, such notification shall have the effect of a request for provisional arrest as provided for in Article 16, and the requesting Party shall submit a formal request for transit;

(b) When it is intended to land, the requesting Party shall submit a formal request for transit.

5. A Party may, however, at the time of signature or of the deposit of its instrument of ratification of, or accession to, this Convention, declare that it will only grant transit of a person on some or all of the conditions on which it grants extradition. In that event, reciprocity may be applied.

6. The transit of the extradited person shall not be carried out through any territory where there is reason to believe that his life or his freedom may be threatened by reason of his race, religion, nationality or political opinion.

Article 22

Procedure

Except where this Convention otherwise provides, the procedure with regard to extradition and provisional arrest shall be governed solely by the law of the requested Party.

Article 23

Language to be Used

The documents to be produced shall be in the language of the requesting or requested Party. The requested Party may require a translation into one of the official languages of the Council of Europe to be chosen by it.

Article 24

Expenses

1. Expenses incurred in the territory of the requested Party by reason of extradition shall be borne by that Party.

2. Expenses incurred by reason of transit through the territory of a Party requested to grant transit shall be borne by the requesting Party.

3. In the event of extradition a non-metropolitan territory of the requested Party, the expenses occasioned by travel between that territory and the metropolitan territory of the requesting Party shall be borne by the latter. The same rule shall apply to expenses occasioned by travel between the non-metropolitan territory of the requested Party and its metropolitan territory.

Article 25

Definition of "Detention Order"

For the purposes of this Convention, the expression "detention order" means any order involving deprivation of liberty which has been made by a criminal court in addition to or instead of a prison sentence.

Article 26

Reservations

1. Any Contracting Party may, when signing this Convention or when depositing its instrument of ratification or accession, make a reservation in respect of any provision or provisions of the Convention.

2. Any Contracting Party which has made a reservation shall withdraw it as soon as circumstances permit. Such withdrawal shall be made by notification to the secretary-General of the Council of Europe.

3. A Contracting Party which has made a reservation in respect of a provision of the Convention may not claim application of the said provision by another Party save in so far as it has itself accepted the provision.

Article 27

Territorial Application

1. This Convention shall apply to the metropolitan territories of the Contracting Parties.

2. In respect of France, it shall also apply to Algeria and to the overseas Departments and, in respect of the United Kingdom of Great Britain and Northern Ireland, to the Channel Islands and to the Isle of Man.

3. The Federal Republic of Germany may extend the application of this Convention to the *Land* of Berlin by notice addressed to the Secretary-General of the Council of Europe, who shall notify the other Parties of such declaration.

4. By direct arrangement between two or more Contracting Parties, the application of this Convention may be extended, subject to the conditions laid down in the arrangement, to any territory of such Parties, other than the territories mentioned in paragraphs 1, 2 and 3 of this Article, for whose international relations any such Party is responsible.

Article 28

Relations between this Convention and Bilateral Agreements

1. This Convention shall, in respect of those countries to which it applies, supersede the provisions of any bilateral treaties, conventions or agreements governing extradition between any two Contracting Parties.

2. The Contracting Parties may conclude between themselves bilateral or multilateral agreements only in order to supplement the provisions of this Convention or to facilitate the application of the principles contained therein.

3. Where, as between two or more Contracting Parties, extradition takes place on the basis of a uniform law, the Parties shall be free to regulate their mutual relations in respect of extradition exclusively in accordance with such a system notwithstanding the provisions of this Convention. The same principle shall apply as between two or more Contracting Parties each of which has in force a law providing for the execution in its territory of warrants of arrest issued in the territory of the other Party or Parties. Contracting Parties which exclude or may in the future exclude the application of this Convention as between themselves in accordance with this paragraph shall notify the Secretary-General of the Council of Europe accordingly. The Secretary-General shall inform the other Contracting Parties of any notification received in accordance with this paragraph.

Article 29

Signature, Ratification and Entry into Force

1. This Convention shall be open to signature by the Members of the Council of Europe. It shall be ratified. The instruments of ratification shall be deposited with the Secretary-General of the Council.

2. The Convention shall come into force 90 days after the date of deposit of the third instrument of ratification.

3. As regards any signatory ratifying subsequently the Convention shall come into force 90 days after the date of the deposit of its instrument of ratification.

Article 30

Accession

1. The Committee of Ministers of the Council of Europe may invite any State not a Member of the Council to accede to this Convention, provided that the resolution containing such invitation receives the unanimous agreement of the Members of the Council who have ratified the Convention.

2. Accession shall be by deposit with the Secretary-General of the Council of an instrument of accession, which shall take effect 90 days after the date of its deposit.

Article 31

Denunciation

Any Contracting Party may denounce this Convention in so far as it is concerned by giving notice to the Secretary-General of the Council of Europe. Denunciation shall take effect six months after the date when the Secretary-General of the Council received such notification.

Article 32

Notifications

The Secretary-General of the Council of Europe shall notify the Members of the Council and the Government of any State which has acceded to this Convention of:

(a) the deposit of any instrument of ratification or accession;

(b) the date of entry into force of this Convention;

(c) any declaration made in accordance with the provisions of Article 6, paragraph 1, and of Article 21, paragraph 5;

(d) any reservation made in accordance with Article 26, paragraph 1;

(e) the withdrawal of any reservation in accordance with Article 26, paragraph 2;

(f) any notification of denunciation received in accordance with the provisions of Article 31 and by the date on which such denunciation will take effect.

(First) Additional Protocol to the European Convention on Extradition (excerpts) (1975)[*]

Strasbourg, 15 October 1975

Chapter I

Article 1

For the application of Article 3 of the Convention, political offences shall not be considered to include the following:

(a) the crimes against humanity specified in the Convention on the Prevention and Punishment of the Crime of Genocide adopted on 9 December 1948 by the General Assembly of the United Nations;

(b) the violations specified in Article 50 of the 1949 Geneva Convention for the Amelioration of the Condition of the Wounded and Sick in Armed Forces in the Field, Article 51 of the 1949 Geneva Convention for the Amelioration of the Condition of Wounded, Sick and Shipwrecked Members of Armed Forces at Sea, Article 130 of the 1949 Geneva Convention relative to the Treatment of Prisoners of War and Article 147 of the 1949 Geneva Convention relative to the Protection of Civilian Persons in Time of War;

(c) any comparable violations of the laws of war having effect at the time when this Protocol enters into force and of customs of war existing at that time, which are not already provided for in the above-mentioned provisions of the Geneva Conventions.

Chapter II

Article 2

1. Article 9 of the Convention shall be supplemented by the following text, the original Article 9 of the Convention becoming paragraph 1 and the under-mentioned provisions becoming paragraphs 2, 3 and 4:

2. The extradition of a person against whom a final judgment has been rendered in a third State, Contracting Party to the Convention, for the offence or offences in respect of which the claim was made, shall not be granted:

(a) if the afore-mentioned judgment resulted in his acquittal;

(b) if the term of imprisonment or other measure to which he was sentenced:

(i) has been completely enforced;

(ii) has been wholly, or with respect to the part not enforced, the subject of a pardon or an amnesty;

(c) if the court convicted the offender without imposing a sanction.

3. However, in the cases referred to in paragraph 2, extradition may be granted:

---

[*] *European Treaty Series*, No.86.

(a) if the offence in respect of which judgment has been rendered was committed against a person, an institution or any thing having public status in the requesting State;

(b) if the person on whom judgment was passed had himself a public status in the requesting State;

(c) if the offence in respect of which judgment was passed was committed completely or partly in the territory of the requesting State or in a place treated as its territory.

4. The provisions of paragraphs 2 and 3 shall not prevent the application of wider domestic provisions relating to the effect of *ne bis in idem* attached to foreign criminal judgments."

[...]

Second Additional Protocol to the European Convention on Extradition (excerpts) (1978)*

Strasbourg, 17 March 1978

Chapter I

Article 1

Paragraph 2 of Article 2 of the Convention shall be supplemented by the following provision: "This right shall also apply to offences which are subject only to pecuniary sanctions."

Chapter II

Article 2

Article 5 of the Convention shall be replaced by the following provisions:

"Fiscal offences

1. For offences in connection with taxes, duties, customs and exchange extradition shall take place between the Contracting Parties in accordance with the provisions of the Convention if the offence, under the law of the requested Party, corresponds to an offence of the same nature.

2. Extradition may not be refused on the ground that the law of the requested Party does not impose the same kind of tax or duty or does not contain a tax, duty, customs or exchange regulation of the same kind as the law of the requesting Party."

Chapter III

Article 3

The Convention shall be supplemented by the following provisions:

"Judgments in absentia

1. When a Contracting Party requests from another Contracting Party the extradition of a person for the purpose of carrying out a sentence or detention order imposed by a decision rendered against him in absentia, the requested Party may refuse to extradite for this purpose if, in its opinion, the proceedings leading to the judgment did not satisfy the minimum rights of defence recognised as due to everyone charged with criminal offence. However, extradition shall be granted if the requesting Party gives an assurance considered sufficient to guarantee to the person claimed the right to a retrial which safeguards the rights of defence. This decision will authorise the requesting Party either to enforce the judgment in question if the convicted person does not make an opposition or, if he does, to take proceedings against the person extradited.

2. When the requested Party informs the person whose extradition has been requested of the judgment rendered against him in absentia, the requesting Party shall not regard this communication as a formal notification for the purposes of the criminal procedure in that State."

---

* *European Treaty Series*, No.98.

Chapter IV

Article 4

The Convention shall be supplemented by the following provisions:

"*Amnesty*

Extradition shall not be granted for an offence in respect of which an amnesty has been declared in the requested State and which that State had competence to prosecute under its own criminal law."

Chapter V

Article 5

Paragraph 1 of Article 12 of the Convention shall be replaced by the following provisions:

"The request shall be in writing and shall be addressed by the Ministry of Justice of the requesting Party to the Ministry of Justice of the requested Party; however, use of the diplomatic channel is not excluded. Other means of communication may be arranged by direct agreement between two or more Parties."

European Convention on the Suppression of Terrorism (1977)[*]

Strasbourg, 27 January 1977

Article 1

For the purposes of extradition between Contracting States, none of the following offenses shall be regarded as a political offence or as an offence connected with a political offence or as an offence inspired by political motives:

(a) an offence within the scope of the Convention for the Suppression of Unlawful Seizure of Aircraft, signed at The Hague on 16 December 1970;

(b) an offence within the scope of the Convention for the Suppression of Unlawful Acts against the Safety of Civil Aviation, signed at Montreal on 23 September 1971;

(c) a serious offence involving an attack against the life, physical integrity or liberty of internationally protected persons, including diplomatic agents;

(d) an offence involving kidnapping, the taking of a hostage or serious unlawful detention;

(e) an offence involving the use of a bomb, grenade, rocket, automatic firearm or letter or parcel bomb if this use endangers persons;

(f) an attempt to commit any of the foregoing offences or participation as an accomplice of a person who commits or attempts to commit such an offence.

Article 2

1. For the purposes of extradition between Contracting States, a Contracting State may decide not to regard as a political offence or as an offence connected with a political offence or as an offence inspired by political motives a serious offence involving an act of violence, other than one covered by Article 1, against the life, physical integrity or liberty of a person.

2. The same shall apply to a serious offence involving an act against property, other than one covered by Article 1, if the act created a collective danger for persons.

3. The same shall apply to an attempt to commit any of the foregoing offences or participation as an accomplice of a person who commits or attempts to commit such an offence.

Article 3

The provisions of all extradition treaties and arrangements applicable between Contracting States, including the European Convention on Extradition, are modified as between Contracting States to the extent that they are incompatible with this Convention.

Article 4

For the purposes of this Convention and to the extent that any offence mentioned in Article 1 or 2 is not listed as an extraditable offence in any extradition convention or treaty existing between Contracting States, it shall be deemed to be included as such therein.

---

[*] *European Treaty Series*, No.90.

Article 5

Nothing in this Convention shall be interpreted as imposing an obligation to extradite if the requested State has substantial grounds for believing that the request for extradition for an offence mentioned in Article 1 or 2 has been made for the purpose of prosecuting or punishing a person on account of his race, religion, nationality or political opinion, or that that person's position may be prejudiced for any of these reasons.

Article 6

1. Each Contracting State shall take such measures as may be necessary to establish its jurisdiction over an offence mentioned in Article 1 in the case where the suspected offender is present in its territory and it does not extradite him after receiving a request for extradition from a Contracting State whose jurisdiction is based on a rule of jurisdiction existing equally in the law of the requested State.

2. This Convention does not exclude any criminal jurisdiction exercised in accordance with national law.

Article 7

A Contracting State in whose territory a person suspected to have committed an offence mentioned in Article 1 is found and which has received a request for extradition under the conditions mentioned in Article 6, paragraph 1, shall, if it does not extradite that person, submit the case, without exception whatsoever and without undue delay, to its competent authorities for the purpose of prosecution. Those authorities shall take their decision in the same manner as in the case of any offence of a serious nature under the law of that State.

Article 8

1. Contracting States shall afford one another the widest measure of mutual assistance in criminal matters in connection with proceedings brought in respect of the offenses mentioned in Article 1 or 2. The law of the requested State concerning mutual assistance in criminal matters shall apply in all cases. Nevertheless this assistance may not be refused on the sole ground that is concerns a political offence or an offence connected with a political offence or an offence inspired by political motives.

2. Nothing in this Convention shall be interpreted as imposing an obligation to afford mutual assistance if the requested State has substantial grounds for believing that the request for mutual assistance in respect of an offence mentioned in Article 1 or 2 has been made for the purpose of prosecuting or punishing a person on account of his race, religion, nationality or political opinion or that that person's position may be prejudiced for any of these reasons.

3. The provisions of all treaties and arrangements concerning mutual assistance in criminal matters applicable between Contracting State, including the European Convention on Mutual Assistance in Criminal Matters, are modified as between Contracting States to the extent that they are incompatible with this Convention.

Article 9

1. The European Committee on Crime Problems of the Council of Europe shall be kept informed regarding the application of this Convention.

2. It shall do whatever is needful to facilitate a friendly settlement of any difficulty which may arise out of its execution.

Article 10

1. Any dispute between Contracting States concerning the interpretation or application of this Convention, which has not been settled in the framework of Article 9, paragraph 2, shall, at the request of any Party to the dispute, be referred to arbitration. Each Party shall nominate an arbitrator and the two arbitrators shall nominate a referee. If any Party has not nomina-

ted its arbitrator within the three months following the request for arbitration, he shall be nominated at the request of the other Party by the President of the European Court of Human Rights. If the latter should be a national of one of the Parties to the dispute, this duty shall be carried out by the Vice-President of the Court or, if the Vice-President is a national of one of the Parties to the dispute. The same procedure shall be observed if the arbitrators cannot agree on the choice of referee.

2. The arbitration tribunal shall lay down its own procedure. Its decisions shall be taken by majority vote. Its award shall be final.

Article 11

1. This Convention shall be open to signature by the member States of the Council of Europe. It shall be subject to ratification, acceptance or approval. Instruments of ratification, acceptance or approval shall be deposited with the Secretary General of the Council of Europe.

2. The Convention shall enter into force three months after the date of the deposit of the third instrument of ratification, acceptance or approval.

3. In respect of a signatory State ratifying, accepting or approving subsequently, the Convention shall come into force three months after the date of the deposit of its instrument of ratification, acceptance or approval.

Article 12

1. Any State may, at the time of signature or when depositing its instrument of ratification, acceptance or approval, specify the territory or territories to which this Convention shall apply.

2. Any State may, when depositing its instrument of ratification, acceptance or approval or at any later date, by declaration addressed to the Secretary General of the Council of Europe, extend this Convention to any other territory or territories specified in the declaration and for whose international relations it is responsible or on whose behalf it is authorised to give undertakings.

3. Any declaration made in pursuance of the preceding paragraph may, in respect of any territory mentioned in such declaration, be withdrawn by means of a notification addressed to the Secretary General of the Council of Europe. Such withdrawal shall take effect immediately or at such later date as may be specified in the notification.

Article 13

1. Any State may, at the time of signature or when its instrument of ratification, acceptance or approval, declare that it reserves the right to refuse extradition in respect of any offence mentioned in Article 1 which it considers to be a political offence, an offence connected with a political offence or an offence inspired by political motives, provided that it undertakes to take into due consideration, when evaluating the character of the offence, any particularly serious aspects of the offence, including:

    (a) that it created a collective danger to the life, physical integrity or liberty of persons; or

    (b) that it affected persons foreign to the motives behind it: or

    (c) that cruel or vicious means have used in the commission of the offence.

2. Any State may wholly or partly withdraw a reservation it has made in accordance with the foregoing paragraph by means of a declaration addressed to the Secretary General of the Council of Europe which shall become effective as from the date of its receipt.

3. A State which has made a reservation in accordance with paragraph 1 of this article may not claim the application of Article 1 by any other State; it may, however, if its reservation is partial or conditional, claim the application of that article in so far as it has itself accepted it.

Article 14

Any Contracting State may denounce this Convention by means of a written notification addressed to the secretary General of the Council of Europe. Any such denunciation shall take effect immediately or at such later date as may be specified in the notification.

Article 15

This Convention ceases to have effect in respect of any Contracting State which withdraws from or ceases to be a Member of the Council of Europe.

Article 16

The Secretary General of the Council of Europe shall notify the member States of the Council of:

(a) any signature;

(b) any deposit of an instrument of ratification, acceptance of approval;

(c) any date of entry into force of this Convention in accordance with Article 11 thereof;

(d) any declaration or notification received in pursuance of the provisions of Article 12;

(e) any reservation made in pursuance of the provisions of Article 13, paragraph 1;

(f) the withdrawal of any reservation effected in pursuance of the provisions of Article 13, paragraph 2;

(g) any notification received in pursuance of Article 14 and the date on which denunciation takes effect;

(h) any cessation of the effects of the Convention pursuant to Article 15.

Recommendation No. R (80) 7 of the Committee of Ministers to Member States Concerning the Practical Application of the European Convention on Extradition (1980)*

Adopted by the Committee of Ministers on 27 June 1980 at the 321st meeting of the Ministers Deputies

The Committee of Ministers, under the terms of Article 15.b of the Statute of the Council of Europe,

Recalling Resolution (75) 12 on the practical application of the European Convention on Extradition;

Desirous of extending and further facilitating the application of this convention, which was opened for signature on 13 December 1957 and entered into force on 18 April 1960,

1. Recommends the governments of member states:

    1. if they are not yet Contracting Parties to the convention, to ratify it as soon as possible;

    2. if they are Contracting Parties to the convention, to be guided in its practical application by the following principles:

        Concerning the use of extradition

        When deciding on whether to request extradition, the requesting state should take into consideration the hardship which might be caused by the extradition procedure to the person concerned and to his family, where this procedure is manifestly disproportionate to the seriousness of the offence and where the penalty likely to be passed will not significantly exceed the minimum period of detention laid down in Article 2, paragraph 1, of the convention, or will not involve deprivation of liberty.

        In the case of enforcement of a sentence or detention order, the requesting state should apply the same principle of proportionality, particularly where the remainder of the sanction to be served does not exceed a period of four months.

        Concerning the extradition procedure

        Irrespective of the administrative or judicial nature of the extradition proceedings, the person concerned:

        (a) should be informed, promptly and in a language which he understands, of the extradition request and the facts on which it is based, of the conditions and the procedure of extradition, and, where applicable, of the reasons for his arrest;

        (b) should be heard on the arguments which he invokes against his extradition;

        (c) should have the possibility to be assisted in the extradition procedure; if he has not sufficient means to pay for the assistance, he should be given it free.

---

* MÜLLER-RAPPARD, E. and BASSIOUNI, M.C. (ed.), *European Inter-State Cooperation in Criminal Matters. The Council of Europe's Legal Instruments*, Dordrecht/ Boston/ London, Martinus Nijhoff Publishers, 1993, 277.

Concerning summary extradition

With a view to expediting extradition and keeping the period of provisional arrest as short as possible, consideration should be given to the use of a summary procedure enabling the rapid surrender of the person sought without following ordinary extradition procedures, provided that the person concerned consents to it.

Concerning provisional arrest (Article 16 of the convention)

(a) The requesting authority should ask for the provisional arrest of the person sought only if there are strong reasons to suggest that otherwise the extradition could not be effected.

(b) The period of provisional arrest should be kept as short as possible. It should exceed the period of eighteen days only in cases of necessity, particularly where the requesting authority indicates difficulties in submitting the documents within that period.

Concerning transit (Article 21 of the convention)

(a) To render the procedure more expeditious, arrangements for obtaining the consent of the transit states should be made, whenever possible, at the time extradition is requested. The requested state should be promptly informed of the means of transit envisaged and whether transit permission is being sought from other Contracting States.

(b) In principle, the requested state should comply with the wishes of the requesting state with regard to the way in which the transit is to be effected. However, in cases of particular difficulty, the two states should consult each other on the appropriate means of transport (rail, road or air) and possibly on the place where the person to be extradited is to be handed over.

(c) A Contracting State which has been asked to grant transit should act on the request and make the necessary arrangements in a way as to avoid any delay.

(d) If, under the conditions mentioned above, the requested state uses a summary extradition procedure, and transit involves the presence of the person concerned in the territory of the transit state for only a short period, the transit state should consider whether transit can be authorised without the production of all the documents mentioned in Article 12 of the convention.

(e) Transit by air should be used as widely as possible because it is likely to facilitate and accelerate the handing over of the person to be extradited. As a general rule, the person to be surrendered should be escorted;

2. Instructs the Secretary General of the Council of Europe to transmit this recommendation to the governments of those Contracting States which are not members of the Council of Europe.

Recommendation No. R (80) 9 of the Committee of Ministers to Member States Concerning Extradition to States not Party to the European Convention on Human Rights*

Adopted by the Committee of Ministers on 27 June 1980 at the 321st meeting of the Ministers' Deputies

The Committee of Ministers, under the terms of Article 15.b of the Statute of the Council of Europe,

Desirous of strengthening the protection of human rights in cases concerning extradition requested by states not party to the Convention for the Protection of Human Rights and Fundamental Freedoms of 4 November 1950;

Having regard to the provisions of Article 3, paragraph 2, of the European Convention on Extradition of 13 December 1957,

Recommends the governments of member states:

1. not to grant extradition where a request for extradition emanates from a state not party to the European Convention on Human Rights and where there are substantial grounds for believing that the request has been made for the purpose of prosecuting or punishing the person concerned on account of his race, religion nationality or political opinion, or that his position may be prejudiced for any of these reasons;

2. to comply with any interim measure which the European Commission of Human Rights might indicate under Rule 36 of its Rules of Procedure, as, for instance, a request to stay extradition proceedings pending a decision on the matter.

---

* MÜLLER-RAPPARD, E. and BASSIOUNI, M.C. (ed.), *European Inter-State Co-operation in Criminal Matters. The Council of Europe's Legal Instruments*, Dordrecht/ Boston/ London, Martinus Nijhoff Publishers, 1993, 278.

2.3. Schengen Group

Schengen Convention - Title III - Chapter IV (excerpts) (1990)*

Schengen, 19 June 1990

Title III

Police and security

Chapter IV

Extradition

Article 59

1. The provisions of this Chapter are intended to supplement the European Convention of 13 September 1957 on Extradition as well as, in relations between the Contracting Parties which are members of the Benelux Economic Union, Chapter I of the Benelux Treaty on Extradition and Mutual Assistance in Criminal Matters of 27 June 1962, as amended by the Protocol of 11 May 1974, and to facilitate the implementation of these agreements.

2. Paragraph 1 shall not affect the application of the broader provisions of the bilateral agreements in force between Contracting Parties.

Article 60

In relations between two Contracting Parties, one of which is not a party to the European Convention on Extradition of 13 September 1957, the provisions of the said Convention shall apply, subject to the reservations and declarations made at the time of ratifying this Convention or, for Contracting Parties which are not parties to the Convention, at the time of ratifying, approving or accepting the present Convention.

Article 61

The French Republic undertakes to extradite, at the request of one of the Contracting Parties, persons against whom proceedings are being taken for offences punishable under French law by deprivation of liberty or under a detention order for a maximum period of at least two years and under the law of the requesting Contracting Party by deprivation of liberty or under a detention order for a maximum period of at least a year.

Article 62

1. As regards interruption of prescription, only the provisions of the requesting Contracting Party shall apply.

2. An amnesty granted by the requested Contracting Party shall not prevent extradition unless the offence falls within the jurisdiction of that Contracting Party.

3. The absence of a charge or an official notice authorizing proceedings necessary only under the legislation of the requested Contracted Party, shall not affect the obligation to extradite.

---

* Convention of 19 June 1990, applying the Schengen Agreement of 14 June 1985 between the Governments of the States of the Benelux Economic Union, the Federal Republic of Germany and the French Republic, on the Gradual Abolition of Checks at their Common Borders, *International Legal Materials*, 1991, 84.

Article 63

The Contracting Parties undertake, in accordance with the Convention and the Treaty referred to in Article 59, to extradite between themselves persons being prosecuted by the legal authorities of the requesting Contracting Party for one of the offenses referred to in Article 50(1), or being sought by them for the purposes of execution of a sentence or detention order imposed in respect of such an offence.

Article 64

A report included in the Schengen Information System in accordance with Article 95 shall have the same force as a request for provisional arrest under Article 16 of the European Convention on Extradition of 13 September 1957 or Article 15 of the Benelux Treaty on Extradition and Mutual Assistance in Criminal Matters of 27 June 1962, as amended by the Protocol of 11 May 1974.

Article 65

1. Without prejudice to the option to use the diplomatic channel, requests for extradition and transit shall be sent by the relevant Ministry of the requesting Contracting Party to the relevant Ministry of the requested Contracting Party.

2. The relevant Ministries shall be:

   - as regards the Kingdom of Belgium: the Ministry of Justice;

   - as regards the Federal Republic of Germany: the Federal Ministry of Justice and the Justice Ministers or Senators of the Federal States;

   - as regards the French Republic: the Ministry of Foreign Affairs;

   - as regards the Grand Duchy of Luxembourg: the Ministry of Justice;

   - as regards the Kingdom of the Netherlands: the Ministry of Justice.

Article 66

1. If the extradition of a wanted person is not obviously prohibited under the laws of the requested Contracting Party, that Contracting Party may authorize extradition without formal extradition proceedings, provided that the wanted person agrees thereto in a statement made before a member of the judiciary after being examined by the latter and informed of his right to formal extradition proceedings. The wanted person may have access to a lawyer during such examination.

2. In cases of extradition under paragraph 1, a wanted person who explicitly states that he will not invoke the rule of speciality may not revoke that statement.

[...]

2.4. Commonwealth

Commonwealth Scheme for the Rendition of Fugitive Offenders (1966)[*]

London, 1966, as amended in 1990

1. The general provisions set out in this Scheme will govern the return of a person from one part of the Commonwealth, in which he is found, to another part thereof, in which he is accused of an offence; and in particular his return will only be precluded by law, or be subject to refusal by the competent executive authority, in the circumstances mentioned in this Scheme.

2. For the purpose of this Scheme a person liable to return as mentioned in paragraph (1) is described as a fugitive offender and each of the following areas is described as constituting a separate part of the Commonwealth, that is to say

   (a) each sovereign and independent country within the Commonwealth together with any dependent territories (which expression, for the purpose aforesaid, includes protectorates and protected States) which that country designates, and

   (b) each country within the Commonwealth, which, though not sovereign and independent, is not a territory designated for the purposes of the preceding subparagraph.

Returnable offences

2. (1) A fugitive will only be returned for a returnable offence.

   (2) For the purpose of this Scheme a returnable offence is an offence however described which is punishable in the part of the Commonwealth where the fugitive is located and the part of the Commonwealth to which return is requested by imprisonment for two years or a greater penalty.

   (3) Offences described in paragraph (2) are returnable offences notwithstanding that any such offences are of a purely fiscal character, where such offences are returnable under the law of the requested part of the Commonwealth.

Warrants, other than provisional warrants

3. (1) A fugitive offender will only be returned if a warrant for his arrest has been issued in that part of the Commonwealth to which his return is requested and either

   (a) that warrant is endorsed by a competent judicial authority in the part in which he is found (in which case, the endorsed warrant will be sufficient authority for his arrest), or

   (b) A further warrant for his arrest is issued by the competent judicial authority in the part in which he is found, not being a provisional warrant issued as mentioned in clause 4.

   (2) The endorsement or issue of a warrant as mentioned in this clause may be made conditional on the competent executive authority having previously issued an order to proceed.

---

[*] *Commonwealth Law Bulletin*, 1990, 1036.

Provisional warrants

4. (1) Where a fugitive offender is, or is suspected of being, in or on his way to any part of the Commonwealth but no warrant has been endorsed as mentioned in clause 3(1)(a) or issued as mentioned in clause 3(1)(b), the competent judicial authority in that part of the Commonwealth may issue a provisional warrant for his arrest on such information and under such circumstances as would, in the authority's opinion, justify the issue of a warrant if the returnable offence of which the fugitive is accused had been an offence committed within the authority's jurisdiction and for the purposes of this paragraph information contained in an international notice issued by the International Criminal Police Organisation (INTERPOL) in respect of a fugitive may be considered by the authority, either alone or with other information, in deciding whether a provisional warrant should be issued for the arrest of that fugitive.

   (2) A report of the issue of such a provisional warrant, together with the information in justification or a certified copy thereof, will be sent to the competent executive authority and, in a case in which that authority decides on the said information and any other information which may have become available that the fugitive should be discharged, that authority may so order.

Committal proceedings

5. (1) A fugitive offender arrested under a warrant endorsed or issued as mentioned in clause 3(1), or under a provisional warrant issued as mentioned in clause 4, will be brought, as soon as practicable, before the competent judicial authority who will hear the case in the same manner and have the same jurisdiction and powers, as nearly as may be, including power to remand and admit to bail, as if the fugitive were charged with an offence committed within that authority's jurisdiction.

   (2) The competent judicial authority will receive any evidence which may be tendered to show that the return of the fugitive offender is precluded by law.

   (3) Where a provisional warrant has been issued as mentioned in clause 4 but, within such reasonable time as with references to the circumstances of the case the competent judicial authority may fix

   (a) a warrant has not been endorsed or issued as mentioned in clause 3(1), or

   (b) where such endorsement or issue of a warrant has been made conditional on the issue of an order to proceed, as mentioned in clause 3(2), no such order has been issued, the competent judicial authority will order the fugitive to be discharged.

   (4) Where a warrant has been endorsed or issued as mentioned in clause 3(1) the competent judicial authority may commit the fugitive to prison to await his return if

   (a) such evidence is produced as establishes a prima facie case that he committed the offence of which he is accused, and
   (b) his return is not precluded by law.

   But, otherwise, will order him to be discharged.

   (5) Where a fugitive offender is committed to prison to await his return as mentioned in the preceding paragraph, notice of the fact will forthwith be given to the competent executive authority in that part of the Commonwealth in which he is committed.

Consent order for return

6. (1) A fugitive offender may waive committal proceedings, and if satisfied that the fugitive offender has voluntarily and with an understanding of its significance requested such waiver, the competent judicial authority may make an order by consent for the committal of the fugitive offender to prison, or for his admission to bail, to await return.

   (2) The competent executive authority may thereafter order return at any time, notwithstanding the provisions of clause 7.

   (3) The provision of clause 15 shall apply in relation to a fugitive offender returned under this Clause unless waived by him.

Return or discharge by executive authority

7. After the expiry of 15 days from the date of the committal of a fugitive offender to prison to await his return, as mentioned in clause 5, or, if a writ of habeas corpus or other like process is issued with reference to him, from the date of the final decision thereon of the competent judicial authority (whichever date is the later), the competent executive authority will order his return unless it appears to that authority that, in accordance with the provisions set out in this Scheme, his return is precluded by law or should be refused, in which case that authority will order his discharge.

Discharge by judicial authority

8. (1) Where after the expiry of the period mentioned in paragraph (2) a fugitive offender has not been returned, an application to the competent judicial authority may be made by or on behalf of the fugitive for his discharge and if

   (a) reasonable notice of the application has been given to the competent executive authority, and

   (b) sufficient cause for the delay is not shown, the competent judicial authority will order his discharge.

   (2) The period referred to in paragraph (1) will be prescribed by law and will be one expiring either

   (a) not later than two months from the fugitive's committal to prison as mentioned in clause 5, or

   (b) not later than one month from the date of the order for his return made as mentioned in clause 7.

Habeas corpus and review

9. (1) It will be provided that an application may be made by or on behalf of a fugitive offender for a writ of habeas corpus or other like process.

   (2) It will be provided that an application may be made by or on behalf of the government of the requesting part of the Commonwealth for review of the decision of the competent judicial authority in committal proceedings.

Circumstances precluding return

10. (1) (a) The return of a fugitive offender will be precluded by law if the competent judicial or executive authority is satisfied that the offence is of a political character.

   (b) Paragraph (a) shall not apply in relation to offences established under any multilateral international convention to which both the requesting and the requested parts of the Commonwealth are parties and which are declared thereby not to be regarded as political offences for the purposes of extradition.

(c) Any part of the Commonwealth may adopt the provisions set out in Annex 1.

(2) The return of a fugitive offender will be precluded by law if it appears to the competent judicial or executive authority

(a) that the request for his surrender although purporting to be made for a returnable offence was in fact made for the purpose of prosecuting or punishing the person on account of his race, religion, nationality or political opinions, or

(b) that he may be prejudiced at his trial or punished, detained, or restricted in his personal liberty by reason of his race, religion, nationality or political opinions.

(3) The return of a fugitive offender, or his return before the expiry of a specified period, will be precluded by law if the competent judicial or executive authority is satisfied that by reason of

(a) the trivial nature of the case, or

(b) the accusation against the fugitive not having been made in good faith or in the interests of justice, or

(c) the passage of time since the commission of the offence, or

(d) any other sufficient cause,

it would, having regard to all the circumstances be unjust or oppressive or too severe a punishment to return the fugitive or, as the case may be, to return him before the expiry of a period specified by that authority.

(4) The return of a fugitive offender will be precluded by law if the competent judicial or executive authority is satisfied that he has been convicted (and is neither unlawfully at large nor at large in breach of a condition of a licence to be at large), or has been acquitted, whether within or outside the Commonwealth, of the offence of which he is accused.

(5) The competent authorities for the purposes of this and the next following clause will include

(a) any judicial authority which hears or is competent to hear such an application as is mentioned in clause 9, and

(b) the executive authority by whom any order for the fugitive's return would fall to be made.

(6) It will be sufficient compliance with any one of the paragraphs (1), (2), (3), (4) and (5) if a country decides that the competent authority for the purposes of that paragraph is exclusively the judicial authority or the executive authority.

(7) If the competent executive authority

(a) is empowered by law to certify that the offence of which a fugitive offender is accused is an offence of a political character, and

(b) in the case of a particular fugitive offender, so certifies, the certificate will be conclusive in the matter and binding upon the competent judicial authority for the purposes mentioned in this clause.

Offences under military law

11. The return of a fugitive offender will either be precluded by law, or be subject to refusal by the competent authority if the competent authority is satisfied that the offence is an offence only under military law or a law relating to military obligations.

Double-criminality rule

12. The return of a fugitive offender will either be precluded by law or be subject to refusal by the competent executive authority if the facts on which the request for his return is grounded do not constitute an offence under the law of the country or territory in which he is found.

Postponement of return of fugitive and temporary transfer of prisoners to stand trial

13. (1) Subject to the following provisions of this clause, where a fugitive offender

    (a) has been charged with an offence triable by a court in that part of the Commonwealth in which he is found, or

    (b) is serving a sentence imposed by a court in that part of the Commonwealth, then until such a time as he has been discharged (whether by acquittal, the expiration or remission of his sentence, or otherwise) his return will either be precluded by law or be subject for refusal by the competent executive authority as the law of the country or territory concerned may provide.

(2) Subject to the provisions of this Scheme, a prisoner serving such a sentence who is also a fugitive offender may, at the discretion of the competent executive authority of that part of the Commonwealth in which the prisoner is held, be returned temporarily to another part of the Commonwealth in which he is accused of a returnable offence to enable proceedings to be brought against the prisoner in relation to that offence on such conditions as are agreed between the respective parts of the Commonwealth.

Priority where two or more requests made

14. Where requests for the return of a fugitive offender to two or more parts of the Commonwealth fall to be dealt with at the same time, the competent executive authority will determine to which part he should be returned and, accordingly, may refuse the other requests; and in determining the matter that authority will consider all the circumstances of the case and in particular:

    (a) the relative seriousness of the offences

    (b) the relative dates on which the requests were made, and

    (c) the citizenship or other national status of the fugitive and his ordinary residence.

Speciality rule

15. (1) This clause relates to a fugitive offender who has been returned from one part of the Commonwealth to another part thereof, so long as he has not had a reasonable opportunity of leaving the second mentioned part.

(2) In the case of a fugitive offender to whom this clause relates, his detention or trial in the part of the Commonwealth to which he has been returned for any

offence committed prior to his return (other than the one for which he was returned or any lesser offence proved by the facts on which that return was grounded or, with the consent of the requested country or territory, any returnable offence) will be precluded by law.

(3) When considering a request for consent under paragraph (2) the executive authority of the requested part of the Commonwealth may call for such particulars as it may require in order that it may be satisfied that such request is otherwise consistent with the principles of this Scheme, and shall not unreasonably withhold consent; but where in the opinion of the requested part of the Commonwealth it appears that, on the facts known of the requesting part of the Commonwealth at the time of the original application for return of the fugitive offender, application should have been made in respect of such offences at that time, that fact may constitute a ground for refusal.

(4) The requesting part of the Commonwealth shall not, without the consent of the requested part, return or surrender to another country or territory a fugitive offender returned to the requesting part and sought by such other country or territory in respect of any offence committed prior to his return; and in considering a request under this paragraph the requested part of the Commonwealth may call for the particulars referred to in paragraph (3) and shall not unreasonably withhold consent.

(5) Nothing in this clause shall prevent a court in the requesting part of the Commonwealth from taking into account at the request of the fugitive any other offence, whether returnable or not under this Scheme, for the purpose of passing sentence on a fugitive convicted of an offence for which he has been returned under this Scheme, where the fugitive desired that such other offence shall be taken into account.

Return of escaped prisoners

16. (1) In the case of a person who

 (a) has been convicted of a returnable offence by a court in any part of the Commonwealth and is unlawfully at large before the expiry of his sentence for that offence, and

 (b) is found in some other part of the Commonwealth, the provisions set out in this Scheme, as applied for the purposes of this clause by paragraph (2), will govern his return to the part of the Commonwealth in which he was convicted.

(2) For the purposes of this clause this Scheme shall be construed, subject to any necessary adaptations or modifications, as though the person unlawfully at large were accused of the offence of which he was convicted and, in particular

 (a) any reference to a fugitive offender shall be construed as including a reference to such a person as is mentioned in paragraph (1), and

 (b) the reference in clause 5(4) to such evidence as establishes a prima facie case that he committed the offence of which he is accused shall be construed as a reference to such evidence as establishes that he has been convicted.

(3) The references in this clause to a person unlawfully at large shall be construed as including reference to a person at large in breach of a condition of a licence to be at large.

Ancillary provisions

17. Each Commonwealth country or territory will take, subject to its constitution, any legislative and other steps which may be necessary or expedient in the circumstances to facilitate and effectuate

    (a) the return of a fugitive offender who is in transit in its territory for that purpose.

    (b) the delivery of property found in the possession of a fugitive offender at the time of his arrest which may be material evidence of the offence at which he is accused, and

    (c) the proof of warrants, certificates of conviction, depositions and other documents.

Alternative arrangements and modifications

18. Nothing in this Scheme shall prevent

    (a) the making of arrangements between two or more parts of the Commonwealth for further or alternative provision for the return of offenders, or

    (b) the application of the Scheme with modifications by any part of the Commonwealth in relation to any other part which has not brought clauses 1 to 17 fully into effect.

Supplementary provisions

19. (1) Any part of the Commonwealth may or may not adopt either or both of the supplementary provisions set out in Annex 1 but, where such a provision is adopted, any other part of the Commonwealth may in relation to the first part reserve its position as to whether it will give effect to clauses 1 to 17 or will give effect to them subject to such exceptions and modifications as appear to it to be necessary or expedient or give effect to any arrangement made under clause 18(a).

    (2) Two or more parts of the Commonwealth may make arrangements under which in matters of rendition between them clause 5(4) will be replaced either by Annex 3 or by other provisions agreed by the Governments of those parts.

Annex 1

Discretion as to definition of political offences

1. It may be provided by a law in any part of the Commonwealth that certain acts shall not be held to be offences of a political character including

    (a) an offence against the life or person of a Head of State or a member of his immediate family or any related offence (i.e. aiding and abetting, or counselling or procuring the commission of, or being an accessory before or after the fact to, or attempting or conspiring to commit such an offence).

    (b) an offence against the life or person of a Head of Government, or of a Minister of a Government, or any related offence as aforesaid,

    (c) murder, or any related offence as aforesaid

    (d) an act declared to constitute an offence under a multilateral international convention whose purpose is to prevent or repress a specific category of offences and which imposes on the parties thereto an obligation either to extradite or prosecute the person sought.

2. Any part of the Commonwealth may restrict the application of any of the provisions made under paragraph 1 to a request from a part of the Commonwealth which has made similar provisions in its law.

Annex 2

Supplementary provisions: discretion as respects return for offences punishable by death

1. (1) The return of a fugitive offender may be refused by the competent executive authority where it appears to that authority that, by reason that:

    (a) if he was returned he would be likely to suffer the death penalty for the offence for which his return is requested, and

    (b) in the country or territory in which he is found or in any part thereof that offence is not punishable by death,

it would, having regard to all the circumstances of the case and to any likelihood that if not returned he would be immune from punishment, be unjust or oppressive or too severe a punishment to return him.

(2) In determining whether a fugitive would be likely to suffer the death penalty, the executive authority shall take into account any representations which the authorities of the requesting part of the Commonwealth may make with regard to the possibility that the death penalty, if imposed, will not be carried out.

Discretion as respects return of citizens etc.

2. (1) The return of a fugitive offender who is a national or permanent resident of the part of the Commonwealth in which he is found

    (a) may be precluded by law, or

    (b) may be refused by the competent executive authority:

Provided that return will not be so refused if the fugitive is also a national of that part of the Commonwealth to which his return is requested.

(2) For the purposes of this paragraph a fugitive shall be treated as a national of a part of the Commonwealth if that part consists of, or includes

    (a) a Commonwealth country of which he is a citizen, or

    (b) a country or territory his connection with which determines his national status,

in either case at the date of the request.

Annex 3

Alternative provisions as to committal proceedings

1. Where a warrant has been endorsed or issued as mentioned in clause 3(1) the competent judicial authority may commit the fugitive to prison to await his return if

    (a) the contents of the record of the case received under this Annex whether or not admissible in evidence, under the law of the requested part, and any other evidence admissible under the law of the requested part, are sufficient to warrant a trial of the charges for which rendition has been requested; and

(b) the fugitive's return is not precluded by law, but otherwise will order the fugitive to be discharged.

2. The competent judicial authority will receive a record of the case prepared by an investigating authority in the requesting part if it is accompanied by

(a) an affidavit of an officer of the investigating authority stating that the record of the case was prepared by or under the direction of that officer, and that the evidence has been preserved for use in court; and

(b) a certificate of the Attorney General of the requesting part that in his opinion the record of the case discloses the existence of evidence under the law of the requesting part sufficient to justify a prosecution.

3. The record of the case will contain

(a) particulars of the description, identity, nationality and, to the extent available, whereabouts of the person sought;

(b) particulars of each offence or conduct in respect of which rendition is requested, specifying the date and place of commission, the legal definition of the offence and the relevant provisions in the law of the requesting part, including a certified copy of any such definition in the written law of that part;

(c) the original or a certified copy of any document of process issued in the requesting part against the person whom it seeks to have committed for rendition;

(d) a recital of the evidence acquired to support the request for rendition of the person sought;

(e) and a certified copy, reproduction or photograph of exhibits or documents evidence.

2.5. Bilateral Extradition Treaties

Convention between Belgium and the United States of America concerning the Mutual Extradition of Fugitive Offenders (1901)[*]

Washington, 26 October 1901

His Majesty the King of the Belgians and the United States of America, having judged it expedient with a view to the better administration of justice and the prevention of crime within their respective territories and jurisdictions that persons charged with or convicted of the crimes and offences hereinafter enumerated, and being fugitives from justice, should, under certain circumstances, be reciprocally delivered up, have resolved to conclude an new Convention for that purpose and have appointed as their Plenipotentiaries:

His Majesty the King of the Belgians, Mr Charles-C. Wauters, chargé d'affaires *ad interim* of Belgium near the Government of the United States; and

The President of the United States, John Hay, Secretary of State of the United States;

Who, after having communicated to each other their respective full powers, found in good and due form, have agreed upon and concluded the following articles:

Article 1

The Government of Belgium and the Government of the United States mutually agree to deliver up persons who, having been charged, as principals or accessories, with or convicted of any of the crimes and offences specified in the following article committed within the jurisdiction of one of the contracting parties, shall seek an asylum or be found within the territories of the other: Provided, that this shall only be done upon such evidence of criminality as, according to the laws of the place where the fugitive or person so charged shall be found, would justify his or her apprehension and commitment for trial if the crime had been there committed.

Article 2

Persons shall be delivered up who shall have been convicted of or be charged, according to the provisions of this Convention, with any of the following crimes:

(a) Murder, comprehending the crimes designated in the Belgian penal code by the terms of parricide, assassination, poisoning and infanticide;

(b) The attempt to commit murder;

(c) Rape, or attempt to commit rape, bigamy, abortion;

(d) Arson;

(e) Piracy, or mutiny on shipboard whenever the crew, or part thereof, shall have taken possession of the vessel by fraud of by violence against the commander;

(f) Larceny; the crime of burglary, defined to be the act of breaking and entering by night into the house of another with the intent to commit felony; and the crime of robbery, defined to be the act of feloniously and forcibly taking from the person of another money or goods by violence or putting him in fear; and the corresponding crimes punished by the Belgian laws under the description of thefts committed in an inhabited house by night, and by breaking in by climbing or forcibly, and thefts committed with violence or by means of threats;

---

[*] *Moniteur belge- Belgisch Staatsblad*, 29 and 30 June 1902.

(g) The crime of forgery, by which is understood the utterance of forged papers and also the counterfeiting of public, sovereign, or governmental acts;

(h) The fabrication or circulation of counterfeit money either coin or paper, or of counterfeit public bonds, coupons of the public debt, banknotes, obligations, or in general anything being a title or instrument of credit: the counterfeiting of seals and dies, impressions, stamps and marks of State and public administrations, and the utterance thereof;

(i) The embezzlement of public moneys committed within the jurisdiction of either party by public officers or depositaries;

(j) Embezzlement by any person or persons hired or salaried to the detriment of their employers, when the crime is subject to punishment by the laws of the place where it was committed;

(k) Wilful and unlawful destruction or obstruction of rail roads which endangers human life;

(l) Obtaining money, valuable securities or other property by false pretences, when such act is made criminal by the laws of both countries and the amount of money or the value of the property fraudulently obtained is not less than two hundred dollars or one thousand francs;

(m) Kidnapping of minors;

(n) Reception of articles obtained by means of one of the crimes or offences provided for by the present Convention.

Extradition may also be granted for the attempt to commit any of the crimes above enumerated when such attempt is punishable by the laws of both contracting parties.

Article 3

1. A person surrendered under this Convention shall not be tried or punished in the country to which his extradition has been granted, nor given up to a third power for a crime or offence, not provided for by the present Convention and committed previously to his extradition, until he shall have been allowed one month to leave the country after having been discharged; and, if he shall have been tried and condemned to punishment, he shall be allowed one month after having suffered his penalty or having been pardoned.

2. He shall moreover not be tried or punished for any crime or offence provided for by this Convention committed previous to his extradition, other than that which gave rise to the extradition, without the consent of the Government which surrendered him, which may, if it think proper, require the production of one of the documents mentioned in article 7 of this Convention.

3. The consent of that Government shall likewise be required for the extradition of the accused to a third country; nevertheless, such consent shall not be necessary when the accused shall have asked of his own accord to be tried or to undergo his punishment, or when he shall not have left within the space of time above specified the territory of the country to which he has been surrendered.

Article 4

1. The provisions of this Convention shall not be applicable to persons guilty of any political crime or offence or of one connected with such a crime or offence. A person who has been surrendered on account of one of the common crimes or offences mentioned in article 2 shall consequently in no case be prosecuted and punished in the State to which his extradition has been granted on account of a political crime or offence committed by him previously to his extradition or on account of an act connected with such a political crime or offence, unless he has been at liberty to leave country for one month after having been tried

and, in case of condemnation, for one month after having suffered his punishment or having been pardoned.

2. An attempt against the life of the head of a foreign government or against that of any member of his family when such attempt comprises the act either of murder or assassination, or, of poisoning, shall not be considered a political offence or an act connected with such an offence.

Article 5

Neither of the contracting parties shall be bound to deliver up its own citizens or subjects under the stipulations of this Convention.

Article 6

If the person whose surrender may be claimed pursuant to the stipulations of the present treaty shall have been arrested for the commission of offences in the country where he has sought an asylum, or shall have been convicted thereof, his extradition may be deferred until he shall have been acquitted or have served the term of imprisonment to which he may have been sentenced.

Article 7

1. Requisitions for the surrender of fugitives from justice shall be made by the respective diplomatic agents of the contracting parties, or, in the event of the absence of these from the country or its seat of government, they may be made by superior consular officers.

2. If the person whose extradition may be asked for shall have been convicted of a crime or offence, a copy of the sentence of the court in which he may have been convicted authenticated under its seal, and attestation of the official character of the judge by the proper executive authority, and of the latter by the minister or consul of Belgium or of the United States, respectively, shall accompany the requisition. When, however, the fugitive shall have been merely charged with crime, a duly authenticated copy of the warrant for his arrest in the country where the crime may have been committed, and of the depositions upon which such warrant may have been issued, must accompany the requisition as aforesaid.

3. It shall be lawful for any competent judicial authority of the United States, upon production of a certificate issued by the secretary of State stating that a request has been made by the Government of Belgium for the provisional arrest of a person convicted or accused of the commission therein of a crime or offence extraditable under the provisions of this Convention, and upon complaint duly made that such crime or offence has been so committed, to issue his warrant for the apprehension of such person.

4. But if the demand for surrender, with the formal proofs herein before mentioned, be not made as aforesaid by the diplomatic agent of the demanding government, or, in his absence, by the competent consular officer, within forty days from the date of the commitment of the fugitive, the prisoner shall be discharged from custody.

5. And the Government of Belgium will, upon request of the Government of the United States, transmitted through the diplomatic agent of the United States, or, in his absence, through the competent consular officer, secure in conformity with law the provisional arrest of persons convicted or accused of the commission therein of crimes or offences extraditable under this Convention. But if the demand for surrender, with the formal proofs hereinbefore mentioned, be not made as aforesaid by the diplomatic agent of the demanding government, or, in his absence, by the competent consular officer, within forty days from the date of the commitment of the fugitive, the prisoner shall be discharged from custody.

Article 8

The expenses of the arrest, detention, examination and delivery of fugitives under this Convention shall be borne by the State in whose name the extradition is sought; provided, that the demanding government shall not be compelled to bear any expense for the services of such officers of the government from which extradition is sought as receive a fixed salary; and provided that the charge for the services of such public officials as receive only fees shall not exceed the fees to which such officials are entitled under the laws of the country for services rendered in ordinary criminal proceedings.

Article 9

Extradition shall not be granted, in pursuance of the provisions of this Convention, if legal proceedings or the enforcement of the penalty for the act committed by the person claimed has become barred by limitation, according to the laws of the country to which the requisition is addressed.

Article 10

All articles found in the possession of the accused party and obtained through the commission of the act with which he is charged, or that may be used as evidence of the crime for which his extradition is demanded, shall be seized if the competent authority shall so order, and shall be surrendered with his person.

The rights of third parties to the articles so found shall nevertheless be respected.

Article 11

The present Convention shall take effect thirty days after the exchange of ratifications.

After it shall have taken effect, the convention of June 13, 1882, shall cease to be in force and shall be superseded by the present convention which shall continue to have binding force for six months after a desire for its termination shall have been expressed in due form by one of the two governments to the other.

It shall be ratified and its ratification shall be exchanged at Washington as soon as possible.

In witness, whereof, the respective plenipotentiaries have signed the above articles both in the English and French languages, and they have thereunto affixed their seals.

Done, in duplicate, at the city of Washington this 26 day of october 1901.

Declaration

The Senate of the United States, by its resolution of January 30, 1902, having given its advice and consent to the ratification of the extradition treaty between Belgium and the United States, signed at Washington on October 26, 1901, with the following amendment:

In article 2 insert after the word "committed" the following: "and the amount of money or the value of the property embezzled is not less than two hundred dollars or one thousand francs." and the said amendment being acceptable to the Government of Belgium, the undersigned Plenipotentiaries before proceeding with the exchange of ratifications of the said treaty, and being duly authorized, have agreed to the following:

Extradition may not be granted for the offences enumerated in paragraph 10, article 2, of the said treaty unless "the amount of money or the value of the property embezzled is not less than two hundred dollars or one thousand francs".

The present declaration shall have the same force and duration as the extradition treaty of which it forms an integral part.

Done in duplicate at Washington, the sixth day of June 1902.

Supplementary Convention concerning the Extradition Convention between Belgium and the United States of America signed on 26 October 1901 (1935)[*]

Washington, 20 June 1935

The Governments of His Majesty the King of the Belgians and the United States of America, being desirous of enlarging the list of crimes on account of which extradition may be granted under the Convention concluded between the two countries on October 26, 1901, have resolved to conclude a Supplementary Convention for this purpose and have appointed as their Plenipotentiaries:

His Majesty the King of the Belgians:

Count Robert van der Straten Ponthoz, His Majesty's Ambassador, Extraordinary and Plenipotentiary to the United States of America, and

The President of the United States of America:

Mr. Cordell Hull, Secretary of State to the United States of America;

Who, after having communicated to each other their respective full powers, which were found to be in due and proper form, have agreed upon the following articles:

Article 1

The following crimes and offences are added to the list of crimes and offences numbered 1 to 14 in Article II of the said Convention of October 26, 1901, on account of which extradition may be granted, that is to say:

15. Crimes and offences committed in violation of legislation on bankruptcy.

16. Fraud or breach of trust on the part of a depositary, banker, agent, middleman, trustee, executor, administrator, guardian, director or agent of any company or corporation, or on the part of any person occupying a position of trust.

Article 2

The present Convention shall be considered as an integral part of the said Extradition Convention of October 26, 1901, and article II of the last mentioned Convention shall be read as if the list of crimes and offences therein contained had originally comprised the additional crimes and offences specified and numbered 15 and 16 in the first article of the present convention.

Article 3

The present Convention shall be ratified by the High Contracting Parties in accordance with their respective constitutional methods and shall go into effect one month after the exchange of ratifications, which shall take place at Brussels, as soon as possible.

In witness whereof, the above named Plenipotentiaries have signed the present Convention, both in the French and English languages, and have hereunto affixed their seals.

Done in duplicata, at Washington, this twentieth day of June, one thousand nine hundred and thirty-five.

---

[*] *Moniteur belge - Belgisch Staatsblad*, 28-29 October 1935.

Supplementary Treaty concerning the Extradition Treaty between the Government of the United States of America and the Government of the United Kingdom of Great Britain and Northern Ireland signed at London on 8 June 1972 (excerpts) (1985)*

Washington, 25 June 1985

The Government of the United States of America and the Government of the United Kingdom of Great Britain and Northern Ireland;

Desiring to make more effective the Extradition Treaty between the Contracting Parties, signed at London on 8 June 1972 (hereinafter referred to as "the Extradition Treaty");

Have resolved to conclude a Supplementary Treaty and have agreed as follows:

Article 1

For the purposes of the Extradition Treaty, none of the following offences shall be regarded as an offence of a political character:

(a) an offence within the scope of the Convention for the Suppression of Unlawful Seizure of Aircraft, opened for signature at The Hague on 16 December 1970;

(b) an offence within the scope of the Convention for the Suppression of Unlawful Acts against the Safety of Civil Aviation, opened for signature at Montreal on 23 September 1971;

(c) an offence within the scope of the Convention on the Prevention and Punishment of Crimes against Internationally Protected Persons, including Diplomatic Agents, opened for signature at New York on 14 December 1973;

(d) an offence within the scope of the International Convention against, the Taking of Hostages, opened for signature at New York on 18 December 1979;

(e) murder;

(f) manslaughter;

(g) maliciously wounding or inflicting grievous bodily harm;

(h) kidnapping, abduction, false imprisonment or unlawful detention, including the taking of a hostages;

(i) the following offences relating to explosives:

  (i) the causing of an explosion likely to endanger life or cause serious damage to property; or

  (ii) conspiracy to cause such an explosion; or

  (iii) the making or possession of an explosive substance by a person who intends either himself or through another person to endanger life or cause serious damage to property;

(j) the following offences relating to firearms or ammunition.

---

* *International Legal Materials*, 1985, 1105.

(i) the possession of a firearm or ammunition by a person who intends either himself or through another person to endanger life; or

(ii) the use of a firearm by a person with intent to resist or prevent the arrest or detention of himself or another person;

(k) damaging property with intent to endanger life or with reckless disregard as to whether the life of another would thereby be endangered;

(l) an attempt to commit any of the foregoing offenses.

[...]

3. MUTUAL ASSISTANCE

3.1. Police Cooperation

Constitution of Interpol (1956) *

Vienna, 1956

GENERAL PROVISIONS

Article 1

The Organization called the "INTERNATIONAL CRIMINAL POLICE COMMISSION" shall henceforth be entitled: "THE INTERNATIONAL CRIMINAL POLICE ORGANIZATION - INTERPOL". Its seat shall be in France.

Article 2

Its aims are:

(a) To ensure and promote the widest possible mutual assistance between all criminal police authorities within the limits of the laws existing in the different countries and in the spirit of the "Universal Declaration of Human Rights";

(b) To establish and develop all institutions likely to contribute effectively to the prevention and suppression of ordinary law crimes.

Article 3

It is strictly forbidden for the Organisation to undertake any intervention or activities of a political, military, religious or racial character.

Article 4

Any country may delegate as a Member to the Organization any official police body whose functions come within the framework of activities of the Organization.

The request for membership shall be submitted to the Secretary General by the appropriate governmental authority.

Membership shall be subject tot approval by a two-thirds majority of the General Assembly.

STRUCTURE AND ORGANIZATION

Article 5

The International Criminal Police Organization - Interpol shall comprise:

- The General Assembly
- The Executive Committee
- The General Secretariat
- The National Central Bureaus
- The Advisers.

---

* Amended version (1964) published by the I.C.P.O.-INTERPOL General Secretariat.

THE GENERAL ASSEMBLY

Article 6

The General Assembly shall be the body of supreme authority in the Organization. It is composed of delegates appointed by the Members of the Organization.

Article 7

Each Member may be represented by one or several delegates; however, for each country there shall be only one delegation head, appointed by the competent governmental authority of that country.

Because of the technical nature of the Organization, Members should attempt to include the following in their delegations:

(a) High officials of departments dealing with police affairs,

(b) Officials whose normal duties are connected with the activities of the Organization,

(c) Specialists in the subjects on the agenda.

Article 8

The functions of the General Assembly shall be the following:

(a) To carry out the duties laid down in the Constitution;

(b) To determine principles and lay down the general measures suitable for attaining the objectives of the Organization as given in Article 2 of the Constitution;

(c) To examine and approve the general programme of activities prepared by the Secretary General for the coming year;

(d) To determine any other regulations deemed necessary;

(e) To elect persons to perform the functions mentioned in the Constitution;

(f) To adopt resolutions and make recommendations to Members on matters with which the Organization is competent to deal;

(g) To determine the financial policy of the Organization;

(h) To examine and approve any agreements to be made with other organizations.

Article 9

Members shall do all within their power, in so far as is compatible with their own obligations, to carry out the decisions of the General Assembly.

Article 10

The General Assembly of the Organization shall meet in ordinary session every year. It may meet in extraordinary session at the request of the Executive Committee or of the majority of Members.

Article 11

The General Assembly may, when in session, set up special committees for dealing with particular matters.

Article 12

During the final meeting of each session, the General Assembly shall choose the place of meeting for the following session. The date of this meeting shall be fixed by agreement between the inviting country and the President after consultation with the Secretary General.

Article 13

Only one delegate from each country shall have the right to vote in the General Assembly.

Article 14

Decisions shall be made by a simple majority except in those cases where a two-thirds majority is required by the Constitution.

THE EXECUTIVE COMMITTEE

Article 15

The Executive Committee shall be composed of the President of the Organization, the three Vice-Presidents and nine Delegates.

The thirteen members of the Executive Committee shall belong to different countries, due weight having been given to geographical distribution.

Article 16

The General Assembly shall elect, from among the delegates, the President and three Vice-Presidents of the Organization.

A two-thirds majority shall be required for the election of the President; should this majority not be obtained after the second ballot, a simple majority shall suffice.

The President and Vice-Presidents shall be from different continents.

Article 17

The President shall be elected for four years. The Vice-Presidents shall be elected for three years. They shall not be immediately eligible for re-election either to the same posts or as Delegates on the Executive Committee.

If, following the election of a President, the provisions of Article 15 (paragraph 2) or Article 16 (paragraph 3) cannot be applied or are incompatible, a fourth Vice-President shall be elected so that all four continents are represented at the Presidency level.

If this occurs, the Executive Committee will, for a temporary period, have fourteen members. The temporary period shall come to an end as soon as circumstances make it possible to apply the provisions of Articles 15 and 16.

Article 18

The President of the Organization shall:

(a) Preside at meetings of the Assembly and the Executive Committee and direct the discussions;

(b) Ensure that the activities of the Organizations are in conformity with the decisions of the General Assembly and the Executive Committee;

(c) Maintain as far as is possible direct and constant contact with the Secretary General of the Organization.

Article 19

The nine Delegates on the Executive Committee shall be elected by the General Assembly for a period of three years. They shall not be immediately eligible for re-election to the same posts.

Article 20

The Executive Committee shall meet at least once each year on being convened by the President of the Organization.

Article 21

In the exercise of their duties, all members of the Executive Committee shall conduct themselves as representatives of the Organization and not as representatives of their respective countries.

Article 22

The Executive Committee shall:

(a) Supervise the execution of the decisions of the General Assembly;

(b) Prepare the agenda for sessions of the General Assembly;

(c) Submit to the General Assembly any programme of work or project which it considers useful;

(d) Supervise the administration and work of the Secretary General;

(e) Exercise all the powers delegated to it by the Assembly.

Article 23

In case of resignation or death of any of the members of the Executive Committee, the General Assembly shall elect another member to replace him and whose term of office shall end on the same date as his predecessor's. No member of the Executive Committee may remain in office should he cease to be a delegate to the Organization.

Article 24

Executive Committee members shall remain in office until the end of the session of the General Assembly held in the year in which their term of office expires.

THE GENERAL SECRETARIAT

Article 25

The permanent departments of the Organization shall constitute the General Secretariat.

Article 26

The General Secretariat shall:

(a) Put into application the decisions of the General Assembly and the Executive Committee;

(b) Serve as an international centre in the fight against ordinary crime;

(c) Serve as a technical and information centre;

(d) Ensure the efficient administration of the Organization;

(e) Maintain contact with national and international authorities, whereas questions relative to the search for criminals shall be dealt with through the National Central Bureaus;

(f) Produce any publications which may be considered useful;

(g) Organize and perform secretariat work at the sessions of the General Assembly, the Executive Committee and any other body of the Organization;

(h) Draw up a draft programme of work for the coming year for the consideration and approval of the General Assembly and the Executive Committee;

(i) Maintain as far as is possible direct and constant contact with the President of the Organization.

Article 27

The General Secretariat shall consist of the Secretary General and a technical and administrative staff entrusted with the work of the Organization.

Article 28

The appointment of the Secretary General shall be proposed by the Executive Committee and approved by the General Assembly for a period of five years. He may be re-appointed for other terms but must lay down office on reaching the age of sixty-five, although he may be allowed to complete his term of office on reaching this age.
He must be chosen from among persons highly competent in police matters.

In exceptional circumstances, the Executive Committee may propose at a meeting of the General Assembly that the Secretary General be removed from office.

Article 29

The Secretary General shall engage and direct the staff, administer the budget, and organize and direct the permanent departments, according to the directives decided upon by the General Assembly or Executive Committee.

He shall submit to the Executive Committee or the General Assembly any propositions or projects concerning the work of the Organisation.

He shall be responsible to the Executive Committee and the General Assembly.

He shall have the right to take part in the discussions of the General Assembly, the Executive Committee and all other dependent bodies.

In the exercise of his duties, he shall represent the Organization and not any particular country.

Article 30

In the exercise of their duties, the Secretary General and the staff shall neither solicit nor accept instructions from any government or authority outside the Organization. They shall abstain from any action which might be prejudicial to their international task.

Each Member of the Organization shall undertake to respect the exclusively international character of the duties of the Secretary General and the staff, and abstain from influencing them in the discharge of their duties.

All Members of the Organization shall do their best to assist the Secretary General and the staff in the discharge of their functions.

NATIONAL CENTRAL BUREAUS

Article 31

In order to further its aims, the Organization need the constant and active co-operation of its Members, who should do all within their power which is compatible with the legislation of their countries to participate diligently in its activities.

Article 32

In order to ensure the above co-operation, each country shall appoint a body which will serve as the National Central Bureau. It shall ensure liaison with:

(a) The various departments in the country;

(b) Those bodies in other countries serving as National Central Bureaus;

(c) The Organization's General Secretariat.

Article 33

In the case of those countries where the provisions of Article 32 are inapplicable or do not permit of effective centralized co-operation, the General Secretariat shall decide, with these countries, the most suitable alternative means of co-operation.

THE ADVISERS

Article 34

On scientific matters, the Organization may consult "Advisers".

Article 35

The role of the Advisers shall be purely advisory.

Article 36

Advisers shall be appointed for three years by the Executive Committee. Their appointment will become definite only after notification by the General Assembly.

They shall be chosen from among those who have a world-wide reputation in some field of interest to the Organization.

Article 37

An Adviser may be removed from office by decision of the General Assembly.

BUDGET AND RESOURCES

Article 38

The Organization's resources shall be provided by:

(a) The financial contributions from Members;

(b) Gifts, bequests, subsidies, grants and other resources after these have been accepted or approved by the Executive Committee.

Article 39

The General Assembly shall establish the basis of Members' subscriptions and the maximum annual expenditure according to the estimate provided by the Secretary General.

Article 40

The draft budget of the Organization shall be prepared by the Secretary General and submitted for approval to the Executive Committee.

It shall come into force after acceptance by the General Assembly.

Should the General Assembly not have had the possibility of approving the budget, the Executive Committee shall take all necessary steps according to the general outlines of the preceding budget.

RELATIONS WITH OTHER ORGANIZATIONS

Article 41

Whenever it deems fit, having regard to the aims and objects provided in the Constitution, the Organization shall establish relations and collaborate with other intergovernmental or non-governmental international organizations.

The general provisions concerning the relations with international, intergovernmental or non-governmental organizations will only be valid after their approval by the General Assembly.

The Organization may, in connection with all matters in which it is competent, take the advice of non-governmental international, governmental national or non-governmental national organizations.

With the approval of the General Assembly, The Executive Committee or, in urgent cases, the Secretary General may accept duties within the scope of its activities and competence either from other international institutions or organizations or in application of international conventions.

APPLICATIONS, MODIFICATION AND INTERPRETATION OF THE CONSTITUTION

Article 42

The present Constitution may be amended on the proposal of either a Member or the Executive Committee.

Any proposal for amendment to this Constitution shall be communicated by the Secretary General to Members of the Organization at least three months before submission to the General Assembly for consideration.

All amendments to this Constitution shall be approved by a two-thirds majority of the Members of the Organizations.

Article 43

The French, English and Spanish texts of this Constitutions shall be regarded as authoritative.

Article 44

The application of this Constitution shall be determined by the General Assembly through the General Regulations and Appendices, whose provisions shall be adopted by a two-thirds majority.

TEMPORARY MEASURES

Article 45

All bodies representing the countries mentioned in Appendix 1 shall be deemed to be Members of the Organization unless they declare through the appropriate governmental authority that they cannot accept this constitution. Such a declaration should be made within six months of the date of the coming into force of the present Constitution.

Article 46

At the first election, lots will be drawn to determine a Vice-President whose term of office will end a year later.

At the first election, lots will be drawn to determine two Delegates on the Executive Committee whose term of office will end a year later, and two others whose term of office will end two years later.

Article 47

Persons having rendered meritorious and prolonged services in the ranks of the ICPO may be awarded by the General Assembly honorary titles in corresponding ranks of the ICPO.

Article 48

All property belonging to the International Criminal Police Commission are transferred to the International Criminal Police Organization.

Article 49

In the present Constitution:

- "Organization", wherever it occurs, shall mean the International Criminal Police Organization;

- "secretary General" shall mean the Secretary General of the International Criminal Police Organization;

- "Committee" shall mean the Executive Committee of the Organization;

- "Assembly" or "General Assembly" shall mean the General Assembly of the Organization;

- "Member" of "Members" shall mean a Member or Members of the International Criminal Police Organization as mentioned in Article 4 of the Constitution;

- "delegate" (in the singular) or "delegates" (in the plural) shall mean a person or persons belonging to a delegation or delegations as defined in Article 7;

- "Delegate" (in the singular) or "Delegates" (in the plural) shall mean a person or persons elected to the Executive Committee in the conditions laid down in Article 19.

Article 50

This Constitution shall come into force on 13th June 1956.

Schengen Convention - Title III - Chapter I and Title IV - Chapters I to IV (excerpts) (1990)[*]

Schengen, 19 June 1990

Title III

Police and security

Chapter I

Police co-operation

Article 39

1. The Contracting Parties undertake to ensure that their police authorities shall, in compliance with national legislation and within the limits of their responsibilities, assist each other for the purposes of preventing and detecting criminal offenses, insofar as national law does not stipulate that the request is to be made to the legal authorities and provided the request or the implementation thereof does not involve the application of coercive measures by the requested Contracting Party. Where the requested police authorities do not have jurisdiction to implement a request, they shall forward it to the competent authorities.

2. The written information provided by the requested Contracting Party under paragraph 1 may not be used by the requesting Contracting Party as evidence of the criminal offence other that with the agreement of the relevant legal authorities of the requested Contracting Party.

3. Requests for assistance referred to in paragraph 1 and the replies to such requests may be exchanged between the central bodies responsible in each Contracting Party for international police co-operation. Where the request cannot be made in good time by the above procedure, it may me addressed by the police authorities of the requesting Contracting Party directly to the competent authorities of the requested Party, which may reply directly. In such cases, the requesting police authority shall as soon as possible inform the central body responsible in the requested Contracting Party for international police co-cooperation of its direct application.

4. In border regions, co-operation may be covered by arrangements between the responsible Ministers of the Contracting Parties.

5. The provisions of this Article shall not preclude more detailed present or future bilateral agreements between Contracting Parties with a common order. The Contracting Parties shall inform each other of such agreements.

Article 40

1. Police officers of one of the Contracting Parties who, within the framework of a criminal investigation, are keeping under observation in their country, a person who is presumed to have taken part in a criminal offence to which extradition may apply, shall be authorized to continue their observation in the territory of another Contracting Party where the latter has authorized cross-border observation in response to a request for assistance which has previously been submitted. Conditions may be attached to the authorization.

---

[*] Convention of 19 June 1990, applying the Schengen Agreement of 14 June 1985 between the Governments of the States of the Benelux Economic Union, the Federal Republic of Germany and the French Republic, on the Gradual Abolition of Checks at their Common Borders, *International Legal Materials*, 1991, 84.

On request, the observation will be entrusted to officers of the Contracting Party in whose territory it is carried out.

The request, for assistance referred to in the first subparagraph must be sent to an authority designated by each of the Contracting Parties and having jurisdiction to grant or to forward the requested authorization.

2. Where, for particularly urgent reasons, prior authorization of the other Contracting Party cannot be requested, the officers conducting the observation shall be authorized to continue beyond the border the observation of a person presumed to have committed offenses listed in paragraph 7, provided that the following conditions are met:

(a) the authorities of the Contracting Party designated under paragraph 5, in whose territory the observation is to be continued, must be notified immediately, during the observation, that the border has been crossed:

(b) A request for assistance submitted in accordance with paragraph 1 and outlining the grounds for crossing the border without prior authorization shall be submitted without delay.

Observation shall cease as soon as the Contracting Party in whose territory it is taking place so requests, following the notification referred to in (a) or the request to in (b) or where authorization has not been obtained five hours after the border was crossed.

3. The observation referred to in paragraph 1 and 2 shall be carried out only under the following general conditions:

(a) The officers conducting the observation must comply with the provisions of this Article and with the law of the Contracting Party in whose territory they are operating: they must obey the instructions of the local responsible authorities.

(b) except in the situations provided for in paragraph 2, the officers shall, during the observation, carry a document certifying that authorization has been granted.

(c) The officers conducting the observation must be able at all times to provide proof that they are acting in an official capacity.

(d) The officers conducting the observation may carry their service weapons during the observation save where specifically otherwise decided by the requested party; their use shall be prohibited save in cases of legitimate self-defence.

(e) Entry into private homes and places not accessible to the public shall be prohibited.

(f) The officers conducting the observation may neither challenge nor arrest the person under observation.

(g) All operations shall be the subject of a report to the authorities of the Contracting Party in whose territory they took place; the officers conducting the observation may be required to appear in person.

(h) The authorities of the Contracting Party from which the observing officers have come shall, when requested by the authorities of the Contracting Party in whose territory the observation took place, assist the enquiry subsequent to the operation in which they took part, including legal proceedings.

4. The officers referred to in paragraphs 1 and 2 shall be:

(a) as regards the Kingdom of Belgium: members of the "police judiciaire près les Parquets", the "gendarmerie" and the "police communale" as well as customs officers, under the conditions laid down in appropriate bilateral agreements referred to in paragraph 6, with respect to their powers regarding illicit traffic in narcotic drugs and psychotropic substances, traffic in arms and explosives, and the illicit carriage of toxic and dangerous waste;

(b) as regards the Federal Republic of Germany, officers of the "Polizeien des Bundes und der Länder" as well as, with respect only to illegal traffic in narcotic drugs and psychotropic substances and arms traffic, officers of the "Zollfahndungsdienst (customs investigation service) in their capacity as auxiliary officers of the public ministry;

(c) as regards the French Republic: officers and criminal police officers of the national police and national "gendarmerie" as well as customs officers, under the conditions laid down in appropriate bilateral agreements referred to in paragraph 6, with respect to their powers regarding illicit traffic in narcotic drugs and psychotropic substances, traffic in arms and explosives, and the illicit carriage of toxic and dangerous waste;

(d) as regards the Grand Duchy of Luxembourg: officers of the "gendarmerie" and the police as well as customs officers, under the conditions laid down in appropriate bilateral agreements referred to in paragraph 6, with respect to their powers regarding illicit traffic in narcotic drugs and psychotropic substances, traffic in arms and explosives, and the illicit carriage of toxic and dangerous waste;

(e) as regards the Kingdom of the Netherlands: officers of the "Rijkspolitie" and the "Gemeentepolitie" as well as, under the conditions laid down in appropriate bilateral agreements referred to in paragraph 6, with respect to their powers regarding illicit traffic in narcotic drugs and psychotropic substances, traffic in arms and explosives and the illicit carriage of toxic and dangerous waste, officers of the fiscal information and research service responsible for entry and excise duties.

5. The authority referred to in paragraphs 1 and 2 shall be:

(a) as regards the Kingdom of Belgium: the "Commissariat général de la Police judiciaire":

(b) as regards the Federal Republic of Germany: the "Bundeskriminalamt";

(c) as regards the French Republic: the "Direction centrale de la Police judiciare";

(d) as regards the Grand Duchy of Luxembourg: the "Procureur général d'Etat";

(e) as regards the Kingdom of the Netherlands: the "Landelijk Officier van Justitie" responsible for cross-border observation.

6. The Contracting Parties may, at bilateral level, extend the scope of this Article and adopt additional measures in implementation thereof.

7. The observation referred to in paragraph 2 may take place only for one of the following criminal offenses:

(a) assassination,

(b) murder,

(c) rape,

(d) arson,

(e) counterfeiting,

(f) armed robbery and receiving of stolen goods,

- (g) extortion,
- (h) kidnapping and hostage taking,
- (i) traffic in human beings,
- (j) illicit traffic in narcotic drugs and psychotropic substances,
- (k) breach of the laws on arms and explosives,
- (l) use of explosives,
- (m) illicit carriage of toxic and dangerous waste.

Article 41

1. Officers of one of the Contracting Parties following, in their country, an individual apprehended in the act of committing one of the offenses referred to in paragraph 4 or participating in one of those offenses, shall be authorized to continue pursuit in the territory of another Contracting Party without prior authorization where given the particular urgency of the situation it was not possible to notify the competent authorities of the other Contracting Party by one of the means provided for in Article 44 prior to entry into that territory or where these authorities have been unable to reach the scene in time to take over the pursuit.

The same shall apply where the person pursued has escaped from provisional custody or while serving a custodial sentence.

The pursuing officers shall, not later than when they cross the border, contact the competent authorities of the Contracting Party in whose territory the pursuit is to take place. The pursuit will cease as soon as the Contracting Party on the territory of which the pursuit is taking place so requests. At the request of the pursuing officers, the competent local authorities shall challenge the pursued person so as to establish his identity or to arrest him.

2. The pursuit shall be carried out in accordance with one of the following procedures, defined by the declaration provided for in paragraph 9:

- (a) The pursuing officers shall not have the right to apprehend.
- (b) If no request to cease the pursuit is made and if the competent local authorities are unable to intervene quickly enough, the pursuing officers may apprehend the person pursued until the officers of the Contracting Party in the territory of which the pursuit is taking place, who must be informed without delay, are able to establish his identity or arrest him.

3. Pursuit shall be carried out in accordance with paragraphs 1 and 2 in one of the following ways as defined by the declaration provided for in paragraph 9:

- (a) in an area or during a period as from the crossing of the border, to be established in the declaration;
- (b) without limit in space or time.

4. In a declaration referred to in paragraph 9, the Contracting Parties shall define the offenses referred to in paragraph 1 in accordance with one of the following procedures:

- (a) The following offences:
    - assassination,
    - murder,
    - rape,

- arson,
- counterfeiting,
- armed robbery and receiving of stolen goods,
- extortion,
- kidnapping and hostage taking,
- traffic in human beings,
- illicit traffic in narcotic drugs and psychotropic substances,
- breach of the laws on arms and explosives,
- use of explosives,
- illicit carriage of toxic and dangerous waste.
- taking to flight after an accident which has resulted in death or serious injury.

(b) Extraditable offences.

5. Pursuit shall be subject to the following general conditions:

(a) The pursuing officers must comply with the provisions of this Article and with the law of the Contracting Party in whose territory they are operating: they must obey the instructions of the competent local authorities.

(b) Pursuit shall be solely over land borders.

(c) Entry into private homes and places not accessible to the public shall be prohibited.

(d) The pursuing officers shall be easily identifiable, either by their uniform or by means of an armband or by a accessories fitted to their vehicle: the use of civilian clothes combined with the use of unmarked vehicles without the aforementioned identification is prohibited; the pursuing officers must at all times be able to prove that they are acting in an official capacity.

(e) The pursuing officers may carry their service weapons: their use shall be prohibited save in cases of legitimate self-defence.

(f) Once the pursued person has been apprehended as provided for in paragraph 2(b), for the purpose of bringing him before the competent local authorities he may be subjected only to a security search; handcuffs may be used during his transfer: objects carried by the pursued person may be seized.

(g) After each operation mentioned in paragraphs 1, 2 and 3 the pursuing officers shall present themselves before the local competent authorities of the Contracting Party in whose territory they were operating and shall give an account of their mission; at the request of those authorities, they must remain at their disposal until the circumstances of their action have been adequately elucidated; this condition shall apply even where the pursuit has not resulted in the arrest of the pursued person.

(h) The authorities of the Contracting Party from which the pursuing officers have come shall, when requested by the authorities of the Contracting Party in whose territory the pursuit took place assist the inquiry subsequent to the operation in which they took part, including legal proceedings.

6. A person who, following the action provided for in paragraph 2, has been arrested by the competent local authorities may, whatever his nationality, be held for questioning. The relevant rules of national law shall apply by analogy.

If the person is not a national of the Contracting Party in the territory of which he was arrested, he shall be released no later that six hours after his arrest, not including the hours between midnight and 9.00 in the morning, unless the competent local authorities have previously received a request for his provisional arrest for the purposes of extradition in any form whatever.

7. The officers referred to in the previous paragraphs shall be:

   (a) as regards the Kingdom of Belgium: members of the "police judiciaire près les Parquets", the "gendarmerie" and the "police communale" as well as customs officers, under the conditions laid down in appropriate bilateral agreements referred to in paragraph 10, with respect to their powers regarding illicit traffic in narcotic drugs and psychotropic substances, traffic in arms and explosives, and the illicit carriage of toxic and dangerous waste;

   (b) as regards the Federal Republic of Germany: officers of the "Polizeien des Bundes und der Länder" as well as, with respect only to illegal traffic in narcotic drugs and psychotropic substances and arms traffic, officers of the "Zollfahndungsdienst" customs investigation service) in their capacity as auxiliary officers of the public ministry;

   (c) as regards the French Republic: officers and criminal police officers of the national police and national "gendarmerie" as well as customs officers, under the conditions laid down in the appropriate bilateral agreements referred to in paragraph 10, with respect to their powers regarding illicit traffic in narcotic drugs and psychotropic substances, traffic in arms and explosives, and the illicit carriage of toxic and dangerous waste:

   (d) as regards the Grand Duchy of Luxembourg: officers of the "gendarmerie" and the police as well as customs officers, under the conditions laid down in the appropriate bilateral agreements referred to in paragraph 10, with respect to their powers regarding illicit traffic in narcotic drugs and psychotropic substances, traffic in arms and explosives, and the illicit carriage of toxic and dangerous waste:

   (e) as regards the Kingdom of the Netherlands: officers of the "Rijkspolitie" and the "Gemeentepolitie" as well as, under the conditions laid down in the appropriate bilateral agreements referred to in paragraph 10, with respect to their powers regarding the illicit traffic in narcotic drugs and psychotropic substances, traffic in arms and explosives and the illicit carriage of toxic and dangerous waste, officers of the fiscal information and research service responsible for entry and excise duties.

8. This Article shall be without prejudice, where the Contracting Parties are concerned, to Article 27 of the Benelux Treaty of 27 June 1962 on Extradition and Mutual Assistance in Criminal Matters as amended by the Protocol of 11 May 1974.

9. On signing this Convention, each Contracting Party shall make a declaration in which it shall define, on the basis of paragraphs 2, 3 and 4 above, the procedures for implementing pursuit in its territory for each of the Contracting Parties with which it has a common border.

A Contracting Party may at any moment replace its declaration by another declaration, provided the latter does not restrict the scope of the former.

Each declaration shall be made after consultations with each of the Contracting Parties concerned and with a view to obtaining equivalent arrangements on both sides of internal borders.

10. The Contracting Parties may, on a bilateral basis, extend the scope of paragraph 1 and adopt additional provisions in implementation of this Article.

Article 42

During the operations referred to in Articles 40 and 41, officers operating on the territory of another Contracting Party shall be regarded as officers of that Party with respect to offences committed against them or by them.

Article 43

1. Where, in accordance with Articles 40 and 41 of this Convention, officers of a Contracting Party are operating in the territory of another Contracting Party, the first Contracting Party shall be responsible for any damage caused by them during the course of their mission, in accordance with the law of the Contracting Party in whose territory they are operating.

2. The Contracting Party in whose territory the damage referred to in paragraph 1 is caused shall repair such damage under the conditions applicable to damage caused by its own officers.

3. The Contracting Party whose officers have caused damage to whomsoever in the territory of another Contracting Party shall reimburse in full to the latter any sums it has paid out to the victims or other entitled persons.

4. Without prejudice to the exercise of its rights vis-à-vis third parties and without prejudice to paragraph 3, each Contracting Party shall refrain, in the case provided for in paragraph 1, from requesting reimbursement of the amount of the damages it has sustained from another Contracting Party.

Article 44

1. In accordance with the relevant international agreements and account being taken of local circumstances and the technical possibilities, the Contracting Parties shall set up, in particular in border areas, telephone, radio, and telex lines and other direct links to facilitate police and customs co-operation, in particular for the transmission of information in good time for the purposes of cross-border observation and pursuit.

2. In addition to these short-term measures, they will in particular examine the following possibilities:

   (a) the exchange of equipment or the assignment of liaison officials provided with appropriate radio equipment;

   (b) the widening of the frequency bands used in border areas;

   (c) the establishment of a common link for police and customs services operating in these same areas;

   (d) co-ordination of their programmes for the procurement of communications equipment, with a view to achieving the introduction of standardized compatible communications systems.

Article 45

1. The Contracting Parties undertake to take the measures required to guarantee that:

   (a) the managers of establishments providing lodging or their employees ensure that aliens accommodated therein, including nationals of the other Contracting Parties as well as those of other Member States of the European Communities, with the exception of accompanying spouses or minors or members of travel groups, personally complete and sign declaration forms and confirm their identity by the production of a valid identity document:

(b) the declaration forms thus completed will be kept for the competent authorities or forwarded to them where such authorities deem this necessary for the prevention of threats, for criminal proceedings or to ascertain what has happened to persons who have disappeared or who have been the victim of an accident, save where national law provides otherwise.

2. Paragraph 1 shall apply by analogy to persons staying in any accommodation provided by professional lessors, in particular tents, caravans and boats.

Article 46

1. In particular cases, each Contracting Party may, in compliance with its national legislation and without being asked, send the Contracting Party concerned any information which may be of interest to it in helping prevent future crime and to prevent offences against or threats to public order and security.

2. Information shall be exchanged, without prejudice to the arrangements for co-operation in border areas referred to in Article 39(4), through a central body to be designated. In particularly urgent cases, the exchange of information within the meaning of this Article may take place directly between the police authorities concerned, save where national provisions provide otherwise. The central body shall be informed of this as soon as possible.

Article 47

1. The Contracting Parties may conclude bilateral agreements providing for the secondment, for a specified or unspecified period, of liaison officers from one Contracting Party to the Police authorities of the other Contracting Party.

2. The secondment of liaison officers for a specified or unspecified period is intended to promote and to accelerate co-operation between the Contracting Parties, particularly by providing assistance.

(a) in the form of the exchange of information for the purposes of fighting crime by means both of prevention and of punishment.

(b) in complying with requests for mutual police assistance and legal assistance in criminal matters;

(c) for the purposes of missions carried out by the authorities responsible for the surveillance of external borders.

3. Liaison officers shall have the task of giving advice and assistance. They shall not be competent to take independent police action. They shall supply information and perform their duties in accordance with the instructions given to them by the Contracting Party of origin and by the Contracting Party to which they are seconded. They shall make report regularly to the head of the police service to which they are seconded.

4. The Contracting Parties may agree within a bilateral or multilateral framework that liaison officers from a Contracting Party seconded to third States shall also represent the interests of one or more other Contracting Parties. Under such agreements, liaison officers seconded to third States shall supply information to other Contracting Parties when requested to do so or on their own initiative and shall, within the limits of their powers, perform duties on behalf of such Parties. The Contracting Parties shall inform one another of their intentions as regards the secondment of liaison officers to third States.

[...]

Title IV

The Schengen Information System

Chapter I

Letting up of the Schengen Information System

Article 92

1. The Contracting Parties shall set up and maintain a joint information system, hereinafter referred to as the Schengen Information System, consisting of a national section in each of the Contracting Parties and a technical support function. The Schengen Information System shall enable the authorities designated by the Contracting Parties, by means of an automated search procedure, to have access to reports on persons and objects for the purposes of border checks and controls and other police and customs checks carried out within the country in accordance with national law and, in the case of the single category of report referred to in Article 96, for the purposes of issuing visas, the issue of residence permits and the administration of aliens in the context of the application of the provisions of this Convention relating to the movement of persons.

2. Each Contracting Party shall set up and maintain, for its own account and at its own risk, its national section of the Schengen information System, the data file of which shall be made materially identical to the data files of the national sections of each of the other Contracting Parties using the technical support function. To ensure the rapid and effective transmission of data as referred to in paragraph 3, each Contracting Party shall observe when creating its national section, the protocols and procedures which the Contracting Parties have jointly established for the technical support function. Each national section´s data file shall be available for the purposes of automated search in the territory of each of the Contracting Parties. It shall not be possible to search the data files of other Contracting Parties´national sections.

3. The Contracting Parties shall set up and maintain jointly and with joint liability for risks, the technical support function of the Schengen Information System, the responsibility for which shall be assumed by the French Republic: the technical support function shall be located in Strasbourg. The technical support function shall comprise a data file which ensures that the data files of the national sections are kept identical by the on-line transmission of information. The data file of the technical support function shall contain reports on persons and objects where these concern all the Contracting Parties. The data file of the technical support function shall contain no data other than those referred to in this paragraph and in Article 113(2).

Chapter II

Operation and utilization of the Schengen Information System

Article 93

The purpose of the Schengen Information System shall be in accordance with this Convention to maintain public order and security, including State security, and to apply the provisions of this Convention relating to the movement of persons, in the territories of the Contracting Parties, using information transmitted by the system.

Article 94

1. The Schengen Information System shall contain only the categories of data which are supplied by each of the Contracting Parties and are required for the purposes laid down in Articles 95 to 100. The Contracting Party providing a report shall determine whether the importance of the case warrants the inclusion of the report in the Schengen Information System.

2. The categories of data shall be as follows:

(a) persons reported

(b) objects referred to in Article 100 and vehicles referred to in Article 99.

3. The items included in respect of persons, shall be no more than the following:

(a) name and forename, any aliases possible registered separately;

(b) any particular objective and permanent physical features;

(c) first letter of second forename

(d) date and place of birth;

(e) sex;

(f) nationality;

(g) whether the persons concerned are armed;

(h) whether the persons concerned are violent;

(i) reason for the report;

(j) action to be taken.

Other references, in particular the data listed in Article 6, first sentence of the Council of Europe Convention of 28 January 1981 for the Protection of individuals with regard to Automatic Processing of Personal Data, shall not be authorized.

4. Insofar as a Contracting Party considers that a report in accordance with Articles 95, 97 or 99 is incompatible with its national law, its international obligations or essential national interests, it may subsequently add to the report in the data file of the national section of the Schengen Information System a note to the effect that the action referred to will not be taken in its territory in connection with the report. Consultations must be held in this connection with the other Contracting Parties. If the reporting Contracting Party does not withdraw the report it will continue to apply in full for the other Contracting Parties.

Article 95

1. Data relating to persons wanted for arrest for extradition purposes shall be included at the request of the judicial authority of the requesting Contracting Party.

2. Prior to making a report, the reporting Contracting Party shall check whether the arrest is authorized by the national law of the requested Contracting Parties. If the reporting Contracting Party has doubts, it must consult the other Contracting Parties concerned.

The reporting Contracting Party shall send the requested Contracting Parties together with the report, by the swiftest means, the following essential information relating to the case:

(a) the authority which issued the request for arrest;

(b) whether there is an arrest warrant or a document having the same force, or an enforceable judgment;

(c) the nature and legal classification of the offence;

(d) a description of the circumstances in which the offence was committed, including the time, place and degree of participation in the offence by the person reported;

(e) as far as possible the consequences of the offence.

3. A requested Contracting Party may add to the report in the file of the national section of the Schengen Information System a note prohibiting arrest in connection with the report, until such time as the note is deleted. The note shall be deleted no later than 24 hours after the report is included, unless the Contracting Party refuses to make the requested arrest on legal grounds or for special reasons of expediency. Where, in particularly exceptional cases, this is justified by the complexity of the facts underlying the report, the above time limit may be extended to one week. Without prejudice to a qualifying note or a decision to refuse arrest, the other Contracting Parties may make the arrest requested in the report.

4. If, for particularly urgent reasons, a Contracting Party requests an immediate search, the Party requested shall examine whether it is able to withdraw its note. The Contracting Party requested shall take the necessary steps to ensure that the action to be taken can be carried out without delay if the report is validated.

5. If the arrest cannot be made because an investigation has not been completed or owing to a refusal by the requested Contracting Party, the latter must regard the report as being a report for the purposes of communicating the place of residence of the person concerned.

6. The requested Contracting Parties shall carry out the action to be taken as requested in the report in compliance with extradition Conventions in force and with national law. They shall not be required to carry out the action requested where one of their nationals is involved, without prejudice to the possibility of making the arrest in accordance with national law.

Article 96

1. Data relating to aliens who are reported for the purposes of being refused entry shall be included on the basis of a national report resulting from decisions taken, in compliance with the rules of procedure laid down by national legislation, by the administrative authorities or courts responsible.

2. Decisions may be based on a threat to public order or national security and safety which the presence of an alien in national territory may pose.

Such may in particular be the case with:

(a) an alien who has been convicted of an offence carrying a custodial sentence of at least one year;

(b) an alien who, there are serious grounds for believing, has committed serious offences, including those referred to in Article 71, or against whom there is genuine evidence of an intention to commit such offences in the territory of a Contracting Party.

3. Decisions may also be based on the fact that the alien has been the subject of a deportation, removal or expulsion measure which has not been rescinded or suspended, including or accompanied by a prohibition on entry or, where appropriate, residence, based on non-compliance with national regulations on the entry or residence of aliens.

Article 97

Data relating to persons who have disappeared or to persons who, in the interests of their own protection or in order to prevent threats, need to be placed provisionally in a place of safety at the request of the competent authority or the competent judicial authority of the reporting Party, shall be included in order that the police authorities can communicate their whereabouts to the reporting Party or can remove the person to a place of safety for the purposes of preventing him from continuing his journey, if so authorized by national legislation. This shall apply in particular to minors and to persons who must be interned by decision of a competent authority. Communication of the information shall be subject to the consent of the person who has disappeared, if of full age.

Article 98

1. Data relating to witnesses, to persons summoned to appear before the judicial authorities in connection with criminal proceedings in order to account for acts for which they are being prosecuted, or to persons who are to be notified of a criminal judgment or of a summons to appear in order to serve a custodial sentence, shall be included, at the request of the competent judicial authorities, for the purposes of communicating their place of residence or domicile.

2. Information requested shall be communicated to the requesting Party in accordance with national legislation and with the Conventions in force concerning mutual judicial assistance in criminal matters.

Article 99

1. Data relating to persons or vehicles shall be included in compliance with the national lay of the reporting Contracting Party, for the purposes of discreet surveillance or specific checks, in accordance with paragraph 5.

2. Such a report may be made for the purposes of prosecuting criminal offences and for the prevention of threats to public safety:

   (a) where there are real indications to suggest that the person concerned intends to commit or is committing numerous and extremely serious offences, or

   (b) where an overall evaluation of the person concerned, in particular on the basis of offences committed hitherto, gives reason to suppose that he will also commit extremely seriously offences in future.

3. In addition, a report may be made in accordance with national law, at the request of the authorities responsible for State security, where concrete evidence gives reason to suppose that the information referred to in paragraph 4 is necessary for the prevention of a serious threat by the person concerned or other serious threats to internal or external State security. The reporting Contracting Party shall be required to consult the other Contracting Parties beforehand.

4. For the purposes of discreet surveillance, the following information may in whole or in part be collected and transmitted to the reporting authority when border checks or other police and customs checks are carried out within the country:

   (a) the fact that the person reported or the vehicle reported has been found:

   (b) the place, time or reason for the check:

   (c) the route and destination of the journey:

   (d) persons accompanying the person concerned or occupants of the vehicle:

   (e) the vehicle used:

   (f) objects carried:

   (g) the circumstances under which the person or the vehicle was found.

When such information is collected, steps must be taken to ensure that the discreet nature of the surveillance is not jeopardized.

5. In the context of the specific checks referred to in paragraph 1, persons, vehicles and objects carried may be searched in accordance with national law, in order to achieve the purpose referred to in paragraphs 2 and 3. If the specific check is not authorized in accordance with the law of a Contracting Party, it shall automatically be converted, for that Contracting Party, into discreet surveillance.

6. A requested Contracting Party may add to the report in the file of the national section of the Schengen Information System a note prohibiting, until the note is deleted, performance of the action to be taken pursuant to the report for the purposes of discreet surveillance or specific checks. The note must be deleted no later than 24 hours after the report has been included unless the Contracting Party refuses to take the action requested on legal grounds or for special reasons of expediency. Without prejudice to a qualifying note or a refusal decision, the other Contracting Parties may carry out the action requested in the report.

Article 100

1. Data relating to objects sought for the purposes of seizure or of evidence in criminal proceedings shall be included in the Schengen Information System.

2. If a search brings to light the existence of a report on an item which has been found the authority noticing the report shall contact the reporting authority in order to agree on the requisite measures. For this purpose personal data may also be transmitted in accordance with this Convention. The measures to be taken by the Contracting Party which found the object must comply with its national law.

3. The categories of objects listed below shall be included:

   (a) motor vehicles with a capacity in excess of 50cc which have been stolen, misappropriated or lost;

   (b) trailers and caravans with an unladen weight in excess of 750 kg which have been stolen, misappropriated or lost;

   (c) firearms which have been stolen, misappropriated or lost;

   (d) blank documents which have been stolen, misappropriated or lost;

   (e) identification documents issued (passports, identity cards driving licences) which have been stolen, misappropriated or lost;

   (f) bank notes (registered notes).

Article 101

1. Access to data included in the Schengen Information System and the right to search such data directly shall be reserved exclusively for the authorities responsible for

   (a) border checks;

   (b) other police and customs checks carried out within the country, and the co-ordination of such checks.

2. In addition, access to data included in accordance with Article 96 and the right to search such data directly may be exercised by the authorities responsible for issuing visas, the central authorities responsible for examining visa applications and the authorities responsible for issuing residence permits and the administration of aliens within the framework of the application of the provisions on the movement of persons under this Convention. Access to data shall be governed by the national law of each Contracting Party.

3. Users may only search data which are necessary for the performance of their tasks.

4. Each of the Contracting Parties shall communicate to the Executive Committee a list of the competent authorities which are authorized to search the data included in the Schengen Information System directly. That list shall indicate for each authority the data which it may search, and for what purposes.

Chapter III

Protection of personal data and security of data under the Schengen Information System

Article 102

1. The Contracting Parties may use the data provided for in Articles 95 to 100 only for the purposes laid down for each type referred to in those Articles.

2. Data may be duplicated only for technical purposes, provided that such duplication is necessary for direct searching by the authorities referred to in Article 101. Reports by other Contracting Parties may not be copied from the national section of the Schengen Information System in other national data files.

3. In connection with the types of report provided for in Article 95 to 100 of this Convention, any derogation from paragraph 1 in order to change from one type of report to another must be justified by the need to prevent an imminent serious threat to public order and safety, for serious reasons of State security or for the purposes of preventing a serious offence. The prior authorization of the reporting Contracting Party must be obtained for this purpose.

4. Data may not be used for administrative purposes. By way of derogation, data included in accordance with Article 96 may be used, in accordance with the national law of each of the Contracting Parties, only for the purposes of Article 101(2).

5. Any use of data which does not comply with paragraphs 1 to 4 shall be considered as a misuse in relation to the national law of each Contracting Party.

Article 103

Each Contracting Party shall ensure that, on average, every tenth transmission of personal data is recorded in the national section of the Schengen Information System by the data file managing authority for the purpose of checking the admissibility of searching. The recording may be used only for this purpose and shall be deleted after six months.

Article 104

1. The law applying to reports shall be the national law of the reporting Contracting Party, unless more rigorous conditions are laid down in this Convention.

2. Insofar as this Convention does not lay down specific provisions the law of each Contracting Party shall apply to data included in the national section of the Schengen Information System.

3. Insofar as this Convention does not lay down specific provisions concerning performance of the action requested in the report, the national law of the Contracting Party requested which carries out the action shall apply. Insofar as this Convention lays down specific provisions concerning performance of the action requested in the report, responsibility for the action to be taken shall be governed by the national law of the requested Contracting Party. If the action requested cannot be performed, the requested Contracting Party shall inform the reporting Contracting Party without delay.

Article 105

The reporting Contracting Party shall be responsible for the accuracy, up-to-dateness and lawfulness of the inclusion of data in the Schengen Information System.

Article 106

1. Only the reporting Contracting Party shall be authorized to amend, supplement, correct or delete data which it has introduced.

2. If one of the Contracting Parties which has not made the report has evidence to suggest that an item of data is legally or factually inaccurate, it shall advise the reporting Contracting Party thereof as soon as possible; the latter must check the communication and, if necessary, correct or delete the item in question without delay.

3. If the Contracting Parties are unable to reach agreement, the Contracting Party which did not generate the report shall submit the case to the joint supervisory authority referred to in Article 115(1) for its opinion.

Article 107

Where a person has already been the subject of a report in the Schengen Information System, a Contracting Party which introduces a further report shall come to an agreement on the inclusion of the reports with the Contracting Party which introduced the first report. The Contracting Parties may also adopt general provisions to this end.

Article 108

1. Each of the Contracting Parties shall designate an authority which shall have central responsibility for the national section of the Schengen Information System.

2. Each of the Contracting Parties shall make its reports via that authority.

3. The said authority shall be responsible for the correct operation of the national section of the Schengen Information System and shall take the measures necessary to ensure compliance with the provisions of this Convention.

4. The Contracting Parties shall inform one another, via the Depositary, of the authority referred to in paragraph 1.

Article 109

1. The right of any person to have access to data relating to him which are included in the Schengen Information System shall be exercised in accordance with the law of the Contracting Party before which it invokes that right. If the national law so provides the national supervisory authority provided for in Article 114 (1) shall decide whether information shall be communicated and by what procedures. A Contracting which has not made the report may communicate information concerning such data only if it has previously given the reporting Contracting Party an opportunity to state its position.

2. Communication of information to the person concerned shall be refused if it may undermine the performance of the legal task specified in the report, or in order to protect the rights and freedoms of others. It shall be refused in any event during the period of reporting for the purposes of discreet surveillance.

Article 110

Any person may have factually inaccurate data relating to him corrected or have legally inaccurate data relating to him deleted.

Article 111

1. Any person may, in the territory of each Contracting Party, bring before the courts or the authority competent under national law an action to correct, delete or provide information or obtain compensation in connection with a report concerning him.

2. The Contracting Parties shall undertake amongst themselves to execute final decisions taken by the courts or authorities referred to in paragraph 1, without prejudice to the provisions of Article 116.

Article 112

1. Personal data included in the Schengen Information System for the purposes of locating persons shall be kept only for the time required to achieve the purposes for which they were supplied. No later than three years after their inclusion, the need for their retention must be reviewed by the reporting Contracting Party. This period shall be one year in the case of reports referred to in Article 99.

2. Each of the Contracting Parties shall, where appropriate, set shorter review periods in accordance with its national law.

3. The technical support function of the Schengen Information System shall automatically inform the Contracting Parties of a scheduled deletion of data from the system, giving one month's notice.

4. The reporting Contracting Party may, within the review period, decide to retain the report if its retention is necessary for the purposes for which the report was made. Any extension of the report must be communicated to the technical support function. The provisions of paragraph 1 shall apply to report extension.

Article 113

1. Data other than those referred to in Article 112 shall be retained for a maximum of ten years, data relating to identity documents issued and to registered bank notes for a maximum of five years and those relating to motor vehicles, trailers and caravans for a maximum of three years.

2. Data deleted shall continue to be retained for one year in the technical support function. During that period they may be consulted only for the purposes of subsequently checking their accuracy and the lawfulness of their inclusion. Afterwards they must be destroyed.

Article 114

1. Each Contracting Party shall designate a supervisory authority responsible, in compliance with national law, for carrying out independent supervision of the data file of the national section of the Schengen Information System and for checking that the processing and utilization of data included in the Schengen Information System are not in violation of the rights of the person concerned. For this purpose the supervisory authority shall have access to the data file of the national section of the Schengen Information System.

2. Any person shall have the right to ask the supervisory authorities to check the data concerning him which are included in the Schengen Information System and the use which is made of such data. That right shall be governed by the national law of the Contracting Party to which the request is made. If the data have been included by another Contracting Party, the check shall be carried out in close co-ordination with that Contracting Party's supervisory authority.

Article 115

1. A joint supervisory authority shall be set up, with responsibility for supervising the technical support function of the Schengen Information System. This authority shall consist of two representatives of each national supervisory authority. Each Contracting Party shall have one vote. Supervision shall be carried out in accordance with the provisions of this Convention, of the Council of Europe Convention of 28 January 1981 for the Protection of Individuals with regard to the Automatic Processing of Personal Data, taking into account Recommendation R (87) 15 of 17 September 1987 of the Committee of Ministers of the Council of Europe regulating the use of personal data in the police sector, and in accordance with the national law of the Contracting Party responsible for the technical support function.

2. As regards the technical support function of the Schengen Information System, the joint supervisory authority shall have the task of checking that the provisions of this Convention

are properly implemented. For this purpose it shall have access to the technical support function.

3. The joint supervisory authority shall also be competent to examine any difficulties of application or interpretation which may arise during the operation of the Schengen Information System, to study problems which may arise with the exercise of independent supervision by the national supervisory authorities of the Contracting Parties or in the exercise of the right of access to the system, and to draw up harmonized proposals for the purpose of finding joint solutions to problems.

4. Reports drawn up by the joint supervisory authority shall be forwarded to the authorities to which the national supervisory authorities submit their reports.

Article 116

1. Each Contracting Party shall be responsible, in accordance with its national law, for any injury caused to a person through the use of the national data file of the Schengen Information System. This shall also be the case where the injury was caused by the reporting Contracting Party, where the latter included legally or factually inaccurate data.

2. If the Contracting Party against which an action is brought is not the reporting Contracting Party, the latter shall be required to reimburse, on request, sums paid out as compensation, unless the data were used by the requested Contracting Party in contravention of this Convention.

Article 117

1. With regard to the automatic processing of personal data which are transmitted pursuant to this Title, each Contracting Party shall, not later than when this Convention enters into force, make the national arrangements necessary to achieve a level of protection of personal data at least equal to that resulting from the principles of the Council of Europe Convention of 28 January 1981 for the Protection of Individuals with regard to the Automatic Processing of Personal Data, and in compliance with Recommendation R (87) 15 of 17 September 1987 of the Committee of Ministers of the Council of Europe regulating the use of personal data in the police sector.

2. The transmission of personal data provided for in this Title may take place only where the arrangements for the protection of personal data provided for in paragraph 1 have entered into force in the territory of the Contracting Parties concerned by the transmission.

Article 118

1. Each of the Contracting Parties shall undertake, in respect of the national section of the Schengen Information System, to take the measures necessary to:

    (a) prevent any unauthorized person from having access to installations used for the processing of personal data (checks at the entrance to installations);

    (b) prevent data media from being read, copied, modified or removed by unauthorized persons (control of data media);

    (c) prevent the unauthorized entry of data into the file and any unauthorized consultation, modification or deletion of personal data included in the file (control of data entry);

    (d) prevent automated data processing systems from being used by unauthorized persons by means of data transmissions equipment (control of utilization);

    (e) guarantee that, with respect to the use of an automated data processing system, authorized persons have access only to data for which they are responsible (control of access);

(f) guarantee that it is possible to check and establish to which authorities personal data may be transmitted by data transmission equipment (control of transmission);

(g) guarantee that it is possible to check and establish a posteriori what personal data has been introduced into automated data processing systems, when and by whom (control of data introduction);

(h) prevent the unauthorized reading, copying, modification or deletion of personal data during the transmission of data and the transport of data media (control of transport).

2. Each Contracting Party must take special measures to ensure the security of data when it is being transmitted to services located outside the territories of the Contracting Parties. Such measures must be communicated to the joint supervisory authority;

3. Each Contracting Party may designate for the processing of data in its national section of the Schengen Information System only specially qualified persons subject to security checks.

4. The Contracting Party responsible for the technical support function of the Schengen Information System shall take the measures laid down in paragraphs 1 to 3 in respect of the latter.

Chapter IV

Apportionment of the costs of the Schengen Information System

Article 119

1. The costs of setting up and using the technical support function referred to in Article 92 (3), including the cost of cabling for connecting the national sections of the Schengen Information System to the technical support function, shall be defrayed jointly by the Contracting Parties. Each Contracting Party's share shall be determined on the basis of the rate for each Contracting Party applied to the uniform basis of assessment of value-added tax within the meaning of Article 2(1) (c) of the Decision of the Council of the European Communities of 24 June 1988 on the system of the Communities' own resources.

2. The costs of setting up and using the national section of the Schengen Information System shall be borne by each Contracting Party individually.

[...]

Europol Convention (1995)[*]

Brussels, 26 July 1995

The Council of the European Union,

HAVING REGARD to the Treaty on European Union, and in particular Article K.3(2)(c) and Article K.1(9) thereof,

WHEREAS for the purposes of achieving the objectives of the Union the Member States regard the establishment of a European Police Office as a matter of common interest;

HAS DECIDED on the drawing up of the Convention, the text of which is annexed, which has been signed today by the Representatives of the Governments of the Member States of the Union;

RECOMMENDS that it be adopted by the Member States in accordance with their respective constitutional requirements.

ANNEX

CONVENTION
BASED ON ARTICLE K.3 OF THE TREATY ON EUROPEAN UNION, ON THE ESTABLISHMENT OF A EUROPEAN POLICE OFFICE
(EUROPOL CONVENTION)

THE HIGH CONTRACTING PARTIES to the present Convention, Member States of the European Union,

REFERRING to the Council act of 26 July 1995;

AWARE of the urgent problems arising from terrorism, unlawful drug trafficking and other serious forms of international crime;

WHEREAS there is a need for progress in solidarity and co-operation between the Member States of the European Union, particularly through an improvement in police cooperation between the Member States;

WHEREAS such progress should enable the protection of security and public order to be further improved;

WHEREAS the establishment of a European Police Office (Europol) was agreed in the Treaty on European Union of 7 February 1992;

IN VIEW of the decision of the European Council of 29 October 1993 that Europol should be established in the Netherlands and have its seat in The Hague;

MINDFUL of the common objective of improving police cooperation in the field of terrorism, unlawful drug trafficking and other serious forms of international crime through a constant, confidential and intensive exchange of information between Europol and Member States' national units;

---

[*] Council Act of 26 July Drawing up the Convention based on Article K.3 of the Treaty on European Union, on the Establishment of a European Police Office, *Official Journal of the European Communities* No C 316, 27.11.1995, p.1.

ON THE UNDERSTANDING that the forms of cooperation laid down in this Convention should not affect other forms of bilateral or multilateral cooperation;

CONVINCED that in the field of police co-operation, particular attention must be paid to the protection of the rights of individual, and in particular to the protection of their personal data;

WHEREAS the activities of Europol under this Convention are without prejudice to the powers of the European Communities; whereas Europol and the Communities have a mutual interest, in the framework of the European Union, in establishing types of cooperation enabling each of them to perform their respective tasks as effectively as possible,

HAVE AGREED as follows:

Title I

Establishment and tasks

Article 1

Establishment

1. The Member States of the European Union, hereinafter referred to as "Member States", hereby establish a European Police Office, hereinafter referred to as "Europol".

2. Europol shall liaise with a single national unit in each Member State, to be established or designated in accordance with Article 4.

Article 2

Objective

1. The objective of Europol shall be, within the framework of cooperation between the Member States pursuant to Article K.1(9) of the Treaty on European Union, to improve, by means of the measures referred to in this Convention, the effectiveness and cooperation of the competent authorities in the Member States in preventing and combating terrorism, unlawful drug trafficking and other serious forms of international crime where there are factual indications that an organized criminal structure is involved and two or more Member States are affected by the forms of crime in question in such a way as to require a common approach by the Member States owing to the scale, significance and consequences of the offences concerned.

2. In order to achieve progressively the objective mentioned in paragraph 1, Europol shall initially act to prevent and combat unlawful drug trafficking, trafficking in nuclear and radioactive substances, illegal immigrant smuggling, trade in human beings and motor vehicle crime.

Within two years at the latest following the entry into force of this Convention, Europol shall also deal with crimes committed or likely to be committed in the course of terrorist activities against life, limb, personal freedom or property. The Council, acting unanimously in accordance with the procedure laid down in Title VI of the Treaty on European Union, may decide to instruct Europol to deal with such terrorist activities before that period has expired.

The Council, acting unanimously in accordance with the procedure laid down in Title VI of the Treaty on European Union, may decide to instruct Europol to deal with other forms of crime listed in the Annex to this Convention or specific manifestations thereof. Before acting, the Council shall instruct the Management Board to prepare its decision and in particular to set out the budgetary and staffing implications for Europol.

3. Europol's competence as regards a form of crime or specific manifestations thereof shall cover both:

(a) illegal money-laundering activities in connection with these forms of crime or specific manifestations thereof;

(b) related criminal offences.

The following shall be regarded as related and shall be taken into account in accordance with the procedures set out in Articles 8 and 10:

- criminal offences committed in order to procure the means for perpetrating acts within the sphere of competence of Europol;

- criminal offences committed in order to facilitate or carry out acts within the sphere of competence of Europol;

- criminal offences committed to ensure the impunity of acts within the sphere of competence of Europol.

4. For the purposes of this Convention, "competent authorities" means all public bodies existing in the Member States which are responsible under national law for preventing and combating criminal offences.

5. For the purposes of paragraphs 1 and 2, "unlawful drug trafficking" means the criminal offences listed in Article 3(1) of the United Nations Convention of 20 December 1988 against Illicit Traffic in Narcotic Drugs and Psychotropic Substances and in the provisions amending or replacing that Convention.

Article 3

Tasks

1. In the framework of its objective pursuant to Article 2(1), Europol shall have the following principal tasks:

(a) to facilitate the exchange of information between the Member States;

(b) to obtain, collate and analyse information and intelligence;

(c) to notify the competent authorities of the Member States without delay via the national units referred to in Article 4 of information concerning them and of any connections identified between criminal offences;

(d) to aid investigations in the Member States by forwarding all relevant information to the national units;

(e) to maintain a computerized system of collected information containing data in accordance with Articles 8, 10 and 11.

2. In order to improve the cooperation and effectiveness of the competent authorities in the Member States through the national units with a view to fulfilling the objective set out in Article 2(1), Europol shall furthermore have the following additional tasks:

(a) to develop specialist knowledge of the investigative procedures of the competent authorities in the Member States and to provide advice on investigations;

(b) to provide strategic intelligence to assist with and promote the efficient and effective use of the resources available at national level for operational activities;

(c) to prepare general situation reports.

3. In the context of its objective under Article 2(1) Europol may, in addition, in accordance with its staffing and the budgetary resources at its disposal and within the limits set by the Management Board, assist Member States through advice and research in the following areas:

(a) training of members of their competent authorities;

(b) organization and equipment of those authorities;

(c) crime prevention methods;

(d) technical and forensic police methods and investigative procedures.

Article 4

National units

1. Each Member State shall establish or designate a national unit to carry out the tasks listed in this Article.

2. The national unit shall be the only liaison body between Europol and the competent national authorities. Relationships between the national unit and the competent authorities shall be governed by national law, and, in particular the relevant national constitutional requirements.

3. Member States shall take the necessary measures to ensure that the national units are able to fulfil their tasks and, in particular, have access to relevant national data.

4. It shall be the task of the national units to:

(a) supply Europol on their own initiative with the information and intelligence necessary for it to carry out its tasks;

(b) respond to Europol's requests for information, intelligence and advice;

(c) keep information and intelligence up to date;

(d) evaluate information and intelligence in accordance with national law for the competent authorities and transmit this material to them;

(e) issue requests for advice, information, intelligence and analysis to Europol;

(f) supply Europol with information for storage in the computerized system;

(g) ensure compliance with the law in every exchange of information between themselves and Europol.

5. Without prejudice to the exercise of the responsibilities incumbent upon Member States as set out in Article K.2(2) of the Treaty on European Union, a national unit shall not be obliged in a particular case to supply the information and intelligence provided for in paragraph 4, points 1, 2 and 6 and in Articles 7 and 10 if this would mean:

(a) harming essential national security interests; or

(b) jeopardizing the success of a current investigation or the safety of individuals;

(c) involving information pertaining to organizations or specific intelligence activities in the field of State security.

6. The costs incurred by the national units for communications with Europol shall be borne by the Member States and, apart from the costs of connection, shall not be charged to Europol.

7. The Heads of national units shall meet as necessary to assist Europol by giving advice.

Article 5

Liaison officers

1. Each national unit shall second at least one liaison officer to Europol. The number of liaison officers who may be sent by Member States to Europol shall be laid down by unanimous decision of the Management Board; the decision may be altered at any time by unanimous decision of the Management Board. Except as otherwise stipulated in specific provisions of this Convention, liaison officers shall be subject to the national law of the seconding Member State.

2. The liaison officers shall be instructed by their national units to represent the interests of the latter within Europol in accordance with the national law of the seconding Member State and in compliance with the provisions applicable to the administration of Europol.

3. Without prejudice to Article 4(4) and (5), the liaison officers shall, within the framework of the objective laid down in Article 2(1), assist in the exchange of information between the national units which have seconded them and Europol, in particular by:

   (a) providing Europol with information from the seconding national unit;

   (b) forwarding information from Europol to the seconding national unit; and

   (c) cooperating with the officials of Europol by providing information and giving advice as regards analysis of the information concerning the seconding Member State.

4. At the same time, the liaison officers shall assist in the exchange of information from their national units and the coordination of the resulting measures in accordance with their national law and within the framework of the objective laid down in Article 2(1).

5. To the extent necessary for the performance of the tasks under paragraph 3 above, the liaison officers shall have the right to consult the various files in accordance with the appropriate provisions specified in the relevant Articles.

6. Article 25 shall apply mutatis mutandis to the activity of the liaison officers.

7. Without prejudice to the other provisions of this Convention, the rights and obligations of liaison officers in relation to Europol shall be determined unanimously by the Management Board.

8. Liaison officers shall enjoy the privileges and immunities necessary for the performance of their tasks in accordance with Article 41(2).

9. Europol shall provide Member States free of charge with the necessary premises in the Europol building for the activity of their liaison officers. All other costs which arise in connection with seconding liaison officers shall be borne by the seconding Member State; this shall also apply to the costs of equipment for liaison officers, to the extent that the Management Board does not unanimously recommend otherwise in a specific case when drawing up the budget of Europol.

Article 6

Computerized system of collected information

1. Europol shall maintain a computerized system of collected information consisting of the following components:

   (a) an information system as referred to in Article 7 with restricted and precisely defined content which allows rapid reference to the information available to the Member States and Europol;

(b) work files as referred to in Article 10 established for variable periods of time for the purposes of analysis and containing comprehensive information and

(c) an index system containing certain particulars from the analysis files referred to in point 2, in accordance with the arrangements laid down in Article 11.

2. The computerized system of collected information operated by Europol must under no circumstances be linked to other automated processing systems, except for the automated processing systems of the national units.

Title II

Information system

Article 7

Establishment of the information system

1. In order to perform its tasks, Europol shall establish and maintain a computerized information system. The information system, into which Member States, represented by their national units and liaison officers, may directly input data in compliance with their national procedures, and into which Europol may directly input data supplied by third States and third bodies and analysis data, shall be directly accessible for consultation by national units, liaison officers, the Director, the Deputy Directors and duly empowered Europol officials.

Direct access by the national units to the information system in respect of the persons referred to in Article 8(1), point 2 shall be restricted solely to the details of identity listed in Article 8(2). If needed for a specific enquiry, the full range of data shall be accessible to them via the liaison officers.

2. Europol shall:

(a) have the task of ensuring compliance with the provisions governing cooperation on and operation of the information system, and

(b) be responsible for the proper working of the information system in technical and operational respects. Europol shall in particular take all necessary measures to ensure that the measures referred to in Article 21 and 25 regarding the information system are properly implemented.

(c) The national unit in each Member State shall be responsible for communication with the information system. It shall, in particular, be responsible for the security measures referred to in Article 25 in respect of the data-processing equipment used within the territory of the Member State in question, for the review in accordance with Article 21 and, insofar as required under the laws, regulations, administrative provisions and procedures of that Member State, for the proper implementation of this Convention in other respects.

Article 8

Content of the information system

1. The information system may be used to store, modify and utilize only the data necessary for the performance of Europol's tasks, with the exception of data concerning related criminal offences as referred to in the second subparagraph of Article 2(3). Data entered shall relate to:

(a) persons who, in accordance with the national law of the Member State concerned, are suspected of having committed or having taken part in a criminal offence for which Europol is competent under Article 2 or who have been convicted of such an offence;

(b) persons who there are serious grounds under national law for believing will commit criminal offences for which Europol is competent under Article 2.

2. Personal data as referred to in paragraph 1 may include only the following details:

(a) surname, maiden name, given names and any alias or assumed name;

(b) date and place of birth;

(c) nationality;

(d) sex, and

(e) where necessary, other characteristics likely to assist in identification, including any specific objective physical characteristics not subject to change.

3. In addition to the data referred to in paragraph 2 and data on Europol or the inputting national unit, the information system may also be used to store, modify and utilize the following details concerning the persons referred to in paragraph 1:

(a) criminal offences, alleged crimes and when and where they were committed;

(b) means which were or may be used to commit the crimes;

(c) departments handling the case and their filing references;

(d) suspected membership of a criminal organization;

(e) convictions, where they relate to criminal offences for which Europol is competent under Article 2.

These data may also be input when they do not yet contain any references to persons. Where Europol inputs the data itself, as well as giving its filing reference it shall also indicate whether data were provided by a third party of are the result of its own analyses.

4. Additional information held by Europol or national units concerning the groups of persons referred to in paragraph 1 may be communicated to any national unit or Europol should either so request. National units shall do so in compliance with their national law.

Where the additional information concerns one or more related criminal offences as defined in the second subparagraph of Article 2(3), the data stored in the information system shall be marked accordingly to enable units and Europol to exchange information on the related criminal offences.

5. If proceedings against the person concerned are dropped or if that person is acquitted, the data relating to either decision shall be deleted.

Article 9

Right of access to the information system

1. Only national units, liaison officers, and the Director, Deputy Directors or duly empowered Europol officials shall have the right to input data directly into the information system and retrieve it therefrom. Data may be retrieved where this is necessary for the performance of Europol's tasks in a particular case; retrieval shall be effected in accordance with the laws, regulations, administrative provisions and procedures of the retrieving unit, subject to any additional provisions contained in this Convention.

2. Only the unit which entered the data may modify, correct or delete such data. Where a unit has reason to believe that data as referred to in Article 8(2) are incorrect or wishes to supplement them, it shall immediately inform the inputting unit; the latter shall examine such notification without delay and if necessary modify, supplement, correct or delete the data

immediately. Where the system contains data as referred to in Article 8(3) concerning a person any unit may enter additional data as referred to in Article 8(3). Where there is an obvious contradiction between the data input, the units concerned shall consult each other and reach agreement. Where a unit intends to delete altogether data as referred to in Article 8(2) which is has input on a person and where data as referred to in Article 8(3) are held on the same person but input by other units, responsibility in terms of data protection legislation pursuant to Article 15(1) and the right to modify, supplement, correct and delete such data pursuant to Article 8(2) shall be transferred to the next unit to have entered data as referred to in Article 8(3) on that person. The unit intending to delete shall inform the unit to which responsibility in terms of data protection is transferred of its intention.

3. Responsibility for the permissibility of retrieval from, input into and modifications within the information system shall lie with the retrieving, inputting or modifying unit; it must be possible to identify that unit. The communication of information between national units and the competent authorities in the Member States shall be governed by national law.

Title III

Work files for the purposes of analysis

Article 10

Collection, processing and utilization of personal data

1. Where this is necessary to achieve the objective laid down in Article 2(1), Europol, in addition to data of a non-personal nature, may store, modify, and utilize in other files data on criminal offences for which Europol is competent under Article 2(2), including data on the related criminal offences provided for in the second subparagraph of Article 2(3) which are intended for specific analyses, and concerning:

(a) persons as referred to in Article 8(1);

(b) persons who might be called on to testify in investigations in connection with the offences under consideration or in subsequent criminal proceedings;

(c) persons who have been the victims of one of the offences under consideration or with regard to whom certain facts give reason for believing that they could be the victims of such an offence;

(d) contacts and associates, and

(e) persons who can provide information on the criminal offences under consideration.

The collection, storage and processing of the data listed in the first sentence of Article 6 of the Council of Europe Convention of 28 January 1981 with regard to Automatic Processing of Personal Data shall not be permitted unless strictly necessary for the purposes of the file concerned and unless such data supplement other personal data already entered in that file. It shall be prohibited to select a particular group of persons solely on the basis of the data listed in the first sentence of Article 6 of the Council of Europe Convention of 28 January 1981 in breach of the aforementioned rules with regard to purpose.

The Council, acting unanimously, in accordance with the procedure laid down in Title VI of the Treaty on European Union, shall adopt implementing rules for data files prepared by the Management Board containing additional details, in particular with regard to the categories of personal data referred to in this Article and the provisions concerning the security of the data concerned and the internal supervision of their use.

2. Such files shall be opened for the purposes of analysis defined as the assembly, processing or utilization of data with the aim of helping a criminal investigation. Each analysis project shall entail the establishment of an analysis group closely associating the following participants in accordance with the tasks defined in Article 3(1) and (2) and Article 5(3):

(a) analysts and other Europol officials designated by the Europol Directorate: only analysts shall be authorized to enter data into retrieve data from the file concerned;

(b) the liaison officers and/or experts of the Member States supplying the information or concerned by the analysis within the meaning of paragraph 6.

3. At the request of Europol or on their own initiative, national units shall, subject to Article 4(5), communicate to Europol all the information which it may require for the performance of its tasks under Article 3(1), point 2. The Member States shall communicate such data only where processing thereof for the purposes of preventing, analysing or combating offences is also authorized by their national law.

Depending on their degree of sensitivity, data from national units may be routed directly, and by whatever means may be appropriate to the analysis groups, whether via the liaison officers concerned or not.

4. If, in addition to the data referred to in paragraph 3, it would seem justified for Europol to have other information for the performance of tasks under Article 3(1), point 2, Europol may request that:

(a) the European Communities and bodies governed by public law established under the Treaties establishing those Communities;

(b) other bodies governed by public law established in the framework of the European Union;

(c) bodies which are based on an agreement two or more Member States of the European Union;

(d) third States;

(e) international organizations and their subordinate bodies governed by public law;

(f) other bodies governed by public law which are based on an agreement between two or more States, and

(g) the International Criminal Police Organization,

forward the relevant information to it by whatever means may be appropriated. It may also, under the same conditions and by the same means, accept information provided by those various bodies on their own initiative. The Council, acting unanimously in accordance with the procedure laid down in Title VI of the Treaty on European Union and after consulting the Management Board, shall draw up the rules to be observed by Europol in this respect.

5. Insofar as Europol is entitled under other Conventions to gain computerized access to data from other information systems, Europol may retrieve personal data by such means if this is necessary for the performance of its tasks pursuant to Article 3(1), point 2.

6. If an analysis is of a general nature and of a strategic type, all Member States, through liaison officers and/or experts, shall be fully associated in the findings thereof, in particular through the communication of reports drawn up by Europol.

If the analysis bears on specific cases not concerning all Member States and has a direct operational aim, representatives of the following Member States shall participate therein:

(a) Member States which were the source of the information giving rise to the decision to open the analysis file, or those which are directly concerned by that information and Member States subsequently invited by the analysis group to take part in the analysis because they are also becoming concerned;

(b) Member States which learn from consulting the index system that they need to be informed and assert that need to know under the conditions laid down in paragraph 7.

7. The need to be informed may be claimed by authorized liaison officers. Each Member State shall nominate and authorize a limited number of such liaison officers. It shall forward the list thereof to the Management Board.

A liaison officer shall claim the need to be informed as defined in paragraph 6 by means of a written reasoned statement approved by the authority to which he is subordinate in his Member State and forwarded to all the participants in the analysis. He shall then be automatically associated in the analysis in progress.

If an objection is raised in the analysis group, automatic association shall be deferred until completion of a conciliation procedure, which may comprise three stages as follows:

(a) the participants in the analysis shall endeavour to reach agreement with the liaison officer claiming the need to be informed; they shall have no more than eight days for that purpose;

(b) if no agreement is reached, the heads of the national units concerned and the Directorate of Europol shall meet within three days;

(c) if the disagreement persists, the representatives of the parties concerned on the Management Board shall meet within eight days. If the Member State concerned does not waive its need to be informed, automatic association of that Member State shall be decided by consensus.

8. The Member State communicating an item of data to Europol shall be the sole judge of the degree of its sensitivity and variations thereof. Any dissemination or operational use of analysis data shall be decided on in consultation with the participants in the analysis. A Member State joining an analysis in progress may not, in particular, disseminate or use the data without the prior agreement of the Member States initially concerned.

Article 11

Index system

1. An index system shall be created by Europol for the data stored on the files referred to in Article 10(1).

2. The Director, Deputy Directors and duly empowered officials of Europol and liaison officers shall have the right to consult the index system. The index system shall be such that it is clear to the liaison officers consulting it, from the data being consulted, that the files referred to in Article 6(1), point 2 and Article 10(1) contain data concerning the seconding Member State.

Access by liaison officers shall be defined in such a way that it is possible to determine whether or not an item of information is stored, but that it is not possible to establish connections or further conclusions regarding the content of the files.

3. The detailed procedures for the design of the index system shall be defined by the Management Board acting unanimously.

Article 12

Order opening a data file

1. For every computerized data file containing personal data operated by Europol for the purpose of performing its tasks referred to in Article 10, Europol shall specify in an order opening the file, which shall require the approval of the Management Board:

(a) the file name;

(b) the purpose of the file;

(c) the groups of persons on whom data are stored;

(d) the nature of the data to be stored, and any of the data listed in the first sentence of Article 6 of the Council of Europe Convention of 28 January 1981 which are strictly necessary;

(e) the type of personal data used to open the file;

(f) the supply or input of the data to be stored;

(g) the conditions under which the personal data stored in the file name may be communicated, to which recipients and under what procedure;

(h) the time-limits for examinations and duration of storage;

(i) the method of establishing the audit log.

The joint supervisory body provided for in Article 24 shall immediately be advised by the Director of Europol of the plan to order the opening of such a data file and shall receive the dossier so that it may address any comments it deems necessary to the Management Board.

2. If the urgency of the matter is such as to preclude obtaining the approval of the Management Board as required under paragraph 1, the Director, on his own initiative or at the request of the Member States concerned, may by a reasoned decision, order the opening of a data file. At the same time he shall inform the members of the Management Board of his decision. The procedure pursuant to paragraph 1 shall then be set in motion without delay and completed as soon as possible.

Title IV

Common provisions on information processing

Article 13

Duty to notify

Europol shall promptly notify the national units and also their liaison officers if the national units so request, of any information concerning their Member State and of connections identified between criminal offences for which Europol is competent under Article 2. Information and intelligence concerning other serious criminal offences, of which Europol becomes aware in the course of its duties, may also be communicated.

Article 14

Standard of data protection

1. By the time of the entry into force of this Convention at the latest, each Member State shall, under its national legislation, take the necessary measures in relation to the processing of personal data in data files in the framework of this Convention to ensure a standard of data protection which at least corresponds to the standard resulting from the implementation of the principles of the Council of Europe Convention of 28 January 1981, and, in doing so, shall take account of Recommendation No R(87) 15 of the Committee of Ministers of the Council of Europe of 17 September 1987 concerning the use of personal data in the police sector.

2. The communication of personal data provided for in this Convention may not begin until the data protection rules laid down in paragraph 1 above have entered into force on the territory of each of the Member States involved in such communication.

3. In the collection, processing and utilization of personal data Europol shall take account of the principles of the Council of Europe Convention of 28 January 1981 and of Recommendation No R(87) 15 of the Committee of Ministers of the Council of Europe of 17 September 1987.

Europol shall also observe these principles in respect of non-automated data held in the form of data files, i.e. any structured set of personal data accessible in accordance with specific criteria.

Article 15

Responsibility in data protection matters

1. Subject to other provisions in this Convention, the responsibility for data stored at Europol, in particular as regards the legality, of the collection, the transmission to Europol and the input of data, as well as their accuracy, their up-to-date nature and verification of the storage time-limits, shall lie with:

(a) the Member State which input or otherwise communicated the data;

(b) Europol in respect of data communicated to Europol by third parties or which result from analyses conducted by Europol.

2. In addition, subject to other provisions in this Convention, Europol shall be responsible for all data received by Europol and processed by it, whether such data be in the information system referred to in Article 8, in the data files opened for the purposes of analysis referred to in Article 10, or in the index system referred to in Article 11, or in the data files referred to in Article 14(3).

3. Europol shall store data in such a way that it can be established by which Member State or third party the data were transmitted or whether they are the result of an analysis by Europol.

Article 16

Provisions on the drawing up of reports

On average, Europol shall draw up reports for at least one in ten retrievals of personal data - and for each retrieval made within the information system referred to in Article 7 - in order to check whether they are permissible under law. The data contained in the reports shall only be used for that purpose by Europol and the supervisory bodies referred to in Articles 23 and 24 and shall be deleted after six months, unless the data are further required for ongoing control. The details shall be decided upon by the Management Board following consultation with the joint supervisory body.

Article 17

Rules on the use of data

1. Personal data retrieved from the information system, the index system or data files opened for the purposes of analysis and data communicated by any other appropriate means, may be transmitted or utilized only by the competent authorities of the Member States in order to prevent and combat crimes falling within the competence of Europol and to combat other serious forms of crime.

The data referred to in the first paragraph shall be utilized in compliance with the law of the Member State responsible for the authorities which utilized the data.

Europol may utilize the data referred to in paragraph 1 only for the performance of its tasks as referred to in Article 3.

2. If, in the case of certain data, the communicating Member State or the communicating third State or third body as referred to in Article 10(4) stipulates particular restrictions on use to which such data is subject in that Member State or by third parties, such restrictions shall also be complied with by the user of the data except in the specific case where national law lays down that the restrictions on use be waived for judicial authorities, legislative bodies or any other independent body set up under the law and made responsible for supervising the national competent authorities within the meaning of Article 2(4). In such cases, the data may only be used after prior consultation of the communicating Member State whose interests and opinions must be taken into account as far as possible.

3. Use of the data for other purposes or by authorities other than those referred to in Article 2 of this Convention shall be possible only after prior consultation of the Member State which transmitted the data insofar as the national law of that Member State permits.

Article 18

Communication of data to third states and third bodies

1. Europol may under the conditions laid down in paragraph 4 communicate personal data which it holds to third states and third bodies within the meaning of Article 10(4), where:

   (a) this is necessary in individual cases for the purposes of preventing or combating criminal offences for which Europol is competent under Article 2;

   (b) an adequate level of data protection is ensured in that State or that body, and

   (c) this is permissible under the general rules within the meaning of paragraph 2.

2. In accordance with the procedure in Title VI of the Treaty on European Union, and taking into account the circumstances referred to in paragraph 3, the Council, acting unanimously, shall determine the general rules of the communication of personal data by Europol to the Third States and third bodies within the meaning of Article 10(4). The Management Board shall prepare the Council decision and consult the joint supervisory body referred to in Article 24.

3. The adequacy of the level of data protection afforded by third States and third bodies within the meaning of Article 10(4) shall be assessed taking into account all the circumstances which play a part in the communication of personal data; in particular, the following shall be taken into account:

   (a) the nature of the data;

   (b) the purpose for which the data is intended;

   (c) the duration of the intended processing, and

   (d) the general or specific provisions applying to the third States and third bodies within the meaning of Article 10(4).

4. If the data referred to have been communicated to Europol by a Member State, Europol may communicate them to third States and third bodies only with the Member State's consent. The Member State may give its prior consent, in general or other terms, to such communication; that consent may be withdrawn at any time.

If the data have not been communicated by a Member State, Europol shall satisfy itself that communication of those data is not liable to:

   (a) obstruct the proper performance of the tasks falling within a Member State's sphere of competence;

   (b) jeopardize the security and public order of a Member State or otherwise prejudice its general welfare.

5. Europol shall be responsible for the legality of the authorizing communication. Europol shall keep a record of communications of data and of the grounds for such communications. The communication of data shall be authorized only if the recipient gives an undertaking that the data will be used only for the purpose for which it was communicated. This shall not apply to the communication of personal data required for a Europol inquiry.

6. Where the communication provided for in paragraph 1 concerns information subject to the requirement of confidentiality, it shall be permissible only insofar as an agreement on confidentiality exists between Europol and the recipient.

Article 19

Right of access

1. Any individual wishing to exercise his right of access to data relating to him which have been stored within Europol or to have such data checked may make a request to that effect free of charge to the national competent authority in any Member State he wishes, and that authority shall refer it to Europol without delay and inform the enquirer that Europol will reply to him directly.

2. The request must be fully dealt with by Europol within three months following its receipt by the national competent authority of the Member State concerned.

3. The right of any individual to have access to data relating to him or to have such data checked shall be exercised in accordance with the law of the Member State where the right is claimed, taking into account the following provisions:

Where the law of the Member State applied to provides for a communication concerning data, such communication shall be refused if such refusal is necessary to:

(a) enable Europol to fulfil its duties properly;

(b) protect security and public order in the Member States or to prevent crime;

(c) protect the rights and freedoms of third parties,

considerations which it follows cannot be overridden by the interests of the person concerned by the communication of the information.

4. The right to communication of information in accordance with paragraph 3 shall be exercised to the following procedures:

(a) as regards data entered within the information system defined in Article 8, a decision to communicate such data cannot be taken unless the Member State which entered the data and the Member States directly concerned by communication of such data have first had the opportunity of stating their position, which may extend to a refusal to communicate the data. The data which may be communicated and the arrangements for communicating such data shall be indicated by the Member State which entered the data;

(b) as regards data entered within the information system by Europol, the Member States directly concerned by communication of such data must first have had the opportunity of stating their position, which may extend to a refusal to communicate the data;

(c) as regards data entered within the work files for the purposes of analysis as defined in Article 10, the communication of such data shall be conditional upon the consensus of Europol and the Member States participating in the analysis, within the meaning of Article 10(2), and the consensus of the Member State(s) directly concerned by the communication of such data.

Should one or more Member State or Europol have objected to a communication concerning data, Europol shall notify the person concerned that it has carried out the checks, without giving any information which might reveal to him whether or not he is known.

5. The right to the checking of information shall be exercised in accordance with the following procedures:

Where the national law applicable makes no provision for a communication concerning data or in the case of a simple request for a check, Europol, in close cooperation with the national authorities concerned, shall carry out the checks and notify the enquirer that it has done so without giving any information which might reveal to him whether or not he is known.

6. In its reply to a request for a check or for access to data, Europol shall inform the enquirer that he may appeal to the joint supervisory body if he is not satisfied with the decision. The latter may also refer the matter to the joint supervisory body if there has been no response to his request within the time-limits laid down in this Article.

7. If the enquirer lodges an appeal to the joint supervisory body provided for in Article 24, the appeal shall be examined by that body.

Where the appeal relates to a communication concerning data entered by a Member State in the information system, the joint supervisory body shall take its decision in accordance with the national law of the Member State in which the application was made. The joint supervisory body shall first consult the national supervisory body or the competent judicial body in the Member State which was the source of the data. Either national body shall make the necessary checks, in particular to establish whether the decision to refuse was taken in accordance with paragraphs 3 and 4(1) of this Article. On confirmation of that, the decision, which may extend to a refusal to communicate any information, shall be taken by the joint supervisory body in close cooperation with the national supervisory body or competent judicial body.

Where the appeal relates to a communication concerning data entered by Europol in the information system or data stored in the work files for the purposes of analysis, the joint supervisory body, in the event of persistent objections from Europol or a Member State, may not overrule such objections unless by a majority of two-thirds of its members after having heard Europol or the Member State concerned. If there is no such majority, the joint supervisory body shall notify the enquirer that it has carried out the checks, without giving any information which might reveal to him whether or not he is known.

Where the appeal concerns the checking of data entered by a Member State in the information system, the joint supervisory body shall ensure that the necessary checks have been carried out correctly in close cooperation with the national supervisory body of the Member State which entered the data. The joint supervisory body shall notify the enquirer that it has carried out the checks, without giving any information which might reveal to him whether or not he is known.

Where the appeal concerns the checking of data entered by Europol in the information system or of data stored in the work files for the purposes of analysis, the joint supervisory body shall ensure that the necessary checks have been carried out by Europol. The joint supervisory body shall notify the enquirer that it has carried out the checks, without giving any information which might reveal to him whether or not he is known.

8. The above provisions shall apply mutatis mutandis to non-automated data held by Europol in the form of data files, i.e. any structured set of personal data accessible in accordance with specific criteria.

Article 20

Correction and deletion of data

1. If it emerges that data held by Europol which have been communicated to it by third States or third bodies or which are the result of its own analyses are incorrect or that their input or storage contravenes this Convention, Europol shall correct òr delete such data.

2. If data that are incorrect or that contravene this Convention have been passed directly to Europol by Member States, they shall be obliged to correct or delete them in collaboration with Europol. If incorrect data are transmitted by another appropriate means or if the errors in the data supplied by Member States are due to faulty transmission or have been transmitted in breach of the provisions of this Convention or if they result from their being entered, taken over or stored in an incorrect manner or in breach of the provisions of this Convention by Europol, Europol shall be obliged to correct them or delete them in collaboration with the Member States concerned.

3. In the case referred to in paragraphs 1 and 2, the Member States which are recipients of the data shall be notified forthwith. The recipient Member States shall also correct or delete those data.

4. Any person shall have the right to ask Europol to correct or delete incorrect data concerning him.

Europol shall inform the enquirer that data concerning him have been corrected or deleted. If the enquirer is not satisfied with Europol's reply or if he has received no reply within three months, he may refer the matter to the joint supervisory body.

Article 21

Time limits for the storage and deletion of data files

1. Data in data files shall be held by Europol only for as long as is necessary for the performance of its tasks. The need for continued storage shall be reviewed no later than three years after the input of data. Review of data stored in the information system and its deletion shall be carried out by the inputting unit. Review of data stored in other Europol data files and their deletion shall be carried out by Europol. Europol shall automatically inform the Member States three months in advance of the expiry of the time limits for reviewing the storage of data.

2. During the review, the units referred to in the third and fourth sentences of paragraph 1 above may decide on continued storage of data until the next review if this is still necessary for the performance of Europol's tasks. If no decision is taken on the continued storage of data, those data shall automatically be deleted.

3. Storage of personal data relating to individuals as referred to in point 1 of the first subparagraph of Article 10(1) may not exceed a total of three years. Each time limit shall begin to run afresh on the date on which an event leading to the storage of data relating to that individual occurs. The need for continued storage shall be reviewed annually and the review documented.

4. Where a Member State deletes from its national data files data communicated to Europol which are stored in other Europol data files, it shall inform Europol accordingly. In such cases, Europol shall delete the data unless it has further interest in them, based on intelligence that is more extensive than that possessed by the communicating Member State. Europol shall inform the Member State concerned of the continued storage of such data.

5. Deletion shall not occur if it would damage the interests of the data subject which require protection. In such cases, the data may be used only with the consent of the data subject.

Article 22

Correction and storage of data in paper files

1. If it emerges that an entire paper file or data included in that file held by Europol are no longer necessary for the performance of Europol's tasks, or if the information concerned is overall in contravention of this Convention, the paper file or data concerned shall be destroyed. The paper file or data concerned must be marked as not for use until they have been effectively destroyed.

Destruction may not take place if there are grounds for assuming that the legitimate interests of the data subject would otherwise be prejudiced. In such cases, the paper file must bear the same note prohibiting all use.

2. If it emerges that data contained in the Europol paper files are incorrect, Europol shall be obliged to correct them.

3. Any person covered by a Europol paper file may claim the right vis-à-vis Europol to correction or destruction of paper files or the inclusion of a note. Article 20(4) and Article 24(2) and (7) shall be applicable.

Article 23

National supervisory body

1. Each Member State shall designate a national supervisory body, the task of which shall be to monitor independently, in accordance with its respective national law, the permissibility of the input, the retrieval and any communication to Europol of personal data by the Member State concerned and to examine whether this violates the rights of the data subject. For this purpose, the supervisory body shall have access at the national unit or at the liaison officers' premises to the data entered by the Member State in the information system and in the index system in accordance with the relevant national procedures.

For their supervisory purposes, national supervisory bodies shall have access to the offices and documents of their respective liaison officers at Europol.

In addition, in accordance with the relevant national procedures, the national supervisory bodies shall supervise the activities of national units under Article 4(4) and the activities of liaison officers under Article 5(3), points 1 and 3 and Article 5(4) and (5), insofar as such activities are of relevance to the protection of personal data.

2. Each individual shall have the right to request the national supervisory body to ensure that the entry or communication of data concerning him to Europol in any form and the consultation of the data by the Member State concerned are lawful.

This right shall be exercised in accordance with the national law of the Member State to the national supervisory body of which the request is made.

Article 24

Joint supervisory body

1. An independent joint supervisory body shall be set up, which shall have the task of reviewing, in accordance with this Convention, the activities of Europol in order to ensure that the rights of the individual are not violated by the storage, processing and utilization of the data held by Europol. In addition, the joint supervisory body shall monitor the permissibility of the transmission of data originating from Europol. The joint supervisory body shall be composed of not more than two members or representatives (where appropriate assisted by alternates) of each of the national supervisory bodies guaranteed to be independent and having the necessary abilities, and appointed for five years by each Member State. Each delegation shall be entitled to one vote.

The joint supervisory body shall appoint a chairman from among its members.

In the performance of their duties, the members of the joint supervisory body shall not receive instructions from any other body.

2. Europol must assist the joint supervisory body in the performance of the latter's tasks. In doing so, it shall, in particular:

(a) supply the information it requests, give it access to all documents and paper files as well as access to the data stored in the system, and

(b) allow it free access at any time to all its premises.

(c) carry out the joint supervisory body's decisions on appeals in accordance with the provisions of Articles 19(7) and 20(4).

3. The joint supervisory body shall also be competent for the examination of questions relating to implementation and interpretation in connection with Europol's activities as regards the processing and utilization of personal data, for the examination of questions relating to checks carried out independently by the national supervisory bodies of the Member States or relating to the exercise of the right to information, as well as for drawing up harmonized proposals for common solutions to existing problems.

4. Each individual shall have the right to request the joint supervisory body to ensure that the manner in which his personal data have been collected, stored, processed and utilized by Europol is lawful and accurate.

5. If the joint supervisory body notes any violations of the provisions of this Convention in the storage, processing or utilization of personal data, it shall make any complaints it deems necessary to the Director of Europol and shall request him to reply within a time limit to be determined by it. The Director shall keep the Management Board informed of the entire procedure. In the event of any difficulty, the joint supervisory body shall refer the matter to the Management Board.

6. The joint supervisory body shall draw up activity reports at regular intervals. In accordance with the procedure laid down in Title VI of the Treaty on European Union, these shall be forwarded to the Council; the Management Board shall first have the opportunity to deliver an opinion, which shall be attached to the reports.

The joint supervisory body shall decide whether or not to publish its activity report, and, if it decides to do so, determine how it should be published.

7. The joint supervisory body shall unanimously adopt its rules of procedure, which shall be submitted for the unanimous approval of the Council. It shall set up internally a committee comprising one qualified representative from each Member State with entitlement to a vote. The committee shall have the task of examining the appeals provided for in Articles 19(7) and 20(4) by all appropriate means. Should they so request, the parties, assisted by their advisers if they so wish, shall be heard by the committee. The decisions taken in this context shall be final as regards all the parties concerned.

8. It may also set up one or more other committees.

9. It shall be consulted on that part of the budget which concerns it. Its opinion shall be annexed to the draft budget in question.

10. It shall be assisted by a secretariat, the tasks of which shall be defined in the rules of procedure.

Article 25

Data security

1. Europol shall take the necessary technical and organizational measures to ensure the implementation of this Convention. Measures shall only be necessary where the effort they involve is proportionate to the objective they are designed to achieve in terms of protection.

2. In respect of automated data processing at Europol each Member State and Europol shall implement measures designed to:

   (a) deny unauthorized persons access to data processing equipment used for processing personal data (equipment access control);

   (b) prevent the unauthorized reading, copying, modification or removal of data media (data media control);

   (c) prevent the unauthorized input of data and the unauthorized inspection, modification or deletion of stored personal data (storage control);

   (d) prevent the use of automated data processing systems by unauthorized persons using data communication equipment (user control);

   (e) ensure that persons authorized to use an automated data processing system only have access to the data covered by their access authorization (data access control);

   (f) ensure that it is possible to verify and establish to which bodies personal data may be transmitted using data communication equipment (communication control);

   (g) ensure that it is subsequently possible to verify and establish which personal data have been input into automated data processing systems and when and by whom the data were input (input control);

   (h) prevent unauthorized reading, copying, modification or deletion of personal data during transfers of personal data or during transportation of data media (transport control);

   (i) ensure that installed systems may, in case of interruption, be immediately restored (recovery);

   (j) ensure that the functions of the system perform without fault, that the appearance of faults in the functions is immediately reported (reliability) and that stored data cannot be corrupted by means of a malfunctioning of the system (integrity).

Title V

Legal status, organization and financial provisions

Article 26

Legal capacity

1. Europol shall have legal personality.

2. Europol shall enjoy in each Member State the most extensive legal and contractual capacity available to legal persons under that State's law. Europol may in particular acquire and dispose of movable or immovable property and be a party to legal proceedings.

3. Europol shall be empowered to conclude a headquarters agreement with the Kingdom of the Netherlands and to conclude with third bodies within the meaning of Article 10(4) the

necessary confidentiality agreements pursuant to Article 18(6) as well as other arrangements in the framework of the rules laid down unanimously by the Council on the basis of this Convention and of Title VI of the Treaty on European Union.

Article 27

Organs of Europol

The organs of Europol shall be:

1) the Management Board;

2) the Director;

3) the Financial Controller;

4) the Financial Committee.

Article 28

Management board

1. Europol shall have a Management Board. The Management Board:

    (a) shall take part in the extension of Europol's objective (Article 2(2));

    (b) shall define unanimously liaison officers' rights and obligations towards Europol (Article 5);

    (c) shall decide unanimously on the number of liaison officers the Member States may send to Europol (Article 5);

    (d) shall prepare the implementing rules governing data files (Article 10);

    (e) shall take part in the adoption of rules governing Europol's relations with third States and third bodies within the meaning of Article 10(4) (Articles 10, 18 and 42);

    (f) shall unanimously decide on details concerning the design of the index system (Article 11);

    (g) shall approve by a two-thirds majority orders opening data files (Article 12);

    (h) may deliver opinions on the comments and reports of the joint supervisory body (Article 24);

    (i) shall examine problems which the joint supervisory body brings to its attention (Article 24(5));

    (j) shall decide on the details of the procedure for checking the legal character of retrievals in the information system (Article 16);

    (k) shall take part in the appointment and dismissal of the Director and Deputy Directors (Article 29);

    (l) shall oversee the proper performance of the Director's duties (Articles 7 and 29);

    (m) shall take part in the adoption of staff regulations (Article 30);

    (n) shall take part in the preparation of agreements on confidentiality and the adoption of provisions on the protection of confidentiality (Articles 18 and 31);

- (o) shall take part in the drawing up of the budget, including the establishment plan, the auditing and the discharge to be given to the Director (Articles 35 and 36);

- (p) shall adopt unanimously the five-year financing plan (Article 35);

- (q) shall appoint unanimously the financial controller and oversee the performances of his duties (Article 35);

- (r) shall take part in the adoption of the financial regulation (Article 35);

- (s) shall unanimously approve the conclusion of the headquarters agreement (Article 37);

- (t) shall adopt unanimously the rules for the security clearance of Europol officials;

- (u) shall act by a two-thirds majority in disputes between a Member State and Europol or between Member States concerning compensation paid under the liability for unauthorized or incorrect processing of data (Article 38);

- (v) shall take part in any amendment of this Convention (Article 43);

- (w) shall be responsible for any other tasks assigned to it by the Council particularly in provisions for the implementation of this Convention.

2. The Management Board shall be composed of one representative of each Member State. Each member of the Management Board shall have one vote.

3. Each member of the Management Board may be represented by an alternate member; in the absence of the full member, the alternate member may exercise his right to vote.

4. The Commission of the European Communities shall be invited to attend meetings of the Management Board with non-voting status. However, the Management Board may decide to meet without the Commission representative.

5. The members or alternate members shall be entitled to be accompanied and advised by experts from their respective Member States at meetings of the Management Board.

6. The Management Board shall be chaired by the representative of the Member State holding the Presidency of the Council.

7. The Management Board shall unanimously adopt its rules of procedure.

8. Abstentions shall not prevent the Management Board from adopting decisions which must be taken unanimously.

9. The Management Board shall meet at least twice a year.

10. The Management Board shall adopt unanimously each year:

- (a) a general report on Europol's activities during the previous year;

- (b) a report on Europol's future activities taking into account Member States' operational requirements and budgetary and staffing implications for Europol.

These reports shall be submitted to the Council in accordance with the procedure laid down in Title VI of the Treaty on European Union.

Article 29

Director

1. Europol shall be headed by a Director appointed by the Council, acting unanimously in accordance with the procedure laid down in Title VI of the Treaty on European Union after obtaining the opinion of the Management Board, for a four-year period renewable once.

2. The Director shall be assisted by a number of Deputy Directors as determined by the Council and appointed for a four-year period renewable once, in accordance with the procedure laid down in paragraph 1. Their tasks shall be defined in greater detail by the Director.

3. The Director shall be responsible for:

   (a) performance of the tasks assigned to Europol;

   (b) day-to-day administration;

   (c) personnel management;

   (d) proper preparation and implementation of the Management Board's decisions;

   (e) preparing the draft budget, draft establishment plan and draft five-year financing plan and implementing Europol's budget

   (f) all other tasks assigned to him in this Convention or by the Management Board.

4. The Director shall be accountable to the Management Board in respect of the performance of his duties. He shall attend its meetings.

5. The Director shall be Europol's legal representative.

6. The Director and the Deputy Directors may be dismissed by a decision of the Council, to be taken in accordance with the procedure laid down in Title VI of the Treaty on European Union by a two-thirds majority of the Member States, after obtaining the opinion of the Management Board.

7. Notwithstanding paragraphs 1 and 2, the first term of office after entry into force of this Convention shall be five years for the Director, four years for his immediate Deputy and three years for the second Deputy Director.

Article 30

Staff

1. The Director, Deputy Directors and the employees of Europol shall be guided in their actions by the objectives and tasks of Europol and shall not take or seek orders from any government, authority, organization or person outside Europol, save as otherwise provided in this Convention and without prejudice to Title VI of the Treaty on European Union.

2. The Director shall be in charge of the Deputy Directors and employees of Europol. He shall engage and dismiss employees. In selecting employees, in addition to having regard to personal suitability and professional qualifications, he shall take into account the need to ensure the adequate representation of nationals of all Member States and of the official languages of the European Union.

3. Detailed arrangements shall be laid down in staff regulations which the Council shall, after obtaining the opinion of the Management Board, adopt unanimously in accordance with the procedure laid down in Title VI of the Treaty on European Union.

Article 31

Confidentiality

1. Europol and the Member States shall take appropriate measures to protect information subject to the requirement of confidentiality which is obtained by or exchanged with Europol on the basis of this Convention. To this end the Council shall unanimously adopt appropriate rules on confidentiality prepared by the Management Board and submitted to the Council in accordance with the procedure laid down in Title VI of the Treaty on European Union.

2. Where Europol has entrusted persons with a sensitive activity, Member States shall undertake to arrange, at the request of the Director of Europol, for security screening of their own nationals to be carried out in accordance with their national provisions and to provide each other with mutual assistance for the purpose. The relevant authority under national provisions shall inform Europol only of the results of the security screening, which shall be binding on Europol.

3. Each Member State and Europol may entrust with the processing of data at Europol, only those persons who have had special training and undergone security screening.

Article 32

Obligation of discretion and confidentiality

1. Europol organs, their members, the Deputy Directors, employees of Europol and liaison officers shall refrain from any action and any expression of opinion which might be harmful to Europol or prejudice its activities.

2. Europol organs, their members, the Deputy Directors, employees of Europol and liaison officers, as well as any other person under a particular obligation of discretion or confidentiality, shall be bound not to disclose any facts or information which come to their knowledge in the performance of their duties or the exercise of their activities to any unauthorized person or to the public. This shall not apply to facts or information too insignificant to require confidentiality. The obligation of discretion and confidentiality shall apply even after leaving office or employment, or after termination of activities. The particular obligation laid down in the first sentence shall be notified by Europol, and a warning given of the legal consequences of any infringement; a written record shall be drawn up of such notification.

3. Europol organs, their members, the Deputy Directors, employees of Europol and liaison officers, as well as persons under the obligation provided for in paragraph 2, may not give evidence in or outside court or make any statements on any facts or information which come to their knowledge in the performance of their duties or the exercise of their activities, without reference to the Director or, in the case of the Director himself, to the Management Board.

The Director or Management Board, depending on the case, shall approach the judicial body or any other competent body with a view to taking the necessary measures under the national law applicable to the body approached; such measures may either be to adjust the procedures for giving evidence in order to ensure the confidentiality of the information, or, provided that the national law concerned so permits, to refuse to make any communication concerning data insofar as is vital for the protection of the interests of Europol or of a Member State.

Where a Member State's legislation provides for the right to refuse to give evidence, persons asked to give evidence must obtain permission to do so. Permission shall be granted by the Director and, as regards evidence to be given by the Director, by the Management Board. Where a liaison officer is asked to give evidence concerning information he receives from Europol such permission shall be given after the agreement of the Member State responsible for the officer concerned has been obtained.

Furthermore, if the possibility exists that the evidence may extend to information and knowledge which a Member State has communicated to Europol or which clearly involve a

Member State, the position of that Member State concerning the evidence must be sought before permission is given.

Permission to give evidence may be refused only insofar as this is necessary to protect overriding interests of Europol or of a Member State or States that need protection.

This obligation shall apply even after leaving office or employment or after termination of activities.

4. Each Member State shall treat any infringement of the obligation of discretion or confidentiality laid down in paragraphs 2 and 3 as a breach of the obligations imposed by its law on official or professional secrets or its provisions for the protection of confidential material.

Where appropriate, each Member State shall introduce, no later than the date of entry into force of this Convention, the rules under national law or the provisions required to proceed against breaches of the obligations of discretion or confidentiality referred to in paragraphs 2 and 3. It shall ensure that the rules and provisions concerned apply also to its own employees who have contact with Europol in the course of their work.

Article 33

Languages

1. Reports and all other papers and documentation placed before the Management Board shall be submitted in all official languages of the European Union; the working languages of the Management Board shall be the official languages of the European Union.

2. The translations required for Europol's work shall be provided by the translation centre of the European Union institutions.

Article 34

Informing the European parliament

1. The Council Presidency shall each year forward a special report to the European Parliament on the work of Europol. The European Parliament shall be consulted should this Convention be amended in any way.

2. The Council Presidency or its representative appointed by the Presidency shall, with respect to the European Parliament, take into account the obligations of discretion and confidentiality.

3. The obligations laid down in this Article shall be without prejudice to the rights of national parliaments, to Article K.6 of the Treaty on European Union and to the general principles applicable to relations with the European Parliament pursuant to Title VI of the Treaty on European Union.

Article 35

Budget

1. Estimates shall be drawn up of all of Europol's income and expenditure including all costs of the joint supervisory body and of the secretariat set up by it under Article 22 for each financial year and these items entered in the budget; an establishment plan shall be appended to the budget. The financial year shall begin on 1 January and end on 31 December.

The income and expenditure shown in the budget shall be in balance.

A five-year financing plan shall be drawn up together with the budget.

2. The budget shall be financed from Member States' contributions and by other incidental income. Each Member State's financial contribution shall be determined according to the proportion of its gross national product to the sum total of the gross national products of the Member States for the year preceding the year in which the budget is drawn up. For the purposes of this paragraph, "gross national product" shall mean gross national product as determined in accordance with Council Directive 89/130/EEC, Euratom of 13 February 1989 on the harmonization of the compilation of gross national product at market prices.

3. By 31 March each year at the latest, the Director shall draw up the draft budget and draft establishment plan for the following financial year and shall submit them, after examination by the Financial Committee, to the Management Board together with the draft five-year financing plan.

4. The Management Board shall take a decision on the five-year financing plan. It shall act unanimously.

5. After obtaining the opinion of the Management Board, the Council shall, in accordance with the procedure laid down in Title VI of the Treaty on European Union, adopt Europol's budget by 30 June of the year preceding the financial year at the latest. It shall act unanimously. The adoption of the budget by the Council shall entail the obligation for each Member State to make available promptly the financial contribution due from it.

6. The Director shall implement the budget in accordance with the financial regulation provided for in paragraph 9.

7. Monitoring of the commitment and disbursement of expenditure and of the establishment and collection of income shall be carried out by a financial controller from an official audit body of one of the Member States who shall be appointed by the Management Board, acting unanimously, and shall be accountable to it. The financial regulation may make provision for ex-post monitoring by the financial controller in the case of certain items of income or expenditure.

8. The Financial Committee shall be composed of one budgetary representative from each Member State. Its task shall be to prepare for discussions on budgetary and financial matters.

9. The Council shall, in accordance with the procedure laid down in Title VI of the Treaty on European Union, unanimously adopt the financial regulation, specifying in particular the detailed rules for drawing up, amending and implementing the budget and for monitoring its implementation as well as for the manner of payment of financial contributions by the Member States.

Article 36

Auditing

1. The accounts in respect of all income and expenditure entered in the budget together with the balance sheet showing Europol's assets and liabilities shall be subject to an annual audit in accordance with the financial regulation. For this purpose the Director shall submit a report on the annual accounts by 31 May of the following year at the latest.

2. The audit shall be carried out by a joint audit committee composed of three members, appointed by the Court of Auditors of the European Communities on a proposal from its President. The term of office of the members shall be three years; these shall alternate in such a way that each year the member who has been on the audit committee for three years shall be replaced. Notwithstanding the provisions of the second sentence, the term of office of the member that, after drawing lots:

- is first, shall be two years;

- is second, shall be three years;

- is third, shall be four years,

in the initial composition of the joint audit committee after Europol has begun to operate.

Any costs arising from the audit shall be charged to the budget provided for in Article 35.

3. The joint audit committee shall in accordance with the procedure laid down in Title VI of the Treaty on European Union submit to the Council an audit report on the annual accounts; prior thereto the Director and Financial Controller shall be given an opportunity to express an opinion on the audit report and the report shall be discussed by the Management Board.

4. The Europol Director shall provide the members of the joint audit committee with all information and every assistance which they require in order to perform their task.

5. A decision on the discharge to be given to the Director in respect of budget implementation for the financial year in question shall be taken by the Council, after examination of the report on the annual accounts.

6. The detailed rules for performing audits shall be laid down in the Financial Regulation.

Article 37

Headquarters agreement

The necessary arrangements concerning the accommodation to be provided for Europol in the headquarters State and the facilities to be made available by that State as well as the particular rules applicable in the Europol headquarters State to members of Europol's organs, its Deputy Directors, employees and members of their families shall be laid down in a headquarters agreement between Europol and the Kingdom of the Netherlands to be concluded after obtaining the unanimous approval of the Management Board.

Title VI

Liability and legal protection

Article 38

Liability for unauthorized or incorrect data processing

1. Each Member State shall be liable, in accordance with its national law, for any damage caused to an individual as a result of legal or factual errors in data stored or processed at Europol. Only the Member State in which the event which gave rise to the damage occurred may be the subject of an action for compensation on the part of the injured party, who shall apply to the courts having jurisdiction under the national law of the Member State involved. A Member State may not plead that another Member State had transmitted inaccurate data in order to avoid its liability under its national legislation vis-à-vis an injured party.

2. If these legal or factual errors occurred as a result of data erroneously communicated or of failure to comply with the obligations laid down in this Convention on the part of one or more Member States or as a result of unauthorized or incorrect storage or processing by Europol, Europol or the other Member State in question shall be bound to repay, on request, the amounts paid as compensation unless the data were used by the Member State in the territory of which the damage was caused in breach of this Convention.

3. Any dispute between that Member State and Europol or another Member State over the principle or amount of the repayment must be referred to the Management Board, which shall settle the matter by a two-thirds majority.

Article 39

Other liability

1. Europol's contractual liability shall be governed by the law applicable to the contract in question.

2. In the case of non-contractual liability, Europol shall be obliged, independently of any liability under Article 38, to make good any damage caused through the fault of its organs, of its Deputy Directors or of its employees in the performance of their duties, insofar as it may be imputed to them and regardless of the different procedures for claiming damages which exist under the law of the Member States.

3. The injured party shall have the right to demand that Europol refrain from or drop any action.

4. The national courts of the Member States competent to deal with disputes involving Europol's liability as referred to in this Article shall be determined by reference to the relevant provisions of the Brussels Convention of 27 September 1968 on Jurisdiction and the Enforcement of Judgments on Civil and Commercial Matters, as later amended by Accession Agreements.

Article 40

Settlement of disputes

1. Disputes between Member States on the interpretation or application of this Convention shall in an initial stage be discussed by the Council in accordance with the procedure set out in Title VI of the Treaty on European Union with the aim of finding a settlement.

2. When such disputes are not so settled within six months, the Member States who are parties to the dispute shall decide, by agreement among themselves, the modalities according to which they shall be settled.

3. The provisions on appeals referred to in the rules relating to the conditions of employment applicable to temporary and auxiliary staff of the European Communities shall apply, mutatis mutandis, to Europol staff.

Article 41

Privileges and immunities

1. Europol, the members of its organs and the Deputy Directors and employees of Europol shall enjoy the privileges and immunities necessary for the performance of their tasks in accordance with a Protocol setting out the rules to be applied in all Member States.

2. The Kingdom of the Netherlands and the other Member States shall agree in the same terms that liaison officers seconded from the other Member States as well as members of their families shall enjoy those privileges and immunities necessary for the proper performance of the tasks of the liaison officers at Europol.

3. The Protocol referred to in paragraph 1 shall be adopted by the Council acting unanimously in accordance with the procedure laid down in Title VI of the Treaty on European Union and approved by the Member States in accordance with their respective constitutional requirements.

Title VII

Final provisions

Article 42

Relations with third states and third bodies

1. Insofar as is relevant for the performance of the tasks described in Article 3, Europol shall establish and maintain cooperative relations with third bodies within the meaning of Article 10(4), points 1 to 3. The Management Board shall unanimously draw up rules governing such relations. This provision shall be without prejudice to Article 10(4) and (5) and Article 18(2); exchanges of personal data shall take place only in accordance with the provisions of Titles II to IV of this Convention.

2. Insofar as is required for the performance of the tasks described in Article 3, Europol may also establish and maintain relations with third States and third bodies within the meaning of Article 10(4), points 4, 5, 6 and 7. Having obtained the opinion of the Management Board, the Council, acting unanimously in accordance with the procedure laid down in Title VI of the Treaty on European Union, shall draw up rules governing the relations referred to in the first sentence. The third sentence of paragraph 1 shall apply mutatis mutandis.

Article 43

Amendment of the convention

1. In accordance with the procedure laid down in Title VI of the Treaty on European Union, the Council, acting on a proposal from a Member State and, after consulting the Management Board, shall unanimously decide, within the framework of Article K.1(9) of the Treaty on European Union, on any amendments to this Convention which it shall recommend to the Member States for adoption in accordance with their respective constitutional requirements.

2. The amendments shall enter into force in accordance with Article 45(2) of this Convention.

3. However, the Council, acting unanimously in accordance with the procedure laid down in Title VI of the Treaty on European Union, may decide, on the initiative of a Member State and after the Management Board has discussed the matter, to amplify, amend or supplement the definitions of forms of crime contained in the Annex. It may in addition decide to introduce new definitions of the forms of crime listed in the Annex.

4. The Secretary-General of the Council of the European Union shall notify all Member States of the date of entry into force of the amendments.

Article 44

Reservations

Reservations shall not be permissible in respect of this Convention.

Article 45

Entry into force

1. This Convention shall be subject to adoption by the Member States in accordance with their respective constitutional requirements.

2. Member States shall notify the depositary of the completion of their constitutional requirements for adopting this Convention.

3. This Convention shall enter into force on the first day of the month following the expiry of a three-month period after the notification, referred to in paragraph 2, by the Member State which, being a member of the European Union on the date of adoption by the Council of the act drawing up this Convention, is the last to fulfil that formality.

4. Without prejudice to paragraph 2, Europol shall not take up its activities under this Convention until the last of the acts provided for in Articles 5(7), 10(1), 24(7), 30(3), 31(1), 35(9), 37 and 41(1) and (2) enters into force.

5. When Europol takes up its activities, the activities of the Europol Drugs Unit under the joint action concerning the Europol Drugs Unit of 10 March 1995 shall come to an end. At the same time, all equipment financed from the Europol Drugs Unit joint budget, developed or produced by the Europol Drugs Unit of placed at its disposal free of charge by the headquarters State for its permanent use, together with that Unit's entire archives and independently administered data files shall become the property of Europol.

6. Once the Council has adopted the act drawing up this Convention, Member States, acting either individually or in common, shall take all preparatory measures under their national law which are necessary for the commencement of Europol activities.

Article 46

Accession by new member states

1. This Convention shall be open to accession by any State that becomes a member of the European Union.

2. The text of this Convention in the language of the acceding State, drawn up by the Council of the European Union, shall be authentic.

3. Instruments of accession shall be deposited with the depositary.

4. This Convention shall enter into force with respect to any State that accedes to it on the first day of the month following expiry of a three-month period following the date of deposit of its instrument of accession or on the date of entry into force of the Convention if it has not already entered into force at the time of expiry of the said period.

Article 47

Depositary

1. The Secretary-General of the Council of the European Union shall act as depositary of this Convention.

2. The depositary shall publish in the Official Journal of the European Communities the notifications, instruments or communications concerning this Convention.

IN WITNESS WHEREOF the undersigned Plenipotentiaries have signed this Convention.

DONE at Brussels, this twenty-sixth day of July in the year one thousand nine hundred and ninety-five, in a single original in the Danish, Dutch, English, Finnish, French, German, Greek, Irish, Italian, Portuguese, Spanish and Swedish languages, each text being equally authentic; it shall be deposited with the Secretary-General of the Council of the European Union, which shall transmit a certified copy to each of the Member States.

ANNEX

Referred to in article 2

List of other serious forms of international crime which Europol would deal with in addition to those already provided for in Article 2(2) in compliance with Europol's objective as set out in Article 2(1).

Against life, limb or personal freedom:

- murder, grievous bodily injury
- illicit trade in human organs and tissue
- kidnapping, illegal restraint and hostage-taking
- racism and xenophobia

Against property or public goods including fraud:

- organized robbery
- illicit trafficking in cultural goods, including antiquities and works of art
- swindling and fraud
- racketeering and extortion
- counterfeiting and product piracy
- forgery of administrative documents and trafficking therein
- forgery of money and means of payment
- computer crime
- corruption

Illegal trading and harm to the environment:

- illicit trafficking in arms, ammunition and explosives
- illicit trafficking in endangered animals species
- illicit trafficking in endangered plant species and varieties
- environmental crime
- illicit trafficking in hormonal substances and other growth promotors.

In addition, in accordance with Article 2(2), the act of instructing Europol to deal with one of the forms of crime listed above implies that it is also competent to deal with the related money-laundering activities and the related criminal offences.

With regard to the forms of crime listed in Article 2(2) for the purpose of this Convention:

- "crime connected with nuclear and radioactive substances" means the criminal offences listed in Article 7(1) of the Convention on the Physical Protection of Nuclear Material, signed at Vienna and New York on 3 March 1980, and relating to the nuclear and/or radioactive materials defined in Article 197 of the Euratom Treaty and Directive 80/836 Euratom of 15 July 1980;

- "illegal immigrant smuggling" means activities intended deliberately to facilitate, for financial gain, the entry into, residence or employment in the territory of the Member States of the European Union, contrary to the rules and conditions applicable in the Member States;

- "traffic in human beings" means subjection of a person to the real and illegal sway of other persons by using violence or menaces or by abuse of authority or intrigue with a view to the exploitation of prostitution, forms of sexual exploitation and assault of minors or trade in abandoned children;

- "motor vehicle crime" means the theft or misappropriation of motor vehicles, lorries, semi-trailers, the loads of lorries or semi-trailers, buses, motorcycles, caravans and agricultural vehicles, works vehicles, and the spare parts for such vehicles, and the receiving and concealing of such objects;

- "illegal money-laundering activities" means the criminal offences listed in Article 6(1) to (3) of the Council of Europe Convention on Laundering, Search, Seizure and Confiscation of the Proceeds from Crime, signed at Strasbourg on 8 November 1990.

The forms of crime referred to in Article 2 and in this Annex shall be assessed by the competent national authorities in accordance with the national law of the Member States to which they belong.

Declarations

Article 40(2)

"The following Member States agree that in such cases they will systematically submit the dispute in question to the Court of Justice of the European Communities:

- Kingdom of Belgium
- Kingdom of Denmark
- Federal Republic of Germany
- Hellenic Republic
- Kingdom of Spain
- French Republic
- Ireland
- Italian Republic
- Grand Duchy of Luxembourg
- Kingdom of the Netherlands
- Republic of Austria
- Portuguese Republic
- Republic of Finland
- Kingdom of Sweden".

3.2. Administrative Cooperation

EC Council Regulation No 1468/81 of 19 May 1981 on Mutual Assistance between the Administrative Authorities of the Member States and Cooperation between the Latter and the Commission to Ensure the Correct Application of the Law on Customs or Agricultural Matters (1981)[*]

Brussels, 19 May 1981, as amended 30 March 1987.

THE COUNCIL OF THE EUROPEAN COMMUNITIES,

HAS ADOPTED THIS REGULATION:

Article 1

1. This Regulation lays down the ways in which the administrative authorities responsible in the Member States for the application of the law on customs or agricultural matters shall cooperate with those in the other Member States and with the Commission in order to ensure compliance with the law.

2. The provisions of this Regulation shall not apply to the extent that they overlap with those of Regulations (EEC) No 283/72 and (EEC) No 359/79.

Article 2

1. For the purposes of this Regulation:

 (a) 'the law on customs matters' shall mean all Community provisions and provisions which contribute to the application of Community rules governing the import, export, transit and presence of goods forming the subject of trade between the Member States and between the latter and third countries.

 (b) 'the law on agricultural matters' shall mean all provisions adopted in the context of the common agricultural policy and all specific rules adopted, pursuant to Article 235 of the Treaty, with regard to goods resulting from the processing of agricultural products.

 (c) 'applicant authority' shall mean the competent authority of a Member State which makes a request for assistance.

 (d) 'requested authority' shall mean the competent authority of a Member State to which a request for assistance is made.

2. Each Member State shall communicate to the other Member States and to the Commission a list of the competent authorities which are appointed to act as correspondents for the purposes of applying this Regulation.

In this Regulation 'competent authorities' shall mean those authorities appointed to act as correspondents under the first subparagraph.

---

[*] *Official Journal of the European Communities*, No L 144, 2.6.1981, p.1 and *Official Journal of the European Communities*, No L 90, 2.4.1987, p.3 (amendments).

Article 3

The obligation to provide assistance laid down by this Regulation shall not cover the provision of information or documents obtained by the administrative authorities referred to in Article 1 (1) under powers exercised by them at the request of the judicial authority.

However, in the case of an application for assistance, such information or documents shall be provided in all cases where the judicial authority, which must be consulted to that effect, gives its consent.

Title 1

Assistance on request

Article 4

1. At the request of the applicant authority, the requested authority shall communicate to it all information likely to enable the former to ensure compliance with the provisions laid down by the law on customs or agricultural matters and in particular those concerning:

(a) the application of customs duties and charges having equivalent effect as well as agricultural levies and other charges laid down within the framework of the common agricultural policy or of the specific arrangements applicable, pursuant to Article 235 of the Treaty, to certain goods resulting from the processing of agricultural products.

(b) operations forming part of the system of financing by the European Agricultural Guidance and Guarantee Fund.

2. In order to obtain this information, the requested authority or the administrative authority which it has addressed shall proceed as though it were acting on its own account or at the request of another authority in its own country.

Article 5

At the request of the applicant authority, the requested authority shall supply to it any attestation, document or official copy of a document which it has or which it obtains in the manner referred to in Article 4 (2) and which relates to operations covered by the law on customs or agricultural matters.

Article 6

1. At the request of the applicant authority, the requested authority shall, while observing the rules in force in the Member State in which it is situated, notify the addressee or have him notified of all instruments or decisions which emanate from the administrative authorities and concern the application of the law on customs or agricultural matters.

2. Requests for notification, mentioning the subject of the act or decision to be communicated, shall be accompanied by a translation in the official language or one of the official languages of the Member State in which the requested authority is situated, without prejudice to the latter's right to waive such a translation.

Article 7

At the request of the applicant authority, the requested authority shall as far as possible keep a special watch or arrange for a special watch to be kept within its operational area:

(a) on persons of whom there are reasonable grounds for believing that they are contraveners of the law on customs or agricultural matters and, more particularly, on the movements of such persons;

(b) on places where stocks of goods have been assembled in such a way that there are reasonable grounds for supposing that they are intended as supplies for operations contrary to the law on customs or agricultural matters;

(c) on movements of goods notified as possibly constituting operations contrary to the law on customs or agricultural matters;

(d) on means of transport for which there are reasonable grounds for believing that they are used for carrying out operations contrary to the law on customs or agricultural matters.

Article 8

At the request of the applicant authority, the requested authority shall supply to it any information in its possession or which it can obtain as prescribed in Article 4 (2), in particular in the form of reports and other documents or official copies of or extracts from such reports or documents, concerning operations detected or planned which are or appear to the applicant authority to be contrary to the law on customs or agricultural matters.

However, such communication shall be in the form of original documents and property only if the provisions in force in the Member States in which the requested authority has its headquarters do not preclude this.

Article 9

1. At the request of the applicant authority, the requested authority shall carry out appropriate enquiries or arrange for such enquiries to be carried out concerning operations which are or appear to the applicant authority to be contrary to the law on customs or agricultural matters.

In order to carry out these enquiries the requested authority or the administrative authority which it has addressed shall proceed as though it were acting on its own account or at the request of another authority in its own country.

The requested authority shall communicate the results of these enquiries to the applicant authority.

2. By agreement between the applicant authority and the requested authority, officials designated by the applicant authority may be present at the enquiries referred to in paragraph 1.

Article 10

By agreement between the applicant authority and the requested authority and in accordance with the arrangements laid down by the latter, officials duly authorized by the applicant authority may obtain, from the offices where the administrative authorities of the Member State in which the requested authority is situated exercise their functions, information concerning the application of the law on customs or agricultural matters which is needed by the applicant authority and which is derived from documentation to which the staff of those offices have access. These officials shall be authorised to take copies of the said documentation.

Title 2

Spontaneous assistance

Article 11

The competent authorities of each Member State shall, as laid down in Articles 12 and 13, provide assistance to the competent authorities of the other Member States without prior request of the latter.

Article 12

Where they consider it useful in connection with compliance with the law on customs or agricultural matters, the competent authorities of each Member State shall:

(a) as far as possible keep the special watch provided for in Article 7 or arrange for such watch to be kept;

(b) communicate to the competent authorities of the other Member States concerned all available information, in particular in the form of reports and other documents or copies of or extracts from such reports or documents, concerning operations which are or appear to be contrary to the law on customs or agricultural matters.

Article 13

The competent authorities of each Member State shall immediately send to the competent authorities of the other Member States concerned all information of use in connection with operations which are contrary or appear to them to be contrary to the law on customs or agricultural matters and in particular information concerning goods that are covered by it and new means or methods used to carry out such operations.

Title 3

Final provisions

Article 14

1. The competent authorities of each Member State shall communicate to the Commission as soon as it is available to them:

(a) any information they consider useful concerning:

(i) goods which have been or are suspected of having been the subject of transactions contrary to the law on customs or agricultural matters;

(ii) the methods or processes used or suspected of having been used to contravene the law on customs or agricultural matters;

(b) any information on deficiencies of, or lacunae in, the rules on customs or agricultural matters which their application has revealed or suggested.

2. The Commission shall communicate to the competent authorities of each Member State, as soon as it is available to it, any information which is such as to enable compliance with the law on customs or agricultural matters to be enforced.

Article 14a

1. Where the competent authorities of a Member State become aware of operations which are, or appear to be, contrary to the law on customs or agricultural matters and which are of particular interest at Community level, and in particular:

(a) where they have, or might have, ramifications in other Member States, or

(b) where it appears to the said authorities likely that similar operations have been also carried out in other Member States,

they shall pass on to the Commission as quickly as possible, either on their own initiative or at the reasoned request of the Commission, all relevant information, where appropriate in the form of documents or copies or extracts from documents, necessary to determine the facts so as to enable the Commission to coordinate the action undertaken by the Member States.

The Commission shall pass this information on to the competent authorities of the other Member States.

2. Information relating to natural or legal persons shall be communicated as provided for in paragraph 1 only to the extent strictly necessary to enable operations which are contrary to the law on customs or agricultural matters to be noted.

3. Where the competent authorities of a Member State make use of paragraph 1, they need not communicate information as provided in Article 12 (b) and in Article 13 to the competent authorities of the other Member States concerned'.

Article 15

The Commission shall organize meetings with the representatives of the Member States during which:

- (a) the operation of the mutual assistance arrangements provided for in this Regulation shall be examined in general terms,

- (b) a practical procedure for forwarding the information referred to in Articles 14 and 14a shall be laid down,

- (c) the information sent to the Commission pursuant to Articles 14 and 14a shall be examined with a view to drawing the relevant conclusions, determining the measures required to put an end to any operations found to be contrary to the law on customs or agricultural matters and, where necessary, suggesting amendments to existing Community provisions or the drawing up of additional ones.

Article 15a

Provided the third country concerned has given a legal undertaking to provide the assistance required to gather proof of the irregular nature of operations which appear to be contrary to the law on customs or agricultural matters or to determine the scope, of operations which have been noted as being contrary to such law, the information obtained pursuant to Article 14a may be communicated to the third country concerned, with the agreement of the competent authorities of the Member State which supplied it and, if necessary, with the agreement of the person concerned in so far as this does not jeopardize the successful outcome of the investigation.

The communication may be made by the Commission, which in that case shall by appropriate means ensure protection equivalent to that laid down in Article 19 (1).

Article 15b

1. For the purposes of attaining the objectives of this Regulation the Commission may, under the conditions laid down in Article 15a, carry out Community administrative and investigative missions in third countries in coordination and close cooperation with the competent authorities of the Member States.

2. The Community missions in third countries referred to in paragraph 1 shall be carried out under the following conditions:

- (a) missions may be undertaken on the Commission's initiative or at the request of one or more Member States;

- (b) missions shall be carried out by Commission representatives designated for that purpose and by officials designated for that purpose by the Member State or Member States concerned;

- (c) a mission may also, with the agreement of the Commission and the Member States concerned, be carried out in the Community interest by officials of a Member State, in particular under a bilateral assistance agreement with a third country; in that event the Commission shall be informed of the results of the mission;

(d) mission expenses shall be paid by the Commission.

3. The Commission shall inform the Member States of the results of missions carried out in pursuance of this Article.

Article 15c

The findings established and the information obtained in the context of the Community missions referred to in Article 15b, particularly in the form of documents passed on by the competent authorities of the third countries concerned, shall be dealt with in accordance with Article 19.

Original documents obtained or certified copies thereof shall be delivered by the Commission to the competent authorities of the Member States, at the said authorities' request, for use in connection with judicial proceedings or proceedings instituted for failure to comply with the law on customs or agricultural matters'.

Article 16

For the purposes of applying this Regulation, Member States shall take all the necessary steps to:

(a) ensure sound internal coordination between the administrative authorities referred to in Article 1 (1);

(b) establish direct cooperation in their mutual relations as necessary, between the authorities specially empowered to this end;

(c) decide jointly, to the extent necessary, on suitable arrangements for ensuring the smooth operation of the mutual assistance arrangements provided for in this Regulation.

Article 17

1. This Regulation shall not bind the administrative authorities of the Member States to grant each other assistance where to do so would be likely to prejudice public policy or any other fundamental interests of the State in which they are situated.

2. Reasons shall be stated for any refusal to grant assistance.

Article 18

The documents provided for in this Regulation may be replaced by computerized information produced in any form for the same purpose.

Article 19

1. Any information communicated in whatever form pursuant to this Regulation shall be of a confidential nature. It shall be covered by the obligation of professional secrecy and shall enjoy the protection extended to like information under both the national law of the Member State which received it and the corresponding provisions applying to the Community authorities.

The information referred to in the first subparagraph may not in particular be sent to persons other than those in the Member States or within the Community institutions whose duties require that they have access to it. Nor may it be used for purposes other than those provided for in this Regulation, unless the authority supplying it has expressly agreed and in so far as the provisions in force in the Member State where the authority which received it is situated do not preclude such communication or use.

2. Paragraph 1 shall not impede the use, in any legal actions or proceedings subsequently instituted in respect of non-compliance with the law on customs or agricultural matters, of information obtained pursuant to this Regulation.

The Competent authority of the Member State which supplied this information shall be informed forthwith of such utilization.

Article 20

Member States shall communicate to the Commission the bilateral mutual assistance agreements between customs administrations concluded with third countries.

Article 21

Member States shall waive all claims for the reimbursement of expenses incurred pursuant to this Regulation except, as appropriate, in respect of fees paid to experts.

Article 22

This Regulation shall not affect the application in the Member States of the rules on mutual assistance in criminal matters.

Article 23

This Regulation shall enter into force on 1 July 1981.

This Regulation shall be binding in its entirety and directly applicable in all Member States.

3.3. Judicial Cooperation

UN Model Treaty on Mutual Assistance in Criminal Matters (1990)[*]

New York, 14 December 1990

Article 1

Scope of application [1]

1. The Parties shall, in accordance with the present Treaty, afford to each other the widest possible measure of mutual assistance in investigations or court proceedings in respect of offences the punishment of which at the time of the request for assistance, falls within the jurisdiction of the judicial authorities of the requesting State.

2. Mutual assistance to be afforded in accordance with the present Treaty may include:

   (a) Taking evidence or statements from persons;

   (b) Assisting in the availability of detained persons or others to give evidence or assist in investigations;

   (c) Effecting service of judicial documents;

   (d) Executing searches and seizures;

   (e) Examining objects and sites;

   (f) Providing information and evidentiary items;

   (g) Providing originals or certified copies of relevant documents and records, including bank, financial, corporate or business records.

3. The present Treaty does not apply to:

   (a) The arrest or detention of any person with a view to the extradition of that person;

   (b) The enforcement in the requested State of criminal judgements imposed in the requesting State except to the extent permitted by the law of the requested State and the Optional Protocol to the present Treaty;

   (c) The transfer of persons in custody to serve sentences;

   (d) The transfer of proceedings in criminal matters.

---

[*] General Assembly resolution 45/117 of 14 December 1990, *Compendium of United Nations Standards and Norms in Crime Prevention and Criminal Justice*, New York, United Nations, 1992, 61; *International Legal Materials*, 1991, 1421.

[1] Additions to the scope of assistance to be provided, such as provisions covering information on sentences passed on nationals of the Parties, can be considered bilaterally. Obviously, such assistance must be compatible with the law of the requested State.

Article 2 [2]

Other arrangements

Unless the Parties decide otherwise, the present Treaty shall not affect obligations subsisting between them whether pursuant to other treaties or arrangements or otherwise.

Article 3

Designation of competent authorities

Each Party shall designate and indicate to the other Party an authority or authorities by or through which requests for the purpose of the present Treaty should be made or received.

Article 4 [3]

Refusal of assistance

1. Assistance may be refused if: [4]

    (a) The requested State is of the opinion that the request, if granted, would prejudice its sovereignty, security, public order (*ordre public*) or other essential public interests;

    (b) The offence is regarded by the requested State as being of a political nature;

    (c) There are substantial grounds for believing that the request for assistance has been made for the purpose of prosecuting a person on account of that person's race, sex, religion, nationality, ethnic origin or political opinions or that that person's position may be prejudiced for any of those reasons;

    (d) The request relates to an offence that is subject to investigation or prosecution in the requested State or the prosecution of which in the requesting State would be incompatible with the requested State's law on double jeopardy (*ne bis in idem*);

    (e) The assistance requested requires the requested State to carry out compulsory measures that would be inconsistent with its law and practice had the offence been the subject of investigation or prosecution under its own jurisdiction;

    (f) The act is an offence under military law, which is not also an offence under ordinary criminal law.

2. Assistance shall not be refused solely on the ground of secrecy of banks and similar financial institutions.

3. The requested State may postpone the execution of the request if its immediate execution would interfere with an ongoing investigation or persecution in the requested State.

---

[2] Article 2 recognizes the continuing role of informal assistance between law enforcement agencies and associated agencies in different countries.

[3] Article 4 provides an illustrative list of the grounds for refusal.

[4] Some countries may wish to delete or modify some of the provisions or include other grounds for refusal, such as those related to the nature of the offence (e.g. fiscal), the nature of the applicable penalty (e.g. capital punishment), requirements of shared concepts (e.g. double jurisdiction, no lapse of time) or specific kinds of assistance (e.g. interception of telecommunications, performing deoxyribonucleic-acid (DNA) tests). In particular, some countries may wish to include as grounds for refusal the fact that the act on which the request is based would not be an offence if committed in the territory of the requested State (dual criminality).

4. Before refusing a request or postponing its execution, the requested State shall consider whether assistance may be granted subject to certain conditions. If the requesting State accepts assistance subject to these conditions, it shall comply with them.

5. Reasons shall be given for any refusal or postponement of mutual assistance.

Article 5

Contents of requests

1. Requests for assistance shall include: [5]

   (a) The name of the requesting office and the competent authority conducting the investigation or court proceedings to which the request relates;

   (b) The purpose of the request and a brief description of the assistance sought;

   (c) A description of the facts alleged to constitute the offence and a statement or text of the relevant laws, except in cases of a request for service of documents;

   (d) The name and address of the person to be served, where necessary;

   (e) The reasons for and details of any particular procedure or requirement that the requesting State wishes to be followed, including a statement as to whether sworn or affirmed evidence or statements are required;

   (f) Specification of any time-limit within which compliance with the request is desired;

   (g) Such other information as is necessary for the proper execution of the request.

2. Requests, supporting documents and other communications made pursuant to the present Treaty shall be accompanied by a translation into the language of the requested State or another language acceptable to that State.

3. If the requested State considers that the information contained in the request is not sufficient to enable the request to be dealt with, it may request additional information.

Article 6

Execution of requests [6]

Subject to article 19 of the present Treaty, requests for assistance shall be carried out promptly, in the manner provided for by the law and practice of the requested State. To the extent consistent with its law and practice, the requested State shall carry out the request in the manner specified by the requesting State.

Article 7

Return of material to the requested State

Any property, as well as original records or documents, handed over to the requesting State under the present Treaty shall be returned to the requested State as soon as possible unless the latter waives its right of return thereof.

---

[5] This list can be reduced or expanded in bilateral negotiations.

[6] More detailed provisions may be included concerning the provision of information on the time and place of execution of the request and requiring the requested State to inform promptly the requesting State in cases where significant delay is likely to occur or where a decision is made not to comply with the request and the reasons for refusal.

Article 8 [7]

Limitation on use

The requesting State shall not, without the consent of the requested State, use or transfer information or evidence provided by the requested State for investigations or proceedings other than those stated in the request. However, in cases where the charge is altered, the material provided may be used in so far as the offence, as charged, is an offence in respect of which mutual assistance could be provided under the present Treaty.

Article 9

Protection of confidentiality [8]

Upon request:

(a) The requested State shall use its best endeavours to keep confidential the request for assistance, its contents and its supporting documents as well as the fact of granting of such assistance. If the request cannot be executed without breaching confidentiality, the requested State shall so inform the requesting State, which shall then determine whether the request should nevertheless be executed;

(b) The requesting State shall keep confidential evidence and information provided by the requested State, except to the extent that the evidence and information is needed for the investigation and proceedings described in the request.

Article 10

Service of documents [9]

1. The requested State shall effect service of documents that are transmitted to it for this purpose by the requesting State.

2. A request to effect service of summonses shall be made to a requested State not less than [...] [10] days before the date on which the appearance of a person is required. In urgent cases, the requested State may waive the time requirement.

---

[7] Some countries may wish to omit article 8 or modify it, e.g. restrict it to fiscal offences.

[8] Provisions relating to confidentiality will be important for many countries but may present problems to others. The nature of the provisions in individual treaties can be determined in bilateral negotiations.

[9] More detailed provisions relating to the service of documents, such as writs and judicial verdicts, can be determined bilaterally. Provisions may be desired for the service of documents by mail or other manner and for the forwarding of proof of service of the documents. For example, proof of service could be given by means of a receipt dated and signed by the person served or by means of a declaration made by the requested State that service has been effected, with an indication of the form and date of such service. One or other of these documents could be sent promptly to the requesting State. The requested State could, if the requesting State so requests, state whether service has been effected in accordance with the law of the requested State. If service could not be effected, the reasons could be communicated promptly by the requested State to the requesting State.

[10] Depending on travel distance and related arrangements.

Article 11 [11]

Obtaining of evidence

1. The requested State shall, in conformity with its law and upon request, take the sworn or affirmed testimony, or otherwise obtain statements of persons or require them to produce items of evidence for transmission to the requesting State.

2. Upon the request of the requesting State, the parties to the relevant proceedings in the requesting State, their legal representatives and representatives of the requesting State may, subject to the laws and procedures of the requested State, be present at the proceedings.

Article 12

Right or obligation to decline to give evidence

1. A person who is required to give evidence in the requested or requesting State may decline to give evidence where either:

    (a) The law of the requested State permits or requires that person to decline to give evidence in similar circumstances in proceedings originating in the requested State; or

    (b) The law of the requesting State permits or requires that person to decline to give evidence in similar circumstances in proceedings originating in the requesting State.

2. If a person claims that there is a right or obligation to decline to give evidence under the law of the other State, the State where that person is present shall, with respect thereto, rely on a certificate of the competent authority of the other State as evidence of the existence or non-existence of that right or obligation.

Article 13

Availability of persons in custody to give evidence or to assist in investigations [12]

1. Upon the request of the requesting State, and if the requested State agrees and its law so permits, a person in custody in the latter State may, subject to his or her consent, be temporarily transferred to the requesting State to give evidence or to assist in the investigations.

2. While the person transferred is required to be held in custody under the law of the requested State, the requesting State shall hold that person in custody and shall return that person in custody to the requested State at the conclusion of the matter in relation to which transfer was sought or at such earlier time as the person's presence is no longer required.

3. Where the requested State advises the requesting State that the transferred person is no longer required to be held in custody, that person shall be set at liberty and be treated as a person referred to in article 14 of the present Treaty.

---

[11] Article 11 is concerned with the obtaining of evidence in judicial proceedings, the taking of a person's statement by a less formal process and the production of items of evidence.

[12] In bilateral negotiations, provisions may also be introduced to deal with such matters as the modalities and time of restitution of evidence and the setting of a time-limit for the presence of the person in custody in the requesting State.

Article 14

Availability of other persons to give evidence or assist in investigations [13]

1. The requesting State may request the assistance of the requested State in inviting a person:

    (a) To appear in proceedings in relation to a criminal matter in the requesting State unless that person is the person charged; or

    (b) To assist in the investigations in relation to a criminal matter in the requesting State.

2. The requested State shall invite the person to appear as a witness or expert in proceedings or to assist in the investigations. Where appropriate, the requested State shall satisfy itself that satisfactory arrangements have been made for the person's safety.

3. The request or the summons shall indicate the approximate allowances and the travel and subsistence expenses payable by the requesting State.

4. Upon request, the requested State may grant the person an advance, which shall be refunded by the requesting State.

Article 15 [14]

Safe conduct

1. Subject to paragraph 2 of the present article, where a person is in the requesting State pursuant to a request made under article 13 or 14 of the present Treaty:

    (a) That person shall not be detained, prosecuted, punished or subjected to any other restrictions of personal liberty in the requesting State in respect of any acts or omissions or convictions that preceded the person's departure from the requested State;

    (b) That person shall not, without that person's consent, be required to give evidence in any proceeding or to assist in any investigation other than the proceeding or investigation to which the request relates.

2. Paragraph 1 of the present article shall cease to apply if that person, being free to leave, has not left the requesting State within a period of [15] consecutive days, or any longer period otherwise agreed on by the Parties, after that person has been officially told or notified that his or her presence is no longer required or, having left, has voluntarily returned.

3. A person who does not consent to a request pursuant to article 13 or accept an invitation pursuant to article 14 shall not, by reason thereof, be liable to any penalty or be subjected to any coercive measure, notwithstanding any contrary statement in the request or summons.

---

[13] Provisions relating to the payment of the expenses of the person providing assistance are contained in paragraph 3 of article 14. Additional details, such as provision for the payment of costs in advance, can be the subject of bilateral negotiations.

[14] The provisions in article 15 may be required as the only way of securing important evidence in proceedings involving serius national and transnational crime. However, as they may raise difficulties for some countries, the precise content of the article, including any additions or modifications, can be determined in bilateral negotiations.

Article 16

Provision of publicly available documents and other records [15]

1. The requested State shall provide copies of documents and records in so far as they are open to public access as part of a public register or otherwise, or in so far as they are available for purchase or inspection by the public.

2. The requested State may provide copies of any other document or record under the same conditions as such document or record may be provided to its own law enforcement and judicial authorities.

Article 17

Search and seizure [16]

The requested State shall, in so far as its law permits, carry out requests for search and seizure and delivery of any material to the requesting State for evidentiary purposes, provided that the rights of *bona fide* third parties are protected.

Article 18

Certification and authentication [17]

A request for assistance and the documents in support thereof, as well as documents or other material supplied in response to such a request, shall not require certification or authentication.

Article 19

Costs [18]

The ordinary costs of executing a request shall be borne by the requested State, unless otherwise determined by the Parties. If expenses of a substantial or extraordinary nature are or will be required to execute the request, the Parties shall consult in advance to determine the terms and conditions under which the request shall be executed as well as the manner in which the costs shall be borne.

---

[15] The question may arise as to whether this should be discretionary. This provision can be the subject of bilateral negotiations.

[16] Bilateral arrangements may cover the provision of information on the results of search and seizure and the observance of conditions imposed in relation to the delivery of seized property.

[17] The laws of some countries require authentication before documents transmitted from other countries can be admitted in their courts, and, therefore, would require a clause setting out the authentication required.

[18] More detailed provisions may be included, for example, the requested State would meet the ordinary cost of fulfilling the request for assistance except that the requesting State would bear (a) the exceptional or extraordinary expenses required to fulfil the request, where required by the requested State and subject to previous consultations; (b) the expenses associated with conveying any person to or from the territory of the requested State, and any fees, allowances or expenses payable to that person while in the requesting State pursuant to a request under article 11, 13 or 14; (c) the expenses associated with conveying custodial or escorting officers; and(d) the expenses involved in obtaining reports of experts.

Article 20

Consultation

The Parties shall consult promptly, at the request of either, concerning the interpretation, the application or the carrying out of the present Treaty either generally or in relation to a particular case.

Article 21

Final provisions

1. The present Treaty is subject to (ratification, acceptance or approval). The instruments of [ratification, acceptance or approval] shall be exchanged as soon as possible.

2. The present Treaty shall enter into force on the thirtieth day after the day on which the instruments of [ratification, acceptance or approval] are exchanged.

3. The present Treaty shall apply to requests made after its entry into force, even if the relevant acts or omissions occurred prior to that date.

4. Either Contracting Party may denounce the present Treaty by giving notice in writing to the other Party. Such denunciation shall take effect six months following the date on which it is received by the other Party.

Optional Protocol to the UN Model Treaty on Mutual Assistance in Criminal Matters concerning the Proceeds of Crime (1990)[*][1]

New York, 14 December 1990

1. In the present Protocol "proceeds of crime" means any property suspected, or found by a court, to be property directly or indirectly derived or realized as a result of the commission of an offence or to represent the value of property and other benefits derived from the commission of an offence.

2. The requested State shall, upon request, endeavour to ascertain whether any proceeds of the alleged crime are located within its jurisdiction and shall notify the requesting State of the results of its inquiries. In making the request, the requesting State shall notify the requested State of the basis of its belief that such proceeds may be located within its jurisdiction.

3. In pursuance of a request made under paragraph 2 of the present Protocol, the requested State shall endeavour to trace assets, investigate financial dealings, and obtain other information or evidence that may help to secure the recovery of proceeds of crime.

4. Where, pursuant to paragraph 2 of the present Protocol, suspected proceeds of crime are found, the requested State shall upon request take such measures as are permitted by its law to prevent any dealing in, transfer or disposal of, those suspected proceeds of crime, pending a final determination in respect of those proceeds by a court of the requesting State.

5. The requested State shall, to the extent permitted by its law, give effect to or permit enforcement of a final order forfeiting or confiscating the proceeds of crime made by a court of the requesting State or take other appropriate action to secure the proceeds following a request by the requesting State. [2]

6. The Parties shall ensure that the rights of *bona fida* third parties shall be respected in the application of the present Protocol.

---

[*] General Assembly resolution 45/117 of 14 December 1990, *Compendium of United Nations Standards and Norms in Crime Prevention and Criminal Justice*, New York, United Nations, 1992, 74; *International Legal Materials*, 1991, 1432.

[1] The present Optional Protocol is included on the ground that questions of forfeiture are conceptually different from, although closely related to, matters generally accepted as falling within the description of mutual assistance. However, States may wish to include these provisions in the text because of their importance in dealing with organized crime. Moreover, assistance in forfeiting the proceeds of crime has now emerged as a new instrument in international co-operation. Provisions similar to those outlined in the present Protocol appear in many bilateral assistance treaties. Further details can be provided in bilateral arrangements. One matter that could be considered is the need for other provisions dealing with issues related to bank secrecy. An addition could, for example, be made to paragraph 4 of the present Protocol providing that the requested State shall, upon request, take such measures as are permitted by its law to require compliance with monitoring orders by financial institutions. Provision could be made for the sharing of the proceeds of crime between the Contracting States or for consideration of the disposal of the proceeds on a case-by-case basis.

[2] The Parties might consider widening the scope of the present Protocol by the inclusion of references to victims' restitution and the recovery of fines imposed as a sentence in a criminal prosecution.

European Convention on Mutual Assistance in Criminal Matters (1959)[*]

Strasbourg, 20 April 1959

Chapter I

General Provisions

Article 1

1. The Contracting Parties undertake to afford each other, in accordance with the provisions of this Convention, the widest measure of mutual assistance in proceedings in respect of offences the punishment of which, at the time of the request for assistance, falls within the jurisdiction of the judicial authorities of the requesting Party.

2. This convention does not apply to arrests, the enforcement of verdicts or offences under military law which are not offences under ordinary criminal law.

Article 2

Assistance may be refused:

(a) if the request concerns an offence which the requested Party considers a political offence, an offence connected with a political offence, or a fiscal offence;

(b) if the requested Party considers that execution of the request is likely to prejudice the sovereignty, security, ordre public or other essential interests of its country.

Chapter II

Letters rogatory

Article 3

1. The requested Party shall execute in the manner provided for by its law any letters rogatory relating to a criminal matter and addressed to it by the judicial authorities of the requesting Party for the purpose of procuring evidence or transmitting articles to be produced in evidence, records or documents.

2. If the requesting Party desires witnesses or experts to give evidence on oath, it shall expressly so request, and the requested Party shall comply with the request if the law of its country does not prohibit it.

3. The requested Party may transmit certified copies or certified photostat copies of records or documents requested, unless the requesting Party expressly requests the transmission of originals, in which case the requested Party shall make every effort to comply with the request.

Article 4

On the express request of the requesting Party the requested Party shall state the date and place of execution of the letters rogatory. Officials and interested persons may be present if the requested Party consents.

---

[*] *European Treaty Series*, No.30.

Article 5

1. Any Contracting Party may, by a declaration addressed to the Secretary-General of the Council of Europe, when signing this Convention or depositing its instrument of ratification or accession, reserve the right to make the execution of letters rogatory for search or seizure of property dependent on one or more of the following conditions:

- (a) that the offence motivating the letters rogatory is punishable under both the law of the requesting Party and the law of the requested Party;
- (b) that the offence motivating the letters rogatory is an extraditable offence in the requested country;
- (c) that execution of the letters rogatory is consistent with the law of the requested Party.

2. Where a Contracting Party makes a declaration in accordance with paragraph 1 of this Article, any other Party may apply reciprocity.

Article 6

1. The requested Party may delay the handing over of any property, records or documents requested, if it required the said property, records or documents in connection with pending criminal proceedings.

2. Any property, as well as original records or documents, handed over in execution of letters rogatory shall be returned by the requesting Party to the requested Party as soon as possible unless the latter Party waives the return thereof.

Chapter III

Service of Writs and Records of Judicial Verdicts - Appearance of Witnesses, Experts and Prosecuted Persons

Article 7

1. The requested Party shall effect service of writs and records of judicial verdicts which are transmitted to it for this purpose by the requesting Party.

Service may be effected by simple transmission of the writ or record to the person to be served. If the requesting Party expressly so requests, service shall be effected by the requested Party in the manner provided for the service of analogous documents under its own law or in a special manner consistent with such law.

2. Proof of service shall be given by means of a receipt dated and signed by the person served or by means of a declaration made by the requested Party that service has been effected and stating the form an date of such service. One or other of these documents shall be sent immediately to the requesting Party. The requested Party shall, if the requesting Party so requests, state whether service has been effected in accordance with the law of the requested Party. If service cannot be effected, the reasons shall be communicated immediately by the requested Party to the requesting Party.

3. Any Contracting Party may, by a declaration addressed to the Secretary-General of the Council of Europe, when signing this Convention or depositing its instrument of ratification or accession, request that service of a summons on an accused person who is in its territory be transmitted to its authorities by a certain time before the date set for appearance. This time shall be specified in the aforesaid declaration and shall not exceed 50 days.

This time shall be taken into account when the date of appearance is being fixed and when the summons is being transmitted.

Article 8

A witness or expert who has failed to answer a summons to appear, service of which has been requested, shall not, even if the summons contains a notice of penalty, be subjected to any punishment or measure of restraint, unless subsequently he voluntarily enters the territory of the requesting Party and is there again duly summoned.

Article 9

The allowances, including subsistence, to be paid and the travelling expenses to be refunded to a witness or expert by the requesting Party shall be calculated as from his place of residence and shall be at rates at least equal to those provided for in the scales and rules in force in the country where the hearing is intended to take place.

Article 10

1. If the requesting Party considers the personal appearance of a witness or expert before its judicial authorities especially necessary, it shall so mention in its request for service of the summons and the requested Party shall invite the witness or expert to appear.

The requested Party shall inform the requesting Party of the reply of the witness or expert.

2. In the case provided for under paragraph 1 of this Article the request or the summons shall indicate the approximate allowances payable and the travelling and subsistence expenses refundable.

3. If a specific request is made, the requested Party may grant the witness or expert an advance. The amount of the advance shall be endorsed on the summons and shall be refunded by the requesting Party.

Article 11

1. A person in custody whose personal appearance as a witness or for purposes of confrontation is applied for by the requesting Party, shall be temporarily transferred to the territory where the hearing is intended to take place, provided that he shall be sent back within the period stipulated by the requested Party and subject to the provisions of Article 12 in so far as these are applicable.

Transfer may be refused:

(a) if the person in custody does not consent,

(b) if his presence is necessary at criminal proceedings pending in the territory of the requested Party,

(c) if transfer is liable to prolong his detention, or

(d) if there are other overriding grounds for not transferring him to the territory of the requesting Party.

2. Subject to the provisions of Article 2, in a case coming within the immediately preceding paragraph, transit of the person in custody through the territory of a third State, Party to this Convention, shall be granted on application, accompanied by all necessary documents, addressed by the Ministry of Justice of the requesting Party to the Ministry of Justice of the Party through whose territory transit is requested.

A Contracting Party may refuse to grant transit to its own nationals.

3. The transferred person shall remain in custody in the territory of the requesting Party and, where applicable, in the territory of the Party through which transit is requested, unless the Party from whom transfer is requested applies for this release.

Article 12

1. A witness or expert, whatever his nationality, appearing on a summons before the judicial authorities of the requesting Party shall not be prosecuted or detained or subjected to any other restriction of his personal liberty in the territory of that Party in respect of acts or convictions anterior to his departure from the territory of the requested Party.

2. A person, whatever his nationality, summoned before the judicial authorities of the requesting Party to answer for acts forming the subject of proceedings against him, shall not be prosecuted or detained or subjected to any other restriction of his personal liberty for acts or convictions anterior to his departure from the territory of the requested Party and not specified in the summons.

3. The immunity provided for in this article shall cease when the witness or expert or prosecuted person, having had for a period of fifteen consecutive days from the date when his presence is no longer required by the judicial authorities an opportunity of leaving, has nevertheless remained in the territory, or having left it, has returned.

Chapter IV

Judicial Records

Article 13

1. A requested Party shall communicate extracts from and information relating to judicial records, requested from it by the judicial authorities of a Contracting Party and needed in a criminal matter, to the same extent that these may be made available to its own judicial authorities in like case.

2. In any case other than that provided for in paragraph 1 of this Article the request shall be complied with in accordance with the conditions provided for by the law, regulations or practice of the requested Party.

Chapter V

Procedure

Article 14

1. Requests for mutual assistance shall indicate as follows:

   (a) the authority making the request,

   (b) the object of and the reason for the request,

   (c) where possible, the identity and the nationality of the person concerned, and

   (d) where necessary, the name and address of the person to be served.

2. Letters rogatory referred to in Articles 3, 4 and 5 shall, in addition, state the offence and contain a summary of the facts.

Article 15

1. Letters rogatory referred to in Articles 3, 4 and 5 as well as the applications referred to in Article II shall be addressed by the Ministry of Justice of the requesting Party to the Ministry of Justice of requested Party and shall be returned through the same channels.

2. In case of urgency, letters rogatory may be addressed directly by the judicial authorities of the requesting Party to the judicial authorities of the requested Party. They shall be returned together with the relevant documents through the channels stipulated in paragraph 1 of this article.

3. Requests provided for in paragraph 1 of Article 13 may be addressed directly by the judicial authorities concerned to the appropriate authorities of the requested Party, and the replies may be returned directly by those authorities. Requests provided for in paragraph 2 of Article 13 shall be addressed by the Ministry of Justice of the requesting Party to the Ministry of Justice of the requested Party.

4. Requests for mutual assistance, other than those provided for in paragraphs 1 and 3 of this article and, in particular, requests for investigation preliminary to prosecution, may be communicated directly between the judicial authorities.

5. In cases where direct transmission is permitted under this Convention, it may take place through the International Criminal Police Organisation (Interpol).

6. A Contracting Party may, when signing this Convention or depositing its instrument of ratification or accession, by a declaration addressed to the Secretary-General of the Council of Europe, give notice that some or all requests for assistance shall be sent to it through channels other than those provided for in this article, or require that, in a case provided for in paragraph 2 of this article, a copy of the letters rogatory shall be transmitted at the same time to its Ministry of Justice.

7. The provisions of this article are without prejudice to those of bilateral agreements or arrangements in force between Contracting Parties which provide for the direct transmission of requests for assistance between their respective authorities.

Article 16

1. Subject to paragraph 2 of this article, translations of requests and annexed documents shall not be required.

2. Each Contracting Party may, when signing or depositing its instrument of ratification or accession, by means of a declaration addressed to the Secretary-General of the Council of Europe, reserve the right to stipulate that requests and annexed documents shall be addressed to it accompanied by a translation into its own language or into either of the official languages of the Council of Europe or into one of the latter languages, specified by it. The other Contracting Parties may apply reciprocity.

3. This article is without prejudice to the provisions concerning the translation of requests or annexed documents contained in the agreements or arrangements in force or to be made, between two or more Contracting Parties.

Article 17

Evidence or documents transmitted pursuant to this Convention shall not require any form of authentication.

Article 18

When the authority which receives a request for mutual assistance has no jurisdiction to comply therewith, it shall, *ex officio*, transmit the request to the competent authority of its country and shall so inform the requesting Party through the direct channels, if the request has been addressed through such channels.

Article 19

Reasons shall be given for any refusal of mutual assistance

Article 20

Subject to the provisions of Article 9, execution of requests for mutual assistance shall not entail refunding of expenses except those incurred by the attendance of experts in the territory of the requested Party or the transfer of a person in custody carried out under Article 11.

Chapter VI

Laying of Information in Connection with Proceedings

Article 21

1. Information laid by one Contracting Party with a view to proceedings in the courts of another Party shall be transmitted between the Ministries of Justice concerned unless a Contracting Party avails itself of the option provided for in paragraph 6 of Article 15.

2. The requested Party shall notify the requesting Party of any action taken on such information and shall forward a copy of the record of any verdict pronounced.

3. The provisions of Article 16 shall apply to information laid under paragraph 1 of this article.

Chapter VII

Exchange of Information from Judicial Records

Article 22

Each Contracting Party shall inform any other Party of all criminal convictions and subsequent measures in respect of nationals of the latter Party, entered in the judicial records. Ministries of Justice shall communicate such information to one another at least once a year. Where the person concerned is considered a national of two or more other Contracting Parties, the information shall be given to each of these Parties, unless the person is a national of the Party in the territory of which he was convicted.

Chapter VIII

Final Provisions

Article 23

1. Any Contracting Party may, when signing this Convention or when depositing its instrument of ratification or accession, make a reservation in respect of any provisions of the Convention.

2. Any Contracting Party which has made a reservation shall withdraw it as soon as circumstances permit. Such withdrawal shall be made by notification to the Secretary-General of the Council of Europe.

3. A Contracting Party which has made a reservation in respect of a provision of the Convention may not claim application of the said provision by another Party save in so far as it has itself accepted the provision.

Article 24

A Contracting Party may, when signing the Convention or depositing its instrument of ratification or accession, by a declaration addressed to the Secretary-General of the Council of Europe, define what authorities it will, for the purposes of the Convention, deem judicial authorities.

Article 25

1. This Convention shall apply to the metropolitan territories of the Contracting Parties.

2. In respect of France, it shall also apply to Algeria and to the overseas Departments, and, in respect of Italy, it shall also apply to the territory of Somaliland under Italian administration.

3. The Federal Republic of Germany may extend the application of this Convention to the Land of Berlin by notice addressed to the Secretary-General of the Council of Europe.

4. In respect of the Kingdom of the Netherlands, the Convention shall apply to its European territory. The Netherlands may extend the application of this Convention to the Netherlands Antilles, Surinam and Netherlands New Guinea by notice addressed to the Secretary-General of the Council of Europe.

5. By direct arrangement between two or more Contracting Parties and subject to the conditions laid down in the arrangement, the application of this Convention may be extended to any territory, other than the territories mentioned in paragraphs 1, 2, 3 and 4 of this article, of one of these Parties, for the international relations of which any such Party is responsible.

Article 26

1. Subject to the provisions of Article 15, paragraph 7 and Article 16, paragraph 3, this Convention shall, in respect of those countries to which it applies, supersede the provisions of any treaties, conventions or bilateral agreements governing mutual assistance in criminal matters between any two Contracting Parties.

2. This Convention shall not affect obligations incurred under the terms of any other bilateral or multilateral international convention which contains or may contain clauses governing specific aspects of mutual assistance in a given field.

3. The Contracting Parties may conclude between themselves bilateral or multilateral agreements on mutual assistance in criminal matters only in order to supplement the provisions of this Convention or to facilitate the application of the principles contained therein.

4. Where, as between two or more Contracting Parties, mutual assistance in criminal matters is practised on the basis of uniform legislation or of a special system providing for the reciprocal application in their respective territories of measures of mutual assistance, these Parties shall, notwithstanding the provisions of this Convention, be free to regulate their mutual relations in this field exclusively in accordance with such legislation or system. Contracting Parties which, in accordance with this paragraph, exclude as between themselves the application of this Convention shall notify the Secretary-General of the Council of Europe accordingly.

Article 27

1. This Convention shall be open to signature by the Members of the Council of Europe. It shall be ratified. The instruments of ratification shall be deposited with the Secretary-General of the Council.

2. The Convention shall come into force 90 days after the date of deposit of the third instrument of ratification.

3. As regards any signatory ratifying subsequently the Convention shall come into force 90 days after the date of the deposit of its instrument of ratification.

Article 28

1. The Committee of Ministers of the Council of Europe may invite any State not a Member of the Council to accede to this Convention, provided that the resolution containing such invitation obtains the unanimous agreement of the Members of the Council who have ratified the Convention.

2. Accession shall be by deposit with the Secretary-General of the Council of an instrument of accession which shall take effect 90 days after the date of its deposit.

Article 29

Any Contracting Party may denounce this Convention in so far as it is concerned by giving notice to the Secretary-General of the Council of Europe. Denunciation shall take effect six months after the date when the Secretary-General of the Council received such notification.

Article 30

The Secretary-General of the Council of Europe shall notify the Members of the Council and the Government of any State which has acceded to this Convention of:

(a) the names of the Signatories and the deposit of any instrument of ratification or accession;

(b) the date of entry into force of this Convention;

(c) any notification received in accordance with the provisions of Article 5 - paragraph I, Article 7 - paragraph 3, Article 15 - paragraph 6, Article 16 - paragraph 2, Article 24, Article 25 - paragraphs 3 and 4, or Article 26 - paragraph 4;

(d) any reservation made in accordance with Article 23, paragraph I;

(e) the withdrawal of any reservation in accordance with Article 23, paragraph 2;

(f) any notification of denunciation received in accordance with the provisions of Article 29 and the date on which such denunciation will take effect.

Additional Protocol to the European Convention on Mutual Assistance in Criminal Matters (excerpts) (1978)[*]

Strasbourg, 17 March 1978

Chapter I

Article 1

The Contracting Parties shall not exercise the right provided for in Article 2 (a) of the Convention to refuse assistance solely on the ground that the request concerns an offence which the requested Party considers a fiscal offence.

Article 2

1. In the case where a Contracting Party has made the execution of letters rogatory for search or seizure of property dependent on the condition that the offence motivating the letters rogatory is punishable under both the law of the requesting Party and the law of the requested Party, this condition shall be fulfilled, as regards fiscal offences, if the offence is punishable under the law of the requesting Party and corresponds to an offence of the same nature under the law of the requested Party.

2. The request may not be refused on the ground that the law of the requested Party does not impose the same kind of tax or duty or does not contain a tax, duty, customs and exchange regulation of the same kind as the law of the requesting Party.

Chapter II

Article 3

The Convention shall also apply to:

(a) the service of documents concerning the enforcement of a sentence, the recovery of a fine or the payment of costs of proceedings;

(b) measures relating to the suspension of pronouncement of a sentence or if its enforcement, to conditional release, to deferment of the commencement of the enforcement of a sentence or to the interruption of such enforcement.

Chapter III

Article 4

Article 22 of the Convention shall be supplemented by the following text, the original Article 22 of the Convention becoming paragraph 1 and the below-mentioned provisions becoming paragraph 2:

"2. Furthermore, any Contracting Party which has supplied the above-mentioned information shall communicate to the Party concerned, on the latter's request in individual cases, a copy of the convictions and measures in question as well as any other information relevant thereto in order to enable it to consider whether they necessitate any measures at national level. This communication shall take place between the Ministries of Justice concerned."

---

[*] *European Treaty Series*, No.99.

Recommendation No. R (80)8 of the Committee of Ministers to Member States concerning the Practical application of the European Convention on Mutual Assistance in Criminal Matters[*]

Adopted by the Committee of Ministers on 27 June 1980 at the 321st meeting of the Ministers' Deputies

The Committee of Ministers, under the terms of Article 15.b of the Statute of the Council of Europe,

Recalling Resolutions (71) 43 and (77) 36 on the practical application of the European Convention on Mutual Assistance in Criminal Matters;

Desirous of extending and further facilitating the application of this convention, which was opened for signature on 20 April 1959 and entered into force on 12 June 1962.

I. Recommends the governments of member states:

(a) if they are not yet Contracting Parties to the convention, to ratify it as soon as possible;

(b) if they are Contracting Parties to the convention, to be guided in its practical application by the following principles:

Concerning compliance with a request for assistance

In complying with a request for assistance, the competent authority of the requested state should be guided by the principles contained in Article 6 of the European Convention on Human Rights.

In particular, it should comply with a request for assistance as rapidly as possible. Where the requested authority finds that an exceptional length of time is necessary to comply with the request, it should so inform the requesting authority, if possible by indicating at the same time the approximate date on which the reply can be expected.

Concerning the execution of letters rogatory (Article 4 of the convention)

When applying Article 4 of the Convention and subject to its domestic law, the competent authority of the requested state should make generous use of its discretion to allow officials of the requesting state and interested persons to be present at the execution of letters rogatory and to co-operate in these proceedings as actively as possible;

II. Instructs the Secretary General of the Council of Europe to transmit this recommendation to the governments of those Contracting States which are not members of the Council of Europe.

---

[*] MÜLLER-RAPPARD, E. and BASSIOUNI, M.C. (ed.), *European Inter-State Co-operation in Criminal Matters. The Council of Europe's Legal Instruments*, Dordrecht/ Boston/ London, Martinus Nijhoff Publishers, 1993, 64.

Schengen Convention - Title III - Chapters II and III (excerpts) (1990)[*]

Schengen, 19 June 1990

Title III

Police and security

[...]

Chapter II

Mutual assistance in criminal matters

Article 48

1. The provision of this Chapter intended to supplement the European Convention of 20 April 1959 on Mutual Assistance in Criminal Matters as well as, in relations between the Contracting Parties which are members of the Benelux Economic Union, Chapter II of the Benelux Treaty on Extradition and Mutual Assistance in Criminal Matters of 27 June 1962, as amended by the Protocol of 11 May 1974, and to facilitate the implementation of these agreements.

2. Paragraph 1 shall not affect the application of the broader provisions of the bilateral agreements in force between the Contracting Parties.

Article 49

Mutual assistance shall also be afforded:

(a) in proceedings brought by the administrative authorities in respect of offences which are punishable in one of the two Contracting Parties or in both Contracting Parties by virtue of being infringements of the rules of law, where the decision may give rise to proceedings before a criminal court:

(b) in proceedings for compensation in respect of unjustified prosecution or conviction:

(c) in proceedings in non-contentious matters;

(d) in civil proceedings joined to criminal proceedings, as long as the criminal court has not yet given a final ruling in the criminal proceedings.

(e) to communicate legal statements relating to the execution of a sentence or measure, the imposition of a fine or the payment of costs or proceedings;

(f) in respect of measures relating to the suspension of delivery of a sentence or measure, conditional release or the postponement or suspension of execution of a sentence or measure.

---

[*] Convention of 19 June 1990, applying the Schengen Agreement of 14 June 1985 between the Governments of the States of the Benelux Economic Union, the Federal Republic of Germany and the French Republic, on the Gradual Abolition of Checks at their Common Borders, *International Legal Materials*, 1991, 84.

Article 50

1. The Contracting Parties undertake to afford each other, in accordance with the Convention and the Treaty referred to in Article 48, mutual assistance as regards infringements of their rules of law with respect to excise duty, value added tax and customs duties. Customs provisions are the rules laid down in Article 2 of the Convention of 7 September 1967 between Belgium, the Federal Republic of Germany, France, Italy, Luxembourg and the Netherlands on mutual assistance between customs administrations, as well as Article 2 of Council Regulation (EEC) No 1468/81 of 19 May 1981.

2. Requests based on evasion of excise duties may not be rejected on the grounds that the country requested does not levy excise duties on the goods referred to in the request.

3. The requesting Contracting Party shall not forward or use information or evidence obtained from the requested Contracting Party for enquiries, proceedings or procedures other than those referred to in its request, without the prior assent of the requested Contracting Party.

4. The mutual assistance provided for in this Article may be refused where the alleged amount of duty underpaid or evaded is no more than ECU 25 000 or where the presumed value of the goods exported or imported without authorization is no more than ECU 100 000, unless, given the circumstances or the identity of the accused, the case is deemed to be extremely serious by the requesting Contracting Party.

5. The provisions of this Article shall also apply when the mutual assistance requested concerns infringements punishable on by a fine as infringements of the rules of law in proceedings brought by the administrative authorities, where the request for assistance emanates from a judicial authority.

Article 51

The Contracting Parties may not make the admissibility of letters rogatory for search or seizure dependent on conditions other than the following:

(a) the offence giving rise to the letters rogatory is punishable under the law of both Contracting Parties by a custodial sentence or a security measure restricting liberty of a maximum of at least six months or is punishable under the law of one of the two Contracting Parties by an equivalent penalty and under the law of the other Contracting Party as an infringement of the regulations which is prosecuted by the administrative authorities where the decision may give rise to proceedings before a criminal court.

(b) execution of the letters rogatory is consistent with the law of the requested Contracting Party.

Article 52

1. Each Contracting Party may address procedural documents directly by post to persons who are in the territory of another Contracting Party. The Contracting Parties shall send the Executive Committee a list of the documents which may be forwarded in this way.

2. Where there is reason to believe that the addressee does not understand the language in which the document is drafted, the document - or at least the important passages in it - must be translated into (one of) the language(s) of the Contracting Party in the territory of which the addressee is staying. If the authority forwarding the document knows that the addressee speaks only another language, the document - or at least the important passages thereof must be translated into that other language.

3. An expert or witness who has failed to answer a summons to appear, sent to him by post, shall not, even if the summons contains a notice of penalty, be subjected to any punishment or measure of restraint, unless subsequently he voluntarily enters the territory of the

requesting Party and is there again duly summoned. The authority sending a summons to appear by post shall ensure that it does not involve penalties. This provision shall be without prejudice to Article 34 of the Benelux Treaty on Extradition and Mutual Assistance in Criminal Matters of 27 June 1962 as amended by the Protocol of 11 May 1974.

4. If the offence on which the request for assistance is based is punishable under law of both Contracting Parties as an infringement of the regulations which is being prosecuted by the administrative authorities where the decision may give rise to proceedings before a criminal court, the procedure outlined in paragraph 1 must in principle be used for the forwarding of procedural documents.

5. Notwithstanding paragraph 1, procedural documents may be forwarded through the legal authorities of the requested Contracting Party where the addressee's address is unknown or where the requesting Contracting Party requires a formal service.

Article 53

1. Requests for assistance may be made directly between legal authorities and returned through the same channels.

2. Paragraph 1 shall not prejudice the possibility of requests being sent and returned between Ministries of Justice or through the intermediary of national central offices of the International Criminal Police Organization.

3. Requests for the temporary transfer or transit of persons provisionally under arrest or detained or who are the subject of a measure depriving them of their liberty, and the periodic or occasional exchange of data from the judicial records must be effected through the Ministries of Justice.

4. Within the meaning of the European Convention of 20 April 1959 on Mutual Assistance in Criminal Matters, Ministry of Justice means, where the Federal Republic of Germany is concerned, the Federal Minister of Justice and the Justice Ministers or Senators of the Federal States.

5. Information laid with a view to proceedings in respect of infringements of the legislation on driving and rest time, in accordance with Article 21 of the European Convention of 20 April 1959 on Mutual Assistance in Criminal Matters or with Article 42 of the Benelux Treaty on Extradition and Mutual Assistance in Criminal Matters of 27 June 1962, as amended by the Protocol of 11 May 1974, may be sent by the legal authorities of the requesting Contracting Party directly to the legal authorities of the requested Contracting Party.

Chapter III

Application of the non bis in idem principle

Article 54

A person who has been finally judged by a Contracting Party may not be prosecuted by another Contracting Party for the same offences provided that, where he is sentenced, the sentence has been served or is currently being served or can no longer be carried out under the sentencing laws of the Contracting Party.

Article 55

1. A Contracting Party may when ratifying, accepting or approving this Convention declare that it is not bound by Article 54 in one or more of the following cases:

    (a) where the acts to which the foreign judgment relates took place in whole or in part in its own territory: in the latter case, this exception shall not however apply if the acts took place in part in the territory of the Contracting Party where the judgment was given:

(b) where the acts to which the foreign judgment relates constitute an offence against State security or other equally essential interests of that Contracting Party;

(c) where the acts to which the foreign judgment relates were committed by an official of that Contracting Party in violation of the obligations of his office.

2. A Contracting Party which has made a declaration regarding the exception referred to in paragraph 1(b) shall specify the categories of offences to which this exception may apply.

3. A Contracting Party may at any moment withdraw a declaration relating to one or more of the exceptions referred to in paragraph 1.

4. The exceptions which were the subject of a declaration under paragraph 1 shall not apply where the Contracting Party concerned has, in respect of the same acts, requested the other Contracting Party to prosecute or has granted the extradition of the person concerned.

Article 56

If further proceedings are brought by a Contracting Party against a person who has been finally judged for the same offences by another Contracting Party, any period of deprivation of liberty served on the territory of the latter Contracting Party on account of the offences in question must be deducted from any sentence handed down. Account will also be taken, to the extent that national legislation permits, of sentences other than periods of imprisonment already undergone.

Article 57

1. Where a Contracting Party accuses an individual of an offence and the competent authorities of that Contracting Party have reason to believe that the accusation relates to the same offences as those for which the individual has already been finally judged by another Contracting Party, these authorities shall, if they deem it necessary, request the relevant information from the competent authorities of the Contracting Party in whose territory judgement has already been delivered.

2. The information requested shall be provided as soon as possible and shall be taken into consideration as regards further action to be taken in the proceedings in progress.

3. At the time of ratification, acceptance or approval of this Convention, each Contracting Party will nominate the authorities which will be authorized to request and receive the information provided for in this Article.

Article 58

The above provisions shall not preclude the application of wider national provisions on the "non bis in idem" effect attached to legal decisions taken abroad.

[...]

Scheme Relating to Mutual Assistance in Criminal Matters within the Commonwealth including Amendments made by Law Ministers in April 1990[*]

Harare, 1986

Purpose and Scope

1. (1) The purpose of this Scheme is to increase the level and scope of assistance rendered between Commonwealth Governments in criminal matters. In augments, and in no way derogates from existing forms of cooperation, both formal and informal; nor does it preclude the development of enhanced arrangements in other fora.

    (2) This Scheme provides for the giving of assistance by the competent authorities of one country (the requested country) in respect of criminal matters arising in another country (the requesting country).

    (3) Assistance in criminal matters under this Scheme includes assistance in

    (a) identifying and locating persons;

    (b) serving documents;

    (c) examining witnesses;

    (d) search and seizure;

    (e) obtaining evidence;

    (f) facilitating the personal appearance of witnesses;

    (g) effecting a temporary transfer of persons in custody to appear as a witness;

    (h) obtaining production of judicial or official records; and

    (i) tracing, seizing and confiscating the proceeds or instrumentalities of crime.

Meaning of Country

2. For the purposes of this Scheme, each of the following is a separate country, that is to say

    (a) each sovereign and independent country within the Commonwealth together with any dependent territories which that country designates; and

    (b) each country within the Commonwealth which, though not sovereign and independent, is not designated for the purposes of the preceding subparagraph.

Criminal Matter

3. (1) For the purposes of this Scheme, a criminal matter arises in a country if the Central Authority of that country certifies that criminal or forfeiture proceedings

---

[*] *Commonwealth Law Bulletin*, 1990, 1043.

have been instituted in a court exercising jurisdiction in that country or that there is reasonable cause to believe that an offence has been committed in respect of which such proceedings could be so instituted.

(2) Offence, in the case of a federal country or a country having more than one legal system, includes an offence under the law of the country or any part thereof.

(3) 'Forfeiture proceedings' means proceedings, whether civil or criminal, for an order -

    (a) restraining dealings with any property in respect of which there is reasonable cause to believe that it has been

        (i) derived or obtained, whether directly or indirectly, from; or

        (ii) used in, or in connection with,

    the commission of an offence;

    (b) confiscating any property derived or obtained as provided in paragraph (a)(i) or used as provided in paragraph (a)(ii); or

    (c) imposing a pecuniary penalty calculated by reference to the value of any property derived or obtained as provided in paragraph (a)(i) or used as provided in paragraph (a)(ii).

Central Authorities

4. Each country shall designate a Central Authority to transmit and to receive requests for assistance under this Scheme.

Action in the Requesting Country

5. (1) A request for assistance under this Scheme may be initiated by any law enforcement agency or public prosecution or judicial authority competent under the law of the requesting country.

(2) The Central Authority of the requesting country shall, if it is satisfied that the request can properly be made under this Scheme, transmit the request to the Central Authority of the requested country and shall ensure that the request contains all the information required by the provisions of this Scheme.

(3) The Central Authority of the requesting country shall provide as far as practicable additional information sought by the Central Authority of the requested country.

Action in the Requested Country

6. (1) Subject to the provisions of this Scheme, the requested country shall grant the assistance requested as expeditiously as practicable.

(2) The Central Authority of the requested country shall, subject to the following provisions of this paragraph, take the necessary steps to ensure that the competent authorities of that country comply with the request.

(3) If the Central Authority of the requested country considers

    (a) that the request does not comply with the provisions of this Scheme, or

    (b) that in accordance with the provisions of this Scheme the request for assistance is to be refused in whole or in part, or

(c) that the request cannot be complied with, in whole or in part, or

(d) that there are circumstances which are likely to cause a significant delay in complying with the request,

it shall promptly inform the Central Authority of the requesting country, giving reasons.

Refusal of Assistance

7. (1) The requested country may refuse to comply in whole or in part with a request for assistance under this Scheme if the criminal matter appears to the Central Authority of that country to concern

   (a) conduct which would not constitute an offence under the law of that country; or

   (b) an offence or proceedings of a political character; or

   (c) conduct which in the requesting country is an offence only under military law or a law relating to military obligations; or

   (d) conduct in relation to which the person accused or suspected of having committed an offence has been acquitted or convicted by a court in the requested country.

   (2) The requested country may refuse to comply in whole or in part with a request for assistance under this Scheme

   (a) to the extent that it appears to the Central Authority of that country that compliance would be contrary to the Constitution of that country, or would prejudice the security, international relations or other essential public interests of that country; or

   (b) where there are substantial grounds leading the Central Authority of that country to believe that compliance would facilitate the prosecution or punishment of any person on account of his race, religion, nationality or political opinions or would cause prejudice for any of these reasons to any person affected by the request.

   (3) The requested country may refuse to comply in whole or in part with a request for assistance to the extent that the steps required to be taken in order to comply with the request cannot under the law of that country be taken in respect of criminal matters arising in that country.

   (4) An offence shall not be an offence of a political character for the purposes of this paragraph if it is an offence within the scope of any international convention to which both the requesting and requested countries are parties and which imposes on the parties thereto an obligation either to extradite or prosecute a person accused of the commission of the offence.

Measures of Compulsion

8. (1) The competent authorities of the requested country shall in complying with a request under this Scheme use only such measures of compulsion as are available under the law of that country in respect of criminal matters arising in that country.

   (2) Where under the law of the requested country measures of compulsion cannot be applied to any person to take the steps necessary to secure compliance with a request under this Scheme but the person concerned is willing to act voluntarily in compliance or partial compliance with the terms of the request, the compe-

tent authorities of the requested country shall make available the necessary facilities.

Scheme not to Cover Arrest or Extradition

9. Nothing in this Scheme is to be construed as authorising the extradition, or the arrest or detention with a view to extradition, of any person.

Confidentiality

10. The Central Authorities and the competent authorities of the requesting and requested countries shall use their best efforts to keep confidential a request and its contents and the information and materials supplied in compliance with a request except for disclosure in criminal proceedings and where otherwise authorised by the Central Authority of the other country.

Limitation of Use of Information or Evidence

11. The requesting country shall not use any information or evidence obtained in response to a request for assistance under this Scheme in connection with any matter other than the criminal matter specified in the request without the prior consent of the Central Authority of the requested country.

Expenses of Compliance

12. (1) Except as provided in the following provisions of this paragraph, compliance with a request under this Scheme shall not give rise to any claim against the requesting country for expenses incurred by the Central Authority or other competent authorities of the requested country.

   (2) The requesting country shall be responsible for the travel and incidental expenses of witnesses travelling to the requesting country, including those of accompanying officials, for fees of experts, and for the costs of any translation required by the requesting country.

   (3) If in the opinion of the requested country the expenses required in order to comply with the request are of an extraordinary nature, the Central Authority of the requested country shall consult with the Central Authority of the requesting country as to the terms and conditions under which compliance with the request may continue, and in the absence of agreement the requested country may refuse to comply further with the request.

Contents of Request for Assistance

13. (1) A request under the Scheme shall

   (a) specify the nature of the assistance requested;

   (b) contain the information appropriate to the assistance sought as specified in the following provisions of this Scheme;

   (c) indicate any time-limit within which compliance with the request is desired, stating reasons;

   (d) contain the following information:

      (i) the identity of the agency or authority initiating the request;

      (ii) the nature of the criminal matter; and

      (iii) whether or not criminal proceedings have been instituted;

(e) where criminal proceedings have been instituted, contain the following information:

   (i) the court exercising jurisdiction in the proceedings;

   (ii) the identity of the accused person;

   (iii) the offences of which he stands accused, and a summary of the facts;

   (iv) the stage reached in the proceedings; and

   (v) any date fixed for further stages in the proceedings;

(f) where criminal proceedings have not been instituted, state the offence which the Central Authority of the requesting country has reasonable cause to believe to have been committed, with a summary of the known facts.

(2) A request shall normally be in writing, and if made orally in case of urgency shall be confirmed in writing forthwith.

Identifying and Locating Persons

14. (1) A request under this Scheme may seek assistance in identifying or locating persons believed to be within the requested country.

(2) The request shall indicate the purpose for which the information is requested and shall contain such information as is available to the Central Authority of the requesting country as to the whereabouts of the person concerned and such other information as it possesses as may facilitate the identification of that person.

Service of documents

15. (1) A request under this Scheme may seek assistance in the service of documents relevant to a criminal matter arising in the requesting country.

(2) The request shall be accompanied by the documents to be served and, where those documents relate to attendance in the requesting country, such notice as the Central Authority of that country is reasonably able to provide of outstanding warrants or other judicial orders in criminal matters against the person to be served.

(3) The Central Authority of the requested country shall endeavour to have the documents served.

   (a) any particular method stated in the request, unless such method is incompatible with the law of that country; or

   (b) by any method prescribed by the law of that country for the service of documents in criminal proceedings.

(4) The requested country shall transmit to the Central Authority of the requesting country a certificate as to the service of the documents or, if they have not been served, as to the reasons which have prevented service.

(5) A person served in compliance with a request with a summons to appear as a witness in the requesting country and who fails to comply with the summons shall not by reason thereof be liable to any penalty or measure of compulsion in either the requesting or the requested country notwithstanding any contrary statement in the summons.

Examination of Witnesses

16. (1) A request under this Scheme may seek assistance in the examination of witnesses in the requested country.

    (2) The request shall specify, as appropriate and so far as the circumstances of the case permit

    (a) the names and addresses or the official designations of the witnesses to be examined;

    (b) the questions to be put to the witnesses or the subject-matter about which they are to be examined;

    (c) whether it is desired that the witnesses be examined orally or in writing;

    (d) whether it is desired that the oath be administered to be witnesses (or, as the law of the requested country allows, that they be required to make their solemn affirmation);

    (e) any provisions of the law of the requesting country as to privilege or exemption from giving evidence which appear especially relevant to the request; and

    (f) any special requirements of the law of the requesting country as to the manner of taking evidence relevant to its admissibility in that country.

    (3) The request may ask that, so far as the law of the requested country permits, the accused person or his legal representative may attend the examination of the witness and ask questions of the witness.

Search and Seizure

17. (1) A request under this Scheme may seek assistance in the search for and seizure of property in the requested country.

    (2) The request shall specify the property to be searched for and seized ad shall contain, so far as reasonably practicable, all information available to the Central Authority of the requesting country which may be required to be adduced in an application under the law of the requested country for any necessary warrant or authorisation to effect the search and seizure.

    (3) The requested country shall provide such certification as may be required by the requesting country concerning the result of any search, the place and circumstances of seizure, and the subsequent custody of the property seized.

Other Assistance in Obtaining Evidence

18. (1) A request under this Scheme may seek other assistance in obtaining evidence.

    (2) The request shall specify, as appropriate and so far as the circumstances of the case permit:

    (a) the documents, records or property to be inspected, preserved, photographed, copied or transmitted;

    (b) the samples of property to be taken, examined or transmitted; and

    (c) the site to be viewed or photographed.

Privilege

19. (1) No person shall be compelled in response to a request under this Scheme to give any evidence in the requested country which he could not be compelled to give

    (a) in criminal proceedings in that country; or

    (b) in criminal proceedings in the requesting country.

    (2) For the purposes of this paragraph any reference to giving evidence includes references to answering any question and to producing any document.

Production of Judicial or Official Records

20. (1) A request under this Scheme may seek the production of judicial or official records relevant to a criminal matter arising in the requesting country.

    (2) For the purposes of this paragraph 'judicial records' means judgments, orders and decisions of courts and other documents held by judicial authorities and 'official records' means documents held by government departments or agencies or prosecution authorities.

    (3) The requested country shall provide copies of judicial or official records which are publicly available.

    (4) The requested country may provide copies of judicial or official records not publicly available, to the same extent and under the same conditions as apply to the provision of such records to its own law enforcement agencies or prosecution or judicial authorities.

Transmission and Return of Material

21. (1) Where compliance with a request under this Scheme would involve the transmission to the requesting country of any document, record or property, the requested country

    (a) may postpone the transmission of the material if it is required in connection with proceedings in that country, and in such a case shall provide certified copies of a document or record pending transmission of the original;

    (b) may require the requesting country to agree to terms and conditions to protect third party interests in the material to be transmitted and may refuse to effect such transmission pending such agreement.

    (2) Where any document, record or property is transmitted to the requesting country in compliance with a request under this Scheme, it shall be returned to the requested country when it is no longer required in connection with the criminal matter specified in the request unless that country has indicated that its return is not desired.

    (3) The requested country shall authenticate material that is to be transmitted by that country.

Authentication

22. A document or other material transmitted for the purposes of or in response to a request under this Scheme shall be deemed to be duly authenticated if it:

    (a) purports to be signed or certified by a judge or magistrate, or to bear the stamp or seal of a Minister, government department or Central Authority; or

(b) is verified by the oath of a witness or of a public officer of the Commonwealth country from which the document or material emanates.

Personal Appearance of Witnesses in the Requesting Country

23. (1) A request under this Scheme may seek assistance in facilitating the personal appearance of witnesses before a court exercising jurisdiction in the requesting country.

(2) The request shall specify

(a) the subject matter upon which it is desired to examine the witnesses;

(b) the reasons for which the personal appearance of the witnesses is required; and

(c) details of the travelling, subsistence and other expenses payable by the requesting country in respect of the personal appearance of the witnesses.

(3) The competent authorities of the requested country shall invite persons whose appearance as witnesses in the requesting country is desired; and

(a) ask whether they agree to appear;

(b) inform the Central Authority of the requesting country of their answer; and

(c) if they are willing to appear, make appropriate arrangements to facilitate the personal appearance of the witnesses.

(4) A person whose appearance as a witness is the subject of a request and who does not agree to appear shall not by reason thereof be liable to any penalty or measure of compulsion in either the requesting or requested country.

Personal Appearance of Persons in Custody

24. (1) A request under this Scheme may seek the temporary transfer of persons in custody in the requested country to appear as witnesses before a court exercising jurisdiction in the requesting country.

(2) The request shall specify

(a) the subject matter upon which it is desired to examine the witnesses;

(b) the reasons for which the personal appearance of the witnesses is required;

(3) The requested country shall refuse to comply with a request for transfer of persons in custody if the persons concerned do not consent to the transfer.

(4) The requested country may refuse to comply with a request for the transfer of persons in custody and shall be under no obligation to inform the requesting country of the reasons for such refusal.

(5) A person in custody whose transfer is the subject of a request and who does not consent to the transfer shall not by reason thereof be liable to any penalty or measure of compulsion in either the requesting or requested country.

(6) Where persons in custody are transferred, the requested country shall notify the requesting country of

(a) the dates upon which the persons are due under the law of the requested country to be released from custody and

(b) the dates by which the requested country requires the return of the persons and shall notify any variations in such dates.

(7) The requesting country shall keep the persons transferred in custody, and shall return the persons to the requested country when their presence as witnesses in the requesting country is no longer required, and in any case by the earlier of the dates notified under sub paragraph (6).

(8) The obligation to return the persons transferred shall subsist notwithstanding the fact that they are nationals of the requesting country.

(9) The period during which the persons transferred are in custody in the requesting country shall be deemed to be service in the requested country of an equivalent period of custody in that country for all purposes.

(10) Nothing in this paragraph shall preclude the release in the requesting country without return to the requested country of any person transferred where the two countries and the person concerned agreed.

Immunity of Persons Appearing

25. (1) Subject to the provisions of paragraph 24, witnesses appearing in the requesting country in response to a request under paragraph 23 or persons transferred to that country in response to a request under paragraph 24 shall be immune in that country from prosecution, detention or any other restriction of personal liberty in respect of criminal acts, omissions or convictions before the time of their departure from the requested country.

(2) The immunity provided for in that paragraph shall cease

(a) in the case of witnesses appearing in response to a request under paragraph 23, when the witnesses having had, for a period of 15 consecutive days from the dates when they were notified by the competent authority of the requesting country that their presence was no longer required by the court exercising jurisdiction in the criminal matter, an opportunity of leaving have nevertheless remained in the requesting country, or having left that country have returned to it;

(b) in the case of persons transferred in response to a request under paragraph 24 and remaining in custody when they have been returned to the requested country.

Tracing the Proceeds or Instrumentalities of Crime

26. (1) A request under this Scheme may seek assistance in identifying, locating, and assessing the value of, property believed to have been derived or obtained, directly or indirectly, from, or to have been used in, or in connection with, the commission of an offence and believed to be within the requested country.

(2) The request shall contain such information as is available to the central Authority of the requesting country as to the nature and location of the property and as to any person in whose possession or control the property is believed to be.

Seizing and Confiscating the Proceeds or Instrumentalities of Crime

27. (1) A request under this Scheme may seek assistance in securing

(a) the making in the requested country of an order relating to the proceeds or instrumentalities of crime; or

(b) the recognition or enforcement in that country of such an order made in the requesting country.

(2) For the purpose of this paragraph, 'an order relating to the proceeds or instrumentalities of crime' means

(a) an order restraining dealings with any property in respect of which there is reasonable cause to believe that it has been derived or obtained, directly or indirectly, from, or used in, or in connection with, the commission of an offence;

(b) an order confiscating property derived or obtained, directly or indirectly, from, or used in or in connection with, the commission of an offence; and

(c) an order imposing a pecuniary penalty calculated by reference to the value of any property so derived, obtained or used.

(3) Where the requested country cannot enforce an order made in the requesting country, the requesting country may request the making of any similar order available under the law of the requested country.

(4) The request shall be accompanied by a copy of any order made in the requesting country and shall contain, so far as reasonably practicable, all information available to the Central Authority of the requesting country which may be required in connection with the procedures to be followed in the requested country.

(5) The law of the requested country shall apply to determine the circumstances and manner in which an order may be made, recognised or enforced in response to the request.

Disposal or Release of Property

28. (1) The law of the requested country shall apply to determine the disposal of any property

(a) forfeited; or

(b) obtained as a result of the enforcement of a pecuniary penalty order

as a result of a request under this Scheme.

(2) The law of the requested country shall apply to determine the circumstances in which property made the subject of interim seizure as a result of a request under this Scheme may be released from the effects of such seizure.

Consultation

29. The Central Authorities of the requested and requesting countries shall consult promptly, at the request of either, concerning matters arising under this Scheme.

Other assistance

30. After consultation between the requesting and the requested countries assistance not within the scope of this Scheme may be given in respect of a criminal matter on such terms and conditions as may be agreed by those countries.

Notification of Designations

31. Designations of dependent territories under paragraph 2 and of Central Authorities under paragraph 4 shall be notified to the Commonwealth Secretary-General.

4. TRANSFER OF PROCEEDINGS, OF EXECUTION AND OF PRISONERS

4.1. Transfer of Proceedings

UN Model Treaty on the Transfer of Proceedings in Criminal Matters (1990)[*]

New York, 14 December 1990

Article 1

Scope of application

1. When a person is suspected of having committed an offence under the law of a State which is a Contracting Party, that State may, if the interests of the proper administration of justice so require, request another State which is a Contracting Party to take proceedings in respect of this offence.

2. For the purpose of applying the present Treaty, the Contracting Parties shall take the necessary legislative measures to ensure that a request of the requesting State to take proceedings shall allow the requested State to exercise the necessary jurisdiction.

Article 2

Channels of communications

A request to take proceedings shall be made in writing. The request, supporting documents and subsequent communication shall be transmitted through diplomatic channels, directly between the Ministries of Justice or any other authorities designated by the Parties.

Article 3

Required documents

1. The request to take proceedings shall contain or be accompanied by the following information:

   (a) The authority presenting the request;

   (b) A description of the act for which transfer of proceedings is being requested, including the specific time and place of the offence;

   (c) A statement on the results of investigations which substantiate the suspicion of an offence;

   (d) The legal provisions of the requesting State on the basis of which the act is considered to be an offence;

   (e) A reasonably exact statement on the identity, nationality and residence of the suspected person.

2. The documents submitted in support of a request to take proceedings shall be accompanied by a translation into the language of the requested State or into another language acceptable to that State.

---

[*] General Assembly resolution 45/118 of 14 December 1990, *Compendium of United Nations Standards and Norms in Crime Prevention and Criminal Justice*, New York, United Nations, 1992, 76; *International Legal Materials*, 1991, 1435.

Article 4

Certification and authentication

Subject to national law and unless the Parties decide otherwise, a request to take proceedings and the documents in support thereof, as well as the documents and other material supplied in response to such a request, shall not require certification or authentication.[1]

Article 5

Decision on the request

The competent authorities of the requested State shall examine what action to take on the request to take proceedings in order to comply, as fully as possible, with the request under their own law, and shall promptly communicate their decision to the requesting State.

Article 6

Dual criminality

A request to take proceedings can be complied with only if the act on which the request is based would be an offence if committed in the territory of the requested State.

Article 7

Grounds for refusal

If the requested State refuses acceptance of a request for transfer of proceedings, it shall communicate the reasons for refusal to the requesting State. Acceptance may be refused if:

(a) The suspected person is not a national of or ordinary resident in the requested State;

(b) The act is an offence under military law, which is not also an offence under ordinary criminal law;

(c) The offence is in connection with taxes, duties, customs or exchange;

(d) The offence is regarded by the requested State as being of a political nature.

Article 8

The position of the suspected person

1. The suspected person may express to either State his or her interest in the transfer of the proceedings. Similarly, such interest may be expressed by the legal representative or close relatives of the suspected person.

2. Before a request for transfer of proceedings is made, the requesting State shall, if practicable, allow the suspected person to present his or her views on the alleged offence and the intended transfer, unless that person has absconded or otherwise obstructed the course of justice.

---

[1] The laws of some countries require authentication before documents transmitted from other countries can be admitted in their courts and, therefore, would require a clause setting out the authentication required.

Article 9

The rights of the victim

The requesting and requested States shall ensure in the transfer of proceedings that the rights of the victim of the offence, in particular his or her right to restitution or compensation, shall not be affected as a result of the transfer. If a settlement of the claim of the victim has not been reached before the transfer, the requested State shall permit the representation of the claim in the transferred proceedings, if its law provides for such a possibility. In the event of the death of the victim, these provisions shall apply to his or her dependants accordingly.

Article 10

Effects of the transfer of proceedings on the requesting State
(ne bis in idem)

Upon acceptance by the requested State of the request to take proceedings against the suspected person, the requesting State shall provisionally discontinue prosecution, except necessary investigation, including judicial assistance to the requested State, until the requested State informs the requesting State that the case has been finally disposed of. From that date on, the requesting State shall definitely refrain from further prosecution of the same offence.

Article 11

Effects of the transfer of proceedings on the requested State

1. The proceedings transferred upon agreement shall be governed by the law of the requested State. When charging the suspected person under its law, the requested State shall make the necessary adjustment with respect to particular elements in the legal description of the offence. Where the competence of the requested State is based on the provision set forth in paragraph 2 of article 1 of the present Treaty, the sanction pronounced in that State shall not be more severe than that provided by the law of the requesting State.

2. As far as compatible with the law of the requested State, any act with a view to proceedings or procedural requirements performed in the requesting State in accordance with its law shall have the same validity in the requested State as if the act had been performed in or by the authorities of that State.

3. The requested State shall inform the requesting State of the decision taken as a result of the proceedings. To this end a copy of any final decision shall be transmitted to the requesting State upon request.

Article 12

Provisional measures

When the requesting State announces its intention to transmit a request for transfer of proceedings, the requested State may, upon a specific request made for this purpose by the requesting State, apply all such provisional measures, including provisional detention and seizure, as could be applied under its own law if the offence in respect of which transfer of proceedings is requested had been committed in its territory.

Article 13

The plurality of criminal proceedings

When criminal proceedings are pending in two or more States against the same suspected person in respect of the same offence, the States concerned shall conduct consultations to decide which of them alone should continue the proceedings. An agreement reached thereupon shall have the consequences of a request for transfer of proceedings.

Article 14

Costs

Any costs incurred by a Contracting Party because of a transfer of proceedings shall not be refunded, unless otherwise agreed by both the requesting and requested States.

Article 15

Final provisions

1. The present Treaty is subject to [ratification, acceptance or approval]. The instruments of [ratification, acceptance, or approval] shall be exchanged as soon as possible.

2. The present Treaty shall enter into force on the thirtieth day after the day on which the instruments of [ratification, acceptance of approval] are exchanged.

3. The present Treaty shall apply to requests made after its entry into force, even if the relevant acts or omissions occurred prior to that date.

4. Either Contracting Party may denounce the present Treaty by giving notice in writing to the other Party. Such denunciation shall take effect six months following the date on which it is received by the other Party.

European Convention on the Transfer of Proceedings in Criminal Matters (1972)[*]

Strasbourg, 15 May 1972

Part I

Definitions

Article 1

For the purpose of this Convention:

(a) "offence" comprises acts dealt with under the criminal law and those dealt with under the legal provisions listed in Appendix III to this Convention on condition that where an administrative authority is competent to deal with the offence it must be possible for the person concerned to have the case tried by a court;

(b) "sanction" means any punishment or other measure incurred or pronounced in respect of an offence or in respect of a violation of the legal provisions listed in Appendix III.

Part II

Competence

Article 2

1. For the purposes of applying this Convention, any Contracting State shall have competence to prosecute under its own criminal law any offence to which the law of another Contracting State is applicable.

2. The competence conferred on a Contracting State exclusively by virtue of paragraph 1 of this Article may be exercised only pursuant to a request for proceedings presented by another Contracting State.

Article 3

Any Contracting State having competence under its own law to prosecute an offence may, for the purposes of applying this Convention, waive or desist from proceedings against a suspected person who is being or will be prosecuted for the same offence by another Contracting State. Having regard to Article 21, paragraph 2, any such decision to waive or to desist from proceedings shall be provisional pending a final decision in the other Contracting State.

Article 4

The requested State shall discontinue proceedings exclusively grounded on Article 2 when to its knowledge the right of punishment is extinguished under the law of the requesting State for a reason other than time-limitation, to which Articles 10 (c), 11 (f) and (g), 22, 23 and 26 in particular apply.

Article 5

The provisions of Part III of this Convention do not limit the competence given to a requested State by its municipal law in regard to prosecutions.

---

[*] *European Treaty Series*, No.73.

Part III

Transfer of Proceedings

Section I

Request for Proceedings

Article 6

1. When a person is suspected of having committed an offence under the law of a Contracting State, that State may request another Contracting State to take proceedings in the cases and under the conditions provided for in this Convention.

2. If under the provisions of this Convention a Contracting State may request another Contracting State to take proceedings, the competent authorities of the first State shall take that possibility into consideration.

Article 7

1. Proceedings may not be taken in the requested State unless the offence in respect of which the proceedings are requested would be an offence if committed in its territory and when, under these circumstances, the offender would be liable to sanction under its own law also.

2. If the offence was committed by a person of public status or against a person, an institution or any thing of public status in the requesting State, it shall be considered in the requested State as having been committed by a person of public status or against such a person, an institution or any thing corresponding, in the latter State, to that against which it was actually committed.

Article 8

1. A Contracting State may request another Contracting State to take proceedings in any one or more of the following cases:

    (a) if the suspected person is ordinarily resident in the requested State;

    (b) if the suspected person is a national of the requested State or if that State is his State of origin

    (c) if the suspected person is undergoing or is to undergo a sentence involving deprivation of liberty in the requested State;

    (d) if proceedings for the same or other offences are being taken against the suspected person in the requested State;

    (e) if it considers that transfer of the proceedings is warranted in the interests of arriving at the truth and in particular that the most important items of evidence are located in the requested State;

    (f) if it considers that the enforcement in the requested State of a sentence if one were passed is likely to improve the prospects for the social rehabilitation of the person sentenced.

    (g) if it considers that the presence of the suspected person cannot be ensured at the hearing of proceedings in the requesting State and that his presence in person at the hearing of proceedings in the requested State can be ensured.

    (h) if it considers that it could not itself enforce a sentence if one were passed, even by having recourse to extradition, and that the requested State could do so.

2. Where the suspected person has been finally sentenced in a Contracting State, that State may request the transfer of proceedings in one or more of the cases referred to in paragraph 1 of this Article only if it cannot itself enforce the sentence, even by having recourse to extradition, and if the other Contracting State does not accept enforcement of a foreign judgment as a matter of principle or refuses to enforce such sentence.

Article 9

1. The competent authorities in the requested State shall examine the request for proceedings made in pursuance of the preceding Articles. They shall decide, in accordance with their own law, what action to take thereon.

2. Where the law of the requested State provides for the punishment of the offence by an administrative authority, that State shall, as soon as possible, so inform the requesting State unless the requested State has made a declaration under paragraph 3 of this Article.

3. Any Contracting State may at the time of signature, or when depositing its instrument of ratification, acceptance or accession, or at any later date indicate, by declaration addressed in the Secretary General of the Council of Europe, the conditions under which its domestic law permits the punishment of certain offences by an administrative authority. Such a declaration shall replace the notification envisaged in paragraph 2 of this Article.

Article 10

The requested State shall not take action on the request:

(a) if the request does not comply with the provisions of Articles 6, paragraph 1, and 7, paragraph 1;

(b) if the institution of proceedings is contrary to the provisions of Article 35;

(c) if, at the date on the request, the time-limit for criminal proceedings has already expired in the requesting State under the legislation of that State.

Article 11

Save as provided for in Article 10 the requested State may not refuse acceptance of the request in whole or in part, except in any one or more of the following cases:

(a) if it considers that the grounds on which the request is based under Article 8 are not justified;

(b) if the suspected person is not ordinarily resident in the requested State:

(c) if the suspected person is not a national of the requested State and was not ordinarily resident in the territory of that State at the time of the offence;

(d) if it considers that the offence for which proceedings are requested is an offence of a political nature or a purely military or fiscal one;

(e) if it considers that there are substantial grounds for believing that the request for proceedings was motivated by considerations of race, religion, nationality or political opinion.

(f) if its own law is already applicable to the offence and if at the time of the receipt of the request proceedings were precluded by lapse of time according to that law; Article 26, paragraph 2, shall not apply in such a case;

(g) if its competence is exclusively grounded on Article 2 and if at the time of the receipt of the request proceedings would be precluded by lapse of time according to its law, the prolongation of the time-limit by six months under the terms of Article 23 being taken into consideration;

(h) if the offence was committed outside the territory of the requesting State;

(i) if proceedings would be contrary to the international undertakings of the requested State;

(j) if proceedings would be contrary to the fundamental principles of the legal system of the requested State;

(k) if the requesting State has violated a rule of procedure laid down in this Convention.

Article 12

1. The requested State shall withdraw its acceptance of the request if, subsequent to this acceptance, a ground mentioned in Article 10 of this Convention for not taking action on the request becomes apparent.

2. The requested State may withdraw its acceptance of the request:

(a) if it becomes apparent that the presence in person of the suspected person cannot be ensured at the hearing of proceedings in that State or that any sentence, which might be passed, could not be enforced in that State;

(b) if one of the grounds for refusal mentioned in Article 11 becomes apparent before the case is brought before a court: or

(c) in other cases, if the requesting State agrees.

Section II

Transfer Procedure

Article 13

1. All requests specified in this Convention shall be made in writing. They, and all communications necessary for the application of this Convention, shall be sent either by the Ministry of Justice of the requesting State to the Ministry of Justice of the requested State or, by virtue of special mutual arrangements, direct by the authorities of the requesting State to those of the requested State; they shall be returned by the same channel.

2. In urgent cases, requests and communications may be sent through the International Criminal Police Organisation (INTERPOL).

3. Any Contracting State may, by declaration addressed to the Secretary General of the Council of Europe, give notice of its intention to adopt insofar as it itself is concerned rules of transmission other than those laid down in paragraph 1 of this Article.

Article 14

If a Contracting Party considers that the information supplied by another Contracting State is not adequate to enable it to apply this Convention, it shall ask for the necessary additional information, it may prescribe a date for the receipt of such information.

Article 15

1. A request for proceedings shall be accompanied by the original, or a certified copy, of the criminal file and all other necessary documents. However, if the suspected person is remanded in custody in accordance with the provisions of Section 5 and if the requesting State is unable to transmit these documents at the same time as the request for proceedings, the documents may be sent subsequently.

2. The requesting State shall also inform the requested State in writing of any procedural acts performed or measures taken in the requesting State after the transmission of the request which have a bearing on the proceedings. This communication shall be accompanied by any relevant documents.

Article 16

1. The requested State shall promptly communicate its decision on the request for proceedings to the requesting State.

2. The requested State shall also inform the requesting State of a waiver of proceedings or of the decision taken as a result of proceedings. A certified copy of any written decision shall be transmitted to the requesting State.

Article 17

If the competence of the requested State is exclusively grounded on Article 2 that State shall inform the suspected person of the request for proceedings with a view to allowing him to present his views on the matter before that State has taken a decision on the request.

Article 18

1. Subject to paragraph 2 of this Article, no translation of the documents relating to the application of this Convention shall be required.

2. Any Contracting State may, at the time of signature or when depositing its instrument of ratification, acceptance or accession, by declaration addressed to the Secretary General of the Council of Europe, reserve the right to require that, with the exception of the copy of the written decision referred to in Article 16, paragraph 2, the said documents be accompanied by a translation. The other Contracting States shall send the translations in either the national language of the receiving State or such one of the official languages of the Council of Europe as the receiving State shall indicate. However, such an indication is not obligatory. The other Contracting States may claim reciprocity.

3. This Article shall be without prejudice to any provisions concerning translation of requests and supporting documents that may be contained in agreements or arrangements now in force or that may be concluded between two or more Contracting States.

Article 19

Documents transmitted in application of this Convention need not be authenticated.

Article 20

Contracting Parties shall not claim from each other the refund of any expenses resulting from the application of this Convention.

Section III

Effects in the requesting State of a request for proceedings.

Article 21

1. When the requesting State has requested proceedings, it can no longer prosecute the suspected person for the offence in respect of which the proceedings have been requested or enforce a judgment which has been pronounced previously in that State against him for that offence. Until the requested State's decision on the request for proceedings has been received, the requesting State shall, however, retain its right to take all steps in respect of prosecution, short of bringing the case to trial, or, as the case may be, allowing the competent administrative authority to decide on the case.

2. The right of prosecution and of enforcement shall revert to the requesting State:

(a) if the requested State informs it of a decision in accordance with Article 10 not to take action on the request;

(b) if the requested State informs it of a decision in accordance with Article 11 to refuse acceptance of the request;

(c) if the requested State informs it of a decision in accordance with Article 12 to withdraw acceptance of the request;

(d) if the requested State informs it of a decision not to institute proceedings or discontinue them;

(e) if it withdraws its request before the requested State has informed it of a decision to take action on the request.

Article 22

A request for proceedings, made in accordance with the provisions of this Part, shall have the effect in the requesting State of prolonging the time-limit for proceedings by six months.

Section IV

Effects in the requested State of a request for proceedings.

Article 23

If the competence of the requested State is exclusively grounded on Article 2 the time-limit for proceedings in that State shall be prolonged by six months.

Article 24

1. If proceedings are dependent on a complaint in both States the complaint brought in the requesting State shall have equal validity with that brought in the requested State.

2. If a complaint is necessary only in the requested State, that State may take proceedings even in the absence of a complaint if the person who is empowered to bring the complaint has not objected within a period of one month from the date of receipt by him of notice from the competent authority informing him of his right to object.

Article 25

In the requested State the sanction applicable to the offence shall be that prescribed by its own law unless that law provides otherwise. Where the competence of the requested State is exclusively grounded on Article 2, the sanction pronounced in that State shall not be more severe than that provided for in the law of the requesting State.

Article 26

1. Any act with a view to proceedings, taken in the requesting State in accordance with its law and regulations, shall have the same validity in the requested State as if it had been taken by the authorities of that State, provided that assimilation does not give such act a greater evidential weight than it has in the requesting State.

2. Any act which interrupts time-limitation and which has been validly performed in the requesting State shall have the same effects in the requested State and vice versa.

Section V

Provisional measures in the requested State

Article 27

1. When the requesting State announces its intention to transmit a request for proceedings, and if the competence of the requested State would be exclusively grounded on Article 2, the requested State may, on application by the requesting State and by virtue of this Convention, provisionally arrest the suspected person:

   (a) if the law of the requested State authorises remand in custody for the offence, and

   (b) if there are reasons to fear that the suspected person will abscond or that he will cause evidence to be suppressed.

2. The application for provisional arrest shall state that there exists a warrant of arrest or other order having the same effect, issued in accordance with the procedure laid down in the law of the requesting State; it shall also state for what offence proceedings will be requested and when and where such offence was committed and it shall contain as accurate a description of the suspected person as possible. It shall also contain a brief statement of the circumstances of the case.

3. An application for provisional arrest shall be sent direct by the authorities in the requesting State mentioned in Article 13 to the corresponding authorities in the requested State, by post or telegram or by any other means affording evidence in writing or accepted by the requested State. The requesting State shall be informed without delay of the result of its application.

Article 28

Upon receipt of a request for proceedings accompanied by the documents referred to in Article 15, paragraph 1, the requested State shall have jurisdiction to apply all such provisional measures, including remand in custody of the suspected person and seizure of property, as could be applied under its own law if the offence in respect of which proceedings are requested had been committed in its territory.

Article 29

1. The provisional measures provided in Articles 27 and 28 shall be governed by the provisions of this Convention and the law of the requested State. The law of that State, or the Convention shall also determine the conditions on which the measures may lapse.

2. These measures shall lapse in the cases referred to in Article 21, paragraph 2.

3. A person in custody shall in any event be released if he is arrested in pursuance of Article 27 and the requested State does not receive the request for proceedings within 18 days from the date of the arrest.

4. A person in custody shall in any event be released if he is arrested in pursuance of Article 27 and the documents which should accompany the request for proceedings have not been received by the requested State within 15 days from the receipt of the request for proceedings.

5. The period of custody applied exclusively by virtue of Article 27 shall not in any event exceed 40 days.

Part IV

Plurality of Criminal Proceedings

Article 30

1. Any Contracting State which, before the institution or in the course of proceedings for an offence which it considers to be neither of a political nature nor a purely military one, is aware of proceedings pending in another Contracting State against the same person in respect of the same offence shall consider whether it can either waive or suspend its own proceedings, or transfer them to the other State.

2. If it deems it advisable in the circumstances not to waive or suspend its own proceedings it shall so notify the other State in good time and in any event before judgment is given on the merits.

Article 31

1. In the eventuality referred to in Article 30, paragraph 2, the States concerned shall endeavour as far as possible to determine, after evaluation in each case of the circumstances mentioned in Article 8, which of them alone shall continue to conduct proceedings. During this consultative procedure the States concerned shall postpone judgment on the merits without however being obliged to prolong such postponement beyond a period of 30 days as from the despatch of the notification provided for in Article 30, paragraph 2.

2. The provisions of paragraph 1 shall not be binding:

   (a) on the State despatching the notification provided for in Article 30, paragraph 2, if the main trial has been declared open there in the presence of the accused before despatch of the notification;

   (b) on the State to which the notification is addressed, if the main trial has been declared open there in the presence of the accused before receipt of the notification.

Article 32

In the interests of arriving at the truth and with a view to the application of an appropriate sanction, the States concerned shall examine whether it is expedient that one of them alone shall conduct proceedings and, if so, endeavour to determine which one, when:

   (a) several offences which are materially distinct and which fall under the criminal law of each of those States are ascribed either to a single person or to several persons having acted in unison;

   (b) a single offence which falls under the criminal law of each of those States is ascribed to several persons having acted in unison.

Article 33

All decisions reached in accordance with Articles 31 paragraph 1, and 32 shall entail, as between the States concerned, all the consequences of a transfer of proceedings as provided for in this Convention. The State which waives its own proceedings shall be deemed to have transferred them to the other State.

Article 34

The transfer procedure provided for in Section 2 of Part III shall apply in so far as its provisions are compatible with those contained in the present Part.

Part V

Ne bis in idem

Article 35

1. A person in respect of whom a final enforceable criminal judgment has been rendered may for the same act neither be prosecuted nor sentenced nor subjected to enforcement of a sanction in another Contracting State:

 (a) is he was acquitted;

 (b) if the sanction imposed:

 (i) has been completely enforced or is being enforced, or

 (ii) has been wholly, or with respect to the part not enforced, the subject of a pardon or an amnesty, or

 (iii) can no longer be enforced because of lapse of time;

 (c) if the court convicted the offender without imposing a sanction.

2. Nevertheless, a Contracting State shall not, unless it has itself requested the proceedings, be obliged to recognise the effect of *ne bis in idem* if the act which gave rise to the judgment was directed against either a person or an institution or any thing having public status in that State, or if the subject of the judgment had himself a public status in that State.

3. Furthermore, a Contracting State where the act was committed or considered as such according to the law of that State shall not be obliged to recognise the effect of *ne bis in idem* unless that State has itself requested the proceedings.

Article 36

If new proceedings are instituted against a person who in another Contracting State has been sentenced for the same act, then any period of deprivation of liberty arising from the sentence enforced shall be deducted from the sanction which may be imposed.

Article 37

This part shall not prevent the application of wider domestic provisions relating to the effect of *ne bis in idem* attached to foreign criminal judgments.

Part VI

Final Clauses

Article 38

1. This Convention shall be open to signature by the member States of the Council of Europe. It shall be subject to ratification or acceptance. Instruments of ratification or acceptance shall be deposited with the Secretary General of the Council of Europe.

2. This Convention shall enter into force there months after the date of the deposit of the third instrument of ratification or acceptance.

3. In respect of a signatory State ratifying or accepting subsequently, the Convention shall come into force three months after the date of the deposit of its instrument of ratification or acceptance.

Article 39

1. After the entry into force of this Convention, the Committee of Ministers of the Council of Europe may invite any non-member State to accede thereto provided that the resolution containing such invitation receives the unanimous agreement of the Members of the Council who have ratified the Convention.

2. Such accession shall be effected by depositing with the Secretary General of the Council of Europe an instrument of accession which shall take effect three months after the date of its deposit.

Article 40

1. Any Contracting State may, at the time of signature or when depositing its instrument of ratification, acceptance or accession, specify the territory or territories to which this Convention shall apply.

2. Any Contracting State may, when depositing its instruments of ratification, acceptance or accession or at any later date, by declaration addressed to the Secretary General of the Council of Europe, extend this Convention to any other territory or territories specified in the declaration and for whose international relations it is responsible or on whose behalf it is authorised to give undertakings.

3. Any declaration made in pursuance of the preceding paragraph may, in respect of any territory mentioned in such declaration, be withdrawn according to the procedure laid down in Article 45 of this Convention.

Article 41

1. Any Contracting State may, at the time of signature or when depositing its instrument of ratification, acceptance or accession, declare that it avails itself of one or more of the reservations provided for in Appendix I or make a declaration provided for in Appendix II to this Convention.

2. Any Contracting State may wholly or partly withdraw a reservation or declaration it has made in accordance with the foregoing paragraph by means of a declaration addressed to the Secretary General of the Council of Europe which shall become effective as from the date of its receipt.

3. A Contracting State which has made a reservation in respect of any provision of this Convention may not claim the application of that provision by any other Contracting State; it may, however, if its reservation is partial or conditional, claim the application of that provision insofar as it has itself accepted it.

Article 42

1. Any Contracting State may at any time, by declaration addressed to the Secretary General of the Council of Europe, set out the legal provisions to be included in Appendix III to this Convention.

2. Any Change of the national provisions listed in Appendix III shall be notified to the Secretary General of the Council of Europe if such a change renders the information in this Appendix incorrect.

3. Any changes made in Appendix III in application of the preceding paragraphs shall take effect in each Contracting State one month after the date of their notification by the Secretary General of the Council of Europe.

Article 43

1. This Convention affects neither the rights and the undertakings derived from extradition treaties and international multilateral conventions concerning special matters, nor provisions

concerning matters which are dealt with in the present Convention and which are contained in other existing conventions between Contracting States.

2. The Contracting States may not conclude bilateral or multilateral agreements with one another on the matters dealt with in this Convention, except in order to supplement its provisions or facilitate application of the principles embodied in it.

3. Should two or more Contracting States, however, have already established their relations in this matter on the basis of uniform legislation, or instituted a special system of their own, or should they in future do so, they shall be entitled to regulate those relations accordingly, notwithstanding the terms of this Convention.

4. Contracting States ceasing to apply the terms of this Convention to their mutual relations in this matter in accordance with the provisions of the preceding paragraph shall notify the Secretary General of the Council of Europe to that effect.

Article 44

The European Committee on Crime Problems of the Council of Europe shall be kept informed regarding the application of this Convention and shall do whatever is needful to facilitate a friendly settlement of any difficulty which may arise out of its execution.

Article 45

1. This Convention shall remain in force indefinitely.

2. Any Contracting State may, insofar as it is concerned, denounce this Convention by means of a notification addressed to the Secretary General of the Council of Europe.

3. Such denunciation shall take effect six months after the date of receipt by the Secretary General of such notification.

Article 46

The secretary General of the Council of Europe shall notify the member States of the Council and any State which has acceded to this Convention of:

(a) any signature;

(b) any deposit or an instrument of ratification, acceptance or accession;

(c) any date of entry into force of this Convention in accordance with Article 38 thereof;

(d) any declaration received in pursuance of the provisions of Article 9, paragraph 3;

(e) any declaration received in pursuance of the provisions of Article 13, paragraph 3;

(f) any declaration received in pursuance of the provisions of Article 18, paragraph 2;

(g) any declaration received in pursuance of the provisions of Article 40, paragraphs 2 and 3;

(h) any reservation or declaration made in pursuance of the provisions of Article 41, paragraph 1;

(i) the withdrawal of any reservation or declaration carried out in pursuance of the provisions of Article 41, paragraph 2;

(j) any declaration received in pursuance of the provisions of Article 42, paragraph 1, and any subsequent notification received in pursuance of paragraph 2 of that Article;

(k) any notification received in pursuance of the provisions of Article 43, paragraph 4;

(l) any notification received in pursuance of the provisions of Article 45 and the date on which denunciation takes effect.

Article 47

This Convention and the notifications and declarations authorised thereunder shall apply only to offences committed after the Convention comes into effect for the Contracting States involved.

4.2. Transfer of Execution

European Convention on the International Validity of Criminal Judgments (1970)[*]

The Hague, 28 May 1970

Part I

Definitions

Article 1

For the purposes of this Convention:

(a) "European criminal judgment" means any final decision delivered by a criminal court of a Contracting State as a result of criminal proceedings;

(b) "Offence" comprises, apart from acts dealt with under the criminal law, those dealt with under the legal provisions listed in Appendix II to the present Convention on condition that where these provisions give competence to an administrative authority there must be opportunity for the person concerned to have the case tried by a court;

(c) "Sentence" means the imposition of a sanction;

(d) "Sanction" means any punishment or other measure expressly imposed on a person, in respect of an offence, in a European criminal judgment, or in an "ordonnance pénale";

(e) "Disqualification" means any loss or suspension of a right or any prohibition or loss of legal capacity;

(f) "Judgment rendered in absentia" means any decision considered as such under Article 21, paragraph 2;

(g) "Ordonnance pénale" means any of the decisions delivered in another Contracting State and listed in Appendix III to this Convention.

Part II

Enforcement of European criminal judgments

Section I

General provisions

(a) General conditions of enforcement

Article 2

This Part is applicable to:

(a) sanctions involving deprivation of liberty;

(b) fines or confiscation;

---

[*] *European Treaty Series*, No.70.

(c)   disqualifications.

Article 3

1.   A Contracting State shall be competent in the cases and under the conditions provided for in this Convention to enforce a sanction imposed in another Contracting State which is enforceable in the latter State.

2.   This competence can only be exercised following a request by the other Contracting State.

Article 4

1.   The sanction shall not be enforced by another Contracting State unless under its law the act for which the sanction was imposed would be an offence if committed on its territory and the person on whom the sanction was imposed liable to punishment if he had committed the act there.

2.   If the sentence relates to two or more offences, not all of which fulfil the requirements of paragraph 1, the sentencing State shall specify which part of the sanction applies to the offences that satisfy those requirements.

Article 5

The sentencing State may request another Contracting State to enforce the sanction only if one or more of the following conditions are fulfilled:

(a)   if the person sentenced is ordinarily resident in the other State;

(b)   if the enforcement of the sanction in the other State is likely to improve the prospects for the social rehabilitation of the person sentenced;

(c)   if, in the case of a sanction involving deprivation of liberty, the sanction could be enforced following the enforcement of another sanction involving deprivation of liberty which the person sentenced is undergoing or is to undergo in the other State;

(d)   if the other State is the State of origin of the person sentenced and has declared itself willing to accept responsibility for the enforcement of that sanction;

(e)   if it considers that it cannot itself enforce the sanction, even by having recourse to extradition, and that the other State can.

Article 6

Enforcement requested in accordance with the foregoing provisions may not be refused, in whole or in part, save:

(a)   where enforcement would run counter to the fundamental principles of the legal system of the requested State;

(b)   where the requested State considers the offence for which the sentence was passed to be of a political nature or a purely military one;

(c)   where the requested State considers that there are substantial grounds for believing that the sentence was brought about or aggravated by considerations of race, religion, nationality or political opinion;

(d)   where enforcement would be contrary to the international undertakings of the requested State;

(e) where the act is already the subject of proceedings in the requested State or where the requested State decides to institute proceedings in respect of the act;

(f) where the competent authorities in the requested State have decided not to take proceedings or to drop proceedings already begun, in respect of the same act;

(g) where the act was committed outside the territory of the requesting State;

(h) where the requested State is unable to enforce the sanction;

(i) where the request is grounded on Article 5 (e) and none of the other conditions mentioned in that Article is fulfilled;

(j) where the requested State considers that the requesting State is itself able to enforce the sanction;

(k) where the age of the person sentenced at the time of the offence was such that he could not have been prosecuted in the requested State;

(l) where under the law of the requested State the sanction imposed can no longer be enforced because of the lapse of time;

(m) where and to the extent that the sentence imposes a disqualification.

Article 7

A request for enforcement shall not be complied with if enforcement would run counter to the principles recognised in the provisions of Section I of Part III of this Convention.

(b) Effects of the transfer of enforcement

Article 8

For the purposes of Article 6, paragraph 1 and the reservation mentioned under (c) of Appendix I of the present Convention any act which interrupts or suspends a time limitation validly performed by the authorities of the sentencing State shall be considered as having the same effect for the purpose of reckoning time limitation in the requested State in accordance with the law of that State.

Article 9

1. A sentenced person detained in the requesting State who has been surrendered to the requested State for the purpose of enforcement shall not be proceeded against, sentenced or detained with a view to the carrying out of a sentence or detention order for any offence committed prior to his surrender other than that for which the sentence to be enforced was imposed, nor shall he for any other reason be restricted in his personal freedom, except in the following cases:

    (a) when the State which surrendered him consents. A request for consent shall be submitted, accompanied by all relevant documents and a legal record of any statement made by the convicted person in respect of the offence concerned. Consent shall be given when the offence for which it is requested would itself be subject to extradition under the law of the State requesting enforcement or when extradition would be excluded only by reason of the amount of the punishment;

    (b) when the sentenced person, having had an opportunity to leave the territory of the State to which he has been surrendered, has not done so within 45 days of his final discharge, or if he has returned to that territory after leaving it.

2. The State requested to enforce the sentence may, however, take any measure necessary to remove the person from its territory, or any measures necessary under its law, including proceedings by default, to prevent any legal effects of lapse of time.

Article 10

1. The enforcement shall be governed by the law of the requested State and that State alone shall be competent to take all appropriate decisions, such as those concerning conditional release.

2. The requesting State alone shall have the right to decide on any application for review of sentence.

3. Either State may exercise the right of amnesty or pardon.

Article 11

1. When the sentencing State has requested enforcement it may no longer itself begin the enforcement of a sanction which is the subject of that request. The sentencing State may, however, begin enforcement of a sanction involving deprivation of liberty when the sentenced person is already detained on the territory of that State at the moment of the presentation of the request.

2. The right of enforcement shall revert to the requesting State:

(a) if it withdraws its request before the requested State has informed it of an intention to take action on the request;

(b) if the requested State notifies a refusal to take action on the request;

(c) if the requested State expressly relinquishes its right of enforcement. Such relinquishment shall only be possible if both the States concerned agree or if enforcement is no longer possible in the requested State. In the latter case, a relinquishment demanded by the requesting Sate shall be compulsory.

Article 12

1. The competent authorities of the requested State shall discontinue enforcement as soon as they have knowledge of any pardon, amnesty or application for review of sentence or any other decision by reason of which the sanction ceases to be enforceable. The same shall apply to the enforcement of a fine when the person sentenced has paid it to the competent authority in the requesting State.

2. The requesting State shall without delay inform the requested State of any decision or procedural measure taken on its territory that causes the right of enforcement to lapse in accordance with the preceding paragraph.

(c) Miscellaneous provisions

Article 13

1. The transit through the territory of a Contracting State of a detained person, who is to be transferred to a third Contracting State in application of this Convention, shall be granted at the request of the State in which the person is detained. The State of transit may require to be supplied with any appropriate document before taking a decision on the request. The person being transferred shall remain in custody in the territory of the State of transit, unless the state from which he is being transferred requests his release.

2. Except in cases where the transfer is requested under Article 34 any Contracting State may refuse transit:

(a) on one of the grounds mentioned in Article 6 (b) and (c);

(b) on the ground that the person concerned is one of its own nationals.

3. If air transport is used, the following provisions shall apply:

(a) when it is not intended to land, the State from which the person is to be transferred may notify the State over whose territory the flight is to be made that the person concerned is being transferred in application of this Convention. In the case of an unscheduled landing such notification shall have the effect of a request for provisional arrest as provided for in Article 32, paragraph 2, and a formal request for transit shall be made;

(b) where it is intended to land, a formal request for transit shall be made.

Article 14

Contracting States shall not claim from each other the refund of any expenses resulting from the application of this Convention.

Section II

Requests for enforcement

Article 15

1. All requests specified in this Convention shall be made in writing. They, and all communications necessary for the application of this Convention, shall be sent either by the Ministry of Justice of the requesting State to the Ministry of Justice of the requested State or, if the Contracting States so agree, direct by the authorities of the requesting State to those of the requested State; they shall be returned by the same channel.

2. In urgent cases, requests and communications may be sent through the International Criminal Police Organisation (INTERPOL).

3. Any Contracting State may, by declaration addressed to the Secretary General of the Council of Europe, give notice of its intention to adopt other rules in regard to the communications referred to in paragraph 1 of this Article.

Article 16

The request for enforcement shall be accompanied by the original, or a certified copy, of the decision whose enforcement is requested and all other necessary documents. The original, or a certified copy, of all or part of the criminal file shall be sent to the requested State, if it so requires. The competent authority of the requesting State shall certify the sanction enforceable.

Article 17

If the requested State considers that the information supplied by the requesting State is not adequate to enable it to apply this Convention, it shall ask for the necessary additional information. It may prescribe a date for the receipt of such information.

Article 18

1. The authorities of the requested State shall promptly inform those of the requesting State of the action taken on the request for enforcement.

2. The authorities of the requested State shall, where appropriate, transmit to those of the requesting State a document certifying that the sanction has been enforced.

Article 19

1. Subject to paragraph 2 of this Article, no translation of requests or of supporting documents shall be required.

2. Any Contracting State may, at the time of signature of when depositing its instrument of ratification, acceptance or accession, by a declaration addressed to the Secretary General of the Council of Europe, reserve the right to require that requests and supporting documents be accompanied by a translation into its own language or into one of the official languages of the Council of Europe or into such one of those languages as it shall indicate. The other Contracting States may claim reciprocity.

3. This Article shall be without prejudice to any provisions concerning translation of requests and supporting documents that may be contained in agreements or arrangements now in force or that may be concluded between two or more Contracting States.

Article 20

Evidence and documents transmitted in application of this Convention need not be authenticated.

Section III

Judgments rendered in absentia and "ordonnances pénales"

Article 21

1. Unless otherwise provided in this Convention, enforcement of judgments rendered in absentia and of "ordonnances pénales" shall be subject to the same rules as enforcement of other judgments.

2. Except as provided in paragraph 3, a judgment in absentia for the purposes of this Convention means any judgment rendered by a court in a Contracting State after criminal proceedings at the hearing of which the sentenced person was not personally present.

3. Without prejudice to Articles 25, paragraph 2, 26, paragraph 2 and 29, the following shall be considered as judgments rendered after a hearing of the accused:

(a) any judgment in absentia and any "ordonnance pénale" which have been confirmed or pronounced in the sentencing State after opposition by the person sentenced;

(b) any judgment rendered in absentia on appeal, provided that the appeal from the judgment of the court of first instance was lodged by the person sentenced.

Article 22

Any judgments rendered in absentia and any "ordonnances pénales" which have not yet been the subject of appeal or opposition may, as soon as they have been rendered, be transmitted to the requested State for the purpose of notification and with a view to enforcement.

Article 23

1. If the requested State sees fit to take action on the request to enforce a judgment rendered in absentia or an "ordonnance pénale", it shall cause the person sentenced to be personally notified of the decision rendered in the requesting State.

2. In the notification to the person sentenced information shall also be given:

(a) that a request for enforcement has been presented in accordance with this Convention;

(b) that the only remedy available is an opposition as provided for in Article 24 of this Convention;

(c) that the opposition must be lodged with such authority as may be specified; that for the purposes of its admissibility the opposition is subject to the provisions of Article 24 of this Convention; and that the person sentenced may ask to be heard by the authorities of the sentencing State;

(d) that, if no opposition is lodged within the prescribed period, the judgment will, for the entire purposes of this Convention, be considered as having been rendered after a hearing of the accused.

3. A copy of the notification shall be sent promptly to the authority which requested enforcement.

Article 24

1. After notice of the decision has been served in accordance with Article 23, the only remedy available to the person sentenced shall be an opposition. Such opposition shall be examined, as the person sentenced chooses, either by the competent court in the requesting State or by that in the requested State. If the person sentenced expresses no choice, the opposition shall be examined by the competent court in the requested State.

2. In the cases specified in the preceding paragraph, the opposition shall be admissible if it is lodged with the competent authority of the requested State within a period of 30 days from the date on which the notice was served. This period shall be reckoned in accordance with the relevant rules of the law of the requested State. The competent authority of that State shall promptly notify the authority which made the request for enforcement.

Article 25

1. If the opposition is examined in the requesting State, the person sentenced shall be summoned to appear in that State at the new hearing of the case. Notice to appear shall be personally served not less than 21 days before the new hearing. This period may be reduced with the consent of the person sentenced. The new hearing shall be held before the court which is competent in the requesting State and in accordance with the procedure of that State.

2. If the person sentenced fails to appear personally or is not represented in accordance with the law of the requesting State, the court shall declare the opposition null and void and its decision shall be communicated to the competent authority of the requested State. The same procedure shall be followed if the court declares the opposition inadmissible. In both cases, the judgment rendered in absentia or the "ordonnance pénale" shall, for the entire purposes of this Convention, be considered as having been rendered after a hearing of the accused.

3. If the person sentenced appears personally or is represented in accordance with the law of the requesting State and if the opposition is declared admissible, the request for enforcement shall be considered as null and void.

Article 26

1. If the opposition is examined in the requested State the person sentenced shall be summoned to appear in that State at the new hearing of the case. Notice to appear shall be personally served not less than 21 days before the new hearing. This period may be reduced with the consent of the person sentenced. The new hearing shall be held before the court which is competent in the requested State and in accordance with the procedure of that State.

2. If the person sentenced fails to appear personally or is not represented in accordance with the law of the requested State, the court shall declare the opposition null and void. In that event, and if the court declares the opposition inadmissible, the judgment rendered in absentia or the "ordonnance pénale" shall, for the entire purposes of this Convention, be considered as having been rendered after a hearing of the accused.

3. If the person sentenced appears personally or is represented in accordance with the law of the requested State, and if the opposition is admissible, the act shall be tried as if it had been committed in that State. Preclusion of proceedings by reason of lapse of time shall, however, in no circumstances be examined. The judgment rendered in the requesting State shall be considered null and void.

4. Any step with a view to proceedings or a preliminary enquiry, taken in the sentencing State in accordance with its law and regulations, shall have the same validity in the requested State as if it had been taken by the authorities of that State, provided that assimilation does not give such steps a greater evidential weight than they have in the requesting State.

Article 27

For the purpose of lodging an opposition and for the purpose of the subsequent proceedings, the person sentenced in absentia or by an "ordonnance pénale" shall be entitled to legal assistance in the cases and on the conditions prescribed by the law of the requested State and, where appropriate, of the requesting State.

Article 28

Any judicial decisions given in pursuance of Article 26, paragraph 3, and enforcement thereof, shall be governed solely by the law of the requested State.

Article 29

If the person sentenced in absentia or by an "ordonnance pénale" lodges no opposition, the decision shall, for the entire purposes of this Convention, be considered as having been rendered after the hearing of the accused.

Article 30

National legislations shall be applicable in the matter of reinstatement if the sentenced person, for reasons beyond his control, failed to observe the time-limits laid down in Articles 24, 25 and 26 or to appear personally at the hearing fixed for the new examination of the case.

Section IV

Provisional measures

Article 31

If the sentenced person is present in the requesting State after notification of the acceptance of its request for enforcement of a sentence involving deprivation of liberty is received, that State may, if it deems it necessary in order to ensure enforcement, arrest him with a view to his transfer under the provisions of Article 43.

Article 32

1. When the requesting State has requested enforcement, the requested State may arrest the person sentenced:

   (a) if, under the law of the requested State, the offence is one which justifies remand in custody, and

   (b) if there is a danger of abscondence or, in case of a judgment rendered in absentia, a danger of secretion of evidence.

2. When the requesting State announces its intention to request enforcement, the requested State may, on application by the requesting State, arrest the person sentenced, provided that requirements under (a) and (b) of the preceding paragraph are satisfied. The said application

shall state the offence which led to the judgment and the time and place of its perpetration, and contain as accurate a description as possible of the person sentenced. It shall also contain a brief statement of the facts on which the judgment is based.

Article 33

1. The person sentenced shall be held in custody in accordance with the law of the requested State; the law of that State shall also determine the conditions on which he may be released.

2. The person in custody shall in any event be released;

   (a) after a period equal to the period of deprivation of liberty imposed in the judgment;

   (b) if he was arrested in pursuance of Article 32, paragraph 2, and the requested State did not receive, within 18 days from the date of the arrest, the request together with the documents specified in Article 16.

Article 34

1. A person held in custody in the requested State in pursuance of Article 32 who is summoned to appear before the competent court in the requesting State in accordance with Article 25 as a result of the opposition he has lodged, shall be transferred for that purpose to the territory of the requesting State.

2. After transfer, the said person shall not be kept in custody by the requesting State if the condition set out in Article 33, paragraph 2 (a), is met or if the requesting State does not request enforcement of a further sentence. The person shall be promptly returned to the requested State unless he has been released.

Article 35

1. A person summoned before the competent court of the requesting State as a result of the opposition he has lodged shall not be proceeded against, sentenced or detained with a view to the carrying out of a sentence or detention order nor shall he for any other reason be restricted in his personal freedom for any act or offence which took place prior to his departure from the territory of the requested State and which is not specified in the summons unless he expressly consents in writing. In the case referred to in Article 34, paragraph 1, a copy of the statement of consent shall be sent to the State from which he has been transferred.

2. The effects provided for in the preceding paragraph shall cease when the person summoned, having had the opportunity to do so, has not left the territory of the requesting State during 15 days after the date of the decision following the hearing for which he was summoned to appear or if he returns to that territory after leaving it without being summoned anew.

Article 36

1. If the requesting State has requested enforcement of a confiscation of property, the requested State may provisionally seize the property in question, on condition that its own law provides for seizure in respect of similar facts.

2. Seizure shall be carried out in accordance with the law of the requested State which shall also determine the conditions on which the seizure may be lifted.

Section V

Enforcement of sanctions

(a) General clauses

Article 37

A sanction imposed in the requesting State shall not be enforced in the requested State except by a decision of the court of the requested State. Each Contracting State may, however, empower other authorities to take such decisions if the sanction to be enforced is only a fine or a confiscation and if these decisions are susceptible of appeal to a court.

Article 38

The case shall be brought before the court or the authority empowered under Article 37 if the requested State sees fit to take action on the request for enforcement.

Article 39

1. Before a court takes a decision upon a request for enforcement the sentenced person shall be given the opportunity to state his views. Upon application he shall be heard by the court either by letters rogatory or in person. A hearing in person must be granted following his express request to that effect.

2. The court may, however, decide on the acceptance of the request for enforcement in the absence of a sentenced person requesting a personal hearing if he is in custody in the requesting State. In these circumstances any decision as to the substitution of the sanction under Article 44 shall be adjourned until, following his transfer to the requested State, the sentenced person has been given the opportunity to appear before the court.

Article 40

1. The court, or in the cases referred to in Article 37, the authority empowered under the same Article, which is dealing with the case shall satisfy itself:

    (a) that the sanction whose enforcement is requested was imposed in a European criminal judgment;

    (b) that the requirements of Article 4 are met;

    (c) that the condition laid down in Article 6 (a) is not fulfilled or should not preclude enforcement;

    (d) that enforcement is not precluded by Article 7;

    (e) that, in case of a judgment rendered in absentia or in "ordonnance pénale" the requirements of Section 3 of this Part are met.

2. Each Contracting State may entrust to the court or the authority empowered under Article 37 the examination of other conditions of enforcement provided for in this Convention.

Article 41

The judicial decisions taken in pursuance of the present section with respect to the requested enforcement and those taken on appeal from decisions by the administrative authority referred to in Article 37, shall be appealable.

Article 42

The requested State shall be bound by the findings as to the facts insofar as they are stated in the decision or insofar as it is impliedly based on them.

(b) Clauses relating specifically to enforcement of sanctions involving deprivation of liberty

Article 43

When the sentenced person is detained in the requesting State he shall, unless the law of that State otherwise provides, be transferred to the requested State as soon as the requesting State has been notified of the acceptance of the request for enforcement.

Article 44

1. If the request for enforcement is accepted, the court shall substitute for the sanction involving deprivation of liberty imposed in the requesting State a sanction prescribed by its own law for the same offence. This sanction may, subject to the limitations laid down in paragraph 2, be of a nature or duration other than that imposed in the requesting State. If this latter sanction is less than the minimum which may be pronounced under the law of the requested State, the court shall not be bound by that minimum and shall impose a sanction corresponding to the sanction imposed in the requesting State.

2. In determining the sanction, the court shall not aggravate the penal situation of the person sentenced as it results from the decision delivered in the requesting State.

3. Any part of the sanction imposed in the requesting State and any term of provisional custody, served by the person sentenced subsequent to the sentence shall be deducted in full. The same shall apply in respect of any period during which the person sentenced was remanded in custody in the requesting State before being sentenced insofar as the law of that State so requires.

4. Any Contracting State may, at any time, deposit with the Secretary General of the Council of Europe a declaration which confers on it in pursuance of the present Convention the right to enforce a sanction involving deprivation of liberty of the same nature as that imposed in the requesting State even if the duration of that sanction exceeds the maximum provided for by its national law for a sanction of the same nature. Nevertheless, this rule shall only be applied in cases where the national law of this State allows, in respect of the same offence, for the imposition of a sanction of at least the same duration as that imposed in the requesting State but which is of a more severe nature. The sanction imposed under this paragraph may, if its duration and purpose so require, be enforced in a penal establishment intended for the enforcement of sanctions of another nature.

(c) Clauses relating specifically to enforcement of fines and confiscations

Article 45

1. If the request for enforcement of a fine or confiscation of a sum of money is accepted, the court or the authority empowered under Article 37 shall convert the amount thereof into the currency of the requested State at the rate of exchange ruling at the time when the decision is taken. It shall thus fix the amount of the fine, or the sum to be confiscated, which shall nevertheless not exceed the maximum sum fixed by its own law for the same offence, or failing such a maximum, shall not exceed the maximum amount customarily imposed in the requested State in respect of a like offence.

2. However, the court or the authority empowered under Article 37 may maintain up to the amount imposed in the requesting State the sentence of a fine or of a confiscation when such a sanction is not provided for by the law of the requested State for the same offence, but this law allows for the imposition of more severe sanctions. The same shall apply if the sanction imposed in the requesting State exceeds the maximum laid down in the law of the

requested State for the same offence, but this law allows for the imposition of more severe sanctions.

3. Any facility as to time of payment or payment by instalments, granted in the requesting State, shall be respected in the requested State.

Article 46

1. When the request for enforcement concerns the confiscation of a specific object, the court or the authority empowered under Article 37 may order the confiscation of that object only insofar as such confiscation is authorised by the law of the requested State for the same offence.

2. However, the court or the authority empowered under Article 37 may maintain the confiscation ordered in the requesting State when this sanction is not provided for in the law of the requested State for the same offence but this law allows for the imposition of more severe sanctions.

Article 47

1. The proceeds of fines and confiscations shall be paid into the public funds of the requested State without prejudice to any rights of third parties.

2. Property confiscated which is of special interest may be remitted to the requesting State if it so requires.

Article 48

If a fine cannot be exacted, a court of the requested State may impose an alternative sanction involving deprivation of liberty insofar as the laws of both States so provide in such cases unless the requesting State expressly limited its request to exacting of the fine alone. If the court decides to impose an alternative sanction involving deprivation of liberty, the following rules shall apply:

(a) If conversion of a fine into a sanction involving deprivation of liberty is already prescribed either in the sentence pronounced in the requesting Sate or directly in the law of that State, the court of the requested State shall determine the nature and length of such sanction in accordance with the rules laid down by its own law. If the sanction involving deprivation of liberty already prescribed in the requesting State is less than the minimum which may be imposed under the law of the requested State, the court shall not be bound by that minimum and shall impose a sanction corresponding to the sanction prescribed in the requesting State. In determining the sanction the court shall not aggravate the penal situation of the person sentenced as it results from the decision delivered in the requesting State.

(b) In all other cases the court of the requested State shall convert the fine in accordance with its own law, observing the limits prescribed by the law of the requesting State.

(d) Clauses relating specifically to enforcement of disqualification

Article 49

1. Where a request for enforcement of a disqualification is made such disqualification imposed in the requesting Sate may be given effect in the requested State only if the law of the latter State allows for disqualification for the offence in question.

2. The court dealing with the case shall appraise the expediency of enforcing the disqualification in the territory of its own State.

Article 50

1. If the court orders enforcement of the disqualification it shall determine the duration thereof within the limits prescribed by its own law, but may not exceed the limits laid down in the sentence imposed in the requesting State.

2. The court may order the disqualification to be enforced in respect of some only of the rights whose loss or suspension has been pronounced.

Article 51

Article 11 shall not apply to disqualifications.

Article 52

The requested State shall have the right to restore to the person sentenced the rights of which he has been deprived in accordance with a decision taken in application of this section.

Part III

International Effects of European Criminal Judgments

Section I

Ne bis in idem

Article 53

1. A person in respect of whom a European criminal judgment has been rendered may for the same act neither be prosecuted nor sentenced nor subjected to enforcement of a sanction in another Contracting State:

    (a) if he was acquitted;

    (b) if the sanction imposed:
        (i) has been completely enforced or is being enforced, or

        (ii) has been wholly, or with respect to the part not enforced, the subject of a pardon or an amnesty, or

        (iii) can no longer be enforced because of lapse of time;

    (c) if the court convicted the offender without imposing a sanction.

2. Nevertheless, a Contracting State shall not, unless it has itself requested the proceedings, be obliged to recognise the effect of ne bis in idem if the act which gave rise to the judgment was directed against either a person or an institution or any thing having public status in that State, or if the subject of the judgment had himself a public status in that State.

3. Furthermore, any Contracting State where the act was committed or considered as such according to the law of that State shall not be obliged to recognise the effect of ne bis in idem unless that State has itself requested the proceedings.

Article 54

If new proceedings are instituted against a person who in another Contracting State has been sentenced for the same act, then any period of deprivation of liberty arising from the sentence enforced shall be deducted from the sanction which may be imposed.

Article 55

This Section shall not prevent the application of wider domestic provisions relating to the effect of ne bis in idem attached to foreign criminal judgments.

Section II

Taking into consideration

Article 56

Each Contracting State shall legislate as it deems appropriate to enable its courts when rendering a judgment to take into consideration any previous European criminal judgment rendered for another offence after a hearing of the accused with a view to attaching to this judgment all or some of the effects which its law attaches to judgments rendered in its territory. It shall determine the conditions in which this judgment is taken into consideration.

Article 57

Each Contracting State shall legislate as it deems appropriate to allow the taking into consideration of any European criminal judgment rendered after a hearing of the accused so as to enable application of all or part of a disqualification attached by its law to judgments rendered in its territory. It shall determine the conditions in which this judgment is taken into consideration.

Part IV

Final provisions

Article 58

1. This Convention shall be open to signature by the member States represented on the Committee of Ministers of the Council of Europe. It shall be subject to ratification or acceptance. Instruments of ratification or acceptance shall be deposited with the Secretary General of the Council of Europe.

2. This Convention shall enter into force three months after the date of the deposit of the third instrument of ratification or acceptance.

3. In respect of a signatory State ratifying or accepting subsequently, the Convention shall come into force three months after the date of the deposit of its instrument of ratification or acceptance.

Article 59

1. After the entry into force of this Convention, the Committee of Ministers of the Council of Europe may invite any non-member State to accede thereto, provided that the resolution containing such invitation receives the unanimous agreement of the members of the Council who have ratified the Convention.

2. Such accession shall be effected by depositing with the Secretary General of the Council of Europe an instrument of accession which shall take effect three months after the date of its deposit.

Article 60

1. Any Contracting State may, at the time of signature or when depositing its instrument of ratification, acceptance or accession, specify the territory or territories to which this Convention shall apply.

2. Any Contracting State may, when depositing its instrument of ratification, acceptance or accession or at any later date by declaration addressed to the Secretary General of the Council of Europe, extend this Convention to any other territory or territories specified in the declaration and for whose international relations it is responsible or on whose behalf it is authorised to give undertakings.

3. Any declaration made in pursuance of the preceding paragraph may, in respect of any territory mentioned in such declaration, be withdrawn according to the procedure laid down in Article 66 of this Convention.

Article 61

1. Any Contracting State may, at the time of signature or when depositing its instrument of ratification, acceptance or accession, declare that it avails itself of one or more of the reservations provided for in Appendix I to this Convention.

2. Any Contracting State may wholly or partly withdraw a reservation it has made in accordance with the foregoing paragraph by means of a declaration addressed to the Secretary General of the Council of Europe which shall become effective as from the date of its receipt.

3. A Contracting State which has made a reservation in respect of any provision of this Convention may not claim the application of that provision by any other State: it may, however, if its reservation is partial or conditional, claim the application of that provision in so far as it has itself accepted it.

Article 62

1. Any Contracting State may at any time, by declaration addressed to the Secretary General of the Council of Europe, set out the legal provisions to be included in Appendices II or III to this Convention.

2. Any change of the national provisions listed in Appendices II or III shall be notified to the Secretary General of the Council of Europe if such a change renders the information in these Appendices incorrect.

3. Any changes made in Appendices II or III in application of the preceding paragraphs shall take effect in each Contracting State one month after the date of their notification by the Secretary General of the Council of Europe.

Article 63

1. Each Contracting State shall, at the time of depositing its instrument of ratification, acceptance or accession supply the Secretary General of the Council of Europe with relevant information on the sanctions applicable in that State and their enforcement, for the purposes of the application of this Convention.

2. Any subsequent change which renders the information supplied in accordance with the previous paragraph incorrect, shall also be notified to the Secretary General of the Council of Europe.

Article 64

1. This Convention affects neither the rights and the undertakings derived from extradition treaties and international multilateral Conventions concerning special matters, nor provisions concerning matters which are dealt with in the present Convention and which are contained in other existing Conventions between Contracting States.

2. The Contracting States may not conclude bilateral or multilateral agreements with one another on the matters dealt with in this Convention, except in order to supplement its provisions or facilitate application of the principles embodied in it.

3. Should two or more Contracting States, however, have already established their relations in this matter on the basis of uniform legislation, or instituted a special system of their own, or should they in future do so, they shall be entitled to regulate those relations accordingly, notwithstanding the terms of this Convention.

4. Contracting States ceasing to apply the terms of this Convention to their mutual relations in this matter shall notify the Secretary General of the Council of Europe to that effect.

Article 65

The European Committee on Crime Problems of the Council of Europe shall be kept informed regarding the application of this Convention and shall do whatever is needful to facilitate a friendly settlement of any difficulty which may arise out of its execution.

Article 66

1. This Convention shall remain in force indefinitely.

2. Any Contracting State may, insofar as it is concerned, denounce this Convention by means of a notification addressed to the Secretary General of the Council of Europe.

3. Such denunciation shall take effect six months after the date of receipt by the Secretary General of such notification.

Article 67

The Secretary General of the Council of Europe shall notify the member States represented on the Committee of Ministers of the Council, and any State that has acceded to this Convention, of:

(a) any signature;

(b) any deposit of an instrument of ratification, acceptance or accession;

(c) any date of entry into force of this Convention in accordance with Article 58 thereof;

(d) any declaration received in pursuance of Article 19, paragraph 2;

(e) any declaration received in pursuance of Article 44, paragraph 4;

(f) any declaration received in pursuance of Article 60;

(g) any reservation made in pursuance of the provisions of Article 61, paragraph 1, and the withdrawal of such reservation;

(h) any declaration received in pursuance of Article 62, paragraph 1, and any subsequent notification received in pursuance of that Article, paragraph 2;

(i) any information received in pursuance of Article 63, paragraph 1, and any subsequent notification received in pursuance of that Article, paragraph 2;

(j) any notification concerning the bilateral or multilateral agreements concluded in pursuance of Article 64, paragraph 2, or concerning uniform legislation introduced in pursuance of Article 64, paragraph 3;

(k) any notification received in pursuance of Article 66, and the date on which denunciation takes effect.

Article 68

This Convention and the declarations and notifications authorised thereunder shall apply only to the enforcement of decisions rendered after the entry into force of the Convention between the Contracting States concerned.

APPENDIX I

Each Contracting State may declare that it reserves the right:

(a) to refuse enforcement, if it considers that the sentence relates to a fiscal or religious offence;

(b) to refuse enforcement of a sanction for an act which according to the law of the requested State could have been dealt with only by an administrative authority;

(c) to refuse enforcement of a European criminal judgment which the authorities of the requesting State rendered on a date when, under its own law, the criminal proceedings in respect of the offence punished by the judgment would have been precluded by the lapse of time;

(d) to refuse the enforcement of sanctions rendered in absentia and "ordonnances pénales" or of one of these categories of decisions only;

(e) to refuse the enforcement of the provisions of Article 8 where this Sate has an original competence and to recognise in these cases only the equivalence of acts interrupting or suspending time limitation which have been accomplished in the requesting State;

(f) to accept the application of Part III in respect of its two sections only.

APPENDIX II

List of offences other than offences dealt with under criminal law

The following offences shall be assimilated to offences under criminal law:

- in France: Any unlawful behaviour sanctioned by a "contravention de grande voirie".

- in the Federal Republic of Germany:

    Any unlawful behaviour dealt with according to the procedure laid down in Act on violations of Regulations (Gesetz über Ordnungswidrigkeiten) of 24 May 1968 (BGBL 1968, I, 481).

- in Italy: Any unlawful behaviour to which is applicable Act No. 317 of 3 March 1967.

APPENDIX III

List of "Ordonnances Pénales"

AUSTRIA

Strafverfügung (Articles 460-62 of the Code of Criminal Procedure).

DENMARK

Bodeforelae or *Udenretlig bodevedtagelse* (Article 931 of the Administration of Justice Act).

FRANCE

1. *Amende de Composition* (Articles 524-528 of the Code of Criminal Procedure supplemented by Articles R 42 - R 50).

2. *Ordonnance pénale* applied only in the departments of the Bas-Rhin, the Haut-Rhin and the Moselle.

FEDERAL REPUBLIC OF GERMANY

1. *Strafbefehl* (Articles 407-412 of the Code of Criminal Procedure).

2. *Strafverfügung* (Article 413 of the Code of Criminal Procedure).

3. *Bussgeldbescheid* (Articles 65-66 of Act of 24 May 1968 - BGBL 1968 I, 481).

ITALY

1. *Decreto penale* (Articles 506-10 of the Code of Criminal Procedure).

2. *Decreto penale* in fiscal maters (Act of 7 January 1929, No. 4).

3. *Decreto penale* in navigational matters (Articles 1242-43 of the Code of Navigation).

4. Decision rendered in pursuance of Act No. 317 of 3 March 1967.

LUXEMBOURG

1. *Ordonnance pénale* (Act of 31 July 1924 on the organisation of "ordonnances pénales").

2. *Ordonnance pénale* (Article 16 of Act of 14 February 1955 on the Traffic on Public Highways).

NORWAY

1. *Forelegg* (Articles 287-290 of the Act on Judicial Procedure in Penal Cases).

2. *Forenklet forelegg* (Article 31 B of Traffic Code of 18 June 1965).

SWEDEN

1. *Strafföreläggande* (Chapter 48 of the Code of Procedure).

2. *Föreläggande av ordningsbot* (Chapter 48 of the Code of Procedure).

SWITZERLAND

1. *Strafbefehl* (Aargau, Bâle-Country, Bâle-Town, Schaffhausen, Schwys, Uri, Zug, Zurich). *Ordonnance pénale* (Fribourg, Valais).

2. *Strafantrag* (Lower Unterwalden).

3. *Strafbescheid* (St. Gallen).

4. *Strafmandat* (Bern, Graubünden, Solothurn, Upper Unterwalden).

5. *Strafverfügung* (Appenzell Outer Rhoden, Glarus, Schaffhausen, Thurgau).

6. *Abwandlungserkenntnis* (Lucerne).

7. *Bussenentscheid* (Appenzell Inner Rhoden).

8. *Ordonnance de condamnation* (Vaud).

9. *Mandat de répression* (Neuchâtel)

10. *Avis de contravention* (Geneva, Vaud).

11. *Prononcé préfectoral* (Vaud).

12. *Prononcé de contravention* (Valais).

13. *Decreto di accusa* (Ticino).

TURKEY

Ceza Kararnamesi (Articles 386-91 of the Code of Criminal Procedure) and all other decisions by which administrative authorities impose sanctions.

4.3. Transfer of Prisoners

UN Model Agreement on the Transfer of Foreign Prisoners*

New York, 13 December 1985

I. General principles

1. The social resettlement of offenders should be promoted by facilitating the return of persons convicted of crime abroad to their country of nationality or of residence to serve their sentence at the earliest possible stage. In accordance with the above, States should afford each other the widest measure of co-operation.

2. A transfer of prisoners should be effected on the basis of mutal respect for national sovereignty and jurisdiction.

3. A transfer of prisoners should be effected in cases where the offence giving rise to conviction is punishable by deprivation of liberty by the judicial authorites of both the sending (sentencing) State and the State to which the transfer is to be effected (administering State) according to their national laws.

4. A transfer may be requested by either the sentencing or the administering State. The prisoner, as well as close relatives, may express to either State their interest in the transfer. To that end, the contracting State shall inform the prisoner of their competent authorities.

5. A transfer shall be dependent on the agreement of both the sentencing and the administering State, and should also be based on the consent of the prisoner.

6. The prisoner shall be fully informed of the possibility and of the legal consequences of a transfer, in particular whether or not he might be prosecuted because of other offences committed before his transfer.

7. The administering State should be given the opportunity to verify the free consent of the prisoner.

8. Any regulation concerning the transfer of prisoners shall be applicable to sentences of imprisonment as well as to sentences imposing measures involving deprivation of liberty because of the commission of a criminal act.

9. In cases of the person's incapability of freely determining his will, his legal representative shall be competent to consent to the transfer.

II. Other requirements

10. A transfer shall be made only on the basis of a final and definitive sentence having executive force.

11. At the time of the request for a transfer, the prisoner shall, as a general rule, still have to serve at least six months of the sentence; a transfer should, however, be granted also in cases of indeterminate sentences.

12. The decision whether to transfer a prisoner shall be taken wihout any delay.

13. The person transferred for the enforcement of a sentence passed in the sentencing State may not be tried again in the administering State for the same act upon which the sentence to be executed is based.

---

* General Assembly Resolution 40/146, *Compendium of United Nations Standards and Norms in Crime Prevention and Criminal Justice*, New York, United Nations, 1992, 106.

III. Procedural regulations

14. The competent authorities of the administering State shall: (a) continue the enforcement of the sentence immediately or through a court or administrative order; or (b) convert the sentence, thereby substituting for the sanction imposed in the sentencing State a sanction prescribed by the law of the administering State for a corresponding offence.

15. In the case of continued enforcement, the administering State shall be bound by the legal nature and duration of the sentence as determined by the sentencing State. If, however, this sentence is by its nature or duration incompatible with the law of the administering State, this State may adapt the sanction to the punishment or measure prescribed by its own law for a corresponding offence.

16. In the case of conversion of sentence, the administering State shall be entitiled to adapt the sanction as to its nature or duration according to its national law, taking into due consideration the sentence passed in the sentencing State. A sanction involving deprivation of liberty shall, however, not be converted to a pecuniary sanction.

17. The administering State shall be bound by the findings as to the facts in so far as they appear from the judgement imposed in the sentencing State. Thus the sentencing State has the sole competence for a review of the sentence.

18. The period of deprivation of liberty already served by the sentenced person in either State shall be fully deducted from the final sentence.

19. A transfer shall in no case lead to an aggravation of the situation of the prisoner.

20. Any costs incurred because of a transfer and related to transportation should be borne by the administering State, unless otherwise decided by both the sentencing and administering States.

IV. Enforcement and pardon

21. The enforcement of the sentence shall be governed by the law of the administering State.

22. Both the sentencing and the administering State shall be competent to grant pardon and amnesty.

V. Final causes

23. This agreement shall be applicable to the enforcement of sentences imposed either before or after its entry into force.

24. This agreement is subject to ratification. The instruments of ratification shall be deposited as soon as possible in ...

25. This agreement shall enter into force on the thirtieth day after the day on which the instruments of ratification are exchanged.

26. Either Contracting Party may denounce this agreement in writing to the ... Denunciation shall take effect six months following the date on which the notification is received by the...

In witness whereof the undersigned, being duly authorized thereto by the respective Governments, have signed this treaty.

UN Model Treaty on the Transfer of Supervision of Offenders Conditionally Sentenced or Conditionally Released (1990)*

New York, 14 December 1990

Article 1

Scope of application

1. The present Treaty shall be applicable, if, according to a final court decision, a person has been found guilty of an offence and has been:

   (a) Placed on probation without sentence having been pronounced;

   (b) Given a suspended sentence involving deprivation of liberty;

   (c) Given a sentence, the enforcement of which has been modified (parole) or conditionally suspended, in whole or in part, either at the time of the sentence or subsequently.

2. The State where the decision was taken (sentencing State) may request another State (administering State) to take responsibility for applying the terms of the decision (transfer of supervision).

Article 2

Channels of communications

A request for the transfer of supervision shall be made in writing. The request, supporting documents and subsequent communication shall be transmitted through diplomatic channels, directly between the Ministries of Justice or any other authorities designated by the Parties.

Article 3

Required documents

1. A request for the transfer or supervision shall contain all necessary information on the identity, nationality and residence of the sentenced person. The request shall be accompanied by the original or a copy of any court decision referred to in article 1 of the present Treaty and a certificate that this decision if final.

2. The documents submitted in support of a request for transfer of supervision shall be accompanied by a translation into the language of the requested State or into another language acceptable to that State.

Article 4

Certification and authentication

Subject to national law and unless the Parties decide otherwise, a request for transfer of supervision and the documents in support thereof, as well as the documents and other

---

* General Assembly Resolution 45/119 of 14 December 1990, *Compendium of United Nations Standards and Norms in Crime Prevention and Criminal Justice*, New York, United Nations, 1992, 126; *International Legal Materials*, 1991, 1443.

material supplied in response to such a request, shall not require certification or authentication. [1]

Article 5

Decision on the request

The competent authorities of the administering State shall examine what action to take on the request for supervision in order to comply, as fully as possible, with the request under their own law, and shall promptly communicate their decision to the sentencing State.

Article 6

Dual criminality [2]

A request for transfer of supervision can be complied with only if the act on which the request is based would constitute an offence if committed in the territory of the administering State.

Article 7

Grounds for refusal [3]

If the administering State refuses acceptance of a request for transfer of supervision, it shall communicate the reasons for refusal to the sentencing State. Acceptance may be refused where:

(a) The sentenced person is not an ordinary resident in the administering State;

(b) The act is an offence under military law, which is not also an offence under ordinary criminal law;

(c) The offence is in connection with taxes, duties, customs or exchange;

(d) The offence is regarded by the administering State as being of a political nature;

(e) The administering State, under its own law, can no longer carry out the supervision or enforce the sanction in the event of revocation because of lapse of time.

Article 8

The position of the sentenced person

Whether sentenced or standing trial, a person may express to the sentencing State his or her interest in a transfer of supervision and his or her willingness to fulfil any conditions to be imposed. Similarly, such interest may be expressed by his or her legal representative or close relatives. Where appropriate, the Contracting States shall inform the offender or his or her close relatives of the possibilities under the present Treaty.

---

[1] The laws of some countries require authentication before documents transmitted from other countries can be admitted in their courts and, therefore, would require a clause setting out the authentication required;

[2] When negotiating on the basis of the present Model Treaty, States may wish to waive the requirement of dual criminality.

[3] When negotiating on the basis of the present Model Treaty, States may wish to add other grounds for refusal or conditions to this list, relating, for example, to the nature or gravity of the offence, to the protection of fundamental human rights, or to consideration of public order.

Article 9

The rights of the victim

The sentencing State and the administering State shall ensure in the transfer of supervision that the rights of the victims of the offence, in particular his or her rights to restitution or compensation, shall not be affected as a result of the transfer. In the event of the death of the victim, this provision shall apply to his or her dependants accordingly.

Article 10

The effects of the transfer of supervision on the sentencing State

The acceptance by the administering State of the responsibility for applying the terms of the decision rendered in the sentencing State shall extinguish the competence of the latter State to enforce the sentence.

Article 11

The effects of the transfer of supervision on the administering State

1. The supervision transferred upon agreement and the subsequent procedure shall be carried out in accordance with the law of the administering State. That State alone shall have the right of revocation. That State may, to the extent necessary, adapt to its own law the conditions or measures prescribed, provided that such conditions or measures are, in terms of their nature or duration, not more severe than those pronounced in the sentencing State.

2. If the administering State revokes the conditional sentence or conditional release, it shall enforce the sentence in accordance with its own law without, however, going beyond the limits imposed by the sentencing State.

Article 12

Review, pardon and amnesty

1. The sentencing State alone shall have the right to decide on any application to reopen the case.

2. Each Party may grant pardon, amnesty or commutation of the sentence in accordance with the provisions of its Constitution or other laws.

Article 13

Information

1. The Contracting Parties shall keep each other informed, in so far as it is necessary, of all circumstances likely to affect measures of supervision or enforcement in the administering State. To this end they shall transmit to each other copies of any relevant decisions in this respect.

2. After expiration of the period of supervision, the administering State shall provide to the sentencing State, at its request, a final report concerning the supervised person's conduct and compliance with the measures imposed.

Article 14

Costs

Supervision and enforcement costs incurred in the administering State shall not be refunded, unless otherwise agreed by both the sentencing State and the administering State.

Article 15

Final provisions

1. The present Treaty is subject to [ratification, acceptance or approval]. The instruments of [ratification, acceptance or approval] shall be exchanged as soon as possible.

2. The present Treaty shall enter into force on the thirtieth day after the day on which the instruments of [ratification, acceptance or approval] are exchanged.

3. The present Treaty shall apply to requests made after its entry into force, even if the relevant acts or omissions occurred prior to that date.

4. Either Contracting Party may denounce the present Treaty by giving notice in writing to the other Party. Such denunciation shall take effect six months following the date on which it is received by the other Party.

Convention on the Transfer of Sentenced Persons (1983)[*]

Strasbourg, 21 March 1983

Article 1

Definitions

For the purposes of this Convention:

(a) "sentence" means any punishment or measure involving deprivation of liberty ordered by a court for a limited or unlimited period of time on account of a criminal offence;

(b) "judgment" means a decision or order of a court imposing a sentence;

(c) "sentencing State" means the State in which the sentence was imposed on the person who may be, or has been, transferred;

(d) "administering State" means the State to which the sentenced person may be, or has been, transferred in order to serve his sentence.

Article 2

General principles

1. The Parties undertake to afford each other the widest measure of co-operation in respect of the transfer of sentenced persons in accordance with the provisions of this Convention.

2. A person sentenced in the territory of a Party may be transferred to the territory of another Party, in accordance with the provisions of this Convention, in order to serve the sentence imposed on him. To that end, he may express his interest to the sentencing State or to the administering State in being transferred under this Convention.

3. Transfer may be requested by either the sentencing State or the administering State.

Article 3

Conditions for transfer

1. A sentenced person may be transferred under this Convention only on the following conditions:

(a) if that person is a national of the administering State;

(b) if the judgment is final;

(c) if, at the time of receipt of the request for transfer, the sentenced person still has at least six months of the sentence to serve or if the sentence is indeterminate;

(d) if the transfer is consented to by the sentenced person or, where in view of his age or his physical or mental condition one of the two States considers it necessary, by the sentenced person's legal representative;

---

[*] *European Treaty Series*, No.112.

(e) if the acts or omissions on account of which the sentence has been imposed constitute a criminal offence according to the law of the administering State or would constitute a criminal offence if committed on its territory; and

(f) if the sentencing and administering States agree to the transfer.

2. In exceptional cases, Parties may agree to a transfer even if the time to be served by the sentenced person is less than that specified in paragraph 1.c.

3. Any State may, at the time of signature or when depositing its instrument of ratification, acceptance, approval or accession, by a declaration addressed to the Secretary General of the Council of Europe, indicate that it intends to exclude the application of one of the procedures provided in Article 9.1.a and b in its relations with other Parties.

4. Any State may, at any time, by a declaration addressed to the Secretary General of the Council of Europe, define, as far as it is concerned, the term "national" for the purposes of this Convention.

Article 4

Obligation to furnish information

1. Any sentenced person to whom this Convention may apply shall be informed by the sentencing State of the substance of this Convention.

2. If the sentenced person has expressed an interest to the sentencing State in being transferred under this Convention, that State shall so inform the administering State as soon as practicable after the judgment becomes final.

3. The information shall include:

(a) the name, date and place of birth of the sentenced person;

(b) his address, if any, in the administering State;

(c) a statement of the facts upon which the sentence was based;

(d) the nature, duration and date of commencement of the sentence.

4. If the sentenced person has expressed his interest to the administering State, the sentencing State shall, on request, communicate to that State the information referred to in paragraph 3 above.

5. The sentenced person shall be informed, in writing, of any action taken by the sentencing State or the administering State under the preceding paragraphs, as well as of any decision taken by either State on a request for transfer.

Article 5

Requests and replies

1. Requests for transfer and replies shall be made in writing.

2. Requests shall be addressed by the Ministry of Justice of the requesting state to the Ministry of Justice of the requested State. Replies shall be communicated through the same channels.

3. Any Party may, by a declaration addressed to the Secretary General of the Council of Europe, indicate that it will use other channels of communication.

4. The requested State shall promptly inform the requesting State of its decision whether or not to agree to the requested transfer.

Article 6

Supporting documents

1. The administering State, if requested by the sentencing State, shall furnish it with:

    (a) a document or statement indicating that the sentenced person is a national of that State;

    (b) a copy of the relevant law of the administering State which provides that the acts or omissions on account of which the sentence has been imposed in the sentencing State constitute a criminal offence according to the law of the administering State, or would constitute a criminal offence if committed on its territory;

    (c) a statement containing the information mentioned in Article 9.2.

2. If a transfer is requested, the sentencing State shall provide the following documents to the administering State, unless either State has already indicated that it will not agree to the transfer:

    (a) a certified copy of the judgment and the law on which it is based;

    (b) a statement indicating how much of the sentence has already been served, including information on any pre-trial detention, remission, and any other factor relevant to the enforcement of the sentence;

    (c) a declaration containing the consent to the transfer as referred to in Article 3.1.d; and

    (d) whenever appropriate, any medical or social reports on the sentenced person, information about his treatment in the sentencing State, and any recommendation for his further treatment in the administering State.

3. Either State may ask to be provided with any of the documents or statements referred to in paragraphs 1 or 2 above before making a request for transfer or taking a decision on whether or not to agree to the transfer.

Article 7

Consent and its verification

1. The sentencing State shall ensure that the person required to give consent to the transfer in accordance with Article 3.1.d does so voluntarily and with full knowledge of the legal consequences thereof. The procedure for giving such consent shall be governed by the law of the sentencing State.

2. The sentencing State shall afford an opportunity to the administering State to verify, through a consul or other official agreed upon with the administering State, that the consent is given in accordance with the conditions set out in paragraph 1 above.

Article 8

Effect of transfer for sentencing State

1. The taking into charge of the sentenced person by the authorities of the administering State shall have the effect of suspending the enforcement of the sentence in the sentencing State.

2. The sentencing State may no longer enforce the sentence if the administering State considers enforcement of the sentence to have been completed.

Article 9

Effect of transfer for administering State

1. The competent authorities of the administering State shall:

    (a) continue the enforcement of the sentence immediately or through a court or administrative order, under the conditions set out in Article 10, or

    (b) convert the sentence, through a judicial or administrative procedure, into a decision of that State, thereby substituting for the sanction imposed in the sentencing State a sanction prescribed by the law of the administering State for the same offence, under the conditions set out in Article 11.

2. The administering State, if requested, shall inform the sentencing State before the transfer of the sentenced person as to which of these procedures it will follow.

3. The enforcement of the sentence shall be governed by the law of the administering State and that State alone shall be competent to take all appropriate decisions.

4. Any State which, according to its national law, cannot avail itself of one of the procedures referred to in paragraph 1 to enforce measures imposed in the territory of another Party on persons who for reasons of mental condition have been held not criminally responsible for the commission of the offence, and which is prepared to receive such persons for further treatment may, by way of a declaration addressed to the Secretary General of the Council of Europe, indicate the procedures it will follow in such cases.

Article 10

Continued enforcement

1. In the case of continued enforcement, the administering State shall be bound by the legal nature and duration of the sentence as determined by the sentencing State.

2. If, however, this sentence is by its nature or duration incompatible with the law of the administering State, or its law so requires, that State may, by a court or administrative order, adapt the sanction to the punishment or measure prescribed by its own law for a similar offence. As to its nature, the punishment or measure shall, as far as possible, correspond with that imposed by the sentence to be enforced. It shall not aggravate, by its nature or duration, the sanction imposed in the sentencing State, nor exceed the maximum prescribed by the law of the administering State.

Article 11

Conversion of sentence

1. In the case of conversion of sentence, the procedures provided for by the law of the administering State apply. When converting the sentence, the competent authority:

    (a) shall be bound by the findings as to the facts insofar as they appear explicitly by or implicitly from the judgment imposed in the sentencing State;

    (b) may not convert a sanction involving deprivation of liberty to a pecuniary sanction;

    (c) shall deduct the full period of deprivation of liberty served by the sentenced person; and

    (d) shall not aggravate the penal position of the sentenced person, and shall not be bound by any minimum which the law of the administering State may provide for the offence or offences committed.

2. If the conversion procedure takes place after the transfer of the sentenced person, the administering State shall keep that person in custody or otherwise ensure his presence in the administering State pending the outcome of that procedure.

Article 12

Pardon, amnesty, commutation

Each Party may grant pardon, amnesty or commutation of the sentence in accordance with its Constitution or other laws.

Article 13

Review of judgment

The sentencing State alone shall have the right to decide on any application for review of the judgment.

Article 14

Termination of enforcement

The administering State shall terminate enforcement of the sentence as soon as it is informed by the sentencing State of any decision or measure as a result of which the sentence ceases to be enforceable.

Article 15

Information on enforcement

The administering State shall provide information to the sentencing State concerning the enforcement of the sentence:

(a) when it considers enforcement of the sentence to have been completed;

(b) if the sentenced person has escaped from custody before enforcement of the sentence has been completed; or

(c) if the sentencing State requests a special report.

Article 16

Transit

1. A Party shall, in accordance with its law, grant a request for transit of a sentenced person through its territory if such a request is made by another Party and that State has agreed with another Party or with a third State to the transfer of that person to or from its territory.

2. A Party may refuse to grant transit:

(a) if the sentenced person is one of its nationals, or

(b) if the offence for which the sentence was imposed is not an offence under its own law.

3. Requests for transit and replies shall be communicated through the channels referred to in the provisions of Article 5.2 and 3.

4. A Party may grant a request for transit of a sentenced person through its territory made by a third State if that State has agreed with another Party to the transfer to or from its territory.

5. The Party requested to grant transit may hold the sentenced person in custody only for such time as transit through its territory requires.

6. The Party requested to grant transit may be asked to give an assurance that the sentenced person will not be prosecuted, or, except as provided in the preceding paragraph, detained, or otherwise subjected to any restriction on his liberty in the territory of the transit State for any offence committed or sentence imposed prior to his departure from the territory of the sentencing State.

7. No request for transit shall be required if transport is by air over the territory of a Party and no landing there is scheduled. However, each State may, by a declaration addressed to the Secretary General of the Council of Europe at the time of signature or of deposit of its instrument of ratification, acceptance, approval or accession, require that it be notified of any such transit over its territory.

Article 17

Language and costs

1. Information under Article 4, paragraphs 2 to 4, shall be furnished in the language of the Party to which it is addressed or in one of the official languages of the Council of Europe.

2. Subject to paragraph 3 below, no translation of requests for transfer or of supporting documents shall be required.

3. Any State may, at the time of signature or when depositing its instrument of ratification, acceptance, approval or accession, by a declaration addressed to the Secretary General of the Council of Europe, require that requests for transfer and supporting documents be accompanied by a translation into its own language or into one of the official languages of the Council of Europe or into such one of these languages as it shall indicate. It may on that occasion declare its readiness to accept translations in any other language in addition to the official language or languages of the Council of Europe.

4. Except as provided in Article 6.2.a, documents transmitted in application of this Convention need not be certified.

5. Any costs incurred in the application of this Convention shall be borne by the administering State, except costs incurred exclusively in the territory of the sentencing State.

Article 18

Signature and entry into force

1. This Convention shall be open for signature by the member States of the Council of Europe and non-member States which have participated in its elaboration. It is subject to ratification, acceptance or approval. Instruments of ratification, acceptance or approval shall be deposited with the Secretary General of the Council of Europe.

2. This Convention shall enter into force on the first day of the month following the expiration of a period of three months after the date on which three member States of the Council of Europe have expressed their consent to be bound by the Convention in accordance with the provisions of paragraph 1.

3. In respect of any signatory State which subsequently expresses its consent to be bound by it, the Convention shall enter into force on the first day of the month following the expiration of a period of three months after the date of the deposit of the instrument of ratification, acceptance or approval.

Article 19

Accession by non-member States

1. After the entry into force of this Convention, the Committee of Ministers of the Council of Europe, after consulting the Contracting States, may invite any State not a member of the Council and not mentioned in Article 18.1 to accede to this Convention, by a decision taken by the majority provided for in Article 20.d of the Statute of the Council of Europe and by the unanimous vote of the representatives of the Contracting States entitled to sit on the Committee.

2. In respect of any acceding State, the Convention shall enter into force on the first day of the month following the expiration of a period of three months after the date of deposit of the instrument of accession with the Secretary General of the Council of Europe.

Article 20

Territorial application

1. Any State may at the time of signature or when depositing its instrument of ratification, acceptance, approval or accession, specify the territory or territories to which this Convention shall apply.

2. Any State may at any later date, by a declaration addressed to the Secretary General of the Council of Europe, extend the application of this Convention to any other territory specified in the declaration. In respect of such territory the Convention shall enter into force on the first day of the month following the expiration of a period of three months after the date of receipt of such declaration by the Secretary General.

3. Any declaration made under the two preceding paragraphs may, in respect of any territory specified in such declaration, be withdrawn by a notification addressed to the Secretary General. The withdrawal shall become effective on the first day of the month following the expiration of a period of three months after the date of receipt of such notification by the Secretary General.

Article 21

Temporal application

This Convention shall be applicable to the enforcement of sentences imposed either before or after its entry into force.

Article 22

Relationship to other Conventions and Agreements

1. This Convention does not affect the rights and undertakings derived from extradition treaties and other treaties on international co-operation in criminal matters providing for the transfer of detained persons for purposes of confrontation or testimony.

2. If two or more Parties have already concluded an agreement or treaty on the transfer of sentenced persons or otherwise have established their relations in this matter, or should they in future do so, they shall be entitled to apply that agreement or treaty or to regulate those relations accordingly, in lieu of the present Convention.

3. The present Convention does not affect the right of States party to the European Convention on the International Validity of Criminal Judgments to conclude bilateral or multilateral agreements with one another on matters dealt with in that Convention in order to supplement its provisions or facilitate the application of the principles embodied in it.

4. If a request for transfer falls within the scope of both the present Convention and the European Convention on the International Validity of Criminal Judgments or another agree-

ment or treaty on the transfer of sentenced persons, the requesting State shall, when making the request, indicate on the basis of which instrument it is made.

Article 23

Friendly settlement

The European Committee on Crime Problems of the Council of Europe shall be kept informed regarding the application of this Convention and shall do whatever is necessary to facilitate a friendly settlement of any difficulty which may arise out of its application.

Article 24

Denunciation

1. Any Party may at any time denounce this Convention by means of a notification addressed to the Secretary General of the Council of Europe.

2. Such denunciation shall become effective on the first day of the month following the expiration of a period of three months after the date of receipt of the notification by the Secretary General.

3. The present Convention shall, however, continue to apply to the enforcement of sentences of persons who have been transferred in conformity with the provisions of the Convention before the date on which such a denunciation takes effect.

Article 25

Notifications

The Secretary General of the Council of Europe shall notify the member States of the Council of Europe, the non-member States which have participated in the elaboration of this Convention and any State which as acceded to this Convention of:

(a) any signature;

(b) the deposit of any instrument of ratification, approval or accession;

(c) any date of entry into force of this Convention in accordance with Articles 18.2 and 3, 19.2 and 20.2 and 3;

(d) any other act, declaration, notification or communication relating to this Convention.

Schengen Convention - Title III - Chapter V (excerpts) (1990)*

Schengen, 19 June 1990

Title III

Police and security

Chapter V

Transfer of the execution of criminal judgements

Article 67

The following provisions shall apply between the Contracting Parties who are parties to the Council of Europe Convention of 21 March 1983 on the Transfer of Sentenced Persons, for the purposes of supplementing that Convention.

Article 68

1. The Contracting Party in whose territory a sentence of deprivation of liberty or a detention order has been imposed in a judgment which has obtained the force of res judicata in respect of a national of another Contracting Party who, by escaping to his own country, has avoided the execution of that sentence or detention order, may request the latter Contracting Party, if the escaped person is in its territory, to take over the execution of the sentence or of the detention order.

2. The requested Contracting Party may, at the request of the requesting Contracting Party, prior to the arrival of the documents supporting the request that the execution of the sentence or of the detention order or part of the sentence be taken over, and prior to the decision on that request, take the convicted person into police custody or take other measures to ensure that he remains in the territory of the requested Contracting Party.

Article 69

The transfer of execution under Article 68 shall not require the consent of the person on whom the sentence or the detention order has been imposed. The other provisions of the Council of Europe Convention of 21 March 1983 on the Transfer of Sentenced Persons shall apply by analogy.

[...]

---

* Convention of 19 June 1990, applying the Schengen Agreement of 14 June 1985 between the Governments of the States of the Benelux Economic Union, the Federal Republic of Germany and the French Republic, on the Gradual Abolition of Checks at their Common Borders, *International Legal Materials*, 1991, 84.

5. INTERNATIONAL CRIMINAL COURT

Nuremberg Charter: Charter of International Military Tribunal, adopted by the Big Four Powers (1945)[*]

London, 8 August 1945.

Part I

Constitution of the international military tribunal

Article 1

In pursuance of the Agreement signed on the 8th August, 1945, by the Government of the United Kingdom of Great Britain and Northern Ireland, the Government of the United States of America, the Provisional Government of the French Republic and the Government of the Union of Soviet Socialist Republics, there shall be established an International Military Tribunal (hereinafter called 'the Tribunal') for the just and prompt trial and punishment of the major war criminals of the European Axis.

Article 2

The Tribunal shall consist of four members each with an alternate. One member and one alternate shall be appointed by each of the Signatories. The alternates shall, so far as they are able, be present at all sessions of the Tribunal. In case of illness of any member of the Tribunal or his incapacity for some other reason to fulfill his functions, his alternate shall take his place.

Article 3

Neither the Tribunal, its members nor their alternates can be challenged by the prosecution, or by the Defendants or their Counsel. Each Signatory may replace its member of the Tribunal or his alternate for reasons of health or for other good reasons, except that no replacement may take place during a Trial, other than by an alternate.

Article 4

(a) The presence of all four members of the Tribunal or the alternate for any absent member shall be necessary to constitute the quorum.

(b) The members of the Tribunal shall, before any trial begins, agree among themselves upon the selection from their number of a President, and the President shall hold office during that trial, or as many otherwise be agreed by a vote of not less than three members. The principle of rotation of presidency for successive trials is agreed. If, however, a session of the Tribunal takes place on the territory of one of the four Signatories, the representative of that Signatory on the Tribunal shall preside.

(c) Save as aforesaid the Tribunal shall take decisions by a majority vote and in case the votes are evenly divided, the vote of the President shall be decisive: provided always that convictions and sentences shall only be imposed by affirmative votes of a least three members of the Tribunal.

---

[*] *United Nations Treaty Series*, vol.82, 279.

Article 5

In case of need and depending on the number of the matters to be tried, other Tribunals may be set up: and the establishment, functions, and procedure of each Tribunal shall be identical, and shall be governed by this Charter.

Part II

Jurisdiction and general principles.

Article 6

The Tribunal established by the Agreement referred to in Article 1. hereof for the trial and punishment of the major war criminals of the European Axis countries shall have the power to try and punish persons who, acting in the interests of the European Axis countries, whether as individuals or as members of organizations, committed any of the following crimes. The following acts, or any of them are crimes coming within the jurisdiction of the Tribunal for which there shall be individual responsibility:

(a) Crimes against peace: namely, planning, preparation, initiation or waging of a war of aggression, or a war in violation of international treaties, agreements or assurances, or participation in a common plan or conspiracy for the accomplishment of any of the foregoing:

(b) War crimes: namely, violations of the laws or customs of war. Such violations shall include, but not be limited to, murder, ill-treatment or deportation to slave labour or for any other purpose of civilian population of or in occupied territory, murder or ill-treatment of prisoners of war or persons on the seas, killing of hostages, plunder of public or private property, wanton destruction of cities, towns or villages, or devastation not justified by military necessity;

(c) Crimes against humanity: namely, murder, extermination, enslavement, deportation, and other inhumane acts committed against any civilian population, before or during the war; or persecutions on political, racial or religious grounds in execution of or in connection with any crime within the jurisdiction of the Tribunal, whether or not in violation of the domestic law of the country where perpetrated. Leaders, organisers, instigators and accomplices participating in the formulation or execution of a common plan or conspiracy to commit any of the foregoing crimes are responsible for all acts performed by any persons in execution of such plan.

Article 7

The official position of defendants, whether as Heads of State or responsible officials in Government Departments, shall not be considered as freeing them from responsibility or mitigating punishment.

Article 8

The fact that the Defendant acted pursuant to order of his Government or of a superior shall not free him from responsibility, but may be considered in mitigation of punishment if the Tribunal determines that justice so requires.

Article 9

At the trial of any individual member of any group or organisation the Tribunal may declare (in connection with any act of which the individual may be convicted) that the group or organisation of which the individual was a member was a criminal organisation. After receipt of the Indictment the Tribunal shall give such notice as it thinks fit that the prosecution intends to ask the Tribunal to make such declaration and any member of the organisation will be entitled to apply to the Tribunal for leave to be heard by the Tribunal upon the question of the criminal character of the organisation. The Tribunal shall have power to allow or reject the application. If the application is allowed, the Tribunal may direct in what manner the applicants shall be represented and heard.

Article 10

In cases where a group or organisation is declared criminal by the Tribunal, the competent national authority of any Signatory shall have the right to bring individuals to trial for membership therein before national, military, or occupation courts. In any such case the criminal nature of the group or organisation is considered proved and shall not be questioned.

Article 11

Any person convicted by the Tribunal may be charged before a national, military or occupation court, referred to in Article 10 of this Charter, with a crime other than of membership in a criminal group or organisation and such court may, after convicting him, impose upon him punishment independent of and additional to the punishment imposed by the Tribunal for participation in the criminal activities of such group or organisation.

Article 12

The Tribunal shall have the right to take proceedings against a person charged with crimes set out in Article 6 of this Charter in his absence, if he has not been found or if the Tribunal, for any reason, finds it necessary, in the interests of justice, to conduct the hearing in his absence.

Article 13

The Tribunal shall draw up rules for its procedure. These rules shall not be inconsistent with the provisions of this Charter.

Part III

Committee for the investigation and prosecution of major war criminals

Article 14

Each Signatory shall appoint a Chief Prosecutor for the Investigation of the charges against and the prosecution of major war criminals.

The Chief Prosecutors shall act as a committee for the following purposes:

(a) to agree upon a plan of the individual work of each of the Chief Prosecutors and his staff,

(b) to settle the final designation of major war criminals to be tried by the Tribunal,

(c) to approve the Indictment and the documents to be submitted therewith,

(d) to lodge the Indictment and the accompanying documents with the Tribunal,

(e) to draw up and recommended to the Tribunal for its approval draft rules of procedure, contemplated by Article 13 of this Charter. The Tribunal shall have power to accept, with or without amendments, or to reject, the rules so recommended. The Committee shall act in all the above matters by a majority vote and shall appoint a Chairman as may be convenient and in accordance with the principle of rotation: provided that if there is an equal division of vote concerning the designation of a Defendant to be tried by the Tribunal, or the crimes with which he shall be charged, that proposal will be adopted which was made by the party which proposed that the particular Defendant be tried or the particular charges be preferred against him.

Article 15

The Chief Prosecutors shall individually, and acting in collaboration with one another, also undertake the following duties:

(a) investigation, collection and production before or at the Trial of all necessary evidence.

(b) the preparation of the Indictment for approval by the Committee in accordance with paragraph (c) of Article 14, hereof,

(c) the preliminary examination of all necessary witnesses and of the Defendants,

(d) to act as prosecutor at the Trial,

(e) to appoint representatives to carry out such duties as may be assigned to them,

(f) to undertake such other matters as may appear necessary to them for the purposes of the preparation for and conduct of the Trial.

It is understood that no witness or Defendant detained by any Signatory shall be taken out of the possession of that Signatory without its assent.

Part IV

Fair trial for defendants

Article 16

In order to ensure fair trail for the Defendants, the following procedure shall be followed;

(a) The Indictment shall include full particulars specifying in detail the charges against the Defendants. A copy of the Indictment and of all the documents lodged with the Indictment, translated into a language which he understands, shall be furnished to the Defendant at a reasonable time before the Trial.

(b) During any preliminary examination or trial of a Defendant be shall have the right to give any explanation relevant to be charges made against him.

(c) A preliminary examination of a Defendant and his Trial shall be conducted in, or translated into, a language which the Defendant understands.

(d) A Defendant shall have the right to conduct his own defence before the Tribunal or to have the assistance of Counsel,

(e) A Defendant shall have the right through himself or through his Counsel to present evidence at the Trial in support of his defence, and to cross-examine any witness called by the Prosecution.

Part V

Powers of the tribunal and conduct of the trial

Article 17

The Tribunal shall have the power:

(a) to summon witnesses to the Trial and to require their attendance and testimony and to put questions to them.

(b) to interrogate any Defendant,

(c) to require the production of documents and other evidentiary material,

(d) to administer oaths to witnesses,

(e) to appoint officers for the carrying out of any task designated by the Tribunal including the power to have evidence taken on commission.

Article 18

The Tribunal shall:

(a) confine the Trial strictly to an expeditious hearing of the issues raised by the charges,

(b) take strict measures to prevent any action which will cause unreasonable delay, and rule out irrelevant issues and statements of any kind whatsoever,

(c) deal summarily with any contumacy, imposing appropriate punishment, including exclusions of any Defendant or his Counsel from some or all further proceedings, but without prejudice to the determination of the charges.

Article 19

The Tribunal shall not be bound by technical rules of evidence. It shall adopt and apply to the greatest possible extent expeditious and non-technical procedure, and shall admit any evidence which it deems to have probative value.

Article 20

The Tribunal may require to be informed of the nature of any evidence before it is offered so that it may rule upon the relevance thereof.

Article 21

The Tribunal shall not require proof of facts of common knowledge but shall take judicial notice thereof. It shall also take judicial notice of official governmental documents and reports of the United Nations, including the acts and documents of the committees set up in the various Allied countries for the investigation of war crimes and the records and findings of military or other Tribunals of any of the United Nations.

Article 22

The permanent seat of the Tribunal shall be in Berlin. The first meetings of the members of the Tribunal and of the Chief Prosecutors shall be held at Berlin in a place to be designated by the Control Council for Germany. The first trial shall be held at Nuremberg, and any subsequent trials shall be held at such places as the Tribunal may decide.

Article 23

One or more of the Chief Prosecutors may take part in the prosecution at each Trial. The function of any Chief Prosecutor may be discharged by him personally, or by any person or persons authorized by him.

The function of Counsel for a Defendant may be discharged at the Defendant's request by any Counsel professionally qualified to conduct cases before the Courts of his own country, or by any other person who may be specially authorised thereto by the Tribunal.

Article 24

The proceedings at the Trial shall take the following course:

(a) The Indictment shall be read in court.

(b) The Tribunal shall ask each Defendant whether he pleads 'guilty' of 'not guilty'.

(c) The Prosecution shall make an opening statement.

(d) The Tribunal shall ask the Prosecution and the Defence what evidence (if any) they wish to submit to the Tribunal, and the Tribunal shall rule upon the admissibility of any such evidence.

(e) The witnesses for the Prosecution shall be examined and after that the witnesses for the Defence. Thereafter such rebutting evidence as may be held by the Tribunal to be admissible shall be called by either the Prosecution or the Defence.

(f) The Tribunal may put any question to any witness and to any Defendant, at any time.

(g) The Prosecution and the Defence shall interrogate and may cross-examine any witnesses and any Defendant who gives testimony.

(h) The Defence shall address the court.

(i) The Prosecution shall address the court.

(j) Each Defendant may make a statement to the Tribunal.

(k) The Tribunal shall deliver judgement and pronounce sentence.

Article 25

All official documents shall be produced, and all court proceedings conducted, in English, French and Russian, and in the language of the Defendant. So much of the record and of the proceedings may also by translated into the language of any country in which the Tribunal is sitting, as the Tribunal considers desirable in the interests of justice and public opinion.

Part VI

Judgement and sentence

Article 26

The Judgement of the Tribunal as to the guilt or the innocence of any Defendant shall give the reasons on which it is based, and shall be final and not subject to review.

Article 27

The Tribunal shall have the right to impose upon a Defendant, on conviction, death or such other punishment as shall be determined by it to be just.

Article 28

In addition to any punishment imposed by it, the Tribunal shall have the right to deprive the convicted person of any stolen property and order its delivery to the Control Council for Germany.

Article 29

In case of guilt, sentences shall be carried out in accordance with the orders of the Control Council for Germany, which may at any time reduce or otherwise after the sentences, but may not increase the severity thereof. If the Control Council for Germany, after any Defendant has been convicted and sentenced, discovers fresh evidence which, in its opinion, would found a fresh charge against him, the Council shall report accordingly to the Committee established under Article 14 hereof for such action as they may consider proper, having regard to the interests of justice.

Part VII

Expenses

Article 30

The expenses of the Tribunal and of the Trials, shall be charged by the Signatories against the funds allotted for maintenance of the Control Council for Germany.

Statute of the International Tribunal for the Former Yugoslavia (1993)[*]

New York, 25 May 1993

Statute of the International Tribunal

Having been established by the Security Council acting under Chapter VII of the Charter of the United Nations, the International Tribunal for the Prosecution of Persons Responsible for Serious Violations of International Humanitarian Law Committed in the Territory of the Former Yugoslavia since 1991 (hereinafter referred to as "the International Tribunal") shall function in accordance with the provisions of the present Statute.

Article 1

Competence of the International Tribunal

The International Tribunal shall have the power to prosecute persons responsible for serious violations of international humanitarian law committed in the territory of the former Yugoslavia since 1991 in accordance with the provisions of the present Statute.

Article 2

Grave breaches of the Geneva Conventions of 1949

The International Tribunal shall have the power to prosecute persons committing or ordering to be committed grave breaches of the Geneva Conventions of 12 August 1949, namely the following acts against persons or property protected under the provisions of the relevant Geneva Convention:

(a) wilful killing;

(b) torture or inhuman treatment, including biological experiments;

(c) wilfully causing great suffering or serious injury to body or health;

(d) extensive destruction and appropriation of property, not justified by military necessity and carried out unlawfully and wantonly;

(e) compelling a prisoner of war or a civilian to serve in the forces of a hostile power;

(f) wilfully depriving a prisoner of war or a civilian of the rights of fair and regular trial;

(g) unlawful deportation or transfer or unlawful confinement of a civilian;

(h) taking civilians as hostages.

---

[*] Security Council Resolution 827 (1993) on Establishing an International Tribunal for the Prosecution of Persons Responsible for Serious Violations of International Humanitarian Law Committed in the Territory of the Former Yugoslavia, *International Legal Materials*, 1993, 1192 (text statute) and 1203 (text resolution).

Article 3

Violations of the laws or customs of war

The International Tribunal shall have the power to prosecute persons violating the laws or customs of war. Such violations shall include, but not be limited to:

(a) employment of poisonous weapons or other weapons calculated to cause unnecessary suffering;

(b) wanton destruction of cities, towns or villages, or devastation not justified by military necessity;

(c) attack, or bombardment, by whatever means, of undefended towns, villages, dwellings, or buildings;

(d) seizure of, destruction or wilful damage done to institutions dedicated to religion, charity and education, the arts and sciences, historic monuments and works of art and science;

(e) plunder of public or private property.

Article 4

Genocide

1. The International Tribunal shall have the power to prosecute persons committing genocide as defined in paragraph 2 of this article or of committing any of the other acts enumerated in paragraph 3 of this article.

2. Genocide means any of the following acts committed with intent to destroy, in whole or in part, a national, ethnical, racial or religious group, as such:

(a) killing members of the group;

(b) causing serious bodily or mental harm to members of the group;

(c) deliberately inflicting on the group conditions of life calculated to bring about its physical destruction in whole or in part;

(d) imposing measures intended to prevent births within the group;

(e) forcibly transferring children of the group to another group.

3. The following acts shall be punishable:

(a) genocide;

(b) conspiracy to commit genocide;

(c) direct and public incitement to commit genocide;

(d) attempt to commit genocide;

(e) complicity in genocide.

Article 5

Crimes against humanity

The International Tribunal shall have the power to prosecute persons responsible for the following crimes when committed in armed conflict, whether international or internal in character, and directed against any civilian population:

(a) murder;

(b) extermination;

(c) enslavement;

(d) deportation;

(e) imprisonment;

(f) torture;

(g) rape;

(h) persecutions on political, racial and religious grounds;

(i) other inhumane acts.

Article 6

Personal jurisdiction

The International Tribunal shall have jurisdiction over natural persons pursuant to the provisions of the present Statute.

Article 7

Individual criminal responsibility

1. A person who planned, instigated, ordered, committed or otherwise aided and abetted in the planning, preparation or execution of a crime referred to in articles 2 to 5 of the present Statute, shall be individually responsible for the crime.

2. The official position of any accused person, whether as Head of State or Government or as a responsible Government official, shall not relieve such person of criminal responsibility nor mitigate punishment.

3. The fact that any of the acts referred to in articles 2 to 5 of the present Statute was committed by a subordinate does not relieve his superior of criminal responsibility if he knew or had reason to know that the subordinate was about to commit such acts or had done so and the superior failed to take the necessary and reasonable measures to prevent such acts or to punish the perpetrators thereof.

4. The fact that an accused person acted pursuant to an order of a Government or of a superior shall not relieve him of criminal responsibility, but may be considered in mitigation of punishment if the International Tribunal determines that justice so requires.

Article 8

Territorial and temporal jurisdiction

The territorial jurisdiction of the International Tribunal shall extend to the territory of the former Socialist Federal Republic of Yugoslavia, including its land surface, airspace and territorial waters. The temporal jurisdiction of the International Tribunal shall extend to a period beginning on 1 January 1991.

Article 9

Concurrent jurisdiction

1. The International Tribunal and national courts shall have concurrent jurisdiction to prosecute persons for serious violations of international humanitarian law committed in the territory of the former Yugoslavia since 1 January 1991.

2. The International Tribunal shall have primacy over national courts. At any stage of the procedure, the International Tribunal may formally request national courts to defer to the competence of the International Tribunal in accordance with the present Statute and the Rules of Procedure and Evidence of the International Tribunal.

Article 10

Non-bis-in-idem

1. No person shall be tried before a national court for acts constituting serious violations of international humanitarian law under the present Statute, for which he or she has already been tried by the International Tribunal.

2. A person who has been tried by a national court for acts constituting serious violations of international humanitarian law may be subsequently tried by the International Tribunal only if:

 (a) the act for which he or she was tried characterized as an ordinary crime; or

 (b) the national court proceedings were not impartial or independent, were designed to shield the accused from international criminal responsibility, or the case was not diligently prosecuted.

3. In considering the penalty to be imposed on a person convicted of a crime under the present Statute, the International Tribunal shall take into account the extent to which any penalty imposed by a national court on the same person for the same act has already been served.

Article 11

Organization of the International Tribunal

The International Tribunal shall consist of the following organs:

 (a) The Chambers, comprising two Trial Chambers and an Appeals Chamber;

 (b) The Prosecutor, and

 (c) A Registry, servicing both the Chambers and the Prosecutor.

Article 12

Composition of the Chambers

The Chambers shall be composed of eleven independent judges, no two of whom may be nationals of the same State, who shall serve as follows:

(a) Three judges shall serve in each of the Trial Chambers;

(b) Five judges shall serve in the Appeals Chamber.

Article 13

Qualifications and election of judges

1. The judges shall be persons of high moral character, impartiality and integrity who possess the qualifications required in their respective countries for appointment to the highest judicial offices. In the overall composition of the Chambers due account shall be taken of the experience of the judges in criminal law, international law, including international humanitarian law and human rights law.

2. The judges of the International Tribunal shall be elected by the General Assembly from a list submitted by the Security Council, in the following manner:

(a) The Secretary-General shall invite nominations for judges of the International Tribunal from States Members of the United Nations and non-member States maintaining permanent observer missions at United Nations Headquarters;

(b) Within sixty days of the date of the invitation of the Secretary-General, each State may nominate up to two candidates meeting the qualifications set out in paragraph 1 above, no two of whom shall be of the same nationality;

(c) The Secretary-General shall forward the nominations received to the Security Council. From the nominations received the Security Council shall establish a list of not less than twenty-two and not more than thirty-three candidates, taking due account of the adequate representation of the principal legal systems of the world;

(d) The President of the Security Council shall transmit the list of candidates to the President of the General Assembly. From that list the General Assembly shall elect the eleven judges of the International Tribunal. The candidates who receive an absolute majority of the votes of the States Members of the United Nations and of the non-Member States maintaining permanent observer missions at United Nations Headquarters, shall be declared elected. Should two candidates of the same nationality obtain the required majority vote, the one who received the higher number of votes shall be considered elected.

3. In the event of a vacancy in the Chambers, after consultation with the Presidents of the Security Council and of the General Assembly, the Secretary-General shall appoint a person meeting the qualifications of paragraph 1 above, for the remainder of the term of office concerned.

4. The judges shall be elected for a term of four years. The terms and conditions of service shall be those of the judges of the International Court of Justice. They shall be eligible for re-election.

Article 14

Officers and members of the Chambers

1. The judges of the International Tribunal shall elect a President.

2. The President of the International Tribunal shall be a member of the Appeals Chamber and shall preside over its proceedings.

3. After consultation with the judges of the International Tribunal, the President shall assign the judges to the appeals Chamber and to the Trial Chambers. A judge shall serve only in the Chamber to which he or she was assigned.

4. The judges of each Trial Chamber shall elect a Presiding Judge, who shall conduct all of the proceedings of the Trial Chamber as a whole.

Article 15

Rules of procedure and evidence

The judges of the International Tribunal shall adopt rules of procedure and evidence for the conduct of the pre-trial phase of the proceedings, trials and appeals, the admission of evidence, the protection of victims and witnesses and other appropriate matters.

Article 16

The Prosecutor

1. The Prosecutor shall be responsible for the investigation and prosecution of persons responsible for serious violations of international humanitarian law committed in the territory of the former Yugoslavia since 1 January 1991.

2. The Prosecutor shall act independently as a separate organ of the International Tribunal. He or she shall not seek or receive instructions from any Government or from any other source.

3. The Office of the Prosecutor shall be composed of a Prosecutor and such other qualified staff as may be required.

4. The Prosecutor shall be appointed by the Security Council on nomination by the Secretary-General. He or she shall be of high moral character and possess the highest level of competence and experience in the conduct of investigations and prosecutions of criminal cases. The Prosecutor shall serve for a four-year term and be eligible for reappointment. The terms and conditions of service of the Prosecutor shall be those of an Under-Secretary-General of the United Nations.

5. The staff of the Office of the Prosecutor shall be appointed by the Secretary-General on the recommendation of the Prosecutor.

Article 17

The Registry

1. The Registry shall be responsible for the administration and servicing of the International Tribunal.

2. The Registry shall consist of a Registrar and such other staff as may be required.

3. The Registrar shall be appointed by the Secretary-General after consultation with the President of the International Tribunal. He or she shall serve for a four-year term and be eligible for reappointment. The terms and conditions of service of the Registrar shall be those of an Assistant Secretary-General of the United Nations.

4. The staff of the Registry shall be appointed by the Secretary-General on the recommendation of the Registrar.

Article 18

Investigation and preparation of indictment

1. The Prosecutor shall initiate investigations ex officio or on the basis of information obtained from any source, particularly from Governments, United Nations organs, intergovernmental and non-governmental organizations. The Prosecutor shall assess the information received or obtained and decide whether there is sufficient basis to proceed.

2. The Prosecutor shall have the power to question suspects, victims and witnesses, to collect evidence and to conduct on-site investigations. In carrying out these tasks, the Prosecutor may, as appropriate, seek the assistance of the State authorities concerned.

3. If questioned, the suspect shall be entitled to be assisted by counsel of his own choice, including the right to have legal assistance assigned to him without payment by him in any such case if he does not have sufficient means to pay for it, as well as to necessary translation into and from a language he speaks and understands.

4. Upon a determination that a prima facie case exists, the Prosecutor shall prepare an indictment containing a concise statement of the facts and the crime or crimes with which the accused is charged under the Statute. The indictment shall be transmitted to a judge of the Trial Chamber.

Article 19

Review of the indictment

1. The judge of the Trial Chamber to whom the indictment has been transmitted shall review it. If satisfied that a prima facie case has been established by the Prosecutor, he shall confirm the indictment. If not so satisfied, the indictment shall be dismissed.

2. Upon confirmation of an indictment, the judge may, at the request of the Prosecutor, issue such orders and warrants for the arrest, detention, surrender or transfer of persons, and any other orders as may be required for the conduct of the trial.

Article 20

Commencement and conduct of trial proceedings

1. The Trial Chambers shall ensure that a trial is fair and expeditious and that proceedings are conducted in accordance with the rules of procedure and evidence, with full respect for the rights of the accused and due regard for the protection of victims and witnesses.

2. A person against whom an indictment has been confirmed shall, pursuant to an order or an arrest warrant of the International Tribunal, be taken into custody, immediately informed of the charges against him and transferred to the International Tribunal.

3. The Trial Chamber shall read the indictment, satisfy itself that the rights of the accused are respected, confirm that the accused understands the indictment, and instruct the accused to enter a plea. The Trial Chamber shall then set the date for trial.

4. The hearings shall be public unless the Trial Chamber decides to close the proceedings in accordance with its rules of procedure and evidence.

Article 21

Rights of the accused

1. All persons shall be equal before the International Tribunal.

2. In the determination of charges against him, the accused shall be entitled to a fair and public hearing, subject to article 22 of the Statute.

3. The accused shall be presumed innocent until proved guilty according to the provisions of the present Statute.

4. In the determination of any charge against the accused pursuant to the present Statute, the accused shall be entitled to the following minimum guarantees, in full equality:

   (a) to be informed promptly and in detail in a language which he understands of the nature and cause of the charge against him;

   (b) to have adequate time and facilities for the preparation of his defence and to communicate with counsel of his own choosing;

   (c) to be tried without undue delay;

   (d) to be tried in his presence, and to defend himself in person or through legal assistance of his own choosing; to be informed, if he does not have legal assistance, of this right; and to have legal assistance assigned to him, in any case where the interests of justice so require, and without payment by him in any such case if he does not have sufficient means to pay for it;

   (e) to examine, or have examined, the witnesses against him and to obtain the attendance and examination of witnesses on his behalf under the same conditions as witnesses against him;

   (f) to have the free assistance of an interpreter if he cannot understand or speak the language used in the International Tribunal;

   (g) not to be compelled to testify against himself or to confess guilt.

Article 22

Protection of victims and witnesses

The International Tribunal shall provide in its rules of procedure and evidence for the protection of victims and witnesses. Such protection measures shall include, but shall not be limited to, the conduct of *in camera* proceedings and the protection of the victim's identity.

Article 23

Judgement

1. The Trial Chambers shall pronounce judgements and impose sentences and penalties on persons convicted of serious violations of international humanitarian law.

2. The judgement shall be rendered by a majority of the judges of the Trial Chamber, and shall be delivered by the Trial Chamber in public. It shall be accompanied by a reasoned opinion in writing, to which separate or dissenting opinions may be appended.

Article 24

Penalties

1. The penalty imposed by the Trial Chamber shall be limited to imprisonment. In determining the terms of imprisonment, the Trial Chambers shall have recourse to the general practice regarding prison sentences in the courts of the former Yugoslavia.

2. In imposing the sentences, the Trial Chambers should take into account such factors as the gravity of the offence and the individual circumstances of the convicted person.

3. In addition to imprisonment, the Trial Chambers may order the return of any property and proceeds acquired by criminal conduct, including by means of duress, to their rightful owners.

Article 25

Appellate proceedings

1. The Appeals Chamber shall hear appeals from persons convicted by the Trial Chambers or from the Prosecutor on the following grounds:

   (a) an error on a question of law invalidating the decision; or

   (b) an error of fact which has occasioned a miscarriage of justice.

2. The Appeals Chamber may affirm, reverse or revise the decisions taken by the Trial Chambers.

Article 26

Review proceedings

Where a new fact has been discovered which was not known at the time of the proceedings before the Trial Chambers or the Appeals Chamber and which could have been a decisive factor in reaching the decision, the convicted person or the Prosecutor may submit to the International Tribunal an application for review of the judgement.

Article 27

Enforcement of sentences

Imprisonment shall be served in a State designated by the International Tribunal from a list of States which have indicated to the Security Council their willingness to accept convicted persons. Such imprisonment shall be in accordance with the applicable law of the State concerned, subject to the supervision of the International Tribunal.

Article 28

Pardon or commutation of sentences

If, pursuant to the applicable law of the State in which the convicted person is imprisoned, he or she is eligible for pardon or commutation of sentence, the State concerned shall notify the International Tribunal accordingly. The President of the International Tribunal, in consultation with the judges, shall decide the matter on the basis of the interests of justice and the general principles of law.

Article 29

Cooperation and judicial assistance

1. States shall cooperate with the International Tribunal in the investigation and prosecution of persons accused of committing serious violations of international humanitarian law.

2. States shall comply without undue delay with any request for assistance or an order issued by a Trial Chamber, including, but not limited to:

   (a) the identification and location of persons;

   (b) the taking of testimony and the production of evidence;

   (c) the service of documents;

   (d) the arrest or detention of persons;

   (e) the surrender or the transfer of the accused to the International Tribunal.

Article 30

The status, privileges and immunities of the International Tribunal

1. The Convention on the Privileges and Immunities of the United Nations of 13 February 1946 shall apply to the International Tribunal, the judges, the Prosecutor and his staff, and the Registrar and his staff.

2. The judges, the Prosecutor and the Registrar shall enjoy the privileges and immunities, exemptions and facilities accorded to diplomatic envoys, in accordance with international law.

3. The staff of the Prosecutor and of the Registrar shall enjoy the privileges and immunities accorded to officials of the United Nations under articles V and VII of the Convention referred to in paragraph 1 of this article.

4. Other persons, including the accused, required at the seat of the International Tribunal shall be accorded such treatment as is necessary for the proper functioning of the International Tribunal.

Article 31

Seat of the International Tribunal

The International Tribunal shall have its seat at The Hague.

Article 32

Expenses of the International Tribunal

The expenses of the International Tribunal shall be borne by the regular budget of the United Nations in accordance with Article 17 of the Charter of the United Nations.

Article 33

Working languages

The working languages of the International Tribunal shall be English and French.

Article 34

Annual report

The President of the International Tribunal shall submit an annual report of the International Tribunal to the Security Council and to the General Assembly.

Rules of Procedure and Evidence of the International Tribunal for the Former Yugoslavia (1994)

The Hague, adopted on 11 February 1994, as amended 5 May 1994[*]

Part I

General provisions

Rule 1

Entry into Force

These Rules of Procedures and Evidence, adopted pursuant to Article 15 of the Statute of the Tribunal, shall come into force on 14 March 1994.

Rule 2

Definitions

(a) In the Rules, unless the context otherwise requires, the following terms shall mean:

Rules: The Rules referred to in Rule 1;

Statute: The Statute of the Tribunal adopted by Security Council resolution 827 of 25 May 1993;

Tribunal: The International Tribunal for the Prosecution of Persons Responsible for Serious Violations of International Humanitarian Law Committed in the Territory of the Former Yugoslavia since 1991, established by Security Council resolution 827 of 25 May 1993.

Accused: A person against whom an indictment has been submitted in accordance with Rule 47;

Arrest: The act of taking a suspect or an accused into custody by a national authority;

Bureau: A body composed of the President, the Vice-President and the Presiding Judges of the Trial Chambers;

Investigation: All activities undertaken by the Prosecutor under the Statute and the Rules for the collection of information and evidence;

Party: The Prosecutor or the accused;

President: The President of the Tribunal;

Prosecutor: The Prosecutor appointed pursuant to Article 16 of the Statute;

---

[*] Rules of Procedure and Evidence of the International Tribunal for the Prosecution of Persons Responsible for Serious Violations of International Humanitarian Law Committed in the Territory of the Former Yugoslavia since 1991, *International Legal Materials*, 1994, 484.

Suspect: A person concerning whom the Prosecutor possesses information which tends to show that he may have committed a crime over which the Tribunal has jurisdiction;

Victim: A person against whom a crime over which the Tribunal has jurisdiction has allegedly been committed.

(b) In the Rules, the masculine shall include the feminine and the singular the plural, and vice-versa.

Rule 3

Languages

(a) The working languages of the Tribunal shall be English and French.

(b) An accused shall have the right to use his own language.

(c) Any other person appearing before the Tribunal may, subject to Sub-rule (d), use his own language if he does not have sufficient knowledge of either of the two working languages.

(d) Counsel for an accused may apply to the Presiding Judge of a Chamber for leave to use a language other than the two working ones or the language of the accused. If such leave is granted, the expenses of interpretation and translation shall be borne by the Tribunal to the extent, if any, determined by the President, taking into account the rights of the defence and the interests of justice.

(e) The Registrar shall make any necessary arrangements for interpretation and translation into and from the working languages.

Rule 4

Meetings away from the Seat of the Tribunal

A Chamber may exercise its functions at a place other than the seat of the Tribunal, if so authorised by the President in the interests of justice.

Rule 5

Non-compliance with Rules

Any objection by a party to an act of another party on the ground of non-compliance with the Rules shall be raised at the earliest opportunity; it shall be upheld, and the act declared null, only if the act was inconsistent with the fundamental principles of fairness and has occasioned a miscarriage of justice.

Rule 6

Amendment of the Rules

(a) Proposals for amendment of the Rules may be made by a Judge, the Prosecutor or the Registrar and shall be adopted if agreed to by not less than seven Judges at a plenary meeting of the Tribunal convened with notice of the proposal addressed to all Judges.

(b) An amendment to the Rules may be otherwise adopted, provided it is unanimously approved by the Judges.

(c) An amendment shall enter into force immediately, but shall not operate to prejudice the rights of the accused in any pending case.

Rule 7

Authentic Texts

The English and French texts of the Rules shall be equally authentic. In case of discrepancy, the version which is more consonant with the spirit of the Statute and the Rules shall prevail.

Part II

Primacy of the tribunal

Rule 8

Request for Information

Where it appears to the Prosecutor that a crime within the jurisdiction of the Tribunal is or has been the subject of investigations or criminal proceedings instituted in the national courts of any State, he may request the State to forward to him all relevant information in that respect, and the State shall transmit to him such information forthwith in accordance with Article 29 (1) of the Statute.

Rule 9

Prosecutor's Request for Deferral

Where it appears to the Prosecutor that in any such investigations or criminal proceedings instituted in the national courts of any State:

(i) the act being investigated or which is the subject of those proceedings is characterized as an ordinary crime:

(ii) there is a lack of impartiality or independence, or the investigations or proceedings are designed to shield the accused from international criminal responsibility, or the case is not diligently prosecuted; or

(iii) what is in issue is closely related to, or otherwise involves, significant factual or legal questions which may have implications for investigations or prosecutions before the Tribunal,

the Prosecutor may propose to the Trial Chamber designated by the President that a formal request be made that the national court defer to the competence of the Tribunal.

Rule 10

Formal Request for Deferral

(a) If it appears to the Trial Chamber seised of a proposal for deferral that, on any of the grounds specified in Rule 9, deferral is appropriate, the Trial Chamber may issue a formal request to the State concerned that its national court defer to the competence of the Tribunal.

(b) A request for deferral shall include a request that the results of the investigation and a copy of the court's records and the judgement, if already delivered, be forwarded to the Tribunal.

(c) Where deferral to the Tribunal has been requested by a Trial Chamber, any subsequent proceedings shall be held before the other Trial Chamber.

Rule 11

Non-compliance with a Request for Deferral

If, within sixty days after a request for deferral has been notified by the Registrar to the State under whose jurisdiction the investigations or criminal proceedings have been instituted, the State fails to file a response which satisfies the Trial Chamber that the State has taken or is taking adequate steps to comply with the order, the Trial Chamber may request the President to report the matter to the Security Council.

Rule 12

Determinations of National Courts

Subject to Article 10(2) of the Statute, determinations of national courts are not binding on the Tribunal.

Rule 13

Non Bis in Idem

When the President receives reliable information to show that criminal proceedings have been instituted against a person before a national court for a crime for which that person has already been tried by the Tribunal, a Trial Chamber shall, following *mutatis mutandis* the procedure provided in Rule 10, issue a reasoned order requesting the national court permanently discontinue its proceedings. If the national court fails to do so, the President may report the matter to the Security Council.

Part III

Organization of the tribunal

Section 1

The Judges

Rule 14

Solemn Declaration

(a) Before taking up his duties each Judge shall make the following solemn declaration:

"I solemnly declare that I will perform my duties and exercise my powers as a Judge of the International Tribunal for the Prosecution of Persons Responsible for Serious Violations of International Humanitarian Law Committed in the Territory of the Former Yugoslavia since 1991 honourably, faithfully, impartially and conscientiously".

(b) The declaration, signed by the Judge and witnessed by the Secretary-General of the United Nations or his representative, shall be kept in the records of the Tribunal.

Rule 15

Disqualification of Judges

(a) A Judge may not sit on a trial or appeal in any case in which he has a personal interest or concerning which he has or has had any association which might affect his impartiality. He shall in any such circumstance withdraw, and the President shall assign another Judge to sit in his place.

(b) Any party may apply to the Presiding Judge of a Chamber for the disqualification and withdrawal of a Judge of that Chamber from a trial upon the above grounds. The Presiding Judge shall confer with the Judge in question, and if necessary the Bureau shall determine the matter. If the Bureau upholds the application, the President shall assign another Judge to sit in place of the disqualified Judge.

(c) The Judge of the Trial Chamber who reviews an indictment against an accused, pursuant to Article 19 of the Statute and Rule 47, shall not sit as a member of the Trial Chamber for the trial of that accused.

(d) No member of the Appeals Chamber shall sit on any appeal in a case in which he sat as a member of the Trial Chamber.

(e) If a Judge is, for any reason, unable to continue sitting in a part-heard case, the Presiding Judge may, if that inability seems likely to be of short duration, adjourn the proceedings; otherwise he shall report to the President who may assign another Judge to the case and order either a rehearing or, with the consent of the accused, continuation of the proceedings from that point.

Rule 16

Resignation

A Judge who decides to resign shall communicate his resignation in writing to the President who shall transmit it to the Secretary-General of the United Nations.

Rule 17

Precedence

(a) All Judges are equal in the exercise of their judicial functions, regardless of dates of election, appointment, age or period of service.

(b) The Presiding Judges of the Trial Chambers shall take precedence according to age after the President and the Vice-President.

(c) Judges elected or appointed on different dates shall take precedence according to the dates of their election or appointment; Judges elected or appointed on the same date shall take precedence according to age.

(d) In case of re-election, the total period of service as a Judge of the Tribunal shall be taken into account.

Section 2

The Presidency

Rule 18

Election of the President

(a) The President shall be elected for a term of two years, or such shorter term as shall coincide with the duration of his term of office as a Judge. He may be re-elected once.

(b) If the President ceases to be a member of the Tribunal or resigns his office before the expiration of his term, the Judges shall effect from among their number a successor for the remainder of the term.

(c) The President shall be elected by a majority of the votes of the Judges composing the Tribunal. If no Judge obtains such a majority, the second ballot shall be limited to the two Judges who obtained the greatest number of votes on the first ballot. In the case of equality of votes on the second ballot, the Judge who takes precedence in accordance with Rule 17 shall be declared elected.

Rule 19

Functions of the President

The President shall preside at all plenary meetings of the Tribunal; he shall coordinate the work of the Chambers and supervise the activities of the Registry as well as exercise all the other functions conferred on him by the Statute and the Rules.

Rule 20

The Vice-President

(a) The Vice-President shall be elected for a term of two years, or such shorter term as shall coincide with the duration of his term of office as a Judge. He may be re-elected once.

(b) The Vice-President may sit as a member of a Trial Chamber or of the Appeals Chamber.

(c) Sub-rules 18(b) and (c) shall apply *mutatis mutandis* to the Vice-President.

Rule 21

Functions of the Vice-President

Subject to Sub-rule 22(b), the Vice President shall exercise the functions of the President in case of his absence or inability to act.

Rule 22

Replacements

(a) If neither the President nor the Vice-President can carry out the functions of the President, these shall be assumed by the senior Judge, determined in accordance with Rule 17.

(b) If the President is unable to exercise his functions as Presiding Judge of the Appeals Chamber, that Chamber shall elect a Presiding Judge from among its number.

Section 3

Internal Functioning of the Tribunal

Rule 23

The Bureau

(a) The Bureau shall be composed of the President, the Vice-President and the Presiding Judges of the Trial Chambers.

(b) The President shall consult the other members of the bureau on all major questions relating to the functioning of the Tribunal.

(c) A Judge may draw the attention of any member of the Bureau to issues that in his opinion ought to be discussed by the Bureau or submitted to a plenary meeting of the Tribunal.

Rule 24

Plenary Meetings of the Tribunal

The Judges shall meet in plenary to:

(i) elect the President and Vice-President;

(ii) adopt and amend the Rules;

(iii) adopt the Annual Report provided for in Article 34 of the Statute;

(iv) decide upon matters relating to the internal functioning of the Chambers and the Tribunal;

(v) determine or supervise the conditions of detention;

(vi) exercise any other functions provided for in the Statute or in the Rules.

Rule 25

Dates of Plenary Sessions

(a) The dates of the plenary sessions of the Tribunal shall normally be agreed upon in July of each year for the following calendar year.

(b) Other plenary meetings shall be convened by the President if so requested by at least six Judges, and may be convened whenever the exercise of his functions under the Statute or the Rules so requires.

Rule 26

Quorum and Vote

(a) The quorum for each plenary meeting of the Tribunal shall be seven Judges.

(b) Subject to Sub-rules 6(a) and (b) and Sub-rule 18 (c), the decisions of the plenary meetings of the Tribunal shall be taken by the majority of the Judges present. In the event of an equality of votes, the President or the Judge who acts in his place shall have a casting vote.

Section 4

The Chambers

Rule 27

Rotation

(a) Judges shall rotate on a regular basis between the Trial Chambers and the Appeals Chamber. Rotation shall take into account the efficient disposal of cases.

(b) The Judges shall take their places in their new Chamber as soon as the President thinks it convenient, having regard to the disposal of part-heard cases.

(c) The President may at any time temporarily assign a member of a Trial Chamber or of the Appeals Chamber to another Chamber.

Rule 28

Assignment to Review Indictments

The President shall, in July of each year and after consultation with the Judges, assign for each month of the next calendar year a Judge of a Trial Chamber as the Judge to whom indictments shall be transmitted for review under Rule 47, and shall publish the list of assignments.

Rule 29

Deliberations

The deliberations of the Chambers shall take place in private and remain secret.

Section 5

The Registry

Rule 30

Appointment of the Registrar

The President shall seek the opinion of the Judges on the candidates for the post of Registrar, before consulting with the Secretary-General of the United Nations pursuant to Article 17(3) of the Statute.

Rule 31

Appointment of the Deputy Registrar and Registry Staff

The Registrar, after consultation with the Bureau, shall make his recommendations to the Secretary-General of the United Nations for the appointment of the Deputy Registrar and other Registry staff.

Rule 32

Solemn Declaration

(a) Before taking up his duties, the Registrar shall make the following declaration before the President:

"I solemnly declare that I will perform the duties incumbent upon me as Registrar of the International Tribunal for the Prosecution of Persons Responsible for Serious Violations of International Humanitarian Law Committed in the Territory of the Former Yugoslavia since 1991 in all loyalty, discretion and good conscience and that I will faithfully observe all the provisions of the Statute and the Rules of Procedure and Evidence of the Tribunal".

(b) Before taking up his duties, the Deputy Registrar shall make a similar declaration before the President.

(c) Every staff member of the Registry shall make a similar declaration before the Registrar.

Rule 33

Functions of the Registrar

The Registrar shall assist the Chambers, the plenary meetings of the Tribunal, the Judges and the Prosecutor in the performance of their functions. Under the authority of the

President, he shall be responsible for the administration and servicing of the Tribunal and shall serve as its channel of communication.

Rule 34

Victims and Witnesses Unit

(a) There shall be set up under the authority of the Registrar a Victims and Witnesses Unit consisting of qualified staff to:

    (i) recommend protective measures for victims and witnesses in accordance with Article 22 of the Statute; and

    (ii) provide counselling and support for them, in particular in cases of rape and sexual assault.

(b) Due consideration shall be given, in the appointment of staff, to the employment of qualified women.

Rule 35

Minutes

Except where a full record is made under Rule 81, the Registrar, or Registry staff designated by him, shall take minutes of the plenary meetings of the Tribunal and of the sittings of the Chambers, other than private deliberations.

Rule 36

Record Book

The Registrar shall keep a Record Book which shall list all the particulars of each case brought before the Tribunal. The Record Book shall be open to the public.

Section 6

The Prosecutor

Rule 37

Functions

(a) The Prosecutor shall exercise all the functions provided by the Statute in accordance with the Rules and such Regulations as may be framed by him.

(b) His powers under Parts Four to Eight of the Rules may be exercised by staff members of the Office of the Prosecutor authorised by him, or by any person acting under his direction.

Rule 38

Deputy Prosecutor

(a) The Prosecutor shall make his recommendations to the Secretary-General of the United Nations for the appointment of a Deputy Prosecutor.

(b) The Deputy Prosecutor shall exercise the functions of the Prosecutor in the event of his absence of inability to act or upon the Prosecutor's express instructions.

Part IV

Investigations and Rights of Suspects

Section 1

Investigations

Rule 39

Conduct of Investigations

In the conduct of an investigation, the Prosecutor may:

(i) summon and question suspects, victims and witnesses and record their statements, collect evidence and conduct on-site investigations;

(ii) undertake such other matters as may appear necessary for completing the investigation and the preparation and conduct of the prosecution at the trial;

(iii) seek, to that end, the assistance of any State authority concerned, as well as of any relevant international body including the International Criminal Police Organization (INTERPOL); and

(iv) request such orders as may be necessary from a Trial Chamber or a Judge.

Rule 40

Provisional Measures

In case of urgency, the Prosecutor may request any State;

(i) to arrest a suspect provisionally;

(ii) to seize physical evidence;

(iii) to take all necessary measures to prevent the escape of a suspect or an accused, injury to or intimidation of a victim or witness, or the destruction of evidence.

Rule 41

Retention of Information

The Prosecutor shall be responsible for the retention, storage and security of information and physical evidence obtained in the course of his investigations.

Rule 42

Rights of Suspects during Investigation

(a) A suspect who is to be questioned by the Prosecutor shall have the following rights, of which he shall be informed by the Prosecutor prior to questioning, in a language he speaks and understands:

(i) the right to be assisted by counsel of his choice or to have legal assistance assigned to him without payment if he does not have sufficient means to pay for it; and

(ii) the right to have the free assistance of an interpreter if he cannot understand or speak the language to be used for questioning.

(b) Questioning of a suspect shall not proceed without the presence of counsel unless the suspect has voluntarily waived his right to counsel. In case of waiver, if the suspect subsequently expresses a desire to have counsel, questioning shall thereupon cease, and shall only resume when the suspect has obtained or has been assigned counsel.

Rule 43

Recording Questioning of Suspects

Whenever the Prosecutor questions a suspect, the questioning shall be tape-recorded or video-recorded, in accordance with the following procedure:

(i) the suspect shall be informed in a language he speaks and understands that the questioning is being tape-recorded or video-recorded;

(ii) in the event of a break in the course of the questioning, the fact and the time of the break shall be recorded before tape-recording or video-recording ends and the time of resumption of the questioning shall also be recorded;

(iii) at the conclusion of the questioning the suspect shall be offered the opportunity to clarify anything he has said, and to add anything he may wish, and the time of conclusion shall be recorded;

(iv) the tape shall then be transcribed and a copy of the transcript supplied to the suspect, together with a copy of the recorded tape or, if multiple recording apparatus was used, one of the original recorded tapes; and

(v) after a copy has been made, if necessary, of the recorded tape for purposes of transcription, the original recorded tape or one of the original tapes shall be sealed in the presence of the suspect under the signature of the Prosecutor and the suspect.

Section 2

Of Counsel

Rule 44

Appointment and Qualifications of Counsel

Counsel engaged by a suspect or an accused shall file his power of attorney with the Registrar at the earliest opportunity. A counsel shall be considered qualified to represent a suspect or accused if he satisfies the Registrar that he is admitted to the practice of law in a State, or is a University professor of law.

Rule 45

Assignment of Counsel

(a) A list of counsel who speak one or both of the working languages of the Tribunal, meet the requirements of Rule 44 and have indicated their willingness to be assigned by the Tribunal to indigent suspects or accused, shall be kept by the Registrar.

(b) The criteria for determination of indigence shall be established by the Registrar and approved by the Judges.

(c) In assigning counsel to an indigent suspect or accused, the following procedure shall be observed:

   (i) a request for assignment of counsel shall be made to the Registrar;

   (ii) the Registrar shall enquire into the means of the suspect or accused and determine whether the criteria of indigence are met;

   (iii) if he decides that the criteria are met, he shall assign counsel from the list; if he decides to the contrary, he shall inform the suspect or accused that the request is refused.

(d) If a request is refused, a further request may be made by a suspect or an accused to the Registrar upon showing a change in circumstances.

(e) The Registrar shall assign counsel to a suspect or an accused who fails to obtain counsel or to request assignment of counsel, unless the suspect or the accused elects in writing to conduct his own defence.

(f) The Registrar shall, in consultation with the Judges, establish the criteria for the payment of fees to assigned counsel.

Rule 46

Misconduct of Counsel

(a) A Chamber may, after a warning, refuse audience to counsel if, in its opinion, his conduct is offensive, abusive or otherwise obstructs the proper conduct of the proceedings.

(b) A Judge or a Chamber may also, with the approval of the President, communicate any misconduct of counsel to the professional body regulating the conduct of counsel in his State of admission or, if a professor and not otherwise admitted to the profession, to the governing body of his University.

Part V

Pre-trial Proceedings

Section 1

Indictments

Rule 47

Submission of Indictment by the Prosecutor

(a) If in the course of an investigation the Prosecutor is satisfied that there is sufficient evidence to provide reasonable grounds for believing that a suspect has committed a crime within the jurisdiction of the Tribunal, he shall prepare and forward to the Registrar an indictment for confirmation by a Judge, together with supporting material.

(b) The indictment shall set forth the name and particulars of the suspect, and a concise statement of the facts of the case and of the crime with which the suspect is charged.

(c) The Registrar shall forward the indictment and accompanying material to the Judge currently assigned under Rule 28, who will inform the Prosecutor of the date fixed for review of the indictment.

(d) On reviewing the indictment, the Judge shall hear the Prosecutor, who may present additional material in support of any count. The Judge may confirm or dismiss each count or may adjourn the review.

(e) The dismissal of a count in an indictment shall not preclude the Prosecutor from subsequently bringing a new indictment based on the acts underlying that count if supported by additional evidence.

Rule 48

Joinder of Accused

Persons accused of the same or different crimes committed in the course of the same transaction may be jointly charged and tried.

Rule 49

Joinder of Crimes

Two or more crimes may be joined in one indictment if the series of acts committed together form the same transaction, and the said crimes were committed by the same accused.

Rule 50

Amendment of Indictment

The Prosecutor may amend an indictment, without leave, at any time before its confirmation, but thereafter only with leave of the Judge who confirmed it or, if at trial, with leave of the Trial Chamber. If leave to amend is granted, the amended indictment shall be transmitted to the accused and to his counsel and where necessary the date for trial shall be postponed to ensure adequate time for the preparation of the defence.

Rule 51

Withdrawal of Indictment

(a) The Prosecutor may withdraw an indictment, without leave, at any time before its confirmation, but thereafter only with leave of the Judge who confirmed it or, if at trial, only with leave of the Trial Chamber.

(b) The withdrawal of the indictment shall be promptly notified to the suspect or the accused and to his counsel.

Rule 52

Public Character of Indictment

Subject to Rule 53, upon confirmation by a Judge of a Trial Chamber, the indictment shall be made public.

Rule 53

Non-disclosure of Indictment

(a) When confirming an indictment the Judge may, in consultation with the Prosecutor, order that there be no public disclosure of the indictment until it is served on the accused, or, in the case of joint accused, on all the accused.

(b) A Judge or Trial Chamber may, in consultation with the Prosecutor, also order that there be no public disclosure of an indictment, or part thereof, or of any particular document or information, if satisfied that the making of such an order is in the interests of justice.

Section 2

Orders and Warrants

Rule 54

General Rule

At the request of either party or *proprio motu*, a Judge or a Trial Chamber may issue such orders, summonses and warrants as may be necessary for the purposes of an investigation or for the preparation or conduct of the trial.

Rule 55

Execution of Arrest Warrants

(a) A warrant of arrest shall be signed by a Judge and shall bear the seal of the Tribunal. It shall be accompanied by a copy of the indictment, and a statement of the rights of the accused. These rights include those set forth in Article 21 of the Statute, and in Rules 42 and 43 *mutatis mutandis*, together with the right of the accused to remain silent, and to be cautioned that any statement he makes shall be recorded and may be used in evidence.

(b) A warrant for the arrest of the accused and his surrender to the Tribunal shall be transmitted by the Registrar to the national authorities of the State in whose territory or under whose jurisdiction or control the accused resides, or was last known to be, together with instructions that at the time of arrest the indictment and the statement of the rights of the accused be read to him in a language he understands and that he be cautioned in that language.

(c) When an arrest warrant issued by the Tribunal is executed, a member of the Prosecutor's Office may be present as from the time of arrest.

Rule 56

Cooperation of States

The State to which a warrant of arrest is transmitted shall act promptly and with all due diligence to ensure proper and effective execution thereof, in accordance with Article 29 of the Statute.

Rule 57

Procedure after Arrest

Upon the arrest of the accused, the State concerned shall detain him, and shall promptly notify the Registrar. The transfer of the accused to the seat of the Tribunal shall be arranged between the State authorities concerned and the Registrar.

Rule 58

National Extradition Provisions

The obligations laid down in Article 29 of the Statute shall prevail over any legal impediment to the surrender or transfer of the accused to the Tribunal which may exist under the national law or extradition treaties of the State concerned.

Rule 59

Failure to Execute a Warrant

(a) Where the State to which a warrant of arrest has been transmitted has been unable to execute the warrant, it shall rapport forthwith its inability to the Registrar, and the reasons therefor.

(b) If, within a reasonable time after the warrant of arrest has been transmitted to the State, no report is made on action taken, this shall be deemed a failure to execute the warrant of arrest and the Tribunal, through the President, may notify the Security Council accordingly.

Rule 60

Advertisement of Indictment

At the request of the Prosecutor, a form of advertisement shall be transmitted by the Registrar to the national authorities of any State or States in whose territory the Prosecutor has reason to believe that the accused may be found, for publication in newspapers having wide circulation in that territory, intimating to the accused that service of an indictment against him is sought.

Rule 61

Procedure in Case of Failure to Execute a Warrant

(a) If a warrant of arrest has not been executed, and personal service of the indictment has consequently not been effected, and the Prosecutor satisfies a Judge of a Trial Chamber that:

　(i) he has taken all reasonable steps to effect personal service, including recourse to the appropriate authorities of the State in whose territory or under whose jurisdiction and control the person to be served resides or was last known to him to be; and

　(ii) he has otherwise tried to inform the accused of the existence of the indictment by seeking publication of newspaper advertisements pursuant to Rule 60, the Judge shall order that the indictment be submitted by the Prosecutor to the Trial Chamber.

(b) Upon obtaining such an order the Prosecutor shall submit the indictment to the Trial Chamber in open court, together with all the evidence that was before the Judge who initially confirmed the indictment.

(c) If the Trial Chamber is satisfied on that evidence, together with such additional evidence as the Prosecutor may tender, that there are reasonable grounds for believing that the accused has committed all or any of the crimes charged in the indictment, it shall so determine. The Trial Chamber shall have the relevant parts of the indictment read out by the Prosecutor together with an account of the efforts to effect service referred to in Sub-rule (a) above.

(d) The Trial Chamber shall also issue an international arrest warrant in respect of the accused which shall be transmitted to all States.

(e) If the Prosecutor satisfies the Trial Chamber that the failure to effect personal service was due in whole or in part to a failure or refusal of a State to cooperate with the Tribunal in accordance with Article 29 of the Statute, the Trial Chamber shall so certify, in which event the President shall notify the Security Council.

Rule 62

Initial Appearance of Accused

Upon his transfer to the seat of the Tribunal, the accused shall be brought before a Trial Chamber without delay, and shall be formally charged. The Trial Chamber shall:

(i) satisfy itself that the right of the accused to counsel is respected;

(ii) read or have the indictment read to the accused in a language he speaks and understands, and satisfy itself that the accused understands the indictment;

(iii) call upon the accused to enter a plea of guilty or not guilty; should the accused fail to do so, enter a plea of not guilty on his behalf;

(iv) instruct the Registrar to set a date for trial.

Rule 63

Questioning of Accused

After the initial appearance of the accused the Prosecutor shall not question him unless his counsel is present and the questioning is tape-recorded or video-recorded in accordance with the procedure provided for in Rule 43. The Prosecutor shall at the beginning of the questioning caution the accused that he is not obliged to say anything unless he wishes to do so but that whatever he says may be given in evidence.

Rule 64

Detention of Remand

Upon his transfer to the seat of the Tribunal, the accused shall be detained in facilities provided by the host country, or by another country. The President may, on the application of a party, request modification of the conditions of detention of an accused.

Rule 65

Provisional Release

(a) Once detained, an accused may not be released except upon an order of a Trial Chamber.

(b) Release may be ordered by a Trial Chamber only in exceptional circumstances, and only if it is satisfied that the accused will appear for trial and, if released, will not pose a danger to any victim, witness or other person.

(c) The Trial Chamber may impose such conditions upon the release of the accused as it may determine appropriate, including the execution of a bail bond and the observance of such conditions as are necessary to ensure his presence for trial and the protection of others.

(d) If necessary, the Trial Chamber may issue a warrant of arrest to secure the presence of an accused who has been released or is for any other reason at liberty.

Section 3

Production of Evidence

Rule 66

Disclosure by the Prosecutor

(a) The Prosecutor shall make available to the defence, as soon as practicable after the initial appearance of the accused, copies of the supporting material which accompanied the indictment when confirmation was sought.

(b) The Prosecutor shall on request permit the defence to inspect any books, documents, photographs and tangible objects in his custody or control, which are material to the preparation of the defence, or are intended for use by the Prosecutor as evidence at trial or were obtained from or belonged to the accused.

Rule 67

Reciprocal Disclosure

(a) As early as reasonably practicable and in any event prior to the commencement of the trial:

   (i) The Prosecutor shall notify the defence of the names of the witnesses that he intends to call in proof of the guilt of the accused and in rebuttal of any defence plea of which the Prosecutor has received notice in accordance with Sub-rule (ii) below,

   (ii) the defence shall notify the Prosecutor of its intent to offer:

   (iii) the defence of alibi; in which case the notification shall specify the place or places at which the accused claims to have been present at the time of the alleged crime and the names and addresses of witnesses and any other evidence upon which the accused intends to rely to establish the alibi;

   (iv) any special defence, including that of diminished or lack of mental responsibility; in which case the notification shall specify the names and addresses of witnesses and any other evidence upon which the accused intends to rely to establish the special defence.

(b) Failure of the defence to provide notice under this Rule shall not limit the right of the accused to testify on the above defences.

(c) If the defence makes a request pursuant to Sub-rule 66(b), the Prosecutor shall be entitled to inspect any books, documents, photographs and tangible objects, which are within the custody or control of the defence and which it intends to use as evidence at the trial.

(d) If either party discovers additional evidence or material which should have been produced earlier pursuant to the Rules, that party shall promptly notify the other party and the Trial Chamber of the existence of the additional evidence or material.

Rule 68

Disclosure of exculpatory Evidence

The Prosecutor shall, as soon as practicable, disclose to the defence the existence of evidence known to the Prosecutor which in any way tends to suggest the innocence or mitigate the guilt of the accused of a crime charged in the indictment.

Rule 69

Protection of Victims and Witnesses

(a) In exceptional circumstances, the Prosecutor may apply to a Trial Chamber to order the non-disclosure of the identity of a victim or witness who may be in danger or at risk until such person is brought under the protection of the Tribunal.

(b) Subject to Rule 75, the identity of the victim or witness shall be disclosed in sufficient time prior to the trial to allow adequate time for preparation of the defence.

Rule 70

Matters not Subject to Disclosure

Notwithstanding the provisions of Rules 66 and 67, reports, memoranda, or other internal documents prepared by a party, its assistants or representatives in connection with the investigation or preparation of the case, are not subject to disclosure or notification under those Rules.

Section 4

Depositions

Rule 71

Depositions

(a) At the request of either party, a Trial Chamber may, in exceptional circumstances and in the interests of justice, order that a deposition be taken for use at trial, and appoint, for that purpose, a Presiding Officer.

(b) The motion for the taking of a deposition shall be in writing and shall indicate the name and whereabouts of the person whose deposition is sought, the date and place at which the deposition is to be taken, a statement of the matters on which the person is to be examined, and of the exceptional circumstances justifying the taking of the deposition.

(c) If the motion is granted, the party at whose request the deposition is to be taken shall give reasonable notice to the other party, who shall have the right to attend the taking of the deposition and cross-examine the person whose deposition is being taken.

(d) Deposition evidence may also be given by means of a video-conference.

(e) The Presiding Officer shall ensure that the deposition is taken in accordance with the Rules and that a record is made of the deposition, including cross-examination and objections raised by either party for decision by the Trial Chamber. He shall transmit the record to the Trial Chamber.

Section 5

Preliminary Motions

Rule 72

General Provisions

(a) After the initial appearance of the accused, either party may move before a Trial Chamber for appropriate relief or ruling. Such motions may be written or oral, at the discretion of the Trial Chamber.

(b) The Trial Chamber shall dispose of preliminary motions in *limine litis*.

Rule 73

Preliminary Motions by Accused

(a) Preliminary motions by the accused shall include:

(i) objections based on lack of jurisdiction;

(ii) objections based on defects in the form of the indictment;

(iii) applications for the exclusion of evidence obtained from the accused or having belonged to him;

(iv) applications for severance of crimes joined in one indictment under Rule 49, or for separate trials under Sub-rule 82 (b);

(v) objections based on the denial of request for assignment of counsel.

(b) Any of the motions by the accused referred to in Sub-rule (a) shall be brought within sixty days after his initial appearance, and in any case before the hearing on the merits.

(c) Failure to apply within the time-limit prescribed shall constitute a waiver of the right. Upon a showing of good cause, the Trial Chamber may grant relief from the waiver.

Part VI

Proceedings before Trial Chambers

Section 1

General Provisions

Rule 74

Amicus Curiae

A Chamber may, if it considers it desirable for the proper determination of the case, invite or grant leave to a State, organization or person to appear before it and make submissions on any issue specified by the Chamber.

Rule 75

Protection of Victims and Witnesses

(a) A Judge or a Chamber may, *proprio motu* or at the request of either party, or of the victim or witness concerned, order appropriate measures for the privacy and protection of victims and witnesses, provided that the measures are consistent with the rights of the accused.

(b) A Chamber may hold an *ex parte (non-contradictoire)* proceeding to determine whether to order:

(i) measures to prevent disclosure to the public or the media of the identity or whereabouts of a victim or a witness, or of persons related to or associated with him by such means as:

- expunging names and identifying information from the Chamber's public records;
- non-disclosure to the public of any records identifying the victim;
- giving of testimony through image- or voice-altering devices or closed circuit television; and
- assignment of a pseudonym;

(ii) closed sessions, in accordance with Rule 79;

(iii) appropriate measures to facilitate the testimony of vulnerable victims and witnesses, such as one-way closed circuit television.

(c) A Chamber shall, whenever necessary, control the manner of questioning to avoid any harassment or intimidation.

Rule 76

Solemn Declaration by Interpreters and Translators

Before performing any duties, an interpreter or a translator shall solemnly declare to do so faithfully, independently, impartially and with full respect for the duty of confidentiality.

Rule 77

Contempt of Court

(a) Subject to the provisions of Sub-rule 90 (d), a witness who refuses or fails contumaciously to answer a question relevant to the issue before a Chamber may be found in contempt of the Tribunal. The Chamber may impose a fine not exceeding US$10,000 or a term of imprisonment not exceeding six months.

(b) The Chamber may, however, relieve the witness of the duty to answer, for reasons which it deems appropriate.

(c) Payment of a fine shall be made to the Registrar to be held in a separate account.

Rule 78

Open Sessions

All proceedings before a Trial Chamber, other than deliberations of the Chamber, shall be held in public, unless otherwise provided.

Rule 79

Closed Sessions

(a) The Trial Chamber may order that the press and the public be excluded from all or part of the proceedings for reasons of:

- (i) public order or morality;
- (ii) safety, security or non-disclosure of the identity of a victim or witness as provided in Rule 75; or
- (iii) the protection of the interests of justice.

(b) The Trial Chamber shall make public the reasons for its order.

Rule 80

Control of Proceedings

(a) The Trial Chamber may exclude a person from the courtroom in order to protect the right of the accused to a fair and public trial, or to maintain the dignity and decorum of the proceedings.

(b) The Trial Chamber may order the removal of an accused from the courtroom and continue the proceedings in his absence if he has persisted in disruptive conduct following a warning that he may be removed.

Rule 81

Records of Proceedings and Evidence

(a) The Registrar shall cause to be made and preserve a full and accurate record of all proceedings, including audio recordings, transcripts and, when deemed necessary by the Trial Chamber, video recordings.

(b) The Trial Chamber may order the disclosure of all or part of the record of closed proceedings when the reasons for ordering its non-disclosure no longer exist.

(c) The Registrar shall retain and preserve all physical evidence offered during the proceedings.

(d) Photography, video-recording or audio-recording of the trial, otherwise than by the Registry, may be authorised at the discretion of the Trial Chamber.

Section 2

Case Presentation

Rule 82

Joint and Separate Trials

(a) In joint trials, each accused shall be accorded the same rights as if he were being tried separately.

(b) The Trial Chamber may order that persons accused jointly under Rule 48 be tried separately if it considers it necessary in order to avoid a conflict of interests that might cause serious prejudice to an accused, or to protect the interests of justice.

Rule 83

Instruments of Restraint

Instruments of restraints, such as handcuffs, shall not be used except as a precaution against escape during transfer or for security reasons, and shall be removed when the accused appears before a Chamber.

Rule 84

Opening Statements

Before presentation of evidence by the Prosecutor, each party may make an opening statement. The defence may however elect to make its statement after the Prosecutor has concluded his presentation of evidence and before the presentation of evidence for the defence.

Rule 85

Presentation of Evidence

(a) Each party is entitled to call witnesses and present evidence. Unless otherwise directed by the Trial Chamber in the interests of justice, evidence at the trial shall be presented in the following sequence:

   (i) evidence for the prosecution;

   (ii) evidence for the defence;

   (iii) prosecution evidence in rebuttal;

   (iv) defence evidence in rejoinder;

   (v) evidence ordered by the Trial Chamber pursuant to Rule 98.

(b) Examination-in-chief, cross-examination and re-examination shall be allowed in each case. It shall be for the party calling a witness to examine him in chief, but a Judge may at any stage put any question to the witness.

(c) The accused may, if he so desires, appear as a witness in his own defence.

Rule 86

Closing Arguments

After the presentation of all the evidence, the Prosecutor may present an initial argument, to which the defence may reply. The Prosecutor may, if he wishes, present a rebuttal argument, to which the defence may present a rejoinder.

Rule 87

Deliberations

(a) When both parties have completed their presentation of the case, the Presiding Judge shall declare the hearing closed, and the Trial Chamber shall deliberate in private. A finding of guilt may be reached only when a majority of the Trial Chamber is satisfied that guilt has been proved beyond reasonable doubt.

(b) The Trial Chamber shall vote separately on each charge contained in the indictment. If two or more accused are tried together under Rule 48, separate findings shall be made as to each accused.

Rule 88

Judgement

(a) The judgement shall be pronounced in public and in the presence of the accused, on a date of which notice shall have been given to the parties and counsel.

(b) If the Trial Chamber finds the accused guilty of a crime and concludes from the evidence that unlawful taking of property by the accused was associated with it, it shall make a specific finding to that effect in its judgement. The Trial Chamber may order restitution as provided in Rule 105.

(c) A Judge of the Trial Chamber may append a separate or dissenting opinion to the judgement.

Section 3

Rules of Evidence

Rule 89

General Provisions

(a) The rules of evidence set forth in this Section shall govern the proceedings before the Chambers. The Chambers shall not be bound by national rules of evidence.

(b) In cases not otherwise provided for in this Section, a Chamber shall apply rules of evidence which will best favour a fair determination of the matter before it and are consonant with the spirit of the Statute and the general principles of law.

(c) A Chamber may admit any relevant evidence which it deems to have probative value.

(d) A Chamber may exclude evidence if its probative value is substantially outweighed by the need to ensure a fair trial.

(e) A Chamber may request verification of the authenticity of evidence obtained out of court.

Rule 90

Testimony of Witnesses

(a) Witnesses shall, in principle, be heard directly by the Chambers. In cases, however, where it is not possible to secure the presence of a witness, a Chamber may order that the witness be heard by means of a deposition as provided for in Rule 71.

(b) Every witness shall, before giving evidence, make the following solemn declaration: "I solemnly declare that I will speak the truth, the whole truth and nothing but the truth".

(c) A witness, other than an expert, who has not yet testified shall not be present when the testimony of another witness is given. However, a witness who has heard the testimony of another witness shall not for that reason alone be disqualified from testifying.

(d) A witness may decline to make any statement which might tend to incriminate him.

Rule 91

False Testimony under Solemn Declaration

(a) A Chamber, on its own initiative or at the request of a party, may warn a witness of the duty to tell the truth and the consequences that may result from a failure to do so.

(b) If a Chamber has strong grounds for believing that a witness has knowingly and wilfully given false testimony, it may direct the Prosecutor to investigate the matter with a view to the preparation and submission of an indictment for false testimony.

(c) The rules of procedure and evidence in Parts Four to Eight shall apply *mutatis mutandis* to proceedings under this Rule.

(d) No Judge who sat as a member of the Trial Chamber before which the witness appeared shall sit for the trial of the witness for false testimony.

(e) The maximum penalty for false testimony under solemn declaration shall be a fine of US$10,000 or a term of imprisonment of twelve months, or both. The payment of any fine imposed shall be made to the Registrar to be held in the account referred to in Sub-rule 77(c).

Rule 92

Confessions

A confession by the accused given during questioning by the Prosecutor shall, provided the requirements of Rule 63 were strictly complied with, be presumed to have been free and voluntary unless the contrary is proved.

Rule 93

Evidence of Consistent Pattern of Conduct

Evidence of a consistent pattern of conduct may be admissible in the interests of justice.

Rule 94

Judicial Notice

A Trial Chamber shall not require proof of facts of common knowledge but shall take judicial notice thereof.

Rule 95

Evidence Obtained by Means Contrary to Internationally Protected Human Rights

Evidence obtained directly or indirectly by means which constitute a serious violation of internationally protected human rights shall not be admissible.

Rule 96

Evidence in Cases of Sexual Assault

In cases of sexual assault:

(i) no corroboration of the victims's testimony shall be required;

(ii) consent shall not be allowed as a defence if the victim

- has been subjected to or threatened with or has had reason to fear violence, duress, detention of psychological oppression, or

- reasonably believed that if she did not submit, another might be so subjected, threatened or put in fear;

(iii) prior sexual conduct of the victim shall not be admitted in evidence.

Rule 97

Lawyer-Client Privilege

All communications between lawyer and client shall be regarded as privileged, and consequently not subject to disclosure at trial, unless:

(i) the client consents to such disclosure; or

(ii) the client has voluntarily disclosed the content of the communication to a third party, and that third party then gives evidence of that disclosure.

Rule 98

Power of Chambers to Order Production of Additional Evidence

A Trial Chamber may order either party to produce additional evidence. It may itself summon witnesses and order their attendance.

Section 4

Sentencing Procedure

Rule 99

Status of the Acquitted Person

(a) In case of acquittal, the accused shall be released immediately.

(b) If, at the time the judgement is pronounced, the Prosecutor advises the Trial Chamber in open court of his intention to file notice of appeal pursuant to Rule 108, the Trial Chamber may, at the request of the Prosecutor, issue a warrant for the arrest of the accused to take effect immediately.

Rule 100

Pre-sentencing Procedure

If a Trial Chamber finds the accused guilty of a crime, the Prosecutor and the defence may submit any relevant information that may assist the Trial Chamber in determining an appropriate sentence.

Rule 101

Penalties

(a) A convicted person may be sentenced to imprisonment for a term up to and including the remainder of his life.

(b) In determining the sentence, the Trial Chamber shall take into account the factors mentioned in Article 24(2) of the Statute, as well as such factors as:

(i) any aggravating circumstances;

(ii) any mitigating circumstances including the substantial cooperation with the Prosecutor by the convicted person before or after conviction;

(iii) the general practice regarding prison sentences in the courts of the former Yugoslavia;

(iv) the period, if any, during which the convicted person was detained in custody pending his surrender to the Tribunal or pending trial;

(v) the extent to which any penalty imposed by a national court on the convicted person for the same act has already been served, as referred to in Article 10(3) of the Statute.

(c) The Trial Chamber shall indicate whether multiple sentences shall be served consecutively or concurrently.

(d) The sentence shall be pronounced in public and in the presence of the convicted person, subject to Sub-rule 102(b).

Rule 102

Status of the Convicted Person

(a) The sentence shall begin to run from the day it is pronounced under Sub-rule 101(d). However, as soon as notice of appeal is given, the enforcement of the judgement shall thereupon be stayed until the decision on the appeal has been delivered, the convicted person meanwhile remaining in detention, as provided in Rule 64.

(b) If, by a previous decision of the Trial Chamber, the convicted person has been released, or is for any other reason at liberty, and he is not present when the judgement is pronounced, the Trial Chamber shall issue a warrant for his arrest. On arrest, he shall be notified of the conviction and sentence, and the procedure provided in Rule 103 shall be followed.

Rule 103

Place of Imprisonment

(a) Imprisonment shall be served in a State designated by the Tribunal from a list of States which have indicated their willingness to accept convicted persons.

(b) Transfer of the convicted person to that State shall be effected as soon as possible after the time-limit for appeal has elapsed.

Rule 104

Supervision of Imprisonment

All sentences of imprisonment shall be supervised by the Tribunal or a body designated by it.

Rule 105

Restitution of Property

(a) After a judgement of conviction containing a specific finding as provided in Sub-rule 88(b), the Trial Chamber shall, at the request of the Prosecutor, or may, at its own initiative, hold a special hearing to determine the matter of the restitution of the property or the proceeds thereof, and may in the meantime order such provisional measures for the preservation and protection of the property or proceeds as it considers appropriate.

(b) The determination may extend to such property or its proceeds, even in the hands of third parties not otherwise connected with the crime of which the convicted person has been found guilty.

(c) Such third parties shall be summoned before the Trial Chamber and be given an opportunity to justify their claim to the property or its proceeds.

(d) Should the Trial Chamber be able to determine the rightful owner on the balance of probabilities, it shall order the restitution either of the property or the proceeds as appropriate.

(e) Should the Trial Chamber not be able to determine ownership, it shall notify the competent national authorities and request them so to determine.

(f) The Registrar shall transmit to the competent national authorities any summonses, orders and requests issued by a Trial Chamber pursuant to Sub-rules (c), (d), (e).

Rule 106

Compensation to Victims

(a) The Registrar shall transmit to the competent authorities of the States concerned the judgement finding the accused guilty of a crime which has caused injury to a victim.

(b) Pursuant to the relevant national legislation, a victim or persons claiming through him may bring an action in a national court or other competent body to obtain compensation.

(c) For the purposes of a claim made under Sub-rule (b) the judgement of the Tribunal shall be final and binding as to the criminal responsibility of the convicted person for such injury.

Part VII

Appellate Proceedings

Rule 107

General Provision

The rules of procedure and evidence that govern proceedings in the Trial Chambers shall apply *mutatis mutandis* to proceedings in the Appeals Chamber.

Rule 108

Notice of Appeal

A party seeking to appeal a judgement shall, not more than thirty days from the date on which the judgement was pronounced, file with the Registrar and serve upon the other party a written notice of appeal, setting forth the grounds.

Rule 109

Record on Appeal

(a) The record on appeal shall consist of the parts of the trial record, as certified by the Registrar, designated by the parties.

(b) The parties, within thirty days of the certification of the trial record by the Registrar, may be agreement designate the parts of that record which, in their opinion, are necessary for the decision on the appeal.

(c) Should the parties fail so to agree within that time, the Appellant and the Respondent shall each designate to the Registrar, within sixty days of the certification, the parts of the trial record which he considers necessary for the decision on the appeal.

(d) The Appeals Chamber shall remain free to call for the whole of the trial record.

Rule 110

Copies of Record

The Registrar shall make a sufficient number of copies of the record on appeal for the use of the Judges of the Appeals Chamber and of the parties.

Rule 111

Appellant's Brief

An Appellant's brief of argument and authorities shall be served on the other party and filed with the Registrar within ninety days of the certification of the record.

Rule 112

Respondent's Brief

A Respondent's brief of argument and authorities shall be served on the other party and filed with the Registrar within thirty days of the filing of the Appellant's brief.

Rule 113

Brief in Reply

An Appellant may file a brief in reply within fifteen days after the filing of the Respondent's brief.

Rule 114

Date of Hearing

After the expiry of the time-limits for filing the briefs provided for in Rules 111, 112 and 113, the Appeals Chamber shall set the date for the hearing and the Registrar shall notify the parties.

Rule 115

Additional Evidence

(a) A party may apply by motion to present before the Appeals Chamber additional evidence which was not available to it at the trial. Such motion must be served on the other party and filed with the Registrar not less than fifteen days before the date of the hearing.

(b) The Appeals Chamber shall authorise the presentation of such evidence if it considers that the interests of justice so require.

Rule 116

Extension of Time-limits

The Appeals Chamber may grant a motion to extend to time-limit upon a showing of good cause.

Rule 117

Judgement

(a) The Appeals Chamber shall pronounce judgement on the basis of the record on appeal together with such additional evidence as has been presented to it.

(b) The judgement shall be pronounced in public, and in the presence of the accused, on a date of which notice shall have been given to the parties and counsel.

Rule 118

Status of the Accused Following Appeal

(a) A sentence pronounced by the Appeals Chamber shall be enforced immediately.

(b) Where the accused is not present when the judgement is due to be delivered, either as having been acquitted on all charges or as a result of an order issued pursuant to Rule 65, or for any other reason, the Appeals Chamber may deliver its judgement in the absence of the accused and shall, unless it pronounces his acquittal, order his arrest or surrender to the Tribunal.

Part VIII

Review Proceedings

Rule 119

Request for Review

Where a new fact has been discovered which was not known to the moving party at the time of the proceedings before a Trial Chamber or the Appeals Chamber, and could not have been discovered through the exercise of due diligence, the defence or, within one year after the final judgement has been pronounced, the Prosecutor, may make a motion to that Chamber for review of the judgement.

Rule 120

Preliminary Examination

If a majority of Judges of the Chamber that pronounced the judgement agree that the new fact, if proved, could have been a decisive factor in reaching a decision, the Chamber shall review the judgement, and pronounce a further judgement after hearing the parties.

Rule 121

Appeals

The judgement of a Trial Chamber on review may be appealed in accordance with the provisions of Part Seven.

Rule 122

Return of Case to Trial Chamber

If the judgement to be reviewed is under appeal at the time the motion for review is filed, the Appeals Chamber may return the case to the Trial Chamber for disposition of the motion.

Part IX

Pardon and Commutation of Sentence

Rule 123

Notification by States

If, according to the law of the State in which a convicted person is imprisoned, he is eligible for pardon or commutation of sentence, the State shall, in accordance with Article 28 of the Statute, notify the Tribunal of such eligibility.

Rule 124

Determination by the President

The President shall, upon such notice, determine, in consultation with the Judges, whether pardon or commutation is appropriate.

Rule 125

General Standards for Granting Pardon or Commutation

In determining whether pardon or commutation is appropriate, the President shall take into account, *inter alia*, the gravity of the crime or crimes for which the prisoner was convicted, the treatment of similarly-situated prisoners, the prisoner's demonstration of rehabilitation, as well as any substantial cooperation of the prisoner with the Prosecutor.

Statute of the International Tribunal for Rwanda (1994)[*]

New York, 8 November 1994

Having been established by the Security Council acting under Chapter VII of the Charter of the United Nations, the International Criminal Tribunal for the Prosecution of Persons Responsible for Genocide and Other Serious Violations of International Humanitarian Law Committed in the Territory of Rwanda and Rwandan citizens responsible for genocide and other such violations committed in the territory of neighbouring States, between 1 January 1994 and 31 December 1994 (hereinafter referred to as "the International Tribunal for Rwanda") shall function in accordance with the provisions of the present Statute.

Article 1

Competence of the International Tribunal for Rwanda

The International Tribunal for Rwanda shall have the power to prosecute persons responsible for serious violations of international humanitarian law committed in the territory of Rwanda and Rwandan citizens responsible for such violations committed in the territory of neighbouring States, between 1 January 1994 and 31 December 1994, in accordance with the provisions of the present Statute.

Article 2

Genocide

1. The International Tribunal for Rwanda shall have the power to prosecute persons committing genocide as defined in paragraph 2 of this article or of committing any of the other acts enumerated in paragraph 3 of this article.

2. Genocide means any of the following acts committed with intent to destroy, in whole or in part, a national, ethnical, racial or religious group, as such:

   (a) Killing members of the group;

   (b) Causing serious bodily or mental harm to members of the group;

   (c) Deliberately inflicting on the group conditions of life calculated to bring about its physical destruction in whole or in part;

   (d) Imposing measures intended to prevent births within the group;

   (e) Forcibly transferring children of the group to another group.

3. The following acts shall be punishable:

   (a) Genocide;

   (b) Conspiracy to commit genocide;

   (c) Direct and public incitement to commit genocide;

   (d) Attempt to commit genocide;

   (e) Complicity in genocide.

---

[*] Security Council Resolution 955 establishing the International Tribunal for Rwanda, *International Legal Materials*, 1994, 1598.

Article 3

Crimes against humanity

The International Tribunal for Rwanda shall have the power to prosecute persons responsible for the following crimes when committed as part of a widespread or systematic attack against any civilian population on national, political, ethnic, racial or religious grounds:

(a) Murder;

(b) Extermination;

(c) Enslavement;

(d) Deportation;

(e) Imprisonment;

(f) Torture;

(g) Rape;

(h) Persecutions on political, racial and religious grounds;

(i) Other inhumane acts.

Article 4

Violations of Article 3 common to the Geneva Conventions and of Additional Protocol II

The International Tribunal for Rwanda shall have the power to prosecute persons committing or ordering to be committed serious violations of Article 3 common to the Geneva Conventions of 12 August 1949 for the Protection of War Victims, and of Additional Protocol II thereto of 8 June 1977. These violations shall include, but shall not be limited to:

(a) Violence to life, health and physical or mental well-being of persons, in particular murder as well as cruel treatment such as torture, mutilation or any form of corporal punishment;

(b) Collective punishments;

(c) Taking of hostages;

(d) Acts of terrorism;

(e) Outrages upon personal dignity, in particular humiliating and degrading treatment, rape, enforced prostitution and any form of indecent assault;

(f) Pillage;

(g) The passing of sentences and the carrying out of executions without previous judgement pronounced by a regularly constituted court, affording all the judicial guarantees which are recognized as indispensable by civilized peoples;

(h) Threats to commit any of the foregoing acts.

Article 5

Personal jurisdiction

The International Tribunal for Rwanda shall have jurisdiction over natural persons pursuant to the provisions of the present Statute.

Article 6

Individual criminal responsibility

1. A person who planned, instigated, ordered, committed or otherwise aided and abetted in the planning, preparation or execution of a crime referred to in articles 2 to 4 of the present Statute, shall be individually responsible for the crime.

2. The official position of any accused person, whether as Head of State or Government or as a responsible Government official, shall not relieve such person of criminal responsibility nor mitigate punishment.

3. The fact that any of the acts referred to in articles 2 to 4 of the present Statute was committed by a subordinate does not relieve his or her superior of criminal responsibility if he or she knew or had reason to know that the subordinate was about to commit such acts or had done so and the superior failed to take the necessary and reasonable measures to prevent such acts or to punish the perpetrators thereof.

4. The fact that an accused person acted pursuant to an order of a Government or of a superior shall not relieve him or her of criminal responsibility, but may be considered in mitigation of punishment if the International Tribunal for Rwanda determines that justice so requires.

Article 7

Territorial and temporal jurisdiction

The territorial jurisdiction of the International Tribunal for Rwanda shall extend to the territory of Rwanda including its land surface and airspace a well as to the territory of neighbouring States in respect of serious violations of international humanitarian law committed by Rwandan citizens. The temporal jurisdiction of the International Tribunal for Rwanda shall extend to a period beginning on 1 January 1994 and ending on 31 December 1994.

Article 8

Concurrent jurisdiction

1. The International Tribunal for Rwanda and national courts shall have concurrent jurisdiction to prosecute persons for serious violations of international humanitarian law committed in the territory of Rwanda and Rwandan citizens for such violations committed in the territory of neighbouring States, between 1 January 1994 and 31 December 1994.

2. The International Tribunal for Rwanda shall have primacy over the national courts of all States. At any stage of the procedure, the International Tribunal for Rwanda may formally request national courts to defer to its competence in accordance with the present Statute and the Rules of Procedure and Evidence of the International Tribunal for Rwanda.

Article 9

Non bis in idem

1. No person shall be tried before a national court for acts constituting serious violations of international humanitarian law under the present Statute, for which he or she has already been tried by the International Tribunal for Rwanda.

2. A person who has been tried by a national court for acts constituting serious violations of international humanitarian law may be subsequently tried by the International Tribunal for Rwanda only if:

(a) The act for which he or she was tried was characterized as an ordinary crime; or

(b) The national court proceedings were not impartial or independent, were designed to shield the accused from international criminal responsibility, or the case was not diligently prosecuted.

3. In considering the penalty to be imposed on a person convicted of a crime under the present Statute, the International Tribunal for Rwanda shall take into account the extent to which any penalty imposed by a national court on the same person for the same act has already been served.

Article 10

Organization of the International Tribunal for Rwanda

The International Tribunal for Rwanda shall consist of the following organs:

(a) The Chambers, comprising two Trial Chambers and an Appeals Chamber;

(b) The Prosecutor; and

(c) A Registry.

Article 11

Composition of the Chambers

The Chambers shall be composed of eleven independent judges, no two of whom may be nationals of the same State, who shall serve as follows:

(a) Three judges shall serve in each of the Trial Chambers;

(b) Five judges shall serve in the Appeals Chamber.

Article 12

Qualification and election of judges

1. The judges shall be persons of high moral character, impartiality and integrity who possess the qualifications required in their respective countries for appointment to the highest judicial offices. In the overall composition of the Chambers due account shall be taken of the experience of the judges in criminal law, international law, including international humanitarian law and human rights law.

2. The members of the Appeals Chamber of the International Tribunal for the Prosecution of Persons Responsible for Serious Violations of International Law Committed in the Territory of the Former Yugoslavia since 1991 (hereinafter referred to as "the International Tribunal for the Former Yugoslavia") shall also serve as the members of the Appeals Chamber of the International Tribunal for Rwanda.

3. The judges of the Trial Chambers of the International Tribunal for Rwanda shall be elected by the General Assembly from a list submitted by the Security Council, in the following manner:

(a) The Secretary-General shall invite nominations for judges of the Trial Chambers from States Members of the United Nations and non-member States maintaining permanent observer missions at United Nations Headquarters;

(b) Within thirty days of the date of the invitation of the Secretary-General, each State may nominate up to two candidates meeting the qualifications set out in paragraph 1 above, no two of whom shall be of the same nationality and neither of whom shall be of the same nationality as any judge on the Appeals Chamber;

(c) The Secretary-General shall forward the nominations received to the Security Council. From the nominations received the Security Council shall establish a list of not less than twelve and not more than eighteen candidates, taking due account of adequate representation on the International Tribunal for Rwanda of the principal legal systems of the world;

(d) The President of the Security Council shall transmit the list of candidates to the President of the General Assembly. From that list the General Assembly shall elect the six judges of the Trial Chambers. The candidates who receive an absolute majority of the votes of the States Members of the United Nations and of the non-Member States maintaining permanent observer missions at United Nations Headquarters, shall be declared elected. Should two candidates of the same nationality obtain the required majority vote, the one who received the higher number of votes shall be considered elected.

4. In the event of a vacancy in the Trial Chambers, after consultation with the Presidents of the Security Council and of the General Assembly, the Secretary-General shall appoint a person meeting the qualifications of paragraph 1 above, for the remainder of the term of office concerned.

5. The judges of the Trial Chambers shall be elected for a term of four years. The terms and conditions of service shall be those of the judges of the International Tribunal for the Former Yugoslavia. They shall be eligible for re-election.

Article 13

Officers and members of the Chambers

1. The judges of the International Tribunal for Rwanda shall elect a President.

2. After consultation with the judges of the International Tribunal for Rwanda, the President shall assign the judges to the Trial Chambers. A judge shall serve only in the Chamber to which he or she was assigned.

3. The judges of each Trial Chamber shall elect a Presiding Judge, who shall conduct all of the proceedings of that Trial Chamber as a whole.

Article 14

Rules of procedure and evidence

The judges of the International Tribunal for Rwanda shall adopt, for the purpose of proceedings before the International Tribunal for Rwanda, the rules of procedure and evidence for the conduct of the pre-trial phase of the proceedings, trials and appeals, the admission of evidence, the protection victims and witnesses and other appropriate matters of the International Tribunal for the Former Yugoslavia with such changes as they deem necessary.

Article 15

The Prosecutor

1. The Prosecutor shall be responsible for the investigation and prosecution of persons responsible for serious violations of international humanitarian law committed in the territory of Rwanda and Rwandan citizens responsible for such violations committed in the territory of neighbouring States, between 1 January 1994 and 31 December 1994.

2. The Prosecutor shall act independently as a separate organ of the International Tribunal for Rwanda. He or she shall not seek or receive instructions from any Government or from any other source.

3. The Prosecutor of the International Tribunal for the Former Yugoslavia shall also serve as the Prosecutor of the International Tribunal for Rwanda. He or she shall have additional staff, including an additional Deputy Prosecutor, to assist with prosecutions before the International Tribunal for Rwanda. Such staff shall be appointed by the Secretary-General on the recommendation of the Prosecutor.

Article 16

The Registry

1. The Registry shall be responsible for the administration and servicing of the International Tribunal for Rwanda.

2. The Registry shall consist of a Registrar and such other staff as may be required.

3. The Registrar shall be appointed by the Secretary-General after consultation with the President of the International Tribunal for Rwanda. He or she shall serve for a four-year term and be eligible for reappointment. The terms and conditions of service of the Registrar shall be those of an Assistant Secretary-General of the United Nations.

4. The staff of the Registry shall be appointed by the Secretary-General on the recommendation of the Registrar.

Article 17

Investigation and preparation of indictment

1. The Prosecutor shall initiate investigations ex officio or on the basis of information obtained from any source, particularly from Governments, United Nations organs, intergovernmental and non-governmental organizations. The Prosecutor shall assess the information received or obtained and decide whether there is sufficient basis to proceed.

2. The Prosecutor shall have the power to question suspects, victims and witnesses, to collect evidence and to conduct on-site investigations. In carrying out these tasks, the Prosecutor may, as appropriate, seek the assistance of the State authorities concerned.

3. If questioned, the suspect shall be entitled to be assisted by counsel of his or her own choice, including the right to have legal assistance assigned to the suspect without payment by him or her in any such case if he or she does not have sufficient means to pay for it, as well as to necessary translation into and from a language he or she speaks and understands.

4. Upon a determination that a prima facie case exists, the Prosecutor shall prepare an indictment containing a concise statement of the facts and the crime or crimes with which the accused is charged under the Statute. The indictment shall be transmitted to a judge of the Trial Chamber.

Article 18

Review of the indictment

1. The judge of the Trial Chamber to whom the indictment has been transmitted shall review it. If satisfied that a prima facie case has been established by the Prosecutor, he or she shall confirm the indictment. If not so satisfied, the indictment shall be dismissed.

2. Upon confirmation of an indictment, the judge may, at the request of the Prosecutor, issue such orders and warrants for the arrest, detention, surrender or transfer of persons, and any other orders as may be required for the conduct of the trial.

Article 19

Commencement and conduct of trial proceedings

1. The Trial Chambers shall ensure that a trial is fair and expeditious and that proceedings are conducted in accordance with the rules of procedure and evidence, with full respect for the rights of the accused and due regard for the protection of victims and witnesses.

2. A person against whom an indictment has been confirmed shall, pursuant to an order or an arrest warrant of the International Tribunal for Rwanda, be taken into custody, immediately informed of the charges against him or her and transferred to the International Tribunal for Rwanda.

3. The Trial Chamber shall read the indictment, satisfy itself that the rights of the accused are respected, confirm that the accused understands the indictment, and instruct the accused to enter a plea. The Trial Chamber shall then set the date for trial.

4. The hearings shall be public unless the Trial Chamber decides to close the proceedings in accordance with its rules of procedure and evidence.

Article 20

Rights of the accused

1. All persons shall be equal before the International Tribunal for Rwanda.

2. In the determination of charges against him or her, the accused shall be entitled to a fair and public hearing, subject to article 21 of the Statute.

3. The accused shall be presumed innocent until proved guilty according to the provisions of the present Statute.

4. In the determination of any charge against the accused pursuant to the present Statute, the accused shall be entitled to the following minimum guarantees, in full equality:

- (a) To be informed promptly and in detail in a language which he or she understands of the nature and cause of the charge against him or her;

- (b) To have adequate time and facilities for the preparation of his or her defence and to communicate with counsel of his or her own choosing;

- (c) To be tried without undue delay;

- (d) To be tried in his or her presence, and to defend himself or herself in person or through legal assistance of his or her own choosing; to be informed, if he or she does not have legal assistance, of this right; and to have legal assistance assigned to him or her, in any case where the interests of justice so require, and without payment by him or her in any such case if he or she does not have sufficient means to pay for it;

- (e) To examine, or have examined, the witnesses against him or her and to obtain the attendance and examination of witnesses on his or her behalf under the same conditions as witnesses against him or her;

- (f) To have the free assistance of an interpreter if he or she cannot understand or speak the language used in the International Tribunal for Rwanda;

- (g) Not to be compelled to testify against himself or herself or to confess guilt.

Article 21

Protection of victims and witnesses

The International Tribunal for Rwanda shall provide in its rules of procedure and evidence for the protection of victims and witnesses. Such protection measures shall include, but shall not be limited to, the conduct of in camera proceedings and the protection of the victim's identity.

Article 22

Judgement

1. The Trial Chambers shall pronounce judgements and impose sentences and penalties on persons convicted of serious violations of international humanitarian law.

2. The judgement shall be rendered by a majority of the judges of the Trial Chamber, and shall be delivered by the Trial Chamber in public. It shall be accompanied by a reasoned opinion in writing, to which separate or dissenting opinions may be appended.

Article 23

Penalties

1. The penalty imposed by the Trial Chamber shall be limited to imprisonment. In determining the terms of imprisonment, the Trial Chambers shall have recourse to the general practice regarding prison sentences in the courts of Rwanda.

2. In imposing the sentences, the Trial Chambers should take into account such factors as the gravity of the offence and the individual circumstances of the convicted person.

3. In addition to imprisonment, the Trial Chambers may order the return of any property and proceeds acquired by criminal conduct, including by means of duress, to their rightful owners.

Article 24

Appellate proceedings

1. The Appeals Chamber shall hear appeals from persons convicted by the Trial Chambers or from the Prosecutor on the following grounds:

    (a) An error on a question of law invalidating the decision; or

    (b) An error of fact which has occasioned a miscarriage of justice.

2. The Appeals Chamber may affirm, reverse or revise the decisions taken by the Trial Chambers.

Article 25

Review proceedings

Where a new fact has been discovered which was not known at the time of the proceedings before the Trial Chambers or the Appeals Chamber and which could have been a decisive factor in reaching the decision, the convicted person or the Prosecutor may submit to the International Tribunal for Rwanda an application for review of the judgement.

Article 26

Enforcement of sentences

Imprisonment shall be served in Rwanda or any of the States on a list of States which have indicated to the Security Council their willingness to accept convicted persons, as designated by the International Tribunal for Rwanda. Such imprisonment shall be accordance with the applicable law of the State concerned, subject to the supervision of the International Tribunal for Rwanda.

Article 27

Pardon or commutation of sentences

If, pursuant to the applicable law of the State in which the convicted person is imprisoned, he or she is eligible for pardon or commutation of sentence, the State concerned shall notify the International Tribunal for Rwanda accordingly. There shall only be pardon or commutation of sentence if the President of the International Tribunal for Rwanda, in consultation with the judges, so decides on the basis of the interests of justice and the general principles of law.

Article 28

Cooperation and judicial assistance

1. States shall cooperate with the International Tribunal for Rwanda in the investigation and prosecution of persons accused of committing serious violations of international humanitarian law.

2. States shall comply without undue delay with any request for assistance or an order issued by a Trial Chamber, including, but not limited to:

   (a) The identification and location of persons;

   (b) The taking of testimony and the production of evidence;

   (c) The service of documents;

   (d) The arrest or detention of persons;

   (e) The surrender or the transfer of the accused to the International Tribunal of Rwanda.

Article 29

The status, privileges and immunities of the International Tribunal for Rwanda

1. The Convention on the Privileges and Immunities of the United Nations of 13 February 1946 shall apply to the International Tribunal for Rwanda, the judges, the Prosecutor and his or her staff, and the Registrar and his or her staff.

2. The judges, the Prosecutor and the Registrar shall enjoy the privileges and immunities, exemptions and facilities accorded to diplomatic envoys, in accordance with international law.

3. The staff of the Prosecutor and of the Registrar shall enjoy the privileges and immunities accorded to officials of the United Nations under articles V and VII of the Convention referred to in paragraph 1 of this article.

4. Other persons, including the accused, required at the seat or meeting place of the International Tribunal for Rwanda shall be accorded such treatment as is necessary for the proper functioning of the International Tribunal for Rwanda.

Article 30

Expenses of the International Tribunal for Rwanda

The expenses of the International Tribunal for Rwanda shall be expenses of the Organization in accordance with Article 17 of the Charter of the United Nations.

Article 31

Working languages

The working languages of the International Tribunal shall be English and French.

Article 32

Annual report

The President of the International Tribunal for Rwanda shall submit an annual report of the International Tribunal for Rwanda to the Security Council and to the General Assembly.

International Law Commission - Draft Statute for an International Criminal Court (1994)[*]

Part I

Establishment of the Court

Article 1

The Court

There is established an International Criminal Court ("the Court"), whose jurisdiction and functioning shall be governed by the provisions of this Statute.

Article 2

Relationship of the Court to the United Nations

The President, with the approval of the States parties to this Statute ("States parties"), may conclude an agreement establishing an appropriate relationship between the Court and the United Nations.

Article 3

Seat of the Court

1. The seat of the Court shall be established at ... in ... ("the host State").

2. The President, with the approval of the States parties, may conclude an agreement with the host State establishing the relationship between that State and the Court.

3. The Court may exercise its powers and functions on the territory of any State party and, by special agreement, on the territory of any other State.

Article 4

Status and legal capacity

1. The Court is a permanent institution open to States parties in accordance with this Statute. It shall act when required to consider a case submitted to it.

2. The Court shall enjoy in the territory of each State party such legal capacity as may be necessary for the exercise of its functions and the fulfilment of its purposes.

---

[*] *Report of the International Law Commission*, 46th Session, *U.N.G.A.O.R.*, 49th Session, Supp.No.10, UN Doc.A/49/10 (1994).

Part II

Composition and Administration of the Court

Article 5

Organs of the Court

The Court consists of the following organs:

(a)   a Presidency, as provided in article 8;

(b)   an Appeals Chamber, Trial Chambers and other chambers, as provided in article 9;

(c)   a Procuracy, as provided in article 12; and

(d)   a Registry, as provided in article 13.

Article 6

Qualification and election of judges

1.   The judges of the Court shall be persons of high moral character, impartiality and integrity who possess the qualifications required in their respective countries for appointment to the highest judicial offices, and have, in addition:

(a)   criminal trial experience;

(b)   recognized competence in international law.

2.   Each State party may nominate for election not more than two persons, of different nationality, who possess the qualification referred to in paragraph (1) (a) or that referred to in paragraph 1 (b), and who are willing to serve as may be required on the Court.

3.   Eighteen judges shall be elected by an absolute majority vote of the States parties by secret ballot. Ten judges shall first be elected, from among the persons nominated as having the qualification referred to in paragraph 1 (a). Eight judges shall then be elected, from among the persons nominated as having the qualification referred to in paragraph 1 (b).

4.   No two judges may be nationals of the same State.

5.   States parties should bear in mind in the election of the judges that the representation of the principal legal systems of the world should be assured.

6.   Judges hold office for a term of nine years and, subject to paragraph 7 and article 7 (2), are not eligible for re-election. A judge shall, however, continue in office in order to complete any case the hearing of which has commenced.

7.   At the first election, six judges chosen by lot shall serve for a term of three years and are eligible for re-election; six judges chosen by lot shall serve for a term of six years; and the remainder shall serve for a term of nine years.

8.   Judges nominated as having the qualification referred to in paragraph 1 (a) or 1 (b), as the case may be, shall be replaced by persons nominated as having the same qualification.

Article 7

Judicial vacancies

1. In the event of a vacancy, a replacement judge shall be elected in accordance with article 6.

2. A judge elected to fill a vacancy shall serve for the remainder of the predecessor's term, and if that period is less than five years is eligible for re-election for a further term.

Article 8

The Presidency

1. The President, the first and second Vice-Presidents and two alternate Vice-Presidents shall be elected by an absolute majority of the judges. They shall serve for a term of three years or until the end of their term of office as judges, whichever is earlier.

2. The first or second Vice-President, as the case may be, may act in place of the President in the event that the President is unavailable or disqualified. An alternate Vice-President may act in place of either Vice-President as required.

3. The President and the Vice-Presidents shall constitute the Presidency which shall be responsible for:

　(a)　the due administration of the Court; and

　(b)　the other functions conferred on it by this Statute.

4. Unless otherwise indicated, pre-trial and other procedural functions conferred under this Statute on the Court may be exercised by the Presidency in any case where a chamber of the Court is not seized of the matter.

5. The Presidency may, in accordance with the Rules, delegate to one or more judges the exercise of a power vested in it under articles 26 (3), 27 (5), 28, 29 or 30 (3) in relation to a case, during the period before a Trial Chamber is established for that case.

Article 9

Chambers

1. As soon as possible after each election of judges to the Court, the Presidency shall in accordance with the Rules constitute an Appeals Chamber consisting of the President and six other judges, of whom at least three shall be judges elected from among the persons nominated as having the qualification referred to in article 6 (1) (b). The President shall preside over the Appeals Chamber.

2. The Appeals Chamber shall be constituted for a term of three years. Members of the Appeals Chamber shall, however, continue to sit on the Chamber in order to complete any case the hearing of which has commenced.

3. Judges may be renewed as members of the Appeals Chamber for a second or subsequent term.

4. Judges not members of the Appeals Chamber shall be available to serve on Trial Chambers and other chambers required by this Statute, and to act as substitute members of the Appeals Chamber, in the event that a member of that Chamber is unavailable or disqualified.

5. The Presidency shall nominate in accordance with the Rules five such judges to be members of the Trial Chamber for a given case. A Trial Chamber shall include at least three

judges elected from among the persons nominated as having the qualification referred to in article 6 (1) (a).

6. The Rules may provide for alternate judges to be nominated to attend a trial and to act as members of the Trial Chamber in the event that a judge dies or becomes unavailable during the course of the trial.

7. No judge who is a national of a complainant State or of a State of which the accused is a national shall be a member of a chamber dealing with the case.

Article 10

Independence of the judges

1. In performing their functions, the judges shall be independent.

2. Judges shall not engage in any activity which is likely to interfere with their judicial functions or to affect confidence in their independence.
In particular, they shall not while holding the office of judge be a member of the legislative or executive branches of the Government of a State, or of a body responsible for the investigation or prosecution of crimes.

3. Any question as to the application of paragraph 2 shall be decided by the Presidency.

4. On the recommendation of the Presidency, the States parties may by a two-thirds majority decide that the work-load of the Court requires that the judges should serve on a full-time basis. In that case:

(a) existing judges who elect to serve on a full-time basis shall not hold any other office or employment; and

(b) judges subsequently elected shall not hold any other office or employment.

Article 11

Excusing and disqualification of judges

1. The Presidency at the request of a judge may excuse that judge from the exercise of a function under this Statute.

2. Judges shall not participate in any case in which they have previously been involved in any capacity or in which their impartiality might reasonably be doubted on any ground, including an actual, apparent or potential conflict of interest.

3. The Prosecutor or the accused may request the disqualification of a judge under paragraph 2.

4. Any question as to the disqualification of a judge shall be decided by an absolute majority of the members of the Chamber concerned. The challenged judge shall not take part in the decision.

Article 12

The Procuracy

1. The Procuracy is an independent organ of the Court responsible for the investigation of complaints brought in accordance with this Statute and for the conduct of prosecutions. A member of the Procuracy shall not seek or act on instructions from any external source.

2. The Procuracy shall be headed by the Prosecutor, assisted by one or more Deputy Prosecutors, who may act in place of the Prosecutor in the event that the Prosecutor is

unavailable. The Prosecutor and the Deputy Prosecutors shall be of different nationalities. The Prosecutor may appoint such other qualified staff as may be required.

3. The Prosecutor and Deputy Prosecutors shall be persons of high moral character and have high competence and experience in the prosecution of criminal cases. They shall be elected by secret ballot by an absolute majority of the States parties, from among candidates nominated by States parties. Unless a shorter term is otherwise decided on at the time of their election, they shall hold office for a term of five years and are eligible for re-election.

4. The States parties may elect the Prosecutor and Deputy Prosecutor on the basis that they are willing to serve as required.

5. The Prosecutor and Deputy Prosecutors shall not act in relation to a complaint involving a person of their own nationality.

6. The Presidency may excuse the Prosecutor or a Deputy Prosecutor at their request from acting in a particular case, and shall decide any question raised in a particular case as to the disqualification of the Prosecutor or a Deputy Prosecutor.

7. The staff of the Procuracy shall be subject to Staff Regulations drawn up by the Prosecutor, so far as possible in conformity with the United Nations Staff Regulations and Staff Rules and approved by the Presidency.

Article 13

The Registry

1. On the proposal of the Presidency, the judges by an absolute majority by secret ballot shall elect a Registrar, who shall be the principal administrative officer of the Court. They may in the same manner elect a Deputy Registrar.

2. The Registrar shall hold office for a term of five years, is eligible for re-election and shall be available on a full-time basis. The Deputy Registrar shall hold office for a term of five years or such shorter term as may be decided on, and may be elected on the basis that the Deputy Registrar will be available to serve as required.

3. The Presidency may appoint or authorize the Registrar to appoint such other staff of the Registry as may be necessary.

4. The staff of the Registry shall be subject to Staff Regulations drawn up by the Registrar so far as possible in conformity with the United Nations Staff Regulations and Staff Rules, and approved by the Presidency.

Article 14

Solemn undertaking

Before first exercising their functions under this Statute, judges and other officers of the Court shall make a public and solemn undertaking to do so impartially and conscientiously.

Article 15

Loss of office

1. A judge, the Prosecutor or other officer of the Court who is found to have committed misconduct or a serious breach of this Statute, or to be unable to exercise the functions required by this Statute because of long-term illness or disability, shall cease to hold office.

2. A decision as to the loss of office under paragraph 1 shall be made by secret ballot:

(a) in the case of the Prosecutor or a Deputy Prosecutor, by an absolute majority of the States parties;

(b) in any other case, by a two-thirds majority of the judges.

3. The judge, the Prosecutor or any other officer whose conduct or fitness for office is impugned shall have full opportunity to present evidence and to make submissions but shall not otherwise participate in the discussion of the question.

Article 16

Privileges and immunities

1. The judges, the Prosecutor, the Deputy Prosecutors and the staff of the Procuracy, the Registrar and the Deputy Registrar shall enjoy the privileges, immunities and facilities of a diplomatic agent within the meaning of the Vienna Convention on Diplomatic Relations of 16 April 1961.

2. The staff of the Registry shall enjoy the privileges, immunities and facilities necessary to the performance of their functions.

3. Counsel, experts and witnesses before the Court shall enjoy the privileges and immunities necessary to the independent exercise of their duties.

4. The judges may by an absolute majority decide to revoke a privilege or waive an immunity conferred by this article, other than an immunity of a judge, the Prosecutor or Registrar as such. In the case of other officers and staff of the Procuracy or Registry, they may do so only on the recommendation of the Prosecutor or Registrar, as the case may be.

Article 17

Allowances and expenses

1. The President shall receive an annual allowance.

2. The Vice-Presidents shall receive a special allowance for each day they exercise the functions of the President.

3. Subject to paragraph 4, the judges shall receive a daily allowance during the period in which they exercise their functions. They may continue to receive a salary payable in respect of another position occupied by them consistently with article 10.

4. If it is decided under article 10 (4) that judges shall thereafter serve on a full-time basis, existing judges who elect to serve on a full-time basis, and all judges subsequently elected, shall be paid a salary.

Article 18

Working languages

The working languages of the Court shall be English and French.

Article 19

Rules of the Court

1. Subject to paragraphs 2 and 3, the judges may by an absolute majority make rules for the functioning of the Court in accordance with this Statute, including rules regulating:

(a) the conduct of investigations;

(b) the procedure to be followed and the rules of evidence to be applied;

(c) any other matter which is necessary for the implementation of this Statute.

2. The initial Rules of the Court shall be drafted by the judges within six months of the first elections for the Court, and submitted to a conference of States parties for approval. The judges may decide that a rule subsequently made under paragraph 1 should also be submitted to a conference of States parties for approval.

3. In any case to which paragraph 2 does not apply, rules made under paragraph 1 shall be transmitted to States parties and may be confirmed by the Presidency unless, within six months after transmission, a majority of States parties have communicated in writing their objections.

4. A rule may provide for its provisional application in the period prior to its approval or confirmation. A rule not approved or confirmed shall lapse.

Part III

Jurisdiction of the Court

Article 20

Crimes within the jurisdiction of the Court

The Court has jurisdiction in accordance with this Statute with respect to the following crimes:

(a) the crime of genocide;

(b) the crime of aggression;

(c) serious violations of the laws and customs applicable in armed conflict;

(d) crimes against humanity;

(e) crimes, established under or pursuant to the treaty provisions listed in the Annex, which, having regard to the conduct alleged, constitute exceptionally serious crimes of international concern.

Article 21

Preconditions to the exercise of jurisdiction

1. The Court may exercise its jurisdiction over a person with respect to a crime referred to in article 20 if:

(a) in a case of genocide, a complaint is brought under article 25 (1);

(b) in any other case, a complaint is brought under article 25 (2) and the jurisdiction of the Court with respect to the crime is accepted under article 22:

(i) by the State which has custody of the suspect with respect to the crime ("the custodial State"); and

(ii) by the State on the territory of which the act or omission in question occurred.

2. If, with respect to a crime to which paragraph 1 (b) applies, the custodial State has received, under an international agreement, a request from another State to surrender a suspect for the purposes of prosecution, then, unless the request is rejected, the acceptance by the requesting State of the Court's jurisdiction with respect to the crime is also required.

Article 22

*Acceptance of the jurisdiction of the Court
for the purposes of article 21*

1. A State party to this Statute may:

    (a) at the time it expresses its consent to be bound by the Statute, by declaration lodged with the depositary; or

    (b) at a later time, by declaration lodged with the Registrar;

    accept the jurisdiction of the Court with respect to such of the crimes referred to in article 20 as it specifies in the declaration.

2. A declaration may be of general application, or may be limited to particular conduct or to conduct committed during a particular period of time.

3. A declaration may be made for a specified period, in which case it may not be withdrawn before the end of that period, or for an unspecified period, in which case it may be withdrawn only upon giving six months' notice of withdrawal to the Registrar. Withdrawal does not affect proceedings already commenced under this Statute.

4. If under article 21 the acceptance of a State which is not a party to this Statute is required, that State may, by declaration lodged with the Registrar, consent to the Court exercising jurisdiction with respect to the crime.

Article 23

Action by the Security Council

1. Notwithstanding article 21, the Court has jurisdiction in accordance with this Statute with respect to crimes referred to in article 20 as a consequence of the referral of a matter to the Court by the Security Council acting under Chapter VII of the Charter of the United Nations.

2. A complaint of or directly related to an act of aggression may not be brought under this Statute unless the Security Council has first determined that a State has committed the act of aggression which is the subject of the complaint.

3. No prosecution may be commenced under this Statute arising from a situation which is being dealt with by the Security Council as a threat to or breach of the peace or an act of aggression under Chapter VII of the Charter, unless the Security Council otherwise decides.

Article 24

Duty of the Court as to jurisdiction

The Court shall satisfy itself that it has jurisdiction in any case brought before it.

Part IV

Investigation and Prosecution

Article 25

Complaint

1. A State party which is also a Contracting Party to the Convention on the Prevention and Punishment of the Crime of Genocide of 9 December 1948 may lodge a complaint with the Prosecutor alleging that a crime of genocide appears to have been committed.

2. A State party which accepts the jurisdiction of the Court under article 22 with respect to a crime may lodge a complaint with the Prosecutor alleging that such a crime appears to have been committed.

3. As far as possible a complaint shall specify the circumstances of the alleged crime and the identity and whereabouts of any suspect, and be accompanied by such supporting documentation as is available to the complainant State.

4. In a case to which article 23 (1) applies, a complaint is not required for the initiation of an investigation.

Article 26

Investigation of alleged crimes

1. On receiving a complaint or upon notification of a decision of the Security Council referred to in article 23 (1), the Prosecutor shall initiate an investigation unless the Prosecutor concludes that there is no possible basis for a prosecution under this Statute and decides not to initiate an investigation, in which case the Prosecutor shall so inform the Presidency.

2. The Prosecutor may:

   (a) request the presence of and question suspects, victims and witnesses;

   (b) collect documentary and other evidence;

   (c) conduct on-site investigations;

   (d) take necessary measures to ensure the confidentiality of information or the protection of any person;

   (e) as appropriate, seek the cooperation of any State or of the United Nations.

3. The Presidency may, at the request of the Prosecutor, issue such subpoenas and warrants as may be required for the purposes of an investigation, including a warrant under article 28 (1) for the provisional arrest of a suspect.

4. If, upon investigation and having regard, *inter alia*, to the matters referred to in article 35, the Prosecutor concludes that there is no sufficient basis for a prosecution under this Statute and decides not to file an indictment, the Prosecutor shall so inform the Presidency giving details of the nature and basis of the complaint and of the reasons for not filing an indictment.

5. At the request of a complainant State or, in a case to which article 23 (1) applies, at the request of the Security Council, the Presidency shall review a decision of the Prosecutor not to initiate an investigation or not to file an indictment, and may request the Prosecutor to reconsider the decision.

6. A person suspected of a crime under this Statute shall:

   (a) prior to being questioned, be informed that the person is a suspect and of the rights:

      (i) to remain silent, without such silence being a consideration in the determination of guilt or innocence; and

      (ii) to have the assistance of counsel of the suspect's choice or, if the suspect lacks the means to retain counsel, to have legal assistance assigned by the Court;

   (b) not be compelled to testify or to confess guilt; and

(c) if questioned in a language other than a language the suspect understands and speaks, be provided with competent interpretation services and with a translation of any document on which the suspect is to be questioned.

Article 27

Commencement of prosecution

1. If upon investigation the Prosecutor concludes that there is a prima facie case, the Prosecutor shall file with the Registrar an indictment containing a concise statement of the allegations of fact and of the crime or crimes with which the suspect is charged.

2. The Presidency shall examine the indictment and any supporting material and determine:

 (a) whether a prima facie case exists with respect to a crime within the jurisdiction of the Court; and

 (b) whether, having regard, *inter alia*, to the matters referred to in article 35, the case should on the information available be heard by the Court.

If so, it shall confirm the indictment and establish a trial chamber in accordance with article 9.

3. If, after any adjournment that may be necessary to allow additional material to be produced, the Presidency decides not to confirm the indictment, it shall so inform the complainant State or, in a case to which article 23 (1) applies, the Security Council.

4. The Presidency may at the request of the Prosecutor amend the indictment, in which case it shall make any necessary orders to ensure that the accused is notified of the amendment and has adequate time to prepare a defence.

5. The Presidency may make any further orders required for the conduct of the trial, including an order:

 (a) determining the language or languages to be used during the trial;

 (b) requiring the disclosure to the defence, within a sufficient time before the trial to enable the preparation of the defence, of documentary or other evidence available to the Prosecutor, whether or not the Prosecutor intends to rely on that evidence;

 (c) providing for the exchange of information between the Prosecutor and the defence, so that both parties are sufficiently aware of the issues to be decided at the trial;

 (d) providing for the protection of the accused, victims and witnesses and of confidential information.

Article 28

Arrest

1. At any time after an investigation has been initiated, the Presidency may at the request of the Prosecutor issue a warrant for the provisional arrest of a suspect if:

 (a) there is probable cause to believe that the suspect may have committed a crime within the jurisdiction of the Court; and

 (b) the suspect may not be available to stand trial unless provisionally arrested.

2. A suspect who has been provisionally arrested is entitled to release from arrest if the indictment has not been confirmed within 90 days of the arrest, or such longer time as the Presidency may allow.

3. As soon as practicable after the confirmation of the indictment, the Prosecutor shall seek from the Presidency a warrant for the arrest and transfer of the accused. The Presidency shall issue such a warrant unless it is satisfied that:

    (a) the accused will voluntarily appear for trial; or

    (b) there are special circumstances making it unnecessary for the time being to issue the warrant.

4. A person arrested shall be informed at the time of arrest of the reasons for the arrest and shall be promptly informed of any charges.

Article 29

Pre-trial detention or release

1. A person arrested shall be brought promptly before a judicial officer of the State where the arrest occurred. The judicial officer shall determine, in accordance with the procedures applicable in that State, that the warrant has been duly served and that the rights of the accused have been respected.

2. A person arrested may apply to the Presidency for release pending trial. The Presidency may release the person unconditionally or on bail if it is satisfied that the accused will appear at the trial.

3. A person arrested may apply to the Presidency for a determination of the lawfulness under this Statute of the arrest or detention. If the Presidency decides that the arrest or detention was unlawful, it shall order the release of the accused, and may award compensation.

4. A person arrested shall be held, pending trial or release on bail, in an appropriate place of detention in the arresting State, in the State in which the trial is to be held or if necessary, in the host State.

Article 30

Notification of the indictment

1. The Prosecutor shall ensure that a person who has been arrested is personally served, as soon as possible after being taken into custody, with certified copies of the following documents, in a language understood by that person:

    (a) in the case of a suspect provisionally arrested, a statement of the grounds for the arrest;

    (b) in any other case, the confirmed indictment;

    (c) a statement of the accused's rights under this Statute.

2. In any case to which paragraph (1) (a) applies, the indictment shall be served on the accused as soon as possible after it has been confirmed.

3. If, 60 days after the indictment has been confirmed, the accused is not in custody pursuant to a warrant issued under article 28 (3), or for some reason the requirements of paragraph 1 cannot be complied with, the Presidency may on the application of the Prosecutor prescribe some other manner of bringing the indictment to the attention of the accused.

Article 31

Designation of persons to assist in a prosecution

1. A State party may, at the request of the Prosecutor, designate persons to assist in a prosecution.

2. Such persons should be available for the duration of the prosecution, unless otherwise agreed. They shall serve at the direction of the Prosecutor, and shall not seek or receive instructions from any Government or source other than the Prosecutor in relation to their exercise of functions under this article.

3. The terms and conditions on which persons may be designated under this article shall be approved by the Presidency on the recommendation of the Prosecutor.

Part V

The Trial

Article 32

Place of trial

Unless otherwise decided by the Presidency, the place of the trial will be the seat of the Court.

Article 33

Applicable law

The Court shall apply:

(a) this Statute;

(b) applicable treaties and the principles and rules of general international law; and

(c) to the extent applicable, any rule of national law.

Article 34

Challenges to jurisdiction

Challenges to the jurisdiction of the Court may be made, in accordance with the Rules:

(a) prior to or at the commencement of the hearing, by an accused or any interested State; and

(b) at any later stage of the trial, by an accused.

Article 35

Issues of admissibility

The Court may, on application by the accused or at the request of an interested State at any time prior to the commencement of the trial, or of its own motion, decide, having regard to the purposes of this Statute set out in the preamble, that a case before it is inadmissible on the ground that the crime in question:

(a) has been duly investigated by a State with jurisdiction over it, and the decision of that State not to proceed to a prosecution is apparently well-founded;

(b) is under investigation by a State which has or may have jurisdiction over it, and there is no reason for the Court to take any further action for the time being with respect to the crime; or

(c) is not of such gravity to justify further action by the Court.

Article 36

Procedure under articles 34 and 35

1. In proceedings under articles 34 and 35, the accused and the complainant State have the right to be heard.

2. Proceedings under articles 34 and 35 shall be decided by the Trial Chamber, unless it considers, having regard to the importance of the issues involved, that the matter should be referred to the Appeals Chamber.

Article 37

Trial in the presence of the accused

1. As a general rule, the accused should be present during the trial.

2. The Trial Chamber may order that the trial proceed in the absence of the accused if:

(a) the accused is in custody, or has been released pending trial, and for reasons of security or the ill-health of the accused it is undesirable for the accused to be present;

(b) the accused is continuing to disrupt the trial; or

(c) the accused has escaped from lawful custody under this Statute or has broken bail.

3. The Chamber shall, if it makes an order under paragraph 2, ensure that the rights of the accused under this Statute are respected, and in particular:

(a) that all reasonable steps have been taken to inform the accused of the charge; and

(b) that the accused is legally represented, if necessary by a lawyer appointed by the Court.

4. In cases where a trial cannot be held because of the deliberate absence of an accused, the Court may establish, in accordance with the Rules, an Indictment Chamber for the purpose of:

(a) recording the evidence;

(b) considering whether the evidence establishes a *prima facie* case of a crime within the jurisdiction of the Court; and

(c) issuing and publishing a warrant of arrest in respect of an accused against whom a *prima facie* case is established.

5. If the accused is subsequently tried under this Statute:

(a) the record of evidence before the indictment Chamber shall be admissible;

(b) any judge who was a member of the Indictment Chamber may not be a member of the Trial Chamber.

Article 38

Functions and powers of the Trial Chamber

1. At the commencement of the trial, the Trial Chamber shall:

    (a) have the indictment read;

    (b) ensure that articles 27 (5) (b) and 30 have been complied with sufficiently in advance of the trial to enable adequate preparation of the defence;

    (c) satisfy itself that the other rights of the accused under this Statute have been respected; and

    (d) allow the accused to enter a plea of guilty or not guilty.

2. The Chamber shall ensure that a trial is fair and expeditious, and is conducted in accordance with this Statute and the Rules, with full respect for the rights of the accused and due regard for the protection of victims and witnesses.

3. The Chamber may, subject to the Rules, hear charges against more than one accused arising out of the same factual situation.

4. The trial shall be held in public, unless the Chamber determines that certain proceedings be in closed session in accordance with article 43, or for the purpose of protecting confidential or sensitive information which is to be given in evidence.

5. The Chamber shall, subject to this Statute and the Rules have, *inter alia*, the power on the application of a party or of its own motion, to:

    (a) issue a warrant for the arrest and transfer of an accused who is not already in the custody of the Court;

    (b) require the attendance and testimony of witnesses;

    (c) require the production of documentary and other evidentiary materials;

    (d) rule on the admissibility or relevance of evidence;

    (e) protect confidential information; and

    (f) maintain order in the course of a hearing.

6. The Chamber shall ensure that a complete record of the trial, which accurately reflects the proceedings, is maintained and preserved by the Registrar.

Article 39

Principle of legality (nullum crimen sine lege)

An accused shall not be held guilty:

(a) in the case of a prosecution with respect to a crime referred to in article 20 (a) to (d), unless the act or omission in question constituted a crime under international law;

(b) in the case of a prosecution with respect to a crime referred to in article 20 (e), unless the treaty in question was applicable to the conduct of the accused;

at the time the act or omission occurred.

Article 40

Presumption of innocence

An accused shall be presumed innocent until proved guilty in accordance with law. The onus is on the Prosecutor to establish the guilt of the accused beyond reasonable doubt.

Article 41

Rights of the accused

1. In the determination of any charge under this Statute, the accused is entitled to a fair and public hearing, subject to article 43, and to the following minimum guarantees:

   (a) to be informed promptly and in detail, in a language which the accused understands, of the nature and cause of the charge;

   (b) to have adequate time and facilities for the preparation of the defence, and to communicate with counsel of the accused's choosing;

   (c) to be tried without undue delay;

   (d) subject to article 37 (2), to be present at the trial, to conduct the defence in person or through legal assistance of the accused's choosing, to be informed, if the accused does not have legal assistance, of this right and to have legal assistance assigned by the Court, without payment if the accused lacks sufficient means to pay for such assistance;

   (e) to examine, or have examined, the prosecution witnesses and to obtain the attendance and examination of witnesses for the defence under the same conditions as witnesses for the prosecution;

   (f) if any of the proceedings of or documents presented to the Court are not in a language the accused understands and speaks, to have, free of any cost, the assistance of a competent interpreter and such translations as are necessary to meet the requirements of fairness;

   (g) not to be compelled to testify or to confess guilt.

2. Exculpatory evidence that becomes available to the Procuracy prior to the conclusion of the trial shall be made available to the defence. In case of doubt as to the application of this paragraph or as to the admissibility of the evidence, the Trial Chamber shall decide.

Article 42

Non bis in idem

1. No person shall be tried before any other court for acts constituting a crime of the kind referred to in article 20 for which that person has already been tried by the Court.

2. A person who has been tried by another court for acts constituting a crime of the kind referred to in article 20 may be tried under this Statute only if:

   (a) the acts in question were characterized by that court as an ordinary crime and not as a crime which is within the jurisdiction of the Court; or

   (b) the proceedings in the other court were not impartial or independent or were designed to shield the accused from international criminal responsibility or the case was not diligently prosecuted.

3. In considering the penalty to be imposed on a person convicted under this Statute, the Court shall take into account the extent to which a penalty imposed by another court on the same person for the same act has already been served.

Article 43

Protection of the accused, victims and witnesses

The Court shall take necessary measures available to it to protect the accused, victims and witnesses and may to that end conduct closed proceedings or allow the presentation of evidence by electronic or other special means.

Article 44

Evidence

1. Before testifying, each witness shall, in accordance with the Rules, give an undertaking as to the truthfulness of the evidence to be given by that witness.

2. States parties shall extend their laws of perjury to cover evidence given under this Statute by their nationals, and shall cooperate with the Court in investigating and where appropriate prosecuting any case of suspected perjury.

3. The Court may require to be informed of the nature of any evidence before it is offered so that it may rule on its relevance or admissibility.

4. The Court shall not require proof of facts of common knowledge but may take judicial notice of them.

5. Evidence obtained by means of a serious violation of this Statute or of other rules of international law shall not be admissible.

Article 45

Quorum and judgment

1. At least four members of the Trial Chamber must be present at each stage of the trial.

2. The decisions of the Trial Chamber shall be taken by a majority of the judges. At least three judges must concur in a decision as to conviction or acquittal and as to the sentence to be imposed.

3. If after sufficient time for deliberation a Chamber which has been reduced to four judges is unable to agree on a decision, it may order a new trial.

4. The deliberations of the Court shall be and remain secret.

5. The judgment shall be in writing and shall contain a full and reasoned statement of the findings and conclusions. It shall be the sole judgment issued, and shall be delivered in open court.

Article 46

Sentencing

1. In the event of a conviction, the Trial Chamber shall hold a further hearing to hear any evidence relevant to sentence, to allow the Prosecutor and the defence to make submissions and to consider the appropriate sentence to be imposed.

2. In imposing sentence, the Trial Chamber should take into account such factors as the gravity of the crime and the individual circumstances of the convicted person.

Article 47

Applicable penalties

1. The Court may impose on a person convicted of a crime under this Statute one or more of the following penalties:

   (a) a term of life imprisonment, or of imprisonment for a specified number of years;

   (b) a fine.

2. In determining the length of a term of imprisonment or the amount of a fine to be imposed, the Court may have regard to the penalties provided for by the law of:

   (a) the State of which the convicted person is a national;

   (b) the State where the crime was committed; and

   (c) the State which had custody of and jurisdiction over the accused.

3. Fines paid may be transferred, by order of the Court, to one or more of the following:

   (a) the Registrar, to defray the costs of the trial;

   (b) a State the nationals of which were the victims of the crime;

   (c) a trust fund established by the Secretary-General of the United Nations for the benefit of victims of crime.

Part VI

Appeal and Review

Article 48

Appeal against judgment or sentence

1. The Prosecutor and the convicted person may, in accordance with the Rules, appeal against a decision under articles 45 or 47 on grounds of procedural unfairness, error of fact or of law, or disproportion between the crime and the sentence.

2. Unless the Trial Chamber otherwise orders, a convicted person shall remain in custody pending an appeal.

Article 49

Proceedings on appeal

1. The Appeals Chamber has all the powers of the Trial Chamber.

2. If the Appeals Chamber finds that the proceedings appealed from were unfair or that the decision is vitiated by error of fact or law, it may:

   (a) if the appeal is brought by the convicted person, reverse or amend the decision, or, if necessary, order a new trial;

   (b) if the appeal is brought by the Prosecutor against an acquittal, order a new trial.

3. If in an appeal against sentence the Chamber finds that the sentence is manifestly disproportionate to the crime, it may vary the sentence in accordance with article 47.

4. The decision of the Chamber shall be taken by a majority of the judges, and shall be delivered in open court. Six judges constitute a quorum.

5. Subject to article 50, the decision of the Chamber shall be final.

Article 50

Revision

1. The convicted person or the Prosecutor may, in accordance with the Rules, apply to the Presidency for revision of a conviction on the ground that evidence has been discovered which was not available to the applicant at the time the conviction was pronounced or affirmed and which could have been a decisive factor in the conviction.

2. The Presidency shall request the Prosecutor or the convicted person, as the case may be, to present written observations on whether the application should be accepted.

3. If the Presidency is of the view that the new evidence could lead to the revision of the conviction, it may:

   (a) reconvene the Trial Chamber;

   (b) constitute a new Trial Chamber; or

   (c) refer the matter to the Appeals Chamber;

with a view to the Chamber determining, after hearing the parties, whether the new evidence should lead to a revision of the conviction.

Part VII

International Cooperation and Judicial Assistance

Article 51

Cooperation and judicial assistance

1. States parties shall cooperate with the Court in connection with criminal investigations and proceedings under this Statute.

2. The Registrar may transmit to any State a request for cooperation and judicial assistance with respect to a crime, including, but not limited to:

   (a) the identification and location of persons;

   (b) the taking of testimony and the production of evidence;

   (c) the service of documents;

   (d) the arrest or detention of persons; and

   (e) any other request which may facilitate the administration of justice, including provisional measures as required.

3. Upon receipt of a request under paragraph 2:

   (a) in a case covered by article 21 (1) (a), all States parties;

   (b) in any other case, States parties which have accepted the jurisdiction of the Court with respect to the crime in question;

shall respond without undue delay to the request.

Article 52

Provisional measures

1. In case of need, the Court may request a State to take necessary provisional measures, including the following:

(a) to provisionally arrest a suspect;

(b) to seize documents or other evidence; or

(c) to prevent injury to or the intimidation of a witness or the destruction of evidence.

2. The Court shall follow up a request under paragraph 1 by providing, as soon as possible and in any case within 28 days, a formal request for assistance complying with article 57.

Article 53

Transfer of an accused to the Court

1. The Registrar shall transmit to any State on the territory of which the accused may be found a warrant for the arrest and transfer of an accused issued under article 28, and shall request the cooperation of that State in the arrest and transfer of the accused.

2. Upon receipt of a request under paragraph 1:

(a) all States parties:

  (i) in a case covered by article 21 (1) (a), or

  (ii) which have accepted the jurisdiction of the Court with respect to the crime in question;

shall, subject to paragraphs 5 and 6, take immediate steps to arrest and transfer the accused to the Court;

(b) in the case of a crime to which article 20 (e) applies, a State party which is a party to the treaty in question but which has not accepted the Court's jurisdiction with respect to that crime shall, if it decides not to transfer the accused to the Court, forthwith take all necessary steps to extradite the accused to a requesting State or refer the case to its competent authorities for the purpose of prosecution;

(c) in any other case, a State party shall consider whether it can, in accordance with its legal procedures, take steps to arrest and transfer the accused to the Court, or whether it should take steps to extradite the accused to a requesting State or refer the case to its competent authorities for the purpose of prosecution.

3. The transfer of an accused to the Court constitutes, as between States parties which accept the jurisdiction of the Court with respect to the crime, sufficient compliance with a provision of any treaty requiring that a suspect be extradited or the case referred to the competent authorities of the requested State for the purpose of prosecution.

4. A State party which accepts the jurisdiction of the Court with respect to the crime shall, as far as possible, give priority to a request under paragraph 1 over requests for extradition from other States.

5. A State party may delay complying with paragraph 2 if the accused is in its custody or control and is being proceeded against for a serious crime, or serving a sentence imposed by

a court for a crime. It shall within 45 days of receiving the request inform the Registrar of the reasons for the delay. In such cases, the requested State:

(a) may agree to the temporary transfer of the accused for the purpose of standing trial under this Statute; or

(c) shall comply with paragraph 2 after the prosecution has been completed or abandoned or the sentence has been served, as the case may be.

6. A State party may, within 45 days of receiving a request under paragraph 1, file a written application with the Registrar requesting the Court to set aside the request on specified grounds. Pending a decision of the Court on the application, the State concerned may delay complying with paragraph 2, but shall take any provisional measures requested by the Court.

Article 54

Obligation to extradite or prosecute

In a case of a crime referred to in article 20 (e), a custodial State party to this Statute which is a party to the treaty in question but which has not accepted the Court's jurisdiction with respect to the crime for the purposes of article 21 (1) (b) (i) shall either take all necessary steps to extradite the suspect to a requesting State for the purpose of prosecution or refer the case to its competent authorities for that purpose.

Article 55

Rule of speciality

1. A person transferred to the Court under article 53 shall not be subject to prosecution or punishment for any crime other than that for which the person was transferred.

2. Evidence provided under this Part shall not, if the State when providing it so requests, be used as evidence for any purpose other than that for which it was provided, unless this is necessary to preserve the right of an accused under article 41 (2).

3. The Court may request the State concerned to waive the requirements of paragraphs 1 or 2, for the reasons and purposes specified in the request.

Article 56

Cooperation with States not parties to this Statute

States not parties to this Statute may assist in relation to the matters referred to in this Part on the basis of comity, a unilateral declaration, an ad hoc arrangement or other agreement with the Court.

Article 57

Communications and documentation

1. Requests under this Part shall be in writing, or be forthwith reduced to writing, and shall be between the competent national authority and the Registrar. States parties shall inform the Registrar of the name and address of their national authority for this purpose.

2. When appropriate, communications may also be made through the International Criminal Police Organization.

3. A request under this Part shall include the following, as applicable:

(a) a brief statement of the purpose of the request and of the assistance sought, including the legal basis and grounds for the request;

(b) information concerning the person who is the subject of the request on the evidence sought, in sufficient detail to enable identification;

(c) a brief description of the essential facts underlying the request; and

(d) information concerning the complaint or charge to which the request relates and of the basis for the Court's jurisdiction.

4. A requested State which considers the information provided insufficient to enable the request to be complied with may seek further particulars.

Part VIII

Enforcement

Article 58

Recognition of judgments

States parties undertake to recognize the judgments of the Courts.

Article 59

Enforcement of sentences

1. A sentence of imprisonment shall be served in a State designated by the Court from a list of States which have indicated to the Court their willingness to accept convicted persons.

2. If no State is designated under paragraph 1, the sentence of imprisonment shall be served in a prison facility made available by the host State.

2. A sentence of imprisonment shall be subject to the supervision of the Court in accordance with the Rules.

Article 60

Pardon, parole and commutation of sentences

1. If, under a generally applicable law of the State of imprisonment, a person in the same circumstances who had been convicted for the same conduct by a court of that State would be eligible for pardon, parole or commutation of sentence, the State shall so notify the Court.

2. If a notification has been given under paragraph 1, the prisoner may apply to the Court in accordance with the Rules, seeking an order for pardon, parole or commutation of the sentence.

3. If the Presidency decides that an application under paragraph 2 is apparently well-founded, it shall convene a Chamber of five judges to consider and decide whether in the interests of justice the person convicted should be pardoned or paroled or the sentence commuted, and on what basis.

4. When imposing a sentence of imprisonment, a Chamber may stipulate that the sentence is to be served in accordance with specified laws as to pardon, parole or commutation of sentence of the State of imprisonment. The consent of the Court is not required to subsequent action by that State in conformity with those laws, but the Court shall be given at least 45 days' notice of any decision which might materially affect the terms or extent of the imprisonment.

5. Except as provided in paragraphs 3 and 4, a person serving a sentence imposed by the Court is not to be released before the expiry of the sentence.

ANNEX

Crimes pursuant to Treaties (see art. 20 (e))

1. Grave breaches of:

    (i) the Geneva Convention for the Amelioration of the Condition of the Wounded and Sick in Armed Forces in the Field of 12 August 1949, as defined by Article 50 of that Convention;

    (ii) the Geneva Convention for the Amelioration of the Condition of Wounded, Sick and Shipwrecked Members of Armed Forces at Sea of 12 August 1949, as defined by Article 51 of that Convention;

    (iii) the Geneva Convention relative to the Treatment of Prisoners of War of 12 August 1949, as defined by Article 130 of that Convention;

    (iv) the Geneva Convention relative to the Protection of Civilian Persons in Time of War of 12 August 1949, as defined by Article 147 of that Convention;

    (v) Protocol I Additional to the Geneva Conventions of 12 August 1949 and relating to the Protection of Victims of International Armed Conflicts of 8 June 1977, as defined by Article 85 of that Protocol.

2. The unlawful seizure of aircraft as defined by Article 1 of the Hague Convention for the Suppression of Unlawful Seizure of Aircraft of 16 December 1970.

3. The crimes defined by Article 1 of the Montreal Convention for the Suppression of Unlawful Acts against the Safety of Civil Aviation of 23 September 1971.

4. Apartheid and related crimes as defined by Article II of the International Convention on the Suppression and Punishment of the Crime of Apartheid of 30 November 1973.

5. The crimes defined by Article 2 of the Convention on the Prevention and Punishment of Crimes against Internationally Protected Persons, including Diplomatic Agents of 14 December 1973.

6. Hostage-taking and related crimes as defined by Article 1 of the International Convention against the Taking of Hostages of 17 December 1979.

7. The crime of torture made punishable pursuant to Article 4 of the Convention against Torture and Other Cruel, Inhuman or Degrading Treatment or Punishment of 10 December 1984.

8. The crimes defined by Article 3 of the Convention for the Suppression of Unlawful Acts against the Safety of Maritime Navigation of 10 March 1988 and by Article 2 of the Protocol for the Suppression of Unlawful Acts against the Safety of Fixed Platforms Located on the Continental Shelf of 10 March 1988.

9. Crimes involving illicit traffic in narcotic drugs and psychotropic substances as envisaged by Article 3 (1) of the United Nations Convention against Illicit Traffic in Narcotic Drugs and Psychotropic Substances of 20 December 1988 which, having regard to Article 2 of the Convention, are crimes with an international dimension.

6. INTERNATIONAL CRIMINAL CODE

Nuremberg Principles: Principles of International Law Recognized in the Charter of the Nuremberg Tribunal and in the Judgment of the Tribunal (1950)[*]

Principle 1

Any person who commits an act which constitutes a crime under international law is responsible therefor and liable to punishment.

Principle 2

The fact that internal law does not impose a penalty for an act which constitutes a crime under international law does not relieve the person who committed the act from responsibility under international law.

Principle 3

The fact that a person who committed an act which constitutes a crime under international law acted as Head of State or responsible government official does not relieve him from responsibility under international law.

Principle 4

The fact that a person acted pursuant to order of his government or of a superior does not relieve him from responsibility under international law, provided a moral choice was in fact possible to him.

Principle 5

Any person charged with a crime under international law has the right to a fair trial on the facts and law.

Principle 6

The crime hereinafter set out are punishable as crimes under international law:

(a) Crimes Against Peace:

  (i) Planning, preparation, initiation or waging of a war of aggression or a war in violation of international treaties, agreements or assurances;

  (ii) Participation in a common plan or conspiracy for the accomplishment of any of the acts mentioned under (i).

(b) War Crimes:

  Violations of the laws or customs of war which include, but are not limited to, murder, ill-treatment or deportation to slave labour of for any other purpose of civilian population of or in occupied territory, murder or ill-treatment of prisoners of war, of persons on the seas, killing of hostages, plunder of public or private property, wanton destruction of cities, towns, or villages, or devastation not justified by military necessity.

---

[*] *U.N.G.A.O.R.*, 5th Session, Supp.No.12, UN Doc.A/1316 (1950).

(c) Crimes Against Humanity

Murder, extermination, enslavement, deportation and other inhuman acts done against any civilian population, or persecutions on political, racial or religious grounds, when such acts are done or such persecutions are carried on in execution of or in connection with any crime against peace or any war crime.

Principle 7

Complicity in the commission of a crime against peace, a war crime, or a crime against humanity as set forth in Principle VI is a crime under international law.

International Law Commission - Draft Code of Offences against the Peace and Security of Mankind (excerpts) (1954)*

Paris, 28 July 1954

Article 1

Offences against the peace and security of mankind, as defined in this code, are crimes under international law, for which the responsible individuals shall be punished.

Article 2

The following acts are offences against the peace and security of mankind:

1. Any act of aggression, including the employment by the authorities of a State of armed force against another State for any purpose other than national or collective self-defence or in pursuance of a decision or recommendation of a competent organ of the United Nations.

2. Any threat by the authorities of a State to resort to an act of aggression against another State.

3. The preparation by the authorities of a State of the employment of armed force against another State for any purpose other than national or collective self-defence or in pursuance of a decision or recommendations of a competent organ of the United Nations.

4. The organization, or the encouragement of the organization, by the authorities of a State, or armed bands within its territory or any other territory for incursions into the territory of another State, or the toleration of the organization of such bands in its own territory, or the toleration of the use by such armed bands of its territory as a base of operations or as a point of departure for incursions into the territory of another State, as well as direct participation in or support of such incursions.

5. The undertaking or encouragement by the authorities of a State of activities calculated to foment civil strife in another State, or the toleration by the authorities of a State of organized activities calculated to foment civil strife in another State.

6. The undertaking or encouragement by the authorities of a State of terrorist activities in another State, or the toleration by the authorities of a State of organized activities calculated to carry out terrorist acts in another State.

7. Acts by the authorities of a State in violation of its obligations under a treaty which is designed to ensure international peace and security by means of restrictions or limitations on armaments, or on military training, or on fortifications, or of other restrictions of the same character.

8. The annexation by the authorities of a State of territory belonging to another State, by means of acts contrary to international law.

9. The intervention by the authorities of a State in the internal or external affairs of another State, by means of coercive measures of an economic or political character in order to force its will and thereby obtain advantages of any kind.

10. Acts by the authorities of a State or by private individuals committed with intent to destroy, in whole or in part, a national, ethnic, racial or religious group a such, including:

    (a) Killing members of the group;

---

* *Yearbook of the International Law Commission*, 1954, 151.

(b) Causing serious bodily or mental harm to members of the group;

(c) Deliberately inflicting on the group conditions of life calculated to bring about its physical destruction in whole or in part;

(d) Imposing measures intended to prevent births within the group;

(e) Forcibly transferring children of the group to another group.

11. Inhuman acts such as murder, extermination, enslavement, deportation on persecutions, committed against any civilian population on social, political, racial religious or cultural grounds by the authorities of a State or by private individuals acting at the instigation or with the toleration of such authorities.

12. Acts in violation of the laws or customs of war.

13. Acts which constitute:

(a) Conspiracy to commit any of the offences defined in the preceding paragraphs of this article; or

(b) Direct incitement to commit any of the offences defined in the preceding paragraphs of this article; or

(c) Complicity in the commission of any of the offences defined in the preceding paragraphs of this article; or

(d) Attempts to commit any of the offences defined in the preceding paragraph of this article.

Article 3

The fact that a person acted as Head of State or as responsible government official does not relieve him of responsibility for committing any of the offences defined in the code.

Article 4

The fact that a person charged with an offence defined in this code acted pursuant to an order of his Government or of a superior does not relieve him of responsibility in international law if, in the circumstances at the time, if was possible for him not to comply with that order.

[...]

International Law Commission - Draft Code of Crimes against the Peace and Security of Mankind (1991)[*]

Part I

Chapter 1

Definition and Characterization

Article 1

Definition

The crimes (under international law) defined in this Code constitute crimes against the peace and security of mankind.

Article 2

Characterization

The characterization of an act or omission as a crime against the peace and security of mankind is independent of internal law. The fact that an act or omission is or is not punishable under internal law does not affect this characterization.

Chapter 2

General Principles

Article 3

Responsibility and punishment

1. An individual who commits a crime against the peace and security of mankind is responsible therefor and is liable to punishment.

2. An individual who aids, abets or provides the means for the commission of a crime against the peace and security of mankind or conspires in or directly incites the commission of such a crime is responsible therefor and is liable to punishment.

3. An individual who commits an act constituting an attempt to commit a crime against the peace and security of mankind (as set out in arts.) is responsible therefor and is liable to punishment. Attempt means any commencement of execution of a crime that failed or was halted only because of circumstances independent of the perpetrator's intention.

Article 4

Motives

Responsibility for a crime against the peace and security of mankind is not affected by any motives invoked by the accused which are not covered by the definition of the crime.

---

[*] *Report of the International Law Commision*, 43d Session, *U.N.G.A.O.R.*, 46th Session, Supp.No.10, A/46/10 (1991).

Article 5

Responsibility of States

Prosecution of an individual for a crime against the peace and security of mankind does not relieve a State of any responsibility under international law for an act or omission attributable to it.

Article 6

Obligation to try to extradite

1. A State in whose territory an individual alleged to have committed a crime against the peace and security of mankind is present shall either try or extradite him.

2. If extradition is requested by several States, special consideration shall be given to the request of the State in whose territory the crime was committed.

3. The provisions of paragraphs 1 and 2 do not prejudge the establishment and the jurisdiction of an international criminal court.

Article 7

Non-applicability of statutory limitations

No statutory limitation shall apply to crimes against the peace and security of mankind.

Article 8

Judicial guarantees

An individual charged with a crime against the peace and security of mankind shall be entitled without discrimination to the minimum guarantees due to all human beings with regard to the law and the facts. In particular, he shall have the right to be presumed innocent until proved guilty and have the rights;

(a) in the determination of any charge against him, to have a fair and public hearing by a competent, independent and impartial tribunal duly established by law or by treaty;

(b) to be informed promptly and in detail in a language which he understands of the nature and cause of the charge against him;

(c) to have adequate time and facilities for the preparation of his defence and to communicate with counsel of his own choosing;

(d) to be tried without undue delay;

(e) to be tried in his presence, and to defend himself in person or through legal assistance of his own choosing; to be informed, if he does not have legal assistance, of this right; and to have legal assistance assigned to him and without payment by him in any case if he does not have sufficient means to pay for it;

(f) to examine, or have examined, the witnesses against him and to obtain the attendance and examination of witnesses on his behalf under the same conditions as witnesses against him;

(g) to have the free assistance of an interpreter if he cannot understand or speak the language used in court;

(h) not to be compelled to testify against himself or to confess guilt.

Article 9

Non bis in idem

1. No one shall be tried or punished for a crime under this Code for which he has already been finally convicted or acquitted by an international criminal court.

2. Subject to paragraphs 3, 4 and 5, no one shall be tried or punished for a crime under this Code in respect of an act for which he has already been finally convicted or acquitted by a national court, provided that, if a punishment was imposed, it has been enforced or is in the process of being enforced.

3. Notwithstanding the provisions of paragraph 2, an individual may be tried and punished by an international criminal court or by a national court for a crime under this Code if the act which was the subject of a trial and judgment as an ordinary crime corresponds to one of the crimes characterized in this Code.

4. Notwithstanding the provisions of paragraph 2, an individual may be tried and punished by a national court of another State for a crime under this Code:

   (a) if the act which was the subject of the previous judgment took place in the territory of that State; or

   (b) if that State has been the main victim of the crime.

5. In the case of a subsequent conviction under this Code, the court, in passing sentence, shall deduct any penalty imposed and implemented as a result of a previous conviction for the same act.

Article 10

Non-retroactivity

1. No one shall be convicted under this Code for acts committed before its entry into force.

2. Nothing in this article shall preclude the trial and punishment of anyone for any act which, at the time when it was committed, was criminal in accordance with international law or domestic law applicable in conformity with international law.

Article 11

Order of a Government or a superior

The fact that an individual charged with a crime against the peace and security of mankind acted pursuant to an order of a Government or a superior does not relieve him of criminal responsibility if, in the circumstances at the time, it was possible for him not to comply with that order.

Article 12

Responsibility of the superior

The fact that a crime against the peace and security of mankind was committed by a subordinate does not relieve his superiors of criminal responsibility, if they knew or had information enabling them to conclude, in the circumstances at the time, that the subordinate was committing or was going to commit such a crime and if they did not take all feasible measures within their power to prevent or repress the crime.

Article 13

Official position and responsibility

The official position of an individual who commits a crime against the peace and security of mankind, and particularly the fact that he acts as head of State or Government, does not relieve him of criminal responsibility.

Article 14

Defences and extenuating circumstances

1. The competent court shall determine the admissibility of defences under the general principles of law, in the light of the character of each crime.

2. In passing sentence, the court shall, where appropriate, take into account extenuating circumstances.

Part II

Crimes Against the Peace and Security of Mankind

Article 15

Aggression

1. An individual who as leader or organizer plans, commits or orders the commission of an act of aggression shall, on conviction thereof, be sentenced (to ...).

2. Aggression is the use of armed force by a State against the sovereignty, territorial integrity or political independence of another State, or in any other manner inconsistent with the Charter of the United Nations.

3. The first use of armed force by a State in contravention of the Charter shall constitute *prima facie* evidence of an act of aggression, although the Security Council may, in conformity with the Charter, conclude that a determination that an act of aggression has been committed would not be justified in the light of other relevant circumstances, including the fact that the acts concerned or their consequences are not of sufficient gravity.

4. Any of the following acts, regardless of a declaration of war, constitutes an act of aggression, due regard being paid to paragraphs 2 and 3:

   (a) the invasion or attack by the armed forces of a State of the territory of another State, or any military occupation, however temporary, resulting from such invasion or attack, or any annexation by the use of force of the territory of another State or part thereof;

   (b) bombardment by the armed forces of a State against the territory of another State or the use of any weapons by a State against the territory of another State;

   (c) the blockade of the ports or coasts of a State by the armed forces of another State;

   (d) an attack by the armed forces of a State on the land, sea or air forces, or marine and air fleets of another State;

   (e) the use of armed forces of one State which are within the territory of another State with the agreement of the receiving State, in contravention of the conditions provided for in the agreement, or any extension of their presence in such territory beyond the termination of the agreement;

(f) the action of a State in allowing its territory, which it has placed at the disposal of another State, to be used by that other State for perpetrating an act of aggression against a third State;

(g) the sending by or on behalf of a State or armed bands, groups, irregulars or mercenaries, which carry out acts of armed force against another State of such gravity as to amount to the acts listed above, or its substantial involvement therein;

(h) any other acts determined by the Security Council as constituting acts of aggression under the provisions of the Charter;

5. Any determination by the Security Council as to the existence of an act of aggression is binding on national courts.

6. Nothing in this article shall be interpreted as in any way enlarging or diminishing the scope of the Charter of the United Nations including its provisions concerning cases in which the use of force is lawful.

7. Nothing in this article could in any way prejudice the right to self-determination, freedom and independence, as derived from the Charter, of peoples forcibly deprived of that right and referred to in the Declaration on Principles of International Law concerning Friendly Relations and Cooperation among States in accordance with the Charter of the United Nations, particularly peoples under colonial and racist regimes or other forms of alien domination; nor the right of these peoples to struggle to that end and to seek and receive support, in accordance with the principles of the Charter and in conformity with the above-mentioned Declaration.

Article 16

Threat of aggression

1. An individual who as leader or organizer commits or orders the commission of a threat of aggression shall, on conviction thereof, be sentenced (to ...).

2. Threat of aggression consists of declarations, communications, demonstrations of force or any other measures which would give good reason to the Government of a State to believe that aggression is being seriously contemplated against that State.

Article 17

Intervention

1. An individual who as leader or organizer commits or orders the commission of an act of intervention in the internal or external affairs of a State shall, on conviction thereof, be sentenced (to ...).

2. Intervention in the internal or external affairs of a State consists of fomenting (armed) subversive or terrorist activities or by organizing, assisting or financing such activities, or supplying arms for the purpose of such activities, thereby (seriously) undermining the free exercise by that State of its sovereign rights.

3. Nothing in this article shall in any way prejudice the right of peoples to self-determination as enshrined in the Charter of the United Nations.

Article 18

Colonial domination and other forms of alien domination

An individual who as leader or organizer establishes or maintains by force or orders the establishment or maintenance by force of colonial domination or any other form of alien domination contrary to the right of peoples to self-determination as enshrined in the Charter of the United Nations shall, on conviction thereof, be sentenced (to ...).

Article 19

Genocide

1. An individual who commits or orders the commission of an act of genocide shall, on conviction thereof, be sentenced (to ...).

2. Genocide means any of the following acts committed with intent to destroy, in whole or in part, a national, ethnic, racial or religious group as such:

 (a) killing members of the group;

 (b) causing seriously bodily or mental harm to members of the group;

 (c) deliberately inflicting on the group conditions of life calculated to bring about its physical destruction in whole or in part;

 (d) imposing measures intended to prevent births within the group;

 (e) forcibly transferring children of the group to another group.

Article 20

Apartheid

1. An individual who as leader or organizer commits or orders the commission of the crime of *apartheid* shall, on conviction thereof, be sentenced (to ...).

2. *Apartheid* consists of any of the following acts based on policies and practices of racial segregation and discrimination committed for the purpose of establishing or maintaining domination by one racial group over any other racial group and systematically oppressing it:

 (a) denial to a member of members of a racial group of the right to life and liberty of person;

 (b) deliberate imposition on a racial group of living conditions calculated to cause its physical destruction in whole or in part;

 (c) any legislative measures and other measures calculated to prevent a racial group from participating in the political, social, economic and cultural life of the country and the deliberate creation of conditions preventing the full development of such a group;

 (d) any measures, including legislative measures, designed to divide the population along racial lines, in particular by the creation of separate reserves and ghettos for the members of a racial group, the prohibition of marriages among members of various racial groups or the expropriation of landed property belonging to a racial group or to members thereof;

 (e) exploitation of the labour of the members of a racial group, in particular by submitting them to forced labour;

 (f) persecution of organizations and persons, by depriving them of fundamental rights and freedoms, because they oppose *apartheid*.

Article 21

Systematic or mass violations of human rights

An individual who commits or orders the commission of any of the following violations of human rights:

- murder

- torture

- establishing or maintaining over persons a status of slavery, servitude or forced labour

- persecution on social, political, racial, religious or cultural grounds in a systematic manner or on a mass scale; or

- deportation of forcible transfer of population shall, on conviction thereof, be sentenced (to ...).

Article 22

Exceptionally serious war crimes

1. An individual who commits or orders the commission of an exceptionally serious war crime shall, on conviction thereof, be sentenced (to ...).

2. For the purposes of this Code, an exceptionally serious war crime is an exceptionally serious violation of principles and rules of international law applicable in armed conflict consisting of any of the following acts:

(a) acts of inhumanity, cruelty or barbarity directed against the life, dignity or physical or mental integrity of persons (in particular wilful killing, torture, mutilation, biological experiments, taking of hostages, compelling a protected person to serve in the forces of a hostile Power, unjustifiable delay in the repatriation of prisoners of war after the cessation of active hostilities, deportation or transfer of the civilian population and collective punishment);

(b) establishment of settlers in an occupied territory and changes to the demographic composition of an occupied territory;

(c) use of unlawful weapons;

(d) employing methods or means of warfare which are intended or may be expected to cause widespread, long-term and severe damage to the natural environment;

(e) large-scale destruction of civilian property;

(f) wilful attacks on property of exceptional religious, historical or cultural value.

Article 23

Recruitment, use, financing and training of mercenaries

1. An individual who as an agent or representative of a State commits or orders the commission of any of the following acts:

- recruitment, use, financing or training of mercenaries for activities directed against another State or for the purpose of opposing the legitimate exercise of the inalienable right of peoples to self-determination as recognized under international law shall, on conviction thereof, be sentenced (to ...).

2. A mercenary is any individual who:

   (a) is especially recruited locally or abroad in order to fight in an armed conflict;

   (b) is motivated to take part in the hostilities essentially by the desire for private gain and, in fact, is promised, by or on behalf of a party to the conflict, material compensation substantially in excess of that promised or paid to combatants of similar rank and functions in the armed forces of that party;

   (c) is neither a national of a party to the conflict nor a resident of territory controlled by a party to the conflict;

   (d) is not a member of the armed forces of a party to the conflict; and

   (e) has not been sent by a State which is not a party to the conflict on official duty as a member of its armed forces.

3. A mercenary is also any individual who, in any other situation:

   (a) is specially recruited locally or abroad for the purpose of participating in a concerted act of violence aimed at:

   (i) overthrowing a Government or otherwise undermining the constitutional order of a State; or

   (ii) undermining the territorial integrity of a State;

   (b) is motivated to take part therein essentially by the desire for significant private gain and is prompted by the promise or payment of material compensation;

   (c) is neither a national nor a resident of the State against which such an act is directed;

   (d) has not been sent by a State on official duty; and

   (e) is not a member of the armed forces of the State in whose territory the act is undertaken.

Article 24

International terrorism

An individual who as an agent or representative of a State commits or orders the commission of any of the following acts:

- undertaking, organizing, assisting, financing, encouraging or tolerating acts against another State directed at persons or property and of such a nature as to create a state of terror in the minds of public figures, groups of persons or the general public shall, on conviction thereof, be sentenced (to ...).

Article 25

Illicit traffic in narcotic drugs

1. An individual who commits or orders the commission of any of the following acts:

   - undertaking, organizing, facilitating, financing or encouraging illicit traffic in narcotic drugs on a large scale, whether within the confines of a State or in a transboundary context shall, on conviction thereof, be sentenced (to ...).

2. For the purposes of paragraph 1, facilitating or encouraging illicit traffic in narcotic drugs includes the acquisition, holding, conversion or transfer of property by an individual

who knows that such property is derived from the crime described in this article in order to conceal or disguise the illicit origin of the property.

3. Illicit traffic in narcotic drugs means any production, manufacture, extraction, preparation, offering, offering for sale, distribution, sale, delivery on any terms whatsoever, brokerage, dispatch, dispatch in transit, transport, importation or exportation of any narcotic drug or any psychotropic substance contrary to internal or international law.

Article 26

Wilful and severe damage to the environment

An individual who wilfully causes or orders the causing of widespread, long-term and severe damage to the natural environment shall, on conviction thereof, be sentenced (to ...).

[...]

International Law Commission - Draft Code of Crimes against the Peace and Security of Mankind (1996)[*]

Geneva, 31 May 1996

PART I. GENERAL PROVISIONS

Section 1

Article 1

Scope and application of the present Code

1. The present Code applies to the crimes against the peace and security of mankind set out in Part II.

2. Crimes against the peace and security of mankind are crimes under international law and punishable as such, whether or not they are punishable under national law.

Section 2

Article 2

Individual responsibility

1. A crime against the peace and security of mankind entails individual responsibility.

2. An individual shall be responsible for the crime of aggression in accordance with article 16.

3. An individual shall be responsible for a crime set out in articles 17, 18, 19 or 20 if that individual:

    (a)   intentionally commits such a crime;

    (b)   orders the commission of such a crime which in fact occurs or is attempted;

    (c)   fails to prevent or repress the commission of such a crime in the circumstances set out in article 6;

    (d)   knowingly aids, abets or otherwise assists, directly and substantially, in the commission of such a crime, including providing the means for its commission;

    (e)   directly participates in planning or conspiring to commit such a crime which in fact occurs;

    (f)   directly and publicly incites another individual to commit such a crime which in fact occurs;

    (g)   attempts to commit such a crime by taking action commencing the execution of a crime which does not in fact occur because of circumstances independent of his intentions

---

[*] *International Law Commission*, 48th Session, UN Doc.A/CN.4/L.522 of 31 May 1996, as adopted with amendments on 5 July 1996. The amended version of this document had not yet been published when the manuscript for this book was finalised.

Article 3

Punishment

An individual who is responsible for a crime against the peace and security of mankind shall be liable to punishment. The punishment shall be commensurate with the character and gravity of the crime.

Article 4

Responsibility of States

The fact that the present Code provides for the responsibility of individuals for crimes against the peace and security of mankind is without prejudice to any question of the responsibility of States under international law.

Article 5

Order of a Government or a superior

The fact that an individual charged with a crime against the peace and security of mankind acted pursuant to an order of a Government or a superior does not relieve him of criminal responsibility, but may be considered in mitigation of punishment if justice so requires.

Article 6

Responsibility of the superior

The fact that a crime against the peace and security of mankind was committed by a subordinate does not relieve his superiors of criminal responsibility, if they knew or had reason to know, in the circumstances at the time, that the subordinate was committing or was going to commit such a crime and if they did not take all necessary measures within their power to prevent or repress the crime.

Article 7

Official position and responsibility

The official position of an individual who commits a crime against the peace and security of mankind, even if he acted as head of State or Government, does not relieve him of criminal responsibility or mitigate punishment.

Article 8

Establishment of jurisdiction

Without prejudice to the jurisdiction of an international criminal court, each State Party shall take such measures as may be necessary to establish its jurisdiction over the crimes set out in articles 17, 18, 19 and 20, irrespective of where or by whom those crimes were committed. Jurisdiction over the crime set out in article 16 shall rest with an international criminal court. However, a State Party is not precluded from trying its nationals for the crime set out in article 16.

Article 9

Obligation to extradite or prosecute

Without prejudice to the jurisdiction of an international criminal court, the State Party in the territory of which an individual alleged to have committed a crime set out in articles 17, 18, 19 or 20 is found shall extradite or prosecute that individual.

Article 10

Extradition of alleged offenders

1. To the extent that the crimes set out in articles 17, 18, 19 and 20 are not extraditable offences in any extradition treaty existing between states parties, they shall be deemed to be included as such therein. States parties undertake to include those crimes as extraditable offences in every extradition treaty to be concluded between them.

2. If a State party which make extradition conditional on the existence of a treaty receives a request for extradition from another State Party with which it has no extradition treaty, it may at its option consider the present Code as the legal basis for extradition in respect of those crimes.
Extradition shall be subject to the conditions provided in the law of the requested State.

3. States Parties which do not make extradition conditional on the existence of a treaty shall recognize those crimes as extraditable offences between themselves subject to the conditions provided in the law of the requested State.

4. Each of those crimes shall be treated, for the purpose of extradition between States Parties, as if it had been committed not only in the place in which it occurred but also in the territory of any other State Party.

Article 11

Judicial guarantees

1. An individual charged with a crime against the peace and security of mankind shall be presumed innocent until proved guilty and shall be entitled without discrimination to the minimum guarantees due to all human beings with regard to the law and the facts and shall have the rights:

- (a) in the determination of any charge against him, to have a fair and public hearing by a competent, independent and impartial tribunal duly established by law;

- (b) to be informed promptly and in detail in a language which he understands of the nature and cause of the charge against him;

- (c) to have adequate time and facilities for the preparation of his defence and to communicate with counsel of his own choosing;

- (d) to be tried without undue delay;

- (e) to be tried in his presence, and to defend himself in person or through legal assistance of his own choosing; to be informed, if he does not have legal assistance, of this right; and to have legal assistance assigned to him and without payment by him if he does not have sufficient means to pay for it;

- (f) to examine, or have examined, the witnesses against him and to obtain the attendance and examination of witnesses on his behalf under the same conditions as witnesses against him;

- (g) to have the free assistance of an interpreter if he cannot understand or speak the language used in court;

- (h) not to be compelled to testify against himself or to confess guilt.

2. An individual convicted of a crime shall have the right to his conviction and sentence being reviewed according to law.

Article 12

Non bis in idem

1. No one shall be tried for a crime against the peace and security of mankind of which he has already been finally convicted or acquitted by an international criminal court.

2. An individual may not be tried again for a crime of which he has been finally convicted or acquitted by a national court except in the following cases:

 (a) by an international criminal court, if:

 (i) the act which was the subject of the judgment in the national court was characterized by that court as an ordinary crime and not as a crime against the peace and security of mankind; or

 (ii) the national court proceedings were not impartial or independent or were designed to shield the accused from international criminal responsibility or the case was not diligently prosecuted;

 (b) by a national court of another State, if:

 (i) the act which was the subject of the previous judgment took place in the territory of that State; or

 (ii) that State was the main victim of the crime.

3. In the case of a subsequent conviction under the present Code, the court, in passing sentence, shall take into account the extent to which any penalty imposed by a national court on the same person for the same act has already been served.

Article 13

Non-retroactivity

1. No one shall be convicted under the present Code for acts committed before its entry into force.

2. Nothing in this article precludes the trial of anyone for any act which, at the time when it was committed, was criminal in accordance with international law or national law.

Article 14

Defences

The competent court shall determine the admissibility of defences in accordance with the general principles of law, in the light of the character of each crime.

Article 15

Extenuating circumstances

In passing sentence, the court shall, where appropriate, take into account extenuating circumstances in accordance with the general principles of law.

PART II. CRIMES AGAINST THE PEACE AND SECURITY OF MANKIND

Article 16

Crime of aggression

An individual, who, as leader or organizer, actively participates in or orders the planning, preparation, initiation or waging of aggression committed by a State, shall be responsible for a crime of aggression.

Article 17

Crime of genocide

A crime of genocide means any of the following acts committed with intent to destroy, in whole or in part, a national, ethnic, racial or religious group, as such:

(a) killing members of the group;

(b) causing serious bodily or mental harm to members of the group;

(c) deliberately inflicting on the group conditions of life calculated to bring about its physical destruction in whole or in part;

(d) imposing measures intended to prevent births within the group;

(e) forcibly transferring children of the group to another group.

Article 18

Crimes against humanity

A crime against humanity means any of the following acts, when committed in a systematic manner or on a large scale and instigated or directed by a government or by any organization or group:

(a) murder;

(b) extermination;

(c) torture;

(d) enslavement;

(e) persecution on political, racial, religious or ethnic grounds;

(f) institutionalized discrimination on racial, ethnic or religious grounds involving the violation of fundamental human rights and freedoms and resulting in seriously disadvantaging a part of the population;

(g) arbitrary deportation or forcible transfer of population;

(h) forced disappearance of persons;

(i) rape, enforced prostitution and other forms of sexual abuse;

(j) other inhumane acts which severely damage physical or mental integrity, health or human dignity, such as mutilation and severe bodily harm.

Article 19

Crimes against United Nations and associated personnel

1. The following crimes constitute crimes against the peace and security of mankind when committed intentionally and in a systematic manner or on a large scale against United Nations and associated personnel involved in a United Nations operation with a view to preventing or impeding that operation from fulfilling its mandate:

    (a) murder, kidnapping or other attack upon any such personnel;

    (b) violent attack upon the official premises, the private accomodation or the means of transportation of any such personnel likely to endanger his or her person or liberty.

2. This article shall not apply to a United Nations operation authorized by the Security Council as an enforcement action under Chapter VII of the Charter of the United Nations in which any of the personnel are engaged as combatants against organized armed forces and to which the law of international armed conflict applies.

Article 20

War crimes

Any of the following war crimes constitutes a crime against the peace and security of mankind when committed in a systematic manner or on a large scale:

(a) any of the following acts committed in violation of international humanitarian law;

    (i) wilful killing;

    (ii) torture or inhuman treatment, including biological experiments;

    (iii) wilfully causing great suffering or serious injury to body or health;

    (iv) extensive destruction and appropriation of property, not justified by military necessity and carried out unlawfully and wantonly;

    (v) compelling a prisoner of war or other protected person to serve in the forces of a hostile Power;

    (vi) wilfully depriving a prisoner of war or other protected person of the rights of fair and regular trial;

    (vii) unlawful deportation or transfer or unlawful confinement of protected persons;

    (viii) taking of hostages;

(b) any of the following acts committed wilfully in violation of international humanitarian law and causing death or serious injury to body or health:

    (i) making the civilian population or individual civilians the object of attack;

    (ii) launching an indiscriminate attack affecting the civilian population or civilian objects in the knowledge that such attack will cause excessive loss of life, injury to civilians or damage to civilian objects;

    (iii) launching an attack against works or installations containing dangerous forces in the knowledge that such attack will cause excessive loss of life, injury to civilians or damage to civilian objects;

(iv) making a person the object of attack in the knowledge that he is *hors de combat*;

(v) the perfidious use of the distinctive emblem of the red cross, red crescent or red lion and sun or of other recognized protective signs;

(c) any of the following acts committed wilfully in violation of international humanitarian law:

(i) the transfer by the Occupying Power of parts of its own civilian population into the territory it occupies;

(ii) unjustifiable delay in the repatriation of prisoners of war or civilians;

(d) outrages upon personal dignity in violation of international humanitarian law, in particular humiliating and degrading treatment, rape, enforced prostitution and any form of indecent assault;

(e) any of the following acts committed in violation of the laws or customs of war:

(i) employment of poisonous weapons or other weapons calculated to cause unnecessary suffering;

(ii) wanton destruction of cities, towns or villages, or devastation not justified by military necessity;

(iii) attack, of bombardment, by whatever means, of undefended towns, villages, dwellings or buildings or of demilitarized zones;

(iv) seizure of, destruction of or wilful damage done to institutions dedicated to religion, charity and education, the arts and sciences, historic monuments and works of art and science;

(v) plunder of public or private property;

(f) any of the following acts committed in violation of international humanitarian law applicable in armed conflict not of an international character.

(i) violence to the life, health and physical or mental well-being of persons, in particular murder as well as cruel treatment such as torture, mutilation or any form of corporal punishment;

(ii) collective punishments;

(iii) taking of hostages;

(iv) acts of terrorism;

(v) outrages upon personal dignity, in particular humiliating and degrading treatment, rape, enforced prostitution and any form of indecent assault;

(vi) pillage;

(vii) the passing of sentences and the carrying out of executions without previous judgment pronounced by a regularly constituted court, affording all the judicial guarantees which are generally recognized as indispensable;

(g) in the case of armed conflict, using methods or means of warfare not justified by military necessity with the intent to cause widespread, long-term and severe damage to the natural environment and thereby gravely prejudice the health or survival of the population and such damage occurs.

International Law Commission - Draft Articles on State Responsibilty (excerpts) (1976)[*]

Article 19

International crimes and international delicts

1. An act of a State which constitutes a breach of an international obligation is an internationally wrongful act, regardless of the subject-matter of the obligation breached.

2. An internationally wrongful act which results from the breach by a State of an international obligation so essential for the protection of fundamental interests of the international community that its breach is recognized as a crime by that community as a whole constitutes an international crime.

3. Subject to paragraph 2. and on the basis of the rules of international law in force, an international crime may results, *inter alia*, from:

   (a) a serious breach of an international obligation of essential importance for the maintenance of international peace and security, such as that prohibiting aggression;

   (b) a serious breach of an international obligation of essential importance for safeguarding the right of self-determination of peoples, such as that prohibiting the establishment or maintenance by force of colonial domination;

   (c) a serious breach on a widespread scale of an international obligation of essential importance for safeguarding the human being, such as those prohibiting slavery, genocide and *apartheid*;

   (d) a serious breach of an international obligation of essential importance for the safeguarding and preservation of the human environment, such as those prohibiting massive pollution of the atmosphere or of the seas.

4. Any internationally wrongful act which is not an international crime in accordance with paragraph 2 constitutes an international delict.

---

[*] *Report of the International Law Commission*, 28th Session, *U.N.G.A.O.R.*, 31st Session, Supp.No.10, A/31/10 (1976).

7. THE EUROPEAN UNION AND THE CRIMINAL LAW

EEC-Treaty (excerpts) (1957)

Brussels, 25 March 1957

Article 5

Member States shall take all appropriate measures, whether general or particular, to ensure fulfillment of the obligations arising out of this Treaty or resulting from action taken by the institutions of the Community. They shall facilitate the achievement of the Community's tasks.

They shall abstain from any measure which could jeopardize the attainment of the objectives of this Treaty.

[...]

Article 85

1. The following shall be prohibited as incompatible with the common market: all agreements between undertakings, decision by associations of undertakings and concerted practices which may affect trade between Member States and which have as their object or effect the prevention, restriction, or distortion of competition within the common market, and in particular those which:

    (a) directly of indirectly fix purchase or selling prices or any other trading conditions;

    (b) limit or control production, markets, technical development, or investment;

    (c) share markets or sources of supply;

    (d) apply dissimilar conditions to equivalent transactions with other trading parties, thereby placing them at a competitive disadvantage;

    (e) make the conclusion of contracts subject to acceptance by the other parties of supplementary obligations which, by their nature or according to commercial usage, have no connection with the subject of such contracts.

2. Any agreements of decisions prohibited pursuant to this Article shall be automatically void.

3. The provisions of paragraph 1 may, however, be declared inapplicable in the case of:

    - any agreement or category of agreements between undertakings;

    - any decision or category of decisions by associations of undertakings;

    - any concerted practice or category of concerted practices, which contributes to improving the production or distribution of goods or to promoting technical or economic progress, while allowing consumers a fair share of the resulting benefit, and which does not:

    (a) Impose on the undertakings concerned restrictions which are not indispensable to the attainment of these objectives;

    (b) afford such undertakings the possibility of eliminating competition in respect of a substantial part of the products in question.

Article 86

Any abuse by one or more undertakings of a dominant position within the common market or in a substantial part of it shall be prohibited as incompatible with the common market in so far as it may affect trade between Member States.

Such abuse may, in particular, consist in:

(a) Directly or indirectly imposing unfair purchase or selling prices or other unfair trading conditions;

(b) Limiting production, markets or technical development to the prejudice of consumers;

(c) Applying dissimilar conditions to equivalent transactions with other trading parties, thereby placing them at a competitive disadvantage;

(d) Making the conclusion of contracts subject to acceptance by the other parties of supplementary obligations which, by their nature or according to commercial usage, have no connection with the subject of such contracts.

Article 87

1. Within three years, of the entry into force of this Treaty the Council shall, acting unanimously on a proposal from the Commission and after consulting the European Parliament, adopt any appropriate regulations or directives to give effect to the principles set out in Articles 85 and 86.

If such provisions have not been adopted within the period mentioned, they shall be laid down by the Council, acting by a qualified majority on a proposal from the Commission and after consulting the European Parliament.

2. The regulations and directives referred to in paragraph 1 shall be designed in particular:

(a) to ensure compliance with the prohibitions laid down in Article 85(1) and Article 86 by making provision for fines and periodic penalty payments;

(b) to lay down detailed rules for the application of Article 85(3), taking into account the need to ensure effective supervision on the one hand, and to simplify administration to the greatest possible extent on the other;

(c) to define, if need be, in the various branches of the economy, the scope of the provisions of Articles 85 and 86;

(d) to define the respective functions of the Commission and of the Court of Justice in applying the provisions laid down in this paragraph;

(e) to determine the relationship between national laws and the provisions contained in this Section or adopted pursuant to this Article.

[...]

Article 129

1. The Community shall contribute towards ensuring a high level of human health protection by encouraging cooperation between the Member States and, if necessary, lending support to their action.

Community action shall be directed towards the prevention of diseases, in particular the major health scourges, including drug dependence, by promoting research into their causes and their transmission, as well as health information and education.

Health protection requirements shall form a constituent part of the Community's other policies.

2. Member States shall, in liaison with the Commission, coordinate among themselves their policies and programmes in the areas referred to in paragraph I. The Commission may, in close contact with the Member States, take any useful initiative to promote such coordination.

3. The Community and the Member States shall foster cooperation with third countries and the competent international organizations in the sphere of public health.

4. In order to contribute to the achievement of the objectives referred to in this Article, the Council:

 (a) acting in accordance with the procedure referred to in Article 189b, after consulting the Economic and Social Committee, and the Committee of the Regions, shall adopt incentive measures, excluding any harmonization of the laws and regulations of the Member States;

 (b) acting by a qualified majority on a proposal from the Commission, shall adopt recommendations.

[...]

Article 209a

1. Member States shall take the same measures to counter fraud affecting the financial interests of the Community as they take to counter fraud affecting their own financial interests.

2. Without prejudice to other provisions of this Treaty, Member States shall co-ordinate their action aimed at protecting the financial interests of the Community against fraud. To this end they shall organize, with the help of the Commission, close and regular co-operation between the competent departments of their administrations.

[...]

Treaty on the European Union (excerpts) (1992)*

Maastricht, 7 February 1992

Title I

Common Provisions

Article A

By this Treaty, the High Contracting Parties establish among themselves a European Union, hereinafter called 'The Union'.

This Treaty marks a new stage in the process of creating an ever closer union among the peoples of Europe, in which decisions are taken as closely as possible to the citizen.

The Union shall be founded on the European Communities, supplemented by the policies and forms of cooperation established by this Treaty. Its task shall be to organize, in a manner demonstrating consistency and solidarity, relations between the Member States and between their peoples.

Article B

The Union shall set itself the following objectives:

- to promote economic and social progress which is balanced and sustainable, in particular through the creation of an area without internal frontiers, through the strengthening of economic and social cohesion and through the establishment of economic and monetary union, ultimately including a single currency in accordance with the provisions of this Treaty;

- to assert its identity on the international scene, in particular through the implementation of a common foreign and security policy including the eventual framing of a common defence policy, which might in time lead to a common defence;

- to strengthen the protection of the rights and interests of the nationals of its Member States through the introduction of a citizenship of the Union;

- to develop close cooperation on justice and home affairs;

- to maintain in full the 'acquis communautaire' and build on it with a view to considering, through the procedure referred to in Article N (2), to what extent the policies and forms of cooperation introduced by this Treaty may need to be revised with the aim of ensuring the effectiveness of the mechanisms and the institutions of the Community.

The objectives of the Union shall be achieved as provided in this Treaty and in accordance with the conditions and the timetable set out therein while respecting the principle of subsidiarity as defined in Article 3b of the Treaty establishing the European Community.

---

* *Official Journal of the European Communities*, No C 191, 29.07.1992, p.1.

Article C

The Union shall be served by a single institutional framework which shall ensure the consistency and the continuity of the activities carried out in order to attain its objectives while respecting and building upon the 'acquis communautaire'.

The Union shall in particular ensure the consistency of its external activities as a whole in the context of its external relations, security, economic and development policies. The Council and the Commission shall be responsible for ensuring such consistency. They shall ensure the implementation of these policies, each in accordance with its respective powers.

Article D

The European Council shall provide the Union with the necessary impetus for its development and shall define the general political guidelines thereof.

The European Council shall bring together the Heads of State or of Government of the Member States and the President of the Commission.

They shall be assisted by the Ministers for Foreign Affairs of the Member States and by a Member of the Commission. The European Council shall meet at least twice a year, under the chairmanship of the Head of State or of Government of the Member State which holds the Presidency of the Council.

The European Council shall submit to the European Parliament a report after each of its meetings and a yearly written report on the progress achieved by the Union.

Article E

The European Parliament, the Council, the Commission and the Court of Justice shall exercise their powers under the conditions and for the purposes provided for, on the one hand, by the provisions of the Treaties establishing the European Communities and of the subsequent Treaties and Acts modifying and supplementing them and, on the other hand, by the other provisions of this Treaty.

Article F

1. The Union shall respect the national identities of its Member States, whose systems of government are founded on the principles of democracy.

2. The Union shall respect fundamental rights, as guaranteed by the European Convention for the Protection of Human Rights and Fundamental Freedoms signed in Rome on 4 November 1950 and as they result from the constitutional traditions common to the Member States, as general principles of Community law.

3. The Union shall provide itself with the means necessary to attain its objectives and carry through its policies.

[...]

Title VI

Provisions on cooperation in the fields of justice and home affairs

Article K

Cooperation in the fields of justice and home affairs shall be governed by the following provisions.

Article K.1

For the purposes of achieving the objectives of the Union, in particular the free movement of persons, and without prejudice to the powers of the European Community, Member States shall regard the following areas as matters of common interest:

1. asylum policy

2. rules governing the crossing by persons of the external borders of the Member States and the exercise of controls thereon;

3. immigration policy and policy regarding nationals of third countries;

    (a) conditions of entry and movement by nationals of third countries on the territory of Member States;

    (b) conditions of residence by nationals of third countries on the territory of Member States, including family reunion and access to employment;

    (c) combatting unauthorized immigration, residence and work by nationals of third countries on the territory of Member States;

4. combatting drug addiction in so far as this is not covered by 7 to 9;

5. combatting fraud on an international scale in so far as this is not covered by 7 to 9;

6. judicial cooperation in civil matters;

7. judicial cooperation in criminal matters;

8. customs cooperation;

9. police cooperation for the purposes of preventing and combatting terrorism, unlawful drug trafficking and other serious forms of international crime, including if necessary certain aspects of customs cooperation, in connection with the organization of a Union-wide system for exchanging information within a European Police Office (Europol).

Article K.2

1. The matters referred to in Article K.1 shall be dealt with in compliance with the European Convention for the Protection of Human Rights and Fundamental Freedoms of 4 November 1950 and the Convention relating to the Status of Refugees of 28 July 1951 and having regard to the protection afforded by Member States to persons persecuted on political grounds.

2. This Title shall not affect the exercise of the responsibilities incumbent upon Member States with regard to the maintenance of law and order and the safeguarding of internal security.

Article K.3

1. In the areas referred to in Article K.1, Member States shall inform and consult one another within the Council with a view to co-ordinating their action. To that end, they shall establish collaboration between the relevant departments of their administrations.

2. The Council may:
   - on the initiative of any Member State or of the Commission, in the areas referred to in Article K.1 (1) to (6);

- on the initiative of any Member State, in the areas referred to in Article K1(7) to (9):

    (a) adopt joint positions and promote, using the appropriate form and procedures, any cooperation contributing to the pursuit of the objectives of the Union;

    (b) adopt joint action is so far as the objectives of the Union can be attained better by joint action than by the Member States acting individually on account of the scale or effects of the action envisaged, it may decide that measures implementing joint action are to be adopted by a qualified majority;

    (c) without prejudice to Article 220 of the Treaty establishing the European Community, draw up conventions which it shall recommend to the Member States for adoption in accordance with their respective constitutional requirements.

Unless otherwise provided by such conventions, measures implementing them shall be adopted within the Council by a majority of two-thirds of the High Contracting Parties.

Such conventions may stipulate that the Court of Justice shall have jurisdiction to interpret their provisions and to rule on any disputes regarding their application, in accordance with such arrangements as they may lay down.

Article K.4

1. A Coordinating Committee shall be set up consisting of senior officials. In addition to its coordinating role, it shall be the task of the Committee to:

    - give opinions for the attention of the Council, either at the Council's request or on its own initiative;

    - contribute, without prejudice to Article 151 of the Treaty establishing the European Community, to the preparation of the Council's discussions in the areas referred to in Article K.1 and, in accordance with the conditions laid down in Article 100d of the Treaty establishing the European Community, in the areas referred to in Article 100c of that Treaty.

2. The Commission shall be fully associated with the work in the areas referred to in this Title.

3. The Council shall act unanimously, except on matters of procedure and in cases where Article K.3 expressly provides for other voting rules.

Where the Council is required to act by a qualified majority, the votes of its members shall be weighted as laid down in Article 148(2) of the Treaty establishing the European Community, and for their adoption, acts of the Council shall require at least fifty-four votes in favour, cast by at least eight members.

Article K.5

Within international organizations and at international conferences in which they take part, Member States shall defend the common positions adopted under the provisions of this Title.

Article K.6

The Presidency and the Commission shall regularly inform the European Parliament of discussions in the areas covered by this Title. The Presidency shall consult the European Parliament on the principal aspects of activities in the areas referred to in this Title and shall ensure that the views of the European Parliament are duly taken into consideration. The

European Parliament may ask questions of the Council or make recommendations to it. Each year, it shall hold a debate on the progress made in implementation of the areas referred to in this Title.

Article K.7

The provisions of this Title shall not prevent the establishment or development of closer cooperation between two or more Member States in so far as such cooperation does not conflict with, or impede, that provided for in this Title.

Article K.8

1. The provisions referred to in Articles 137, 138, 139 to 142, 146, 147, 150 to 153, 157 to 163 and 217 to the Treaty establishing the European Community shall apply to the provisions relating to the areas referred to in this Title.

2. Administrative expenditure which the provisions relating to the areas referred to in this Title entail for the institutions shall be charged to the budget of the European Communities.

The Council may also:
- either decide unanimously that operational expenditure to which the implementation of those provisions gives rise is to be charged to the budget of the European Communities; in that event, the budgetary procedure laid down in the Treaty establishing the European Community shall be applicable;
- or determine that such expenditure shall be charged to the Member States, where appropriate in accordance with a scale to be decided.

Article K.9

The Council, acting unanimously on the initiative of the Commission or a Member State, may decide to apply Article 100c of the Treaty establishing the European Community to action in areas referred to in Article K.1(1) to (6), and at the same time determine the relevant voting conditions relating to it. It shall recommend the Member States to adopt that decision in accordance with their respective constitutional requirements.

Title VII

Final provisions

Article L

The provisions of the Treaty establishing the European Community, the Treaty establishing the European Coal and Steel Community and the Treaty establishing the European Atomic Energy Community concerning the powers of the Court of Justice of the European Communities and the exercise of those powers shall apply only to the following provisions of this Treaty:

(a) provisions amending the Testablishing the European Economic Community with a view to establishing the European Community, the Treaty establishing the European Coal and Steel Community and the Treaty establishing the European Atomic Energy Community;

(b) the third subparagraph of Article K.3(2)(c);

(c) Articles L to S.

Article M

Subject to the provisions amending the Treaty establishing the European Economic Community with a view to establishing the European Community, the Treaty establishing the European Coal and Steel Community and the Treaty establishing the European Atomic Community, and to these final provisions, nothing in this Treaty shall affect the Treaties establishing the European Communities or the subsequent Treaties and Acts modifying or supplementing them.

Article N

1. The government of any Member State or the Commission may submit to the Council proposals for the amendment of the Treaties on which the Union is founded.

If the Council, after consulting the European Parliament and, where appropriate, the Commission, delivers an opinion in favour of calling a conference of representatives of the governments of the Member States, the conference shall be convened by the President of the Council for the purpose of determining by common accord the amendments to be made to those Treaties. The European Central Bank shall also be consulted in the case of institutional changes in the monetary area.

The amendments shall enter into force after being ratified by all the Member States in accordance with their respective constitutional requirements.

2. A conference of representatives of the governments of the Member States shall be convened in 1996 to examine those provisions of this Treaty for which revision is provided, in accordance with the objectives set out in Articles A and B.

Article O

Any European State may apply to become a Member of the Union. It shall address its application to the Council, which shall act unanimously after consulting the Commission and after receiving the assent of the European Parliament, which shall act by an absolute majority of its component members.

The conditions of admission and the adjustments to the Treaties on which the Union is founded which such admission entails shall be the subject of an agreement between the Member States and the applicant State. This agreement shall be submitted for ratification by all the Contracting States in accordance with their respective constitutional requirements.

Article P

1. Articles 2 to 7 and 10 to 19 of the Treaty establishing a single Council and a single Commission of the European Communities, signed in Brussels on 8 April 1965, are hereby repealed.

2. Article 2, Article 3(2) and Title III of the Single European Act signed in Luxembourg on 17 February 1986 and in The Hague on 28 February 1986 are hereby repealed.

Article Q

This Treaty in concluded for an unlimited period.

Article R

1. This Treaty shall be ratified by the High Contracting Parties in accordance with their respective constitutional requirements. The instruments of ratification shall be deposited with the government of the Italian Republic.

2. This Treaty shall enter into force on 1 January 1993, provided that all the instruments of ratification have been deposited, or, failing that, on the first day of the month following the deposit of the instrument of ratification by the last signatory State to take this step.

Article S

This Treaty, drawn up in a single original in the Danish, Dutch, English, French, German, Greek, Irish, Italian, Portuguese and Spanish languages, the texts in each of these languages being equally authentic, shall be deposited in the archives of the government of the Italian Republic, which will transmit a certified copy to each of the governments of the other signatory States.

In witness whereof, the undersigned Plenipotentiaries have signed this Treaty.

[...]

DECLARATION OF ASYLUM

1. The Conference agrees that, in the context of the proceedings provided for in Articles K.1 and K.3 of the provisions on cooperation in the fields of justice and home affairs, the Council will consider as a matter of priority questions concerning Member States' asylum policies, with the aim of adopting, by the beginning of 1993, common action to harmonize aspects of them, in the light of the work programme and timetable contained in the report on asylum drawn up at the request of the European Council meeting in Luxembourg on 28 and 29 June 1991.

2. In this connection, the Council will also consider, by the end of 1993, on the basis of a report, the possibility of applying Article K.9 to such matters.

DECLARATION ON POLICE COOPERATION

The Conference confirms the agreement of the Member States on the objectives underlying the German delegation's proposals at the European Council meeting in Luxembourg on 28 and 29 June 1991.

For the present, the Member States agree to examine as a matter of priority the drafts submitted to them, on the basis of the work programme and timetable agreed upon in the report drawn up at the request of the Luxembourg European Council, and they are willing to envisage the adoption of practical measures in areas such as those suggested by the German delegation, relating to the following functions in the exchange of information and experience:

- support for national criminal investigation and security authorities, in particular in the coordination of investigations and search operations;

- Creation of data bases;

- central analysis and assessment of information in order to take stock of the situation and identify investigative approaches;

- collection and analyses of national prevention programmes for forwarding to Member States and for drawing up Europe-wide prevention strategies;

- measures relating to further training, research, forensic matters and criminal records departments.

Member States agree to consider on the basis of a report, during 1994 at the latest, whether the scope of such cooperation should be extended.

[...]

8. GENERAL HUMAN RIGHTS INSTRUMENTS AND INTERNATIONAL CRIMINAL LAW

8.1. United Nations

International Covenant on Civil and Political Rights (1966)[*]

New York, 16 December 1966

Part I

Article 1

1. All peoples have the right of self-determination. By virtue of that right they freely determine their political status and freely pursue their economic, social and cultural development.

2. All peoples may, for their own ends, freely dispose of their natural wealth and resources without prejudice to any obligations arising out of international economic co-operation, based upon the principle of mutual benefit, and international law. In no case may a people be deprived of its own means of subsistence.

3. The States Parties to the present Covenant, including those having responsibility for the administration of Non-Self-Governing and Trust Territories, shall promote the realization of the right of self-determination, and shall respect that right, in conformity with the provisions of the Charter of the United Nations.

Part II

Article 2

1. Each State Party to the present Covenant undertakes to respect and to ensure to all individuals within its territory and subject to its jurisdiction the rights recognized in the present Covenant, without distinction of any kind, such as race, colour, sex, language, religion, political or other opinion, national or social origin, property, birth or other status.

2. Where not already provided for by existing legislative or other measures, each State Party to the present Covenant undertakes to take the necessary steps, in accordance with its constitutional processes and with the provisions of the present Covenant, to adopt such legislative or other measures as may be necessary to give effect to the rights recognized in the present Covenant.

3. Each State Party to the present Covenant undertakes:

   (a) To ensure that any person whose rights or freedoms as herein recognized are violated shall have an effective remedy, notwithstanding that the violation has been committed by persons acting in an official capacity;

   (b) To ensure that any person claiming such a remedy shall have his right thereto determined by competent judicial, administrative or legislative authorities, or by any other competent authority provided for by the legal system of the State, and to develop the possibilities of judicial remedy;

   (c) To ensure that the competent authorities shall enforce such remedies when granted.

Article 3

The States Parties to the present Covenant undertake to ensure the equal right of men and women to the enjoyment of all civil and political rights set forth in the present Covenant.

---

[*] *International Legal Materials*, 1967, 368.

Article 4

1. In time of public emergency which threatens the life of the nation and the existence of which is officially proclaimed, the States Parties to the present Covenant may take measures derogating from their obligations under the present Covenant to the extent strictly required by the exigencies of the situation, provided that such measures are not inconsistent with their other obligations under international law and do not involve discrimination solely on the ground of race, colour, sex, language, religion or social origin.

2. No derogation from articles 6, 7, 8 (paragraphs 1 and 2), 11, 15, 16 and 18 may be made under this provision.

3. Any State Party to the present Covenant availing itself of the right of derogation shall immediately inform the other States Parties to the present Covenant, through the intermediary of the Secretary-General of the United Nations, of the provisions from which it has derogated and of the reasons, by which it was actuated. A further communication shall be made, through the same intermediary, on the date on which it terminates such derogation.

Article 5

1. Nothing in the present Covenant may be interpreted as implying for any State, group or person any right to engage in any activity or perform any act aimed at the destruction of any of the rights and freedoms recognized herein or at their limitation to a greater extent than is provided for in the present Covenant.

2. There shall be no restriction upon or derogation from any of the fundamental human rights recognized or existing in any State Party to the present Covenant pursuant to law, conventions, regulations or custom on the pretext that the present Covenant does not recognize such rights or that it recognizes them to a lesser extent.

Part III

Article 6

1. Every human being has the inherent right to life. This right shall be protected by law. No one shall be arbitrarily deprived of his life.

2. In countries which have not abolished the death penalty, sentence of death may be imposed only for the most serious crimes in accordance with the law in force at the time of the commission of the crime and not contrary to the provisions of the present Covenant and to the Convention on the Prevention and Punishment of the crime of Genocide. This penalty can only be carried out pursuant to a final judgement rendered by a competent court.

3. When deprivation of life constitutes the crime of genocide, it is understood that nothing in this article shall authorize any State Party to the present Covenant to derogate in any way from any obligation assumed under the provisions of the Convention on the Prevention and Punishment of the Crime of Genocide.

4. Anyone sentenced to death shall have the right to seek pardon or commutation of the sentence. Amnesty, pardon or commutation of the sentence of death may be granted in all cases.

5. Sentence of death shall not be imposed for crimes committed by persons below eighteen years of age and shall not be carried out on pregnant women.

6. Nothing in this article shall be invoked to delay or to prevent the abolition of capital punishment by any State Party to the present Covenant.

Article 7

No one shall be subjected to torture or to cruel, inhuman or degrading treatment or punishment. In particular, no one shall be subjected without his free consent to medical or scientific experimentation.

Article 8

1. No one shall be held in slavery; slavery and the slave-trade in all their forms shall be prohibited.

2. No one shall be held in servitude.

3. (a) No one shall be required to perform forced or compulsory labour;

    (b) Paragraph 3 (a) shall not be held to preclude, in countries where imprisonment with hard labour may be imposed as a punishment for a crime, the performance of hard labour in pursuance of a sentence to such punishment by a competent court;

    (c) For the purpose of this paragraph the term (forced or compulsory labour' shall not include:

    (i) Any work or service, not referred to in sub-paragraph (b), normally required of a person who is under detention in consequence of a lawful order of a court, or of a person during conditional release from such detention;
    (ii) Any service of a military character and, in countries where conscientious objection is recognized, any national service required by law of conscientious objectors;
    (iii) Any service exacted in cases of emergency or calamity threatening the life or well-being of the community;
    (iv) Any work or service which forms part of normal civil obligations.

Article 9

1. Everyone has the right to liberty and security of person. No one shall be subjected to arbitrary arrest or detention. No one shall be deprived of his liberty except on such grounds and in accordance with such procedure as are established by law.

2. Anyone who is arrested shall be informed, at the time of arrest, of the reasons for his arrest and shall be promptly informed of any charges against him.

3. Anyone arrested or detained on a criminal charge shall be brought promptly before a judge or other officer authorized by law to exercise judicial power and shall be entitled to trial within a reasonable time or to release. It shall not be the general rule that persons awaiting trial shall be detained in custody, but release may be subject to guarantees to appear for trial, at any other stage of the judicial proceedings, and, should occasion arise, for execution of the judgment.

4. Anyone who is deprived of his liberty by arrest or detention shall be entitled to take proceedings before a court, in order that that court may decide without delay on the lawfulness of his detention and order his release if the detention is not lawful.

5. Anyone who has been the victim of unlawful arrest or detention shall have an enforceable right to compensation.

Article 10

1. All persons deprived of their liberty shall be treated with humanity and with respect for the inherent dignity of the human person.

2. (a) Accused persons shall, save in exceptional circumstances, be segregated from convicted persons and shall be subject to separate treatment appropriate to their status as unconvicted persons;

   (b) Accused juvenile persons shall be separated from adults and brought as speedily as possible for adjudication.

3. The penitentiary system shall comprise treatment of prisoners the essential aim of which shall be their reformation and social rehabilitation. Juvenile offenders shall be segregated from adults and be accorded treatment appropriate to their age and legal status.

Article 11

No one shall be imprisoned merely on the ground of inability to fulfil a contractual obligation.

Article 12

1. Everyone lawfully within the territory of a State shall, within that territory, have the right to liberty of movement and freedom to choose his residence.

2. Everyone shall be free to leave any country, including his own.

3. The above-mentioned rights shall not be subject to any restrictions except those which are provided by law, are necessary to protect national security, public order (ordre public), public health or morals or the rights and freedoms of others, and are consistent with the other rights recognized in the present Covenant.

4. No one shall be arbitrarily deprived of the right to enter his own country.

Article 13

An alien lawfully in the territory of a State Party to the present Covenant may be expelled therefrom only in pursuance of a decision reached in accordance with law and shall, except where compelling reasons of national security otherwise require, be allowed to submit the reasons against his expulsion and to have his case reviewed by, and be represented for the purpose before, the competent authority or a person or persons especially designated by the competent authority.

Article 14

1. All persons shall be equal before the courts and tribunals. In the determination of any criminal charge against him, or of his rights and obligations in a suit at law, everyone shall be entitled to a fair and public hearing by a competent, independent and impartial tribunal established by law. The Press and the public may be excluded from all or part of a trial for reasons of morals, public order (ordre public) or national security in a democratic society, or when the interest of the private lives of the parties so requires, or to the extent strictly necessary in the opinion of the court in special circumstances where publicity would prejudice the interests of justice; but any judgment rendered in a criminal case or in a suit of law shall be made public except where the interest of juvenile persons otherwise requires or the proceedings concern matrimonial disputes or the guardianship of children.

2. Everyone charged with a criminal offence shall have the right to be presumed innocent until proved guilty according to law.

3. In the determination of any criminal charge against him, everyone shall be entitled to the following minimum guarantees, in full equality:

(a) To be informed promptly and in detail in a language which he understands of the nature and cause of the charge against him;

(b) To have adequate time and facilities for the preparation of his defence and to communicate with counsel of his own choosing;

(c) To be tried without undue delay;

(d) To be tried in his presence, and to defend himself in person or through legal assistance of his own choosing; to be informed, if he does not have legal assistance, of this right; and to have legal assistance assigned to him, in any case where the interests of justice so require, and without payment by him in any such case if he does not have sufficient means to pay for it;

(e) To examine, or have examined, the witnesses against him and to obtain the attendance and examination of witnesses on his behalf under the same conditions as witnesses against him;

(f) To have the free assistance of an interpreter if he cannot understand or speak the language used in court;

(g) Not to be compelled to testify against himself or to confess guilt.

4. In the case of juvenile persons, the procedure shall be such as will take account of their age and the desirability of promoting their rehabilitation.

5. Everyone convicted of a crime shall have the right to his conviction and sentence being reviewed by a higher tribunal according to law.

6. When a person has by a final decision been convicted of a criminal offence and when subsequently his conviction has been reversed or he has been pardoned on the ground that a new or newly discovered fact shows conclusively that there has been a miscarriage of justice, the person who has suffered punishment as a result of such conviction shall be compensated according to law, unless it is proved that the non-disclosure of the unknown fact in time is wholly or partly attributable to him.

7. No one shall be liable to be tried or punished again for an offence for which he has already been finally convicted or acquitted in accordance with the law and penal procedure of each country.

Article 15

1. No one shall be held guilty of any criminal offence on account of any act or omission which did not constitute a criminal offence, under national or international law, at the time when it was committed. Nor shall a heavier penalty be imposed than the one that was applicable at the time when the criminal offence was committed. If, subsequent to the commission of the offence, provision is made by law for the imposition of a lighter penalty, the offender shall benefit thereby.

2. Nothing in this article shall prejudice the trial and punishment of any person for any act or omission which, at the time when it was committed, was criminal according to the general principles of law recognized by the community of nations.

Article 16

Everyone shall have the right to recognition everywhere as a person before the law.

Article 17

1. No one shall be subjected to arbitrary or unlawful interference, with his privacy, family, home or correspondence, nor to unlawful attacks on his honour and reputation.

2. Everyone has the right to the protection of the law against such interference or attacks.

Article 18

1. Everyone shall have the right to freedom of thought, conscience and religion. This right shall include freedom to have or to adopt a religion or belief of his choice, and freedom, either individually or in community with others and in public or private, to manifest his religion or belief in worship, observance, practice and teaching.

2. No one shall be subject to coercion which would impair his freedom to have or to adopt a religion or belief of his choice.

3. Freedom to manifest one's religion or beliefs may be subject only to such limitations as are prescribed by law and are necessary to protect public safety, order, health, or morals or the fundamental rights and freedoms of others.

4. The States Parties to the present Covenant undertake to have respect for the liberty of parents and, when applicable, legal guardians to ensure the religious and moral education of their children in conformity with their own convictions.

Article 19

1. Everyone shall have the right to hold opinions without interference.

2. Everyone shall have the right to freedom of expression; this right shall include freedom to seek, receive and impart information and ideas of all kinds, regardless of frontiers, either orally, in writing or in print, in the form of art, or through any other media of his choice.

3. The exercise of the rights provided for in paragraph 2 of this article carries with it special duties and responsibilities. It may therefore be subject to certain restrictions, but these shall only be such as are provided by law and are necessary:

   (a) For respect of the rights or reputations of others;

   (b) For the protection of national security or of public order (ordre public), or of public health or morals.

Article 20

1. Any propaganda for war shall be prohibited by law.

2. Any advocacy of national, racial or religious hatred that constitutes incitement to discrimination, hostility or violence shall be prohibited by law.

Article 21

The right of peaceful assembly shall be recognized. No restrictions may be placed on the exercise of this right other than those imposed in conformity with the law and which are necessary in a democratic society in the interests of national security or public safety, public order (ordre public), the protection of public health or morals or the protection of the rights and freedoms of others.

Article 22

1. Everyone shall have the right to freedom of association with others, including the right to form and join trade unions for the protection of his interests.

2. No restrictions may be placed on the exercise of this right other than those which are prescribed by law and which are necessary in a democratic society in the interests of national security or public safety, public order (ordre public), the protection of public health or morals or the protection of the rights and freedoms of others. This article shall not prevent the

imposition of lawful restrictions on members of the armed forces and of the police in their exercise of this right.

3. Nothing in this article shall authorize States Parties to the International Labour Organization Convention of 1948 concerning Freedom of Association and Protection of the Right to Organize to take legislative measures which would prejudice, or to apply the law in such a manner as to prejudice, the guarantees provided for in that Convention.

Article 23

1. The family is the natural and fundamental group unit of society and is entitled to protection by society and the State.

2. The right of men and women of marriageable age to marry and to found a family shall be recognized.

3. No marriage shall be entered into without the free and full consent of the intending spouses.

4. States Parties to the present Covenant shall take appropriate steps to ensure equality of rights and responsibilities of spouses as to marriage, during marriage and at its dissolution. In the case of dissolution, provision shall be made for the necessary protection of any children.

Article 24

1. Every child shall have, without any discrimination as to race, colour, sex, language, religion, national or social origin, property or birth, the right to such measures of protection as are required by his status as a minor, on the part of his family, society and the State.

2. Every child shall be registered immediately after birth and shall have a name.

3. Every child has the right to acquire a nationality.

Article 25

Every citizen shall have the right and the opportunity, without any of the distinctions mentioned in article 2 and without unreasonable restrictions:

(a) To take part in the conduct of public affairs, directly or through freely chosen representatives;

(b) To vote and to be elected at genuine periodic elections which shall be by universal and equal suffrage and shall be held by secret ballot, guaranteeing the free expression of the will of the electors;

(c) To have access, on general terms of equality, to public service in his country.

Article 26

All persons are equal before the law and are entitled without any discrimination to the equal protection of the law. In this respect, the law shall prohibit any discrimination and guarantee to all persons equal and effective protection against discrimination on any ground such as race, colour, sex, language, religion, political or other opinion, national or social origin, property, birth or other status.

Article 27

In those States in which ethnic, religious or linguistic minorities exist, persons belonging to such minorities shall not be denied the right, in community with the other members of their group, to enjoy their own culture, to profess and practise their own religion, or to use their own language.

Part IV

Article 28

1. There shall be established a Human Rights Committee (hereafter referred to in the present Covenant as the Committee). It shall consist of eighteen members and shall carry out the functions hereinafter provided.

2. The Committee shall be composed of nationals of the States Parties to the present Covenant who shall be persons of high moral character and recognized competence in the field of human rights, consideration being given to the usefulness of the participation of some persons having legal experience.

3. The members of the Committee shall be elected and shall serve in their personal capacity.

Article 29

1. The members of the Committee shall be elected by secret ballot from a list of persons possessing the qualifications prescribed in article 28 and nominated for the purpose by the States Parties to the present Covenant.

2. Each State Party to the present Covenant may nominate not more than two persons. These persons shall be nationals of the nominating State.

3. A person shall be eligible for renomination.

Article 30

1. The initial election shall be held no later than six months after the date of the entry into force of the present Covenant.

2. At least four months before the date of each election to the Committee, other than an election to fill a vacancy declared in accordance with article 34, the Secretary-General of the United Nations shall address a written invitation to the States Parties to the present Covenant to submit their nominations for membership of the Committee within three months.

3. The Secretary-General of the United Nations shall prepare a list in alphabetical order of all the persons thus nominated, with an indication of the States Parties which have nominated them, and shall submit it to the States Parties to the present Covenant no later than one month before the date of each election.

4. Elections of the members of the Committee shall be held at a meeting of the States Parties to the present Covenant convened by the Secretary-General of the United Nations at the Headquarters of the United Nations. At that meeting, for which two thirds of the States Parties to the present Covenant shall constitute a quorum, the persons elected to the Committee shall be those nominees who obtain the largest number of votes and an absolute majority of the votes of the representatives of States Parties present and voting.

Article 31

1. The Committee may not include more than one national of the same State.

2. In the election of the Committee, consideration shall be given to equitable geographical distribution of membership and to the representation of the different forms of civilization and of the principal legal systems.

Article 32

1. The members of the Committees shall be elected for a term of four years. They shall be eligible for re-election if renominated. However, the terms of nine of the members elected at the first election shall expire at the end of two years; immediately after the first election,

the names of these nine members shall be chosen by lot by the Chairman of the meeting referred to in article 30, paragraph 4.

2. Elections at the expiry of office shall be held in accordance with the preceding articles of this part of the present Covenant.

Article 33

1. If, in the unanimous opinion of the other members, a member of the Committee has ceased to carry out his functions for any cause other than absence of a temporary character, the Chairman of the Committee shall notify the Secretary-General of the United Nations, who shall then declare the seat of that member to be vacant.

2. In the event of the death or the resignation of a member of the Committee, the Chairman shall immediately notify the Secretary-General of the United Nations, who shall declare the seat vacant from the date of death or the date on which the resignation takes effect.

Article 34

1. When a vacancy is declared in accordance with article 33 and if the term of office of the member to be replaced does not expire within six months of the declaration of the vacancy, the Secretary-General of the United Nations shall notify each of the States Parties to the present Covenant, which may within two months submit nominations in accordance with article 29 for the purpose of filling the vacancy.

2. The Secretary-General of the United Nations shall prepare a list in alphabetical order of the persons thus nominated and shall submit it to the States Parties to the present Covenant. The election to fill the vacancy shall then take place in accordance with the relevant provisions of this part of the present Covenant.

3. A member of the Committee elected to fill a vacancy declared in accordance with article 33 shall hold office for the remainder of the term of the member who vacated the seat on the Committee under the provisions of that article.

Article 35

The members of the Committee shall, with the approval of the General Assembly of the United Nations, receive emoluments from United Nations resources on such terms and conditions as the General Assembly may decide, having regard to the importance of the Committee's responsibilities.

Article 36

The Secretary-General of the United Nations shall provide the necessary staff and facilities for the effective performance of the functions of the Committee under the present Covenant.

Article 37

1. The Secretary-General of the United Nations shall convene the initial meeting of the Committee at the Headquarters of the United Nations.

2. After its initial meeting, the Committee shall meet at such times as shall be provided in its rules of procedure.

3. The Committee shall normally meet at the Headquarters of the United Nations or at the United Nations Office at Geneva.

Article 38

Every member of the Committee shall, before taking up his duties, make a solemn declaration in open committee that he will perform his functions impartially and conscientiously.

Article 39

1. The Committee shall elect its officers for a term of two years. They may be re-elected.

2. The Committee shall establish its own rules of procedure, but these rules shall provide, inter alia, that:

(a) Twelve members shall constitute a quorum;

(b) Decisions of the Committee shall be made by a majority vote of the members present.

Article 40

1. The States Parties to the present Covenant undertake to submit reports on the measures they have adopted which give effect to the rights recognized herein and on the progress made in the enjoyment of those rights:

(a) Within one year of the entry into force of the present Covenant for the States Parties concerned;

(b) Thereafter whenever the Committee so requests.

2. All reports shall be submitted to the Secretary-General of the United Nations, who shall transmit them to the Committee for consideration. Reports shall indicate the factors and difficulties, if any, affecting the implementation of the present Covenant.

3. The Secretary-General of the United Nations may, after consultation with the Committee, transmit to the specialized agencies concerned copies of such parts of the report as may fall within their field of competence.

4. The Committee shall study the reports submitted by the States Parties to the present Covenant. It shall transmit its reports, and such general comments as it may consider appropriate, to the States Parties. The Committee may also transmit to the Economic Social Council these comments along with the copies of the reports it has received from States Parties to the present Covenant.

5. The States Parties to the present Covenant may submit to the Committee observations on any comments that may be made in accordance with paragraph 4 of this article.

Article 41

1. A State Party to the present Covenant may at any time declare under this article that it recognizes the competence of the Committee to receive and consider communications to the effect that a State Party claims that another State Party is not fulfilling its obligations under the present Covenant. Communications under this article may be received and considered only if submitted by a State Party which has made a declaration recognizing in regard to itself the competence of the Committee. No communication shall be received by the Committee if it concerns a State Party which has not made such a declaration. Communications received under this article shall be dealt with in accordance with the following procedure:

(a) If a State Party to the present Covenant considers that another State Party is not giving effect to the provisions of the present Covenant, it may, by written communication, bring the matter to the attention of that State Party. Within three months after the receipt of the communication, the receiving State shall afford the State which sent the communication an explanation or any other statement in writing clarifying the matter, which should include, to the extent possible and pertinent, reference to domestic procedures and remedies taken, pending, or available in the matter.

(b) If the matter is not adjusted to the satisfaction of both States Parties concerned within six months after the receipt by the receiving State of the initial communication, either State shall have the right to refer the matter to the Committee, by notice given to the Committee and to the other State.

(c) The Committee shall deal with a matter referred to it only after it has ascertained that all available domestic remedies have been invoked and exhausted in the matter, in conformity with the generally recognized principles of international law. This shall not be the rule where the application of the remedies is unreasonably prolonged.

(d) The Committee shall hold closed meetings when examining communications under this article.

(e) Subject to the provisions of sub-paragraph (c), the Committee shall make available its good offices to the States Parties concerned with a view to a friendly solution of the matter on the basis of respect for human rights and fundamental freedoms as recognized in the present Covenant.

(f) In any matter referred to it, the Committee may call upon the States Parties concerned, referred to in sub-paragraph (b), to supply any relevant information.

(g) The States Parties concerned, referred to in sub-paragraph (b), shall have the right to be represented when the matter is being considered in the Committee and to make submissions orally and/or in writing.

(h) The Committee shall, within twelve months after the date of receipt of notice under sub-paragraph (b), submit a report:

(i) If a solution within the terms of sub-paragraph (e) is reached, the Committee shall confine its report to a brief statement of the facts and of the solution reached;

(ii) If a solution within the terms of sub-paragraph (e) is not reached, the Committee shall confine its report to a brief statement of the facts; the written submissions and record of the oral submissions made by the States Parties concerned shall be attached to the report.

In every matter, the report shall be communicated to the States Parties concerned.

2. The provisions of this article shall come into force when ten States Parties to the present Covenant have made declarations under paragraph 1 of this article. Such declarations shall be deposited by the States Parties with the Secretary-General of the United Nations, who shall transmit copies thereof to the other States Parties. A declaration may be withdrawn at any time by notification to the Secretary-General. Such a withdrawal shall not prejudice the consideration of any matter which is the subject of a communication already transmitted under this article; no further communication by any State Party shall be received after the notification of withdrawal of the declaration has been received by the Secretary-General unless the State Party concerned has made a new declaration.

Article 42

1. (a) If a matter referred to the Committee in accordance with article 41 is not resolved to the satisfaction of the States Parties concerned, the Committee may, with the prior consent of the States Parties concerned, appoint an ad hoc Conciliation Commission (hereinafter referred to as the Commission). The good offices of the Commission shall be made available to the States Parties concerned with a

view to an amicable solution of the matter on the basis of respect for the present Covenant;

(b) The Commission shall consist of five persons acceptable to the States Parties concerned. If the States Parties concerned fail to reach agreement within three months on all or part of the composition of the Commission, the members of the Commission concerning whom no agreement has been reached shall be elected by secret ballot by a two-thirds majority vote of the Committee from among its members.

2. The members of the Commission shall serve in their personal capacity. They shall not be nationals of the States Parties concerned, or of a State not party to the present Covenant, or of a State Party which has not made a declaration under article 41.

3. The Commission shall elect its own Chairman and adopt its own rules of procedure.

4. The meetings of the Commission shall normally be held at the Headquarters of the United Nations or at the United Nations Office at Geneva. However, they may be held at such other convenient places as the Commission may determine in consultation with the Secretary-General of the United Nations and the States Parties concerned.

5. The secretariat provided in accordance with article 36 shall also service the commissions appointed under this article.

6. The information received and collated by the Committee shall be made available to the Commission and the Commission may call upon the States Parties concerned to supply any other relevant information.

7. When the Commission has fully considered the matter, but in any event not later than twelve months after having been seized of the matter, it shall submit to the Chairman of the Committee a report for communication to the States Parties concerned:

(a) If the Commission is unable to complete its consideration of the matter within twelve months, it shall confine its report to a brief statement of the status of its consideration of the matter;

(b) If an amicable solution to the matter on the basis of respect for human rights as recognized in the present Covenant is reached, the Commission shall confine its report to a brief statement of the facts and of the solution reached;

(c) If a solution within the terms of sub-paragraph (b) is not reached, the Commission's report shall embody its findings on all questions of fact relevant to the issues between the States Parties concerned, and its views on the possibilities of an amicable solution of the matter. This report shall also contain the written submissions and a record of the oral submissions made by the States Parties concerned;

(d) If the Commission's report is submitted under sub-paragraph (c), the States Parties concerned shall, within three months of the receipt of the report, notify the Chairman of the Committee whether or not they accept the contents of the report of the Commission.

8. The provisions of this article are without prejudice to the responsibilities of the Committee under article 41.

9. The States Parties concerned shall share equally all the expenses of the members of the Commission in accordance with estimates to be provided by the Secretary-General of the United Nations.

10. The Secretary-General of the United Nations shall be empowered to pay the expenses of the members of the Commission, if necessary, before reimbursement by the States Parties concerned, in accordance with paragraph 9 of this article.

Article 43

The members of the Committee, and of the ad hoc conciliation commissions which may be appointed under article 42, shall be entitled to the facilities, privileges and immunities of experts on mission for the United Nations as laid down in the relevant sections of the Convention on the Privileges and Immunities of the United Nations.

Article 44

The provisions for the implementation of the present Covenant shall apply without prejudice to the procedures prescribed in the field of human rights by or under the constituent instruments and the conventions of the United Nations and of the specialized agencies and shall not prevent the States Parties to the present Covenant from having resource to other procedures for settling a dispute in accordance with general or special international agreements in force between them.

Article 45

The Committee shall submit to the General Assembly of the United Nations, through the Economic and Social Council, an annual report on its activities.

Part V

Article 46

Nothing in the present Covenant shall be interpreted as impairing the provisions of the Charter of the United Nations and of the constitutions of the specialized agencies which define the respective responsibilities of the various organs of the United Nations and of the specialized agencies in regard to the matters dealt within the present Covenant.

Article 47

Nothing in the present Covenant shall be interpreted as impairing the inherent right of all peoples to enjoy and utilize fully and freely their natural wealth and resources.

Part VI

Article 48

1. The present Covenant is open for signature by any State Member of the United Nations or member of any of its specialized agencies, by any State Party to the Statute of the International Court of Justice, and by any other State which has been invited by the General Assembly of the United Nations to become a party to the present Covenant.

2. The present Covenant is subject to ratification. Instruments of ratification shall be deposited with the Secretary-General of the United Nations.

3. The present Covenant shall be open to accession by any State referred to in paragraph 1 of this article.

4. Accession shall be effected by the deposit of an instrument of accession with the Secretary-General of the United Nations.

5. The Secretary-General of the United Nations shall inform all States which have signed this Covenant or acceded to it of the deposit of each instrument of ratification or accession.

Article 49

1. The present Covenant shall enter into force three months after the date of the deposit with the Secretary-General of the United Nations of the thirty-fifth instrument of ratification or instrument of accession.

2. For each State ratifying the present Covenant or acceding to it after the deposit of the thirty-fifth instrument of ratification or instrument of accession, the present Covenant shall enter into force three months after the date of the deposit of its own instrument of ratification or instrument of accession.

Article 50

The provisions of the present Covenant shall extend to all parts of federal States without any limitations or exceptions.

Article 51

1. Any State Party to the present Covenant may propose an amendment and file it with the Secretary-General of the United Nations. The Secretary-General of the United Nations shall thereupon communicate any proposed amendments to the States Parties to the present Covenant with a request that they notify him whether they favour a conference of States Parties for the purpose of considering and voting upon the proposals. In the event that at least one third of the States Parties favours such a conference, the Secretary-General shall convene the conference under the auspices of the United Nations. Any amendment adopted by a majority of the States Parties present and voting at the conference shall be submitted to the General Assembly of the United Nations for approval.

2. Amendments shall come into force when they have been approved by the General Assembly of the United Nations and accepted by a two-thirds majority of the States Parties to the present Covenant in accordance with their respective constitutional processes.

3. When amendments come into force, they shall be binding on those State Parties which have accepted them, other States Parties still being bound by the provisions of the present Covenant and any earlier amendment which they have accepted.

Article 52

Irrespective of the notifications made under article 48, paragraph 5, the Secretary-General of the United Nations shall inform all States referred to in paragraph 1 of the same article of the following particulars:

  (a) Signatures, ratifications and accessions under article 48;

  (b) The date of the entry into force of the present Covenant under article 49 and the date of the entry into force of any amendments under article 51.

Article 53

1. The present Covenant, of which the Chinese, English, French, Russian and Spanish texts are equally authentic, shall be deposited in the archives of the United Nations.

2. The Secretary-General of the United Nations shall transmit certified copies of the present Covenant to all States referred to in article 48.

Second Optional Protocol to the International Covenant on Civil and Political Rights, aiming at the Abolition of the Death Penalty (1989)[*]

Adopted and proclaimed by General Assembly resolution 44/128 of 15 December 1989

Article 1

1. No one within the jurisdiction of a State Party to the present Protocol shall be executed.

2. Each State Party shall take all necessary measures to abolish the death penalty within its jurisdiction.

Article 2

1. No reservation is admissible to the present Protocol, except for a reservation made at the time of ratification or accession that provides for the application of the death penalty in time of war pursuant to a conviction for a most serious crime of a military nature committed during wartime.

2. The State Party making such reservation shall at the time of ratification or accession communicate to the Secretary-General of the United Nations the relevant provisions of its national legislation applicable during wartime.

3. The State Party having made such a reservation shall notify the Secretary-General of the United Nations of any beginning or ending of a state of war applicable to its territory.

Article 3

The States Parties to the present Protocol shall include in the reports they submit to the Human Rights Committee, in accordance with article 40 of the Covenant, information on the measures that they have adopted to give effect to the present Protocol.

Article 4

With respect to the States Parties to the Covenant that have made a declaration under article 41, the competence of the Human Rights Committee to receive and consider communications when a State Party claims that another State Party is not fulfilling its obligations shall extend to the provisions of the present Protocol, unless the State Party concerned has made a statement to the contrary at the moment of ratification or accession.

Article 5

With respect to the States Parties to the first Optional Protocol to the International Covenant on Civil and Political Rights adopted on 16 December 1966, the competence of the Human Rights Committee to receive and consider communications from individuals subject to its jurisdiction shall extend to the provisions of the present Protocol, unless the State Party concerned has made a statement to the contrary at the moment of ratification or accession.

Article 5

1. The provisions of the present Protocol shall apply as additional provisions to the Covenant.

---

[*] *International Legal Materials*, 1990, 1464.

2. Without prejudice to the possibility of a reservation under article 2 of the present Protocol, the right guaranteed in article 1, paragraph 1, of the present Protocol shall not be subject to any derogation under article 4 of the Covenant.

Article 7

1. The present Protocol is open for signature by any State that has signed the Covenant.

2. The present Protocol is subject to ratification by any State that has ratified the Covenant or acceded to it. Instruments of ratification shall be deposited with the Secretary-General of the United Nations.

3. The present Protocol shall be open to accession by any State that has ratified the Covenant or acceded to it.

4. Accession shall be effected by the deposit of an instrument of accession with the Secretary-General of the United Nations.

5. The Secretary-General of the United Nations shall inform all States that have signed the present Protocol or acceded to it of the deposit of each instrument of ratification or accession.

Article 8

1. The present Protocol shall enter into force three months after the date of the deposit with the Secretary-General of the United Nations of the tenth instrument of ratification or accession.

2. For each State ratifying the present Protocol or acceding to it after the deposit of the tenth instrument of ratification or accession, the present Protocol shall enter into force three months after the date of the deposit of its own instrument of ratification or accession.

Article 9

The provisions of the present Protocol shall extend to all parts of federal States without any limitations or exceptions.

Article 10

The Secretary-General of the United Nations shall inform all States referred to in article 48, paragraph 1, of the Covenant of the following particulars:

(a) Reservations, communications and notifications under article 2 of the present Protocol;

(b) Statements made under articles 4 or 5 of the present Protocol;

(c) Signatures, ratifications and accessions under article 7 of the present Protocol:

(d) The date of the entry into force of the present Protocol under article 8 thereof.

Article 11

1. The present Protocol, of which the Arabic, Chinese, English, French, Russian and Spanish texts are equally authentic, shall be deposited in the archives of the United Nations.

2. The Secretary-General of the United Nations shall transmit certified copies of the present Protocol to all States referred to in article 48 of the Covenant.

8.2. Council of Europe

European Convention on the Protection of Human Rights and Fundamental Freedoms (1950)[*]

Rome, 4 November 1950

Article 1

The High Contracting Parties shall secure to everyone within their jurisdiction the rights and freedoms defined in Section I of this Convention.

Section I

Article 2

1. Everyone's right to life shall be protected by law. No one shall by deprived of his life intentionally save in the execution of a sentence of a court following his conviction of a crime for which this penalty is provided by law.

2. Deprivation of life shall not be regarded as inflicted in contravention of this Article when it results from the use of force which is no more that absolutely necessary:

   (a) in defence of any person from unlawful violence;

   (b) in order to effect a lawful arrest or to prevent the escape of a person lawfully detained;

   (c) in action lawfully taken for the purpose of quelling a riot or insurrection.

Article 3

No one shall be subjected to torture or to inhuman or degrading treatment or punishment.

Article 4

1. No one shall be held in slavery or servitude.

2. No one shall be required to perform forced or compulsory labour.

3. For the purpose of this Article the term "forced or compulsory labour" shall not include:

   (a) any work required to be done in the ordinary course of detention imposed according to the provisions of Article 5 of this Convention or during conditional release from such detention;

   (b) any service of a military character or, in case of conscientious objectors in countries where they are recognised, service exacted instead of compulsory military service;

   (c) any service exacted in case of an emergency or calamity threatening the life or well-being of the community;

   (d) any work or service which forms part of normal civic obligations.

---

[*] *United Nations Treaty Series*, vol.213, 221.

Article 5

1. Everyone has the right to liberty and security of person. No one shall be deprived of his liberty save in the following cases and in accordance with a procedure prescribed by law:

    (a) the lawful detention of a person after conviction by a competent court;

    (b) the lawful arrest or detention of a person for non-compliance with the lawful order of a court or in order to secure the fulfilment of any obligation prescribed by law.

    (c) the lawful arrest or detention of a person effected for the purpose of bringing him before the competent legal authority on reasonable suspicion of having committed an offence or when it is reasonably considered necessary to prevent his committing an offence or fleeing after having done so;

    (d) the detention of a minor by lawful order for the purpose of educational supervision or his lawful detention for the purpose of bringing him before the competent legal authority;

    (e) the lawful detention of persons for the prevention of the spreading of infectious diseases, of persons of unsound mind, alcoholics or drug addicts or vagrants;

    (f) the lawful arrest or detention of a person to prevent his effecting an unauthorised entry into the country or of a person against whom action is being taken with a view to deportation or extradition.

2. Everyone who is arrested shall be informed promptly, in a language which he understands, of the reasons for his arrest and of any charge against him.

3. Everyone arrested or detained in accordance with the provisions of paragraph 1(c) of this Article shall be brought promptly before a judge or other officer authorised by law to exercise judicial power and shall be entitled to trial a reasonable time or to release pending trial. Release may conditioned by guarantees to appear for trial.

4. Everyone who is deprived of this liberty by arrest or detention shall be entitled to take proceedings by which the lawfulness of his detention shall be decided speedily by a court and his release ordered of the detention is not lawful.

5. Everyone who has been the victim of arrest or detention in contravention of the provisions of this Article shall have an enforceable right to compensation.

Article 6

1. In the determination of his civil rights and obligations or of any criminal charge against him, everyone is entitled to a fair and public hearing within a reasonable time by an independent and impartial tribunal established by law. Judgment shall be pronounced publicly but the press and public may be excluded from all or part of the trial in the interests of morals, public order or national security in a democratic society, where the interests of juveniles or the protection of the private life of the parties so require, or to the extent strictly necessary in the opinion of the court in special circumstances where publicity would prejudice the interests of justice.

2. Everyone charged with a criminal offence shall be presumed innocent until proved guilty according to law.

3. Everyone charged with a criminal offence has the following minimum rights:

    (a) to be informed promptly, in a language which he understands and in detail, of the nature and cause of the accusation against him;

    (b) to have adequate time and facilities for the preparation of his defence;

(c) to defend himself in person or through legal assistance of his own choosing or, if he has not sufficient means to pay for legal assistance, to be given it free when the interests of justice so require;

(d) to examine or have examined witnesses against him and to obtain the attendance and examination of witnesses on his behalf under the same conditions as witnesses against him;

(e) to have the free assistance of an interpreter if he cannot understand or speak the language used in court.

Article 7

1. No one shall be held guilty of any criminal offence on account of any act or omission which did not constitute a criminal offence under national or international law at the time when it was committed. Nor shall a heavier penalty be imposed than the one that was applicable at the time the criminal offence was committed.

2. This Article shall not prejudice the trial and punishment of any person for any act or omission which, at the time when it was committed, was criminal according to the general principles of law recognised by civilised nations.

Article 8

1. Everyone has the right to respect for his private and family life, his home and his correspondence.

2. There shall be no interference by a public authority with the exercise of this right except such as is in accordance with the law and is necessary in a democratic society in the interests of national security, public safety or the economic well-being of the country, for the prevention of disorder or crime, for the protection of health or morals, or for the protection of the rights and freedoms of others.

Article 9

1. Everyone has the right to freedom of thought, conscience and religion; this right includes freedom to change his religion or belief and freedom, either alone or in community with others and in public or private, to manifest his religion or belief, in worship, teaching, practice and observance.

2. Freedom to manifest one's religion or beliefs shall be subject only to such limitations as are prescribed by law and are necessary in a democratic society in the interests of public safety, for the protection of public order, health or morals, or for the protection of the rights and freedoms of others.

Article 10

1. Everyone has the right to freedom of expression. This right shall include freedom to hold opinions and to receive and impart information and ideas without interference by public authority and regardless of frontiers. This Article shall not prevent States from requiring the licensing of broadcasting, television or cinema enterprises.

2. The exercise of these freedoms, since it carries with it duties and responsibilities, may be subject to such formalities, conditions, restrictions or penalties as are prescribed by law and are necessary in a democratic society, in the interests of national security, territorial integrity or public safety, for the prevention of disorder or crime, for the protection of health or morals, for the protection of the reputation or rights of others, for preventing the disclosure of information received in confidence, or for maintaining the authority and impartiality of the judiciary.

Article 11

1. Everyone has the right to freedom of peaceful assembly and to freedom of association with others, including the right to form and to join trade unions for the protection of his interests.

2. No restrictions shall be placed on the exercise of these rights other than such as are prescribed by law and are necessary in a democratic society in the interests of national security or public safety, for the prevention of disorder or crime, for the protection of health or morals or for the protection of the rights and freedoms of others. This Article shall not prevent the imposition of lawful restrictions on the exercise of these rights, by members of the armed forces, of the police or of the administration of the State.

Article 12

Men and women of marriageable age have the right to marry and to found a family, according to the national laws governing the exercise of this right.

Article 13

Everyone whose rights and freedoms as set forth in this Convention are violated shall have an effective remedy before a national authority notwithstanding that the violation has been committed by persons acting in an official capacity.

Article 14

The enjoyment of the rights and freedoms set forth in this Convention shall be secured without discrimination on any ground such as sex, race, colour, language, religion, political or other opinion, national or social origin, association with a national minority, property, birth or other status.

Article 15

1. In time of war or other public emergency threatening life of the nation any High Contracting Party may take measures derogating from its obligations under this Convention to the extent strictly required by the exigencies of the situation, provided that such measures are not inconsistent with its other obligations under international law.

2. No derogation from Article 2, except in respect of deaths resulting form lawful acts of war, or from Articles 3, 4 (paragraph 1) and 7 shall be made under this provision.

3. Any High Contracting Party availing itself of this right of derogation shall keep the Secretary-General of the Council of Europe fully informed of the measures which it has taken and the reasons therefor. It shall also inform the Secretary-General of the Council of Europe when such measures have ceased to operate and the provisions of the Convention are again being fully executed.

Article 16

Nothing in Articles 10, 11, and 14 shall be regarded as preventing the High Contracting Parties from imposing restrictions on the political activity of aliens.

Article 17

Nothing in this Convention may be interpreted as implying for any State, group or person any right to engage in any activity or perform any act aimed at the destruction of any of the rights and freedoms set forth herein or at their limitation to a greater extent than is provided for in the Convention.

Article 18

The restrictions permitted under this Convention to the said right and freedoms shall not be applied for any purpose other then those for which they have been prescribed.

Section II

Article 19

To ensure the observance of the engagements undertaken by the High Contracting Parties in the present Convention, there shall be set up:

(a) A European Commission of Human Rights hereinafter referred to as "the Commission";

(b) European Court of Human Rights, hereinafter referred to as "the Court".

Section III

Article 20

The commission shall consist of a number of members equal to that of the High Contracting Parties. No two members of the Commission may be nationals of the same State.

Article 21

1. The members of the Commission shall be elected by the Committee of Ministers by an absolute majority of votes, from a list of names drawn up by the Bureau of the Consultative Assembly; each group of the Representatives of the High Contracting Parties in the Consultative Assembly shall put forward three candidates, of whom two at least shall be its nationals.

2. As far as applicable, the same procedure shall be followed to complete the Commission in the event of other States subsequently becoming Parties to this Convention, and in filling casual vacancies.

Article 22

1. The members of the Commission shall be elected for a period of six years. They may be re-elected. However, of the members elected at the first election, the terms of seven members shall expire at the end of three years.

2. The members whose terms are to expire at the end of the initial period of three years shall be chosen by lot by the Secretary-General of the Council of Europe immediately after the first election has been completed.

3. In order to ensure that, as far as possible, one half of the membership of the Commission shall be renewed every three years, the Committee of Ministers may decide, before proceeding to any subsequent election that the term or terms of office of one or more members to be elected shall be for a period other than six years but not more than nine and not less than three years.

4. In cases where more that one term of office is involved and the Committee of Ministers applies the preceding paragraph, the allocation of the terms of office shall be effected by the drawing of lots by the Secretary-General, immediately after the election.

5. A member of the Commission elected to replace a member whose term of office has not expired shall hold office for the remainder of this predecessor's term.

6. The members of the Commission shall hold office until replaced. After having been replaced, they shall continue to deal with such cases as they already have under consideration.

Article 23

The members of the Commission shall sit on the Commission in their individual capacity.

Article 24

Any High Contracting Party may refer to the Commission through the Secretary-General of the Council of Europe, any alleged breach of the provisions of the Convention by another High Contracting Party.

Article 25

1. The Commission may receive petitions addressed to the Secretary-General of the Council of Europe from any person, non-governmental organisation or group of individuals claiming to be the victim of a violation by one of the High Contracting Parties of the rights set forth in this Convention, provided that the High Contracting Party against which the complaint has been lodged has declared that it recognise the competence of the Commission recognises to receive such petitions. Those of the High Contracting Parties who have made such a declaration undertake not to hinder in any way the effective exercise of this right.

2. Such declarations may be made for a specific period.

3. The declarations shall be deposited with the Secretary-General of the Council of Europe who shall transmit copies thereof to the High Contracting Parties and publish them.

4. The Commission shall only exercise the powers provided for in this Article when at least six High Contracting Parties are bound by declarations made in accordance with the preceding paragraphs.

Article 26

The Commission may only deal with the matter after all domestic remedies have been exhausted, according to the generally recognised rules of international law, and within a period of six months from the date on which the final decision was taken.

Article 27

1. The Commission shall not deal with any petition submitted under Article 25 which

   (a) is anonymous, or

   (b) is substantially the same as a matter which has already been examined by the Commission or has already been submitted to another procedure of international investigation or settlement and if it contains no relevant new information.

2. The Commission shall consider inadmissible any petition submitted under Article 25 which it considers incompatible with the provisions of the present Convention, manifestly ill-founded, or an abuse of the right of petition.

3. The Commission shall reject any petition referred to it which it considers inadmissible under Article 26.

Article 28

In the event of the Commission accepting a petition referred to it:

   (a) it shall, with a view to ascertaining the facts, undertake together with the representatives of the parties an examination of the petition and, if need be, an investigation, for the effective conduct of which the States concerned shall furnish all necessary facilities, after an exchange of views with the Commission;

(b) it shall place itself at the disposal of the parties concerned with a view to securing a friendly settlement of the matter on the basis of respect for Human Rights as defined in this Convention.

Article 29

After it has accepted a petition submitted under Article 25, the Commission may nevertheless decide unanimously to reject the petition if, in the course of its examination, it finds that the existence of one of the grounds for non-acceptance provided for in Article 27 has been established.

In such a case, the decision shall be communicated to the parties.

Article 30

If the Commission succeeds in effecting a friendly settlement in accordance with Article 28, it shall draw up a Report which shall be sent to the States concerned, to the Committee of Ministers and to the Secretary-General of the Council of Europe for publication. This Report shall be confined to a brief statement of the facts and of the solution reached.

Article 31

1. If a solution is not reached, the Commission shall draw up a Report on the facts and state its opinion as to whether the facts found disclose a breach by the State concerned of its obligations under the Convention. The opinions of all the members of the Commission on this point may be stated in the Report.

2. The Report shall be transmitted to the Committee of Ministers. It shall also be transmitted to the States concerned, who shall not be at liberty to publish it.

3. In transmitting the Report to the Committee of Ministers the Commission may make such proposals as it thinks fit.

Article 32

1. If the question is not referred to the Court in accordance with Article 48 of this Convention within a period of three months from the date of the transmission of the Report to the Committee of Ministers, the Committee of Ministers shall decide by a majority of two-thirds of the members entitled to sit on the Committee whether there has been a violation of the Convention.

2. In the affirmative case the Committee of Ministers shall prescribe a period during which the High Contracting Party concerned must take the measures required by the decision of the Committee of Ministers.

3. If the High Contracting Party concerned has not taken satisfactory measures within the prescribed period, the Committee of Ministers shall decide by the majority provided for in paragraph (1) above what effect shall be given to its original decision and shall publish the Report.

4. The High Contracting Parties undertake to regard as binding on them any decision which the Committee of Ministers may take in application of the preceding paragraphs.

Article 33

The Commission shall meet in camera.

Article 34

Subject to the provisions of Article 29, the Commission shall take its decisions by a majority of the Members present and voting.

Article 35

The Commission shall meet as the circumstances require. The meetings shall be convened by the Secretary General of the Council of Europe.

Article 36

The Commission shall draw up its own rules of procedure.

Article 37

The secretariat of the Commission shall be provided by the Secretary-General of the Council of Europe.

Section IV

Article 38

The European Court of Human Rights shall consist of a number of judges equal to that of the Members of the Council of Europe. No two judges may be nationals of the same State.

Article 39

1. The members of the Court shall be elected by the Consultative Assembly by a majority of the votes cast from a list of persons nominated by the Members of the Council of Europe; each Member shall nominate three candidates, of whom two at least shall be its nationals.

2. As far as applicable, the same procedure shall be followed to complete the Court in the event of the admission of new Members of the Council of Europe, and in filling casual vacancies.

3. The candidates shall be of high moral character and must either possess the qualifications required for appointment to high judicial office or be jurisconsults of recognised competence.

Article 40

1. The members of the Court shall be elected for a period of nine years. They may be re-elected. However, of the members elected at the first election the terms of four members shall expire at the end of three years, and the terms of four more members shall expire at the end of six years.

2. The members whose terms are to expire at the end of the initial periods of three and six years shall be chosen by lot by the Secretary-General immediately after the first election has been completed.

3. In order to ensure that, as far as possible, one third of the membership of the Court shall be renewed every three years, the Consultative Assembly may decide, before proceeding to any subsequent election, that the term or terms of office of one or more members to be elected shall be for a period other than nine years but not more than twelve and not less than six years.

4. In cases where more than one term of office is involved and the Consultative Assembly applies the preceding paragraph, the allocation of the terms of office shall be effected by the drawing of lots by the Secretary-General immediately after the election.

5. A member of the Court elected to replace a member whose term of office has not expired shall hold office for the remainder of his predecessor's term.

6. The members of the Court shall hold office until replaced. After having been replaced, they shall continue to deal with such cases as they already have under consideration.

Article 41

The Court shall elect its President and Vice-President for a period of three years. They may be re-elected.

Article 42

The members of the Court shall receive for each day of duty a compensation to be determined by the Committee of Ministers.

Article 43

For the consideration of each case brought before it the Court shall consist of a Chamber composed of seven judges. There shall sit as an exofficio member of the Chamber the judge who is a national of any State party concerned, or, if there is none, a person of its choice who shall sit in the capacity of judge; the names of the other judges shall be chosen by lot by the President before the opening of the case.

Article 44

Only the High Contracting Parties and the Commission shall have the right to bring a case before the Court.

Article 45

The jurisdiction of the Court shall extend to all cases concerning the interpretation and application of the present Convention which the High Contracting Parties or the Commission shall refer to it in accordance with Article 48.

Article 46

1. Any of the High Contracting Parties may at any time declare that it recognises as compulsory *ipso facto* and without special agreement the jurisdiction of the Court in all matters concerning the interpretation and application of the present Convention.

2. The declarations referred to above may be made unconditionally or on condition of reciprocity on the part of several or certain other High Contracting Parties or for a specified period.

3. These declarations shall be deposited with the Secretary-General of the Council of Europe who shall transmit copies thereof to the High Contracting Parties.

Article 47

The Court may only deal with a case after the Commission has acknowledged the failure of efforts for a friendly settlement and within the period of three months provided for in Article 32.

Article 48

The following may bring a case before the Court, provided that the High Contracting Party concerned, if there is only one, or the High Contracting Parties concerned, if there is more than one, are subject to the compulsory jurisdiction of the Court or, failing that, with the consent of the High Contracting Party concerned, if there is only one, or of the High Contracting Parties concerned if there is more than one:

(a) the Commission;

(b) a High Contracting Party whose national is alleged to be a victim;

(c) a High Contracting Party which referred the case to the Commission;

(d) a High Contracting Party against which the complaint has been lodged.

Article 49

In the event of dispute as to whether the Court has jurisdiction, the matter shall be settled by the decision of the Court.

Article 50

If the Court finds that a decision or a measure taken by a legal authority or any other authority of a High Contracting Party is completely or partially in conflict with the obligations arising from the present Convention, and if the internal law of the said Party allows only partial reparation to be made for the consequences of this decision or measure, the decision of the Court shall, if necessary, afford just satisfaction to the injured party.

Article 51

1. Reasons shall be given for the judgment of the Court.

2. If the judgment does not represent in whole or in part the unanimous opinion of the judges, any judge shall be entitled to deliver a separate opinion.

Article 52

The judgment of the Court shall be final.

Article 53

The High Contracting Parties undertake to abide by the decision of the Court in any case to which they are parties.

Article 54

The judgment of the Court shall be transmitted to the Committee of Ministers which shall supervise its execution.

Article 55

The Court shall draw up its own rules and shall determine its own procedure.

Article 56

1. The first election of the members of the Court shall take place after the declarations by the High Contracting Parties mentioned in Article 46 have reached a total of eight.

2. No case can be brought before the Court before this election.

Section V

Article 57

On receipt of a request from the Secretary-General of the Council of Europe any High Contracting Party shall furnish an explanation of the manner in which its internal law ensures the effective implementation of any of the provisions of this Convention.

Article 58

The expenses of the Commission and the Court shall be borne by the Council of Europe.

Article 59

The members of the Commission and of the Court shall be entitled, during the discharge of their functions, to the privileges and immunities provided for in Article 40 of the Statute of the Council of Europe and in the agreements made thereunder.

Article 60

Nothing in this Convention shall be construed as limiting or derogating from any of the human rights and fundamental freedoms which may be ensured under the laws of any High Contracting Party or under any other agreement to which it is a Party.

Article 61

Nothing in this Convention shall prejudice the powers conferred on the Committee of Ministers by the Statute of the Council of Europe.

Article 62

The High Contracting Parties agree that, except by special agreement, they will not avail themselves of treaties, conventions or declarations in force between them for purpose of submitting, by way of petition, a dispute arising out of the interpretation or application of this Convention to a means of settlement other than those provided for in this Convention.

Article 63

1. Any State may at the time of its ratification or at any time thereafter declare by notification addressed to the Secretary-General of the Council of Europe that the present Convention shall extend to all or any of the territories for whose international relations it is responsible.

2. The Convention shall extend to the territory or territories named in the notification as from the thirtieth day after the receipt of this notification by the Secretary-General of the Council of Europe.

3. The provisions of this Convention shall be applied in such territories with due regard, however, to local requirements.

4. Any State which has made a declaration in accordance with paragraph 1 of this Article may at any time thereafter declare on behalf of one or more of the territories to which the declaration relates that it accepts the competence of the Commission to receive petitions from individuals, non-governmental organisations or groups of individuals in accordance with Article 25 of the present Convention.

Article 64

1. Any State may, when signing this Convention or when depositing its instrument of ratification, make a reservation in respect of any particular provision of the Convention to the extent that any law then in force in its territory is not in conformity with the provision. Reservations of a general character shall not be permitted under this Article.

2. Any reservation made under this Article shall contain a brief statement of the law concerned.

Article 65

1. A High Contracting Party may denounce the present Convention only after the expiry of five years from the date on which it became a Party to it and after six months' notice contained in a notification addressed to the Secretary-General of the Council of Europe, who shall inform the other High Contracting Parties.

2. Such a denunciation shall not have the effect of releasing the High Contracting Party concerned from its obligations under this Convention in respect of any act which, being capable of constituting a violation of such obligations, may have been performed by it before the date at which the denunciation became effective.

3. Any High Contracting Party which shall cease to be a Member of the Council of Europe shall cease to be a Party to this Convention under the same conditions.

4. The Convention may be denounced in accordance with the provisions of the preceding paragraphs in respect of any territory to which it has been declared to extend under the terms of Article 63.

Article 66

1. This Convention shall be open to the signature of the Members of the Council of Europe. It shall be ratified. Ratification shall be deposited with the Secretary-General of the Council of Europe.

2. The present Convention shall come into force after the deposit of ten instruments of ratification.

3. As regards any signatory ratifying subsequently, the Convention shall come into force at the date of the deposit of its instrument of ratification.

4. The Secretary-General of the Council of Europe shall notify all the Members of the Council of Europe of the entry into force of the Convention, the names of the High Contracting Parties who have ratified it, and the deposit of all instruments of ratification which may be affected subsequently.

First Protocol to the Convention for the Protection of Human Rights and Fundamental Freedoms (1952)[*]

Paris, 20 March 1952

Article 1

1. Every natural or legal person is entitled to the peaceful enjoyment of his possessions. No one shall be deprived of his possessions except in the public interest and subject to the conditions provided for by law and by the general principles of international law.

2. The preceding provisions shall not, however, in any way impair the right of a State to enforce such laws as it deems necessary to control the use of property in accordance with the general interest or to secure the payment of taxes or other contributions or penalties.

Article 2

No person shall be denied the right to education. In the exercise of any functions which it assumes in relation to education and to teaching, the State shall respect the right of parents to ensure such education and teaching in conformity with their own religious and philosophical convictions.

Article 3

The High Contracting Parties undertake to hold free elections at reasonable intervals by secret ballot, under conditions which will ensure the free expression of the opinion of the people in the choice of the legislature.

Article 4

1. Any High Contracting Party may at the time of signature or ratification or at any time thereafter communicate to the Secretary-General of the Council of Europe a declaration stating the extent to which it undertakes that the provisions of the present Protocol shall apply to such of the territories for the international relations of which it is responsible as are named therein.

2. Any High Contracting Party which has communicated a declaration in virtue of the preceding paragraph may from time to time communicate a further declaration modifying the terms of any former declaration or terminating the application of the provisions of this Protocol in respect of any territory.

3. A declaration made in accordance with this Article shall be deemed to have been made in accordance with paragraph (1) of Article 63 of the Convention.

Article 5

As between the High Contracting Parties the provisions of Articles 1, 2, 3 and 4 of this Protocol shall be regarded as additional Articles to the Convention and all the provisions of the Convention shall apply accordingly.

Article 6

1. This Protocol shall be open for signature by the Members of the Council of Europe, who are the signatories of the Convention; it shall be ratified at the same time as or after the ratification of the Convention. It shall enter into force after the deposit of ten instruments of

---

[*] *European Treaty Series*, No.9.

ratification. As regards any signatory ratifying subsequently, the Protocol shall enter into force at the date of the deposit of its instrument of ratification.

2.   The instruments of ratification shall be deposited with the Secretary-General of the Council of Europe, who will notify all Members of the names of those who have ratified.

Protocol No.6 to the Convention for the Protection of Human Rights and Fundamental Freedoms concerning the Abolition of the Death Penalty (1983)[*]

Strasbourg, 28 April 1983

Article 1

The death penalty shall be abolished. No one shall be condemned to such penalty or executed.

Article 2

A State may make provision in its law for the death penalty in respect of acts committed in time of war or of imminent threat of war; such penalty shall be applied only in the instances laid down in the law and in accordance with its provisions. The State shall communicate to the Secretary General of the Council of Europe the relevant provisions of that law.

Article 3

No derogation from the provisions of this Protocol shall be made under Article 15 of the Convention.

Article 4

No reservation may be made under Article 64 of the Convention in respect of the provisions of this Protocol.

Article 5

1. Any State may at the time of signature or when depositing its instrument of ratification, acceptance or approval, specify the territory or territories to which this Protocol shall apply.

2. Any State may at any later date, by a declaration addressed to the Secretary General of the Council of Europe, extend the application of this Protocol to any other territory specified in the declaration. In respect of such territory the Protocol shall enter into force on the first day of the month following the date of receipt of such declaration by the Secretary General.

3. Any declaration made under the two preceding paragraphs may, in respect of any territory specified in such declaration, be withdrawn by a notification addressed to the Secretary General. The withdrawal shall become effective on the first day of the month following the date of receipt of such notification by the Secretary General.

Article 6

As between the States Parties the provisions of Articles 1 of 5 of this Protocol shall be regarded as additional articles to the Convention and all the provisions of the Convention shall apply accordingly.

Article 7

This Protocol shall be open for signature by the member States of the Council of Europe, signatories to the Convention. It shall be subject to ratification, acceptance of approval. A member State of the Council of Europe may not ratify, accept or approve this Protocol

---

[*] *European Treaty Series*, No.114.

unless it has, simultaneously or previously, ratified the Convention. Instruments of ratification, acceptance or approval shall be deposited with the Secretary General of the Council of Europe.

Article 8

1. This Protocol shall enter into force on the first day of the month following the date on which five member States of the Council of Europe have expressed their consent to be bound by the Protocol in accordance with the provisions of Article 7.

2. In respect of any member State which subsequently expresses its consent to be bound by it, the Protocol shall enter into force on the first day of the month following the date of the deposit of the instrument of ratification, acceptance or approval.

Protocol No. 7 to the Convention for the Protection of Human Rights and Fundamental Freedoms (1984)[*]

Strasbourg, 22 November 1984

Article 1

1. An alien lawfully resident in the territory of a State shall not be expelled therefrom except in pursuance of a decision reached in accordance with law and shall be allowed:

   (a) to submit reasons against his expulsion.

   (b) to have his case reviewed, and

   (c) to be represented for these purposes before the competent authority or a person or persons designated by that authority.

2. An alien may be expelled before the exercise of his rights under paragraph 1 a, b and c of this Article, when such expulsion is necessary in the interests of public order or is grounded on reasons of national security.

Article 2

1. Everyone convicted of a criminal offence by a tribunal shall have the right to have this conviction or sentence reviewed by a higher tribunal. The exercise of this right, including the grounds on which it may be exercised, shall be governed by law.

2. This right may be subject to exceptions in regard to offences of a minor character, as prescribed by law, or in cases in which the person concerned was tried in the first instance by the highest tribunal or was convicted following an appeal against acquittal.

Article 3

When a person has by a final decision been convicted of a criminal offence and when subsequently his conviction has been reversed, or he has been pardoned, on the ground that a new or newly discovered fact shows conclusively that there has been a miscarriage of justice, the person who has suffered punishment as a result of such conviction shall be compensated according to the law or the practice of the State concerned, unless it is proved that the non-disclosure of the unknown fact in time is wholly or partly attributable to him.

Article 4

1. No one shall be liable to be tried or punished again in criminal proceedings under the jurisdiction of the same State for an offence for which he has already been finally acquitted or convicted in accordance with the law and penal procedure of that State.

2. The provisions of the preceding paragraph shall not prevent the reopening of the case in accordance with the law and penal procedure of the State concerned, if there is evidence of new or newly discovered facts, or if there has been a fundamental defect in the previous proceedings, which could affect the outcome of the case.

3. No derogation from this Article shall be made under Article 15 of the Convention.

---

[*] *European Treaty Series*, No. 117.

Article 5

Spouses shall enjoy equality of rights and responsibilities of a private law character between them, and in their relations with their children, as to marriage, during marriage and in the event of its dissolution. This Article shall not prevent States from taking such measures as are necessary in the interests of the children.

Article 6

1. Any State may at the time of signature or when depositing its instrument of ratification, acceptance or approval, specify the territory or territories to which this Protocol shall apply and state the extent to which it undertakes that the provisions of this Protocol shall apply to such territory or territories.

2. Any State may at any later date, by a declaration addressed to the Secretary General of the Council of Europe, extend the application of this Protocol to any other territory specified in the declaration. In respect of such territory the Protocol shall enter into force on the first day of the month following the expiration of a period of two months after the date of receipt by the Secretary General of such declaration.

3. Any declaration made under the two preceding paragraphs may, in respect of any territory specified in such declaration, be withdrawn or modified by a notification addressed to the Secretary General. The withdrawal or modification shall become effective on the first day of the month following the expiration of a period of two months after the date of receipt of such notification by the Secretary General.

4. A declaration made in accordance with this Article shall be deemed to have been made in accordance with paragraph 1 of Article 63 of the Convention.

5. The territory of any State to which this Protocol applies by virtue of ratification, acceptance or approval by that State, and each territory to which this Protocol is applied by virtue of a declaration by that State under this Article, may be treated as separate territories for the purpose of the reference in Article 1 to the territory of a State.

Article 7

1. As between the States Parties, the provisions of Article 1 to 6 of this Protocol shall be regarded as additional Articles to the Convention, and all the provisions of the Convention shall apply accordingly.

2. Nevertheless, the right of individual recourse recognised by a declaration made under Article 25 of the Convention, or the acceptance of the compulsory jurisdiction of the Court by a declaration made under Article 46 of the Convention, shall not be effective in relation to this Protocol unless the State concerned has made a statement recognising such right, or accepting such jurisdiction in respect of Articles 1 to 5 of this Protocol.

Article 8

This Protocol shall be open for signature by member States of the Council of Europe which have signed the Convention. It is subject to ratification, acceptance or approval. A member State of the Council of Europe may not ratify, accept or approve this Protocol without previously or simultaneously ratifying the Convention. Instruments of ratification, acceptance or approval shall be deposited with the Secretary General of the Council of Europe.

Article 9

1. This Protocol shall enter into force on the first day of the month following the expiration of a period of two months after the date on which seven member States of the Council of Europe have expressed their consent to be bound by the Protocol in accordance with the provisions of Article 8.

2. In respect of any member State which subsequently expresses its consent to be bound by it, the Protocol shall enter into force on the first day of the month following the expiration of a period of two months after the date of the deposit of the instrument of ratification, acceptance or approval.

Article 10

The Secretary General of the Council of Europe shall notify all the member States of the Council of Europe of:

(a) any signature;

(b) the deposit of any instrument of ratification, acceptance or approval;

(c) any date of entry into force of this Protocol in accordance with Articles 6 and 9;

(d) any other act, notification or declaration relating to this Protocol.

9. TRANSFER OF DATA AND INTERNATIONAL CRIMINAL LAW

Convention for the Protection of Individuals with regard to Automatic Processing of Personal Data (1981)[*]

Strasbourg, 28 January 1981

Chapter I

General provisions

Article 1

Object and purpose

The purpose of this convention is to secure in the territory of each Party for every individual, whatever his nationality or residence, respect for his rights and fundamental freedoms, and in particular his right to privacy, with regard to automatic processing of persona data relating to him ("data protection").

Article 2

For the purposes of this convention:

(a) "personal data" means any information relating to an identified or identifiable individual ("data subject");

(b) "automated data file" means any set of data undergoing automatic processing;

(c) "automatic processing" includes the following operations if carried out in whole or in part by automated means: storage of data, carrying out of logical and/or arithmetical operations on those data, their alteration, erasure retrieval or dissemination;

(d) "controller of the file" means the natural or legal person, public authority, agency or any other body who is competent according to the national law to decide what should be the purpose of the automated data file, which categories of personal data should be stored and which operations should be applied to them.

Article 3

1. The Parties undertake to apply this convention to automated personal data files and automatic processing of personal data in the public and private sectors.

2. Any State may, at the time of signature or when depositing its instrument of ratification, acceptance, approval or accession, or at any later time, give notice by a declaration addressed to the Secretary General of the Council of Europe:

(a) that it will not apply this convention to certain categories of automated personal data files, a list of which will be deposited. In this list it shall not include, however, categories of automated data files subject under its domestic law to data protection provisions. Consequently, it shall amend this list by a new declaration whenever additional categories of automated personal data files are subjected to data protection provisions under its domestic law;

(b) that it will also apply this convention to information relating to groups of persons, associations, foundations, companies, corporations and any other bodies

---

[*] *European Treaty Series*, No.108.

consisting directly or indirectly of individuals, whether or not such bodies possess legal personality;

(c) that it will also apply this convention to personal data files which are not processed automatically.

3. Any State which has extended the scope of this convention by any of the declarations provided for in sub-paragraph 2.b or c above may give notice in the said declaration that such extensions shall apply only to certain categories of personal data files, a list of which will be deposited.

4. Any Party which has excluded certain categories of automated personal data files by a declaration provided for in sub-paragraph 2.a above may not claim the application of this convention to such categories by a Party which has not excluded them.

5. Likewise, a Party which has not made one or other of the extensions provided for in subparagraphs 2.b and c above may not claim the application of this convention on these points with respect to a Party which has made such extensions.

6. The declarations provided for in paragraph 2 above shall take effect from the moment of the entry into force of the convention with regard to the State which has made them if they have been made at the time of signature or deposit of its instrument of ratification, acceptance, approval or accession, or three months after their receipt by the Secretary General of the Council of Europe if they have been made at any later time. These declarations may be withdrawn, in whole or in part, by a notification addressed to the Secretary General of the Council of Europe. Such withdrawals shall take effect three months after the date of receipt of such notification.

Chapter II

Basic principles for data protection

Article 4

Duties of the Parties

1. Each Party shall take the necessary measures in its domestic law to give effect to the basic principles for data protection set out in this chapter.

2. These measures shall be taken at the latest at the time of entry into force of this convention in respect of that Party.

Article 5

Personal data undergoing automatic processing shall be:

(a) obtained and processed fairly and lawfully;

(b) stored for specified and legitimate purposes and not used in a way incompatible with those purposes;

(c) adequate, relevant and not excessive in relation to the purposes for which they are stored;

(d) accurate and, where necessary, kept up to date;

(e) preserved in a form which permits identification of the data subjects for no longer than is required for the purpose for which those data are stored.

Article 6

Special categories of data

Personal data revealing racial origin, political opinions or religious or other beliefs, as well as personal data concerning health or sexual life, may not be processed automatically unless domestic law provides appropriate safeguards. The same shall apply to personal data relating to criminal convictions.

Article 7

Data security

Appropriate security measures shall be taken for the protection of personal data stored in automated data files against accidental or unauthorised destruction or accidental loss as well as against unauthorised access, alteration or dissemination.

Article 8

Additional safeguards for the data subject

Any person shall be enabled:

(a) to establish the existence of an automated personal data file, its main purposes, as well as the identity and habitual residence or principal place of business of the controller of the file;

(b) to obtain at reasonable intervals and without excessive delay or expense confirmation of whether personal data relating to him are stored in the automated data file as well as communication to him of such data in an intelligible form;

(c) to obtain, as the case may be, rectification or erasure of such data if these have been processed contrary to the provisions of domestic law giving effect to the basic principles set out in Articles 5 and 6 of this convention;

(d) to have a remedy if a request for confirmation or, as the case may be, communication, rectification or erasure as referred to in paragraphs b and c of this article is not complied with.

Article 9

Exceptions and restrictions

1. No exceptions to the provisions of Articles 5, 6 and 8 of this convention shall be allowed except within the limits defined in this article.

2. Derogation from the provisions of Article 5, 6 and 8 of this convention shall be allowed when such derogation is provided for by the law of the Party and constitutes a necessary measure in a democratic society in the interests of:

(a) protecting State security, public safety, the monetary interests of the State or the suppression of criminal offences;

(b) protecting the data subject or the rights and freedoms of others.

3. Restrictions on the exercise of the rights specified in Article 8, paragraphs b, c and d, may be provided by law with respect to automated personal data files used for statistics or for scientific research purposes when there is obviously no risk of an infringement of the privacy of the data subjects.

Article 10

Sanctions and remedies

Each Party undertakes to establish appropriate sanctions and remedies for violations of provisions of domestic law giving effect to the basic principles for data protection set out in this chapter.

Article 11

Extended protection

None of the provisions of this chapter shall be interpreted as limiting or otherwise affecting the possibility for a Party to grant data subjects a wider measure of protection than that stipulated in this convention.

Chapter III

Transborder data flows

Article 12

Transborder flows of personal data and domestic law

1. The following provisions shall apply to the transfer across national borders, by whatever medium, of personal data undergoing automatic processing or collected with a view to their being automatically processed.

2. A Party shall not, for the sole purpose of the protection of privacy, prohibit or subject to special authorization transborder flows of personal data going to the territory of another Party.

3. Nevertheless, each Party shall be entitled to derogate from the provisions of paragraph 2:

   (a) insofar as its legislation includes specific regulations for certain categories of personal data or of automated personal data files, because of the nature of those data or those files, except where the regulations of the other Party provide an equivalent protection;

   (b) when the transfer is made from its territory to the territory of a non-Contracting State through the intermediary of the territory of another Party, in order to avoid such transfers resulting in circumvention of the legislation of the Party referred to at the beginning of this paragraph.

Chapter IV

Mutual assistance

Article 13

Co-operation between Parties

1. The Parties agree to render each other mutual assistance in order to implement this convention.

2. For that purpose:

   (a) each Party shall designate one or more authorities, the name and address of each of which it shall communicate to the Secretary General of the Council of Europe;

(b) each Party which has designated more than one authority shall specify in its communication referred to in the previous sub-paragraph the competence of each authority.

3. An authority designated by a Party shall at the request of an authority designated by another Party:

(a) furnish information on its law and administrative practice in the field of data protection;

(b) take, in conformity with its domestic law and for the sole purpose of protection of privacy, all appropriate measures for furnishing factual information relating to specific automatic processing carried out in its territory, with the exception however of the personal data being processed.

Article 14

Assistance to data subjects resident abroad

1. Each Party shall assist any person resident abroad to exercise the rights conferred by its domestic law giving effect to the principles set out in Article 8 of this Convention.

2. When such a person resides in the territory of another Party he shall be given the option of submitting his request through the intermediary of the authority designated by that Party.

3. The request for assistance shall contain all the necessary particulars, relating inter alia to:

(a) the name, address and any other relevant particulars identifying the person making the request;

(b) the automated personal data file to which the request pertains, or its controller;

(c) the purpose of the request.

Article 15

Safeguards concerning assistance rendered by designated authorities

1. An authority designated by a Party which has received information from an authority designated by another Party either accompanying a request for assistance or in reply to its own request for assistance shall not use that information for purposes other than those specified in the request for assistance.

2. Each Party shall see to it that the persons belonging to or acting on behalf of the designated authority shall be bound by appropriate obligations of secrecy or confidentiality with regard to that information.

3. In no case may a designated authority be allowed to make under Article 14, paragraph 2, a request for assistance on behalf of a data subject resident abroad, of its own accord and without the express consent of the person concerned.

Article 16

Refusal of requests for assistance

A designated authority to which a request for assistance is addressed under Articles 13 or 14 of this convention may not refuse to comply with it unless:

(a) the request is not compatible with the powers in the field of data protection of the authorities responsible for replying;

(b) the request does not comply with the provisions of this convention;

(c) compliance with the request would be incompatible with the sovereignty, security or public policy (ordre public) of the Party by which it was designated, or with the rights and fundamental freedoms of persons under the jurisdiction of that Party.

Article 17

Costs and procedures of assistance

1. Mutual assistance which the Parties render each other under Article 13 and assistance they render to data subjects abroad under Article 14 shall not give rise to the payment of any costs or fees other than those incurred for experts and interpreters. The latter costs or fees shall be borne by the Party which has designated the authority making the request for assistance.

2. The data subject may not be charged costs or fees in connection with the steps taken on his behalf in the territory of another Party other than those lawfully payable by residents of that Party.

3. Other details concerning the assistance relating in particular to the forms and procedures and the languages to be used, shall be established directly between the Parties concerned.

Chapter V

Consultative committee

Article 18

Composition of the committee

1. A Consultative Committee shall be set up after the entry into force of this convention.

2. Each Party shall appoint a representative to the committee and a deputy representative. Any member State of the Council of Europe which is not a Party to the convention shall have the right to be represented on the committee by an observer.

3. The Consultative Committee may, by unanimous decision, invite any non-member State of the Council of Europe which is not a Party to the convention to be represented by an observer at a given meeting.

Article 19

Functions of the committee

The Consultative Committee:

(a) may make proposals with a view to facilitating or improving the application of the convention;

(b) may make proposals for amendment of this convention in accordance with Article 21;

(c) shall formulate its opinion on any proposal for amendment of this convention which is referred to it in accordance with Article 21, paragraph 3;

(d) may, at the request of a Party, express an opinion on any question concerning the application of this convention.

Article 20

Procedure

1. The Consultative Committee shall be convened by the Secretary General of the Council of Europe. Its first meeting shall be held within twelve months of the entry into force of this convention. It shall subsequently meet at least once every two years and in any case when one-third of the representatives of the Parties request its convocation.

2. A majority of representatives of the Parties shall constitute a quorum for a meeting of the Consultative Committee.

3. After each of its meetings, the Consultative Committee shall submit to the Committee of Ministers of the Council of Europe a report on its work and on the functioning of the convention.

4. Subject to the provisions of this convention, the Consultative Committee shall draw up its own Rules of Procedure.

Chapter VI

Amendments

Article 21

Amendments

1. Amendments to this convention may be proposed by a Party, the Committee of Ministers of the Council of Europe or the Consultative Committee.

2. Any proposal for amendment shall be communicated by the Secretary General of the Council of Europe to the member States of the Council of Europe and to every non-member State which has acceded to or has been invited to accede to this convention in accordance with the provisions of Article 23.

3. Moreover, any amendment proposed by a Party or the Committee of Ministers shall be communicated to the Consultative Committee, which shall submit to the Committee of Ministers its opinion on that proposed amendment.

4. The Committee of Ministers shall consider the proposed amendment and any opinion submitted by the Consultative Committee and may approve the amendment.

5. The text of any amendment approved by the Committee of Ministers in accordance with paragraph 4 of this article shall be forwarded to the Parties for acceptance.

6. Any amendment approved in accordance with paragraph 4 of this article shall come into force on the thirtieth day after all Parties have informed the Secretary General of their acceptance thereof.

Chapter VII

Final clauses

Article 22

Entry into force

1. This Convention shall be open for signature by the member States of the Council of Europe. It is subject to ratification, acceptance or approval. Instruments of ratification, acceptance or approval shall be deposited with the Secretary General of the Council of Europe.

2. This convention shall enter into force on the first day of the month following the expiration of a period of three months after the date on which five member States of the Council of Europe have expressed their consent to be bound by the convention in accordance with the provisions of the preceding paragraph.

3. In respect of any member State which subsequently expresses its consent to be bound by it, the convention shall enter into force on the first day of the month following the expiration of a period of three months after the date of the deposit of the instrument of ratification, acceptance or approval.

Article 23

Accession by non-member States

1. After the entry into force of this convention, the Committee of Ministers of the Council of Europe may invite any State not a member of the Council of Europe to accede to this convention by a decision taken by the majority provided for in Article 20.d of the Statute of the Council of Europe and by the unanimous vote of the representatives of the Contracting States entitled to sit on the committee.

2. In respect of any acceding State, the convention shall enter into force on the first day of the month following the expiration of a period of three months after the date of deposit of the instrument of accession with the Secretary General of the Council of Europe.

Article 24

Territorial clause

1. Any State may at the time of signature or when depositing its instrument of ratification, acceptance, approval or accession, specify the territory or territories to which this convention shall apply.

2. Any State may at any later date, by a declaration addressed to the Secretary General of the Council of Europe, extend the application of this convention to any other territory specified in the declaration. In respect of such territory the convention shall enter into force on the first day of the month following the expiration of a period of three months after the date of receipt of such declaration by the Secretary General.

3. Any declaration made under the two preceding paragraphs may, in respect of any territory specified in such declaration, be withdrawn by a notification addressed to the Secretary General. The withdrawal shall become effective on the first day of the month following the expiration of a period of six months after the date of receipt of such notification by the Secretary General.

Article 25

Reservations

No reservation may be made in respect of the provisions of this convention.

Article 26

Denunciation

1. Any Party may at any time denounce this convention by means of a notification addressed to the Secretary General of the Council of Europe.

2. Such denunciation shall become effective on the first day of the month following the expiration of a period of six months after the date of receipt of the notification by the Secretary General.

Article 27

Notifications

The Secretary General of the Council of Europe shall notify the member States of the Council and any State which has acceded to this convention of:

(a) any signature;

(b) the deposit of any instrument of ratification, acceptance, approval or accession;

(c) any date of entry into force of this convention in accordance with Articles 22, 23 and 24;

(d) any other act, notification or communication relating to this convention.

In witness whereof the undersigned, being duly authorised thereto, have signed this Convention.

Recommendation No. R(87) 15 of the Committee of Ministers to Member States Regulating the Use of Personal Data in the Police Sector (1987)[*]

Adopted by the Committee of Ministers on 17 September 1987 at the 410th meeting of the Ministers' Deputies

THE COMMITTEE OF MINISTERS, under the terms of Article 15.b of the Statute of the Council of Europe,[1]

CONSIDERING that the aim of the Council of Europe is to achieve a greater unity between its members;

AWARE of the increasing use of automatically processed personal data in the police sector and of the possible benefits obtained through the use of computers and other technical means in this field;

TAKING ACCOUNT also of concern about the possible threat to the privacy of the individual arising through the misuse of automated processing methods;

RECOGNISING the need to balance the interests of society in the prevention and suppression of criminal offences and the maintenance of public order on the one hand and the interests of the individual and his right to privacy on the other;

BEARING IN MIND the provisions of the Convention for the Protection of Individuals with regard to Automatic Processing of Personal Data of 28 January 1981 and in particular the derogations permitted under Article 9;

AWARE also of the provisions of Article 8 of the Convention for the Protection of Human Rights and Fundamental Freedoms,

RECOMMENDS the governments of member states to:

- be guided in their domestic law and practice by the principles appended to this Recommendation, and

- ensure publicity for the provisions appended to this Recommendation and in particular for the rights which its application confers on individuals.

---

[*] COUNCIL OF EUROPE, *Regulating the use of personal data in the police sector*, Strasbourg, 1988.

[1] When this Recommendation was adopted:
 - in accordance with Article 10.2.c of the Rules of Procedure for the meetings of the Ministers' Deputies, the Representative of Ireland reserved the right of his Government to comply with it or not, the Representative of the United Kingdom reserved the right of her Government to comply or not with Principles 2.2 and 2.4 of the Recommendation, and the Representative of the Federal Republic of Germany reserved the right of his Government to comply or not with Principle 2.1 of the Recommendation;
 - in accordance with Article 10.2.d of the said Rules of Procedure, the Representative of Switzerland abstained, stating that he reserved the right of his Government to comply with it or not and underlining that his abstention should not be interpreted as expressing disapproval of the Recommendation as a whole.

APPENDIX TO RECOMMENDATION NO. R(87) 15

Scope and definitions

The principles contained in this Recommendation apply to the collection, storage, use and communication of personal data for police purposes which are the subject of automatic processing.

For the purposes of this Recommendation, the expression "personal data" covers any information relating to an identified or identifiable individual. An individual shall not be regarded as "identifiable" if identification requires an unreasonable amount of time, cost and manpower.

The expression "for police purposes" covers all the tasks which the police authorities must perform for the prevention and suppression of criminal offences and the maintenance of public order.

The expression "responsible body" (controller of the file) denotes the authority, service or any other public body which is competent according to national law to decide on the purpose of an automated file, the categories of personal data which must be stored and the operations which are to be applied to them.

A member state may extend the principles contained in this Recommendation to personal data not undergoing automatic processing.

Manual processing of data should not take place if the aim is to avoid the provisions of this Recommendation.

A member state may extend the principles contained in this Recommendation to data relating to groups of persons, associations, foundations, companies, corporations or any other body consisting directly or indirectly of individuals, whether or not such bodies possess legal personality.

The provisions of this Recommendation should not be interpreted as limiting or otherwise affecting the possibility for a member state to extend, where appropriate, certain of these principles to the collection, storage and use of personal data for purposes of state security.

Basic principles

Principle 1

Control and notification

1.1. Each member state should have an independent supervisory authority outside the police sector which should be responsible for ensuring respect for the principles contained in this Recommendation.

1.2. New technical means for data processing may only be introduced if all reasonable measures have been taken to ensure that their use complies with the spirit of existing data protection legislation.

1.3. The responsible body should consult the supervisory authority in advance in any case where the introduction of automatic processing methods raises questions about the application of this Recommendation.

1.4. Permanent automated files should be notified to the supervisory authority. The notification should specify the nature of each file declared, the body responsible for its processing, its purposes, the type of data contained in the file and the persons to whom the data are communicated.

Ad hoc files which have been set up at the time of particular inquiries should also be notified to the supervisory authority either in accordance with the conditions settled with the latter, taking account of the specific nature of these files, or in accordance with national legislation.

Principle 2

Collection of data

2.1. The collection of personal data for police purposes should be limited to such as is necessary for the prevention of a real danger or the suppression of a specific criminal offence. Any exception to this provisions should be the subject of specific national legislation.

2.2. Where data concerning an individual have been collected and stored without his knowledge, and unless the data are deleted, he should be informed, where practicable, that information is held about him as soon as the object of the police activities is no longer likely to be prejudiced.

2.3. The collection of data by technical surveillance or other automated means should be provided for in specific provisions.

2.4. The collection of data on individuals solely on the basis that they have a particular racial origin, particular religious convictions, sexual behaviour or political opinions or belong to particular movements or organisations which are not proscribed by law should be prohibited. The collection of data concerning these factors may only be carried out if absolutely necessary for the purposes of a particular inquiry.

Principle 3

Storage of data

3.1. As far as possible, the storage of personal data for police purposes should be limited to accurate data and to such data as are necessary to allow police bodies to perform their lawful tasks within the framework of national law and their obligations arising from international law.

3.2. As far as possible, the different categories of data stored should be distinguished in accordance with their degree of accuracy or reliability and, in particular, data based on facts should be distinguished from data based on opinions or personal assessments.

3.3. Where data which have been collected for administrative purposes are to be stored permanently, they should be stored in a separate file. In any case, measures should be taken so that administrative data are not subject to rules applicable to police data.

Principle 4

Use of data by the police

4. Subject to Principle 5, personal data collected and stored by the police for police purposes should be used exclusively for those purposes.

Principle 5

Communication of data

5.1. *Communication within the police sector*

The communication of data between police bodies to be used for police purposes should only be permissible if there exists a legitimate interest for such communication within the framework of the legal powers of these bodies.

5.2.i.   *Communication to other public bodies*

Communication of data to other public bodies should only be permissible if, in a particular case:

- *a.* there exists a clear legal obligation or authorisation or with the authorisation of the supervisory authority, or if

- *b.* these data are indispensable to the recipient to enable him to fulfil his own lawful task and provided that the aim of the collection or processing to be carried out by the recipient is not incompatible with the original processing, and the legal obligations of the communicating body are not contrary to this.

5.2.ii.   Furthermore, communication to other public bodies is exceptionally permissible if, in a particular case:

- *a.* the communication is undoubtedly in the interest of the data subject and either the data subject has consented or circumstances are such as to allow a clear presumption of such consent, or if

- *b.* the communication is necessary so as to prevent a serious and imminent danger.

5.3.i.   *Communication to private parties*

The communication of data to private parties should only be permissible if, in a particular case, there exists a clear legal obligation or authorisation, or with the authorisation of the supervisory authority.

5.3.ii.   Communication to private parties is exceptionally permissible if, in a particular case:

- *a.* the communication is undoubtedly in the interest of the data subject and either the data subject has consented or circumstances are such as to allow a clear presumption of such consent, or if

- *b.* the communication is necessary so as to prevent a serious and imminent danger.

5.4.   *International communication*

Communication of data to foreign authorities should be restricted to police bodies. It should only be permissible:

- *a.* if there exists a clear legal provision under national or international law,

- *b.* in the absence of such a provision, if the communication is necessary for the prevention of a serious and imminent danger or is necessary for the suppression of a serious criminal offence under ordinary law,

and provided that domestic regulations for the protection of the person are not prejudiced.

5.5.i.   *Requests for communication*

Subject to specific provisions contained in national legislation or in international agreements, requests for communication of data should provide indications as to the body or person requesting them as well as the reason for the request and its objective.

5.5.ii.   *Conditions for communication*

As far as possible, the quality of data should be verified at the latest at the time of their communication. As far as possible, in all communications of data, judicial decisions, as well as decisions not to prosecute, should be indicated and data based on opinions or personal assessments, checked at source before being communicated and their degree of accuracy or reliability indicated.

If it is discovered that the data are no longer accurate and up to date, they should not be communicated. If data which are no longer accurate or up to date have been communicated, the communicating body should inform as far as possible all the recipients of the data of their non-conformity.

5.5.iii. *Safeguards for communication*

The data communicated to other public bodies, private parties and foreign authorities should not be used for purposes other than those specified in the request for communication.

Use of the data for other purposes should, without prejudice to paragraphs 5.2 to 5.4 of this principle, be made subject to the agreement of the communicating body.

5.6. *Interconnection of files and on-line access to files*

The interconnection of files with files held for different purposes is subject to either of the following conditions:

a. the grant of an authorisation by the supervisory body for the purposes of an inquiry into a particular offence, or

b. in compliance with a clear legal provision.

Direct access/on-line access to a file should only be allowed if it is in accordance with domestic legislation which should take account of Principles 3 to 6 of this Recommendation.

Principle 6

Publicity, right of access to police files, right of rectification and right of appeal

6.1. The supervisory authority should take measures so as to satisfy itself that the public is informed of the existence of files which are the subject of notification as well as of its rights in regard to these files. Implementation of this principle should take account of the specific nature of *ad hoc* files, in particular the need to avoid serious prejudice to the performance of a legal task of the police bodies.

6.2. The data subject should be able to obtain access to a police file at reasonable intervals and without excessive delay in accordance with the arrangements provided for by domestic law.

6.3. The data subject should be able to obtain, where appropriate, rectification of his data which are contained in a file.

Personal data which the exercise of the right of access reveals to be inaccurate or which are found to be excessive, inaccurate or irrelevant in application of any of the other principles contained in this Recommendation should be erased or corrected or else be the subject of a corrective statement added to the file.

Such erasure or corrective measures should extend as far as possible to all documents accompanying the police file and, if not done immediately, should be carried out, at the latest, at the time of subsequent processing of the data or of their next communication.

6.4. Exercise of the rights of access, rectification and erasure should only be restricted insofar as a restriction is indispensable for the performance of a legal task of the police or is necessary for the protection of the data subject or the rights and freedoms of others.

In the interests of the data subject, a written statement can be excluded by law for specific cases.

6.5. A refusal or a restriction of those rights should be reasoned in writing. It should only be possible to refuse to communicate the reasons insofar as this is indispensable for the performance of a legal task of the police or is necessary for the protection of the rights and freedoms of others.

6.6. Where access is refused, the data subject should be able to appeal to the supervisory authority or to another independent body which shall satisfy itself that the refusal is well founded.

Principle 7

Length of storage and updating of data

7.1. Measures should be taken so that personal data kept for police purposes are deleted if they are no longer necessary for the purposes for which they were stored.

For this purpose, consideration shall in particular be given to the following criteria: the need to retain data in the light of the conclusion of an inquiry into a particular case: a final judicial decision, in particular an acquittal; rehabilitation; spent convictions; amnesties; the age of the data subject; particular categories of data.

7.2. Rules aimed at fixing storage periods for the different categories of personal data as well as regular checks on their quality should be established in agreement with the supervisory authority or in accordance with domestic law.

Principle 8

Data security

8. The responsible body should take all the necessary measures to ensure the appropriate physical and logical security of the data and prevent unauthorised access, communication or alteration.

The different characteristics and contents of files should, for this purpose, be taken into account.

EC Directive No 95/46 of 24 October 1995 of the European Parliament and of the Council on the Protection of Individuals with regard to the Processing of Personal Data and on the Free Movement of such Data (1995)*

Brussels, 24 October 1995

Chapter 1

General provisions

Article 1

Object of the Directive

1. In accordance with this Directive, Member States shall protect the fundamental rights and freedoms of natural persons, and in particular their right to privacy with respect to the processing of personal data.

2. Member States shall neither restrict nor prohibit the free flow of personal data between Member States for reasons connected with the protection afforded under paragraph 1.

Article 2

Definitions

For the purposes of this Directive:

(a) 'personal data' shall mean any information relating to an identified or identifiable natural person ('data subject'); an identifiable person is one who can be identified, directly or indirectly, in particular by reference to an identification number or to one or more factors specific to his physical, physiological, mental, economic, cultural or social identity;

(b) 'processing of personal data'('processing') shall mean any operation or set of operations which is performed upon personal data, whether or not by automatic means, such as collection, recording, organization, storage, adaptation of alteration, retrieval, consultation, use, disclosure by transmission, dissemination or otherwise making available, alignment or combination, blocking erasure or destruction;

(c) 'personal data filing system' ('filing system') shall mean any structured set of personal data which are accessible according to specific criteria, whether centralized, decentralized or dispersed on a functional or geographical basis:

(d) 'controller' shall mean the natural or legal person, public authority, agency or any other body which alone or jointly with others determines the purposes and means of the processing of personal data; where the purposes and means of processing are determined by national or Community laws or regulations, the controller or the specific criteria for his nomination may be designated by national or Community law;

(e) 'processor' shall mean a natural or legal person, public authority, agency or any other body which processes personal data on behalf of the controller;

---

* *Official Journal of the European Communities* No L 281, 23.11.1995, p.31

(f) 'third party' shall mean any natural or legal person, public authority, agency or any other body other than the data subject, the controller, the processor and the persons who, under the direct authority of the controller or the processor, are authorized to process the data;

(g) 'recipient' shall mean a natural or legal person, public authority, agency or any other body to whom data are disclosed, whether a third party or not; however, authorities which may receive data in the framework of a particular inquiry shall not be regarded as recipients;

(h) 'the data subject's consent' shall mean any freely given specific and informed indication of his wishes by which the data subject signifies his agreement to personal data relating to him being processed.

Article 3

Scope

1. This Directive shall apply to the processing of personal data wholly or partly by automatic means, and to the processing otherwise than by automatic means of personal data which form part of a filing system or are intended to form part of a filing system.

2. This Directive shall not apply to the processing of personal data:

- in the course of an activity which falls outside the scope of Community law, such as those provided for by Titles V and VI of the Treaty on European Union and in any case to processing operations concerning public security, defence, State security (including the economic well-being of the State when the processing operation relates to State security matters) and the activities of the State in areas of criminal law,

- by a natural person in the course of a purely personal or household activity.

Article 4

National law applicable

1. Each Member State shall apply the national provisions it adopts pursuant to this Directive to the processing of personal data where:

(a) the processing is carried out in the context of the activities of an establishment of the controller on the territory of the Member State; when the same controller is established on the territory of several Member States, he must take the necessary measures to ensure that each of these establishments complies with the obligations laid down by the national law applicable;

(b) the controller is not established on the Member State's territory, but in a place where its national law applies by virtue of international public law;

(c) the controller is not established on Community territory and, for purposes of processing personal data makes use of equipment, automated or otherwise, situated on the territory of the said Member State, unless such equipment is used only for purposes of transit through the territory of the Community.

2. In the circumstances referred to in paragraph 1 (c), the controller must designate a representative established in the territory of that Member State, without prejudice to legal actions which could be initiated against the controller himself.

Chapter II

General rules on the lawfulness of the processing of personal data

Article 5

Member States shall, within the limits of the provisions of this Chapter, determine more precisely the conditions under which the processing of personal data is lawful.

Section I

Principles relating to data quality

Article 6

1. Member States shall provide that personal data must be:

    (a) processed fairly and lawfully;

    (b) collected for specified, explicit and legitimate purposes and not further processed in a way incompatible with those purposes. Further processing of data for historical, statistical or scientific purposes shall not be considered as incompatible provided that Member States provide appropriate safeguards;

    (c) adequate, relevant and not excessive in relation to the purposes for which they are collected and/or further processed;

    (d) accurate and, where necessary, kept up to date; every reasonable step must be taken to ensure that data which are inaccurate or incomplete, having regard to the purposes for which they were collected or for which they are further processed, are erased or rectified;

    (e) kept in form which permits identification of data subjects for no longer than is necessary for the purposes for which the data were collected or for which they are further processed. Member States shall lay down appropriate safeguards for personal data stored for longer periods for historical, statistical or scientific use.

2. It shall be for the controller to ensure that paragraph 1 is complied with.

Section II

Criteria for making data processing legitimate

Article 7

Member States shall provide that personal data may be processed only if:

(a) the data subject has, unambiguously given his consent; or

(b) processing is necessary for the performance of a contract to which the data subject is party or in order to take steps at the request of the data subject prior to entering into a contract; or

(c) processing is necessary for compliance with a legal obligation to which the controller is subject; or

(d) processing is necessary in order to protect the vital interests of the data subject; or

(e) processing is necessary for the performance of a task carried out in the public interest or in the exercise of official authority vested in the controller or in a third party to whom the data are disclosed; or

(f) processing is necessary for the purposes of the legitimate interests pursued by the controller or by the third party or parties to whom the data are disclosed except where such interests are overridden by the interests for fundamental rights and freedoms of the data subject which require protection under Article 1 (1).

Section III

Special categories of processing

Article 8

The processing of special categories of data

1. Member States shall prohibit the processing of personal data revealing racial or ethnic origin, political opinions, religious or philosophical beliefs, trade-union membership, and the processing of data concerning health or sex life.

2. Paragraph 1 shall not apply where:

(a) the data subject has given his explicit consent to the processing of those data, except where the laws of the Member State provide that the prohibition referred to in paragraph 1 may not be lifted by the data subject's giving his consent; or

(b) processing is necessary for the purposes of carrying out the obligations and specific rights of the controller in the field of employment law in so far as it is authorized by national law providing for adequate safeguards; or

(c) processing is necessary to protect the vital interests of the data subject or of another person where the data subject is physically or legally incapable of giving his consent; or

(d) processing is carried out in the course of its legitimate activities with appropriate guarantees by a foundation, association or any other non-profit-seeking body with a political, philosophical, religious or trade-union aim and on condition that the processing relates solely to the members of the body or to persons who have regular contact with it in connection with its purposes and that the data are not disclosed to a third party without the consent of the data subjects or

(e) the processing relates to data which are manifestly made public by the data subject or is necessary for the establishment, exercise or defence of legal claims.

3. Paragraph 1 shall not apply where processing of the data is required for the purposes of preventive medicine, medical diagnosis, the provision of care or treatment or the management of health-care services, and where those data are processed by a health professional subject under national law or rules established by national competent bodies to the obligation of professional secrecy or by another person also subject to an equivalent obligation of secrecy.

4. Subject to the provision of suitable safeguards, Member States may, for reasons of substantial public interest, lay down exemptions in addition to those laid down in paragraph 2 either by national law or by decision of the supervisory authority.

5. Processing of data relating to offences, criminal convictions or security measures may be carried out only under the control of official authority, or if suitable specific safeguards are provided under national law, subject to derogations which may be granted by the Member State under national provisions providing suitable specific safeguards. However, a complete register of criminal convictions may be kept only under the control of official authority.

Member States may provide that data relating to administrative sanctions or judgements in civil cases shall also be processed under the control of official authority.

6. Derogations from paragraph 1 provided for in paragraphs 4 and 5 shall be notified to the Commission.

7. Member States shall determine the conditions under which a national identification number or any other identifier of general application may be processed.

Article 9

Processing of personal data and freedom of expression

Member States shall provide for exemptions or derogations from the provisions of this Chapter, Chapter IV and Chapter VI for the processing of personal data carried out solely for journalistic purposes or the purpose of artistic or literary expression only if they are necessary to reconcile the right to privacy with the rules governing freedom of expression.

Section IV

Information to be given to the data subject

Article 10

Information in cases of collection of data from the data subject

Member States shall provide that the controller or his representative must provide a data subject from whom data relating to himself are collected with at least the following information, except where he already has it:

(a) the identity of the controller and of his representative, if any;

(b) the purposes of the processing for which the data are intended;

(c) any further information such as

- the recipients or categories of recipients of the data.

- whether replies to the questions are obligatory or voluntary, as well as the possible consequences of failure to reply,

- the existence of the right of access to and the right to rectify the data concerning him

in so far as such further information is necessary, having regard to the specific circumstances in which the data are collected, to guarantee fair processing in respect of the data subject.

Article 11

Information where the data have not bene obtained from the data subject

1. Where the data have not been obtained from the data subject, Member States shall provide that the controller or his representative must at the time of undertaking the recording of personal data or if a disclosure to a third party is envisaged, no later that the time when the data are first disclosed provide the data subject with at least the following information, except where he already has it:

(a) the identity of the controller and of his representative, if any;

(b) the purposes of the processing;

(c) any further information such as

- the categories of data concerned,

- the recipients or categories of recipients,
- the existence of the right of access to and the right to rectify the data concerning him

in so far as such further information is necessary, having regard to the specific circumstances in which the data are processed, to guarantee fair processing in respect of the data subject.

2. Paragraph 1 shall not apply where, in particular for processing for statistical purposes or for the purposes of historical or scientific research, the provision of such information proves impossible or would involve a disproportionate effort or if recording or disclosure is expressly laid down by law. In these cases Member States shall provide appropriate safeguards.

Section V

The data subject's right of access to data

Article 12

Right of access

Member States shall guarantee every data subject the right to obtain from the controller:

(a) without constraint at reasonable intervals and without excessive delay or expense:

- confirmation as to whether or not data relating to him are being processed and information at least as to the purposes of the processing, the categories of data concerned, and the recipients or categories of recipients to whom the data are disclosed,
- communication to him in an intelligible form of the data undergoing processing and of any available information as to their source,
- knowledge of the logic involved in any automatic processing of data concerning him at least in the case of the automated decisions referred to in Article 15 (1);

(b) as appropriate the rectification, erasure or blocking of data the processing of which does not comply with the provisions of this Directive, in particular because of the incomplete or inaccurate nature of the data;

(c) notification to third parties to whom the data have been disclosed of any rectification, erasure or blocking carried out in compliance with (b), unless this proves impossible or involves a disproportionate effort.

Section VI

Exemptions and restrictions

Article 13

Exemptions and restrictions

1. Member States may adopt legislative measures to restrict the scope of the obligations and rights provided for in Articles 6 (1), 10, 11 (1), 12 and 21 when such a restriction constitutes a necessary measure to safeguard:

(a) national security;

(b) defence:

(c) public security;

(d) the prevention, investigation, detection and prosecution of criminal offences, or of breaches of ethics for regulated professions;

(e) an important economic or financial interest of a Member State or of the European Union, including monetary, budgetary and taxation matters;

(f) a monitoring, inspection or regulatory function connected, even occasionally, with the exercise of official authority in cases referred to in (c), (d) and (e);

(g) the protection of the data subject or of the rights and freedoms of others.

2. Subject to adequate legal safeguards, in particular that the data are not used for taking measures or decisions regarding any particular individual, Member States may, where there is clearly no risk of breaching the privacy of the data subject, restrict by a legislative measure the rights provided for in Article 12 when data are processed solely for purposes of scientific research or are kept in personal form for a period which does not exceed the period necessary for the sole purpose of creating statistics.

Section VII

The data subject's right to object

Article 14

The data subject's right to object

Member States shall grant the data subject the right:

(a) at least in the cases referred to in Article 7 (e) and (f), to object at any time on compelling legitimate grounds relating to his particular situation to the processing of data relating to him, save where otherwise provided by national legislation. Where there is a justified objection, the processing instigated by the controller may no longer involve those data;

(b) to object, on request and free of charge, to the processing of personal data relating to him which the controller anticipates being processed for the purposes of direct marketing, or to be informed before personal data are disclosed for the first time to third parties or used on their behalf for the purposes of direct marketing, and to be expressly offered the right to object free of charge to such disclosures or uses.

Member States shall take the necessary measures to ensure that data subjects are aware of the existence of the right referred to in the first subparagraph of (b).

Article 15

Automated individual decisions

1. Member States shall grant the right to every person not to be subject to a decision which produces legal effects concerning him or significantly affects him and which is based solely on automated processing of data intended to evaluate certain personal aspects relating to him, such as his performance at work, creditworthiness, reliability, conduct, etc.

2. Subject to the other Articles of this Directive, Member States shall provide that a person may be subjected to a decision of the kind referred to in paragraph 1 if that decision:

(a) is taken in the course of the entering into or performance of a contract, provided the request for the entering into or the performance of the contract, lodged by the data subject, has been satisfied or that there are suitable measures to safeguard his legitimate interests, such as arrangements allowing him to put his point of view, or

(b) is authorized by a law which also lays down measures to safeguard the data subject's legitimate interests.

Section VIII

Confidentiality and security of processing

Article 16

Confidentiality and security of processing

Any person acting under the authority of the controller or of the processor, including the processor himself, who has access to personal data must not process them except on instructions from the controller, unless he is required to do so by law.

Article 17

Security of processing

1. Member States shall provide that the controller must implement appropriate technical and organizational measures to protect personal data against accidental or unlawful destruction or accidental loss, alteration, unauthorized disclosure or access, in particular where the processing involves the transmission of data over a network, and against all other unlawful forms of processing.

Having regard to the state of the art and the cost of their implementation, such measures shall ensure a level of security appropriate to the risks represented by the processing and the nature of the data to be protected.

2. The Member States shall provide that the controller must, where processing is carried out on his behalf, choose a processor providing sufficient guarantees in respect of the technical security measures and organizational measures governing the processing to be carried out, and must ensure compliance with those measures.

3. The carrying out of processing by way of a processor must be governed by a contract or legal act binding the processor to the controller and stipulating in particular that:

- the processor shall act only on instructions from the controller,

- the obligations set out in paragraph 1, as defined by the law of the Member State in which the processor is established, shall also be incumbent on the processor.

4. For the purposes of keeping proof, the parts of the contract or the legal act relating to data protection and the requirements relating to the measures referred to in paragraph 1 shall be in writing or in another equivalent form.

Section IX

Notification

Article 18

Obligation to notify the supervisory authority

1. Member States shall provide that the controller or his representative, if any, must notify the supervisory authority referred to in Article 28 before carrying out any wholly or partly

automatic processing operation or set of such operations intended to serve a single purpose or several related purposes.

2. Member States may provide for the simplification of or exemption from notification only in the following cases and under the following conditions:

(a) where, for categories of processing operations which are unlikely, taking account of the data to be processed, to affect adversely the rights and freedoms of data subjects, they specify the purposes of the processing, the data or categories of data undergoing processing, the category or categories of data subject, the recipients or categories of recipient to whom the data are to be disclosed and the length of time the data are to be stored, and/or

(b) where the controller, in compliance with the national law which governs him, appoints a personal data protection official, responsible in particular:

- for ensuring in an independent manner the internal application of the national provisions taken pursuant to this Directive

- for keeping the register of processing operations carried out by the controller, containing the items of information referred to in Article 21 (2),

thereby ensuring that the rights and freedoms of the data subjects are unlikely to be adversely affected by the processing operations.

3. Member States may provide that paragraph 1 does not apply to processing whose sole purpose is the keeping of a register which according to laws or regulations is intended to provide information to the public and which is open to consultation either by the public in general or by any person demonstrating a legitimate interest.

4. Member States may provide for an exemption from the obligation to notify or a simplification of the notification in the case of processing operations referred to in Article 8 (2) (d).

5. Member States may stipulate that certain or all non-automatic processing operations involving personal data shall be notified, or provide for these processing operations to be subject to simplified notification.

Article 19

Contents of notification

1. Member States shall specify the information to be given in the notification. It shall include at least:

(a) the name and address of the controller and of his representative, if any;

(b) the purpose or purposes of the processing;

(c) a description of the category or categories of data subject and of the data or categories of data relating to them;

(d) the recipients or categories of recipient to whom the data might be disclosed;

(e) proposed transfers of data to third countries;

(f) a general description allowing a preliminary assessment to be made of the appropriateness of the measures taken pursuant to Article 17 to ensure security of processing.

2. Member States shall specify the procedures under which any change affecting the information referred to in paragraph 1 must be notified to the supervisory authority.

Article 20

Prior checking

1. Member States shall determine the processing operations likely to present specific risks to the rights and freedoms of data subjects and shall check that these processing operations are examined prior to the start thereof.

2. Such prior checks shall be carried out by the supervisory authority following receipt of a notification from the controller or by the data protection official, who, in cases of doubt, must consult the supervisory authority.

3. Member States may also carry out such checks in the context of preparation either of a measure of the national parliament or of a measure based on such a legislative measure, which define the nature of the processing and lay down appropriate safeguards.

Article 21

Publicizing of processing operations

1. Member States shall take measures to ensure that processing operations are publicized.

2. Member States shall provide that a register of processing operations notified in accordance with Article 18 shall be kept by the supervisory authority.

The register shall contain at least the information listed in Article 19 (1) (a) to (e).

The register may be inspected by any person.

3. Member States shall provide, in relation to processing operations not subject to notification, that controllers or another body appointed by the Member States make available at least the information referred to in Article 19 (1) (a) to (e) in an appropriate form to any person on request.

Member States may provide that this provision does not apply to processing whose sole purpose is the keeping of a register which according to laws or regulations is intended to provide information to the public and which is open to consultation either by the public in general or by any person who can provide proof of a legitimate interest.

Chapter III

Judicial remedies, liability and sanctions

Article 22

Remedies

Without prejudice to any administrative remedy for which provisions may be made, inter alia before the supervisory authority referred to in Article 28, prior to referral to the judicial authority, Member States shall provide for the right of every person to a judicial remedy for any breach of the rights guaranteed him by the national law applicable to the processing in question.

Article 23

Liability

1. Member States shall provide that any person who has suffered damage as a result of an unlawful processing operation or of any act incompatible with the national provisions adopted pursuant to this Directive is entitled to receive compensation from the controller for the damage suffered.

2. The controller may be exempted from this liability, in whole or in part, if he proves that he is not responsible for the event giving rise to the damage.

Article 24

Sanctions

The Member States shall adopt suitable measures to ensure the full implementation of the provisions of this Directive and shall in particular lay down the sanctions to be imposed in case of infringement of the provisions adopted pursuant to this Directive.

Chapter IV

Transfer of personal data to third countries

Article 25

Principles

1. The Member States shall provide that the transfer to a third country of personal data which are undergoing processing or are intended for processing after transfer may take place only if, without prejudice to compliance with the national provisions adopted pursuant to the other provisions of this Directive, the third country in question ensures an adequate level of protection.

2. The adequacy of the level of protection afforded by a third country shall be assessed in the light of all the circumstances surrounding a data transfer operation or set of data transfer operations; particular consideration shall be given to the nature of the data, the purpose and duration of the proposed processing operation or operations, the country of origin and country of final destination, the rules of law, both general and sectoral, in force in the third country in question and the professional rules and security measures which are complied with in that country.

3. The Member States and the Commission shall inform each other of cases where they consider that a third country does not ensure an adequate level of protection within the meaning of paragraph 2.

4. Where the Commission finds, under the procedure provided for in Article 31 (2), that a third country does not ensure an adequate level of protection within the meaning of paragraph 2 of this Article, Member States shall take the measures necessary to prevent any transfer of data of the same type to the third country in question.

5. At the appropriate time, the Commission shall enter into negotiations with a view to remedying the situation resulting from the finding made pursuant to paragraph 4.

6. The Commission may find, in accordance with the procedure referred to in Article 31 (2), that a third country ensures an adequate level of protection within the meaning of paragraph 2 of this Article, by reason of its domestic law or of the international commitments it has entered into, particularly upon conclusion of the negotiations referred to in paragraph 5, for the protection of the private lives and basic freedoms and rights of individuals.

Member States shall take the measures necessary to comply with the Commission's decision.

Article 26

Derogations

1. By way of derogation from Article 25 and save where otherwise provided by domestic law governing particular cases, Member States shall provide that a transfer or a set of transfers of personal data to a third country which does not ensure an adequate level of protection within the meaning of Article 25 (2) may take place on condition that:

(a) the data subject has given his consent unambiguously to the proposed transfer; or

(b) the transfer is necessary for the performance of a contract between the data subject and the controller or the implementation of precontractual measures taken in response to the data subject's request; or

(c) the transfer is necessary for the conclusion or performance of a contract concluded in the interest of the data subject between the controller and a third party; or

(d) the transfer is necessary or legally required on important public interest grounds, or for the establishment, exercise or defence of legal claims; or

(e) the transfer is necessary in order to protect the vital interests of the data subject; or

(f) the transfer is made from a register which according to laws or regulations is intended to provide information to the public and which is open to consultation either by the public in general or by any person who can demonstrate legitimate interest, to the extent that the conditions laid down in law for consultation are fulfilled in the particular case.

2. Without prejudice to paragraph 1, a Member State may authorize a transfer or a set of transfers of personal data to a third country which does not ensure an adequate level of protection within the meaning of Article 25 (2), where the controller adduces adequate safeguards with respect to the protection of the privacy and fundamental rights and freedoms of individuals and as regards the exercise of the corresponding rights; such safeguards may in particular result from appropriate contractual clauses.

3. The Member States shall inform the Commission and the other Member States of the authorizations it grants pursuant to paragraph 2.

If a Member State or the Commission objects on justified grounds involving the protection of the privacy and fundamental rights and freedoms of individuals, the Commission shall take appropriate measures in accordance with the procedure laid down in Article 31 (2).

Member States shall take the necessary measures to comply with the Commission's decision.

4. Where the Commission decides, in accordance with the procedure referred to in Article 31 (2), that certain standard contractual clauses offer sufficient safeguards as required by paragraph 2, Member States shall take the necessary measures to comply with the Commission's decision.

Chapter V

Codes of conduct

Article 27

1. The Member States and the Commission shall encourage the drawing up of codes of conduct intended to contribute to the proper implementation of the national provisions adopted by the Member States pursuant to this Directive, taking account of the specific features of the various sectors.

2. Member States shall make provision for trade associations and other bodies representing other categories of controllers which have drawn up draft national codes or which have the intention of amending or extending existing national codes to be able to submit them to the opinion of the national authority.

Member States shall make provision for this authority to ascertain, among other things, whether the drafts submitted to it are in accordance with the national provisions adopt pursuant to this Directive. If it sees fit, the authority shall seek the views of data subjects or their representatives.

3. Draft Community codes, and amendments or extensions to existing Community codes, may be submitted to the Working Party referred to in Article 29. This Working Party shall determine, among other things, whether the drafts submitted to it are in accordance with the national provisions adopted pursuant to this Directive. If it sees fit, the authority shall seek the views of data subjects or their representatives. The Commission may ensure appropriate publicity for the codes which have been approved by the Working Party.

Chapter VI

Supervisory authority and working party on the protection of individuals with regard to the processing of personal data

Article 28

Supervisory authority

1. Each Member State shall provide that one or more public authorities are responsible for monitoring the application within its territory of the provisions adopted by the Member States pursuant to this Directive.

These authorities shall act with complete independence in exercising the functions entrusted to them.

2. Each Member State shall provide that the supervisory authorities are consulted when drawing up administrative measures or regulations relating to the protection of individuals' rights and freedoms with regard to the processing of personal data.

3. Each authority shall in particular be endowed with:

(a) investigative powers, such as powers of access to data forming the subject-matter of processing operations and powers to collect all the information necessary for the performance of its supervisory duties,

(b) effective powers of intervention, such as, for example, that of delivering opinions before processing operations are carried out, in accordance with Article 20, and ensuring appropriate publication of such opinions, of ordering the blocking, erasure or destruction of data, of imposing a temporary or definitive ban on processing, of warning or admonishing the controller, or that of referring the matter to national parliaments or other political institutions,

(c) the power to engage in legal proceedings where the national provisions adopted pursuant to this Directive have been violated or to bring these violations to the attention of the judicial authorities.

Decisions by the supervisory authority which give rise to complaints may be appealed against through the courts.

4. Each supervisory authority shall hear claims lodged by any person, or by an association representing that person, concerning the protection of his rights and freedoms in regard to the processing of personal data. The person concerned shall be informed of the outcome of the claim.

Each supervisory authority shall, in particular, hear claims for checks on the lawfulness of data processing lodged by any person when the national provisions adopted pursuant to Article 13 of this Directive apply. The person shall at any rate be informed that a check has taken place.

5. Each supervisory authority shall draw up a report on its activities at regular intervals. The report shall be made public.

6. Each supervisory authority is competent, whatever the national law applicable to the processing in question, to exercise, on the territory of its own Member State, the powers conferred on it in accordance with paragraph 3. Each authority may be requested to exercise its powers by an authority of another Member State.

The supervisory authorities shall cooperate with one another to the extent necessary for the performance of their duties, in particular by exchanging all useful information.

7. Member States shall provide that the members and staff of the supervisory authority, even after their employment has ended, are to be subject to a duty of professional secrecy with regard to confidential information to which they have access.

Article 29

Working Party on the Protection of Individuals with regard to the Processing of Personal Data

1. A Working Party on the Protection of Individuals with regard to the Processing of Personal Data, hereinafter referred to as ' the Working Party', is hereby set up.

It shall have advisory status and act independently.

2. The Working Party shall be composed of a representative of the supervisory authority or authorities designated by each Member State and of a representative of the authority or authorities established for the Community institutions and bodies, and of a representative of the Commission.

Each member of the Working Party shall be designated by the institution, authority or authorities which he represents. Where a Member State has designated more than one supervisory authority, they shall nominate a joint representative. The same shall apply to the authorities established for Community institutions and bodies.

3. The Working Party shall take decisions by a simple majority of the representatives of the supervisory authorities.

4. The Working Party shall elect its chairman. The chairman's term of office shall be two years. His appointment shall be renewable.

5. The Working Party's secretariat shall be provided by the Commission.

6. The Working Party shall adopt its own rules of procedure.

7. The Working Party shall consider items placed on its agenda by its chairman, either on his own initiative or at the request of a representative of the supervisory authorities or at the Commission's request.

Article 30

1. The Working Party shall:

   (a) examine any question covering the application of the national measures adopted under this Directive in order to contribute to the uniform application of such measures;

   (b) give the Commission an opinion on the level of protection in the Community and in third countries;

   (c) advise the Commission on any proposed amendment of this Directive, on any additional or specific measures to safeguard the rights and freedoms of natural persons with regard to the processing of personal data and on any other proposed Community measures affecting such rights and freedoms;

(d) give an opinion on codes of conduct drawn up at Community level.

2. If the Working Party finds that divergences likely to affect the equivalence of protection for persons with regard to the processing of personal data in the Community are arising between the laws or practices of Member States, it shall inform the Commission accordingly.

3. The Working Party may, on its own initiative, make recommendations on all matters relating to the protection of persons with regard to the processing of personal data in the Community.

4. The Working Party's opinions and recommendations shall be forwarded to the Commission and to the committee referred to in Article 31.

5. The Commission shall inform the Working Party of the action it has taken in response to its opinions and recommendations. It shall do so in a report which shall also be forwarded to the European Parliament and the Council. The report shall be made public.

6. The Working Party shall draw up an annual report on the situation regarding the protection of natural persons with regard to the processing of personal data in the Community and in third countries, which it shall transmit to the Commission, the European Parliament and the Council. The report shall be made public.

Chapter VII

Community implementing measures

Article 31

The Committee

1. The Commission shall be assisted by a committee composed of the representatives of the Member States and chaired by the representative of the Commission.

2. The representative of the Commission shall submit to the committee a draft of the measures to be taken. The committee shall deliver its opinion on the draft within a time limit which the chairman may lay down according to the urgency of the matter.

The opinion shall be delivered by the majority laid down in Article 148 (2) of the Treaty. The votes of the representatives of the Member States within the committee shall be weighted in the manner set out in that Article. The chairman shall not vote.

The Commission shall adopt measures which shall apply immediately. However, if these measures are not in accordance with the opinion of the committee, they shall be communicated by the Commission to the Council forthwith. It that event:

(a) the Commission shall defer application of the measures which it has decided for a period of three months from the date of communication,

(b) the Council, acting by a qualified majority, may take a different decision within the time limit referred to in the first indent.

Final provisions

Article 32

1. Member States shall bring into force the laws, regulations and administrative provisions necessary to comply with this Directive at the latest at the end of a period of three years from the date of its adoption.

When Member States adopt these measures, they shall contain a reference to this Directive or be accompanied by such reference on the occasion of their official publication. The methods of making such reference shall be laid down by the Member States.

2. Member States shall ensure that processing already under way on the date national provisions adopted pursuant to this Directive enter into force, is brought into conformity with these provisions within three years of this date.

By way of derogation from the preceding subparagraph, Member States may provide that the processing of data already held in manual filing systems on the date of entry into force of the national provisions adopted in implementation of this Directive shall be brought into conformity with Articles 6, 7 and 8 of this Directive within 12 years of the date on which it is adopted. Member States shall, however, grant the data subject the right to obtain, at his request and in particular at the time of exercising his right of access, the rectification, erasure or blocking of data which are incomplete, inaccurate or stored in a way incompatible with the legitimate purposes pursued by the controller.

3. By way of derogation from paragraph 2, Member States may provide, subject to suitable safeguards, that data kept for the sole purpose of historical research need not be brought into conformity with Articles 6, 7 and 8 of this Directive.

4. Member States shall communicate to the Commission the text of the provisions of domestic law which they adopt in the field covered by this Directive.

Article 33

1. The Commission shall report to the Council and the European Parliament at regular intervals, starting not later than three years after the date referred to in Article 32 (1), on the implementation of this Directive, attaching to its report, if necessary, suitable proposals for amendments. The report shall be made public.

2. The Commission shall examine, in particular, the application of this Directive to the data processing of sound and image data relating to natural persons and shall submit any appropriate proposals which prove to be necessary, taking account of developments in information technology and in the light of the state of progress in the information society.

Article 34

This Directive is addressed to the Member States.

Index of International Instruments

(First) Additional Protocol to the European Convention on Extradition (excerpts) (1975) 207

Additional Protocol to the European Convention on Mutual Assistance in Criminal Matters (excerpts) (1978)   337

Commonwealth Scheme for the Rendition of Fugitive Offenders (1966) . 225

Constitution of Interpol (1956) . . 249

Convention on the Transfer of Sentenced Persons (1983) 407

Convention against Illicit Traffic in Narcotic Drugs and Psychotropic Substances (1988) 83

Convention against Torture and Other Cruel, Inhuman or Degrading Treatment or Punishment (1984) 65

Convention on the Physical Protection of Nuclear Material 55

Convention on Insider Trading (1989) 169

Convention on the Protection of the European Communities' Financial Interests (1995) 145

Convention on Laundering, Search, Seizure and Confiscation of the Proceeds from Crime (1990) 107

Convention for the Suppression of Unlawful Acts against the Safety of Maritime Navigation (excerpts) (1988) 51

Convention on the Non-applicability of Statutory Limitations to War Crimes and Crimes against Humanity (1968) 27

Convention between Belgium and the United States of America concerning the Mutual Extradition of Fugitive Offenders (1901) 237

Convention for the Protection of Individuals with regard to Automatic Processing of Personal Data (1981) . . . 583

Convention on The Prevention and Suppression of the Crime of Genocide (1948) 35

Convention for the Suppression of Unlawful Seizure of Aircraft (1970)   41

Convention for the Suppression of Unlawful Acts against the Safety of Civil Aviation (excerpts) (1971) . . . 45

Convention on the Prevention and Punishment of Crimes against Internationally Protected Persons including Diplomatic Agents (excerpts) (1973) 49

Council of Europe Draft Convention for the Protection of the Environment through Criminal Law (1996) . . . 135

Council Regulation (EC, EURATOM) No 2988/95 of 18 December 1995 on the Protection of the European Communities' Financial Interests (1995) . 151

Draft Code of Offences against the Peace and Security of Mankind (excerpts) (1954) 503

Draft Code of Crimes against Peace and Security (1996) 515

EC Council Directive No 89/592 of 13 November 1989 coordinating Regulations on Insider Dealing (1989) . . . 177

EC Council Directive No 91/308 of 10 June 1991 on Prevention of the Use of the Financial System for the Purpose of Money Laundering (1991) 125

EC Council Regulation No 1468/81 of 19 May 1981 on Mutual Assistance between the Administrative Authorities of the Member States and Cooperation between the Latter and the Commission to Ensure the Correct Application of the Law on Customs or Agricultural Matters (1981) 309

EC Directive No 95/46 of 24 October 1995 of the European Parliament and of the Council on the Protection of Individuals with regard to the Processing of Personal Data and on the Free Movement of such Data (1995) 599

EEC-Treaty (excerpts) (1957) . . . 527

European Convention on the Transfer of Proceedings in Criminal Matters (1972) 365

European Convention on Mutual Assistance in Criminal Matters (1959) . 329

European Convention on the Non-applicability of Statutory Limitation to Crimes against Humanity and War Crimes (1974) 29

European Convention on the International Validity of Criminal Judgments (1970) 379

European Convention on Extradition (1957) 197

European Convention on the Suppression of Terrorism (1977) 211

European Convention on the Protection of Human Rights and Fundamental Freedoms (1950) 561

European Convention for the Prevention of Torture and Inhuman or Degrading Treatment or Punishment (1987) .. 75

Europol Convention (1995) 275

First Protocol to the Convention for the Protection of Human Rights and Fundamental Freedoms (1952) 573

Geneva Conventions of 12 August 1949 (excerpts) (1949) 5

Inter-American Convention against Corruption (1996) 159

International Convention on the Suppression and Punishment of the Crime of Apartheid (excerpts) (1973) ... 37

International Convention against the Taking of Hostages (excerpts) (1979) 47

International Covenant on Civil and Political Rights (1966) 543

International Law Commission - Draft Articles on State Responsibilty (excerpts) (1976) 523

International Law Commission - Draft Statute for an International Criminal Court (1994) 477

International Law Commission - Draft Code of Crimes against the Peace and Security of Mankind (1991) 505

Nuremberg Charter: Charter of International Military Tribunal, adopted by the Big Four Powers (1945) 419

Nuremberg Principles: Principles of International Law Recognized in the Charter of the Nuremberg Tribunal and in the Judgment of the Tribunal (1950) 501

Optional Protocol to the UN Model Treaty on Mutual Assistance in Criminal Matters concerning the Proceeds of Crime (1990) 327

Protocol No.6 to the Convention for the Protection of Human Rights and Fundamental Freedoms concerning the Abolition of the Death Penalty (1983) . 575

Protocol to the Convention on Insider Trading (1989) 175

Protocol No.7 to the Convention for the Protection of Human Rights and Fundamental Freedoms (1984) 577

Protocol additional to the Geneva Conventions of 12 August 1949, and Relating to the Protection of Victims of Non-International Armed Conflicts (Protocol II) (excerpts) (1977) 25

Protocol additional to the Geneva Conventions of 12 August 1949, and relating to the Protection of Victims of International Armed Conflicts (Protocol I) (excerpts) (1977) 17

Recommendation No. R(87) 15 of the Committee of Ministers to Member States Regulating the Use of Personal Data in the Police Sector (1987) . 593

Recommendation No. R (80)8 of the Committee of Ministers to Member States concerning the Practical application of the European Convention on Mutual Assistance in Criminal Matters 239

Recommendation No. R (80) 7 of the Committee of Ministers to Member States Concerning the Practical Application of the European Convention on Extradition (1980) 215

Recommendation No. R (80) 9 of the Committee of Ministers to Member States Concerning Extradition to States not Party to the European Convention on Human Rights 217

Rules of Procedure and Evidence of the International Tribunal for the Former Yugoslavia (1994) 437

Scheme Relating to Mutual Assistance in Criminal Matters within the Commonwealth including Amendments made by Law Ministers in April 1990 . 345

Schengen Convention - Title III - (excerpts) (1990)   123, 221, 257, 341, 415

Second Additional Protocol to the European Convention on Extradition (excerpts) (1978) 209

Second Optional Protocol to the International Covenant on Civil and Political Rights, aiming at the Abolition of the Death Penalty (1989) 557

Statute of the International Tribunal for the Former Yugoslavia (1993) . . . 427

Statute of the International Tribunal for Rwanda (1994) 467

Supplementary Treaty concerning the Extradition Treaty between the Government of the United States of America and the Government of the United Kingdom of Great Britain and Northern Ireland signed at London on 8 June 1972 (excerpts) (1985) 243

Treaty on the European Union (excerpts) (1992) 531

UN Model Treaty on Mutual Assistance in Criminal Matters (1990) 319

UN Model Treaty on Extradition (1990) 187

UN Model Treaty on the Transfer of Supervision of Offenders Conditionally Sentenced or Conditionally Released (1990) 403

UN Model Agreement on the Transfer of Foreign Prisoners 401

UN Model Treaty on the Transfer of Proceedings in Criminal Matters (1990) 361

Subject Index

Abortion 237
Ad hoc court 189
Advocate
    See   Counsel
            Right to counsel
Aggression 420, 483, 485, 501, 503, 509, 515, 519, 523
Agricultural matters 309-315
Aiding and abetting 85, 108, 128, 135, 231, 469, 505, 515
Aircraft 41-43, 45, 55, 57, 66, 87, 100, 101, 136, 189, 211, 243, 498
Amnesty 26, 188, 207, 210, 221, 373, 382, 391, 405, 411, 544
    See also
        Immunity
Anti-discrimination clause
    See   Discrimination clause
Anti-trust offences
    See   Competition
Apartheid 21, 27, 37, 38, 498, 510, 523
    See also
        Crimes against humanity
Appeal 12, 113, 116, 289, 384, 388, 440, 461-465, 493, 577, 598
Arbitration 43, 59, 73, 105, 212, 213
Armed conflict 5, 17, 25, 429, 483, 512
    See also
        Non-international armed conflict
Arrest 19, 37, 190, 191, 193, 201, 203, 216, 222, 225, 226, 231, 239, 258, 260, 262, 266, 267, 319, 343, 348, 371, 383, 386, 387, 433, 435, 437, 446, 450, 451, 452, 461, 462, 465, 473, 475, 486-487, 490, 495, 545, 561, 562
    See also
        Deprivation of liberty
        Pre-trial detention
        Right to liberty
Arson 237, 259, 261
Asylum 237, 239, 533, 537
Attempt 35, 49, 57, 65, 146, 211, 237-239, 244, 428, 467, 505
Aut dedere aut judicare
    See   Extradite or prosecute
Banks 179, 319, 536
    See also
        Financial institutions

Bank secrecy 88, 91, 108, 113, 164, 320, 327
Bankruptcy 241
Barbarity 511
Benelux 123, 221, 222, 257, 262, 341, 343, 415
Bigamy 237
Blockade 508
Bombardment 428, 508, 520
Border areas 263, 264
Capital punishment 26, 189, 199, 232, 320, 544, 554, 557, 558, 575
Citizens 232, 239, 467, 469, 471, 531, 549
    See also
        Nationals
Civil and political rights 188, 543, 557, 558
Civilian 15, 17, 20, 420, 427, 429, 468, 501, 502, 504, 511, 520
Civilian objects 20, 520
Coercive measures
    See   Arrest
        Deprivation of liberty
        Searches
        Seizure
        Telefax
        Telephone
Command Responsibility 87
    See also
        Superior Orders
Commonwealth 225-232, 345, 352, 355
Commonwealth scheme 225, 345
Compensation 67, 68, 271, 273, 295, 300, 341, 405, 463, 487, 545, 562, 608
Competition 527
Complaint 67, 370, 484-486, 566, 570
Complicity 35, 65, 428, 467, 502, 504
Compulsory labour 545, 561
Compulsory measures 320
Confession 65, 460
Confidentiality 57, 77, 92, 103, 118, 172, 288, 294, 297, 298, 322, 348, 485, 587, 606
    See also
        Bank secrecy
Confiscation 83, 85, 88, 89, 107-114, 116-118, 121, 124, 137, 192, 202, 379, 387-390
    See also
        Seizure
        Tracing

Conspiracy 35, 85, 108, 161, 243, 420, 428, 467, 501, 504
Contempt of court 456
Controlled delivery 83, 95, 124
Conversion of sentence 402, 410, 411
Corporations 583, 594
   See also
      Legal persons
Corruption 159-164, 304
Counsel 11, 419, 422, 423, 433, 434, 438, 447-449, 452, 455, 458, 473, 482, 485, 491, 506, 517, 547
Court of Justice of the European Communities 149, 305, 528, 532, 534
Crimes against humanity 19, 27, 29, 33, 207, 420, 429, 468, 483, 501, 519
   See also
      Apartheid
      Genocide
      International crimes
Crimes against the peace and security of mankind 420, 501, 515, 519
Crimes against United Nations and associated personnel 520
Crimes under international law 35, 490, 501, 502, 503, 515
   See also
      International crimes
Criminal liability of heads of business 147
   See also
      Legal persons
Criminal Organisations 420-421
   See also
      Organised Crime
Criminal Responsibility 38, 429, 439, 469, 470, 491, 507, 515-516, 518
   See also
      Aiding and abetting
      Attempt
      Complicity
      Conspiracy
      Criminal liability of heads of business
      Defences
      Incitement
      Individual responsibility
      Intentional
      Legal persons
      Moral choice
      Natural persons
      Negligence
      Responsibility of corporations
      State responsibility
      Superior orders
Cruel, inhuman or degrading treatment or punisment 545, 561
   See also
      Torture
Customs of war 29, 207, 420, 428, 483, 501, 504, 520
Customs duties 148, 187, 209, 309-315, 337, 342, 362, 404
Customs and excise 80, 94, 97, 99, 123, 198, 258, 259, 262, 263, 265, 268, 269, 533
Damages 118, 263, 301
Data protection 282, 286, 288, 583, 584, 586, 587, 593-598, 599-614
Death penalty
   See   Capital punishment
Decreto penale 397
Defences
   See   Necessity
      Self-defence
      Superior orders
Deprivation of liberty 85, 91, 147, 187, 197, 203, 215, 344, 366, 373, 379, 380, 382, 386, 387, 389, 390, 391, 401, 402, 403, 407, 410, 415
Discrimination clause
   See   Political opinion
Disqualification 379, 381, 390-392, 440, 480
Dossier 286
Double criminality 187, 197, 225, 237, 320, 330, 362, 365, 366, 380, 404, 408
Double jeopardy 320
   See also
      Non bis in idem
Draft Code of Crimes against the Peace and Security of Mankind 505, 515
Draft Code of Offences against the Peace and Security of Mankind 503
Drug trafficking 123, 126, 127, 276-278, 353
Drugs 83-85, 88, 89, 94, 95, 97-99, 101, 123, 124, 126, 132, 259-262, 276-278, 303, 499, 512-513, 528, 533
   See also
      Psychotropic substances

Economic crimes
    See   Anti-trust offences
           Bank secrecy
           Confidentiality
           Corruption
           Double criminality
           Fraud
           Legal persons
           Money laundering
           Responsibility of corporations
EEC
    See   European Community
Effective penal sanctions 7, 9, 13, 15
Emergency 65, 544, 545, 561, 564
    See also
           Necessity
Enslavement
    See   Slavery
Environment 98, 135-141, 304, 511, 513, 521, 523
European Community 125, 151, 152, 177, 180, 309, 527, 599
European Union 145, 151, 275, 525, 531, 600, 605
Evidence 23, 58, 66-68, 91-94, 108, 109, 118, 129-130, 163, 170, 202, 226, 230, 231-233, 240, 257, 268-269, 297, 319, 321-324, 329, 333, 342, 345, 348, 350, 366, 370, 384, 422-424, 432-435, 437-466, 471-475, 482, 485, 486, 489-497
Expenses 23, 69, 93, 203, 239, 314, 315, 325, 331, 333, 348, 353, 383, 425, 436, 476, 482, 554, 570
Expert 68, 77, 93, 324, 331, 330, 342
Extermination 420, 429, 468, 502, 504, 519
Extraditable offence 42, 58, 66, 90, 187, 211, 257, 330, 517
Extradite or prosecute 7, 9, 13, 15, 42, 58, 66, 90, 147, 163, 198, 212, 231, 347, 496, 506, 517
Extradition 22, 27, 36, 42, 43, 58, 66-67, 90, 91, 137, 147-148, 163, 187-193, 197-204, 207, 209-210, 211- 214, 215-217, 221-222, 228, 235, 237, 241, 243, 266, 267, 380, 381, 450, 496, 506, 516, 517, 562
    See also
           Extraditable offence
           Double criminality
           Discrimination clause
           Fiscal offences
           Political offence exception
(Extra)territorial jurisdiction 7, 9, 13, 15, 35, 41, 57, 65-66, 87, 136, 146, 160, 212, 420
Fact-finding commission 22
Failure to act 21
    See also
           Negligence
Fair and public hearing 433, 473, 491, 506, 517, 546, 562
Fair trial
    See   Rights of the accused
Fairness 438, 491
Fauna 136
Financial institutions 126-131
Financial interests of the European Community 145-148, 151-153, 155, 529
Fines 153, 327, 337, 341, 342, 379, 382, 388-390, 456, 460, 493, 528
Fiscal offences 87, 198, 209, 322, 337
Flora 136
Forced labour 38, 511
Fraud 143, 145-148, 151, 241, 304, 529, 533
Fundamental freedoms 75, 217, 532, 533, 543, 561, 573, 575, 577, 583, 588
Fundamental principles 112, 161, 162, 368, 380
Genocide 27, 29, 35, 36, 207, 428, 467, 483-484, 510, 519, 523, 544
    See also
           Crimes against humanity
Grave breaches 7, 9, 13, 15, 20, 21, 27, 427, 498
Habeas corpus 227
Handcuffs 261, 457
Head of State 198, 231, 429, 469, 501, 504, 508, 516
Hors de combat 5, 20, 521
Hostages 5, 15, 18, 47, 212, 243, 260, 261, 304, 420, 427, 468, 498, 501, 511, 520, 521

Hostile Power 13, 15, 427, 512, 519
Humanitarian 6, 189
Humanitarian law 427, 430-432, 434, 437, 467, 470-471, 474, 475, 519, 520
Illegal export of drugs 123
Immunities 72, 78, 80, 279, 301, 436, 475, 482, 555, 571
Immunity 80, 332, 353, 482
See also
Amnesty
Impartiality 22, 25, 77, 431, 440, 470, 478, 480, 563
Imprisonment 37, 67, 85, 91, 112, 137, 187, 207, 225, 239, 243, 344, 401, 429, 434, 435, 456, 460-462, 468, 474, 475, 493, 497, 545
In absentia 112, 113, 188, 209, 379, 384-386, 388, 396, 421, 451
In camera 11, 76, 434, 474, 567
Incitement 35, 428, 467, 504, 548
Indictment 420-423, 433, 437, 441, 449-453, 455, 458, 472, 473, 486-487, 490
Indiscriminate attack 20, 520
Individual responsibility 420, 421, 429, 469, 505, 515
Information processing
See Data protection
Inhumane acts 420, 429, 468, 519
Insider dealing 169, 175, 177
Insider trading
See Insider dealing
Instrumentalities 88, 91, 94, 107, 109, 110, 113, 137, 345, 354
Intentional 29, 49, 57, 135, 145, 153
International Court of Justice 36, 43, 59, 73, 105, 121, 141, 431, 535, 555
International crimes 275, 276, 277, 304, 523, 533,
See also
Agression
Crimes against humanity
Crimes against the peace and security of mankind

Crimes under international law
Genocide
Crimes against United Nations and associated personnel
War crimes
International Criminal Code 499-523
See also
Draft Code of Crimes against the Peace and Security of Mankind
Draft Code of Offences against the Peace and Security of Mankind
International Criminal Court 36, 417, 477, 507, 516, 517
International Criminal Police Organisation 115, 201, 226, 333, 368, 383
International organisations
See Benelux
European Community
European Union
Council of Europe
Schengen group
Organizations of American States
United Nations
International Tribunal for Rwanda 467-476
International Tribunal for the Former Yugoslavia 427-466
Interpol
See International Criminal Police Organisation
Interpreter 11, 434, 447, 456, 473, 491, 506, 517, 547, 563
Invasion 508
Judicial assistance 67, 268, 363, 435, 475, 494
Judicial authority 112, 113, 154, 190, 225-229, 233, 266, 310, 342, 347
Jurisdiction 420, 427-429, 467-469, 483-484, 516
See also
Temporal Jurisdiction
(Extra)territorial Jurisdiction
Justice and home affairs 532, 537
Lapse of time 113, 188, 199, 221, 320, 367, 373, 381, 386, 391, 396, 404, 506
Larceny 237
Laundering
See Money laundering
Legal persons 57, 113, 138, 154, 179, 293, 313, 573, 583, 600

Legality 286, 288, 490
Legality principle 19, 490, 507, 518, 547, 563
See also
   Non-retroactivity
Liaison 77, 254, 263, 297, 302
Liaison officers 94, 264, 279, 291, 292, 294, 297, 302
Major War Criminals 419-421
Manslaughter 243
Maritime 51, 498
Mass violations 65, 511
Mercenaries 509, 511-512
Military law 188, 198, 229, 320, 329, 347, 362, 404
Miscarriage of justice 435, 438, 474, 547, 577
Money laundering 81, 107, 108, 126-133, 277, 305
See also
   Predicate offence
Moral choice 501
Murder 5, 18, 37, 49, 231, 237, 239, 243, 259, 260, 304, 420, 429, 468, 501, 504, 511, 519, 520
Mutual assistance 21, 22, 43, 58, 114, 163, 169, 170, 172, 175, 221-222, 245, 249, 262, 297, 309, 315, 319-326, 327, 329-336, 337, 339, 341-344, 345, 586, 588
Narcotic drugs
   See Drugs
National Authority (Authorities) 115, 123, 128, 152, 278, 287, 288, 451, 463
National Central Bureaus 249-256
National Court(s) 301, 421, 430, 439, 440, 462, 507, 509
National identification number 603
National language 369
National provisions 264, 344, 393, 609, 614
National law(s) 19, 42, 51, 55, 58, 65, 68, 91, 118, 124, 126, 129, 137, 138, 146, 148, 153, 155, 169, 170, 181, 214, 270, 271, 272, 289, 297, 303, 305, 314, 386, 389, 401, 402, 410, 450, 488, 504, 515, 518, 528, 594, 595, 596, 600, 602, 612
National security 267, 278, 546, 548, 562-564, 578, 605

Nationals 6, 23, 66, 68, 69, 75, 87, 91, 137, 147, 148, 160, 161, 193, 198, 263, 267, 297, 319, 331, 334, 353, 366, 367, 383, 408, 409, 411, 415, 431, 470, 478, 480, 492, 503, 510, 512, 531, 533, 550, 554, 565, 568, 569
Natural persons 113, 138, 159, 179, 429, 469, 599, 600, 601, 613, 615
Ne bis in idem
   See Non bis in idem
Necessity 7, 9, 15, 420, 427, 428, 501, 519, 520, 521
See also
   Emergency
Negligence 136, 153
Non bis in idem 19, 112, 148, 152, 199, 208, 320, 343-344, 363, 373, 391, 392, 430, 440, 469-470, 491, 507, 518
Non-international armed conflict 5, 25, 429, 521
See also
   Armed Conflict
Non-retroactivity 165
See also
   Legality principle
Observation 108, 257-259, 263
Omission 17-19, 25, 73, 118, 146, 152, 161, 162, 483, 490, 505, 547, 563
Ordonnance pénale 379, 384-386, 388, 397
Ordre public 92, 112, 114, 171, 320, 329, 546, 548, 588
Organization of American States 162, 165, 166
Organized crime 126, 127, 327
See also
   Criminal organisations
Pardon 207, 373, 382, 391, 402, 405, 411, 435, 466, 475, 498, 544
See also
   Amnesty
Penal institution 86
Penal sanctions 7, 9, 13, 15
Penalties 12, 35, 41, 49, 57, 65, 127, 132, 145-147, 152, 153, 154, 155, 181, 343, 434, 461, 474, 493, 563, 573
Perfidious use 20, 520
Persecution 420, 429, 468, 502, 504, 511, 519

Piracy 237
Police 41, 92, 115, 123, 191, 201, 221, 226, 247, 249, 250, 253, 256-259, 262-265, 267-269, 272, 273, 275, 276, 277, 278, 284, 286, 333, 341, 343, 369, 383, 415, 446, 497, 533, 537, 548, 564, 593-598
Police assistance 264
Police authorities 249, 257, 264, 267, 594
Police officers 257, 259, 262
Political 38, 65, 68, 243, 602
Political activity 564
Political offences 36, 112, 164, 188, 198, 202, 207, 211-214, 227, 228, 231, 238, 239, 243, 320, 329, 347, 362, 367, 372, 380, 404
Political opinion 18, 87, 90, 188, 198, 203, 212, 217, 367, 380, 543, 549, 585, 595
Political rights 557
Pre-trial detention 409, 487
See also
    Arrest
    Deprivation of Liberty
    Right to Liberty
Predicate offence 107-109
Presumption of innocence 19, 434, 473, 491, 546, 562
Prescription
    See   Lapse of time
Prima facie case 7, 9, 13, 15, 226, 230, 433, 472, 486, 489
Prison 197, 203, 226, 227, 232, 434, 462, 474, 497
Prisoner 11-13, 229, 239, 401, 402, 466
Prisoner of war 11-13, 427, 501, 519
Private property 420, 428, 501, 520
Proactive policing
    See   Observation
    Controlled deliveries
    Use of Informers
Product piracy 304
Procuracy 478, 481, 482
Property 7, 9, 13, 15, 38, 83-85, 88, 89, 91, 94, 107, 108-111, 116, 128, 135-137, 159, 161-164, 192, 202, 231, 238, 243, 244, 304, 321, 330, 371, 387, 390, 420, 428, 434, 462, 474, 501, 511-513, 519, 520, 543, 549, 564, 573
Prosecution 19, 25, 29, 58, 86, 90-93, 147, 163, 188-- 189, 212, 320, 363, 421-424, 427, 432, 437, 445, 446, 471, 472, 480, 481, 484-486, 488, 489, 496, 506
Prosecutor 421-423, 430, 432, 433, 438-440, 445, 446, 447-454, 458, 460-462, 465, 466, 470, 472, 481, 482, 485-488, 493, 494
Protection of victims and witnesses 434, 474
Provisional measures
    See   Tracing
        Seizure
    See also
        Confiscation
Psychotropic substances 83-106, 123, 124, 260-261
Public order
    See   Ordre public
Public status 208, 366, 373, 391
Punishment 18, 37-38, 65, 68, 75, 86, 123, 148, 188, 197, 199, 228, 232, 238, 239, 419-421, 423, 424, 501, 506-508, 516, 519, 520, 544, 545, 547, 561, 563
Race, religion, nationality 90, 188, 198, 212, 213, 228, 380
Racial 21, 35, 37, 38, 420, 428, 429, 468, 502, 504, 510, 511, 518, 519, 548, 585, 595, 602
Racial group 37, 38, 511
Radio equipment 263
Rape 237, 259, 260, 429, 445, 468, 469, 520, 521
Red Crescent 20, 520
Red Cross 6, 8, 20, 78, 520
Red Lion 20, 520
Religious 18, 20, 35, 396, 420, 428, 429, 468, 502, 504, 510-512, 518, 519, 548, 549, 573, 585, 595, 602

Remedies
   See   Appeal
            Retrial
            Review
Reservations 120, 140, 165, 203, 302, 374, 393, 557, 571, 590
Residence 38, 80, 87, 161, 267, 331, 361, 401, 533, 546, 583, 585
Resident 232, 362, 366, 380, 404, 512, 513, 577, 587
Responsibility
   See   Criminal responsibility
Responsibility of corporations
   See   Criminal liability of heads of business
           Legal persons
Right to counsel 19, 422, 431, 434, 473, 517, 547, 563
Right to liberty 545, 562
Right to life 37, 510, 544, 561
Rights of the accused 18-20, 215, 339, 422, 433, 491, 506, 517, 546-547, 562-563
Sanctions 7, 9, 13, 15, 84-85, 136-138, 365, 379-383, 388-390, 391, 396, 402, 410, 586, 609
   See also
           Confiscation
           Disqualification
           Fines
           Imprisonment
Schengen Group 219, 221
Searches 91, 100, 101, 113, 164, 170, 171, 261, 319, 314, 320, 325, 337, 345-350, 587
Secrecy of banks
   See   Bank secrecy
Securities 162, 169, 178-180
Seizing 110, 354
Seizure 41, 80, 83, 89, 97, 107, 124, 202, 325, 330, 337, 345, 350, 354, 363, 371, 387, 428, 520
Self-defence 258, 261, 503
Self-determination 17, 510, 523, 543
Sentence of death
   See
           Capital Punishment
Sentencing State 380-382, 384-386, 401, 402, 404-406, 407-412
Severe pain or suffering 65

Settlement of disputes 105, 121, 141, 301
Severe penalties 41
Sex 5, 18, 188, 266, 281, 320, 543, 544, 549, 564
Sex-life 602
Sexual assault 445, 460
Ship 51, 55, 66, 136
Slavery 420, 429, 468, 502, 504, 511, 519, 523, 545, 561
Speciality 192, 200, 229, 496
State responsibility 523
   See also
       Individual Responsibility
Statutes of limitation
   See   Lapse of time
Superior orders 65, 420, 429, 469, 501, 504, 507, 516
Supplementary information 95, 200
Suspension 153, 172, 337, 341
Tax 148, 160, 171, 187, 209, 337, 342
Tax offences
   See   Fiscal offences
Telefax 115
Telephone 263
Temporal jurisdiction 430, 469
Territorial 56, 84, 119, 137, 204, 413, 430, 469, 590
Terrorism 211, 276, 468, 512, 521, 533
   See also
       Aircraft
       Hostages
       Physical protection of nuclear material
       Political offences
Third state 192-193, 200, 207, 287, 331, 411
Time-limits 23, 26, 117, 200, 285, 321, 37, 370, 455, 462, 464
   See also
       Lapse of time
Torture 5, 7, 9, 13, 15, 18, 37, 65-74, 75, 188, 429, 468, 511, 519, 545, 561
   See also
       Cruel, inhuman or degrading treatment or punishment
Tracing 91, 108, 109, 164, 345, 353
Transfer of data 581, 610
Transfer of execution 377, 415
Transit 56, 84, 94, 95, 97, 193, 202, 216, 331, 343, 382, 383, 411, 513
Trivial 228
Truth 459, 460

United Nations 27-29, 59, 68, 69, 71-73, 98, 102-105, 185, 187, 319, 327, 361, 401, 403, 423, 427, 431-433, 441, 442, 445, 467, 471, 472, 476-478, 481-482, 484-485, 493, 499, 503, 541, 544, 550-556, 558, 559, 561
Urgency 115, 170, 191, 201, 260
Use of the mails 101
Victims 17, 25, 263, 405, 432-434, 445, 446, 454-456, 460, 463, 472-474, 485, 487, 492, 493
Waiver 227, 447, 455
War crimes 3, 27, 29, 420, 501, 511, 520
   See also
      Exceptionally serious war crimes
      Grave breaches
      Major war criminals
Witnesses 67, 93, 268, 324, 329, 330, 331, 332, 342, 345, 349-354, 422, 423, 424, 432-434, 445, 447, 453, 454, 456-461, 472-474, 482, 485, 487, 490-492, 495, 507, 517, 547, 563
Women 12, 19, 26, 445, 544, 564
Wounded and sick 5, 6, 29, 207